# CREATIVE PIANO TEACHING

## FOURTH EDITION

**James Lyke**

**Geoffrey Haydon**

**Catherine Rollin**

ISBN: 978-1-60904-054-3

Published by

STIPES PUBLISHING L.L.C.
202-204 West University Avenue
Post Office Box 526
Champaign, Illinois 61824-0526

# Dedication and Acknowledgments

*This book is dedicated to **Robert Pace** (1924-2010) and **Richard Chronister** (1930-1999), two monumental leaders in the field of Piano Pedagogy.*

*A heartfelt thank you to Kevin Lyke for his diligent efforts in regard to reading, typing, editing—and for his overall invaluable support during the construction of this book.*

*Many thanks to Brian McElwain, graphic designer for Stipes Publishing L.L.C. and Christopher Preissing, music engraver for IS Productions. Each has made extraordinary contributions in the preparation of this book.*

Cover design, interior text design, and layout by Brian K. McElwain.

Music Engraving by IS Productions, Chicago, Illinois.

# Preface to the Fourth Edition

The fourth edition of *Creative Piano Teaching* welcomes new co-author Catherine Rollin, award winning composer and independent piano teacher from Bloomfield Hills, Michigan. Her chapters focus on style and technical development. In addition, many new contributing authors address topics such as establishing a studio, getting started with a teaching practice, composing, entrepreneurship, technology, suitable piano literature for the elementary, intermediate and adult student, understanding jazz, and practice techniques. Other topics for advancing pianists include the comprehension of performance practice involving literature from the Baroque, Classical, Romantic and Modern eras. Helpful teaching suggestions from these periods will be useful to piano teachers. Special chapters on pedaling, practice techniques, fingering, memorization, and preparing for a performance at the more advanced level complete the section on the advancing pianist.

Current research on music wellness, the brain and performance anxiety is presented by experts in the field. Several chapters on the amateur adult pianist highlight this special group of students. Important organizations for piano teachers stress the necessity of "belonging" and keeping current with trends in piano teaching. Some historical perspective on American piano teaching round out this new edition.

*Creative Piano Teaching* is intended as a piano pedagogy text for those preparing to become teachers. It also serves as a valuable resource for established teachers in the profession.

# Contributing Authors

Reid Alexander

Gail Berenson

Tony Caramia

Richard Chronister

Ann Collins

Vanessa Cornett-Murtada

Jo Ellen DeVilbiss

Denise Edwards

Lee Evans

Carole Flatau

William Heiles

Steven Hesla

Peter Jutras

Karen Koch

Karen Krieger

George Litterst

Walter Schenkman

Suzanne Schons

Paul Sheftel

Ruth Slenczynska

Christos Tsitsaros

# Table of Contents

# PART ONE
# THE YOUNG PIANIST

# BEGINNINGS

# CHAPTER 1

## Preparing to Become a Piano Teacher

### James Lyke

Mastering the art of piano teaching is a lifelong process, one that requires interacting with students of all ages. What are some of the essentials involved in preparing to become a successful piano teacher? How does one prepare for this career?

The sad fact about the piano teaching profession is that anyone can "hang out a shingle." Too many people with limited training and experience view teaching as a handy means to supplement other income. Many of these "teachers" perpetuate old fashioned conservatory approaches to instruction. Consequently, the "teaching as I was taught" (or mistaught) syndrome is passed on to young students. Times have changed. The excellence of piano teacher training in colleges and universities throughout the United States, as well as the impact of other professional organizations such as the Music Teachers National Association and the National Conference On Keyboard Pedagogy, have forged a new direction. To earn a degree in piano pedagogy offers a viable option for piano students.

To prepare for a career as an independent music teacher, one should consider pursuing a bachelor's degree in piano pedagogy (or in performance with strong pedagogy training.) This entails the following: (1) acceptance to a four year college by audition and examinations, (2) completion of broad liberal arts requirements, (3) completing core courses in music theory and music history and (4) piano performance and study throughout four years with an artist teacher. In conjunction with piano study, the usual exams and recital requirements would need to be passed. And, of course, piano pedagogy classes.

For those teachers already established in communities, numerous study opportunities are available such as college extension courses in piano pedagogy, workshops given by leading publishers and local, state and national meetings that offer various piano sessions on topics helpful to the established teacher.

# College Piano Pedagogy Courses

A series of piano pedagogy courses prepare the future piano teacher to (1) develop a teaching philosophy, (2) read widely in the field from sources including texts, professional magazines and research studies that deal with private and group teaching, (3) observe piano lessons at all levels and evaluate the effectiveness of varied approaches, (4) student teach under supervision in a laboratory program at different levels of instruction with both children and adults, (5) gain experience with both private lessons and group lessons, (6) survey, evaluate and compare selected elementary methods, (7) play and become acquainted with suitable elementary and intermediate piano literature by leading classical and educational composers, (8) participate in field trips to local studios and community music schools to observe precollege students being taught in a variety of styles, (9) learn how to evaluate and judge student performance in examinations and competitive situations, (10) prepare students for recitals, (11) use technology to enhance motivation and learning in the lesson, (12) notate music with software programs such as Finale or Sibelius and learn to record with programs such as Garage Band (13) become acquainted with the basics of piano maintenance and (14) explore the business aspects of operating a studio.

Care should be taken to select a college piano pedagogy program that offers the experiences outlined above. Beware of programs that do not provide "hands on" teaching experience. A pragmatic program far outweighs esoteric courses that primarily consist of lectures only. Seek a well-rounded curriculum, one that addresses all aspects of piano education.

Beyond the four-year degree in piano teaching (or performance/ pedagogy), teachers might consider graduate study leading to a master's degree - MM degrees in piano pedagogy have been granted since about 1980. Doctoral degrees have also been established in leading universities since the latter part of the 20th century.

Future piano teachers are able to take advantage of numerous courses and workshops throughout the United States and in Europe. Self improvement through continuous study should be a constant aim of every piano teacher.

# Some Random Thoughts on Selected Pedagogical Topics

Below are brief thoughts on random pedagogical topics that will be covered in more detail by various authors in this text. They represent a limited overview of subjects important to the novice teacher.

## Choosing a Beginning Piano Method

Becoming acquainted with effective beginning methods of instruction is essential for the inexperienced teacher. Thankfully, we live in a piano teaching world with an abundance of fine methods available. Students should have the opportunity to compare approaches and understand the hallmarks of these approaches: Middle C vs Black Key-Intervallic vs Multi-Key. Modern methods take into account accepted learning principles, broad musicianship, sequenced technical material and repertoire that is attractive to children. Author teams include gifted educational composers whose worth is a far cry from the dull material I waded through as a child. I could not wait to get to the "real stuff."

## Establishing a Learning Climate

Teachers who are sincere about the lessons they give  establish a studio atmosphere conducive to effective learning. They care about their students regardless of ability level. Successful piano teachers help students realize their full musical potential. And they make musical learning exciting. A learning climate must be flexible and always student-centered. It behooves the young teacher to examine major leading learning theories.

## Planning Lessons

Teachers who are serious about their student's progress spend time planning lessons for the coming week with an eye toward the end of term. Assignments guide a student (and the watchful parent) in home practice. Assignment forms simplify the process; computer generated forms are now the norm. Long gone are the days when a teacher would ask: "Let's see— what did I hear last week?" That sort of question confirms the fact that the teacher hasn't given any thought to the next lesson (or to the student.)

## Home Practice - Keeping in Touch

Assignments are often not enough for the student's home practice. The important triangle of teacher/student/parent is often wanting on the parent end. For the younger students, it is good to be in touch with parents during the week. An e-mail message or phone call in the middle of the week prompts a parent to oversee some of the practice and check off items on the assignment. In some of today's studios, sophisticated technology allows computer or video interaction between teach and student.

## Musicianship Training

In the latter half of the 20th century, a movement towards integrating theory instruction into the piano lesson emerged. Traditional piano teaching was largely concentrated on repertoire and technical training. A trend towards incorporating music theory within the lesson was a happy development. Students began to learn about harmony, how to use chords in harmonization studies, how to compose simple pieces, how to detect form in music and so on. Musicianship classes were formed and offered weekly in addition to repertoire and technique lessons. Even in private lessons, some time was devoted to these elements. Musicianship skills are easier to develop in the group lesson. The "integrated" piano lesson had arrived with the goal of developing a well-rounded keyboard musician.

## Sight Reading

No better musical gift than sight reading skill can be developed by a piano student. It is a life-long gift, one that gives pleasure well into old age. But reading must be nurtured from the start and lesson time must be devoted to it. A good teacher has reading material at his or her fingertips and plenty to send some home with the student. Reading in group lessons tends to be highly effective, as there can be no stopping along the way. The reading process is more difficult in a private lesson but the teacher can play along with improvised accompaniments to keep the student moving ahead.

## Technical Training

Another gift passed along to a student involves technical skill. If properly developed, the student will know how to regain facility after long periods of not playing. The teacher takes great pleasure in shaping a hand and showing a student how to use body parts (wrist, forearm, upper arm, elbow, shoulder etc.) always with a view toward avoiding tension. For children, motions can be tied to game playing - bouncing a ball, throwing darts etc. Technical training should be fun, not just boring exercises.

## Repertoire

Many considerations come into play when selecting and assigning repertoire. Once note learning has been grasped, interesting sounding pieces grab the attention of students. The teacher chooses pieces that engage a student's imagination. The piece must be within the student's technical competence - a composition that perhaps sounds more difficult than it really is. Pieces using pedal fascinate children. Composers take this into account when they write "space" pieces (think Star Wars.) The teacher provides many opportunities for students to play for each other and for parents in informal recitals. Teachers are constantly on the lookout for repertoire that teaches specific elements and is fairly easy to learn. Students need to have several pieces ready to play at a moment's notice. Outside the studio, encourage students to play at school and church or at friends' homes. The student should have some choice in selecting material for study; this serves to motivate learning.

## Teach, Don't "Tell"

The great piano educator Frances Clark was known for her expression: "telling is not teaching." How eager is the young teacher to rush into a thorny musical problem that students struggle with. Instead of guiding the student into discovering how to solve a musical problem, the inexperienced teacher wants to explain everything. This sort of teaching deprives the student of discovering solutions on his own. After all, the goal of a piano teacher is to ultimately make the student independent and able to figure out solutions to musical problems.

## Jazz Instruction for the Classical Pianist

A course in beginning jazz improvisation for the pedagogy major assists the future teacher in many ways. A teacher will deal with elements of jazz in many compositions. The teacher must know how to "swing" and how to guide piano students involved in school jazz ensembles. The ability to work from lead sheets and use good voicings becomes essential. And the fact that improvisation is a core element of jazz piano courses will help the teacher develop and pass on this skill to young students.

## How to Give a Workshop

At one time or another, a teacher will be asked to share his expertise on a certain pedagogical topic. He or she will be asked to give a session at a local meeting, regional meeting, state meeting and even at the national level. How to organize and deliver information through lecturing, performing and using technology (such as a PowerPoint presentation) starts in a piano pedagogy class. This is an important assignment for future teachers who will develop special skills that ought to be shared with others.

## Branching Out

The future piano teacher will find that once settled in his studio, he will often be asked to accompany singers and instrumentalists. Therefore, some collaborative piano study along with performance and pedagogy could be very useful. Opportunities to perform at parties, wedding receptions and fashion shows will crop up. Schools often seek the assistance of piano teachers to accompany vocalists and instrumentalists in music contests. Be prepared to play for high school musicals. These sideline jobs offer an opportunity for extra income. Organ study, along with performance and pedagogy, will come in handy with church work. A pedagogy major must be open to diversification.

# References

Agay, Denes (ed.). *The Art Of Teaching Piano*. New York: Yorktown Music Press, 1981.

Baker-Jordan, Martha. *Practical Piano Pedagogy*. Van Nuys, CA: Alfred Publishing Co., Inc., 2005.

Bastien, James. *How To Teach Piano Successfully* (3rd ed.) San Diego: Neil Kjos Music Company, 1988.

Jacobson, Jeanine M. *Professional Piano Teaching*. Van Nuys, CA: Alfred Music Publishing Co., Inc., 2006.

Uszler, Marienne et al. *The Well-Tempered Keyboard Teacher* (2nd ed.) New York: Schirmer Books, 2000.

# CHAPTER 2

# The Independent Piano Studio

### Denise Edwards

The independent piano teacher has many options available when setting up a studio. Lessons can be offered privately, with partners, in small groups, or as a combination of these. Theory instruction can be offered in a class, in a computer lab, or on the student's home computer using commercial software, free internet programs, or commercial internet theory courses. The piano teacher can offer classes in preschool music, such as Kindermusik and Musikgarten. He or she can offer instruction to adults privately and in groups. The studio teacher can also teach a student anywhere in the world via the Internet.

## Professional Preparation

Before opening a piano studio, a teacher should receive as much musical, pianistic, and pedagogical training as possible. The public expects that, in addition to teaching music reading and "classical music," the studio piano teacher is able to teach popular music, jazz, playing by ear, improvisation, composition, and how to use the latest digital keyboards. The prospective studio teacher should choose courses and instructors that will prepare him or her to meet these expectations.

The prospective studio teacher should develop his or her own technical and interpretive skills as much as possible. An extensive repertoire of early advanced piano literature is essential. College studio classes and piano literature classes are helpful, as is the ability to sight read proficiently. Attending recitals and listening to recordings (by borrowing them from a library or downloading performances off the Internet) are other ways to become familiar with the literature.

Piano pedagogy courses will familiarize the prospective studio teacher with the latest teaching materials and technology and will provide opportunities for observation and practice teaching. The courses will assist the teacher in developing a studio curriculum.

Classes in conducting are recommended. This will enable the studio teacher to conduct large ensembles within the studio, or public "monster concerts." The piano teacher will also have another marketable skill, and one that is invaluable for church music and community musical theatre.

Workshops or courses that include instruction in teaching preschool music are essential if the studio teacher is going to tap into this highly lucrative market.

Courses not directly related to the field of piano teaching can be valuable. Short courses in conversational French, German, and Italian, or a vocal diction class, would help the studio teacher pronounce titles and musical terms. A course in human anatomy can aid the teacher in explaining technical principles.

The studio teacher should be "musically literate." In order to prepare fully for a teaching career, the prospective piano teacher should consider remaining in college an additional semester or two beyond the set curriculum, if such an extension would not result in excessive personal debt.

## Choosing the Studio Location

The teacher must decide whether to locate the studio in the home or to locate it elsewhere. Factors to consider are the number of students the teacher expects to have, whether the lessons will be private or group, the space requirements of the pianos and other equipment, and zoning.

Some parents seek out what they believe is the best music instruction for their children, but many parents base their decision on cost and proximity. "Where do you live, and what do you charge?" are sometimes the first questions asked during a phone inquiry. The ease of access to a particular neighborhood, its affluence, and the number of young children living there are factors to consider when choosing a studio location.

## The Home Studio

Locating a studio at home has several advantages. Overhead is low. There is no time lost to commuting. The teacher's school-age children are able to go to their own home after school.

A primary consideration in locating a studio in the home is separating it from the persons, activities, and sounds of the household. This is most easily accomplished when building a home. An existing structure can be modified, however. A separate entrance, a separate restroom, doors, and soundproofing materials in walls and ceilings can help to separate the business from the family. The teacher's family needs privacy, and the teaching environment should have no distractions. A teacher who lives alone may not have to be concerned about separating the business from the home, but he or she should consider the wear and tear on the flooring and furnishings that will occur. It is desirable to keep pets away from the students. Many are allergic to animals, especially cats. Some are afraid of dogs. Of course, keep any pet's shots current.

If "home" is an apartment, the lease should indicate if home occupations such as piano teaching are allowed. An attorney can determine this and also advise you on any zoning restrictions. However, an apartment may not be a suitable location for a studio unless the teaching can be done in a location or at a time that will not disturb the other residents of the building.

Condo associations also have rules regarding the use of the property. Teaching in a condo has some of the same considerations as teaching in an apartment.

Parking has to be adequate and legal. There are sometimes zoning restrictions for home business parking. Even if it doesn't violate any ordinance, neighbors don't appreciate a front yard that has been turned into a parking lot.

## The Studio Outside of the Home

The primary disadvantage of locating the studio outside of the home is overhead. This overhead may be offset by teaching group piano lessons and preschool music classes, which generate more income than do private lessons. Also, space, and therefore expenses, can be shared with other teachers.

A building to house the studio could also be purchased as an investment. Be certain an attorney reads any leases or purchase agreements before you sign anything. You will, most likely, have to make interior changes. You also need to consider the other tenants who occupy the building.

There are several advantages of having a studio located outside of the home. The studio may appear to be more "professional." You have a place to "go to work." You don't have the wear and tear on your personal property, and you have the potential to work with colleagues.

Security, accessibility, parking, and proximity to clientele should all be considered when locating a studio.

Sometimes it is possible to rent space at a school or church and use the institution's instruments. An established teacher might have the room and need for an apprentice.

Another option, especially for a newly-minted teacher, is to teach at a music store. Often, the lesson instruments are new pianos. Sometimes a digital piano lab is in place. Many parents contact music stores for lessons. The teacher pays the store "rent," which is sometimes a per-lesson fee. There must be a clear understanding about the store's policy on students who want to continue with a teacher after he or she quits teaching at the store. Also, the reputations of the other teachers at the store should be considered when affiliating oneself with a particular store. Music stores do not always hire the most qualified instructors.

# Zoning

A piano studio is a business and must comply with local zoning laws. Whether the studio is to be home-based or in another location, before you set up the studio, an attorney should be hired to interpret the zoning laws that apply to piano teaching. An attorney can determine if a zoning variance is necessary and explain the process and expense of obtaining a variance. The expense of hiring an attorney at this point is minor compared to the the cost of zoning problems later. Be certain to inform the attorney of the type of studio you intend to start (i.e. the maximum number of students you will have, whether all of your teaching will be one-on-one, if there will be group teaching necessitating the arrival and departure of several students at once, what equipment will be used, and whether you will hire someone to assist in the studio).

Also, residential subdivisions have "covenants" that may regulate home occupations. The subdivision covenants are on file with the "recorder of deeds," from whom your attorney can obtain a copy.

Even if a city and subdivision allow for the operation of a piano studio, parking is an important consideration. There may be restrictions on on-street and off-street parking for businesses.

# Business Records

The teacher must pay applicable local, state, and federal taxes on studio income. Tax estimates must be paid quarterly. The studio teacher must pay self-employment tax (Social Security). He or she must keep complete records of all studio income and expenditures. Currently, if the home studio is used exclusively for teaching, the percentage of the residence the studio occupies is used to determine deductions for utilities, real estate taxes, and depreciation. Also, depreciation on capital expenditures such as pianos can be deducted from income. Lessons given in exchange for other services or goods are considered "barter" and are subject to income tax.

Tax laws are complicated, and they change. Before you begin teaching, hire a professional to advise you about tax laws and to prepare your tax returns. An accountant or a tax attorney will instruct you on recordkeeping and can recommend computer software to help you in this task. His or her fees can be deducted as a business expense.

If the studio teacher has an employee or employees, income taxes and social security taxes must be withheld from their paychecks and sent to the state and federal revenue services. Receive professional tax advice before you hire an employee.

You may want to incorporate your business. Consult an attorney or an accountant.

Hire professionals for your music business just as you hope the public will seek out professional music instruction. It will save you expense and grief.

## Property Insurance

Be certain all of your instruments and professional equipment are insured against loss due to fire or theft and whatever natural disasters are possible in your geographic area. Immediately inform your insurance agent whenever you purchase or sell an instrument or a piece of equipment, so that the insurance coverage is up to date Of course, if you own the building housing the studio, you will need coverage for that. Seek the advice of a professional insurance agent.

## Liability Insurance

Carry liability insurance for potential accidents or injuries a piano student or an employee might sustain while on the premises. Your insurance agent can advise you as to how much coverage you should obtain. Ask your agent about an umbrella policy, also.

## Equipping the Studio

If possible, money should be set aside and invested during the college years in preparation for the day the studio opens. The new teacher cannot receive a bank loan without collateral. Interest paid to a music store or credit card could be used to purchase equipment and materials for the studio.

Community colleges sometimes offer free assistance for those wishing to start new businesses. A college's "small business development center" might be affiliated with the United States Small Business Administration and state agencies.

The mode of teaching will determine the equipment necessary for the studio, and the financial resources of the new teacher may determine the mode of instruction. The studio teacher should "think big" and plan the ideal studio. He or she can then scale back to a financially manageable size. As income increases, the teacher can "add on."

For private or partner lessons, minimum equipment would include a vertical acoustic piano (studio or taller) that is in tune and well-regulated. "Climate control" of the studio or within the instrument will help to keep the piano in tune and will prolong its useful life.

When finances permit, the teacher should invest in a second piano, perhaps digital, for ensemble work. Also essential are an adjustable bench, adjustable footstool or two or three footstools of different heights, piano lamp, metronome, file cabinet, floor lamps or overhead lighting, coat rack, and seating for waiting. Flash cards, games, and props used to teach technique and musical concepts are helpful.

A library of music and reference books, in either hard copy or digital form, will expand. The ability to record and listen to recordings can be accomplished with digital equipment and internet access.

It is recommended to have a landline telephone. In the case of bad weather or emergency, the landline phone may be more reliable than cell or internet phone services. Also, the landline is a published number.

Group teaching requires additional digital pianos and large boards for theory work.

Preschool music classes have special requirements, especially for space, depending on the preschool curriculum chosen by the teacher.

The studio teacher needs access to a computer for keeping financial and studio records and for word processing and bill preparation. A computer in the studio itself can also be used to print assignments and can be connected to an electronic keyboard for use with music notation and theory programs.

The contemporary teacher will want a wireless internet connection in the studio for access to audio and video recordings and to music scores.

# Computer-Assisted Instruction

Computer-assisted instruction is an effective and efficient way for students to learn music theory. Younger students have grown up in a digital world and often know more about digital media than do their teachers who are much older. Teachers may opt, but no longer need, to have a computer lab or station in the studio for their students to benefit from computer-assisted instruction. Virtually every student has access to a computer at home. There are commercial theory programs that are accessed through the Internet. Also, there are method books and theory courses that include CDs and computer software as part of the theory instruction. Regardless of the mode of the theory instruction, the teacher has to give assignments and track the progress of the students.

## Lessons

The minimum length of a private lesson should be 40 minutes. As a student becomes more advanced, the time should increase. The length for a group lesson should be 50 minutes for young children and progressively longer as the children mature.

Two private lessons or two partner lessons might overlap, allowing for small group activities and ensemble playing.

Some teachers schedule all students for three weeks of private lessons and a group lesson the fourth week. Six weeks of private lessons followed by a group-lesson week is another combination.

## Fees

Lesson fees should be commensurate with the education and experience of the teacher. The prospective teacher should check with other teachers in the community and college preparatory programs to determine "the going rate." While the new teacher doesn't want to price himself out of the market, he must keep in mind that he deserves to be fairly compensated for his education and capital investment in instruments and other equipment. He must pay income taxes and self-employment tax. He will have to pay for his retirement and possibly health insurance.

Most teachers charge by the month. Charging by the term simplifies bookkeeping and commits the student and parents for a longer period of time. Payment should be made in advance. Some teachers charge a fee for late payment. If there is a computer lab, it is recommended that lab use be required and covered by a separate fee, usually 20 percent of the tuition for a 40-minute lesson.

The teacher should charge a nonrefundable registration fee to reserve a place in next school year's schedule. This registration fee can serve as a "music deposit." The teacher keeps an account for each student, with a record of the music that has been purchased for that student. At the end of the year, the total cost of the music is tallied. If that total is greater than the music deposit, the difference is billed to the parents. If it is less, the difference is refunded. The teacher might want to collect a music deposit for each term, ensuring that the music purchases are always covered.

If the teacher buys music for the student, the necessary materials are always available when needed. The disadvantage of this is that the student does not go to the music store, where he or she might purchase additional music for "fun." It has been observed, however, that it is usually the parent who stops at the music store, often without the teacher's written instructions. The music clerk cheerfully tries to help when the parent asks for the "green theory book." In either case, parents should be encouraged to make outings to the music store with their children, just as they might patronize a bookstore.

There are other fees that a teacher can collect at the beginning of the school year or term, such as contest or festival fees and recital fees. A fee can be charged to each student to pay for rental of the hall and the tuning of the recital instrument.

The teacher should provide a sight reading library for students. A nominal fee is charged per term. Music that is lost or damaged is billed to the student's music account.

## Studio Forms

Prior to the beginning of the school year, a printed copy of the studio calendar, fees, and policies of the teacher should be sent to each studio family. Some teachers keep a signed copy on file. Arrange the calendar so that changes are not necessary in mid-year. Occasionally, the teacher is ill or other emergencies arise, but the teacher who asks parents to make schedule changes is put into the position of being obligated to accommodate their requests. Also, parents appreciate the continuity of regularly scheduled lessons.

A student registration form is recommended. Information to be completed on the registration form should include the student's name, address, phone numbers, and emergency contacts; the type and length of lesson desired; and a list of preferred lesson days and times.

Some teachers require that parents sign a "contract" for a specified period of time. Even if the teacher wouldn't want to go to court to enforce the contract, it offers some assurance of a commitment on the part of the parents. They are not likely to quit lessons within the contract period if the student loses interest, takes up a sport, or acquires the points for his festival cup. Other teachers don't have contracts because they think it makes them look as if they can't keep their students without one. Regardless, it is better to have parents at least sign something indicating that they understand all of the studio policies (which they will have received in writing). Occasionally, teachers have needed to go to small claims court when financial obligations were not met by the parents.

The teacher will find it helpful to have forms for interviewing students and for keeping records of student progress and repertoire. A progress report form can be used to keep parents updated. Forms for sequencing computer exercises are essential.

Spreadsheets can help the studio teacher with financial recordkeeping, making tax preparation much easier.

## Attracting Students

Once a teacher is established, new students are usually acquired through referrals from other teachers and families of current students. Occasionally, one satisfied parent can be a boon to business, as in the case of one highly personable teacher whose enrollment skyrocketed when the parent of a student began recommending her to all of her friends. Most new teachers have to build their clientele one student and one family at a time. Social contacts are important in building the studio business. Being active in the community (by being involved in groups such as religious organizations, choral societies, and community theater; accompanying school and church groups; and doing volunteer work) is a way for the teacher to become known. School music teachers, college music departments, and music stores are often asked for teacher recommendations. The new teacher should become acquainted with these people.

Join the local music teachers associations. Most likely, your contact information will be in a booklet and readily accessible for the members who might refer prospective students to you. Sometimes, a mentor from the group will assist new members in negotiating the intricacies of entering students in the group's auditions and contests.

A teacher should always carry a supply of business cards. They might be useful at the least probable times, such as trips to the laundromat or the grocery store. The business cards should include information about the type of instruction offered and the education of the teacher. List phone numbers, e-mail address, and website, if the studio has one. The teacher might want to give the studio a catchy, but not corny, name.

The new teacher can contact the reporter who writes the business column in the local newspaper. New businesses are periodically mentioned in such columns, and this can be free and effective publicity. Be certain to provide the reporter information, in writing, about your background and the services you offer.

Giving a recital is another way to publicize your studio. Be certain to meet the deadline for the calendar of events in the local newspaper. Also, the reporter who writes about the local arts scene for the newspaper might give you a write-up if you contact him. Again, it is best to provide the information in writing rather than solely over the telephone. In addition, student recitals can sometimes be listed in a newspaper's calendar of events.

Some schools, particularly private and parochial schools, welcome the piano teacher to teach lessons on the campus during school hours, releasing students from class to attend lessons. There are some inherent problems with this situation. The piano teacher may be limited to teaching 30-minute private lessons. School assemblies, field trips, and school holidays make it difficult to keep a consistent schedule. A classroom activity or test may have to be accommodated. Also, the school instrument may be less than ideal. This set-up may be worth considering, though.

Daytime lesson slots can sometimes be filled by students who are homeschooled. Speaking at a meeting of a local homeschooling association is a way to connect with that community.

If a teacher is offering preschool classes or instruction for adults, placing flyers (with permission, of course) on the bulletin boards of preschools and senior citizen centers can be effective. Some preschools might even hire a teacher to come into the school and teach music.

It may be possible to rent space at a senior center and provide electronic keyboard instruction. The students can bring their own keyboards, or the teacher can provide them.

Conventional methods of advertising, such as classified newspaper ads and a listing in the yellow pages of the telephone directory, are still valid ways to attract students.

Music teacher organizations often have online directories of their members. The teachers of students who are moving often check these directories to assist the family in finding a qualified teacher in their new geographical area.

A website is a very effective way to attract students. You want to be near the top of the list when someone does a web search for piano lessons in your area. Enlist the help of a friend or student who is website savvy to help you get your website higher on a search engine list. Editing your site frequently will both keep it current and help it appear higher on the list. Try to get your website's link on other websites to draw traffic.

## The Initial Contact

Parents of prospective students will contact the teacher via phone or e-mail. First impressions do make a difference. Be as professional as possible. You are being assessed from the get-go. If a message is left, return the communication promptly. Avoid calling when you are likely to be interrupted or there is background noise in your environment.

Use the initial phone call for screening both the beginning and the transfer student. Ask how the parent or prospective adult student got your name. You'll want to thank the person who recommended you.

There is no need to waste the teacher's and student's time with an interview if you know that you don't want this student. Have other teachers' names and phone numbers readily accessible in case you determine this is not a good match. Sometimes, it is a simple matter such as the age at which you accept students. Or, a father may insist that he wants two of his children to share a lesson because one is in sports and might miss a lesson. If that is not acceptable to you, tell him up front. He will probably go elsewhere, which is fine.

In the case of a more advanced transfer student, find out what his pianistic goals are. They may or may not match your expectations and expertise. If his goal is to play piano bar and you are still trying to find time to go through that jazz method book you picked up at a conference three years ago, give him the name of a teacher who will be able to guide him.

What is very tricky is when, in the course of the phone conversation, you discover that the student has been studying with a teacher whose students you had previously accepted into the studio. You have made a vow to yourself that you will never take another student from that studio. It is easier to get out of this situation if you ask the name of the previous teacher early in the conversation, before you have mentioned possible lesson times, etc. Some teachers like to have a "balance" of ages and advancement in their studios. Perhaps you can use this as an excuse to get out of the situation. If it has been a few years since you had one of that teacher's students, you might have forgotten how difficult it was and you take on this student, only to regret it later.

Be certain to ask about the prospective student's piano. Don't assume that there is a piano in the home or that the piano is an acoustic piano. Often, parents of beginning students do not want to invest in an acoustic piano and instead purchase keyboards. Some teachers will refuse to take a student who does not have an acoustic piano. The new piano teacher may not be able to be that discriminate. The teacher should ask questions about the keyboard. Some are very good and have touch sensitivity. Keyboards that are really just toys are still sold, however. When in doubt, ask the prospective student to bring the keyboard to the interview.

## The Interview: The Beginning Student

Always interview a prospective student before commencing lessons, even if it is a child who is a sibling of a current student. The purpose of the interview is to assess the child's musical ability, interest, and previous training, if any, and to explain policies and expectations to the child and parent(s). Try to make the child feel comfortable by asking him or her some questions that can be answered easily, such as address, phone number, parents' names, etc. Ask the child what books he likes to read and what is his favorite subject in school. Find out in what extracurricular activities the child participates and the time they take. Ask if other family members play any musical instruments. If the child is hesitant when asked about whether he or she wants to take piano lessons, it might indicate only a reluctance to make a commitment to something unknown, not a negative response. A quick musical assessment can include clapbacks, playbacks, and pitch matching in the child's vocal range. You could teach the beginning student a short rote piece. Tell the child and parent(s) your expectations regarding practicing and parental involvement. Demonstrate what the child can realistically be able to do after nine months of instruction and consistent practice.

Give the child and parent(s) a brief demonstration of any electronic equipment in the studio. If you have a computer, set up a game that the child can do easily. While the child is playing the game, you can talk to the parent(s) about whether or not you think the child is ready for lessons, and why. If you have determined the child is ready, provide the parent(s) with a copy of the studio brochure or other printed materials that include the studio calendar, policies, and fees. Give the parent(s) a registration form to return to you should the child and his parents decide to begin lessons. Often the parents want to sign on immediately, but it is better to insist that they go home and talk it over and let you know their decision within a few days.

If the student will be practicing on a keyboard, be certain that the parents know your expectations about how long that will be a suitable instrument, and when they will be expected to purchase an acoustic piano and why.

# Interviewing a Transfer Student

Interviewing a transfer student is similar to interviewing a beginning student. Ask the student to bring to the interview the most recent books and sheet music studied. Tell him that you would like to hear him play a piece or part of a piece at the interview. Let him know that the piece doesn't need to be memorized, and you don't expect it to be polished. A recent recital or contest piece would be fine. The student should also bring the past year's assignment book and any documentation he might have, such a list of repertoire and technical exercises. Unfortunately, few students will have been given that list by the previous teacher. On the phone, inquire about the method books that the student used or is still using. That information alone can sometimes reveal a lot about the quality of the student's previous instruction.

The goal of the interview is to determine skill assessment and whether or not the student and teacher can work together. It is important that the student not be embarrassed, nor the previous teacher(s) disparaged. At first, try to make the student comfortable by chatting with him about his interests and activities. Ask to hear the piece or pieces he has brought to play. Say something positive about the performance. Ask the student if he has a technical routine and, if so, to demonstrate some of it. Select some sight reading that should be easy for the student. Have him play a few blocked chords with syncopated pedal, if his prepared piece had none. Do some easy clapbacks and playbacks.

Inquire about practice habits. Ask him how he learns a new piece. If he leaves out steps that your students are expected to do, ask him specifically if he does those. The idea of counting out loud is often a shock for transfer students. Before you harshly judge the previous teacher(s), remember that students, even your own, don't always do what they are told to do.

Ask the reason for the transfer. Students should have severed all professional ties with the previous teacher. You don't want even the appearance of impropriety. Unfortunately, this is easier said than done. Most parents want to connect with a new teacher before they tell the current teacher their child will not be returning. They are afraid that they will not find a new teacher. The new teacher needs to decide in advance, before the phone call, how he or she will handle these situations. Some teachers will not interview a prospective transfer student who has not officially quit; others will. Regardless, before the transfer student's first lesson with the new teacher, this teacher must be certain that the parents have notified the previous teacher and that there are no unmet financial obligations to the old teacher.

One of the most difficult aspects of accepting a transfer student is the expectation from the student and his parents that the new teacher will pick up exactly where the previous one left off. Often, there is an indication at the interview that the student is playing music beyond his technical and musical abilities. There may be obvious gaps in his training. He could have poor technical and practice habits. During the interview, explain that with every transfer student, "review" is necessary, and that it is better to start with music that is easier than previously learned music and to work up from there. Students and parents do not like the idea of "going back." Also, be clear about your expectations of how much and how to practice.

Parents interpret the "levels" of method books very literally. For a student who needs to be "put back" a little, choosing a different but easier method book with the same or an even higher "level" number is one strategy. Another is to choose solos that sound more difficult than they really are.

Newly educated teachers, especially, enthusiastically want to teach students everything they know. The transfer student can become overwhelmed if his new teacher presents too many concepts or expects too many changes at once. It is better to be selective and systematic when addressing a transfer student's musical problems. You have to be careful to nurture the student's love of music and the piano and not squelch it. Be supportive of his efforts.

There are transfer students who have been well-trained and who are highly motivated to learn. Some teachers prefer working with students who can already play and welcome the opportunity to take a transfer student.

A new teacher will probably accept most of the students interviewed into his or her studio. Besides receiving income, the teacher will gain experience working with all types of students with many different musical backgrounds. When the teacher is established, he or she may be more selective about the students who are accepted into the studio, particularly transfer students. Some transfer students can have seemingly insurmountable poor technical and practice habits. Some teachers welcome the challenge of the transfer student. Others avoid frustration for themselves and the students by recommending the parents contact another teacher. This has to be done tactfully, of course.

Interviewing all prospective students is necessary. There is no other way to determine the materials to be used with the student and whether what is hoped will be a long-term relationship is likely to work out. The parents are investing a significant amount of money. The teacher is investing time and energy in this student. The student, teacher, and parents must all be comfortable with the arrangement before lessons begin.

## The Adult Student

Teaching the adult student requires the teacher to tailor the curriculum specifically to the individual student. There are many method books available for teaching the adult beginner. Adults are usually very specific about what they want out of their lessons. Often, they bring music they wish to learn. An interview will determine if the teacher can meet the needs of a particular adult student.

Recreational Music Making (RMM) programs are very popular. Whether in a private lesson or in a group setting, the goal is a student-centered, stress-free, supportive environment for personal musical expression rather than superior performance. The social, psychological, and physical benefits of learning to play a musical instrument are emphasized. Personal satisfaction and enjoyment are important.

Most studio teachers of adult students have already incorporated the philosophy of Recreational Music Making into their own teaching. Using the term in studio brochures and on a website can be a good marketing tool. Offering group Recreational Music Making classes can tap into the growing market of baby boomer retirees. Classes can be given in locations such as churches, senior centers, retirement communities, and music stores.

The latest information about Recreational Music Making is available online.

## Scheduling Lessons

The prospective teacher must be realistic about the number of hours a week he or she can teach. If the teacher is to have time to sleep, eat, exercise, run errands, do household and personal chores, keep up practicing, and plan lessons, 30 contact hours a week of one-on-one instruction would seem to be the maximum. Group instruction requires more teacher preparation and the expenditure of more energy. Fewer hours should be scheduled.

For the studio teacher with school-age children, one of the most difficult aspects of teaching is the time of day most of the lessons will need to be given, which is after school. The teacher may not be able to drive his or her children to their own lessons and after-school activities. The teacher may miss sporting events and school programs. Dinner may be a rush. There may not be time after dinner to help with homework and to catch up on the day's activities and the children's lives. The piano may be in use when the piano teacher's children need to practice. Sometimes, both parents are piano teachers.

The most obvious solution is for the teacher to teach fewer hours after school. Instead, the teacher might receive training to start a preschool program, although it may need to be taught on the premises of a daycare center or preschool. Renting a church is another option. There are preschool curricula and materials available to teachers who take workshops offered around the United States. Some of the preschool programs offer classes for infants as young as six months. Preschool education is very popular, especially in more affluent areas. Teaching these music classes can be very lucrative and can later provide a pool of good students for the private studio.

With the increased popularity of homeschooling, homeschooled students can be another source of daytime income. Sometimes, the parents of homeschoolers find it difficult to pay the lesson fees of qualified teachers because it is usually a one-income household. Group lessons with these students can alleviate that problem.

Teaching adults who are able to come to lessons during the day, privately or in groups, can offset the loss of after-school teaching hours. If the teacher has the facilities, offering group lessons to children can provide more income per hour than does private instruction.

Carpooling and having family members who are willing and able to assist with household chores can help, also. It is important to have a life partner who understands what a piano teaching career entails and who is supportive of that choice.

Another common scheduling problem is the "make-up lesson." Teachers must have a written policy about make-up lessons. In spite of the best scheduling efforts, conflicts arise. Students become ill. Many travel, even during the school year. Throughout the year, there are after-school meetings, concerts, and programs. Almost every school-age student, from the youngest to the oldest, is involved in organized sports that consume many hours a week in required practices and games. The piano teacher is expected to accommodate the sports schedule. Make-up lesson policies vary from teacher to teacher. Some teachers with tight schedules give no make-up lessons. Others give make-ups only for reasons of illness or emergency. Some teachers limit the number of make-up lessons a student is allowed. Some set aside a time each week for make-ups or have a "make-up day" periodically. Others encourage their students to switch lessons with another student when there is a scheduling conflict. There is a delicate balance between the teacher's wanting to keep the clients happy and the teacher's need to guard his or her own valuable time. It is important that the teacher have a policy, that the parents have a printed copy of that policy, and that the policy is applied equitably to all students.

## Teacher-Parent Communication

The teacher should encourage the parents to contact the teacher anytime there is a concern. Students tend to be more open with their parents than they are with their teachers, and the teacher may not be aware that there is a problem. The teacher should inform the parents as to the best time to call.

Teachers can remind parents and students about recitals, holidays, deadlines, etc., via e-mail, a website, or regular mail.

The teacher can communicate weekly with the parents by having a parent sign a practice record in the student's assignment book. The parent is aware of how much the child has practiced or says she has practiced. The teacher can also write brief notes every week, such as, "Melissa's hand position has improved. She should check it before she begins every piece. Knuckles should be up, joints firm." If the parent drives the child to the lessons or picks her up, the teacher can request that the parent come into the studio every week for a few minutes so that the teacher can speak briefly with the parent or demonstrate a concept. This is especially important with beginning students.

Parents should be encouraged to attend lessons, especially in the beginning stages of instruction. Some teachers require parents to attend lessons. However, some children function better without a parent at the lesson. Also, the teacher has to be careful not to get sidetracked and become "chatty" with the parent during the lesson.

Of course, telephone and e-mail are other ways to communicate with parents. The most common problem is practicing—specifically, the lack of it. The teacher simply has to pick up the phone and say, "Jeremy has not been prepared for his lessons the past three weeks. Is there something we can do to remedy this situation?" It could be that Jeremy's grandfather from Germany has been visiting, and Jeremy didn't tell his piano teacher that fact.

The teacher will want to send the parents a more formal assessment of progress at the end of every term, or at least at the end of the school year. This assessment should include a list of materials used, repertoire learned, and concepts mastered or introduced. Most of the comments should be positive, but suggestions should be made for improvement. This also provides a record for the student to take to his next teacher, if the student should change teachers. Some teachers discuss the year's study at an end-of-the-year "conference lesson."

## The Challenges of Teaching

The two most common frustrations studio teachers express are students' not practicing and the domination of organized sports in the lives of school-age students. Often, there is a correlation between the two.

Students are expected to do so much more academically and at a younger age than in the past. Even early elementary students have daily homework. High school students take advanced placement courses and perform community service, in addition to participating in extracurricular activities. Every activity, including piano lessons, is weighed for its importance in building the college resume. There are many demands on the student's time.

Trying to schedule a recital, let alone lessons, can be difficult. Sunday afternoons are no longer free from games or tutoring sessions. If a teacher scheduled a recital on a Saturday at midnight, undoubtedly someone would be at a "lock-in" and would not be able to come.

There comes a time in almost every piano teacher's professional life when she has to decide what to do when a student is consistently not practicing. After admonishments and possibly probation, some teachers will "fire" a non-practicing student. Other teachers feel that when the student is at the lesson, he is learning something, and so they let the student continue lessons until he or his parents quit them. Parents usually think it is a waste of money when a child doesn't practice. However, the parent is paying for the teacher's time, not the child's practice time. In deciding what to do about the non-practicing student, the teacher has to consider her own tolerance level and her professional satisfaction and reputation. It may not be worth keeping a student who doesn't practice. It is important to part amicably with a student and his family. A published practice policy that includes the consequences of noncompliance will help to prevent hard feelings and might even prevent the problem in the first place.

Some students are able to juggle the demands of school, sports, and music lessons even through high school. For this to happen, however, the piano teacher has to be flexible in scheduling lessons. Some teachers will accommodate students by teaching at odd times and even allowing students to "go on leave" during a particular sport's season.

Today's school-age students are smart, confident, independent, and seemingly fearless. Older teachers remember that they would have never dared to go to their piano lesson unprepared, much less comment on the teacher's hair or attire. It is important to remember that the student is not being impertinent. Her behavior is the norm for her generation. Maintain a sense of humor and be quietly amused when at 5:31 she says, "We only pay you until 5:30."

# Professional Growth

The independent piano teacher needs to plan for his (or her) own professional growth, just as he plans for the musical development of his students. Setting aside time for reading journals, utilizing the Internet, practicing, attending workshops and seminars, and being active in music teacher associations will contribute to the professional success and personal satisfaction of the independent piano teacher.

# Recommended Reading

Baker-Jordan, Martha. *Practical Piano Pedagogy*. Van Nuys, CA: Alfred Publishing Company, Inc., 2005.

Bastien, James. *How to Teach Piano Successfully*. San Diego, CA: Neil A. Kjos Music Company, 1988.

Klingenstein, Beth Gigante. *The Independent Piano Teacher's Studio Handbook*. Milwaukee, WI: Hal Leonard Corporation, 2008.

Twenge, Jean M. *Generation Me*. New York, NY: Free Press, 2007.

Uszler, Marienne; Gordon, Stewart; and Smith, Scott McBride. *The Well-Tempered Keyboard Teacher*. New York, NY: Schirmer Books, 2000.

# CHAPTER 3

## Some Whys, Hows, and Whats of Preschool Piano

### Ann Collins

Years ago preschool piano lessons or classes were offered in very few studios. Educators in general were not nearly so aware of the learning capabilities of three, four and five-year-olds and piano teachers had no idea of how to begin teaching piano to someone who could not read instructions; did not know the alphabet; could not understand how to add and divide beats; and found it difficult to sit still on a piano bench for more than five minutes. Today many teachers have discovered the joys and income benefits of offering piano to preschoolers. There are many approaches to such teaching and piano teachers are continually experimenting to discover the teaching techniques that are most successful with this age level. It is very likely that in the next few years, the "average-age beginner" will be four instead of seven. Are we ready to accept this challenge?

## Why Teach Preschool Piano?

If you are considering starting a preschool piano program, you likely have asked yourself questions such as: if I have to learn new teaching techniques and find new materials, wouldn't it be just as well to wait until the child is seven? Will I need lots of special equipment and teaching aids, and can I fit these into my budget? Let's begin by examining the benefits of preschool piano teaching from both the standpoint of the student and of the teacher.

1. Many children of four and five have a high interest peak in learning new things, including piano, and may have diminished desire at seven when a large variety of other activities make demands on their time and attention.

2.  Parents are becoming more and more aware of the benefits of providing intellectual and aesthetic stimulation during the formative years of preschool and generally show great interest in starting the child in piano. Most parents of bright, active preschoolers are looking for constructive channels for this curiosity and energy.

3.  Any level of piano study is more successful with active parent support and participation on a daily basis, and parents of preschoolers expect to be involved in the learning process by supervising daily practice more than do parents of school-aged children whose training is often felt to be in the hands of the teachers.

4.  The beginning stages of piano can be frustrating to the older student who can understand at a level far beyond his physical development. Preschoolers are used to trying, failing, trying again and again until they get it right. It hasn't been long since they learned to walk and talk and they don't expect themselves to be perfect or to do it right the first time. Practicing is fun, as repetition of action is natural to most preschoolers. Isn't it amazing how many times they want the same bedtime story read to them night after night? Show a preschooler a new thing to do and just try to keep him from doing it over and over and over! Why not get the daily practice habit started early?

5.  After the first excitement of piano study wears off and the student settles into a routine of gradual development, the older student begins to realize that it is going to take many years to reach the level of playing that satisfies him. By the time a student who started at four is eight or nine, he can play a level of literature that really keeps his interest. In other words, the worst of the hurdles are over and he is ready for really interesting and exciting music.

6.  Although extensive research has not been done, there are many indications that preschool piano experiences are of great benefit to the nonmusical development of the child. Learning to listen carefully and critically is important in many areas of learning, and since music occurs in sound, aural sensitivity is greatly enhanced. Preschool piano study, if properly approached, helps bring the physical development of children from large movements to finer and finer small motor skills. Learning left from right is easy when related to low and high on the keyboard. Thinking the alphabet forwards and backwards in preparation for grand staff reading is also good mental practice. The list can go on and on.

7.  Students who start piano study early seem to, upon reaching elementary level, play with greater physical ease; have more secure

rhythmic skills; are far superior listeners to their own playing and the performance of others; have few qualms about public performance; and are better readers than those who have started at seven or eight.

8.  When the teacher would like to add students, and thus income to the studio, the preschool classes are an easy addition. They do not have to be scheduled after school hours and can also be offered as special programs in nursery schools and day-care centers for working parents who cannot bring them to the studio during the day.

9.  The continual curiosity, inexhaustive energies and exuberant enthusiasm of preschoolers are a shot of adrenaline to the teacher who can become weary of pseudo-sophisticated and less than enthusiastic older students. For most teachers, the preschool piano classes become the brightest spot of the teaching week.

## How Can I Get Started?

If preschool piano is new to your studio and new to your community, people need to find out about the program. If preschool piano teaching is new and, frankly, a little frightening to the teacher, some guidelines may be of help and interest.

1.  Recruit a group of four, four- or five-year-olds who are children of your friends and neighbors. Many young mothers have started preschool piano teaching because they wanted to offer the experience to their own children. When teaching your own child, it usually helps to have the child be one member of a small group so that you can assume the role of "teacher" rather than "parent". Preschool piano is usually more successful in a small group than a one-to-one setting as the children learn from watching each other and a group requires the necessary repetition of activity. After all, everyone must have "a turn". Since four-year-olds cannot be expected to spend thirty minutes sitting at the piano, much of the learning occurs through a wide variety of activities that adapt well to group teaching.

2.  Ask the parents to bring the child for an interview before definitely accepting the child as a student. Not all children have the at-home training and maturity to follow instructions, work effectively in a group and pay attention to the teacher. An undisciplined, unruly child can tax your patience to the breaking point and spoil the learning environment for the other children. This can be quickly determined in an interview and the interview will also give you an opportunity to learn more about the child's background of experiences. Some of the things you may want to determine from the interview include:

a. Does the child know his full name, address, telephone number, age and birthdate, etc.? This will indicate how much the parent has worked with the child at home which could be a preview of future support.

b. Has the child been involved in any structured learning environments such as nursery school, Sunday school, Y-Tots, etc.? This is not to mean that you should not accept a child who has not, but will be an indicator of what you might expect of the child in piano class.

c. Have the child sing some songs for you to determine his developmental stage of singing. Does he match any pitches and which ones? Is he in a limited-range stage or a shape-approximation stage or has he had lots of singing experience and is able to sing complete songs on pitch? Because many singing activities will likely be a part of your preschool curriculum, you will be interested in the child's singing development so that you may gear beginning experiences accordingly.

d. Teach the child some basic keyboard geography such as high and low or up and down to see if he pays attention and can follow instructions.

e. Tap rhythm patterns for the child to repeat and observe his ability to assimilate, retain and repeat rhythms. Ask the child to tap or walk to a steady beat as you play the piano to determine his large motor skill development and sensitivity to beat.

f. Hold up cards with each letter of the musical alphabet for the child to identify. Many fours and even some threes have already learned some alphabet letters. Ask the child to place the alphabet cards in order. Ask him to close his eyes while you remove one card and see if he can discover which letter is missing. Not knowing the music alphabet letters is certainly no reason to not accept the child, but you should know if this skill needs to be taught or has already been mastered.

g. Ask the child to draw various alphabet letters and to write his name. The size and regularity of the letters printed and the alignment of those letters in his name are good indicators of the small motor development of the child.

h. Ask the child if he has a piano at his house and if he does, have him play for you what he plays when he goes to the piano. Be sure he feels comfortable playing for you and that you enthusiastically accept "his music".

# SING and PLAY

## SING AND PLAY DEVELOPMENT ASSESSMENT PROFILE

Date _____

NAME (Check boxes if child supplied information) ☐

ADDRESS ☐

MOTHER ☐ _____ PHONE _____

FATHER ☐ _____ PHONE _____

AGE ☐ _____ BIRTHDATE _____

SCHOOL EXPERIENCE _____

WHAT TYPE OF PIANO _____

MUSICAL BACKGROUND OF PARENTS _____

GENERAL COMMENTS _____

PLACEMENT

| | Excellent | Average | Hesitant |
|---|---|---|---|
| **KEYBOARD RESPONSE** | | | |
| White keys and black keys | | | |
| Twos and threes | | | |
| High and low | | | |
| Up and down | | | |
| Any "repertoire" | | | |
| **SINGING RESPONSE** | | | |
| Singing with adult | | | |
| Singing alone | | | |
| Sense of pitch | | | |
| Sense of rhythm | | | |
| Pitch-matching range | | | |
| **RHYTHMIC RESPONSE** | | | |
| Tapping to a beat | | | |
| Walking to a beat | | | |
| Echo tapping | | | |
| Echo playing | | | |
| Finding body parts | | | |
| General coordination | | | |

**LETTER AND NUMBER RECOGNITION**
(Circle correct response)
C   A   F   B   G   E   D
4   2   1   3   5

**WRITING SKILLS**
On the back of this sheet, ask the child to draw letters and numbers and to "write" his name.

3.  If you have recruited more students than comfortably fit into one group or if, after testing, the level seems to be quite disparate, you may want to consider grouping the children into two groups. The most successful groupings tend to be a) those who already know the alphabet and can write their name, and b) those who have yet to learn these skills. Also consider that those children who have highly developed singing skills will likely progress faster and that girls of the same age are generally more highly developed in skills than are boys. Do not use calendar age as the principal factor in grouping but rather look at all the results of the interview and group developmentally rather than by birthdate.

4.  If you wish to advertise for more children than you have contact with, keep in mind that younger siblings of your present students are potential students; advertise through posters in nursery schools, Sunday schools, grocery stores, community centers, etc. Once you have at least one preschool class started, invite interested parents to come visit and observe the class; see if your local newspaper will do an article and pictures of your class (after all, this is new to the community and of newsworthy interest); and rely on word-of-mouth advertising through parent groups, etc.

## What Are the Physical Needs?

1.  Since the students will not spend their class time sitting at the piano, some amount of moving-around space is necessary, but a very large room sometimes invites more movement than you really want to have occur. Most living rooms and many studios have sufficient space for children to sit in a circle on the floor or at a small child-sized table.

2.  One piano is adequate for a group of four as they can stand side-by-side and play groups of two black keys; find a D, etc. or, since the pieces should be quite short, they can also make a line at the piano and take turns. Larger classes work well with two pianos or in a multi-piano electronic laboratory. It is often wise to remove the piano bench and have the preschooler stand at the piano since getting off and on the bench can be time-consuming. If the child sits on the bench, a footstool is needed to prevent dangling feet and uncomfortable weight balance.

3.  Other equipment that you may find especially beneficial for preschool teaching includes:

  a.  Alphabet flashcards—a set for each child
  b.  Large-sized flashcards showing signs and symbols of music
  c.  Rhythm charts and rhythm instruments
  d.  Record player and/or cassette player
  e.  Crayons
  f.  Keyboard paper for coloring all the C's, etc.
  g.  Large-sized staff paper
  h.  Flannel boards, magnetic boards or velcro boards
  i.  A large vinyl floor keyboard or floor grandstaff

## What Kind of Materials Are Appropriate?

Most method books designed for average-age beginners are not appropriate for four and five-year-olds. The pacing is usually too fast and the visual presentation too complex for preschoolers to follow. In choosing materials, the following criteria should be used:

1.  Are the physical demands appropriate to preschoolers? Using all five fingers at the beginning, playing triads, or early requirements for independent hands may make demands beyond the child's physical development.

2.  Does the book give sufficient practice in "experiencing" music and learning the keyboard before introducing staff reading?

3.  Is the visual presentation large and uncluttered? Preschoolers have difficulty in learning to read from left to right and in keeping their eyes focused on the proper place on the page. Too much clutter of symbols that are not absolutely necessary for the immediate task can be distracting. The full color illustrations are attractive to parents and teachers, yet may be visually distractive to the preschooler.

4.  Is the introduction to staff reading gradual, with sufficient time to experience and practice one group of notes before adding new ones? Is the size of the staff large enough and clear enough for the child to differentiate line notes and space notes?

5.  Does the music have words so that the child can sing with his playing? Singing helps keep the flow of music going and prevents undue rhythmic hesitation.

6.  Are the pieces short with repeated word phrases and repeated melodic phrases so that they can be quickly assimilated?

7.  Are suggestions for activities in writing, ear-training, rhythmic movement included?

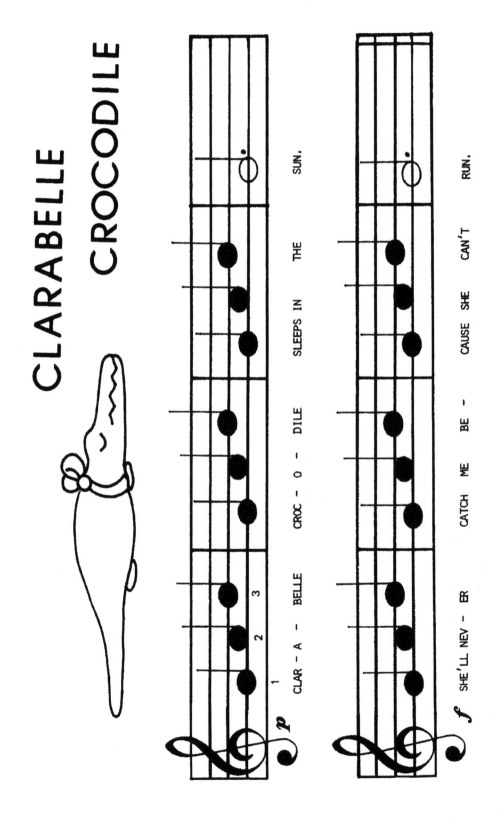

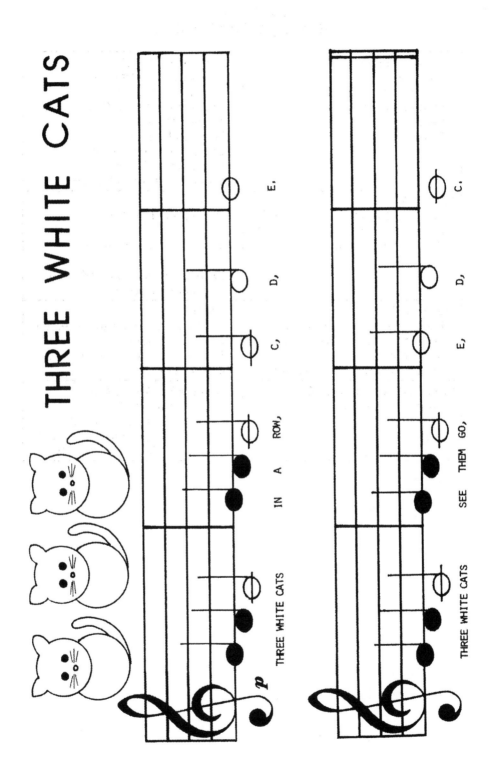

## CONCEPT BLOCK 8
### (Reading G-Clef F and G)

| | |
|---|---|
| **SING AND PLAY**<br>Climbing<br>Line-Space-Line<br>Freddie the Frog<br>Cars<br>Eloise | **WRITE AND LISTEN**<br>Steps Up on the Staff<br>Finger Numbers<br>Steps Up or Steps Down?<br>Naming Notes<br>Lines and Spaces<br>Steps Down on the Staff<br>Steps Up or Down?<br>White Key Names Review |
| **READING**<br>Play and Say Cards: 𝄞 F and G<br>Pattern Cards:         8A, 8B<br>Steps Up and Down | **PLAYING**<br>Closed hand position<br><br>Technic: Finger Numbers<br><br>Exercise: Fingers 1 and 5 together<br>(see parents pages) |
| **LISTENING**<br>Playbacks on C, D, E, F, G<br>Find the half note (rhythmic dictation)<br>Brother John: Continue listening | **MOVING**<br>Rhythm band: Quarter notes and dotted half notes<br>Rhythm sticks jive to recording in 4/4 meter. |
| **SUPPLEMENTARY SONGS**<br>Wiggle (finger numbers) | **SUPPLEMENTARY GAMES**<br>Take a Trip: Staff<br>Mail Man: Play and Say Cards<br>                  Sightreading Pattern<br>                  Cards 7A and 7B |

## STEPS UP OR DOWN?

Listen to the teacher play C D E going up or E D C going down.
Put an X on the box that looks like what you hear.

1.

or

2.

or

3.

or

Block 8

## SKIPPING UP IN THE ALPHABET

Draw a circle around every other letter in the alphabet.

1.

Ⓐ B Ⓒ D E F G A B C D E F G A B

Fill in the alphabet skips.

2.

__ B __ D __ F __ A __ C __ E __ G __ B

Write the Alphabet in skips. Whisper the name of the letter that you skip over.

3.

<u>A</u> <u>C</u> __ __ __ __ __ __ __

**Block 12**

8. Are suggestions for at-home practice or other means of parent communication included?

**CONCEPT BLOCK 12: PARENTS**

**FLASHCARDS:**

**PRACTICE POINTERS:**

- Is this an F-clef song for the left hand or a G-clef song for the right hand?
- What is the first note?
- Which finger goes on the first note?
- Does the melody go up or down from the first note?
- Do you see any other measures just like the first measure?
- Should we play this song piano or forte? Is there only one dynamic marking?
- Get your hand all set to play and count. 1 – 1 – ready – play!

**PATTERN CARDS: 12A and 12B**

**ALPHABET ANTICS:**

- Write the music alphabet several times on one line (A B C D E F G A B C D E F G A B C D E F G).
- Draw a circle around A, then skip the B and draw another circle around the C, and then the E and G, etc.
- Say all the letters that you circled.
- Try to say the music alphabet in skips without looking at the circles.

**RHYTHM RHYMES:**

- Teach the rhyme to the child by rote (not designed for him to read).
- Tap the rhythms of the rhyme, and then do the motions, moving rhythmically.

9. Is the pacing of new concept presentation appropriate to preschoolers? Is there sufficient review of skills and concepts learned and adequate preparation for new ideas?

# What Are the Teacher Qualifications?

What kind of preparation for preschool piano teaching does the teacher need? A pedagogy course at the college or university level is the most desirable preparation, but not always available in all areas of the country. Short-term workshops or extension courses are more accessible and opportunities to watch experienced preschool teachers in action are invaluable. The most difficult task facing the beginning preschool piano teacher is in making crystal-clear presentations that do not assume understandings and abilities beyond the child's developmental level. Although there is not a wealth of pedagogical material about preschool piano teaching, there is a wealth of information about preschool teaching techniques in other subject areas and the creative teacher will be able to apply this knowledge to piano teaching.

Careful lesson planning is more crucial with preschoolers than with older students. Activities need to be varied and the teacher must move quickly from one activity to the next in order to prevent little minds and bodies from wandering or creating their own activity. A good forty-five to sixty minute class plan would include:

1. Songs to sing and play
2. Motor-rhythmic activities
3. Ear-training and listening activities
4. Reading flashcard drills and games
5. Writing or drawing activities
6. Ensemble playing or clapping
7. Short technique exercises
8. Floor keyboard or grandstaff games

Liking and understanding the preschool child and being able to communicate with this age level is really more important than a high level of piano performance proficiency. However, the teacher should have experienced the technical and musical demands of piano performance if he or she is to lay the proper foundation for future pianistic development.

## Suggested Materials

Collins, Ann and Clary, Linda. *Sing and Play (Books 1–3)*, Champaign, Illinois: Stipes Publishing Company, 1981, 1987.

Collins, Ann and Clary, Linda. *Write and Listen (Books 1–3)*, Champaign, Illinois: Stipes Publishing Company, 1984, 1987.

Collins, Ann and Clary, Linda. *Teachers Manual, Sing and Play*. Champaign, Illinois: Stipes Publishing Company, 1981, 1987.

Collins, Ann. *Mother Goose*. Champaign, Illinois: Stipes Publishing Company, 1984.

Collins, Ann. *Partners: Parent-Child Song Duets*. Champaign, Illinois: Stipes Publishing Company, 1984.

Collins, Ann. *Sing and Play, A Holiday*. Champaign, Illinois: Stipes Publishing Company, 1987.

Collins, Ann. *Sing and Play, Flashcards*. Champaign, Illinois: Stipes Publishing Company, 1987.

# CHAPTER 4

## Let's Start at the Very Beginning: First Lessons in the Independent Studio

### Carole Flatau

The first lesson is a memorable event in a student's life, comparable to the first day of first grade or the first day in a new school. First impressions can be hard to override. Of course, by the time the student comes in the door, you've acquired pertinent information. You know how old he is, what grade, whether there are siblings and if so, where he fits in the family lineup. You know that he has access to a piano (or a keyboard if you've agreed to it) and is eager to learn to play. The student doesn't know nearly so much about you! And that's okay. All he needs to know at this point is that you are nice, not intimidating.

Being regarded as nice shouldn't imply being very casual or nonprofessional. There are huge responsibilities that demand that we be disciplined and diligent in our planning and preparation, and structured and fair. We must be all this, and still be flexible.

Here are some teaching precepts that are the same for the first lesson or the fiftieth, whether we've taught for one month or twenty years.

1.  Have a big-picture plan. Think carefully about your teaching philosophy and your intentions for implementing it. Writing a mission statement is a good idea. Know why you're teaching what you're teaching.

2.  Have a plan for each lesson. It need not be charted out as in classroom teaching, but know the focus before the lesson. Be ready to shift gears, adapt, adjust, and sometimes even backtrack in big steps. When everything can't be covered, make note of what was skipped so it can be covered the next week.

3.  Introduce concepts carefully so you don't have to undo what you've already taught. Teachers may have to say the same thing many different ways before the student understands what is meant, but that is clarification, not retraction.

4.  Use appropriate, consistent terminology. Remember that students like to use big words and are generally capable of learning music terms early on.

5.  Beware of TMI (too much information). Don't deprive students of necessary details but don't create overload situations.

We must have overall expectations for our students and ourselves. Is expectation too strong a word? Is goal better? It seems that the real world intrudes on our expectations for our students, despite the fact that we set goals. Too often their expectation of playing piano really well requires more practice and dedication than originally realized.

A logical goal and expectation with our early-level students is to lay a strong foundation. That means that teachers are responsible for incorporating a vast range of skills and awareness along with their reading, rhythm, and technique. How can it all be accomplished? It all starts at the very beginning.

Setting our personal goals requires honesty. Being realistic about our expectations isn't always easy. Independent music teaching is a great profession. We set our own hours and decide how many days a week we'll teach. We decide whom we'll accept into our class; we decide what we'll teach and how we'll do it. We don't turn in lesson plans; we don't deal with academia politics. We set our own fees and do our own collecting and record keeping. We also pay our insurance, pay our piano tuner, and clean our studio.

Why do we do what we do? *Why* is not really the question. What does matter is whether we're teaching with conviction and pride. The rewards can be great and there are always responsibilities. We need to remember why we decided to teach. Finances can be a legitimate reason. But even if initially that was a primary reason, it should never take priority over the love of music.

We need to know our own goals and relate them to the goals of the student. We can't get obsessed with our own ego. Wanting to have a prestigious reputation in the community is fine if it doesn't mean jeopardizing the students' musical well being. Teachers must be aware of their specific capabilities and limitations, and be diligent in maintaining their skills and working toward improving their weak points.

We teach to our specialties. It's up to us to decide what they are. We adjust to the priorities of the time frame, such as a student's contest piece, accompanying project, composition submission deadline, and Christmas or holiday or special-event piece.

# The First Lesson

The following procedures can be observed regardless of the student's age, whether the student is a brand-new beginner or a transfer student. They are an outline of first lessons, developed over many years. (To eliminate the awkwardness of "he or she" wordage, in this section the student will be referred to as *he*.)

Set the scene by saying, "I'm going to pretend that you've never seen a piano." Then tell him what you want him to do.

1. Using a braced finger 3, have him begin at the lowest A, play each key and say the letter name, all the way to the top C. Small students do this most easily by standing and moving, rather than sitting and reaching.

   **Reason:**  We can't assume that students will automatically realize that there is an alphabetical order to the keys. Using the braced third finger is the first step toward a good hand shape.

2. Do it again if it seems like a good idea.

3. Together say **ABCDEFG** then **GFEDCBA.** Say it backwards several times. Then have him start at the top C (telling him if necessary that it's a C) and play and say the name of each key, down to bottom A (or until you're sure he understands the descending music alphabet). It's okay to say names with him.

   **Reason:**  The descending alphabet is a logical requisite for good reading.

4. Have him start again at lowest **A**, saying names. Stop on a higher **A** then have him slowly play **B, C, D,** saying the name of each, repeating **D** a few times.

   **Reason:**  Doing this reinforces locations and introduces the sound of a short pattern, which ends on **D**.

5. Have him find and play another **D**. If he hasn't realized it, help him notice its place between the 2 black keys. He finds all the **D**s.

   **Reason:**  **D** is a great locator key. Finding **D** and going from there makes more sense than finding specific keys by "to the left (or the bottom of) the 2 black keys or "to the right of...."

6. Have him play the **D,** then play and name the key above **D,** then the key above the **E.** Have him say the backward alphabet again, then play and name the key backward from **E,** then backward from **D,** and back to **C, B, A, G.** Repeat in different registers.

   **Reason:**  This reinforces note relationships, especially that of **A G. (F G** is not a problem.)

7.   Have him start at the top **C** and play backwards, saying names. (Say names with him.)

**Note:** Don't scoff at this little drill. It is *not* a frivolous time-taker. It doesn't take long, and it gets the student physically and mentally involved right away, and lays a foundation for keyboard geography skills.

8.   Have him close his eyes. Play a high-pitched key and ask him to play a key somewhere in that neighborhood. (Don't expect the same one!) Repeat in various registers.

> **Reason:** This will give you an immediate clue as to pitch awareness. Don't make a big issue of it. It can grow into later ear-training projects.

*Option* (in addition to, not instead of the drills he's done): Have him play numbers 1, 7 and 8 with <u>**LH**</u> braced finger 3.

9.   Your choice, RH or LH. Have him start on lowest **A**, play and say name, move and hold finger above **B** and without playing, *whisper* its name. Then have him play and name **C**, move to **D**, *whisper* its name, continuing up the keyboard in *skips*, using same procedure. *Option:* play *down* in skips, not saying names.

> **Reason:** Seeing and hearing the skips prepares for reading skips.

This is usually enough of this, and a good time to ask the student if there's anything he already knows how to play. If so, be delighted and listen to it. If not, say that you're glad because it will be so much fun to learn some songs together.

> **Reason:** How else would we know? Maybe he has a great ear for picking out tunes; maybe he's learned from a friend or family member.

10.   Have him cover his eyes while you play and sing "Hot Cross Buns." If he knows it, have him sing along. If he doesn't know it, teach him the words. Then help him play it on the three black keys. If he plays with just the braced 3, that's fine. If not, let him play however he can. That won't do any harm.  Have him find a **B** and play and sing the song, starting there. Then he can start on **E** and play the song.

> **Reason:** He will know a song to play, one that he can play all over the piano. Don't scoff. Kids think it's fun. Some will like hearing the different effects from starting on different keys. This also gets him singing, preparing him for the singing he'll be doing at his lessons. It's also a great rhythm pattern to experience (using quarters, eighths and half notes) with can't-go-wrong words, an excellent rhythm reference point for pieces he'll soon be reading.

You can justify this song segment as preparation for transposition and improvisation, as well as major and minor relationships.

11. If you've planned to incorporate a method book in the first lesson, be sure you've decided exactly how you want to merge it with what you've just taught. Know the page on which you'll start. A piano book is very exciting for the students, the proof that they are learning to play the piano! Later in this chapter, there's a section on choosing a method series.

## Assignments

It's important to be explicit with assignments. A variety of assignment books can be found on the market. Notebooks, either steno or standard 8 x 10 composition notebooks, are highly recommended. Daily assignments from this lesson would include instructions to say the music alphabet forward and backward several times, play and say names up and down at least every-other day, play and say names up and down in skips, play "Hot Cross Buns" at least three different ways. Most students can also play the C warm-up pattern, which I write in the notebook. All students are assigned "make up a song,"— whatever they like—black keys, white keys, high, low, fast, slow, loud, soft—it's their choice. If we've worked in a lesson book, they'll have an assignment for the pages we studied.

They mark their practice time (how many minutes each day) on a chart at the bottom of the notebook page. Be sure the parent or caregiver understands the practice procedure. Assignments, of course, become more specific as we go forward, with number of times to play each piece, specific warm-ups, and all the various things they are to practice. (Warm-ups are explained in the following section.)

> **Five-finger-pattern warm-ups** serve as a foundation for theory and technique. Some books refer to them as pentatonic scales. Teachers can refer to them as warm-ups, a name that lasts forever. Most students can begin them at the first or second lesson, with the pattern introduced by finger numbers, right hand, key of C.

$$\text{RH } 1 \; {}^{2}\; {}^{3}\; {}^{4}\; {}^{5}\; {}^{4}\; {}^{3}\; {}_{2}\; {}_{1} \qquad 3 \qquad {}^{5}\; 3 \qquad {}^{5}\; {}^{3}_{1} \; {}_{1}$$

Teachers can talk about and experiment with hand shape, warning against "popsicle stick" fingers. It's a judgment call about including the chord, as well as whether to play the pattern with the left hand.

The C pattern provides the basis for every major five-finger warm-up. They see that there is only one half step, always from finger 3 to 4 in the right hand. The warm-ups are a part of every early-level assignment.

When fingers are strong enough, students can use the standard warm-up pattern.

With a little guidance, students realize that their full-cadence warm-ups use every note of the scale, another valuable tool for theory and good reading. When they've become proficient (or at least comfortable) in all keys, the assignment can be "warm-ups, white-key starters" or "black-key starters." Minor warm-ups are also a good idea.

Students need not read warm-up patterns. Once learned, they're in the hands to stay.

Students are taught to chant **GBDFACEGBDFACEGBDFACE** regularly. It strengthens note identification, and prepares them for ledger lines and chord spelling. The visual *skips* translate into *3rds*, with *even-number intervals* on either side. Have them point to bottom line G on the staff, then play and say each skip **GBDFA**, middle **C** first line, **EGBDF**, ledger lines **A** and **C**.

A great tool for solidifying this process is the *Wright-Way Note Finder*. It can be found online. It's not new or high tech, but students (including adults) use it willingly, some even eagerly.

Students should do lots tapping of rhythms that occur in new pieces (not clapping), a habit that helps keep the pulse steady as rhythms get more complicated. Tapping allows each hand to "play" its part. It strengthens the reading skills; students learn to see the pitch patterns as well as the rhythms.

## Choosing Piano Methods

On today's market, there is an incredible amount of good teaching material, series that are designed to interest the student and meet the teacher's standards. They are usually divided into four major categories, based on their approach to developing reading skills: middle C, intervallic, multi-key, or an eclectic combination. The majority of recently written methods include some pre-reading non-staff pages.

The recent acquisition of *Clavier* magazine by *Keyboard Companion* attracted the attention of piano teachers across America. The Frances Clark Center for Piano Pedagogy now publishes *Clavier Companion,* a magazine that combines the strengths of both publications. The Center has assembled first-rate editors to head various departments. One of these editors, Rebecca Grooms Johnson, heads a column called *A Survey of Current Methods*. Readers can explore the on-going articles that started in the fall of 2009, available online with reviews by teachers who currently use these methods, as well as discussion of the handling of the areas of research such as reading, rhythm, technique, repertoire, and theory. Some of these methods date back to the mid-twentieth century; others are more recent.

Choosing method books is a challenge for teachers.  Today, most American methods take into account psychological principles of learning that affect sequence and organization as well as discovery. Further, they stress a unified approach to study, one which considers reading, rhythm, technique, repertoire and keyboard skills as a whole. Folk music and repertoire by competent composers for young people are used throughout a quality series.

## Deciding What to Teach

Before we can make decisions about specific materials, we must have a philosophy and know what we want to teach, how we want to teach it, and the end results we want to achieve with our students. Then we will have a basis for selecting appropriate materials to accomplish our aims. A solid elementary series will help students acquire strong basics, leading into successful musical development at the intermediate level.

### Reading

1. Is the reading approach step-by-step?
2. In the beginning, do reading experiences start with non-staff notation and proceed gradually to staff reading?
3. Do reading exercises encompass the entire range of the keyboard?
4. Are landmarks such as bass F, middle C, treble G, or others utilized?
5. Are intervals learned early in the instructional scheme?
6. Do black and white keys receive equal emphasis?
7. Does the repertoire reinforce the reading?
8. Is there adequate reading material throughout the series?
9. Are sharps and flats introduced at a logical time? Or too early?
10. Are key signatures introduced at the proper time and place?
11. Is the approach eclectic?

## Rhythm

1. Are students given progressive rhythm patterns to experience by clapping, tapping and counting?

2. How is counting note values presented? For instance, see Example 3 below.

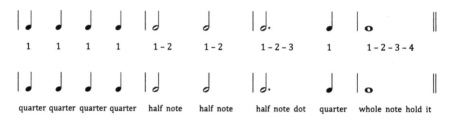

3. Are rests introduced in a clear manner related to note values?

4. Are measures and bar lines delayed until the young student grasps note and rest values?

5. How are time signatures introduced?

6. Are there supporting materials (CDs, Standard MIDI files, etc.) to enhance student's ability to play with good rhythm?

## Technique

1. Do early phases of training involve a balanced hand (starting with fingers 2 or 3)?

2. Is control of sound emphasized from the beginning?

3. Does the left hand get a good workout?

4. Are there short assignments (enabling easy checking)?

5. Do the assignments involve various registers of the keyboard?

6. Are technique studies imaginative?

7. Are two-note slurs introduced as "down-ups"?

8. Are mirror patterns utilized?

9. Do the exercises include transposition?

10. Do the exercises develop the outside of the hands? (fingers 4 and 5)

11. Is there emphasis on the hand arch throughout the series?

12. Are various touches explored? (legato, staccato, portato)

13. Is the pedal introduced early, capitalizing on the student's fascination with it?

14. Is there ample experience in 5-finger major and minor patterns prior to scale playing?

15. Does arpeggiation play an important role? (hand over hand)

16. Is there solid preparation for shifts?

17. Are chromatic figures presented for study?

18. Do the technique assignments relate to and reinforce the music studied in the lesson book?

## Musicianship

1. Does the study of musical elements require an additional theory book?

2. Are writing, notating, and basic composing an integral part of the text, and easy to check at the lesson?

3. Are students taught to identify form in compositions?

4. Do harmonization studies appear in logical sequence?

5. Do students identify and label harmonies?

6. How is ear training developed within the book?

7. Is improvisation encouraged?

8. Are musical signs taught in a systematic way? Are they reinforced through visual and written games and puzzles?

9. Are sounds from twentieth-century repertoire included?

10. Do the compositions facilitate easy memorization?

11. Are CDs and/or Standard MIDI files included? Or available separately?

## Supplementary Music

1. Does the music have appealing sounds?

2. Is the music coherent? Do the various patterns make musical sense? Is there unity in the piece as a whole? Are the elements used in an efficient way?

3. Does the structure of the piece lead to easy memorization?

4. Is the title appropriate for the piece? Does it stimulate the student's imagination?

5. Does the piece feel good under the fingers? Does it reinforce technical development?

One can hardly go wrong when considering supplementary music by fine American composers such as Dennis Alexander, Tony Caramia, Nancy Faber, Mike Kocour, Eugenie Rocherolle, Catherine Rollin, Paul Sheftel, Christos Tsitaros, Lynn Freeman Olson, Jon George, and Robert Vandall.

## Method Books

**Illustrations:** Color has become an absolute in method books, and surely can enhance the attractiveness of the pages. However, it can also be a distraction. The style of illustrations and the brightness of the color can move the books from the plus to the minus column for some students. The illustrations in a book will delight some, while other students consider them garish. It is recommended that teachers stay away from books with illustrations that interfere with focusing on the music. It's important to consider illustrations while choosing books. As keyboard editor for Warner Bros. Publications, I had worked with a revision of the entire Michael Aaron series. The original black-and-white illustrations were retained. They were top quality, and—for the most part—timeless. An excellent artist replaced some, duplicating the style of the originals. A few new ones were added, but selectively. The response from teachers was overwhelmingly positive. When there was a major revision of the Schaum series, color was added throughout the series. There were numerous planning sessions and consultations with the artist who created the illustrations, including opinions from teachers and students. The response to the addition of color and new illustrations was, as expected, overwhelmingly positive.

**Engraving:** There is a trend in the publishing industry today to use a "loose" layout, with notes spaced quite far apart. When notes are s p r e a d f a r   a p a r t , it's hard to see the relationship between them and it's even harder to see patterns. It's like reading a  l e t t e r   a t   a   t i m e   r a t h e r t h a n   a   w o r d   a t   a   t i m e . The loose engraving (apparently letting the computer be responsible for the layout) results in more pages of music, which means not only more pages in the book, but consequently more page turning. There were old editions, of course, where the layout was so tight that notes were difficult to read. Chances are, though, that most of us are still playing some of those from our own libraries. A format in-between serves us well. Fortunately, there are publishers and editors who insist on good spacing.

**Accompaniments:** Most of the newer method series include teacher accompaniments for the pieces. Many of them are excellent. They serve a legitimate purpose in providing a duet experience from the very beginning, and they encourage students to feel the pulse, count carefully, and keep a steady beat—unless, of course, the teacher allows the student to slow down the difficult parts. Teacher accompaniments provide a parent-pleasing recital performance, one that can build performance security. Two not-so-positive points are: 1) Some students are not ready for them. 2) A piece that depends on an accompaniment to sound good can take away the satisfaction of playing an unaccompanied solo piano piece.

**Forewords and Handbooks:** The writers and editors have given careful thought to the forewords of their books; take time to read them. If the publisher offers a handbook for the series, read it. Then use your own judgment. Keep in mind that handbooks serve two purposes: they explain the plan of the series, and they are promotional material.

**Publisher Mailing Lists:** They'll keep you informed about new publications as well as existing ones, and often will offer discounts to entice you to try new things. Check out their websites for information.

**Workshops at Music Stores:** At these workshops, you can meet the writers and/or their designated presenters, giving you an added touch of their philosophy of teaching and learning.

Become familiar with as many series as possible, including the old ones that still exist. The more material that you know, the better chance you have of finding the right fit for your students. Teachers can mix-and-match methods, using two different series with a student. Doing so provides reading reinforcement, specifically allowing for the transfer of learning skills, applying concepts in many ways. It also keeps teachers from getting complacent. Most teachers don't want to teach the same music to student after student. Try to give new methods a hands-on trial. It can be rewarding to find a new publication that works better than originally thought.

Some teachers do use the often-maligned Middle C approach as well as all the other approaches. Superfluous finger numbers have been removed in reprints of most of these series, and teachers always have the right to remove or change fingering in most books or teaching pieces. It's better to be less concerned about possibly allowing a dependency on finger numbers than about becoming locked into positions. The intervallic approach helps students be logically aware of intervals in all their material.

When considering method books, teachers should keep in mind:

1. Is it really the best series, or the best promoted series?

2. Approach all method books with an open mind.

3. Remember that each series presents the philosophies of one writer (or one team) and that of the publisher.

4. There is no such thing as a one-size-fits-all.

5. There is a wealth of excellent pedagogically sound, appealing material available.

6. It's up to us to choose methods that best meet our teaching philosophies.

7. We want our students to be well-rounded musicians, with music a joy in their lives. We do whatever we can to make that happen.

## Coda

Every student should be able to play something by memory at any time, from day one.

Set some immediate small goals.

Set standards high enough to inspire, but low enough to achieve.

Never let yesterday use up today.

People will forget what you said. People will forget what you did. But people will never forget how you made them feel.

# CHAPTER 5

# Naming Notes is Not Reading

## Richard Chronister

It is time for note-spellers to fade away. They foster the notion that naming notes is the way to reading competency. In fact, naming a note is the one thing we could dispense with totally. The name of a note is the one thing we do not have to know, and yet some teachers spend more time on this aspect of note reading than any other.

## What is Note Reading?

At the piano, note reading is the ability to see any note on the staff and simultaneously play its corresponding key on the keyboard. Of course, much more than this is necessary if fluent and musical reading are to result from this ability—understanding direction on the staff as it relates to direction on the keyboard; reading intervals; recognizing note patterns; reading chords as well as melodic phrases; a technic that allows body, arms, hands, and fingers to respond easily to the notation; a tactile sense of the keyboard that allows the eyes to remain on the music when necessary; an aural sense that tells the player what sounds to expect. It is the teacher's responsibility to see that all this is acquired by all their students at the proper point in their development and to see that the materials chosen for the students' home practice support, on a daily basis, the presentations made during the lesson.

## Reading is Not the Beginning of Music Study

When someone says that a child "has begun taking music lessons," it generally means that the child has begun to take lessons in which he or she is taught to *read* music for the first time. This, of course, is not the beginning of music learning. Children have many musical experiences before taking lessons, and many children play the piano before piano lessons begin. There is some question about the effect this prior experience has on learning to read. Regardless of the effect, once reading lessons have begun, it becomes the teacher's responsibility to find a way to make all students literate musicians. Teaching students to read fluently is a primary goal of piano lessons.

## Musical Experience Before Reading

An especially important question is whether or not the student is ready to learn to read music. As with any other language, it is wise to have some practical experience with music before having to deal with the abstract principles involved in reading it. A child's prior musical experience is helpful in learning to read music, provided the teacher finds a way to make use of that experience, and provided there is some connection between the child's prior musical experience and the musical experience in the piano lesson. If a child has learned to play *Chopsticks* by rote before lessons begin, for example, then the *musical* result of the pieces to be *read* in the piano lesson must, to some degree, match the musical result experienced with *Chopsticks*. Most children will not be around long enough to learn to read fluently if the result of their reading is not a satisfying experience.

## When is a Child Ready to Learn to Read?

Whatever a child's musical experience before lessons, it is doubtful that any student should ever embark on the arduous road to fluent reading until old enough to face daily practice alone at the piano. For many children, this is their first experience with the kind of aloneness that is necessary to produce progress. Parents will often agree to sit with the child each day, making sure the assignment is followed, providing some interaction that alleviates the feeling of aloneness that accompanies piano practice. This will enhance the possibilities of success, but too many parents, who begin this assistance with a real sense of responsibility, find themselves too busy to continue it. For children who cannot read the assignment and cannot work alone each day, it is better that they continue their musical experience with more singing, listening, and playing by rote. Even for the child who can read words, the responsibility of daily practice can never be left to the child alone. The failure of students to get to the piano each day is more the cause of the general failure of piano education than the poor practice that might occur once they get there. Good teaching can never overcome a lack of practice, but consistent practice has often overcome poor teaching. The skill of fluent reading develops in direct proportion to the student's adherence to a daily schedule of practice. No other failure can be corrected until the failure to practice is corrected.

There is no particular age at which a child is ready to begin to learn to read music. We must make this judgment for each individual who comes to us for lessons. Ideally, once we have made this judgment, we will find ourselves face to face with a child who has enjoyed singing and listening to music all his or her life, and who has experienced playing rote pieces such as *Chopsticks.* Our decision to begin teaching the student to read music should be based on the student possessing a maturity that includes the ability to follow directions in a lesson and to read and follow the instructions on the home assignment. Students like this are ready to learn to read music. But, just as important, are we ready to teach them to read music?

## From Rote to Note

Our new student, Fred, learned *Chopsticks* by rote long before we met him. This means someone told him and showed him what to play. We now want to teach him to learn pieces *by note,* which means that a picture on a piece of paper will tell him and show him what to play rather than another person—he will be able to tell himself what to play by looking at the picture. This idea will capture Fred's interest if the notation we put in front of him truly tells him and shows him what to do, and if the piece he reads turns out to be a worthwhile musical experience, and especially if all this happens in a short period of time.

It is always hard for advanced musicians to realize that music notation, so clear to all of us, does not speak directly to one who is seeing it for the first time. This picture does, indeed, tell *us* what to play.

This picture does not tell Fred anything the first time he sees it. Just as with a rote piece, we will have to tell him everything and show him everything about how to play this piece. Then, we will hope that he remembers what we told him. We will probably have to tell him again next week when we discover he could not remember everything we told him. And, not only this, the sound of this piece is light years away from the sound of *Chopsticks.* Consider a picture like this:

Before teaching Fred to read this picture, I teach him to play the piece by rote. This will be quick and easy since there is only one pattern, and it is repeated three times on three groups of three black keys. It is played in a steady pulse and it is all loud—just like *Chopsticks*—and can be played by Fred at a tempo to match *Chopsticks*. Using only finger 2 or fingers 2-3-4, it can be played by one hand or by two hands together an octave apart. And, like Chopsticks, it can be played as a solo or as a duet with an accompaniment like this:

In the process of playing the piece—fast and slow, loud and soft, high and low—we talk about what a piece like this could be about. After a discussion of how it sounds and feels, there are a number of possibilities, one of which could be *Hopping Up the Stairway.* This could become the title, as well as the words for each phrase.

After the fun of playing and naming the piece, I tell Fred that I want to be sure he remembers how to play it at home. I tell him that I can draw a picture of this piece that will remind him of what we did at the lesson. It helps if teachers keep in mind that music notation, for anyone, is something that reminds us of what we already know. Music notation is not something new every time we look at it. A new piece simply uses all notational elements we already know, but in an arrangement we may be seeing for the first time.

Teaching Fred to read this piece is done best by leading him, step by step, through an understanding of what this picture can tell him and show him at home. Instead of showing Fred the whole picture, I draw the picture as I talk about it—much like you would draw any picture for a child.

I tell Fred that first comes what musicians call a *clef,* the part of music notation that tells us what keys to play on the keyboard. The piano teacher is required here to accept the fact that *anything* that tells us what keys to play may rightly be called a clef. As I begin to draw the clef—the picture of three black keys—I ask Fred to find all the groups of three blacks on the keyboard, and I ask him if these were the keys we played in *Hopping Up the Stairway.*

Then I ask him if he thinks this picture can remind him at home that we played on the groups of three black keys. He's apt to say, at this point, that he won't forget that! I tell him, "Just in case."

As I complete the clef by drawing the arrow pointing to the first black key, I ask him if this was the first key we played in each group?

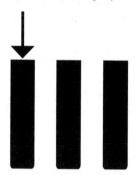

Then, he finds that black key all over the keyboard. So far, the picture on the page is something that is capable of telling Fred what to do, as well as remind him what to do at home if he happens to forget. There is nothing for Fred to memorize, nothing he has to remember when he gets home. The picture will remember for him.

Then, as I draw five lines, I tell Fred that musicians call this a *staff*— that music paper, just like the paper he writes words on, needs lines to help us keep our place.

Now, ready to draw the first note, I tell Fred that a picture of a piece of music does have some things he may never have seen before. As I draw the first note head, I tell him this is one of those things—a note with a line going through its middle, called a line note. I tell him that the arrow in the clef is pointing to the key this note stands for.

Then, as I add the stem, I tell him that the note also has what is called a stem.

Then, we recall together that we played the first key two times, we *repeated* it, so that means we need to draw this note twice so that it will remind him at home to play that key twice. I mention that these are called repeated notes.

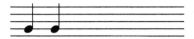

Then, we recall that the next two keys he played were also repeated, but on the second key of the group of three blacks. As I draw the next two notes, I show him that they are higher than the first two notes and they are in the space between two lines, so they are called space notes.

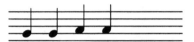

Then, I complete the first phrase by adding the last two notes, higher still, pointing out that they are line notes and that they tell us to play the last black key two times.

While I am going through this with Fred, I casually mention that going from a line note up to the next space note is called a 2nd, which tells him to go up to the next key on the keyboard. Fred will accept this little piece of wisdom, but I know that he will not need to understand this or any of the other little pieces of wisdom I have mentioned as we drew the picture. Up and down on the keyboard and staff, line notes and space notes, 2nds and repeated notes, etc., are things I will mention over and over at each lesson, but I know that it will take some time before Fred begins to really understand what these terms mean.

In the meantime, I will not depend on this understanding to ensure correct practice at home. He may not understand direction on the keyboard as it relates to the staff, but the piece itself is constructed to lead him to move to the right on the keyboard. Since the first two notes are played on the lowest key of the group of three black keys, the only way to go on that group of black keys is up. He may not understand line note and space notes, but he can easily see that the first two notes are exactly alike, the next two exactly alike, and the last two exactly alike, reminding him to play each of the three blacks twice. He may not understand 2nds, but after he plays the first two notes, the natural place to go is the next black key, and then to the last black key.

Since he has already played the whole piece by rote, Fred knows what comes next—the very same thing, only higher. Again, Fred may not yet understand that up on the keyboard is to the right, but that is the direction he is playing, so it is only natural to keep moving in the same direction and find the next group of three black keys. Fred will also see it as natural that the picture of this move will *look* higher on the page. And so, we complete the picture of *Hopping Up the Stairway.*

At the end of the piece, we draw a double bar, naming it and explaining that this is a sign in music that tells us that we have come to the end of the piece. We add the forte sign, naming it and mentioning that this is a sign in music that reminds us that this is a loud piece—certainly something Fred won't need to remember if he's ever hopped up a stairway.

## Notation That is Easy to Read and Fun to Play

This is notation that speaks directly to the student, notation that any child can understand. Notation that reminds Fred of what he already knows is the first step toward fluent reading on the grand staff. Beginning with this picture, the grand staff will emerge, following a step-by-step plan that ensures student understanding along the way. As Fred sees and responds to staff/keyboard direction, he will absorb its meaning just as his body is absorbing its feel. As he sees and responds to line notes, space notes, repeated notes, 2nds, 3rds, 4ths, 5ths, phrases, steady pulse, bar lines, forte, and piano, he will absorb meaning, understanding, sound, and feel.

As mentioned before, an important aspect of this piece is its similarity to *Chopsticks*. Children love to play *Chopsticks* because they enjoy the physical experience of playing it. The non-legato repeated notes and 2nds are played with freedom and a physical motion familiar to the child, rather than the unnatural physical feel of legato, and therefore are easy and fun to do. *Hopping Up the Stairway* has the same physical feel of *Chopsticks*—non legato and a steady pulse.

The note patterns in *Chopsticks* are easy to remember; the note patterns of *Hopping Up the Stairway* are even easier to remember. The rhythm of *Chopsticks* consists of quarter notes only, as does the rhythm of *Hopping Up the Stairway*. All this added together allows for a lively tempo from the very beginning and, finally, adding a big-sounding accompaniment yields a sound and feel to rival the sound and feel of *Chopsticks*.

## Why This Simplified Notation?

The piano teacher's task is to continue to provide these two essential parts of successful piano study: pieces that are fun to play and easy to read.

Students who enjoy playing the pieces we assign, and who can read them easily, will not only want to continue to take lessons, they will learn to read fluently. Students who do not enjoy the sound and feel of the pieces they are asked to practice will not want to take lessons any more. If the pieces they like to play are not easy to read, they will learn them some other way, leaving their reading skills far behind.

The reason to begin with the notation used in *Hopping Up the Stairway* is that this notation allows both of these goals to be realized. There are a few piano methods that employ this kind of pre-grand staff reading, but usually not enough of it to provide a solid background in reading understanding. Teachers who use methods that include some pre-grand staff reading will need to supplement with more pieces of their own making, like *Hopping Up the Stairway*, that make music notation speak directly to the student. Teachers who use methods that begin directly with a piece written on the grand staff, like the Middle-C piece at the beginning of his chapter, will need to make some pieces like *Hopping Up the Stairway* to use *before* beginning the method book. Very few students are ready to begin grand staff reading with understanding until after they understand and can read direction on the staff/keyboard, line notes and space notes, and 2nds and repeated notes.

## From Black Keys to White Keys

Playing pieces using only the groups of black keys prepares Fred to recognize that the white keys are also in groups, even though the white-key groups are not as easy to see. All pianists find white keys on the keyboard by their relationship to the black keys. We think of white keys in two groups—CDE and FGAB; the so-called musical alphabet (ABCDEFG) is not really helpful in learning to read. The logical next step after learning the groups of three black keys is learning the groups of four white keys that touch the groups of three black keys. As I did with *Hopping Up the Stairway*, I teach Fred something like this by rote:

This piece is fun to play and easy to read, especially if you call the piece *Bouncing On the Bed* and say *bounc-ing* on every pair of repeated notes. No child can resist the vicarious experience of bouncing on a bed, especially in the piano teacher's perfectly safe studio. The teacher's accompaniment adds the spice the piece needs, and gives the teacher a chance to bounce on the bed along with the student. Notice the F Clef in front of the first note of each phrase. This clef tells Fred that he can start on any F on the keyboard, so long as there is room to move up two octaves. This letter clef, added to the already self-explanatory picture clef that says play this piece on the FGAB groups of white keys, is one step closer to the traditional treble clef.

Similar pieces can be fashioned using the groups of two blacks and the groups of three whites that touch each of those groups. After a few pieces on each of the four groups of keys, the entire keyboard is learned, as well as a basic understanding of clefs, lines and spaces, repeated notes and 2nds, the basis for learning to read on the grand staff.

## Learning Down

Direction on the keyboard may be one of the most baffling aspects of learning to read. Again, experienced musicians take for granted that to the right is up and to the left is down. This is something young students must *learn,* and up and down are easier to learn if they are not presented at the same time. In fact, learning the harder part—down—comes much more easily if a number of pieces that only go up have already been learned.

Only after learning to read a number of pieces going up is the student ready to learn the more difficult direction of down. Reading notes that go to the right on the page but are played to the left on the keyboard is not something we should introduce lightly. The grand-staff middle-C piece shown at the beginning of this chapter requires the student to read both up and down, just as most beginning pieces do. Students may play that piece correctly, but seldom because they understand up and down. Usually it is the fingering that makes each hand play in the correct direction. Or the fact that, if both thumbs are on middle-C, it is only natural to move up with the right hand and down with the left. Like too much that is connected to the traditional way of teaching reading, the student does the right thing for the wrong reason, and only later does the teacher realize that no real learning stands behind an otherwise acceptable performance of a piece on the assignment.

Up should be separated from down until the student feels comfortable with each of them independently. This following piece continues the idea of providing the student with music that is fun to play and easy to read.

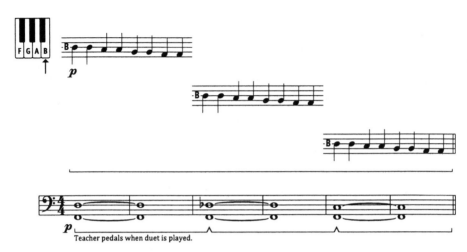

Teacher pedals when duet is played.

Played softly with the damper pedal down, an ideal name for this piece is *Falling Leaves,* and the word *Fall-ing* can be said or sung on each pair of repeated notes. The teacher's accompaniment adds to the calm character of the piece.

Pieces made using only the groups of two blacks, the groups of three whites that touch them, the groups of three blacks, and the groups of four whites that touch them give the student ownership of the keys on the keyboard. If some pieces go up the keyboard and some go down the keyboard, the student will grow to understand the complex idea of direction on the staff as it relates to direction on the keyboard. In the meantime, the clear pictures we draw of each piece make Fred comfortable with the idea that the printed music tells him which key to start on (the pieces we make can start on any black key, using an arrow to indicate the starting note, or on any white key, using a letter clef to indicate the starting note), and the lines and spaces tell Fred when to go up to the next key, when to go down, and when to repeat.

As we make new pieces using these basic fundamentals of pitch-notation reading, we can also go beyond the basic fundamental rhythm we have been teaching. Once the student learns that a piece made of all quarter notes is played in a steady pulse, we can begin to add half notes and then dotted half notes.

## Introducing the Treble Clef

In this piece, Fred sees the treble clef (something he's never seen before) and also a B Clef (something he already knows). I explain to Fred that he can easily see that this piece begins on B, but that the new sign, which is called a Treble Clef, tells musicians that the composer wants this B to be one particular B on the keyboard—the first B going up from Middle C. (While I was teaching the pieces using the groups of black keys and the groups of white keys, I constantly referred to the C in the middle of the keyboard as Middle C in preparation for this moment.)

After a few pieces that start on Treble B and have both the Treble Clef and the B Clef, the B Clef will disappear. While Fred is learning that the Treble Clef names the center line Treble B, the B Clef remains as a reminder, but soon it will no longer be needed. Fred will have taught himself to respond to the Treble Clef.

Each of the pieces preceding this piece was written on one staff and could be played with either hand alone or both hands together playing the same thing an octave apart. With the first piece written on two staffs, Fred is taught that the right hand plays the notes written on the upper staff and the left hand plays the notes written on the lower staff. This is the general rule. Following this general rule, the treble clef does not mean right hand; the bass clef does not mean left hand; up stems do not mean right hand; down stems do not mean left hand. Those cases where the stems do indicate RH and LH are exceptions to the general rule and should not be taught at the beginning of reading.

## The Center Line of a 5-Line Staff as a Guide Line

With this introduction to the treble staff, the center line of the five lines will become the student's guide line (landmark) on the treble staff. When Fred places both his thumbs on Treble B, his ten fingers are lying on all the lines and spaces of the Treble Staff. As he looks at the staff and feels his fingers on the keys, he sees that his left hand fifth finger is lying on the bottom line and the right hand fifth finger is lying on the top line; fingers 1, 3, and 5 are on the line notes; fingers 2 and 4 are on the space notes. Looking at his left hand fifth finger, he sees that the bottom line of the treble staff is E and the top line is F. He sees that his hands, in this position, tell him everything he needs to know about the lines and spaces of the Treble Staff.

## Introducing the Bass Clef

The Bass Staff is introduced in the same way as the Treble Staff, but, like teaching up and down, these two related signs are not taught at the same time. Teaching related items at the same time is almost always a mistake. We end up causing the student to guess rather than respond with understanding. A few wrong guesses can give both the teacher and students many unhappy weeks, even months, of straightening out.

So, Fred sees two Bass Clefs and two D letter clefs when he sees this picture for the first time. In this case, the Bass Clef sign tells him that the composer wants a particular D to be played, the first D below Middle C.

As with the Treble Clef, when Fred puts both thumbs on Bass D, his ten fingers *become* the lines and spaces of the Bass Staff. The Bass Staff becomes something totally comprehensible to Fred, almost immediately.

# The Grand Staff

**SHHH!**

While Fred was learning the Treble Staff and the Bass Staff, it was apparent that there were three keys on the keyboard between the Treble Staff keys and the Bass Staff keys. What about those keys? The introduction of the Grand Staff solves that mystery with a piece that uses those notes as starting notes. Middle C, Middle D, and Middle B are simply the three notes in the middle—between the Treble Staff and the Bass Staff.

During the time Fred was learning pieces using only the Treble Staff or the Bass Staff, I also began to introduce intervals. Many pieces using only 2nds preceded the playing of any other intervals. Since a complete understanding of intervals is determined by a thorough knowledge of 2nds, we wait until we are sure this knowledge has taken hold before proceeding. When Fred was ready, I introduced 3rds, telling Fred that the interval of a 3rd gets its name from the fact that it covers three white keys, leaving out the middle one. 5ths cover five white keys, leaving out all the middle ones, etc. By the time I introduce the Grand Staff, Fred has played a number of pieces that use only 2nds, only 3rds, only 4ths, and only 5ths.

## Reading for Every Child

The Grand Staff is not the beginning of reading. It is, instead, almost the opposite of the beginning. If the student's earliest lessons include a step-by-step understanding of all the components that make up the Grand Staff, the Grand Staff itself can be an exciting culmination, the end of an interesting journey. Students who build their own Grand Staff in the way we have described here are never dependent on the teacher to tell them how to read music. The music itself tells them what to play. Armed with this kind of solid understanding of how printed notation came to be, students are eager to figure out the pieces they want to play. Teachers, then, are left with only one real challenge—finding pieces that children really want to play. It is not enough to give our students the tools for fluent reading, although we face certain failure unless we do. We must continue to turn the reading experience into playing that is exciting and fulfilling for the student. If our students continue to find the same enjoyment in the pieces we assign as they find in playing *Chopsticks,* they will not be bored, they will not hate to practice, and they will look forward to coming to the next lesson because that is the place where it is fun to make music. And perhaps most important of all, this means they will be around long enough to play Bach and Beethoven and Chopin with the same enthusiasm they had for *Chopsticks.*

## Endnote

The musical examples used in this chapter are © copyright by National Keyboard Arts Associates and are reprinted with permission.

# MUSICIANSHIP
# SKILLS

# CHAPTER 6

## Keyboard Theory for the Elementary Student

### James Lyke

There are many keyboard skills that need to be developed while teaching the young pianist. This chapter will focus on five of these skills: harmonizing melodies, playing basic chord patterns, playing by ear, transposing and improvising. These skills can be developed from the beginning lessons and refined throughout the years of elementary level learning.

Undergraduate music theory programs have changed markedly over the past several decades. Where once undergraduates took separate courses in ear training, sight singing, harmony (including perhaps a keyboard harmony class) and analysis, today the various components of music theory have been unified. This trend came to be labeled as a *comprehensive musicianship* approach.

Forward looking piano teachers see the value of relating keyboard theory learning to the piano lesson itself in the early stages of instruction, long before the student reaches college age. Teachers understand the advantage reinforcement plays in music learning. When students identify familiar chords in repertoire or sight reading which have already been built at the keyboard, transposed, and used in harmonization studies and ear training, reinforcement is at work. A sequential program of skill development in keyboard theory is one which constantly relates to repertoire, technical patterns and sight reading. The serious teacher designs an effective program, one which points toward *overall* musicianship skills.

## Chord Patterns

When a beginning student learns tetrachord scale patterns, it is simple to introduce him to the concept of tonic and dominant chords, the two chords used most frequently in music. In addition to learning the meaning of tonic and dominant, the young student gradually attaches other labels, such as Roman numeral and the more practical letter-name symbols. In the technique part of the lesson, scale playing can conclude with the playing of the pattern I-V-I. The student should be encouraged to play the chords in each hand with logical fingering.

Example 1

It is important to teach young students *root position* chords first: the learning of inversions should be delayed until root position chords are thoroughly understood. Too many beginning methods incorrectly identify the first inversion of the dominant seventh as shown below:

Example 2

Many young pianists develop a "feel" for this first inversion dominant seventh chord with very little understanding of its derivation. Later, they must relearn this concept of V⁷ when they find they've been playing its first inversion all this time!

When a student is able to play his tonic and dominant chords in many keys with ease, these chords should be put to use in harmonization exercises. Melodies may be found in several sources (see references at the end of this section) and the teacher will want to either write out melodies or use supplemental books in the musicianship class. Below is a sample melody

Example 3                                                    **Folk Song Melody**

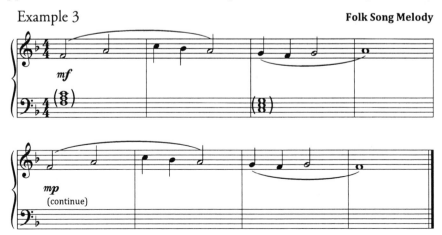

which calls for I and V harmony. Students should be encouraged to identify the harmony in each measure by noting chord outlines and by testing their ears. Good fingering in the melody is essential. Melody harmonization is an excellent group project; when the assignment is satisfactorily completed, students should be encouraged to transpose it to other keys.

If harmonization assignments are available to students in their piano books, it is a good idea to have the students write in harmony because writing will often clarify hazy concepts of notation.

In addition to assigning chord pattern and harmonization exercises, the teacher should maintain a list of tunes which demand only a tonic and dominant (or dominant seventh) background. The teacher should be able to play any of these tunes in any key, while the student supplies an appropriate accompaniment. The accompaniment may be very simple, but the important point is that the student anticipates harmonic change and rapidly shifts to the proper chord without losing the beat. This activity promotes "inner hearing", with the mind slightly ahead of what the fingers actually are playing at the moment. Students should be taught various styles of accompaniment that fit the character of each melody, such as waltz, broken chord, etc.

A partial listing of tunes using tonic and dominant or dominant seventh chords is presented below.

## Tunes Using I and V or V⁷ Harmony

 1. Clementine
 2. Did You Ever See A Lassie?
 3. Down At The Station
 4. Down In The Valley
 5. Hail, Hail, The Gang's All Here
 6. London Bridge
 7. Merrily We Roll Along
 8. Oh, Dear, What Can The Matter Be?
 9. Polly Wolly Doodle
10. Shoo Fly
11. Three Blind Mice
12. The Irish Washerwoman

In example 4, the teacher plays the melody *without showing it to the student;* the melody might also be sung. The student, limited in choice by two chords, decides his harmonies ahead of time. In a group, the next person to play might try another key, or the teacher might use two or three tunes for this brief activity, each tune being in a different key. Note that the student now plays four-voice harmony, a single bass note and three voices the right hand.

Example 4

Example 4 uses the dominant seventh chord rather than the dominant. Students quickly learn that adding another third to the dominant chord forms a seventh. The various inversions of the dominant seventh chord can then be drilled at the keyboard and written for more experience. Students need to be taught the correct labels for the three inversions, both Roman numeral and letter name form, the latter being employed in folk and popular music. The bass in letter name symbols is identified by the letter immediately following the slanted line (G⁷/B, G/D). A good exercise for students involves singing the chord tones up and down. For example, in the key of C, C-E-G-E-C, G-B-D-F-D-B-G and C-E-G-E-C. This is good ear training work and builds chord knowledge. The inversions of the dominant seventh chord may also be sung (up and down) after the root tone is played.

Example 5

Example 6 tests knowledge of inversions. Though the progression remains the same, I V⁷ I (because roots are in the bass), the right hand must adjust to inverted dominant seventh patterns. This occurs because of the various starting positions of the right hand tonic chord. First the 5th is in the soprano, then the root and finally the 3rd. Teach students the proper

RH fingering. Again, have the student sing (up and down) root position, first inversion and second inversion triads.

Example 6

As the subdominant chord is introduced, similar procedures for its keyboard application may be followed. First it is wise to have the student build the IV chord in a setting such as seen in example 7, then transpose it to many keys.

Example 7

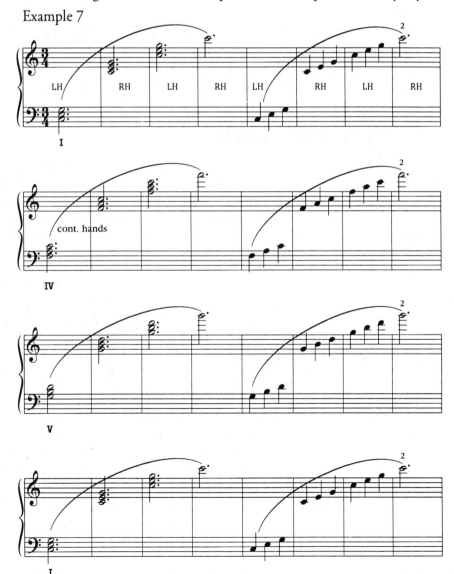

When students have been exposed to the concept of inversion, they will find the six-four position of the subdominant chord a smooth progression from the tonic. A common tone (C) is shared in both chords and the fingering is smooth. Again, students should be encouraged to think out spellings of each chord so as not to rely on finger memory alone.

Example 8

## Melody Harmonization

The knowledge of the subdominant chord may be applied through melody harmonization and playing by ear. Example 9 shows a simple left hand harmonization employing inversions of both the subdominant and dominant seventh chords. Younger students find these left hand harmonizations simple; however, students must be cautioned to make this type of harmonization as musical as possible through proper balance of the hands.

Example 9                                        German Carol

With further experience, students should learn to shift the chord to the right hand and play single bass notes in the left hand; this type of setting provides a more satisfactory sound than example 9. The melody note becomes the top note of the chord; students must fill in other notes of the chord beneath the melody note. This experience provides good "thinking" situations for the keyboard student. Example 10 illustrates chords in the right hand and single bass notes in the left hand or "piano style."

Example 10

Again, a list of tunes having a I IV and V or V$^7$ harmonic background will be helpful to the teacher. The teacher should have students pick various keys and provide an appropriate style of accompaniment, playing chord roots in the left hand and three-note chords in the right hand.

## Tunes Using I, IV and V(7) Harmony

1. Billy Boy
2. Camptown Races
3. Comin' Through The Rye
4. Goodnight, Ladies
5. Happy Birthday
6. Hickory Dickory Dock
7. O Susanna
8. Old Mcdonald
9. Red River Valley
10. When The Saints Come Marching In
11. Yankee Doodle
12. You Are My Sunshine

As the process of playing accompaniments by ear and of melodic harmonization becomes more refined, students should be taught to create more interesting bass lines through inversion and the use of passing tones.

When students are comfortable with I IV V (7) patterns in major, the teacher should introduce the same patterns in minor keys. A typical musicianship activity might entail the following activities:

1. Play I IV I V$^7$ I in d minor.

Example 11

2. Transpose this pattern to a few other minor keys.

3. Harmonize the *British Folk Song* (Ex. 12) using two L.H. chords per measure except in the next to final measure where only one is needed. By ear, find two spots where the subdominant chord (Cm/G) works.

Example 12                                                    **British Folk Song**

Several drills will prove beneficial to students in further keyboard harmony experiences. Teachers should be advised that keyboard harmony goes far beyond familiarity with tonic, subdominant and dominant harmony. A few drills which students can play in teams during the musicianship lesson follow; these drills expand harmonic understanding and push a student beyond a knowledge of only I, IV and V.

1. Build triads on scale degrees. Use both hands. This can be explored in minor keys also. Students should identify each chord by Roman numeral and letter name and quality (major, minor, diminished, etc.) Proceed through a variety of keys in a systematic manner.

Example 13

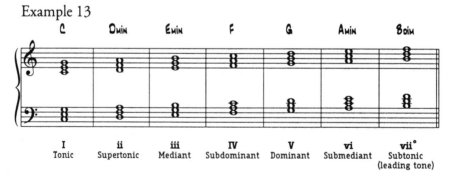

Gradually transpose example 13 to all keys.

2. In example 14, build triads on all twelve notes; change the quality of each chord as shown below. Memorize the order: major, augmented, major, minor, diminished. Chant these qualities while playing the exercise.

Example 14

continue in all keys

3. Build triads and inversions and arpeggiate. Use proper fingering. When all major keys have been completed, repeat in minor keys.

Example 15

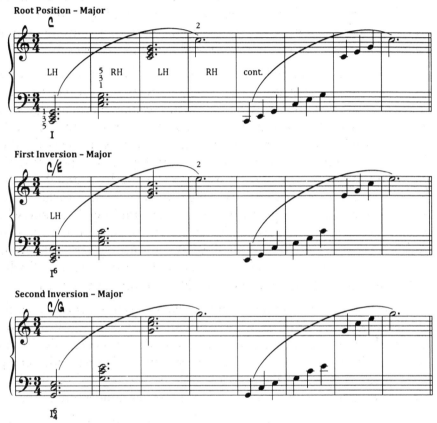

# Transposition

You will notice how the student was encouraged to transpose all the exercises presented. Transposition leads to familiarity of harmonies in many keys. Harmonization studies may also be transposed.

# Improvisation

In past centuries, keyboard improvisational ability for the performer was taken for granted; extemporizing for oneself, or for an audience was a natural process. In the eighteenth century, for example, performer-musicians improvised cadenzas to concerti or sets of variations to a tune suggested by members of an audience. Even contests were held to determine the most skillful performer in the art of improvisation.

In our time, jazz pianists have kept the improvisation tradition alive by elaborating on melodies and skeleton harmonies of standard popular and show tunes. Certain twentieth century styles depend upon improvisational abilities of both soloists and ensembles.

Modern concepts of piano instruction, particularly group teaching, emphasize the development of a student's creative potential through exposure to a variety of improvisational experience. Valuable insights into the basic elements of music are gained through the manipulation of rhythm, melody, harmony and form. This process, if started with the onset of lessons, becomes as natural as other components of musicianship training: sight reading, transposition, and keyboard harmony-related skills.

Some teachers, though they support the idea of improvisational experience, feel inadequate when trying to implement this creative form of expression. There are many reasons for this feeling, but they largely boil down to a lack of background and experience compounded by an "on the spot" feeling when demonstrating ideas. There is no need for these feelings in the group setting; in the musicianship class (a perfect setting for improvisation) students will learn from one another through hearing, comparing, evaluating and emulating the better efforts. The teacher's role is often reduced to supplying ostinato patterns and guiding discussions when students have concluded playing. What often helps is that certain students possess an innate flair for improvising, who intuitively create interesting motives, use repetition, sequence, contrast and aim for cadences. Teachers will learn from students, and students will learn from one another.

One important idea to pursue at elementary levels of instruction is that of having students improvise in every new structure that is presented, from the first few notes and rhythms through more advanced materials. This can be accomplished by inventing interesting ostinato figures and, perhaps, developing a teacher anthology for specific structures such as five-finger major and minor patterns, major and minor scales, modes and so on.

Example 16 shows three notes which might be used as an initial improvisational attempt by the beginning pianist.

Example 16

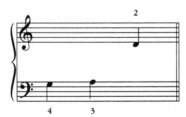

As the teacher provides an ostinato at a second piano, or has the child play the notes in example 16 two octaves higher, if one piano is used, the child should be allowed freedom to experiment with sounds and rhythm. The teacher ostinato is shown in example 17; the chords in this pattern could be employed in various meters and tempi helping to create a march, a slow, dreamy piece, or a waltz.

Example 17

Several points must be aurally grasped when the teacher plays the ostinato a few times as an introduction. The child must determine the meter and the general mood created and he must grasp the beat. The teacher's role is that of guide; he allows complete freedom, offers encouraging comments along the way and directs discussion when each child finishes. Often, as inexperienced children begin to improvise, they wander aimlessly and make incoherent musical statements. Children sometimes use only slow values, such as half notes; with teacher encouragement they begin to employ quarter notes, eighth notes and other values. Often a child uses sophisticated rhythms well beyond his present level of comprehension. All these efforts must be be viewed positively because as the child gains more understanding of melody, phrase structure and cadences, his improvisational efforts will become more musically cohesive and interesting.

If a five-finger (pentachord) approach is used, children should be encouraged to improvise in every five-finger major pattern. Example 18 illustrates an ostinato which immediately suggests several elements to the child: slow tempo, legato mood, expressive lines and three-four meter.

Example 18

As minor five-finger patterns are studied, students should experience improvisation with many of these patterns; ostinato figures should be varied rhythmically and expressively to provide students with imaginative backgrounds which spark creativity. Modern sounds and rhythms, such as suggested in the following bossa nova example, will intrigue students. Teachers should make certain that melodic improvisation occurs with the left hand as well as the right.

Example 19

When students are introduced to scales, either in tetrachord patterns or using conventional fingering, melodies employing all scale steps may be improvised. Example 20, a Latin rhythm, serves as a pattern for scale improvisation. It should be noted that ostinato patterns need to be written so that students experience little clash with harmonies; everything should sound "right." Another point which teachers will notice as improvisation experience progresses is a technical freedom which students will naturally show; arm and finger movements tend to be more free when improvising. This freedom should be pointed out to students and transferred to current pieces and technical studies.

Example 20

In addition to major scales, students need to be exposed to improvising in minor scales and the various modes: dorian, phrygian, lydian, mixolydian, aeolian (natural minor) and locrian. Teachers might provide students with left hand patterns over which right hand melodies could be composed. After several tries in class, students can take the patterns home and notate them. Once the white key forms are learned, transposition of the modes should follow. In example 21 the left hand presents a more structured form of improvisation, but also provides great freedom with the student's scale line.

Example 21

Accidentals often occur along the way in melodic improvising, so-called "mistakes"; these should be incorporated into the improvisation. Students should be guided to resolve quickly to sounds that they find more pleasing.

Other more structured improvisation experiences might include predetermined harmonic schemes. Once chord patterns have been learned, they too (as with melodic structures) should be utilized in improvisational schemes. One student might supply the harmony while another improvises melodies; one or two pianos can be used for this experience. The scheme can be written on a whiteboard or projected. Example 22 shows such a pattern.

Example 22

Student A supplies harmony with simple left hand chords, or roots in the left hand and chords in the right hand as written out below in example 23. Meanwhile, student B improvises a melody which fits with the harmonic structure; each student must feel musical kinship with his partner, aiming toward cadences and coming to a satisfactory close. Aim towards good ensemble.

Example 23

Example 24, a piece by the author, is taken from *Pattern Studies: 20 Original Piano Solos* (Lee Roberts Publications). The L.H. figure could be used as an ostinato figure while the R.H. improvises in the C♯ minor five-finger pattern. Have the student play what is written and then improvise another four or eight bar melody. Patterns such as this may be extracted from literature and used as an impetus to improvise. When coming to the end, aim for the L.H. third in bar 1.

Example 24

**BUSTLING**

James Lyke

continue

# Improvising in Styles

Removing key elements and improvising within a certain style provides a student with valuable insights related to composition. This idea may be carried on throughout piano instruction, from the most simple to advanced levels. Teachers should look for key elements in a student's repertoire which might be taken out for improvisational experience.

One more idea to consider for improvisational activity is that of furnishing students with a few bars of composition and asking that they add on material, keep within the style, and bring the new material to some sort of conclusion. In this way, students are forced to absorb style elements; they cannot mix up classical ideas with those of a modern idiom, for example. Example 25 shows the first four bars of a simple piece by Telemann. Students might be asked to add twelve more bars, after the introductory four bars, using repetition and concluding with a perfect authentic cadence. Bars 9-12 might involve elements of contrast (rhythm, tonality, melody, etc.), and the final four bars, 13-16, might represent some sort of return.

Example 25                                                  **Telemann**

Example 26 illustrates a possibility for the continuation of bars 1-4 above: note the elements of repetition and the perfect authentic cadence as well as the simplicity.

Example 26
(measures 5-8)

Example 27 provides elements of contrast through a temporary shift (transition) to the dominant; the motive of bar 3 is used in a sequential pattern.

Example 27

And finally, example 28 illustrates a possible return using elements from the given opening.

Example 28

It is always interesting to compare a student's improvised example to that of the original piece; the Telemann is easily found in piano collections. Improvisation teaches styles. Simple as the above illustrations appear, one can say he is improvising in a baroque style. Other examples from the classic, romantic and modern eras may be found and used as an impetus for improvising in the style of a certain composer.

Three ideas have been discussed relative to improvisation experience: use of original ostinato figures, excerpts of key elements from a piece used as an ostinato background and continuation of brief musical examples illustrating specific styles. Other ideas currently used in modern piano teaching include improvising melodies to verse, particularly appropriate in elementary study, and telling a musical story at the piano in a completely unstructured way. For example, a young student might want to depict a short space story, from blast-off to landing, utilizing all sorts of sounds like low rumblings and very high pitches. Mention should be made of the relatively easy improvisations on black keys in the pentatonic scale; cowboys, Indians, and bagpipe music are but a few of the possibilities with pentatonic backgrounds.

There are many excellent piano series available with accompanying theory books. These supplementary theory books involve piano students with brief exercises. Various topics include identifying intervals, naming notes, writing and clapping rhythmic figures, recognizing key signatures, naming chords (and their quality), building major and minor scales and so on. Working through these books should develop theoretic understanding and skill with notation. Below is a partial list of piano methods with separate theory books. Browsing on the internet should give a glimpse of the scope of these workbooks.

1. *Alfred's Premier Course Series*: Theory Books, Level 1-6.

2. *Bastien Piano Basics - Theory* and *Bastien Theory Boosters*: Levels 1-5.

3. Clark, Frances. *The Music Tree Activities Book*: Levels 1-4

4. Clark, Frances and Goss, Louise. *Music Maker: Part A, Part B.*

5. *Piano Adventures* by Faber & Faber: Theory books, Primer Level - Level 5.

6. *Hal Leonard Piano Method*: Piano Theory Workbooks, Levels 1-5

7. Pace, Robert. *Music For Piano Series*: Theory Papers, Levels 1-4

# CHAPTER 7

# Elementary Composition for the Young Pianist

### Lee Evans

## Unity and Variety in Musical Composition

When imparting the basics of composition to my piano students, I first teach them the materials that composers utilize in order to create <u>unity</u> in their music; in other words, my students first learn about various compositional devices composers employ that result in musical relationships. These are what make a composer's music sound as though the various musical elements of a work fit together. In order to arrive at that goal, composers employ such compositional devices as *repetition, sequence, retrograde* and *inversion,* among others.

The opposite of unity in music is <u>variety</u>, which is achievable through the use of contrast. A composer needs merely avoid employing compositional devices such as the ones mentioned in the preceding paragraph. Parenthetically, however, I should mention that this is considerably easier said than done, as the natural tendency for a well-trained composer is to utilize techniques that create unifying musical relationships.

The ability to strike a judicious balance between elements of unity and variety in music is one of several considerations in the calculus that separate the wheat from the chaff among composers.

## Composing Within a Musical Form

Once the above unifying compositional devices have been learned by my students, I then teach them how to compose within a specific architectural structure, such as rondo form, theme and variations, sonata allegro form,

12-bar blues, popular-song form, the setting of a poem or lyric to music for voice and piano, etc.

If one wanted to paint a picture, I would think that the first step for that individual would be to visit an art supply store in order to buy a canvas. Choosing a musical structure within which to frame a musical composition is to me the equivalent of a painter purchasing a canvas before beginning to paint.

# Musical Examples of Compositional Techniques

The following are four of the most basic compositional techniques employed by composers to achieve unity in their music. These are taught in workbook format in the book *Learn to Compose and Notate Music* (Hal Leonard Corporation) by Lee Evans and Martha Baker.

REPETITION means repeat a motive (a short musical theme)—note for note—starting on the same pitch.

SEQUENCE means repeat a motive starting on any different pitch. Note that sequences may be accomplished by utilizing white keys only, without regard to the exact interval relationships of the given motive (see measure 2 in the example below); or it may be done by duplicating the exact interval relationships of the given motive (see measures 3 and 4 in the example below.)

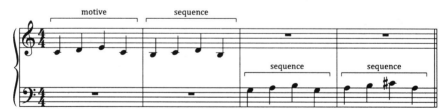

RETROGRADE means play the notes of a motive in backwards order. An even stronger relationship is achieved when the retrograde notes appear in the exact same rhythm as the original motive notes appeared in forwards order.

INVERSION means play the intervals of a motive upside down—in mirror image. For example, if in the original motive an interval goes up a 4th, then to invert it go down a 4th. As another example, if in the original motive the interval goes down a 5th, then to invert it go up a 5th.

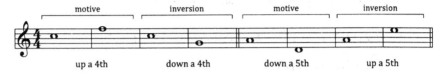

Inversion may be accomplished as a white-key experience, without regard to the exact interval; or it may be done as an exact interval experience.

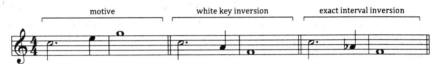

In each of the above examples, the inversion started on the same pitch as the motive. But inversion may start on any other pitch as well.

From the classical literature, my favorite example of inversion appears in Rachmaninoff's *Rhapsody on a Theme of Paganini*. The principal theme of the 18th variation is an inversion of this beautiful and exciting work's opening motive.

From the popular-music repertoire, the following is an example of two compositional devices in combination. Here are the first four pitches of the song

### I Got Rhythm:

In the next phrase, Gershwin presents these notes in both *retrograde* (the pitches in backwards order - in the same rhythm as they appeared in forwards order); and in *inversion* (the intervals upside down—in mirror image):

The result of the employment of these devices in combination is the achievement of a high degree of compositional unity.

# Achieving Unity in the Context of Jazz Performance

I find it especially advantageous when teaching the above unifying devices, to instruct students to utilize *12-bar blues structure*. A basic blues chord progression appears below. (Note: Each of these chords may instead be played as a dominant 7th chord instead of as a triad, in order to achieve a bluesier sound. Examples: Play $I^7$ instead of I; $IV^7$ instead of IV; $V^7$ instead of V.)

I   I or IV   I   I   IV   IV   I   I   V   V or IV   I   I

The following is an example of an initial four measure melodic motive developed exclusively through *repetition and sequence*, in 12-bar blues format. Note the high degree of compositional unity achieved in this piece through the employment of those two compositional devices.

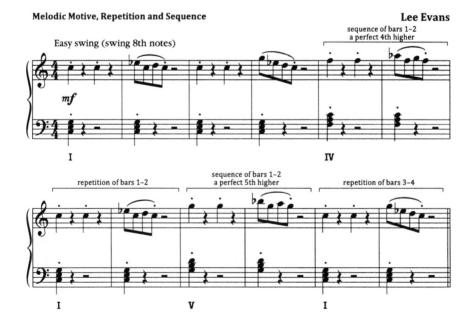

# Criteria for Adjudication of Student Original Compositions

When I adjudicate student piano compositions, I do so principally with an eye on whether students have or have not unified their compositions with compositional devices such as the ones discussed earlier in this chapter. In my written critique I point out specific parts of their compositions that either meet or do not meet this criterion.

I also look for such things as whether students are writing in an anachronistic 18th century harmonic, rhythmic and melodic manner, as many tend to do. If so, I encourage them in their future efforts to compose music that employs a more current musical vocabulary, such as the occasional use of dissonance, the use of chromatic rather than purely diatonic melodic and harmonic materials, the employment of a greater variety of rhythms, and the writing of unequal phrase lengths here and there, among other possibilities, in order to produce more contemporary and less dated sounds.

I also encourage students to occasionally compose using Schoenberg's 12-tone compositional system, as a foolproof way of guaranteeing that their music will have a contemporary sensibility, and as a way of making students comfortable with the sound of unresolved dissonance. (I am the composer/author of an intermediate level book that teaches this approach to composition in a manner that has proven to be extremely effective with students: *Three 12-Tone Waltzes Plus Student 12-Tone Composing Outlines*, published by Hal Leonard Corporation.)

# Musicianship Training

It is important to include musicianship training in each piano lesson. Essential components of this training should include learning how to notate music, learning to interpret jazz and popular music chord symbols at the piano, and making creative use of scales and chords, such as their employment in compositional and/or improvisational experiences.

In this connection, below, from my book *Discovering Blues Improvisation, Book One* (Hal Leonard Corporation), is my 12-bar blues composition, *Blues For Jelly Roll*. It is followed by an opportunity for students to improvise a blues chorus based on this song and its chord structure; utilizing, as suggested pitches for improvisation, the tones of each blues scale compatible with each of the chords of blues structure. In other words, when playing a C chord in the left hand, the right hand might utilize pitches of the C blues scale for melodic improvisation; the F chord will dictate the use of the F blues scale; and the G chord will dictate the use of the G blues scale. The blues scale is typically presented in jazz as follows, or with enharmonic equivalents for ease of reading:

1   $\flat$3   4   $\flat$5   5   $\flat$7   8

## BLUES FOR JELLY ROLL

Lee Evans

*After **Fine**, proceed to the improvisation on the next page.

**Possible compatible melody notes for improvisation**

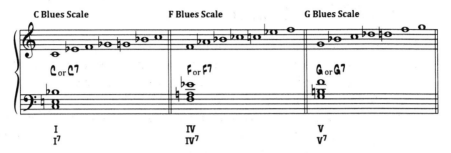

**Format for Improvisation on** *Blues for Jelly Roll*

## Recommended Procedure for Composing an Original Blues Composition

When composing and notating an original 12-bar blues piece, the student should first enter a key signature on every system, then a time signature only at the beginning, followed by a tempo mark above the time signature. Adjacent to the tempo mark, the student should indicate whether the piece is to be played with swing 8ths or straight 8ths interpretation. Then add dynamics, phrasing and articulations (staccatos, accents, etc.) to the entire piece for the benefit of others who play the work.

Follow this with several choruses of improvised solos based on the chord structure of the original, but write out (notate) at least one improvised chorus, remembering to enter a key signature on every system.

Next, return to the original composition for the "out" chorus. This is the procedure most often followed by most jazz practitioners, even for non-blues performances.

## End Word

Playing existing piano repertoire is an extremely satisfying act of re-creation. However, I would like to encourage all pianists and piano students to also engage in the act of creation, by composing music on a regular basis. Let the employment of the compositional techniques described throughout this chapter serve as an introduction and guide to this most exciting and fulfilling of activities.

Additional important compositional techniques and devices appear in a follow-up book, *Composing at the Piano* (Hal Leonard Corporation) by Lee Evans and Martha Baker. These include *altered forms of sequence (such as rhythmic diminution and augmentation, and intervallic diminution and augmentation), pedal point, and ostinato*, among others.

A follow-up volume to *Learn to Compose and Notate Music* and *Composing at the Piano* presents compositional techniques in a jazz context. The book, by Lee Evans, is *Improvise By Learning How To Compose* (Hal Leonard Corporation).

# TECHNICAL DEVELOPMENT

# CHAPTER 8

# Technical Development for the Young Pianist

## Karen Ann Krieger and James Lyke

A great deal of mystery and secrecy often surrounds the topic of piano technique. To an aspiring pianist, the instrument can appear to be an enormous wooden box with a wide grinning set of teeth ready to bite if not treated with great skill. A pianist has only the physical body to coax from this instrument the great gift of beauty that is music.

In the past, many teachers have claimed to have the one and only correct approach to this challenge. As it is impossible to separate technique from sound and musical intention, it is important to set the path toward technical mastery from the very first lesson. Because a pianist must use the whole body, the aim is to find the most natural way of playing that avoids any undue tension in the shoulders, upper arms, forearms, wrists, and hands. Adaptation of these movements will be discussed and illustrated throughout this chapter.

## Position of the Bench

The piano bench is crucial in establishing the correct position at the piano. It must be high enough that the bottom of the student's elbow is level with or slightly higher than the keys. Either an adjustable bench or a firm cushion can make this possible. Since adjustable benches often do not go high enough, another possibility is to place custom-made wooden risers or trays under the legs to raise the bench to the desired height. These are shown in the photograph below. The bench must be far enough away that the knees are just barely under the edge of the keyboard. If the student's feet cannot be flat on the floor, a footrest must be provided. This can be either an adjustable footstool or a pile of rug samples. (Check your local music store or the Internet for available options.)

Since habits, good and bad, are formed during practicing, it is a good idea to send this illustration home with parents and encourage them to take a similar picture of the student at their own piano.

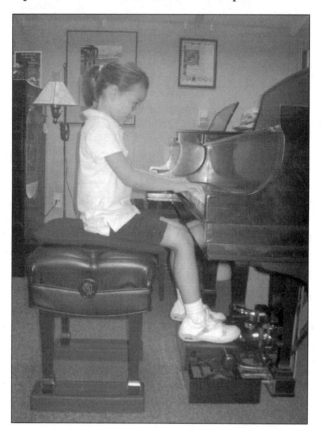

## Sitting Position

The most relaxed position at the piano is a position with the body weight distributed equally between the sit-bones, the feet, and the hands. All students need to become aware of their sit or rocker bones, the two ischial bones of the pelvis, and place them near the edge of the bench so that the bench does not press against the thighs. Pressing on the legs to maintain balance causes tension in the back, while pressing the feet against their support (footstool or floor) provides a natural equilibrium. Tall students can sit farther back if the bench does not press against their legs. Students, unaware of tension in their back, sometimes complain of back pain which can be a result of incorrect balance.

The back should be fairly straight, and the shoulders balanced over the hips, not leaning forward or back. When playing high or low, the body should try to keep a central position between the hands. Shifting the weight from one hip to the other keeps the shoulders level and the arms free to swing as they follow the hands up and down the keyboard. This balance and freedom are not possible if the student is slouching or is too close to the keyboard. The photo illustrates one student too close and one just right.

## The Body

Hand size and body type make technique unique to each student. Teachers can better help a student develop technique by demonstration, but must also occasionally assist by physically adjusting the student's hands and arms. The teacher must remember to respect the student's physical space by asking permission to make adjustments. A simple "May I borrow your arm or play on your back?" should help the student understand the teacher's intentions.

## The Shoulders

Children have loose and supple shoulders but tension can be introduced when teachers or parents constantly say "Sit up!" Students are likely to raise their shoulders, creating muscle tension impeding free arm movement. To make students aware of this tension, they should lift or shrug their shoulders as high as possible, breathing in. Then, during a long exhalation, let the shoulders fall slowly (as though they were being put back or placed on a coat rack). Students will then begin to feel the looseness when moving up and down the keys or when swinging their elbows in small circles. Students must feel the difference that is made when tension is present and when it is not. Only then can they take charge of developing their own technical control. A teacher's gentle touch to the shoulder can determine whether the shoulder is down, relaxed, and resting.

## The Arms

Relaxed shoulders balanced over the hips can easily create space between the upper arms and body, allowing the arms to pivot in wide circles. When students are the correct distance from the keyboard, their arms will be nearly parallel to the floor. If not, the bench needs to be moved in or out or higher or lower. When the position of the bench is correct, the arms gently slope toward the keys.

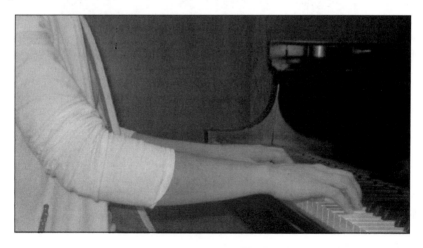

The **upper arms** and **lower arms (or forearms)** must swing freely to play both high and low notes without tension. One forward push to a student's upper arm from behind can determine whether the arm and shoulder are relaxed. Students should remember the arm follows the finger movement. Many pianists forget this and allow the fingers to play without support from the arm.

When playing in front of the body, it is helpful for the student to lean backward to give the arms adequate freedom to move. Weight from the whole body should flow through the arms, wrists and hands into the keys. This creates big sounds that are full and resonant.

The **elbows** bend up and down, but also pivot freely to allow the lower arms to turn the hand in an upward or downward position and every angle in-between. When playing on black keys, raising the elbows along with the upper arms will give the fingertips and wrists room to move up and down between white and black keys. Any tension in the elbows and the forearms will diminish tone quality. An upward push to the bottom of a student's forearm can determine whether there is weight in the forearm. Students should feel as though they can hand the weight of their arm over to their teacher.

## The Wrist

The small bones in the wrist function in a manner similar to ball bearings or shock absorbers in a car. These bones make the hand position totally flexible. They allow the wrist and arm to follow fingers as they negotiate melodic lines, stretch the hand to play a wide interval, or contract the hand for a smaller one. The wrist also makes possible the great variety of touches, such as legato and staccato. Therefore, the wrist must be allowed to rotate freely rather than maintaining a fixed position as was often recommended in the past. Students should move the wrist in a circular motion giving the fingers control in any passage and facilitating legato playing.

**Wrist Rotation:** Students can clearly feel, see, and understand "wrist circle" rotation while playing a 5-finger position or a broken chord. The circular motion should align the forearm behind each finger to facilitate feeling the weight transfer from finger to finger. The elbow reacts in a small circular pattern. Be sure the wrist is lower when the thumb plays, gradually rising as it rotates toward the 5th finger and returns to the thumb around the top of the circle. This gives weaker fingers greater strength. Teachers can assist with rotation by placing their 3rd finger under the wrist and thumb on top, then moving the student's wrist. Play the following rotation exercise hands alone.

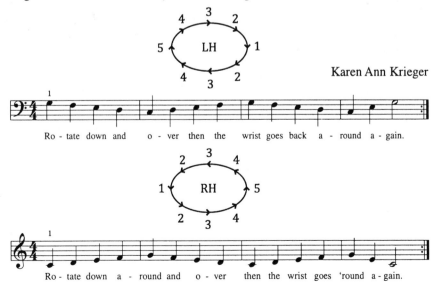

**Slurs:** Another wrist movement involves beginning a slurred passage of any length. The wrist drops and begins the phrase lower regardless of which finger plays first. During the phrase, the wrist adjusts to the length of fingers. At the ends of slurs, the wrist gently rises and hangs loose before proceeding to the next phrase. This is the position of the wrist for just a fraction of time when a pianist "breathes" between phrases. Young students can better understand this wrist movement by thinking of the way birds land feet first (fingers) before relaxing their bodies (hand and wrist). Birds take flight body first (wrist) and their feet (fingers) follow.

 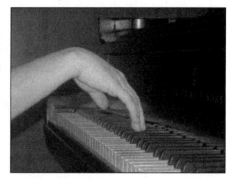

This movement also applies to 2-note slurs, the so-called "down and roll ups." The wrist lowers as the first note is played, not before the initial sound is made. As the second note is played on the pad of the finger, rolling the wrist cuts off the sound. The speed of the wrist roll makes the difference in the sound quality and length of the note when released. The last note is usually softer than the first note. A demonstration of 2-note slurs can be made by allowing the student to place a hand on top of the teacher's.

## The Hand

Forming a good hand position starts with the first lesson. The same relaxed arm and hand that swing to keep you balanced when walking is a good hand shape at the piano. Here are 3 different ways for the teacher to illustrate this position with students:

1. Stand with arms hanging loosely at the side. From the elbows, raise the forearms and turn the still relaxed hands face down over the keyboard, revealing raised knuckles.

2. Grasp the knees while sitting; hold that position while raising the arm to the keyboard.

3. Place the hand flat on a table. Very gradually draw the fingers toward the palm until the second finger almost touches the thumb. The thumb and wrist will be slightly raised.

Take care that the fifth finger doesn't collapse to its side but stands up straight.

Since hands come in all shapes and sizes, remind the student "the end result, the sound coming out of the piano, is what counts," and "careful listening controls improvement of sound." Tone quality of a pianist's playing is the reflection of his own personality and is controlled by the hand position. The teacher's job is to gently correct faulty positions until an excellent hand position becomes second nature to the student. It can often take great patience.

The most important element of a good hand is the arch created by the knuckles. The hand must maintain a strong arch as a bridge between the fingers. The knuckles in a child's hand are not as prominent as an adult's because of the soft fatty tissue that covers them. The strength of this arch can be demonstrated by pressing lightly on it while the fingertips are placed on the keys or a level surface. The student must learn the feeling of keeping that arch, not allowing it to collapse under pressure. This is the first line of defense against collapsing finger joints.

Eminent teacher Richard Chronister advocated a closed hand position in beginning lessons. This is formed by bracing the thumb behind the first joint of finger 2 (brace right above the pad between the fingertip and nail joint).

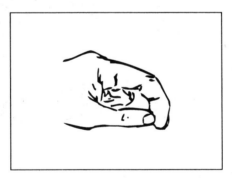

Chronister also believed that in the beginning, non-legato touch should be used because it is easier to play than legato or staccato. It requires a loose fist and free arm action, similar to the beginning Suzuki materials, and allows the other fingers to stay loosely relaxed. Playing with this closed hand position produces rich sounds. It is akin to playing chopsticks in its non-legato character. Chronister also advocated playing five-finger clusters, studying the hand, and making the 5th finger play correctly (standing up on finger 5) in preparation for playing blocked intervals of a fifth. Readers are advised to examine Chapter 12 in the *Piano Teacher's Legacy*.

As Chronister suggested, the correct use of the thumb and 5th finger helps form a good hand position. The wrist and the thumb should be slightly raised, allowing the thumb to be taller and hang loosely near the second finger. The thumb then plays on the side of the tip where the skin meets the nail. If a student plays the thumb elsewhere on its side in an attempt to get a big sound with the first joint, it collapses the high arch of the knuckles and can cause a sagging wrist. Beginning students often let the thumb hang off the keyboard or allow it to pinch the wooden rail while the other fingers play. This can be corrected by having all fingers play on or near black keys.

*The 5th finger* should stand high and play solidly with a sturdy tip. It is the only finger allowed to play on part of the nail near the outside of the pad. Because the 5th finger pad is tiny, many students try to make a stronger finger and bigger sound by playing on the side of the 5th finger like a "karate chop," instead of on the fingertip. This is a bad habit and the result of not aligning the arm with the fingers. When the arm is behind the 5th finger, the fingertips go straight down into the key, just like the other fingers. This will build the muscle on the side of the hand, which is its source of strength. The left photo shows the thumb playing on its side. The one on the right shows both thumb and 5th finger in good positions.

## The Fingers

Most people think of the fingers when piano playing is mentioned. "What fingers!" they exclaim after a brilliant concert, when in reality, playing involves more than just fingers. The muscles inside the palm initiate finger movement from the knuckles but they connect through the arm to the back. When teachers demand "Curve your fingers!" students often tighten all these muscles and play on the nails instead of the pads.

"Fingertips should lead like pilots and fingers should be active, not limp like cooked spaghetti noodles," says Sheila Paige, Associate Faculty of The Dorothy Taubman Seminar and Executive Director of the Piano Wellness Seminar. She suggests playing on the outside of the finger pads—most on 5, less on 4, barely on 3, 2 centered, 1 on the side tip. Once students understand the hidden strength in their fingers and fingertips, weakness, collapsing nail (first) joints, and "flying fingers" seem to disappear.

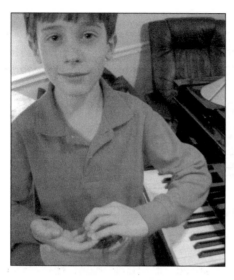

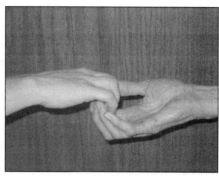

Young students understand their own finger strength when reminded that even a baby can squeeze a person's finger very tightly. They need to learn to transfer that same strength to the tips of their fingers as they play. Dr. Maurice Hinson, author of 12 books including *Guide to the Pianist's Repertoire* and editor of over 270 piano collections, writes "the weight of the hand and arm must go easily from one finger to the next, like walking." Students can understand the concept of keeping the finger joints from collapsing by comparing them to the joints in the legs. The nail joints are the ankles, the second joints are the knees, the hand joints are the hips, and the hands walk from finger to finger. The fingers do not stomp but rather shift the weight of the arm while the other fingers rest loosely on or slightly above the keys in readiness for the next key or step. This also produces a natural legato that is preferable to an overlapping legato. A true legato sound is created by the gradual release of the keys, allowing the damper to settle slowly onto the string as the next note is sounded.

The weakest fingers are usually entrusted to play the two outer voices of any composition, melody and bass. If students don't find the sensation and energy at the end of the fingers, called "fingertip energy," a weak sound is heard. A focused "ping" sound can be achieved by the correct arm weight and finger/hand/arm alignment and by listening and adjusting to every note played. Each fingertip should open and drop a little to take hold of the key. This often translates into a slight gentle pull against the surface of the key, without sliding on the key or pushing the key. Students should activate the grasping muscles to depress, rather than lifting the finger to strike the key. The muscles involved draw their strength from the flexors in the underside of the hand and arm. The extensors on the upper side lift the fingers. Tightness in either set of muscles should be avoided when the other set is in use, since the slightest movement involves a chain of muscles that must contract, relax, and balance at the precise moment. If all these points of control are activated when playing, no one part bears the sole responsibility and fatigue is thus avoided. Wrist rotation is necessary to position the arm in a straight line behind each finger as it plays, so that the muscle doesn't have to pull around a corner. This is called alignment. Study the drawings below.

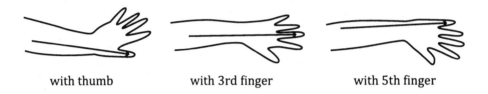

with thumb          with 3rd finger          with 5th finger

The weight of the arm and the speed of attack from the finger determine volume. Less weight and a slower attack produce soft sounds; more weight and a faster attack produce loud sounds. For a crescendo, both are gradually increased to change the sound from soft to loud. The Hungarian-born American pianist Gyorgy Sandor, in his book *On Piano Playing*, discusses at length this process of combining gravity and muscles. Dr. Robert Pace, author of the *Pace Piano Method* and student of Joseph and Rosina Lhevinne at Juilliard, likens this control to Albert Einstein's formula, "energy equals mass times acceleration" or $E=mc^2$. (Mass is the weight and acceleration is the speed of attack.)

# Finger Development

There is frequent disagreement among pianists on the subject of finger exercises. Some say technique can be taught solely through repertoire, which might transform many beautiful pieces of music into gymnastics routines. Others believe it is preferable to first learn a technique, then apply it to learning repertoire. The celebrated pianist/teachers Joseph and Rosina Lhevinne said that one-fourth of a student's practice time should be spent on some type of technique, and they had a number of exercises they practiced daily.

Finger exercises allow students to think about how it feels to maintain control through conscious and careful self-analysis. They can focus on that feeling more easily when not concentrating on musical interpretation of repertoire. Sandor writes that finger-strengthening exercises are both unnecessary and often damaging. However, he does advocate many exercises to develop the habit of controlling a completely natural combination of gravity with muscles throughout all aspects of piano technique. He stressed that any sign of pain or fatigue is evidence of improper technique which should be analyzed and corrected.

## Five-Fingers

The purpose of the following legato exercises by Karen Ann Krieger, co-author of this chapter, is to develop finger independence, the first hurdle for beginners. Students should first play this two-black key exercise on their thighs to feel a gentle shift between fingers. Then, play hands alone slowly (1- = a half note) followed by hands together. Fingers should move from one curved fingertip to the next as if walking. The student's arm should remain quiet and relaxed, and the wrist should stay flexible. The arm and hand should not pump up and down. A teacher's accompaniment is included to provide variety during the many repetitions necessary to achieve progress. Use during the hands alone segment; repeat as needed.

| Left Hand | Right Hand |
|---|---|
| a. 1-2-1-2-1-2-1-1-, 2-1-2-1-2-1-2---. | a. 1-2-1-2-1-2-1-1-, 2-1-2-1-2-1-1---. |
| b. 2-3-2-3-2-3-2-2-, 3-2-3-2-3-2-3---. | b. 2-3-2-3-2-3-2-2-, 3-2-3-2-3-2-2---. |
| c. 3-4-3-4-3-4-3-3-, 4-3-4-3-4-3-4---. | c. 3-4-3-4-3-4-3-3-, 4-3-4-3-4-3-3---. |
| d. 4-5-4-5-4-5-4-4-, 5-4-5-4-5-4-5---. | d. 4-5-4-5-4-5-4-4-, 5-4-5-4-5-4-4---. |

**TWO BLACK KEYS**
Teacher Accompaniment

Karen Ann Krieger

Robert Pace begins technical training with similar exercises in pre-staff notation on black and white keys, while teaching steps and skips in short pentascale melodies. Each of these is transposed to at least four keys and correlated with beginning staff notation and key signatures. By page 12 and 13 of *Finger Builders, Book 1* students can easily play the following exercises called "Tune Ups" in all 12 keys.

With this exercise, the student begins practicing the concepts of "wrist circle" rotation and weight transfer. This multi-key approach provides total

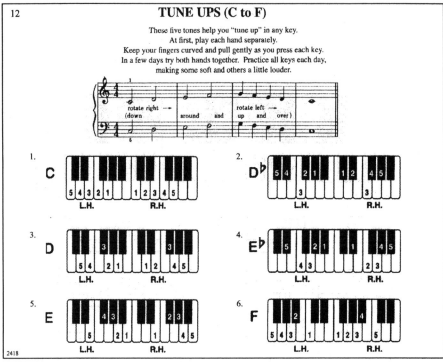

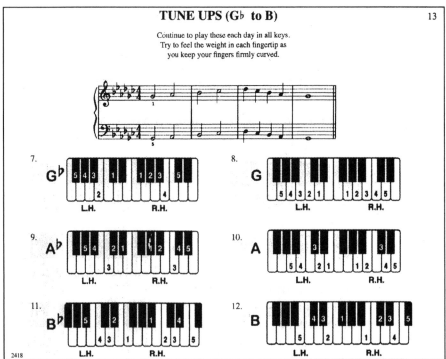

immersion in the entire keyboard and the realization that any melody can be played starting on any key. This knowledge is presented in a manner which corresponds to a child's natural way of learning. Students who play in all keys from the beginning develop a good technique naturally. Curved fingers and a strong arch result from playing on and among black keys. A flexible wrist results from adjusting to different levels of the keys as well as to different lengths of fingers. The thumb learns to function comfortably on black keys as will be required by music of the Romantic Period. Flat fingers and incorrect thumb action, which are so difficult to correct, seldom develop.

## Scales

There are differing schools of thought on the introduction of scales, primarily because of the treatment of the thumb. Some methods introduce tetrachord scales (no thumbs) in all keys around the circle of fifths during the first year of lessons. This allows beginning students to see the full scale under their fingers and explains the key signatures. The LH replaces the RH position to play the next scale. The key signature is formed each time the RH adds a sharp with the 4th finger or drops a flat with the 4th finger. This exercise by James Lyke and Ron Elliston adds rhythmic variety to students' practice.

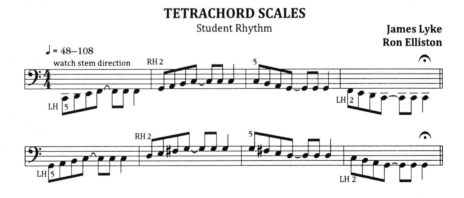

**TETRACHORD SCALES**
Student Rhythm
James Lyke
Ron Elliston

**Tetrachord scales** prepare students to learn all one-octave parallel motion scales in major and harmonic minor during the second year of lessons, while using simple rules of fingering. It should not take years to learn all the scales.

Scale playing has been a pre-occupation of pianists ever since the piano followed the harpsichord as the instrument of choice. The new possibility of legato playing and control of the loudness of every sound dictated both control of touch and careful listening to every note. Pianists used scales to prepare for playing the new repertoire that emerged. Concert pianist John Browning stated, "Technique is not how fast you can play scales, it is the ability to produce many different sounds." Scale technique requires good legato five-finger technique and a flexible thumb. Students must work for evenness of sound and steadiness of rhythm when playing scales.

Smooth passage of the thumb is paramount and is best taught in scales before applying it to arpeggios. Three approaches to this technique are discussed below. Students should try all three to discover which works best for their hand.

In the thumb under approach, the thumb must tuck itself under the hand immediately after playing and stay behind the other fingers until it plays again. When descending, the thumb moves out quickly after playing.

In a second approach, the emphasis is on keeping the thumb relaxed and in constant readiness to play whenever needed. In ascending scales, it should hang near the second finger and move only slightly under to play as the elbow pulls the hand steadily upward, out of the way. The wrist also rotates to align with each finger and rises to adjust to longer fingers. This allows the thumb more freedom to descend vertically. The thumb will move a bit more under the hand to follow the fourth finger but it should never be forced under the hand to play when the arm has not moved. In descending scales, the arm pushes the hand steadily down the keyboard, allowing smooth passage of the third or fourth finger over the thumb without a break. To play fast scales the fingers must be more active, and the fingertips stay closer to the keys. Wasted motion in an up or down direction steals time.

A third approach uses "doorknob" rotation (explained below). This rocking motion can be used in scales to prepare the thumb to play. It is used when the 3rd or 4th fingers precede or follow the thumbs. "The fingers remain active and turn the arm; the arm should not turn the fingers. This type of scale-playing is taught with single and double rotations," according to Sheila Paige and the technique developed by Dorothy Taubman.

## Arpeggios

The concept of arpeggios is often introduced to young students in hand-over-hand style. It is not until late elementary and intermediate level repertoire that students have to deal with melodic or harmonic arpeggios. The technique of playing scales applies equally to arpeggio playing. While the wrist stays basically horizontal, it will rise and rotate as the arm aligns with each longer finger before the thumb plays. In slow playing a true legato may be possible because the wrist and hand can turn sufficiently to allow space for the thumb to descend vertically. In fast playing, a twisting motion is not possible. It is necessary to make a small break between the third or fourth finger and the thumb as the arm moves rapidly over the keys. This break will be unnoticeable to the ear at a fast tempo.

## Chords

The voicing of chords provides subtle harmonic colors by projecting melodies, inner voices, and bass lines. Careful balance of the voicing adds richness to the texture of the music. To develop the necessary finger independence, chord progressions should be practiced with one voice (root, 3$^{rd}$ or 5$^{th}$) loud and the other voices soft. Consequently, the student learns to add weight to a specific finger at any appointed time. Voicing broken chord and Alberti bass patterns also develops individual control of the fingers involved.

## Fingering

The use of consistently correct fingering is an aspect of technical training often misunderstood by students. Teachers would be millionaires if given a dollar every time they say, "Watch your fingering!" If correct fingerings are used, students build good technique and good finger memory. When students practice incorrect fingerings, they are often practicing awkward technical movement. Efficient fingering is essential when learning any repertoire or technical piece. It is important that all students use suggested fingerings in the music and develop good fingering habits from the first playing.

Sometimes students prefer to use a different fingering than what is written. They will begin learning principals of good fingering if they work with the teacher and choose a usable alternative. All changes should be carefully notated in the score. Older students should be taught to write the fingerings in the music themselves. This develops student judgment for future decisions. Changes in fingering should be made within a week or two of beginning study of a piece to avoid making poor choices into nearly indelible habits.

Changes to fingerings may be the best option when the student cannot play a passage after a length of time. Students should be advised that slow practice fingerings sometimes do not work at faster tempi and may need revising after a period of time. The role of the teacher is to facilitate a final product that produces a musical result, with fingerings often modified by the hand shape, student ability, and musical intent.

# Elements of Touch and Sound Quality

## Staccato

There are many different ways to play a staccato depending on the length of the note, the dynamic marking, the use of silence, and context in the tempo of the piece. Some techniques may vary depending on the age of the student. Children are sometimes offered images to better understand staccato such as "imagine popcorn popping." Pretending the key is hot is not recommended because the muscles tighten to prevent burning the fingers. Most beginners can grasp the concept of an equal division of down and up, which produces the Classical Period staccato, where note values are shortened by half. The movement is primarily from the wrist.

The primary question to address in staccato is "how is the key approached?" For example, staccato technique can involve throwing the whole arm into the keys from a loose upper arm, whether playing octaves, chords, or single notes but with varying force. Varying the speed, height of lift, and position of hand also controls the length and amount of sound. Alignment of arm and hand are important for ease of playing. Also, consideration should be given to the amount of motion needed for a staccato as this motion decreases with the increase in speed of the tempo. Students should practice each of the following staccato techniques until comfortable. They involve integrated, simultaneous control of fingers, hand, wrist and arm.

**Finger staccato** is mainly used in single note passages where the musical content demands lightness. Consider "scratching" the keys lightly, or feeling a kind of pulling sensation from the tip of the fingers for a light and close to the key approach. The fingers should rest on the key before striking. Allow the key to ascend, the instant the sound is heard, to carry the hand upward with the key. The key will come up by itself if you give it the chance. The wrist remains fairly quiet during the process. One can also think about the release of the staccato as a fast exit out of the key like jumping on a trampoline.

**Wrist staccato** can more correctly be described as hand staccato because it is the hand that moves and not the wrist. This staccato is useful in parallel or repeated 3ths, 6ths, octaves, and repeated chords, as well as single notes depending on the sound desired. The fingers are the receivers of the wrist and arm movement. The upper arm and forearm remain stationary, and the shoulder is down and relaxed. Students can easily discover the mechanics of wrist staccato by grabbing their right arm with their left hand where the forearm meets the wrist.

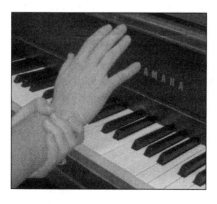 

Move your hand up and down as if you are waving to someone to feel the wrist bend. After a quick downward movement from the wrist, the hand rebounds immediately after touching the key like a bouncing ball. When the same chord is repeated quickly, there is no time to rest between chords, so this rebounding motion resembles a vibration—the fingers never lose contact with the key. When chords are different, remember to adjust the position of the hand and arm to accommodate the new chord with a slight lateral hand and forearm motion.

**Forearm staccato** produces a bigger sound and may be used in chord passages and single or double notes. The forearm and hand, from elbow to fingertip, is used as one lever. The elbow should feel light. Do not bend the wrist while reaching the keyboard or leaving it. The forearm bounces out of the key as the fingers absorb the impact and spring upward.

**Full arm staccato** produces the loudest staccato. The upper arm begins the throw with all other arm/hand parts prepared to absorb the impact and rebound. Throwing the full arm into the keyboard is recommended, but caution must be taken to avoid a build up of tension. Therefore, remember to stay loose and release any tension during the rebound. The fingers absorb the impact and spring upward.

## Rotation

Forearm rotation can be described as "doorknob" rotation. It involves rocking the hand between the low thumb side of the hand (supination) and the higher fifth finger side (pronation). The rotary motion principle resembles the back and forth turning of a doorknob (not to be confused with the motion of moving a door handle). The forearm, wrist, and hand act together as one unit from the elbow; the upper arm doesn't participate in the movement. It is important to keep the upper arm raised and away from the body to allow the forearm to rotate freely and steadily. Students should be reminded the fingers remain active and turn the arm; the arm should not turn the fingers.

Rotation adds power and speed to the fingers and helps maintain a balanced hand. It can be used for trills or Alberti bass, or whenever notes in a series move back and forth, or to play any broken interval within the relaxed span of the fingers. As fingers 2, 3, and 4 travel toward the thumb or toward the 5th finger, the arm should always be in a straight line with or between the fingers involved. The fingers should never stretch for a wide interval. Forearm rotation on wider intervals requires a lateral arc of the hand across the distance between the notes. This motion causes a relaxed upper arm to jiggle when playing repeated wide intervals or broken octaves.

This following exercise, *Rotating 3rds,* by Carolyn and Jamie Shaak, uses rotation. A student should first exaggerate the rotating motion, and then increase the speed so the rotation becomes less obvious. The rotation is a left to right on ascending thirds, and right to left on descending thirds.

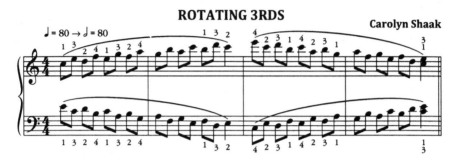

Rotating 3rds from the *Shaak Technique Book, Book 1*. Copyright © Carolyn Shaak—used by permission.

## Full Arm Drop

Forte chords or single notes are effectively produced by using the pull of gravity, the ever-present source of energy. When asked how he could play for hours and not seem tired, famous jazz pianist Duke Ellington replied, "Gravity man, gravity!" Dropping the arm freely produces a powerful resonant sound depending on the strength of the finger joints. Students should practice and master the free fall motion at a slow to moderate tempo where free fall works best. The whole arm is raised to a level no more than 10 inches above the keys, suggests Sandor. The distance can vary with each pianist. With a lowered wrist, the hand forms the chord or prepares the finger in the air. It is important to keep the shoulder down and bring the elbow in so the arm can drop straight down into the keys. The arm must drop, totally relaxed, into the keys. The curved fingers, flexible wrist, hand, elbow, and shoulder joints unite to absorb the impact as a rebound, like a bouncing ball. The letting-go feeling of the rebound releases pressure on the fingertips as the arm rises to be ready for the next drop. This is an ideal way to practice chord inversions in all keys.

## Thrust

This technique is best used for chords with wide stretches as it avoids accidentally landing on the wrong notes. It is well suited for slow to moderately fast chord sequences. Thrust can produce the loudest sound that is possible on the piano, but it can also be used for all levels of dynamics. To adjust the quality of sound and dynamic level, you vary the speed of the muscle contraction which changes the speed of the attack. The fingers remain in constant contact with the keys before, during, and after the sudden muscle contraction that takes place within the body. The chest, stomach, back triceps, and forearm flexors combine to push the keys down instantaneously. The fingers must go vertically into the keys and the hand, wrist, and arm must be firmly fixed during the attack. The entire mechanism must instantly relax to be ready for the next thrust.

## Pedal

Pedal technique should be taught early. Placing the heel on the floor and the ball of the foot on the pedal is important. A pedal extender can be useful for small children. A pedal extender box essentially brings the floor and two pedals, the soft and sustain pedals, up underneath the legs of a young student. The left pedal sits on top of the soft pedal (una corda) and the right pedal sits on top of the sustain or damper pedal. Small children can stand and lean against the edge of the bench when a pedal extender is unavailable.

Careful listening to the effects produced is crucial, because it is the ear that controls pedaling. A beginner will easily blend occasional isolated sections with pedal but, as soon as harmonic changes occur more frequently, the syncopated pedaling technique must be used. The foot presses after the first chord is played, then lifts as the next chord is struck and goes down again after it sounds. This timing can be shown while playing triads moving stepwise to demonstrate the necessity of separating unrelated sounds. With practice, the movement becomes almost as instantaneous as the knee-jerk reaction to a tap on the kneecap. As the student progresses, techniques of half-pedal and flutter pedal are taught.

# Technique Books for Young Pianists

Technique books provide ways to teach various basic technical skills found in piano literature. As a student develops basic fundamental skills, technique studies by Czerny, Hanon, Pischna, Philipp, and Schmitt are often assigned. However, many teachers have their own approach to technical drills or prefer just to teach scales to beginners. For the younger student, most beginning piano methods incorporate technical training either within the main text or in separate books that are referenced to pages within the principal book. The following list explores some examples:

The Alfred Basic Piano Library's *Technic Books* by Lethco, Manus, and Palmer are coordinated with the lesson books and written to support the concepts. The table of contents recommends when to assign the technical exercises.

Alfred's *Premier Piano Course* by Alexander, Kowalchyk, Lancaster, McArthur, and Mier combines technique principals within the lesson book. Short exercises called "Workouts" are included where needed. Technique is developed equally in both hands.

The Bastien Method's *Technic* Books, published by Kjos, are coordinated with the Piano, Theory, and Performance books at each level. *Technic* contains a variety of exercises to develop hand and finger coordination, and to develop control and facility at the keyboard. James and Jane Bastien suggest playing the exercises as warm-ups before beginning to practice pieces.

The Edna-Mae Burnam series *A Dozen a Day,* was first published by the Willis Music Company in 1957 (Hal Leonard/Willis). These preparatory through level 4 books contain short warm-up exercises that address various technical challenges to be played at the beginning of the student's practice session.

*Celebrate Piano!* a method by Albergo, Kolar, and Mrozinski, published by Frederick Harris Music conveniently packages technique within the *Lesson and Musicianship* book.

Frances Clark's *The Music Tree Series for the younger beginner* (Alfred/ Summy-Birchard) incorporates technique within each unit developing finger independence, facility and tonal control. Six *Piano Technic Books* for the early intermediate to early advanced student by Clark and Louis Goss, prepares students for the technical demands in music at that level. These books present musical situations, not mere exercises, to encourage the natural development of a sound basic technique.

The four-book compendium of *Musical Fingers* by pedagogues Frances Clark, Louis Goss, and Sam Holland (Alfred/Summy-Birchard) is another valuable technical source. Book One contains various short exercises in five-finger positions using legato and staccato touch, slurs, extension to the interval of a sixth and contractions involving chromatic scale fragments, and introduction to scales and hand-over-hand arpeggios. Especially helpful are the pictures of the keyboard showing carefully positioned black dotted circles on specific keys to promote rounded shapes and avoid a cramped (curved fingers) approach.

By the time students have completed all four books of *Musical Fingers,* they will have mastered the intricacies of scale and arpeggio playing, diminished seventh chords, thirds, sixths, octaves, scales, voicing, rapid repeated notes and trills. Students will be well grounded in piano technique and able to solve their own technical problems in early to advanced literature.

The Hal Leonard piano method's *Piano Practice Games Book* by Kreader, Kern, Keveren, and Rejino coordinates theory, technique, and creativity with the music in the piano lesson book. The method also has a separate *Piano Technique* book that supports the lesson book.

The FJH Helen Marlais' *Succeeding at the Piano* method integrates technique with the lesson book. Students are encouraged to memorize the exercises so they focus on watching their fingers, hands, and arms, as well as on listening to the sound they create.

The *Pace Keyboard Approach,* Robert Pace's groundbreaking work in multi-key instruction has led gradually to incorporation of interval reading, transposition and improvisation in many piano methods. *Finger Builders*, the technique volumes of his piano method, provide training for all levels of study. Technical exercises with two or three note legato technique, pentascales in all major and minor keys, and tetrachord scales comprise the first year of lessons. The exercises include many varied dynamic levels and multiple legato, staccato, and slurred-note touches. These prepare students to learn one-octave parallel motion scales in all major and relative minor keys in the second year. Scales and arpeggios in two octaves are presented in the third year and four octaves in the fourth year. In every year, scales are accompanied by Hanon-type exercises transposed to each key. This develops thorough knowledge of which notes are unique to that key, and facilitates transposition and improvisation. A student learns that each key has its own language and vocabulary. Chordal voicing and expressive playing are stressed throughout.

*Piano Adventures*, a piano method by Nancy and Randall Faber, includes five levels of *Technique and Artistry Books* that teach technical gesture for artistic playing. Technique "secrets" and exercises give a student tools to play with ease and expression. An artistry hint and piece conclude each unit making the student aware of sound and musicality while developing fluent piano technique. Other topics discussed include good posture, firm fingertips, the use of arm weight, wrist movement, alignment, and rotation. These topics are explained in a simple manner relating the subject matter to everyday life such as blooming flowers, heavy ropes, basketball dribbles, and woodpecker taps.

The Shaak *Technique Book – Book I,* by Carolyn and Jamie Shaak, leading independent teachers in Denver, is packed with useful information, photos and exercises for the beginner and intermediate student. The authors seek to adapt natural movements in life to gestures at the piano. Pedal techniques and scales are included. Exercises in the book include:

1. *Arm as a Unit* (feeling the whole arm behind each gesture to project a focused sound)

2. *Grouping* (shaping a group of notes to give meaning and expressiveness)

3. *Rotation* (the wrist and forearm turn together to achieve a smooth fluid sound)

4. *Letting Go* (resting the arm in a stretched sock as a sling, then releasing the arm to fall freely)

5. *Follow Through* (throwing darts and observing tension vanish)

6. *Rebound/Up* (bouncing ping-pong balls illustrates the springiness needed with staccato touch)

7. *Arm Behind Each Finger* (as fingers move from one key to key, the arm travels along)

John Thompson's *Modern Course for the Piano* Book 1 (Willis/Hal Leonard) includes 16 technical drills in the back of the book. The exercises are intended for use during the study of the book. The drills develop fingers, arms, wrists, and 2 and 3-note slur playing.

## Etudes and Studies

Etudes serve a special purpose in addition to short technical exercises as part of the piano assignment. Etudes represent real music, not exercises, and each address a special technical problem that must be mastered. Etudes by Chopin, Debussy, Liszt, Moszkowski, Rachmaninoff, and Scriabin are fine technical studies for advanced pianists, but finding practical etudes for the younger student is more difficult. This sampling includes both etudes and studies through late-intermediate levels.

Bela Bartok's pieces *For Children*, elementary to intermediate level, are excellent studies of various touches and phrasing, carefully indicated by the composer. These short pieces, based on Hungarian and Slovakian folk music idioms, are musical and beautiful, but require close attention to the composer's detailed markings.

Johann Friedrich Burgmuller's *25 Easy and Progressive Studies, Op. 100*, require the student and teacher to determine what precise technical movements and touches are required. Early technical development should include learning most of these compositions. Working through this volume prepares a student for masterworks of the Classic and Romantic styles.

The Celebration Series' *Piano Studies/Etudes* (Frederick Harris Music) are designed to build technique and musicality and can be used for recitals and competitions. All involve the control of touch--staccato, legato, marcato, accents, slurs, or repeated notes. The first three of ten levels can be used with the younger student. The series *Handbook for Teachers* by Cathy Albergo, Reid Alexander, and Marvin Blickenstaff includes practice suggestions.

The music in the Frances Clark *Piano Etudes* Series in four levels (Alfred/Summy-Birchard) is appropriate for elementary and intermediate students. Practice suggestions by Phyllis Alpert Lehrer focus the student's attention on musical shape through physical sensation, choreography and breathing.

There are several collections by Carl Czerny that are accessible to the younger student. *The Little Pianist, Op. 823*, begins easy and progresses quickly to the intermediate level. *100 Progressive Studies for the Piano, Op. 139*, are primarily one-page, melodic and characteristically repetitious.

Czerny *Selected Piano Studies*, arranged in order of difficulty by Heinrich Germer (50 selected Studies from Op. 139, 261, 599. 821, Volume One) are carefully paced for the young student.

Cornelius Gurlitt's *35 Easy Etudes, Op. 130* are a collection of short character pieces. Gurlitt has written hundreds of pieces for children which are highly idiomatic to the Romantic Period.

Charles-Louis Hanon's *The Virtuoso Pianist 60 Exercises for the Piano,* are well-known white key exercises with the emphases on agility, finger independence, and evenness in the fingers. The collection also includes 12 major and minor scales and arpeggios. The last section is designed to prepare pianists for virtuosic mastery. Transposing these studies teaches students how to navigate black keys. For example, try No. 1 in the key of Db.

The works of Dmitri Kabalevsky, *24 Pieces for Children, Op. 39* and the more challenging *Children's Pieces, Op. 27* are short pieces that begin on the level of a first solo piece, and progress in consecutive order through most aspects of technical development.

*Twenty Short Studies, Op. 91* by Moritz Moszkowski, edited by Maurice Hinson, are short musical pieces that emphasize one aspect of piano technique.

## Conclusion

Remember that children are like sponges—so don't be afraid to show them how to fix their technical problems. There is the old adage "if it ain't broke, don't fix it." However, pain is a sign of incorrect playing and if, indeed, something is broken, it must be fixed. Therefore, students need to be wise when practicing and should be reminded to take needed breaks. Instead of endurance training—a "no pain, no gain" attitude—all pianists must learn to use the most efficient movement and learn to study music away from the piano.

Many teachers agree: when you get inside the music, the technique comes naturally. As C.P.E. Bach suggests in his *Essay on the True Art of Playing Keyboard Instruments,* "A musician cannot move others unless he, too, is moved. He must, of necessity, feel all of the affects that he hopes to arouse in his audience." The technical preparation and achievement of being able to play the piece is only part of the journey. Teaching students how to make music, have fun while doing it, and become their own teachers in practice, is the ultimate destination.

We thank our colleagues and friends Paul Sheftel, Elizabeth Cormier, Anne Hastings Fiedler, Anna White Hayward, Jeffry Peterson, and Carolyn Shaak for talking "technique" with us. This chapter is better thanks to you!

# References

Bach, C.P.E. *Essay on the True Art of Playing Keyboard Instruments,* translated and edited by William J. Mitchell. New York: W.W. Norton, 1949.

Clark, Frances; Goss, Louise; Holland, Sam. *Musical Fingers,* Alfred/ Summy-Birchard, 1983.

Cormier, Elizabeth. Blair School of Music, Vanderbilt University, Emerita; Consultant, International Piano Teaching Foundation, Robert Pace, Director.

Chronister, Richard. *A Piano Teacher's Legacy,* USA: The Frances Clark Center for Keyboard Pedagogy, Inc., 2005.

Hinson, Maurice. *Guide to the Pianist's Repertoire,* Bloomington: Indiana University Press, 1973.

Lyke, James; Elliston, Ron. Champaign, Illinois: Stipes, 1974. "First Year Piano Patterns With Rhythm Background."

Magrath, Jane. *The Pianist's Guide to Standard Teaching and Performance Literature,* California: Alfred Publishing Company, 1995.

Paige, Sheila. Executive Director Keyboard Wellness Seminar Division of Piano Wellness LLC; http://www.KeyboardWellnessSeminar.com.

Sandor, Gyorgy. *On Playing the Piano,* New York: Schirmer Books, 1981; London: Collier Macmillan, 1981.

Sevier, John. Piano bench risers. Technical Services, Blair School of Music, Vanderbilt University. JS.Baritone@gmail.com.

Shaak, Carolyn; Shaak, Jamie. *The Shaak Technique Book "How to Improve your Tone and Technical Skills at the Piano," Book 1.* Denver: Moonstone Music Press, 2006.

# MOTIVATION

# CHAPTER 9

## Preparing Students for Competitions and Fostering a Lifelong Passion for Music

### Catherine Rollin

When I began teaching piano I was a starry eyed optimist who believed 100% in the importance of being true to the musical score and doing everything in ones' power to honor the intentions of the composer. My goal was to always bring the music off the page with authenticity and integrity and to bring the beauty of the music to life. My initial experience as a teacher was one that constantly challenged me to stay true to my beliefs. Because I was a novice teacher, most of the families that were entrusting me with their children were doing so for the wrong reasons—at least by my standards. I would have hoped that the parents would have been interested in my bachelor of musical arts degree with distinction from a well known university. Or perhaps they would like to know that as an undergrad, I was selected to be a collaborative pianist with a prominent violinist on his DMA recital. These facts held no interest for "my families." No one even asked me if I had a degree in music. Their primary concerns were: 1. Do you come to the house? 2. What are your rates? And then knowing that these were both to their liking—the fact that I was young and "perky" was the icing on the cake.

So with a group of students whose families' primary concerns had nothing to do with the musical outcome of the lessons—my career as a piano teacher began. If keeping my high musical standards was going to be important to me, I was in for the challenge of my life. My students' parents were probably my most daunting adversaries in my quest for musical excellence. When I told them that the students had to count, observe the indications on the page and carve out daily practice time—the standard response was: *"We love you, the kids love you, but we don't want our kids to be concert pianists!*" This kind of statement made me realize just how ill informed most families were. To them, even spending time on practicing was not part of their expectation. It really shocked me to realize that my insistence on students differentiating between a quarter and half note made parents think that I was too demanding. But, given my novice standing, I was not about to attract "serious" students and "serious" parents, so I persisted.

One of my first goals was to bring out the students' natural love of music as a motivator. At the time, I was not doing this as a "strategy." It was just what I thought a good teacher should do. Now—I see this as step one in getting students motivated to practice:

1. **Find music that your students love.**

At this early point in my career, most of my students were either beginners or transfer students who had at most a few years of lessons under their belts.

I knew that most method material, while important, was usually not the music that students wanted to play over and over and master. So I began to search for music that was fun, beautiful and inspiring. I found that in the music of William Gillock. Through my acquaintance with William Gillock I not only learned about how good pedagogical music can make a huge difference in a students' love of music and piano, but I also got started on the road to writing pedagogical music myself.

In William Gillock's music I found exactly what I was looking for: pieces that sounded like real music. In his music I found good melodies, rhythms that were fun and lots of written out details that helped students develop musically.

I kept on my path of high standards. In spite of the mine-field like distractions of parents saying they didn't want their kids to be too dedicated (!) I kept insisting on right notes, right counting and even trying to follow every indication on the score. In a remarkably short time, this unmotivated, uncommitted group of students started sounding really musical!

This led to somewhat of a revolution in my little group of uncommitted parents and students. This occurred after the first recital. This revolution leads me to discuss step 2 of the strategy: having many public performance opportunities.

2. **Have your students perform in as many venues as possible.**

My first recital was held in my mother's living room because I didn't have a grand piano in my own home yet. I was so excited to present my students in their debuts as pianists—students who actually sounded musical! I couldn't even wait until the spring. So on a snowy Sunday afternoon in

February, I had my students give their first recital. Miraculously, the recital went extremely well with almost everyone performing at their best. The parents were all asking me who this guy Gillock was. They were animated and proud of their kids and said that this was the best recital that they had ever been to. They gushed that this was the first time that they actually listened to the other students and not just their own kids, etc., etc.

Now I do not want to mislead anyone to think that after that recital everyone became a great student. But many of the students from that recital did "last" as my students for several years. Some of them went on to play through high school and become quite fine players. Especially considering that their families had such low expectations to start with, this was really an impressive result. The most important thing that I witnessed at that first recital was a wonderful change in the parents' attitude. From a state of indifference or even hostility at any demands being placed on their children, their attitude changed to one of one of support and commitment. Strategy number three:

3. **Family support and commitment**.

From that first recital, I learned how helpful it was to have the parents on your side. I found out that what seems like a natural supposition—is not a given. The parents' support of lessons should not be limited to only financial support. It means a great deal if they respect the teacher and the teacher's musical goals. Parents have to realize that they have to help their children carve out time for practice. In fact, it really helps if they practice with them—occasionally or regularly, depending on each individual student.

Once the parents heard this first recital, they realized that having high expectations made a big difference. They realized that if their children were spending any time practicing, they might as well do it correctly. This leads to the next important strategy:

4. **Schedule practice time and make the most of your practice time.**

What I have always tried to impress upon my students from day one is this: you must practice and you must make every moment of your practice count. Parents and students have to realize that without any investment of time, they cannot achieve results. Additionally, the practice sessions have to be productive. It is our job as teachers to show our students how to practice in order to get results. Practice has to be methodical. Slow, hands separate practice is first and continuing hands separate practice to work out all details and trouble spots is imperative. I also stress that as one reads new music, it is important not only to read the notes and the rhythm, but also read all of the other indications. It is absolutely insane to learn the notes and "put the expression in later."

Practice is exactly that. It is practice and preparation for how one eventually will play the piece. Obviously, one cannot feel the true degree of agitato if one is playing it five times slower than the final tempo. But I believe it helps to try to think of all the elements—such as dynamics, touch, etc. in the early stages of learning a piece of music.

Making the most of one's practice time also leads to something that is crucial for successful performances: Focus and concentration. This is the hallmark of the next strategy:

5.  **Practicing with focus, concentration and good listening.**

How you practice is how you will perform. Performance of any kind adds intensity and some stress to the experience of playing a piece. If a student is generally practicing with good concentration and focus, the likelihood that he will stay focused on the music during public performance is increased greatly.

If a student is practicing with mindless repetition, the student will have trouble in performance. For example, the assignment is to *play 3 times hands separately, 3 times hands together* with no other specific thing to focus on. If the student is accustomed to practicing with mindless repetition they are going to revert to that mindless state in performance. At this point, the performer will be relying on sheer motor memory which will lead to a panicky state during performance. If we teachers help our students to understand how to practice, what to listen for and to always listen—chances are that when our students are performing they will also be able to keep up their habit of listening. I believe that the first recital that I had for my students was a success because I drilled listening skills into my first students from the very beginning. I often tell my students—if you listen to yourself, others will listen to you—you will draw in your audience. **Listening also helps reduce the nervousness because we are focused on the music. Focusing on the music takes the attention off of the pure, raw nerves.**

After a fairly short time, I had parents beginning to call me not just because I was perky, coming to the house and the lessons were inexpensive. I started to receive calls for teaching because I was producing good students. Over the years my studio started attracting some of the most talented students in my state. But even with very talented students—the above "strategies" hold true.

The last strategy that I developed over the first decade of my teaching was:

6.  **Developing technical skills that reflect a true understanding of the keyboard and how one's physicality interacts with the instrument.**

Unfortunately, technique is one of the weakest areas for most students. The majority of students don't have a concept of how to produce a good tone, how to play evenly and how to stay physically relaxed. I found that many teachers either classify students as either "those with good fingers" or " those who are pretty hopeless beyond intermediate level." Basically, most teachers pretty much think that "you are what you are" and they might make an effort to give students scales, Czerny and Hanon, but they accept that most people are totally limited by their natural physical gifts. From my very first years of teaching piano I have been exploring the development of arm weight playing, relaxation and the mastery of skills that use larger motor movements rather than finger oriented playing that is totally reliant on small motor skills. This kind of "informed" physicality is important for all students of piano both those with natural "small motor coordination and those with limited small motor skills. Through careful analysis we can get almost any student to play with some degree of artistry that emanates from physical understanding and relaxation.

If students actually understand which physical movements produce which specific sounds, and which physical movements produce tension or relaxation, they are much better equipped to perform a piece. If they have analyzed and practiced their music with a thought-out physical approach, they are much more likely to do well in public performance and competition.

Now that my class of students is comprised of students who generally have above average talent and motivation—I still stress the importance of all of the above strategies. I still spend hours trying to find them repertoire that they truly love. Whether it is a pedagogical piece by Rollin or Gillock or a major masterwork of Chopin or Beethoven, I still think it is my number one priority to find music that the student loves and that is challenging, but also  possible to master. Students **need** to love the music in order to put in the time to truly master it—especially for public performance and competition. There is nothing like drilling a piece for competition that one doesn't even like. Its torture! And really nothing associated with music should ever be torture!

I try to find as many enjoyable and challenging performance and competing opportunities as possible so students will be well experienced in performance itself. The experience of communicating through musical performance is a reward unto itself. But the experience of competitions gives students concrete deadlines and goals. Performing for recitals and competitions gives students external motivation.

With these motivating goals—the practice is always more focused and productive. Students see their peers being rewarded with trophies and commendations for sports, debate teams, etc. It is very helpful to have competitive events that result in similar awards for their work at the piano. While we can tell our children that the music in of itself is the reward, at a young age, it helps to have a real trophy or blue ribbon in hand!

The families that I teach now know that I expect the parents to be active supporters of the lessons. They often come to lessons, video tape them and review them with their children at home. The lesson and even practice often becomes shared family time. This creates a wonderful foundation for the students' love of music. Parents who really invest in lessons through time and not only their check book also become more deeply involved in and dedicated to their children's music study.

All of the above strategies were based on my initial desire to get my students to develop passion for and love of music. Once I saw how important these above steps were, they became my modus operandi and have been the basis for my teaching strategies for over 30 years.

The above strategies form the basis of how I teach and how I instruct students to learn and practice all of the time. These strategies also form the foundation for success at competitions. If your students really love their music, are true to the score, have practiced well with great focus and have the attitude of commitment within themselves and the support of their families, all that they need to do is get out there and perform and most importantly share and communicate their music with an audience. They might not "win" everything, but many times they will. Most judges prize, above all else, a performer's ability to communicate the essence of the music and share the musical experience. A student taught with the above strategies has the best chance at being able to receive the public recognition, the scholarship, blue ribbon or trophy that symbolizes his accomplishment. Win or lose at the actual competition, a musician who has something to say with his music and says it well and with commitment and love, is a lifetime "winner."

# PRACTICING

# CHAPTER 10

## The Young Pianist Practices

### Christos Tsitsaros

The problem of practicing at the elementary level is tightly connected to the more general issue of musical motivation. Based on the assumption that there is no child devoid of the gift of sound, and no child who cannot learn the language of music and develop the ability to play an instrument, we can safely conclude that lack of motivation in children is solely due either to the parents or the teachers.

How and when should musical motivation be cultivated in children? Motivation is not a state of mind that can be expressly implanted in students within a specific span of time, be it one day, one month or even a year. It is rather a disposition that is naturally and systematically nurtured by the child's environment during the formative years. Preferably, sound experiences should take place between the ages of three and five, when the child's excitement, wonder and curiosity are at their peak. Understandably, the natural ability to discover and learn through direct experience, innate in children, carries through in the area of music.

Children who have listened to various kinds of music in their home environment, who have seen their parents or other relatives play a musical instrument, or even better, who have had themselves musical experiences of any nature, such as informally playing an instrument, singing or dancing, are more likely to become motivated and learn to play an instrument. The student's desire to learn an instrument should invariably stem from within, from the internal need and urgency to create, express and communicate by means of sound. Under no circumstance should the student undertake lessons because of external reasons, such as pleasing his parents, or imitating his peers. Lack of this prerequisite condition will invariably create disinterested students. It is therefore the parents' responsibility to prepare the foundations at the right time, should they wish their children to begin and continue studying the piano. This is of course only part of the parents' role in the motivation process; we will return to the family environment, after we shift our attention to the role of the teacher.

How does a teacher direct and channel the beginner's desire to learn to play the piano, and how does he lead him to good practicing habits? Before we attempt to answer this question, it would be helpful to examine some of the characteristics of children's learning psychology. Children's mastery of different skills stems from their curiosity to learn things that capture their excitement and their love of play and fun. This implies learning by direct experience, by means of trial and error, rather than by rationalizing and applying cognitive ideas. This assumption helps us also to trace the origins of children's motivation: essentially the need to express themselves and communicate their thoughts and feelings through the medium of sound, and in return to enjoy and take pleasure in the music they are producing. It is essential for us to bear this in mind, because this is the key to the problem of how to motivate beginners to practice: by making practicing both interesting and fun for them. Something is enjoyable and fun when it is relatively easy and feasible, when it can be mastered with the least amount of effort, and when the results can be enjoyed immediately and appreciated by the student's nearby environment. Something is interesting when it appeals to the student's taste, stirs in him a certain emotion, stimulates his imagination and succeeds in capturing his interest. Constant cooperation between teacher and parents is essential to ensure that the student continues to perceive music learning and practicing as something he looks forward to, rather than something he is obliged to do.

There are several steps that can be taken in the above direction. One of them is the choice of appropriate literature by the teacher. The biggest part of the assigned music should fit the student's musical background and reflect his musical preferences. It should be relevant to the auditory experiences that he has already had, and therefore it should be understandable and appealing to him. A variety of musical idioms, such as folk song, occasional music, jazz, or even famous classic tunes arranged for piano, may be employed here, in conjunction with the standard music literature, in order to maintain the student's level of interest and excitement. Additional duets and four hand pieces are very appropriate because they provide the student with a richer sense of harmony, they help him with the rhythmical aspect and they are fun to play. In terms of content, the pieces should be relevant to the new concepts presented at the lesson, or they should review, and thus reinforce, elements and skills that have already been mastered in previous lessons. Finding appealing and interesting pieces, of appropriate length and level of difficulty, is part of the teacher's responsibility. Good editions containing useful fingerings should be carefully selected. Especially at the elementary level, pieces should always be within reach in a considerably short time. Teachers may therefore need to become updated and flexible in terms of finding materials that are pedagogically useful and at the same time fit the student's needs. We are fortunate today to have an enormous proliferation of such pieces composed by a number of excellent contemporary educational composers with the elementary student in mind.

The presentation phase of a piano lesson is undoubtedly the most important with regard to capturing the student's interest and excitement, and in turn leading him to practice. It is during this initial stage that lies the teacher's responsibility to ignite the spark within the student. There exist a variety of ways that can be employed to attain this, but the most important of all is the enthusiasm shown by the teacher himself. In introducing new pieces, the teacher should present the musical picture in vivid colors, by relating it to its title, an image or a story. This will help the student understand the emotional content of the piece and associate the music with his personal experiences. It will also lead him to perceive music as a means of communication and expression. When introducing new concepts and pieces to beginning students, it is essential to start with the sound, because children understand in a simple, empirical and synthetic way rather than in an analytical one. The teacher should make sure that the student fully understands the newly introduced concepts by recognizing their sound, and by experiencing what it feels like to reproduce the same effects.

These two items, namely the presentation of new pieces and the introduction of new concepts, set the stage for the assignment of the work to be done at home. This is a sensitive point, requiring a good deal of judgment on the part of the teacher, in order to make the assignments as precise, relevant and clear as possible.

One obvious rule that must be followed to arrive at this result is never to assign pieces containing elements that have not been fully explained during the lesson time. The same is true for all assigned practicing suggestions: each activity should be rehearsed and demonstrated by the teacher. In this sense the lesson time should be in large part a step by step demonstration of what the student should practice at home. In doing so, the teacher sets small, precise, short-term goals for the student. Unclear objectives, lack of direction and excessive demands are all factors that will most likely frustrate the beginning student. Along the same lines, it is better to set goals one at a time than to expect multiple aspects of the piece to be mastered from session to session. For example, in presenting a new piece the teacher may explain the pitch, the rhythmic structure and write down important fingerings, expecting the student to master only these aspects by the next session. In subsequent lessons, he may stress other elements such as dynamics and articulation. Dividing the work in such a way can be of great help to beginners, especially in their effort to assimilate new musical and technical skills. Teachers often have the tendency to forget that they themselves view beginning pieces from their perspective, after years of musical study and experience, which is entirely different from the student's perspective. What may seem obvious and easy for the teacher, can be viewed as a mountain by the young student. This pertains to the fact stated earlier, that in order to make students practice, we have to make them perceive practicing as something easily attainable.

Varying and adapting the practicing routine is another important element on which the student's motivation depends for following through and applying the teacher's suggestions at home. While with more advanced students a consistent and predictable practicing routine may prove successful, employing the same standards with elementary students, in a rigid manner, may lead to discouragement. Routine implies repetition of a certain pattern of activities, lack of variation and predictability, and inevitably boredom. Interest through variation is a necessary prerequisite for the maintenance of the level of interest in the process of practicing.

To avoid this mistake the teacher may vary the activities and suggestions according to different items of the practicing agenda. For example, not all pieces should necessarily be practiced first with separate hands. The metronome does not have to be used at all times. Using these techniques, of course, should not be precluded, but rather blended with a multitude of other practicing suggestions, such as blocking melodic and chord patterns, trying different tempos, shifting accents, and playing the piece slowly and expressively from beginning to end. There should be a purpose for any suggested activity, based on the student's needs in a particular piece, and with a projected desired result in mind. Activities involving the singing voice and body movement are especially encouraged at the elementary level because of their potential as a sort of game and a means of variation; also because of their function in helping the student's grasp of concepts and ideas through direct experience.

Such activities may include clapping and singing the melodic line of a piece, swaying or stepping to the rhythm, tapping with one hand and playing with the other. The only precaution here is that each of these activities should not be merely assigned, but rehearsed and demonstrated during the lesson as well.

Finally, practicing should not be approached as a tedious activity, far removed from the final musical result. Children always tend to skip the necessary preparatory steps, attempting to savor the joy of playing the piece in its final form. This tendency can be both beneficial and destructive at the same time. The positive side of it is that children should never lose perspective of the purpose of practicing, that is to obtain maximum results with minimum effort. Often we forget this simple truth as we grow older. The negative side of it is that by skipping the necessary early stages, the mastery of the fine points of the music may become impaired, and the student may acquire bad technical and musical habits. Trying to keep a balance between these two sides is another point where the role of the teacher may be crucial in sustaining the student's interest in practicing. After all, pieces do not need to continue being practiced indefinitely. By allowing certain pieces, especially the ones that the student has already worked on for a while, just to be played in their entity, and enjoyed, the teacher can manage to obtain the sensitive balance between enjoyment and work. As a result of applying this method, the student is more likely to do more of the ground work that is required of him.

For this same reason, a good strategy is always to keep in hand pieces that the student likes, and knows how to play fairly well. Another idea is to provide the student with sight reading materials which he can play fairly easily, and which make use of concepts that he has already encountered in other pieces.

The order of the practicing activities may also be varied in order to maintain the student's interest. Especially at the elementary level, practicing sessions need not always have to start with technical drills or scales. The student may begin with one of his favorite pieces, continue with new assignments, later do some sight reading and so on. In this way, the ice of the dreaded practicing session is broken, and a more pleasant perspective of the time to be spent opens up for the student.

Every teacher knows the use of the assignment book, where the student can glance at a specific and organized plan of the practice session. In filling out the assignment book, teachers may find it useful to involve the student in the process by having him first verbalize and then write down his assignments, preferably as soon as they appear, instead of the end of the lesson. In this way the teacher makes sure that the student understands how each item should be practiced. On the other hand, the student will be more likely not to switch off his attention while the teacher does the work for him.

Even with the best intentions from the part of the teacher, there is always the possibility that the student does not follow up with his practicing in a systematic way. A recurring pattern that can be observed in today's students is their simultaneous involvement in a multitude of activities. In such cases, the teacher may need to find out and embrace the student's problems, ask questions about his daily activities, and help him out in finding time to practice the piano. Setting rigid standards of practicing may discourage a significant amount of students who feel excited about learning to play but cannot manage to keep up with such a routine. Only when the teacher approaches the student in a realistic way, as a person, will the student become willing to cooperate and put in the necessary effort. The teacher will soon discover that there will be days when the student will only be able to spend fifteen minutes at the piano. This is still better than not practicing at all because of feeling unable to stick to the set routine, which will eventually lead to hostility and finally aversion. Young students may be able to fit several small practicing sessions into their daily schedule instead of a long one; bearing in mind the rather short span of attention of young students, this division of practicing may prove to be beneficial.

The right choice of literature, clear and vivid presentation, definition of small attainable goals, and precise and realistic organization of the assignments and the practicing time are all steps to be taken by the teacher in order to ensure that the student follows through at home. This is where the parents can take an active role, by providing the right space and atmosphere during the practice sessions and by constantly supporting the student's efforts with genuine interest and positive reinforcement.

The space where the student practices is important for the quality and consistency of his work. It should be preferably free of distractions, such as noise from TV sets, stereos or other children playing nearby. If possible, it should also be inspiring: pictures of favorite musicians, a small musical library, records and an instrument in decent condition, are all contributing elements to the right musical environment.

An easy and subtle way to have parents follow the student's practicing is to have the student explain his assignments to them as soon as he returns from the lesson. This method has two advantages:

• the student reviews the assignment by verbalizing it.

• the parents show interest in their child's practicing without seeming to supervise him in an authoritative way.

For the elementary student, the sense of recognition of his achievement by his immediate environment is a primary condition for the maintenance of his desire to learn. The parents can provide moral support in ways that are both relevant and realistic. Simply acknowledging the student's work and results is a much needed gesture. This can be done by periodically listening to the student and offering positive comments on the beauty of the music he is practicing and on the way he plays it. Other ways of doing this are singing or humming the tunes after the child has finished practicing, or asking him to play at a special occasion, such as a gathering of friends and family. It is far better for parents to provide motivation of an intrinsic nature, related to the music and the benefits of practicing, than of an extrinsic nature, such as bribing him with material items. If material rewards are to be used, they should remain rewards for achievement and in no case become conditions of practicing. Replacing intrinsic motivational stimuli with extrinsic ones is dangerous, as it may become harmful and have negative effects in the long run.

The lowest form of motivation that can be employed by parents is the threat and fear of punishment. In cases where parents systematically resort to such tactics, they risk discouraging their child and sooner or later seeing him drop out. The reason this may happen is quite simple: when the fun and excitement are replaced by fear and boredom, there is little hope that the student will keep up with his activities and assignments. When students refuse to practice in a reactive manner, it should be time for parents to investigate carefully, both outside and within themselves, in order to find out where the problem lies. Imposing radical solutions will certainly not improve the situation, and are more likely to create feelings of failure and guilt in the student.

The evaluation stage is no less critical for the fostering of a healthy attitude toward practicing, for it is then that the student will eventually feel a sense of accomplishment and more importantly gain confidence in his method of practicing, by seeing the teacher validate his results.

The teacher will have to use firmness combined with discretion, to prompt the student to correct, refine and strengthen different skills, and at the same time send a message to him that his work is worthwhile and productive. More importantly the teacher will have to inspire confidence to the student and the assurance that he can build new skills based on the ones that he has just learned. No matter how far removed the student's product is from the ideal, there is always a way of starting from a positive angle. By stressing what is good in the student's performance and providing specific praise, the teacher validates the results of his work. Even in the event that the student has not worked enough, at least he will not be turned off by feeling inadequate. Similarly, the weak sides and the mistakes should be pointed out to the student in the form of positive suggestions, rather than negative criticism. Comments like "this sounds arrhythmical, too loud, clumsy" etc. can easily become constructive by turning them into comments like "let's try to make this more . . ." or "what if . . .". Another way to do this is to ask the student different questions concerning the piece, and have him determine himself if he has applied what is written on the page. By criticizing his own performance, the student becomes more active in the evaluating process; in addition to this his listening ability will improve considerably.

Apart from providing frequent praise and constructive criticism, rewarding the young student with stars, prizes and certificates may stimulate him to practice more. This is partly due to the elusive and abstract nature of music, the results and rewards of which cannot be observed in material form.

The teacher may find it useful to review the various steps of practicing with the student during the lesson. In this way, the student can realize how his weak spots are related to different parts of the practicing sequence that may have been overlooked or even neglected. By proving to the student that everything he does at the lesson is the result of his practicing, the student will understand the value of practicing and gradually develop a trust in the process.

Providing models for the student is an excellent way to inspire the desire to practice. This can be done in a variety of different ways: the teacher may periodically demonstrate, or have the student listen to recordings, or organize informal studio recitals. Such events form an opportunity for the student to share his own gifts and listen to both his peers and more advanced students.

Finally, the teacher will have to decide how long the student should keep the same pieces and assignments, whether he should continue correcting and perfecting or move on to new things. Especially at the elementary level, it is often necessary to sacrifice refinement for the benefit of general musicianship and advancement. Elements which are encountered in certain pieces will come back in subsequent ones. Hopefully, by that time, the student will be able to integrate them faster and apply them in relation to new concepts. Moving to new pieces in a reasonable amount of time is essential to avoid boredom and disenchantment.

It would be very difficult to come up with one general piece of advice in regards to the complex and multi-faced issue of practicing at the elementary level. A teacher must understand that each young student is a different and unique individual; he will have to tailor his teaching accordingly, and become more versatile, tolerant and above all human. There is nothing that children are more turned off by than the image of a strict and inflexible teacher, sitting next to them, pencil in hand, ready to repeat the same things all over again. The desire to practice is the natural outcome and extension of what is being done and presented at the lesson. The parents, on the other hand, need to learn how to genuinely support and recognize the student's efforts no matter how small they may seem. If the elementary student continues his piano study, the most difficult part of the battle will be won.

# Guiding the Student to Practicing Bach's
## *Minuet 3 from Overture in G Minor, BWV 822*

Menuet 1 da capo

Quality vs. quantity is an essential working principle, which permeates all healthy practicing habits. Notwithstanding a degree of validity in the old saying "no pain, no gain," more recent cognitive trends in educational methodology have demonstrated the importance of training the mind along with the physical means; the brain being the instigator of everything that happens during performance. It is all too common to witness students turning on "automatic pilot" when they practice, i.e., going with what comes naturally to their hands with little or no regards to what is required by the music. Practicing mindlessly and without a specific purpose can be ineffective and, at worst, detrimental as it reinforces bad habits that are persistent and hard to correct. Following are some steps that can help students avoid the pitfalls of mechanical work. Depending on the learning stage of a piece, any of these phases can be bypassed, touched upon briefly, or combined in a different order. With younger students embarking on new pieces, I suggest a four-step approach, every stage requiring different practicing strategies. The first stage is "ground base," a place where the student needs to return occasionally for maintenance and quality control.

1. **Presentation phase**.

This phase includes everything we do when we assign a piece for the first time. It is quite helpful to start with the sound, as all interpretational details (tempo, articulation, dynamics) and notational features are embedded in the sound of the piece. Whether the teacher plays or uses an accompanying CD to demonstrate the music, what matters is the first vivid sound impression that will inform the student and serve as reference point in each step of the way; hopefully, a good performance will also inspire him to embrace the music with more enthusiasm and desire to work.

Organizing the student's work and deciding how much and how he is expected to prepare can save a great deal of time and effort. For the first acquaintance with Bach's *Minuet 3 from Overture in G Minor, BWV 822*, it would be reasonable to break it into two parts, assigning each at a time, while setting small, realistic goals: phrase by phrase, hands alone first, then together. Subsequently, combine more phrases, until the entire section is covered. The amount and order of these analytical practicing techniques will depend on the student's degree of hand coordination and prior exposure to similar pieces.

At this point, it would be helpful to indicate some key fingerings (if they are not already marked in the score), or add to the existing ones. Some editorial fingerings may need to be adjusted to the student's technical level, or to accommodate certain musical features, such as articulation, tempo, and dynamic inflection. Asking the student to sight read part of the piece to make sure that he understands the range, key signature, and basic rhythmic structure will help him feel less overwhelmed when he is off on his own.

Many young students have never learned how to work; therefore just assigning a new piece without precise practicing suggestions may not be sufficient. If a student is to adopt any type of practicing method with integrity and commitment, it is essential that we explain the method's specific purpose and function; often, it is also helpful to spend some time practicing with the student during the lesson. Slow, solid practice is essential particularly at the initial stage; it acquires, though, more meaning when the student understands its importance and usefulness, that is to allow the brain enough time to anticipate the action and to coordinate the physical means necessary for the realization of the musical idea. Thus, the first goal in practicing the *Minuet in G* would be to play the first part from beginning to end distinctly, with the right articulation and fingering, in a mildly slower tempo, rhythmically and smoothly, avoiding "double takes", i.e. correcting wrong notes on the spot. Practicing rhythmically is essential, as rhythm is at the basis of music and propels and orchestrates all physical motions. Every note, shift, and articulation needs to be performed in the right time, within the rhythmic frame structure. Smoothness and solidity of articulation therefore should be stressed against speed.

As soon as the student starts working with these specific goals, he is naturally led to engage in quicker thinking and a deeper level of concentration. "Play slow—think fast" is excellent advice that can benefit pianists of all ages. Evening out everything and feeling comfortable within the rhythmic framework of the work in various tempos, including the actual tempo of the piece, as well as incorporating the dynamic changes and other stylistic features is the subject of the next phase.

2. **Follow through**.

Very rarely will a novice learner achieve a balanced, rhythmic, and accurate reading of a baroque minuet without the help of the teacher. Even the most gifted upper elementary or early intermediate student will be challenged by the linear texture and shifts of position that are a far cry from the rather static, simple-textured pieces found in most beginning piano methods. As soon as the student brings back the piece for the first time, the teacher's task is to help him identify all problem areas, understand why they are occurring, and select an appropriate working approach in order to solve them. Leading the student to identify her own problem areas, isolate and work on them, then integrate them in the long musical line, is the key to achieving permanent results. Simply correcting the actual symptoms as soon as they appear can only serve as a temporary fix. Many problems can be avoided when students understand for themselves the true reasons these occur, and decide accordingly the means and strategies to tackle them. Good practicing is therefore situation-specific and purposeful, in the sense that it aims at certain results.

Typical problems include shifts of position (especially involving both hands simultaneously), wrong notes and articulations, as well as fingerings.

If the student has a hard time shifting in connective points, such as in between phrases (ex. mm. 8-1, 9-10), he should be prompted to go back to the previous measure (m. 8 going to 1, and m. 9 going to 10) and work uniquely on that connection at a slower tempo. The transfer of the hands must happen "in time". Later on, he should start integrating those measures with what comes before and after: practice mm. 7-1 and 7-10, then 7-3, 7-11, and so on. Landing on wrong notes on the downbeat and correcting them as soon as they occur will amount to little if any progress, since the problem lies not in the notes themselves but in the concentration needed to reach them correctly based on what comes before. In other words, the brain has to anticipate the action. The student can only achieve this mental and physical synergy by slowing down the tempo and working evenly within rhythmic boundaries.

It is the same for wrong notes, articulations and fingerings. Unless wrong notes are just accidental slips, they happen again due to a lack of mental preparation and anticipation of the sound. Much like shifts of position, they should be corrected in the context of the entire phrase. An effective way to do this is by asking the student to identify places where she habitually plays a wrong note, then instruct her to go to the beginning of the phrase and practice the passage rhythmically and accurately at a slower tempo, either with separate hands, or together, depending on her needs. If the student repeats the same mistake, she should be discouraged from fixing the note quickly; she will only benefit from returning to the beginning of the phrase and playing at an even slower tempo. As a next step, the student is asked to integrate the problem area to a longer segment, starting from an earlier point (as described in the previous paragraph.) The integration phase is crucial since it exposes all problems and clarifies what needs to be worked on.

Similarly, articulation needs to be consistent, and integral. Right from the start, we have to instruct the student to play with the right articulation. Along with pitch, rhythmic and fingering accuracy, articulation is an indispensable qualifying element that should become part of the student's practicing. Learning the music the way it is meant to sound makes more sense than learning it incorrectly and changing it later.

It is essential that the student employ the right fingering from the start, as fingering translates to connection. Once the appropriate fingering has been decided, it should be required from the student to adhere to it. Fingering needs to be integrated in the practicing process and be treated like the aforementioned problems. Playing a note with an incorrect finger denotes lack of focus; although the teacher may diligently indicate such deviations every time they happen, no real integration will take place unless the student learns to practice with correct fingerings within the content of a phrase at a slower rate first, before increasing the tempo.

Fortunately, things become easier with regular repetition of this practicing technique, which fosters mental alertness, concentration, and intense internal hearing. However, not until the real core of any problem is addressed, will the symptoms dissipate and the playing gain in fluidity and ease. Ultimately, one comes to realize that less of the right type of practicing yields better and more permanent results than more of the wrong kind.

Some other situation-specific ways of practicing include the following:

- Play the piece with a solid tone *(mf to f)* from beginning to end, rhythmically, in a stable tempo, paying extra attention to articulating all the notes distinctly. This works well with students who play with weak fingers.

- Practice all shorter values such as the eighth notes of this minuet, in a short, accented *staccato*. This is another way of addressing the earlier-mentioned problem; it activates the fingertips, and promotes distinct articulation.

- Practice at a moderately slow tempo in a piano dynamic with more arm motion. Students who suffer from tension problems will benefit from this type of work, as it emphasizes more forearm participation. In doing this, we can also modify all staccatos and lengthen them, either as in *legato* or *portato*.

- Play and count out loud, or clap and syllabicate the notes of the melody or the bass line. Occasional practicing with a metronom is also recommended, but students should also learn to assess time without it. These ways of practicing will reinforce rhythm in students who have a weak sense of the beat or have difficulty calculating rhythmic relations.

Such special techniques should be only assigned occasionally and tailored to the student's individual needs. Too much of any type of practicing that deviates from the musical content of the piece can become a habit and, as such, distort the student's correct idea and understanding of the true meaning of the work.

### 3. Musical work and further refinement.

The incorporation of basic dynamics is to start rather early, as soon as the student is able to play the assigned section fairly accurately and comfortably. As long as they are not overwhelmingly complicated and overshadow more pertinent problems, dynamics can be introduced alongside with the type of corrections discussed in the second phase. Learning to play with the right volume and tone quality needs to be integrated early in the student's playing approach; however, this process can be refined in subsequent sessions together with improvements in articulation, overall feel and character, as well as tempo acquisition. Working on dynamics, phrasing, and tempo should occur progressively and while keeping track of the rhythmic integrity, tempo stability, and proper enunciation of all the notes. Often playing with expression equates in young students forgetting about the basic framework of the piece without which everything else collapses. Speeding up in crescendos and slowing down while diminishing is a manifestation of this problem. In the minuet genre, such accelerations are incompatible with the dancing character, which calls for an almost metronomic evenness and regularity. For this reason, it is important to remind the student that while aiming at an expressive performance in a faster tempo, it is necessary to revisit a neutral, even and slower practicing, making sure that all the necessary elements are in place, solid, grounded and comfortable.

Phases two and three can be combined together. For example, once the basic problems (notes, rhythm, fingering, articulation, hand coordination) are addressed, we can assign the second half in the same manner, while adding basic dynamic concepts in the first half. In the following session, it will be easier to transfer some of the expressive elements we incorporated in the first section to the second and add on expressive refinements to the first (which eventually the student will carry on to the second part.) This additive way of working is pedagogically healthy and effective. The student taps into prior knowledge and applies concepts he already knows to other sections within the piece.

4. **Mental work and retention.**

Memorization constitutes the most important step in the learning sequence since it involves thorough understanding of everything within the piece; this includes all melodic, harmonic and textural relations, the form and key structure, as well as rhythmic permutations and variations appearing in similar phrases in corresponding sections. In order for the student to memorize the piece in a permanent and conscious way, we need to guide him to work on understanding. We can promote understanding by engaging the following cognitive methods of work:

• Incorporate theory. Encourage the student to recognize intervals and harmonic progressions implied in the piece, even though it is in two-part texture. Basic theory is quite necessary and should be included in the piano lesson, if the student is to acquire a thorough understanding of the music, which will enable him to retain it in a more permanent way. Can the student name the chords in the first eight measures, either using chord letter symbols or roman numerals?

I-V$^6$-V /I /V (the left-hand G in the downbeat is a suspension) /I-I-V$^7$/ I6 /IV /V /I

Equally, make sure that the student recognizes all chord and passing tones and understands the expressive role of appoggiaturas and suspensions.

- Mix in aural skills exercises. Have the student practice pitch/ interval anticipation by stopping at a certain note and singing the next, especially in places where she has difficulty projecting the sound mentally and therefore does not remember it. This happens frequently in parallel phrases where the melody traces a different path. The student is fixed mentally to the first version, and cannot project that different turn occurring in the next section because she does not hear it internally. The singing exercise works particularly well when such problems occur; not only should the student be able to sing the melody, but the bass line as well. Can the student sing the melody part in mm. 1-4 and then do the same in mm. 18-21 without looking at the notes? Check whether the student is able to sing the left hand in mm. 10-14 right after having played the first half of the piece.

- Involve active understanding. Have the student identify similarities and differences between parallel phrases in the two sections. Then, ask him to describe those in musical terms. For example, ask him to verbalize the differences between measures 7-8 and 24-25.

- Encourage mental practice. Ask the student to look at the score silently, trying to recreate the sound in his mind as vividly as possible. Also, have the student visualize himself playing the piece, while at the same time hearing it internally. These techniques work equally well as warming up sessions before recitals or examinations.

# References

## Articles

Cameron, Joyce. "From Inside Out: Motivation." *Keyboard Companion*, Summer 1992.

Jacobson, Jeanine. "Motivating Students." *Clavier*, February 1993.

Kennell, Richard and Marks, Virginia. "Student Motivation in the Applied Studio." *American Music Teacher*, June/July 1992.

Kolakoski, Dawn, Rowe, Charlotte and Lomax, Elisabeth. "Practice Incentives." *Clavier*, March 1993.

Pearce, Elvina. "Home Practice." *Keyboard Companion*, Winter 1992.

Sitton, Michael. "The Pedagogy of Practice." *American Music Teacher*, April/May 1992.

Widhalm, Betsy, Maudell, Baker and Rabin, Rhoda. "Teaching Preschoolers." *Clavier*, April 1993.

## Books

Agay, Denes (ed.). *Teaching Piano*. New York: Yorktown Press, 1981.

Bach, Johann Sebastian. *Neue Ausgabe Sämtlicher Werke (Neue Bach Ausgabe)*, ed. Johann-Sebastian-Bach-Institute, Göttligen, and Bach Archiv, Leipzig. Kassel and Basle, 1954.

Bach, Johann Sebastian. *First Lessons in Bach*. Schirmer Performance Editions, ed. Christos Tsitsaros, G. Schirmer, Inc., 2009.

Bastien, James. *How to Teach Piano Successfully*. San Diego: Neil A. Kjos Music Company, 1988.

Jersild, Arthur. *Child Psychology*. Fifth Edition, Prentice Hall, Inc. Englewood Cliffs, 1960.

McDonald, Frederick. *Educational Psychology*. Second Edition, 1965, Wadsworth Publishing Company, Inc., 1965.

# TEACHING
# OPTIONS

# CHAPTER 11

# Modes of Instruction: Private, Group or Both?

## James Lyke

Today's piano teacher has a wide choice of instructional modes to consider when auditioning students for lessons. Auditions help determine musicality, learning styles, personality traits, motivation and interaction within the triangle of student, teacher and parent. Auditions also ascertain what sort of piano lesson best suits the child. Some children flourish in the group setting, others in a private lesson. Many teachers offer both group and private lessons. Uppermost in the teacher's mind is what works well for both the teacher and the student.

## Private Lessons

Individual piano instruction is based on the traditional tutorial system. This approach is the most widely used in piano teaching. Stated simply, the piano student prepares a body of work including several pieces, technical assignments and perhaps some theory papers. At the lessons, pieces are critiqued, suggestions made, demonstrations given, and written assignments checked. Certainly the teacher serves as a model and a close relationship is generally fostered between student and teacher.

A research team headed by Benjamin Bloom at the University of Chicago in 1985 reported findings on talented young people. The section on pianists underscored the necessity of private tutoring for the talented student, e.g., the student possessing a high level of ability, achievement and skill in a special field of study such as piano. Bloom's research also pointed out the important role parents played in the nurturing, training and encouragement of the talented young pianist.

Bloom identified five stages in the growth of musical talent in children. Briefly, these steps for the young pianist were described as follows: *First Stage*. The young child tries to copy his parents as they sing or play a musical instrument. The child is bathed in the atmosphere of music. He is encouraged to play and experiment. *Second Stage*. These early experiences give the child a head start in skills and interest. At the age of 5 or 6, he is provided with a *private* teacher, a local person who is good with children and rewards their efforts with candy, gold stars, etc. Much encouragement and praise is given by both teacher and the family. *Third Stage*. The family now tries to obtain instruction from a more highly skilled teacher. One parent often attends lessons and supervises practice. The new instructor realizes the child is unusually motivated and tries to convince him he has great potential. *Fourth Stage*. If the child has been "hooked" by the age of ten or early adolescence, a great change takes place. Higher goals are considered and a better piano is purchased. Still better teachers are required and a period of discipline and mastery begins. *Fifth Stage*. In middle or late adolescence, the family spends a year or two seeking a master teacher for the teenager who is now practicing at least twenty hours a week. He will have to work even harder if he is accepted by the master teacher. Practice and mastery now become a vocation in "the religious sense."

Of course not all private teachers accept only the extremely talented youngster. Ordinary children, those not destined to be singled out with extraordinary talent, can profit from private lessons as well. They certainly can do well in group lessons too, especially during the early years of instruction.

## Group Lessons

In various workshops I've given, I am always astonished by how few teachers are involved in group teaching. There tends to be uneasiness with this method of teaching. It is time to dispel many common myths about teaching piano in groups.

Many private teachers think that group teaching requires a piano lab, or if not a lab, then more than one piano. This is not true and I deliberately demonstrated in workshops with four students using only one piano. Another misconception is that group teaching emphasizes keyboard skills and not performance. Good group teachers weight performance and skills equally. They use the performance situation as a critical listening experience, one in which students are taught to make constructive criticisms about the music being played and decide together what effective practice procedures will improve the piece.

Private teachers fear that group teaching equates with mass production and that group teaching works well only with beginners. Groups can, of course, vary considerably in size anywhere from partner lessons to four and six students, the ideal being four. Class lessons, such as musicianship, generally run from six to eight students. But these lessons focus mainly on keyboard theory skills.

Beginning students work well in a group. But regrouping is bound to occur later, with family moves, schedule conflicts and so on. However, I've had some groups together for as many as five or six years. When students mature, it is wise to cut the size of the group down and even increase the lesson time. This is necessary because of longer pieces and more complex musicianship studies.

Some private teachers have also been led to believe that different rates of learning work against the success of the group. Experts believe the students should be grouped as much as possible by intelligence. This is more important than age, though wide age spans are not advisable. For example, girls aged 7 generally work will with boys aged 8.

Finally, some private teachers have the opinion that parents do not favor group teaching. Parents, they believe, see the lesson time divided by the number of students. When parents are shown the essence of group teaching in a demonstration, they react positively. In my own demonstrations for prospective students, parents have told me afterwards "that's the way I wish I had been taught!" Group teaching does make sense to parents.

# When Group Teaching Works

When groups function well and solid musical learning is taking place within the group, the following essentials have been put into operation by the teacher.

1.  The teacher introduces a broad curriculum which includes an interrelated program of repertoire, technique and keyboard theory.

2.  The teacher groups students by mental and emotional maturity and considers chronological age as well.

3.  The teacher understands group techniques and knows how to plan and implement exciting lessons which result in effective learning. Students are shown and taught good practice habits.

4.  The teacher understands the elements of competition, cooperation, thoughtful criticism and peer interaction.

5.  The teacher knows how to facilitate learning and refrains from "telling."

6.  The teacher find ways to relate theoretic learnings to repertoire study.

7. The teacher becomes a model for students, keeps practicing and introduces new repertoire through competent performances.

8. The teacher offers frequent evaluative opportunities to students such as recitals, competitions and syllabus examinations.

9. The teacher makes sure that students sight read at every lesson and continue to improve this skill.

10. The teacher considers ensemble playing an integral part of lessons and provides opportunities for students to experience two-piano repertoire, duets, accompanying and chamber music, if possible.

11. The teacher communicates with parents frequently through notes, phone calls or e-mails.

12. The teacher develops a healthy learning climate free from threat, helps students solve their musical problems, diagnoses difficulties quickly, listens to students about their lives outside the studio and remains stable and supportive at all times.

## Some Basic Equipment for Group Teaching

1. A piano (one will do, two would be ideal.) A digital piano with a computer should be considered.

2. Adjustable seats (very young students can stand for parts of the lesson.) Footstools become necessary for the younger pianists.

3. Chairs and a table for written theory work (clipboards can take the place of a table.)

4. Various percussion instruments for rhythm activities.

5. Any basic series plus theory-musicianship books.

6. Flashcards (commercial and homemade.)

7. Music paper and pencils.

8. Supplementary music for sight reading.

9. A dry marker board with staff lines, dry marker pens and erasers.

10. Music stands.

## Some Problem Areas

As with any kind of teaching, group teachers will experience some problems which will affect the group. Briefly, these include: (1) the split up of a group caused by a family move or sickness, (2) personality conflicts within a group and (3) too small a pool of students with diverse age ranges making groups impossible. Exceptional children, those with special problems or those who are extremely gifted belong in a private lesson situation where their special needs can be handled more easily.

# The Combination Approach

Many private teachers favor combining the private lesson with a group lesson in musicianship skills. These classes are generally held weekly and additional fees are charged for them. Private teachers can then concentrate on pieces and technique during the individual lesson. In the separate musicianship class, for example, they can gather all the 8 and 9 year old beginners together (as many as about eight) and fill in the musical gaps with activities the private lesson leaves little time for. The larger group develops its own dynamic force. Teachers will want to take advantage of turning many of the activities into games. Here, healthy competition flourishes.

Pre-printed planning forms which fit into a notebook help the teacher organize learning experiences sequentially. The previous week's plan may be consulted to assure smooth continuity and progression in all areas. The pre-printed forms work at *any* level; more advanced students will be involved with experiences requiring deeper musical and intellectual depth. In the sample planning form which follows, note the left-hand column of activities which can be considered ongoing at any level. To the right of this column, the teacher jots down abbreviated notes for each class, page numbers and books for sight reading, sets of flash cards to use, chord patterns to check, etc. On the right side of the page, teachers should indicate by initials which students should read, play patterns, harmonize tunes, etc., so that no one is slighted. Each activity may be numbered in the order of presentation. For example, students might read literature in minor keys, then play chord patterns in minor, then analyze a brief piece in minor, then differentiate major from minor chords. In this way, new knowledge is applied, continuity is assured and the learning process is reinforced. As each activity is completed, the teacher makes a check mark to avoid needless repetition when planning the next class.

The key to conducting successful musicianship classes is rapid movement from one activity to another, with at least a half-dozen or more activities planned for each forty-five minute session. Students should move from chairs to blackboards to the piano and so on. Good teachers recognize the value of varied activities in sustaining student interest and attention in class.

It is important for teachers to relate musicianship activities to the structuring of the piece lesson, and vice versa. Good sight readers who analyze melodic and harmonic patterns in musicianship class learn repertoire in the piece lesson more quickly. Piano students who understand the basics of any given style in the piece lesson improvise in that style more readily in the musicianship class. Again, teachers should try to integrate learning activities in both lessons.

## Repertoire Class

Many teachers organize repertoire classes that meet once a month. These classes offer an opportunity to play for other students and to receive helpful suggestions from class members. It helps to direct listening if the teacher assigns certain tasks to each listener. "Were the staccato marks observed?" "Were dynamic levels well defined?" "Was there good balance between the hands?" Students should be following each performance with scores in hand. The teacher also must guard against cruel comments; a supportive atmosphere must be established from the outset.

## Lab Group Teaching

Group teaching in a lab with multiple digital pianos, a teacher control center and various technological aids is treated in a later chapter. Various techniques and materials are discussed. See the chapter, **The Adult In A College Piano Lab** by James Lyke. All the ideas may be adapted to teaching children.

| MUSICIANSHIP CLASS, LEVEL_____ DATE_____ TERM_____ WEEK_____ | Order | | Initials |
|---|---|---|---|
| SIGHTREADING | | | |
| EAR TRAINING | | | |
| CHORD PATTERNS | | | |
| HARMONIZATION | | | |
| TRANSPOSITION | | | |
| IMPROVISATION | | | |
| WRITING | | | |
| FLASH CARD DRILLS | | | |
| TECHNIQUE | | | |
| PERFORMANCE | | | |

Example 1. Pre-printed Planning Form

# References

Agay, Denes (ed.). *The Art Of Teaching Piano*. New York: Yorktown Music Press, 1981.

Baker-Jordan, Martha. *Practical Piano Pedagogy*. Van Nuys, CA: Alfred Music Publishing Co., Inc., 2005.

Bastien, James. *How To Teach Piano Successfully - 3rd ed*. San Diego: Neil A. Kjos, Publishers, 1988.

Bloom, Benjamin S. (ed.). *Developing Talent In Young People*. New York: Ballantine Books, 1985.

Clark, Frances. *Questions And Answers*. Northfield, IL: The Instrumentalist Company, 1992.

Darling, Edward (ed.). *A Piano Teacher's Legacy (Selected Writings by Richard Chronister)*. Kingston, NJ: The Frances Clark Center For Keyboard Pedagogy, Inc., 2005.

Enoch, Yvonne. *Group Piano Teaching*. London: Oxford University Press, 1974.

Fisher, Christopher. *Teaching Piano In Groups*. New York: Oxford University Press, 2010.

Jacobson, Jeanine M. *Professional Piano Teaching*. Van Nuys, CA: Alfred Music Publishing Co., Inc., 2006.

Uszler, Marienne et al. *The Well-Tempered Keyboard Teacher*. New York: Schirmer Books, 2000.

# PIANO
# TEACHER
# AS
# ENTREPRENEUR

# CHAPTER 12

## Tuning In to Teaching Aids

### Karen Koch

How many times in a career must a music teacher explain basic concepts? "Whole, whole, half, whole" "Be sure to count the rest." "G-major has one sharp." How many times must an individual student receive such information before it is fully learned? How on earth do teachers manage the endless needed repetition without burn-out and boredom for themselves and their students? The probable answer is CREATIVITY!

## Good Teachers Are Creative

Successful teachers engage the senses and the intellect for themselves and their students, and they CREATE: New explanations. Visual demonstrations. Written work. Performance examples. Verbal imagery. Learning Games. Software. Engaging (but not too challenging) drills. Musical compositions. Creativity is vital for a musician, especially for a teaching musician, in order to develop student understanding, motivation and skill. However different learning styles and abilities require different strategies and fresh approaches.

Every teacher must react to the "I don't get it" look in a student's eyes. One of these uh-oh moments occurred for me in the early 1980's. I asked a 10-year-old student if he remembered in which historical period Mozart lived. He replied slowly, "Well, I don't exactly remember the period, but I think it was sometime before Grandpa. . . . (long, thoughtful pause). . .and after Jesus?" His answer showed me that I needed to figure out a better way to teach music history, which resulted in a master's thesis topic, which led to the development of a product, which culminated in the creation of a business. . . which has shaped my subsequent life and made me a better teacher.

# Publishing and Self-Publishing

In order to be profitable, music publishing companies must offer materials likely to appeal to the widest possible market and then promote those selected products with extensive advertising budgets and marketing strategies. Meanwhile teachers in the real world often must improvise additional materials to meet their own students' needs and interests. Teacher creativity pops up everywhere from the nursery to the classroom to the senior center. Often it is shared at workshops, teacher meetings, music stores, conferences and schools. Sometimes the products become published materials.

Lucy Chu (E-Z Notes) and Jane Calder (Making Music Fun) are just two examples of teachers who have grown small companies over many years by selling their unique teaching aids. New self-published materials continue to proliferate, aided by the internet, but not necessarily resulting in sustainable businesses. Internet shopping from home provides convenience and choice for customers, but local brick-and-mortar stores are almost an endangered species due to closures and consolidations as their customers google away.

# Before You Self-Publish. . .

For anyone who may be considering the sale of your fantastic teaching aid creation, you need to know that the easy part is the creation of the materials. The difficult part is in letting the world know that they exist. Without repeated and ongoing expenditures of time and money, the most beautiful and useful materials will collect dust because they are unknown to enough potential customers.

Here are some important considerations for anyone who is thinking of offering a teaching aid for sale:

- Who is your potential target market? Teachers? Parents? Students?
- How will you reach them and how much will your advertising cost?
- How much will it cost to produce your ready-to-ship product?
- Experts recommend adding at least 150-200% above that production cost to allow for the costs of ongoing marketing and a small profit. What will your retail selling price have to be?
- Would you pay that retail price for your product?
- Is there enough leeway in the selling price that you can cover your costs if you wish to offer a sale price or convention special or wholesale discount?

- Would the product have shipping challenges? Heavy? Large size? Odd shape? Require special or protective packaging? Fit into Flat Rate boxes from US Postal Service? You need to consider the cost of shipping boxes, packing materials, and labels. What exactly would it cost to ship it across the country to a customer?

- Is your product a one-time purchase per customer such as a board game or display item, or will you have repeat sales from disposable or sequenced materials such as workbooks. It is much easier to sell to an existing customer than to gain a new one.

- Can your material be easily photocopied? If so, should you raise the price and make it reproducible?

## One Route to Sharing Teaching Aids

"This is great. Why don't you publish it?" were the fateful words from a fellow piano teacher. They inspired a long and often bumpy ride to my own hoped-for destination of a successful product. However after a few years of limited sales, despite some targeted and expensive print advertising, I knew I needed to broaden my exposure. I reasoned that by cooperating with others who had also created and self-published music teaching aids, we could work together to divide our costs and multiply our marketing exposure. At various teacher conferences I had become acquainted with several teacher/creators who had excellent and useful materials but were completely unknown to most of their potential customers.

My son, an accomplished early techie, observed that the only way for us to reach a national audience at a reasonable price was to go online. This was in 1998, and I objected, "I'll bet not one third of piano teachers are even online yet." He replied prophetically, "But they WILL be..."

So a simple plan was developed in which I would continue my teaching, but reach out to colleagues. I would use my existing 800 phone number and credit card merchant account, and pay one of my high school students to create a website to serve as an online showroom for our products. We had no shopping software at that point. I invited sixteen potential marketers to contribute $300 each for an advertising seed fund to advertise our online showroom in professional teacher magazines. Six of them sent a check. I was to process all the sales and when an order came in, I would create the invoice and then email the marketer the order and shipping information. I kept a 45% cut out of each sale to help cover my costs for our promotional expenses. This was a good deal for the marketers because music stores and publishers take commissions from 45% to 60% .

Almost immediately customers—especially those who were not yet online—began requesting a paper catalog, a major expense of several thousand dollars, not counting the cost of postage to mail the catalogs to customers. Shipping was also a problem because if a customer ordered products from more than one marketer, the customer was charged a single shipping fee. However each marketer then had to share that single fee, though they had each incurred full shipping expense from their own location. At that point, I decided I would have to warehouse some products so that I could ship those multiple-item orders from my own location. That was the end of having two cars in my family's garage.

Other self-publishers began to hear about the Music Educators' Marketplace and requested participation. We established a policy of accepting teaching aids, but no sheet music or method books. We also strove to provide personalized customer service that we would expect as a customer. I acquired a webmaster by offering piano lessons to his two daughters in exchange for his services. In eleven years we grew to 200 products from 45 different creators. I continued to teach in my own studio, and the costs of advertising and promotion continued to consume virtually all of the income generated by Music Educators' Marketplace.

In 2010, again looking to technology for marketing assistance and customer service, I partnered with Kevin LaManna at DupleMeter.com, a young technology company, to build a new website. In addition to an updated virtual store, we created an online hub of products, websites, information, content, and communication by and for teachers who wish to share their good ideas.

## First Aids for Teaching

That "I don't get it" look in a student's eyes has inspired some amazing materials. At a university piano pedagogy class, I was asked to "show and tell" some of the self-published materials available from Music Educators' Marketplace. The class had been assigned the task of individually creating a game or teaching aid, and my display was to be an inspiration for them. However at the end of the presentation one student said plaintively, "After seeing this, I think everything has already been invented." I suggested that if she focused on the specific need of one of her most challenging students, she could probably come up with an inspiration. Very often the need of one student is the genesis of creativity.

At Music Educators' Marketplace I frequently hear from teachers who have done just that. Christine Wolf in Minnesota created music alphabet blocks which make theory concepts tactile and visual. Sally Ritchie is a school music and piano teacher in Wisconsin who publishes a bevy of snappy and attractive teaching games for rhythm, intervals, note reading.

Evelyn Westwood (Utah) laid out a Circle of 5ths Scale Fingering Reference Chart. Bonnie Slaughter (Idaho) develops music camp plans. Barbara Rader (Nebraska) and Suzanne Fauser (Wisconsin) created music history table games. Renee Lacey (Idaho) published a complete ear training software course. Brenda Freed (Texas) recorded a practical singing course on CD. Dennis Kobray (New Jersey) filmed five of his composer impersonation presentations for school age children. There are literally hundreds more creative minds at work everywhere.

Even students themselves sometimes create teaching aids to meet their own needs, and these can also be shared. Nine-year-old Nathan DeLong (Ohio) was struggling to learn his scale fingerings when his teacher pointed out that scales have fingering families. With that understanding, he came up with the idea of having a movable template for each family scale group in order to direct the fingers to the proper keys and fingering for that family. Nate's Piano Plates is now a popular aid for tactile scale practice.

Teaching aids can be as individual as the next student who walks through the door, or as universal as printed music itself. The sharing of teacher creativity is a wonderful tendency of our profession. By employing and sharing our creativity, we are assisted,  in the words of the well-known teacher and clinician Suzanne Guy, ". . .in our task of adding to the musical beauty in the world."

# CHAPTER 13

# Establishing a Community Music School

## Jo Ellen DeVilbiss

It was a cold but sunny day in February when I took our then 6-year-old son to his recorder lesson. During that lesson his teacher told me about an idea for a music school that was brewing among some area teachers and supporters of the arts. This small group of people was interested in joining together to reach out into the community with music instruction and activities, something they could not easily accomplish as independent teachers. The concept of community arts education warmed me greatly on that very cold day and not too many weeks went by before I found myself involved in the planning process for a community music school both from the perspective of a parent and as a piano teacher.

There was much to be accomplished before such an organization could move from a glimmering idea to reality. Organizational structure, location, and finding interested community members to support the project were just a few of the topics that occupied time and discussion during the months that followed. The first official Board meeting of this new group was held in June. Things moved quickly over the summer. The doors opened in August for the next school year and a new community music school was born, The Conservatory of Central Illinois. During its first year of operation, instruction in piano, violin, viola, cello, bass, flute, recorder, percussion, early childhood music, and string orchestra was offered by a teaching faculty of 10.

## What is a Community School of the Arts?

Community schools of the arts first found their basis in the settlement house movement of the late 1800s that provided cultural, arts, and language opportunities to those in need. Over a century later, the need still exists. While many such groups are centered in music only, some community arts organizations have offerings in visual arts, drama, dance, and other specialized programs. Education programs reach beyond instruction for children only. Programs designed for special populations such as senior residential centers, individuals with disabilities, and underserved populations are often found in the typical community school of the arts. Statistics from the National Guild for Community Arts Education (NGCAE) reveal that in 2010 there were over 5,000 community arts education organizations in the United States reaching over 1,200,000 students with their programs. The NGCAE alone represents over 450 member organizations with 16,000 instructors of music and other art forms. Egan (1989), in his book about community music schools, provides a wonderful overview of the entire movement, from the early settlement houses to the current guild organizational structure that continues to blossom with new member institutions.

Those who work in the not-for-profit community arts sector possess a passion for the arts and the creative process, along with the belief that in the arts lies the ability to change lives. This passion drives its members to provide accessible opportunities for students to reach for the highest artistic goals at their level and to promote lifelong learning opportunities in the arts. If you believe in this concept and have an interest in entrepreneurship you might want to join with others to begin a community school of the arts.

# How Do You Get There?

What happened during the six months before The Conservatory of Central Illinois opened its doors? First of all, it is important to note that many months of brainstorming and other discussions had taken place before my own personal involvement in the winter of that year. Certain questions must be addressed early on in the process such as:

## Offerings

What will be the instructional offerings—piano only, or many instruments?

Will ensembles such as orchestra, band, or chamber music be included?

What types of instruction will be offered? For example, will there be individual instruction, group classes, or a combination of both?

Will the curriculum be based on a particular method or approach? Or, will instructors be given latitude to teach in their own style utilizing methods and musical materials of their choice?

Will the curricular offerings focus on traditional styles of classically based western music or will many styles be included such as jazz, folk, and world music?

What will the organization do to become community based? How will it provide special services? Such services could include a program of financial aid, free concerts for the public, presentations for community groups and organizations, or special concerts and recitals. Alexander (1997) states:

> Furthermore, these programs [referring to community music programs] often furnish services to the community-at-large. These services can take the form of workshops for area music teachers, partial underwriting of music and arts events in the community, sponsoring music festivals and competitions for area youth, and providing concert and rehearsal facilities for community performing groups, to name only a few (p. 7).

Are there cultural offerings your community needs that could be best provided by such a group? Such a list would vary widely depending upon the geographic location of the organization. For example, an organization being founded in a suburb of a metropolitan city such as St. Louis would be able to provide decidedly different options that one being founded in a less populated area, such as central Kansas.

## Community Support and Advisors

A group of advisors and supporters will need to be identified. Regardless of the structure that is chosen for a community arts organization, certain types of advice will be necessary for success. It is important to identify leaders to provide support and to seek additional input and expertise from individuals in the areas of:

- Legal
- Finance
- Business
- Human Resources
- Marketing

It is useful to develop and cultivate support from area public and private schools, home school networks, and other local organizations that have an interest in the role of music education in the community. It is advisable to seek information from sources that can provide guidance through the process of establishing a community arts organization. The National Guild for Community Arts Education (www.nationalguild.org) makes available a number of publications and other information to assist in this process.

Additional information may be found by checking with organizations such as the Small Business Council of America (www.sbca.net).

## Location and Population Served

Many of the same considerations that relate to setting up an independent music studio will apply to starting a community arts organization. A location may be found in the business sector of the community or in churches. An enterprising group of teachers may find it possible to rent space in a house or office building. When establishing any type of teaching environment it is important to take care to investigate all local zoning laws. Flexibility in teaching hours may be limited by the location. Additionally, acoustical considerations must be weighed in any decision. For the teaching location, an atmosphere that is pleasant and as free as possible from interruptions should be maintained to create a positive learning environment.

In the case of our organization, the first location was in an historic Victorian home that previously had been used as a gift shop and professional offices. Some years later the school moved into former office space in the downtown business section of our community. And, as with establishing an independent studio, decisions will need to be made regarding the acquisition of instruments, equipment, and the availability of teaching materials.

## Other Levels of Involvement

The time and energy to begin such an organization is significant, but well worth the effort. However, there are other  ways to become involved in a community school of the arts. You might find it beneficial to pursue teaching opportunities in one of the many community arts groups spread throughout the United States and Canada. Community schools often employ individuals who help manage and oversee programs or are involved in other programs beyond the main area of expertise. While my initial involvement was as a member of the piano faculty, after some time with the school I was invited by the governing board to become an arts administrator while still maintaining a teaching studio. Those with an interest or skill in such areas as marketing, event planning, development or business planning may find a niche in the community school environment.

# Why Become Involved?

Prior to joining the faculty of The Conservatory of Central Illinois, I managed a successful teaching studio in my home for a number of years. However, I found the concept of reaching out beyond my own walls and working in tandem with others to bring music to our community an intriguing idea. I came to realize that I could provide some very exciting and special opportunities for my students that were more challenging to manage as an independent teacher. For example, each year I am able to introduce the art of collaborative piano to my students through the Chamber Music Festival that is held annually for students in our community school. Even the youngest pianist can undertake the accompaniment for a Suzuki violin friend playing *Twinkle Variations*. Older students have teamed up with their high school instrumental peers to work on more standard repertoire such as Beethoven violin sonatas. While a home studio does not preclude this type of activity, the task is much less challenging when students attend lessons and teachers offer instruction at the same location. Students also have other opportunities to interact with their peers and are exposed to much more music as they wait for lesson or class times. Parents too have some advantages, as they become their own unofficial support group for common issues such as the timeworn question, "How do I get my child to practice on a regular basis?"

Working with students to learn the art of pianism involves the development of musical and technical skills at the instrument. However, it also involves the development of the student in areas that reach far beyond the music making itself. Creative thinking and problem solving, confidence, goal setting, and many other life skills can be developed at the keyboard. The interactive environment of a community music school provides much to help teachers bring out these qualities in their students.

Beyond educational aspects of teaching in a community school of music, certain elements of the business of teaching are altered for the teacher. For example, many aspects of record keeping and billing are eliminated. And, as an employee rather than a self-employed person, certain income tax related issues are altered.

On a personal level, I have found that my own professional horizons have been expanded. As an arts administrator for our community music school faculty I have been afforded the opportunity to work with other organizations in our community. Our students, for example, have been honored by the local United Way for their artistic contributions to the volunteer community. Through daily interaction with other teaching professionals beyond the world of piano I have learned much about other teaching philosophies and approaches thereby enriching my own approach to educational development and performance. Along this path, I have been presented with many opportunities for performance through faculty recitals and other programs presented to the community by our school.

The emergence of community arts education organizations throughout North America is a growing movement that has seen a steady increase in recent years. The National Guild for Community Arts Education alone has grown from approximately 200 programs in the early 1990s to now over 400. If you have a passion for music, enjoy working with other teachers and musicians to share your interests with the community, and believe that music can change lives, you will find that working in the world of community arts education is a very rewarding path to follow.

# References

Alexander, Charles Reid (1997). *Relationships Between Community Music Programs And Their Affiliated Collegiate Music Schools.* Doctoral Dissertation, Vanderbilt University, Nashville, TN.

Egan, Robert F. (1989). *Music and the arts in the community: The community music school in America.* Metuchen, New Jersey: Scarecrow Press.

# Suggested Resources

Americans for the Arts (2003). *Community Schools of the Arts: An Arts Education Resource for Your Community.* Americans for the Arts, Washington, D.C. Website: www.artsusa.org

MacLaughlin, LaMoine (2003). *Ten Steps Toward Starting A Community School of the Arts.* National Guild of Community Schools of the Arts: New York, New York. Website: www.nationalguild.org

Ober/Kaler, Attorneys at Law (2005). *The Nonprofit Legal Landscape.* Board Source, Building Effective Nonprofit Boards. Website: www.boardsource.org/Bookstore.asp

# INTRODUCING
# JAZZ
# STYLE

# CHAPTER 14

## Jazz Style for the Traditional Piano Teacher

### Catherine Rollin

Several years ago, a couple of piano teacher friends of mine called me up and asked if they could have a lesson or two with me to help them teach jazz music. I assured them that if they wanted to teach the jazz style—music that was already written—they didn't need any help from me. They insisted though, that they didn't feel comfortable with jazz style eighth notes (swung eighths) and they would feel a lot better if I could spend a couple of hours with them.

I proceeded to give these friends a couple of lessons. At these lessons I not only convinced them that they were fine to play jazz style eighth notes if they could count in triplets, but I also showed them the rudimentary harmonies that start one on the path to sounding jazzy. Although the pieces were already written out, they felt a lot more comfortable teaching these jazz style pieces, after I demonstrated the swung eighths and pointed out the theory that applied to the harmonies used in the music.

In this chapter, I would like to do just what I did for my friends at those couple of lessons. I have also done this subsequently at many teacher workshops around the country. My goal is to assure all teachers that they can confidently teach written out jazz pieces. Moreover, I am hoping that teachers will pass on the insights presented here to their students. If a student starts understanding the rhythmic and harmonic elements that comprise jazz and blues, they might just get their students to start composing and improvising themselves. What a wonderful side benefit that would be in addition to simply enjoying playing jazz and blues style pieces.

171

# Flatted Thirds and Other Flatted Notes

Almost all of our students start out playing pieces in five-finger positions. In my *Pathways to Artistry* series, I emphasize the importance of students learning **all** of the major and minor white key five-finger positions before venturing into larger intervallic melodies. Students can readily understand the whole, whole, half, whole pattern of the major five-finger position and the whole, half, whole, whole pattern of the minor five-finger position. If we teach our students how to apply this pattern starting on any key, they will understand transposition immediately. They will also build a confident understanding of what a whole and half step are.

One of the first things that a student can hear happening in many easy jazz style pieces are the half step alteration of notes in the five-finger pattern—most notably the flatted third. In *Mr. Jazz Man* (See example 1), the late elementary student can see how the piece alternates using the major third in measure one with the flatted third in measure two.

Example 1

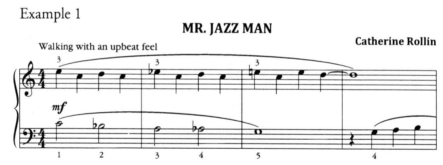

**MR. JAZZ MAN**

Catherine Rollin

This pattern is then transposed in ms. 9–16.

Example 2

# Walking Bass Lines

A walking bass line occurs when the composer, or improvising player "walks" primarily in a step-wise fashion in their left hand, using notes in the scale or five finger position that agree with the current or relevant harmony. In the case of *Mr. Jazzman,* the left hand is walking down first a C scale (ms. 1-4) and then an F scale (ms. 9-12) using flatted 6ths and 7ths for harmonic interest.

# The Twelve Bar Blues Foundation

In my studio, I teach students the concept of chord numbers (I, V, etc.) according to their position in the scale as soon as the student can understand a five-finger pattern. If they are learning a piece in the key of C, have them play that five-finger position; have them play the first, third and fifth note of the position; and explain to them that this is the I chord for that key. Although I do teach the V⁷ chord early on in its standard first inversion (B,F,G in the key of C) I also teach the students the V chord in its root position in my first technique book. (*Pathways to Artistry Technique 1*)

Once a student starts playing major scales (*Pathways to Artistry Technique 2*) I add the IV chord in root position. At this technique level, I emphasize learning what I call the group I major scales—C, G, D, A and E. I then show the students how to play the I, IV and V chords in root position in addition to the standard inversions that they will use as accompaniments. Nothing, however, helps a student to understand the I, IV and V chords in root positions more than playing them in a real piece of music—especially a jazz style piece that is a lot of fun!

In my piece *Blues Train (Jazz a Little Jazz A lot Book I)* measures 1-8 are in the I chord position. (See example 3) (In this piece and in many other pedagogical pieces, the 12 bar blues gets doubled in length because of using quarters, rather than eighth note values.)

Example 3

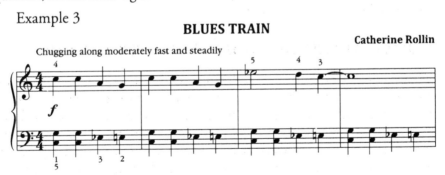

**BLUES TRAIN**

Catherine Rollin

At Measure 9, we move to the IV chord position:

Example 4

At measure 17 we move for two bars to the V chord and then two bars of the IV chord (See example 5); then the piece returns to the I position.

Example 5

I explain to my students that just these three positions (I, IV and V) are used for the basic chords of the blues (see example 6).

Example 6

I  –  I  –  I  –  I
IV  –  IV  –  I  –  I
V  –  IV  –  I  –  I (V)

The students immediately understand this concept when they see it and implement it in the piece of music. Additionally, most of them are so excited about the accessibility that they start trying to make up their own songs using this I, IV, V blues pattern. It is great to teach theory and have it so readily received, absorbed and implemented. Even if the students don't start to do their own improvising and/or composing, they always go home, ready to practice these pieces with their clear-cut and accessible harmonic movement.

## Flatted Thirds in Chord Accompaniments

We have already explored flatted thirds as used in a melody. It is important now to show students how flatted thirds are used extensively as part of chord accompaniments. By the time my students have reached this level, they are usually familiar with all of their major five-finger positions. (If the student is not already conversant with these positions, I would explain the pattern of whole, whole, half, whole to them.) In *Blues Train* (examples 3, 4 and 5)—the student can immediately see how the flatted third is used in each position. (see above I, IV and V positions of this piece). Students love seeing how this easy step of alternating between the major third and the flatted third immediately makes the music sound "jazzy."

For the teacher—you can send the student home to learn this piece and they will have lots of fun. But, you can also show them how this standard blues pattern can be transposed to be played in other keys. They can add into their assignment doing this same accompaniment in the key of G or D. Or they can stay in the key of C and add a new right hand. In other words, the student can simply enjoy the piece and understand the harmony or they can understand it, enjoy it and possibly take it to another level of composition and/or improvisation.

# Jazz Style Eighths or Swinging the Eighths

It was those swing eighths that initially prompted my friends to ask for their jazz style lessons several years ago. For all musicians, I want to assure you that if you can count in triplets, you are fine to play the jazz style eighth notes. The rhythmic division is:

For a student who has not yet had triplets, I will usually forego the introduction of triplets and just demonstrate how to play the eighth note pair as a long short combination.

Example 7

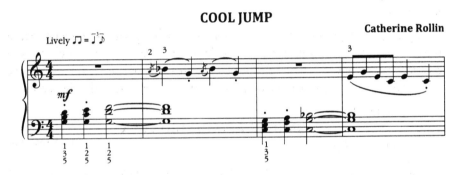

When I teach the jazz style eighths by rote, I always have the student clap it first (see example 7 above).

Even if the student is ready to count with triplet counting, I will usually have them clap the rhythm first before attempting to play the notes. This method frees the student up to concentrate only on the rhythm. In my piece *Jazz Cat*, I wrote out the swung eighths with actual triplets, rather than with regular eighth notes. I would still suggest however, that the student clap or tap the rhythm before playing the actual notes.

Example 8

# Syncopation

Syncopation commonly occurs in traditional Classical music also (see example 9).

Example 9

### ÉCOSSAISE IN G MAJOR

Ludwig van Beethoven

Syncopation is the temporary displacement of the natural strong beats in the music.

Syncopations go against the basic pulse. The challenge of playing syncopation is to create such a clear pulse that the deviation against that pulse is obvious. In *Boogie 'Round the Clock* (see example 10) the student has to create a very strict left hand pulse so the syncopated emphasis in ms. 2 and 4 is clearly heard.

Example 10

### BOOGIE 'ROUND THE CLOCK

Catherine Rollin

I will often help set up a strict pulse by playing a jazz beat with a brush and cymbal in my studio: **quarter, eighth-eighth, quarter, eighth-eighth** (jazz style eighths) Teachers can also use a drum pre-setting on their keyboards.

Example 11

Accompanying a student with a real or keyboard percussion builds a student's sense of pulse – and the feel of the syncopation against it. It is also much more fun than using a metronome. In my teaching studio – the students invariably play their Classical pieces with more strictness and do better syncopations if they have played jazz pieces.

# Building a Vocabulary of Seventh Chords

If a teacher doesn't teach any theory at all, then the following might seem extremely sophisticated. But it is my feeling that all students should readily be able to build major and minor chords. If they can build a major chord (major third [2 whole steps] plus minor third [1&1/2 steps]) or a minor chord (minor third [1&1/2 steps] plus major third [2 whole steps]), most students can easily build the following seventh chords:

Dominant 7th:  Major third, Minor third, Minor third

Major 7th:  Major third, Minor third, Major third

Minor 7th:  Minor third, Major third, Minor third

Diminished 7th:  Minor third, Minor third, Minor third

With this chord vocabulary students can readily understand most of the harmonies used in written out blues and jazz pieces. If teachers point this out to them, they can also start recognizing these seventh chord "colors" almost as easily as they can hear major and minor. Using the above seventh chords adds a new degree of sophistication to the music. Here are some examples of these seventh chords used in very accessible jazz teaching pieces:

Example 12

Example 13

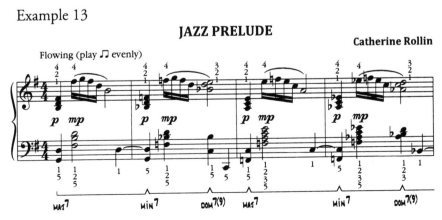

Pedagogical jazz pieces are fun and extremely motivational for our students. Playing jazz pieces helps our students develop better command of rhythm that also translates into their Classical playing. Playing jazz pieces provides an enticing environment for our students to learn theory in a context that is fun and accessible. The joy of teaching jazz pieces will become obvious when teachers see how much students love them, and look forward to practicing and playing them!

# Permissions

Examples 1-2: *Mr. Jazz Man* by Catherine Rollin. © MMVII by Alfred Publishing Co., Inc. All Rights Reserved. Used by Permission.

Examples 3-5: *Blues Train* (from "Jazz A Little, Jazz A Lot 1") by Catherine Rollin. © MCMXCIII by Alfred Publishing Co., Inc. All Right Reserved. Used by Permission.

Example 7: *Cool Jump* (from "Jazz A Little, Jazz A Lot 1") by Catherine Rollin. © MCMXCII by Alfred Publishing Co., Inc. All Rights Reserved. Used by Permission.

Example 8: *Jazz Cat* by Catherine Rollin. © MCMLXXXIV by Alfred Publishing Co., Inc. All Right Reserved. Used by Permission.

Example 10: *Boogie Round The Clock* (from "Jazz A Little, Jazz A Lot 2") by Catherine Rollin. © MMVIII by Alfred Publishing Co., Inc. All Rights Reserved. Used by Permission.

Example 11: *Jam Session* (from "Jazz A Little, Jazz A Lot 1") by Catherine Rollin. © MCMXCIII by Alfred Publishing Co., Inc. All Rights Reserved. Used by Permission.

Example 12: *Jazz Prelude* (from "Jazz A Little, Jazz A Lot 3") by Catherine Rollin. © MMVIII by Alfred Publishing Co., Inc. All Rights Reserved. Used by Permission.

# TECHNOLOGY

# CHAPTER 15

## Technology in My Musical Life

### Paul Sheftel

As I begin to write this I realize that by the time it gets into print much of the technology I will be describing will already be passé if not obsolete—such is the world we currently inhabit. But if the tools change perhaps the concepts and ideas will be valid for a while.

I often think that I am of the wrong generation to be dealing with all this. For most young people growing up in today's world, much technology is complete second nature; computer literacy is a given. For those of us who grew up when the radio, not TV, was our form of information and entertainment, when films were in black and white (not actually a bad thing when you see great old Hitchcock thrillers, for instance), when a long distance phone call cost a fortune (you spoke fast and kept your conversations very short) when airplanes used propellers that you could actually see (and hoped to see in motion when in flight), when all cars had manual transmissions (no I did not grow up in the horse and buggy era)—my how things have changed.

Interestingly in the realm of piano teaching I find that things aren't too different from when I was growing up. The metronome is, in many teaching studios, the most advanced if not the only technology in the room—apart from the piano itself. Now this is not necessarily a bad thing. A fine teacher is always a fine teacher. Fine teachers, with or without technology, are irreplaceable. Still I like to think that advances in technology can enhance many teaching situations, as they certainly have in my teaching. It is with this thought that I offer the following descriptions of the many and varied types of technology that I use in my teaching and attempt to describe the ways in which technology has helped me as a teacher.

Let's begin with three very basic and often asked questions:

1. "I am technologically challenged. I cannot figure out (or perhaps don't wish to bother trying) how to use the remote on my VCR, I cannot figure out how to use my cell phone (I personally must confess to fitting into this category to a degree at least). How am I ever to learn all this stuff?"

2. "Teaching piano may afford me a comfortable enough income but hardly sufficient to cover the costs of all the equipment and software that you are about to describe."

3. "Even if I can overcome the obstacles of 1 and 2, is any of this going to help me be a better teacher—is any or all this of real pedagogical value?"

I'll begin with issues 1 and 2. True confession: I am technologically challenged. My mentor, George Litterst, apart from being a superb musician and inspiring teacher, is, it can be safely argued, one of the most technologically astute and informed people in the universe. So guess what? When I am in challenged mode, George will step in, take control of my screen (thanks to a wonderful capability called "screen sharing") and adroitly (and always generously I must add) solve my problem and thereby save me from throwing myself off a cliff or bridge. My young students, my "un-challenged" wife, my kids, grandkids, my friends are also all there to step into the breach. Finally in desperation I can call Ted, a professional "geek," as such professional folks are sometimes dubbed, who is both kind, patient and brilliant.

Sometimes in life one can have a friendship that can be transformative, that can indeed change the direction of your life. Bob Bachman has been such a friend to me. Many years ago I was teaching Bob's two kids, now quite grown. Bob at the time was working at IBM research. One evening I asked him a very simple question, akin in complexity to something on the order of how to change a light bulb. Bob then proceeded to show me how I could change my whole studio. From that episode there developed a warm and lasting friendship—and a very changed studio. From there Bob proceeded to help me steer my way through a new world of technology. There is no way that I could have navigated the complexities of this totally new world without Bob's amazing guidance. So we all need our Georges, our Bobs, our loving families, friends and students. It's that easy!

With this part taken care of I can be freer to devote myself just to learning and working with the software programs (and come out, by the way, looking quite technologically astute). Learning the software programs is not totally without challenges but many programs are quite intuitive—for me it's still easier than trying to understand the true meaning of gigabytes. There are, in my opinion, two issues: understanding the inner workings (what's under the hood) and understanding how to work the programs (actually driving the car). Perhaps this is obvious but I believe it is important to make this distinction. Another crucial point for all of us teachers to remember is what we perpetually tell our students: don't go too fast and don't do too much at a time.

With the second or financial issue let me say it again: don't go too fast, don't do too much. Remember:

- When you add value to your studio you add value to your teaching.

- Consider tax advantages and professional discounts.

- A tiny increment to your tuition can go very far: if you had, let us say, 25 students a week and were to increase your tuition but by $1 you would have an additional $100 a month and would have added, with little doubt, more than an additional dollar in value to your students.

- Best news of all: many of the items I'll be discussing are within fairly to very easy financial reach.

So now on to the nitty-gritty issue: pedagogical value. In order best to deal with this I offer a description of some of my personal experiences with and views of the following:

- Keyboards
- Sequencers
- Video recording
- Audio
- Distance learning
- Computers: other uses

## Keyboards

This a multi-faceted topic as there are so many different types of electronic keyboards available from the tiny and inexpensive to highly sophisticated and costly. Some advantages:

- Practicing can be done without disturbing others.

- Electronic keyboards can be used as an interface to a computer with many applications.

- Higher end instruments can be remarkably fine with great feel and sound. In many cases they can better an inferior acoustic instrument. It can safely be said that the same money may buy a much better electronic instrument than a comparably priced acoustic piano.

- A second piano can be a valuable asset, particularly in a teaching studio. An electronic instrument can serve as a second piano for relatively modest expense.

- At this writing an excellent quality, touch sensitive electronic instrument with good sound and weighted keys can be obtained for under $1000. (Oops. How will that sound in a year or two—or ten?)

I have an acoustic grand piano and a high-end electronic piano in my studio. I use my second piano to accompany my students, improvise with them, play duets—and teach. My electronic piano has a few sounds other than piano such as harpsichord and organ. This capability affords my students a chance to experience playing their pieces with varieties of sounds.

My electronic keyboard interacts with my computer. Students using the keyboard create music; do interesting exercises of a variety of descriptions and play musical games, all of which add to the value and interest of the lesson.

I myself use the keyboard and computer to create my own musical compositions. I have been able to make piano recordings that are so life-like as to be undistinguishable from recordings made with an acoustic instrument. By using my music writing program (Sibelius), my written music looks thoroughly professional.

Thanks to technology that will be discussed below, it is possible, using internet technology, for two electronic pianos to communicate anywhere in the world—in other words I can play my piano and you can hear it played on your piano, wherever you are. While this can be accomplished with any electronic keyboard, the instrument, par excellence, for doing this kind of work is the Yamaha Disklavier. The Disklavier is a conventional acoustic instrument (it comes in many different sizes from upright to concert grand) equipped with electronics that allow for instant recording and playback without need of microphones: the instrument actually plays back what was just played. The keys and pedals actually move. The same thing occurs on the other end. One of my Juilliard pedagogy students recently performed in my New York living room, on my Disklavier, for an audience in Providence, Rhode Island. The audience in Rhode Island could see the performer on a screen and hear her live. A new world truly awaits us.

## Sequencers

Many years ago, at a convention of music teachers, I learned from a colleague of an arresting new device that the Roland Corporation of America had recently developed and brought to market. The device was called a "sequencer" and carried the exotic name of MT100. I understood dimly that this was some kind of recording/playback device. After a while I became aware of how different this was from a conventional recording device and why it had been given what I thought was the rather peculiar name "sequencer." (Still do find the name a bit peculiar, actually.) Ah but what else to call this device that would enable you to layer track over track using all kinds of different electronic sounds (some most attractive, some perhaps less so and some considerably less so), and then on playback, miracle of miracles, would enable you to slow down or speed up without altering the pitch; a device enabling you to play any or all tracks at a given time, to alter the sound, to transpose any or every track? When I began to think of the implications I was literally blown away. In my teaching, especially with my younger students, I would often improvise an accompaniment to help them keep their playing steady and musical. Now I could create accompaniments ahead of time with all kinds of colors and sounds. I went home from the convention with an MT100 tucked under my arm. Oh but I did need to understand one additional thing: MIDI. It took me a while to grasp but I finally understood. Musical Instrument Digital Interface (MIDI) translated into understandable language simply meant, for my needs, that in order to play the sounds in one device, I needed to hook up an electronic keyboard using this technology called MIDI. (Why couldn't they just call it something like HUYVD (Hook Up Your Various Devices).

I was like a kid with a new toy. I busily started grinding out one MIDI accompaniment after another. Little by little after much trial and error I began to grasp subtleties: the nicer sounds, the value of balancing volume, panning instruments to the left and right—all kinds of things. It was at this time that I got to know Bob Bachman. He became intrigued and suggested that other teachers in possession of MT100s might enjoy using some of my, he thought and I tended to agree, rather fanciful and elegant files. A close friendship developed between the two of us and we actually developed our own little company: SoundStart Electronic Publications. To our sorrow we began to learn that the number of teachers owning MT100s seemed to be minuscule and the number of teachers wishing to acquire this device, even smaller. Not a great business but great, great fun. Roland shortly thereafter brought out an expanded version of the device, the MT200. Then came the 300. I don't know if these are still available, and they have been quite costly (which may understandably have deterred many teachers) but the good news is that there is now a new and infinitely less costly solution, with many features that were not available on the MTs called Home Concert Xtreme. This will be described later in this article. (And yes, SoundStart is alive and well.)

## Video Recording

Here is another piece of equipment that can be of phenomenal value in many and varied ways. Today's digital cameras are tremendously easy to use. They can be easily connected to a computer. Videos can be saved, edited and viewed with great ease. Some uses:

- Feedback. Students (or you yourself) can get much valuable information by watching their own performances.

- Archiving. Whenever a student masters a piece I try to get a recording. Over the years this provides a wonderful scrapbook of a student's pianistic journey. I record all piano parties and have created from these events wonderful little montages with fragments from each student's performances.

- Sharing. It's wonderful to share your images with the families of students. If you are a member of a teacher's organization or, perhaps, teach a pedagogy course, a picture is worth a thousand words.

Very recently I acquired an iPhone with a remarkable video camera capability. Taking videos suddenly has become even easier. And the clips can be emailed on the spot from the phone.

I have two esteemed colleagues who have used video recordings very effectively in different ways:

Ingrid Clarfield who teaches advanced, college level students makes a video recording of each and every lesson—the camera, as I understand it, is on and running at all times. The student then takes the recording home and has the clearest possible record of what transpired at the lesson. Ingrid by the way also uses her Disklavier (see below) in a highly innovated manner. She has her students record their performances and then has them listen to the playback at a greatly reduced speed (yes the Disklavier can do this). Imperfections are magnified, cruelly perhaps, but very clearly detected. Her students reportedly play quite magnificently (well OK undoubtedly more due to Ingrid's masterful teaching than her Disklavier. But still – what a great idea!).

Bruce Berr is another renowned teacher who is a leader in the field of piano pedagogy. Years ago I heard Bruce describe his use of video recordings at a national pedagogy conference. Bruce, like Ingrid, would keep the camera on at all times. He then, quite laboriously I am sure, edited his videos and categorized them. Thus practically at every step in his pedagogy classes he was able to present a video, taken from an actual lesson, to demonstrate almost any given point.

## Audio Recording

Once again, advances in technology open new worlds. Not so very long ago tape recorders were the main resource in this area. They were a blessing in many ways but clunky in others. You could not trust them to be in tune if you wanted to play along with a recording. If you wanted to find or repeat a segment, rewinding and fast-forwarding were tiresome and inaccurate. All that is now a thing of the past. For many years I have used a device called a Superscope for making CDs on the spot. Great advantages: reliably in tune, easy to operate and easy to create a separate track for every thought or idea. But now it has gotten even better. The latest versions of the Superscope are now digital and other superb and very compact digital recorders are now available, many at surprisingly low cost. I have a rather high-end digital recorder. The sound is amazing! Editing and organizing are totally simple. I have it by my side at all times when I teach and can record any segment of a lesson or instructions at will. I then plug this device into my computer. My students come to their lesson with their little flash drives (or I can email the recording to them) and immediately have all the reminders, accompaniments, you name it, that they need for that week. It has been a challenge to arrive at a format for making valid recordings. A solution that seems to work effectively for me is to make a distinction between "information" tracks that can serve as a reminder to the student – possibly only to be listened to once or twice—and "practice" tracks to help guide the student to practice carefully and attentively—and rhythmically!

# Distance Learning

Some years ago the oldest of my four grandchildren, Catherine, began her piano studies. She was thrilled the first year but by the second was already beginning to suffer burnout. I could not bear to see this happen. It was around this time that I discovered that we could connect over the Internet with both picture and sound. Why not try a long distance teaching experiment? Forgot to mention that I live in New York, my two daughters, husbands and grandkids are all in the Boston area. In due time I was doing distance teaching with all four grandkids: Catherine, James, Zoe and Miranda. What a source of joy for me (maybe even for them) and it works! At this time I also continue to work with several students who have moved on to college. I occasionally give distance lessons to students who, for one reason or another, can't make it to their lesson. Even have one student who spends time in Thailand and calls for an occasional lesson.

This season, for the first time, I am teaching a pedagogy course long distance. I am in my New York studio, my class is in Princeton, New Jersey at Westminster Choir College of Rider University. While we have had some birth pains it is proving to be remarkably effective.

All that is needed is a computer, either Skype, available for either Mac or PC or iChat available only on Mac, a built in camera, available on some Mac machines, or a video camera with a firewire to connect to a computer—and a piano, needless to say. It can be a conventional acoustic piano or an electronic keyboard that will afford certain of the advantages mentioned above. As long as you the teacher can see hands and torso, and the student can see your hands (it's also possible, with two cameras, to toggle between hands and face), you are in business. There are some adjustments in teaching styles that must be made, but not as many as one might imagine.

With Mac computers (as of this writing only with Macs) it is possible to do a number of maneuvers such as screen sharing that can be enormously advantageous. Then there is Internet MIDI that enables the teacher on one end to control the keyboard as well as software on the other end. The Yamaha Disklavier opens a new world of possibilities. It is now possible to play a Disklavier in one part of the world and have it play a comparable instrument anywhere else in the world.

Even if a teacher might not be teaching a student at a distance on a regular basis it can be monumentally useful as a resource for teaching students on an occasional basis who might not, for one reason or another, be able to attend a lesson.

## The Piano Lab

This is mostly for teachers working in schools furnished with this kind of equipment. A piano lab is an extraordinary teaching tool for classroom or small group teaching. The teacher can tune into the whole class or individual students from a central instrument. It is the perfect means for combining the dynamics of group teaching with the advantages of one-on-one teaching. There are, in fact, great similarities to teaching in a piano lab and doing distance teaching. Distance may be somewhat easier in the sense that you can see the hands of the student as you teach. In a lab situation you will usually have to move about the room in order to see what the student is doing.

## Computers

So now, even though I have been discussing numerous activities that involve using a computer, let me attempt, in conclusion, to enumerate and briefly describe some of the many other ways in which I utilize computers in my daily professional life. It was not so long ago that there was life without computers but as I look at my list, I realize how monumentally my life as been changed and enriched in this computer age—and continues to be as I learn new things, as new things develop in this rapidly changing world and as I acquire new knowledge and skills. Here is a partial list in no particular order:

1. Record keeping
2. Writing music—Sibelius
3. Creating MIDI files—Cakewalk and Digital Performer
4. Web page
5. Internet
6. Tutorials

## Record Keeping

By record keeping I mean such items as:

- Appointments
- Financial records and billing
- Assignments and records of repertoire

In days of yore I wrote my appointments in an appointment book. It was quite laborious since most of my appointments were recurring. Each week I would essentially copy in the same information as I had for the previous week. Then I discovered that with an electronic organizer I could be spared this tiresome task. Recurring appointments entered only once would appear quite magically every week. I only have to make note of cancellations. My hand organizer is synced to my computer and another portable device so I'm always able at any location to retrieve information.

I use the computer for assignments. Students all have 3 ring binders for holding the assignment of the week. The assignment sheet contains not only the current assignment but a record of repertoire, names of books being used and other pertinent information. Best of all I have a permanent record; a quick glance at last week's assignment and I have an instant reminder that enables me to create an instant new lesson plan.

## Writing Music

There are numerous programs of varying degrees of cost and complexity on the market for this purpose. For many years, Sibelius has been my program of choice. An immensely powerful and complex program, it is also ingeniously designed, and is quite intuitive and user friendly. It must be borne in mind that many, if not most computer software programs are intended for a wide range of users with varying needs. With Sibelius you can score a symphony, write an opera or a pop song with lyrics. If writing simple piano music is your need then the depth and complexity of such a program need not daunt you. Remember that you only need to learn that which serves your purpose. Simple enough but deserves to be stated. It is possible to use the program without the use of an electronic keyboard by simply entering notes one by one from a standard computer keyboard but an electronic piano keyboard affords incredible advantages. I have a seven year old student, admittedly very precocious, whose greatest pleasure at our lesson is to be given time to copy music into Sibelius. He learns vast amounts by doing this. He has not only understood how to work the program but is learning his notes and understanding note values in a very creative manner.

## Sequencing

In the section on sequencing I focused mainly on stand-alone sequencers. George Litterst, my mentor, has been instrumental in developing a remarkable piece of software called *Home Concert Xtreme,* intended for playback of MIDI files that does everything that the old stand-alones could do—and then some. George has also developed two other programs, Classroom Maestro and Internet MIDI, each serving distinct purposes in very remarkable ways. George, in his segment, will expand.

Creating MIDI files is possible using various software programs. The two that I have used are *Cakewalk* for PCs and *Digital Performer* on my Mac.

## Web Pages

Many people these days, for many varieties of reasons, have their own web pages. These can serve a wealth of purposes. On my page I have, for instance,

- A "blog" capability that enables me to post my precious thoughts and announcements at any time.
- A list of all my publications plus recordings of much of my music.
- Links to other sites of interest.
- A "studio" section in which I can post videos of students—or whatever I wish to post.
- Bio and contact info.
- News of activities.

This list could go on. What tools we now have!!! Consider the wealth of the internet as a resource; consider the vast range of specially designed tutorial programs.

Technology can be both spooky and wonderful. The piano teacher in the 21ˢᵗ century has an array of tools as never before. Often voiced concerns:

- Will these tools replace the teacher? Answer: no.
- Are they really necessary? Answer: no. The teacher is really necessary.
- Are they really useful? Answer: used intelligently and creatively—to be sure.
- Should I start using some of these tools? Answer: if you don't want to be left behind but above all if you want to explore ways of becoming yet more effective and innovative in the way you teach.

Educating the young (and not so young) in effective and inspiring ways has to be one of the greatest challenges we have ever faced and continue to face. "Yes we can!"

# CHAPTER 16

# A Window Into My Teaching World

## George F. Litterst

I admit it: I enjoy new technologies. I find it fun to explore new technology-based products, figure out what they can do for my students, and even work with a small team of people to invent new technologies for music education and performance.

In a nutshell, I find the act of figuring out how to exploit new technologies just as interesting as figuring out how to learn a complex musical passage or figuring out the best way to communicate with a student who is having difficulty. The intellectual challenges are similar. That should not sound like a surprising statement. As teachers, we are creative problem solvers, right?

Having made my confession, I should to point out that using technology in a lesson for its own sake is a bad idea. There needs to be a purpose. The focus should be on the musical result; the technology should recede into the background.

## Musical and Pedagogical Objectives

My application of modern technologies to learning, teaching, and music-making is motivated by the following statements:

1. A student should:
   - learn to become his/her own teacher.
   - learn to gain a perspective on his/her own performance.
   - become a good listener and collaborative musician.
   - learn both to read music and to improvise.

2.  Each student comes to the lesson with a variety of learning strengths and weaknesses. A good teacher needs to leverage each student's strengths and work with them on their weak points. In short, the teacher should address the student in a complete manner: visually, aurally, intellectually, kinesthetically, and through the process of discovery.

3.  Although it is great to teach a student in person, students and teachers should be able to overcome obstacles of time and distance.

With these concepts in mind, allow me to open a window to my studio. When you take a peak inside, imagine the ways in which the technologies in my studio serve these goals.

## George's Studio Setup

I teach on a Yamaha Disklavier grand piano. This is a real piano with hammers and strings. It also has a built-in record/playback system, which means that it is a high-tech player piano. Most importantly for me, it connects to my computer.

The biggest benefits of this setup are that I can:

-   record students and let them listen to themselves
-   use the playback feature to play master performances for my students
-   connect the piano to the computer and use interactive software
-   teach long distance

You can obtain many of these features by using a high quality digital piano. The Disklavier, though, has the advantage of being a real piano.

I hasten to note that you can add a MIDI output feature to any acoustic piano rather simply, using a product called PNOscan (www.qrsmusic. com). PNOscan consists of an optical sensor strip that is positioned under the keys. It has no effect on the touch of the piano but does enable you to output MIDI data to a computer. It also comes with sensors for the three pedals.

If you teach using a high-tech player piano, a high quality digital piano, or an acoustic piano with a PNOscan system, you have a modern instrument that can provide your teaching efforts with wings!

# MIDI Accompaniments

Ever since the early 1990s, the major publishers of piano method materials have published MIDI files that coordinate with the various method and supplementary books. These MIDI files consist of a piano part that matches the student's printed music as well as accompaniment tracks. The accompaniment tracks may constitute anything from a classical orchestra to a Broadway ensemble to a rock band.

I have found the use of MIDI accompaniments to be the single most effective application of technology in my studio.

For starters, MIDI accompaniments can function like a metronome. They keep the student in time. But, unlike a traditional metronome, a MIDI accompaniment establishes a musical context for the beat, making it much easier for the student to realize that his/her playing is a little ahead or a little behind.

Beyond providing a pulse, a MIDI accompaniment helps to establish a musical groove and to clarify the rhythmic challenges in the piece. MIDI accompaniments open the student's ear, encouraging the student to listen to other musical parts and to become a facile, collaborative player.

Students who work with MIDI accompaniments very quickly acquire the skill of being able to start anywhere in the piece. Why? The reason is that when they are playing with the accompaniment and accidentally stumble, the accompaniment continues and they get used to the idea of jumping back in again.

Many modern keyboard instruments have the ability to play MIDI files using their built-in sounds. They usually come with features for canceling the playback for the left- or right-hand tracks, canceling any of the accompaniment tracks, setting a slower or faster tempo, and transposing.

One of the wonderful things about MIDI accompaniments is that they are available for all genres of repertoire, including classical themes, Broadway tunes, movie and TV hits, jazz and pop compositions, hymns, Christmas carols, and even piano concertos. If a student comes to a lesson wanting to play a tune from *Pirates of the Caribbean* or one of the *Harry Potter* movies, I can not only provide an arrangement that fits the student's playing level, I can provide a MIDI orchestration that actually sounds like the music in the movie.

Teenage and adult beginners especially benefit from MIDI accompaniments. The reason is pretty simple: These students have a playing level that is much lower than their intellectual level. As a result, it can be challenging to keep them engaged as they slowly progress to more advanced repertoire. Nicely orchestrated MIDI files, however, can provide the student with a more complete musical experience even when the student part is pretty simple.

## Interactive Computer Software

I find that these MIDI accompaniments are even easier and more effective to use with a personal computer. I copy all of my MIDI files to my computer's hard drive and use a program called *Home Concert Xtreme* from TimeWarp Technologies (www.timewarptech.com) to open them. *Home Concert Xtreme* transcribes the piano tracks into music notation on the screen and provides additional interactive features.

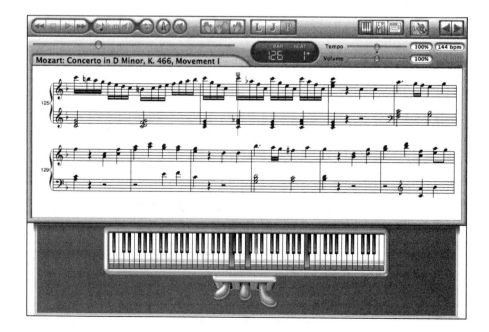

In Learn mode, you set a playback tempo and play along with the accompaniment. If you don't play a note accurately, the program will wait for you to play the note correctly and even show you which one to play.

In Jam mode, the program requires you to keep up with the accompaniment. In Perform mode, the program will actually follow your tempo as it changes, moment to moment. In all modes, the program can respond to how loud you play, adjusting the volume of the accompaniment dynamically, and it will even turn the pages at the right time.

Recently, I have experienced the electronic future of piano teaching while working with some adult students. Each of these students brings a laptop to the lesson and plugs it into my piano. The student reads the music that I have assigned off the computer screen, and I add fingerings and other comments as necessary. At the end of the lesson, the student goes home, plugs the computer into the home piano, and practices independently with all of the interactive features that we used during the lesson. The results have been compelling.

## Long Distance Lessons

Any number of circumstances can separate student and teacher:

- student or teacher moves to another location
- student has a bad cold and doesn't want to share it
- teacher is out of town on tour or attending a conference
- student has a disability that makes travel to a lesson difficult or impossible
- student lives in a location that has no teacher nearby
- teacher lives in a location where there are few students
- student or teacher has scheduling problems that make it impossible for both to be in the same location at the same time

Remarkably, all of these problems can be solved with a long distance lesson given over the Internet.

The basic ingredients for a long distance lesson are a broadband Internet connection and a video conferencing program, such as Skype (which is free). A high quality video conferencing connection requires adequate bandwidth up and down (1-2 Mbps preferred). Using a video conferencing setup, you can see and talk to your student.

The next requirement is a piano-to-piano connection. This can be achieved using another TimeWarp program called *Internet MIDI*. When two pianos are connected via *Internet MIDI*, the person who plays the local piano simultaneously plays the remote piano. *Internet MIDI's* onscreen graphics will show the movement of the keys and the pedals.

You can use *Classroom Maestro*, also from TimeWarp, simultaneously with *Internet MIDI*. *Classroom Maestro* provides a two-way, interactive electronic blackboard that facilitates musical discourse. Use *Classroom Maestro* to illustrate the relationship between notes on the staff with notes on the keyboard, intervals, chords, scales, and hand positions. The program is musically intelligent and understands major and minor keys, key signatures, and even how to spell correctly and analyze intervals, chords, and scales.

## Concluding Thoughts

Many things in life can be complex in their design and powerful in their implementation yet easy to use. Take the automobile, for example. The engineering embedded in an automobile is complex, to be sure. And, the result of that engineering is a powerful result: the miracle of fast, personal transportation. At the same time, it is not particularly difficult for most adults to drive a car.

Although it is not difficult to drive a car, learning to drive does take some devotion to the task. Once you have acquired the skill, you can almost drive one in your sleep (but I caution you not to try!).

Contemporary technologies for the modern piano teacher present a similar situation.

# ENSEMBLE MUSIC

# CHAPTER 17

# Ensemble Music for Elementary and Intermediate Students: Duets, Duos, Concertos and Multiple Pianos

**James Lyke**

## Duets

Piano students benefit from an early introduction to four-hand playing in several ways. Outside of the sheer joy of playing with another musician, children experience the challenge of attempting to make two play as one. This involves listening carefully to a partner, responding with precise rhythm and experiencing the full resources of a single instrument. Four hand playing for pianists parallels quartet playing for string players. The full range of the keyboard with its various colors is manipulated by four hands and twenty fingers. For the pianist, four hand performance represents chamber music in its truest sense.

Besides developing musicianship in branches such as rhythm and listening, four hand repertoire can be used as one type of reading experience. At early levels of instruction, teachers valuing sight reading skill may spend a few minutes of the lesson time having young students read simple primo and secondo parts. By reading with the teacher (or another student), the young pianist is prevented from re-reading or stopping to correct mistakes. The student often experiences reading in two treble, or two bass clefs in registers which often contrast to solo music normally in treble and bass clef.

Many fine composers have written excellent music for young pianists with a limited hand stretch. Therefore, there is an abundance of easy duet music where primo or secondo parts span only five notes in each hand. The teacher (usually harder) part makes the student sound richer. Parents experience pleasure when a student plays duets in recitals. The student will sound more advanced and take pleasure in playing with his teacher or a student partner.

Problems inherent in four hand playing become interesting and challenging for the child to solve. Some of these involve becoming used to sitting left or right of center and learning to practice in that same position at home. Another challenge concerns the question of which partner pedals, one that will crop up when the child's feet become capable of reaching the pedal mechanism. Other considerations include page turns (which partner?), starting and ending together by prearranged signals, becoming used to the closeness of a secondo player's right arm to the primo player's left arm, releasing notes needed by a partner and working out a proper balance in the various piano registers.

Piano teachers are fortunate to be able to select elementary and intermediate duet sheet music and collections from a wealth of well-written four-hand repertoire. Major publishers have engaged first-rate composers and arrangers to provide duet music that teachers can arrange in a developmental plan for their students. The present interest in quality duet music for young pianists stems in large part from the tireless work of the American husband and wife team Weekley and Arganbright. In addition to workshops and teaching, this couple constantly researches, edits and arranges duet music at various levels; their editions (Kjos) reflect admirable scholarship. Moreover, the lay-out of their scores (primo *over* secondo) makes the rehearsing of the music a far simpler task than if the primo and secondo pages faced each other.

At the elementary and intermediate levels, original and arranged four-hand literature by educational composers such as Robert D. Vandall, Lynn Freeman Olson, Dennis Alexander, William Gillock, Eugenie Rocherolle, Paul Sheftel and Catherine Rollin lead the student down the path to a lifetime of musical enjoyment. Moreover, there are notable composers from the classic, romantic and modern eras who have devoted themselves to enriching the literature with original four-hand duo-piano music and concerti (then played on two pianos.) These include figures such as Beethoven, Schumann and Dello Joio. The literature is vast. An excellent reference for the teacher is Weekley and Arganbright's *The Piano Duet: A Learning Guide* (Kjos). This collection is a "must" for all piano teachers teaching at elementary, intermediate and early advanced levels of instruction.

The following list suggests only some of the duet repertoire available for beginning, elementary and intermediate stages of development. It goes without saying that enterprising teachers will always be searching for and evaluating new issues from respected and skilled composers as well as arrangers. Bearing in mind that publishers often merge, teachers should use the internet to check availability.

## Recommended Duet Sheets and Collections for Various Stages of Elementary Instruction

| Composer/Arranger | Composition/Title | Publisher/Distributor |
|---|---|---|
| Agay, Denes | *The First Duets* | Yorktown |
| Alexander, Dennis | *Five Star Folk Duets* | Alfred |
| | *Five Star Sacred Duets* | Alfred |
| | *Five Star Patriotic Duets* | Alfred |
| | *Just for You & Me* (Book 1) | Alfred |
| Bastien, Jane | *Duets for Fun* (1 & 2) | Kjos |
| Bober, Melody | *Grand Duets for Piano* (Books 1 & 2) | Alfred |
| Brackner, Anton | *Three Little Pieces* | Oxford |
| Dello Joio, Norman | *Family Album* | Hal Leonard |
| Diabelli, Anton | *Pleasure of Youth* (Opus 163) | Alfred |
| George, Jon | *Kaleidoscope Duets* (Sets 1 - 3) | Alfred |
| | *Two at One Piano* (Books 1 - 3) | Alfred |
| Haydon, Geoff and Lyke, Jim | *Ensemble Music for Group Piano* (Sections 1 & 2) | Stipes |
| Ikeda, Naoko | *Pandora* | Hal Leonard |
| Maykapar, Samuel | *First Steps* | MCA |
| Olson, Lynn | *Round 'n Round* | Carl Fischer |
| | *The Ash Grove* | Carl Fischer |
| | *Two by Two* | Carl Fischer |
| Pace, Robert | *Duets for Piano* (Sets 1 & 2) | Lee Roberts |
| | *Duets to Play & Play With* | Lee Roberts |
| Resphigi, Ottorino | *Six Children's Pieces* | Associated |
| Rocherolle, Eugénie | *Tour for Two* | Hal Leonard |

| | | |
|---|---|---|
| Rollino, Joseph & Sheftel, Paul | *Festivities*<br>*Further Festivities* | Carl Fischer<br>Carl Fischer |
| Starer, Robert | *First Duets for Young Pianists* | MCA |
| Stravinsky, Igor | *Three Easy Pieces* | Chester Music (Hal Leonard) |
| | *Five Easy Pieces* | Chester Music (Hal Leonard) |
| Tansman, Alexander | *Les Jeunes Au Piano* (Books 1 & 2) | Max Eschig (Hal Leonard) |
| Tsitsaros, Christos | *Tour for Two* | Hal Leonard |
| Tcherepnin, Alexander | *Exploring the Piano* | Alfred |
| Vandall, Robert | *Celebrated Piano Duets* (Books 1 & 2) | Alfred |
| Walton, William | *Duets for Children* (Vols. 1 & 2) | Oxford |
| Weekley & Arganbright | *Primo Light*<br>*Secondo Light*<br>*Primo Progresses*<br>*Easy for Two*<br>*Piano Together* | Kjos<br>Kjos<br>Kjos<br>Kjos<br>Kjos |

# Two Pianos

Equipping a studio with a second piano offers the teacher numerous ways to improve instruction. Besides the obvious advantage of demonstrating from a second piano, the teacher will be able to make two new types of repertoire available to the student: two-piano repertoire and concertos.

The advantages cited for one-piano, four-hand performance apply equally to duo-piano study. These include 1) added interest and enjoyment of partnership, 2) ensemble training of a different nature, 3) becoming acquainted with a new body of literature, 4) sight reading opportunities and 5) rhythmic development. Yet some differences between one-piano, four-hand playing and duo-piano playing need to be examined.

While four hands and twenty fingers are involved in both duet and duo-piano performance, other considerations must be taken into account. Two damper pedals, 176 keys, pianos with somewhat different personalities represent but a few of the new challenges a young pianist meets. Balance and dynamics between two instruments call for the utmost listening skill. Tone and color of instruments which often do not match, plus a wide range of sonorities doubles the problems encountered with two at one piano. Duo-pianists must develop an extraordinary coordination of the ears and eyes.

The fun of two-piano playing comes from the freedom and ease at one keyboard, a normal seating position and each partner having control over a pedal. Interesting antiphonal effects possible on two pianos cannot be accomplished in duet playing.

Unique signal systems for two-piano partners need to be worked out for precise beginnings and endings. This is usually accomplished with a slight upbeat notion of one partner's head. The ever present problem of balance, especially when considering pedaling, might require a third party opinion. And the distance between two pianists certainly calls for a sixth sense to be developed.

Two-piano playing has always fascinated listeners and stunning two-piano teams make a lasting impression on an audience. The two-piano medium has an interesting history and a substantial repertoire by major composers at more advanced levels. If teachers can afford a second piano, students will enjoy and profit from learning and performing original and arranged duo piano music.

In many states, piano festivals are being organized with students being prepared by their teacher, rehearsed by a conductor-pianist and presented in a final concert. As many as perhaps twelve pianos are used for these events. These festivals stem from the popularity of "monster concerts" promoted by the late American pianist, Eugene List. Gottschalk presented such concerts in the latter part of the nineteenth century.

With the advent of piano laboratories used for group piano teaching in schools and colleges, a body of original and arranged music for multiple pianos has emerged. This repertoire has enabled teachers of group piano to provide reading experiences, rehearse and conduct music written for as many as six pianos. In this situation the student pianist, much like the instrumentalist in a bad or orchestra, counts carefully, attempts accurate entrances and blends with many other instruments. Robert Vandall has provided much attractive music for this distinctive setting. Teachers should consult the piano catalogs of Alfred, Kjos, and Hal Leonard for this distinct repertoire.

## Student Concertos

Young piano students respond with excitement when the teacher assigns a concerto. The word concerto conjures up an image of a very big and important piece. Some elementary level concertos are written with a second piano as accompaniment. Others call for a small ensemble or even a full orchestra. It is never too early to pave the way for the learning and performance of Haydn's D major concerto. To set the stage for the high school years, teachers have many elementary and lower intermediate level concertos to teach.

Over these years of searching, learning and teaching concertos for the young, I've established a basic list which will continue to grow over the years. Meanwhile, this list gives me a framework for starting students young and preparing them for the various styles they will encounter later: classic, romantic and modern. They will gain experience with scale passages and ornaments in easier Haydn works (Concertos in C and F); they will learn pedal techniques and romantic configurations (Rowley, *Miniature Concerto*) and they will gain an understanding of modern harmony and how chord configurations can build exciting effects (Vandall, *Concerto in G*). The students will continue along a path of gradual development which includes performing in recitals with a second piano substituting for the orchestra or in school with small instrumental ensembles (Olson, *Celebration* and Haydn, *Concertino*). Further, the students will enter junior-level concerto events to compete for the honor of playing with a symphony orchestra.

The annotated listing of eleven concertos which follows could serve as a basic starting point for the concerto experience starting at the elementary level and proceeding through the junior high school/middle school years. The teacher remains free to choose an appropriate work from the list, and to add to the list as new works become known.

# Suggested Concertos for Children

## Elementary Level

1. Verhaalen, Marion   *Concertino*        Lee Roberts Music Pub. 1978

   All three movements contain modal flavors. The second movement has a 6/8 sicilienne rhythm and the third movement offers some rhythmical and technical challenges with bi-chordal clashes. This concerto, though simple, sounds well and succeeds in a recital format. A second piano provides the accompaniment.

2. Berkovich, I.        *Piano Concerto,*   Associated Music Pub. 1977
                         *Op. 44*

   This concerto represents one of four in a Russian series written especially for student-teacher performance in competitions. Each of the three movements offers lyric writing based on folk literature. The student will be challenged by interesting rhythmic figures and technical hurdles. The second movement is based upon a haunting and beautiful Ukrainian folk song. The third movement features chord outlines exchanged between the hands and a waltz-like middle section before a return to the romping folk song theme upon which the movement is based. Scoring is for second piano only.

3. Sylvanski, N.        *Piano Concerto*    Associated Music Pub. 1977

Sylvanski's *Concerto* makes few technical demands on the student. Much of the writing features melodies between the hands or in unison. The first movement cadenza allows the student to rhythmically build to an effective climax. The D minor middle movement casts a sombre spell and allows the performer freedom of expression. The final movement demands clear articulation in passage work and accuracy with chords. This concerto is scored for two pianos only.

4. Haydn, Josef      *Concertino*      C. F. Peters 1964

This small-scale work contains all the challenges of interpreting classical repertoire. Some technical hurdles include a rapid left hand triplet accompaniment figure in the first movement and right hand trills. A cadenza is supplied; this could be improvised by the performer. The middle movement, *Minuet and Trio*, exudes charm. A small string ensemble could accompany the performer. If string players are unavailable, the second piano part provides an adequate substitute.

5. Olson, Lynn F.      *Celebration!*      Alfred Publishing Co. 1981

*Celebration!* affords the young pianist an opportunity to perform in a school setting accompanied by a rhythmic ensemble, snare drummer and conductor. Its three movements lie easily under the hands of the elementary pianist. The first and third movements feature hand crossings and melodic and chordal patterns which move rapidly. The second movement demands unusual pedal effects and some lengthy glissandi. If a percussion ensemble is not used, the second piano part sounds very well.

6. Kasschau, Howard   *Country Concerto*      G. Schirmer 1971

The first movement opens with a staccato theme alternating with a more lyrical theme. The writing is sparse, but effective. The second movement provides the student with a miniature Romantic movement utilizing scale passages, dotted rhythms, and an opportunity for effective pedaling. The third movement's driving tarantella rhythm builds to an effective climax. Orchestra parts are available from the publisher. The piano reduction serves the student well if orchestra players are not available.

## Lower Intermediate Level

7. Haydn, Josef      *Piano Concerto in C*   Boosey & Hawkes 1955

This concerto must be considered a "classic," one of those "must teach" pieces for young piano students. Clean scale playing, rapid execution of ornaments and smooth left-hand *Alberti* bass configuration make challenges for the performer in this work. The second movement

*Minuet and Trio* is an absolute gem. And the third movement requires rotational skills as well as perfect balance between the hands when outlining harmonies. The first movement cadenza represents a miniature model for study. This work is scored for a small chamber orchestra. The two-piano version serves well if the student does not play with an orchestra.

8.  Haydn, Josef        *Piano Concerto*    International Music Co. 1960
                        *in F*

The F major concerto in some ways presents fewer problems than the C major. The second movement is especially lovely and requires the performer to achieve smooth cantabile playing and perfect balance. The third movement abounds in contrasting touches, broken chord configurations and syncopation. Some beautiful two-part writing highlights secondary dominant harmonies prior to the closing theme. Orchestral parts may be rented from the publisher. The piano reduction is very serviceable.

9.  Rowley, Alec        *Miniature Concerto*    Boosey & Hawkes 1947
                        *for Piano and Orchestra*

Rowley's *Concerto* paves the way for the study of Romantic concerti at later stages of development. The G major first movement opens with a short introduction consisting of rich chords and arpeggiations. This is immediately followed by a working of themes and sections in a variety of keys, moods and styles. The movement is full of scale passages (hands alone and together) and broken chord figures. The second movement is set in D major and requires careful pedaling of chord outlines and principal theme. The 6/8 final movement, *Rondo*, requires precise touch control and agile fingers. The alternating sections provide a relief from the driving rhythm of the *Rondo* theme. The cadenza will teach a student much about *ad libitum* playing. The closing section restates the opening introduction and concludes in a brilliant scale passage prior to the final chords. Orchestra parts are available from the publisher.

## Intermediate Level

10. Vandall, Robert      *Concerto in G*      Alfred Publishing Co., Inc.
                        *Major for Piano*                    1985

Vandall possesses a special gift for combining tuneful melodies and modern harmonies into patterns which feel good under the child's hands. Moreover, the composer gives the young pianist configurations and interesting technical twists which make him sound (and feel) as if he were at a more advanced level than is actually the case. This work begins with a cantabile theme accompanied by broken chords which contrasts with a quicker second theme demanding staccato left-hand single notes and right-hand broken octaves. A short cadenza leads to a brilliant conclusion of the movement. The second movement in E aeolian furnishes the student with long expressive lines as well as some interesting passages with right-hand thirds. The third movement is in the form of a rondo with a toccata flavor. The left-hand especially must be accurate in its crosses over the right-hand. The accompaniment is especially appealing with its interesting harmonic progression and syncopated rhythms. This work appeals to audiences and is a welcome addition to youth concerti repertoire. *Concerto in G* may be played with a student chamber orchestra using the orchestration by Eric Benjamin. Consult with Robert Vandall about obtaining parts. rvandall@tusco.net

11.  Vandall, Robert        *Concertino in C*        Alfred Publishing Co., Inc.
                             *Major*                                           1992

This concerto has been scored for two pianos. It contains all the hallmarks of this composer's style: flowing melodies, interesting rhythms, jazz-like harmonies and technical challenges bound to improve a student's technique. The first movement intermixes a cantabile theme with another more rhythmic idea ♩ ♫ ♩♩ .
There is a nice interplay of scalar material against a slower moving legato theme. The first movement includes a Piano I cadenza. The second movement is a scherzo requiring excellent control over a variety of touches. This 6/8 movement becomes a fine study in rapid five finger passages along with chords and intervals which alternate between the hands. The vivace third movement is toccata-like and demands excellent rhythmic and touch control. Students will find this movement exciting. Syncopation abounds in staccato passages; legato passages provide an opportunity for pedal work and careful listening to contrasts in sound color. This movement is a gem! The *Concertino in C Major* is scored for a chamber orchestra, orchestration by Eric Benjamin. Consult with Robert Vandall about obtaining parts. rvandall@tusco.net

## Other Recommended Concertos

| | | |
|---|---|---|
| Alexander, Dennis | *Concertino in D Major* | Alfred |
| | *Concertante in G Major* | Alfred |
| Edwards, Matthew | *Concerto for Young Pianists* | Hal Leonard |
| | *Concerto #2 in G Major* | Hal Leonard |
| Hummel, Johann Nepomuk | *Concertino for Piano and Orchestra* | Kjos |

| | | |
|---|---|---|
| Peskanov, Alexander | *Concerto #1 for Piano and Strings* | Hal Leonard |
| Rollin, Catherine | *Concerto in C Major* | Alfred |
| | *Concerto Romantique* | Alfred |

A significant and exciting duet and duo piano repertoire awaits the intermediate student. Top notch composers and arrangers provide the intermediate student with a brilliant array of works in many different styles. The following lists merely scratch the surface. The alert teacher who makes piano ensemble an important component of study becomes aware of new works through workshops and conventions.

## Recommended Duet Collections and Sheets for Various Stages of Intermediate Instruction

| Composer | Collection/Sheet | Publisher/Distributor |
|---|---|---|
| Agay, Denes | *The Joy of Duets* | Yorktown |
| Alexander, Dennis | *Festival in Cordoba* | Alfred |
| | *Festival Overture* | Alfred |
| | *Just for You & Me* (Book 2) | Alfred |
| | *Preludium in D Major* | Alfred |
| | *Sacred Portraits* | Alfred |
| | *Touch a Rainbow* | Alfred |
| | *Valse Caprice* | Alfred |
| André, Johann | *Divertimento in A Minor* | C. F. Peters |
| Austin, Glenda | *All-American Ragtime Duets* (Books 1 - 6) | Willis (Hal Leonard) |
| Bach/Hess | *Jesu Joy of Man's Desiring* | Oxford |
| Bober, Melody | *Grand Duets for Piano* (Books 3 & 4) | Alfred |
| Brahms, Johannes | *Waltzes, Op. 39* | G. Henle |
| Casella, Alfredo | *Puppazetti* | Alfred |
| Clark, Sondra | *Florida Fantasy Suite* | Hal Leonard |
| Clementi, Muzio | *Three Rondos* | G. Schirmer (Hal Leonard) |
| Debussy, Claude | *Petite Suite* | International |
| Dello Joio, Norman | *Song of Springtime* | Associated (Hal Leonard) |
| | *Stage Parodies* | Associated (Hal Leonard) |
| Dusek, Josefa | *Three Sonatas* | Elkan-Vogel |

| | | |
|---|---|---|
| Fauré, Gabriel | *Dolly Suite* | International |
| Gershwin, George (arr. James Lyke) | *Rialto Ripples* | Alfred |
| Gershwin, George (arr. Haydon & Lyke) | *By Strauss* | Alfred |
| | *A Gershwin Medley* | Alfred |
| Gillock, William | *Accent on Duets* | Willis |
| Grieg, Edvard | *Norwegian Dances, Op.35* | C. F. Peters |
| Haydon, Geoff & Lyke, Jim | *Ensemble Music for Group Piano* (Section 2) | Stipes |
| Kern, Fred (arr.) | *Joplin Ragtime Duets* | Hal Leonard |
| Kuhlau, Friedrich | *Sonatina in G* | G. Schirmer (Hal Leonard) |
| Lyke, Jim | *Great American Songwriters* | Lee Roberts (Hal Leonard) |
| | *Swing Band Dance Hits* | Lee Roberts (Hal Leonard) |
| | *We Love a Piano* (15 Favorites) | Alfred |
| Matz, Carol | *Piano for Two* (Books 1 - 6) | FJH |
| Milhaud, Darius | *Enfantines* | Max Eschig (Hal Leonard) |
| Moskowski, Moritz | *Spanish Dances* | G. Schirmer (Hal Leonard) |
| Mozart, Wolfgang A. | *Original Compositions* | G. Henle |
| Persichetti, Vincent | *Serenade No. 8* | Elkan-Vogel |
| Poulenc, Francis | *Sonata* | Chester Music (Hal Leonard) |
| Ravel, Maurice (ed. Weekley & Arganbright) | *Ma Mère L'oye* (Mother Goose Suite) | Kjos |
| Rocherolle, Eugénie | *Tour for Two* | Hal Leonard |
| | *Two's Company* | Hal Leonard |
| Rollin, Catherine | *Celebration Overture* | Alfred |
| | *Dances for Two* (Books 1 & 2) | Alfred |
| | *Fiesta for Two* | Alfred |
| | *The Grand Finale* | Alfred |
| | *Valse Sentimentale a Deux* | Alfred |

| Rossi, Wynne-Ann | *Spotlight on Duets* | FJH |
| Satie, Eric | *Trois Morceaux en Forme de Poire* | Salabert (Hal Leonard) |
| Schubert, Franz | *Original Compositions* | G. Henle |
| Schumann, Robert | *Pictures From the East, Op. 66* | C. F. Peters |
| Stravinsky, Soulima | *Music Alphabet* (Vols. 1 & 2) | C. F. Peters |
| Tansman, Alexander | *Les Jeunes au Piano* (Books 3 & 4) | Max Eschig (Hal Leonard) |
| Tschaikovsky, Peter | *Russian Folk Songs* | C. F. Peters |
| Türk, Daniel Gottlieb | *Tonstucke* (Books 1 & 2) | Schott |
| Vandall, Robert | *Allegro Festivo* | Alfred |
| | *Broadway Lights* | Alfred |
| | *Celebrated Piano Duets* (Books 3 - 5) | Alfred |
| | *Celebration Fanfare* | Alfred |
| | *Festival Toccata* | Alfred |
| | *Oakton Toccata* | Alfred |
| | *Ostinato Barbaro* | Alfred |
| | *Turquoise Skies* | Alfred |
| Weekley & Arganbright (arr.) | *Classics for Two* | Kjos |
| | *Five Joplin Rags* | Kjos |
| Weekley & Arganbright (ed.) | *Brahms Waltzes, Op. 39* | Kjos |
| | *Duet Repertoire* | Kjos |

# Recommended Music for Two Pianos and Multiple Pianos: Intermediate to Early Advanced Levels

| Composer | Collection/Sheet | Publisher/Distributor |
| --- | --- | --- |
| Alexander, Dennis | *Fanfare Toccata - Rondo* | Alfred |
| | *Flirtations* | Alfred |
| Bach, J. C. | *Sonata in G* | Schott (Hal Leonard) |
| Bach, J. S. (arr. G. Maier) | *Sicilienne* | Alfred |

| | | |
|---|---|---|
| Benjamin, Arthur | *Jamaican Rumba* | Boosey & Hawkes |
| Berlin, Irving (arr. Heitler & Lyke) | *Alexander's Ragtime Band* *When the Midnight Choo-Choo Leaves for Alabam'* | Alfred Alfred |
| Bowman, Euday (arr. Haydon & Lyke) | *12th Street Rag* | Alfred |
| Clementi, Muzio | *Two Sonatas in B Flat* | C. F. Peters |
| Cohan, George M. (arr. Heitler & Lyke) | *Patriotic Cohan, a Medley* | Alfred |
| Gershwin, George (arr. Haydon & Lyke) | *By Strauss* | Alfred |
| Gould, Morton | *Pavane* | Alfred |
| Grainger, Percy | *Country Gardens* | G. Schirmer (Hal Leonard) |
| Haydon, G & Lyke, J. (arr) | *Ensemble Music for Group Piano* (Section 3) | Stipes |
| Haydon & Lyke, Heitler & Lyke (arr) | *15 Arrangements of American Classic Songs for Two Pianos-Four Hands* | Alfred |
| O'Hearn, Arletta | *Jazz Theme & Variations* *Suite Talk* | Kjos Kjos |
| Pinto, Octavio | *Scenas Infantis* | G. Schirmer (Hal Leonard) |
| Rocherolle, Eugénie | *Jambalaya* | Hal Leonard |
| Thomson, Virgil | *Synthetic Waltzes* *Walking Song* | Elkan-Vogel G. Schirmer (Hal Leonard) |
| Waller, Thomas "Fats" (arr. Heitler & Lyke) | *Ain't Misbehavin'* | Alfred |
| Ward, Samuel A. (arr. Heitler & Lyke) | *America the Beautiful* | Alfred |

## Multiple Pianos

| | | |
|---|---|---|
| Haydon, G. & Lyke, J. (arr) | *Ensemble Music for Group Piano* (Section 3) | Stipes |
| Vandall, Robert | *Celebrated Keyboard Ensembles* | Alfred |

# References

Albergo, Cathy and Alexander, Reid. *Intermediate Piano Repertoire: A Guide for Teaching.* Champaign, IL: Stipes Publishing Company, 2011.

Ferguson, Howard. *Keyboard Duets From the 16th to the 20th Century For One & Two Pianos.* New York: Oxford University Press, 1999.

Ferguson, Howard. *Style and Interpretation, Vols. 5 and 6.* London: Oxford University Press, 1971.

Hinson, Maurice. *Music for More Than One Piano: An Annotated Guide.* Bloomington: Indiana University Press, 1983.

Hinson, Maurice. *Music for Piano and Orchestra: An Annotated Guide.* Bloomington: Indiana University Press, 1981.

Lubin, Ernst. *The Piano Duet: A Guide for Pianists.* New York: Grossman Publishers, 1970.

McGraw, Cameron. *Piano Duet Repertoire: Music Originally Written for One Piano, Four Hands.* Bloomington, Indiana University Press, 1981.

Weekley, Dallas and Arganbright, Nancy. *The Piano Duet: A Learning Guide.* San Diego: Neil A. Kjos Music Company, 1996.

# HOLIDAY MUSIC

# CHAPTER 18

# Holiday Repertoire for Elementary and Intermediate Students

## James Lyke

In the past several years, a significant repertory of music for the Christmas and Hanukkah season has emerged. This arranged and original music can be very useful to the piano teacher during the period which stretches from mid-November to the traditional holiday break in late December.

During these weeks, piano teachers encounter young students who occasionally appear listless and whose practice has become below par. Many of these students' thoughts focus on the break, special family plans or a yearning for a rest from school pressures and preparation for weekly piano lessons. To help students through this low-energy period, piano teachers might consider a plan which takes into account this predictable yearly slump.

One possible solution involves a teaching calendar allowing for a recital in late November, perhaps just prior to the Thanksgiving (November 25) festivity. This would give students a goal, and the fall term would culminate in a program. Immediately after this program, teachers could begin new repertoire, but also assign music of a seasonal nature. This repertoire would need to be selected judiciously since it should be at a level easily learned in about three or four weeks time.

The learning of this special body of original and arranged literature would enable the student to share familiar music with family members. Moreover, a mini-recital could be scheduled for parents and friends at the final lesson prior to the holiday break. Teachers should encourage younger students to play this music in their school, either informally in music classes, or as a part of a special holiday program.

In addition to learning solo and ensemble holiday repertoire for normal educational values, teachers might consider its use in other ways. For example, sight reading this repertoire would be a pleasurable experience for the student, especially because of the familiarity of the melodies. In conjunction with reading, some transposition would promote visual and aural skills. Other musicianship activities might include the assigning of Christmas or Hanukkah melodies with chord symbols. Students could make their own arrangements of these tunes according to their musical and notational ability. Taking dictation or playing back phrases of holiday tunes would be one more way to improve listening skills. More advanced students might try their hand at arranging traditional or popular tunes for piano-four hands, or even for two pianos.

After the Christmas break, students will be ready for a fresh start on new repertoire. The shelved holiday repertoire will be re-discovered at the next season. Students then realize how simple the previous year's work seems. This represents achievement and progress. In future years, the young students' acquaintance with this special repertoire can be broadened with progressively sophisticated music. The following suggested list is by no means complete, but it can serve as a basis for adding and deleting titles as new music appears and other music becomes no longer available.

## Holiday Music: Elementary Level Solo Collections and Sheets

| Composer/Arranger | Title | Publisher |
|---|---|---|
| Alexander, Dennis | *The Magic of Christmas* (Books 1-3) | Alfred |
| Alexander, Kowalchyk, et al. | *Premier Piano Course: Christmas* (Books 1-2 A and 1-2 B) | Alfred |
| Austin, Glenda (arr.) | *More Merry Christmas* | Willis (Hal Leonard) |
| Bastien, James (arr.) | *Popular Christmas Songs* | Kjos |
| Bastien, Jane (arr.) | *Pre-Reading Christmas Party* | Kjos |
| | *Pre-Reading Hanukkah Party* | Kjos |
| Berr, Bruce(arr.) | *Festive Chanukah Songs* (Level 2) | Hal Leonard |
| Coates, Dan (arr.) | *Fun and Jolly Christmas Songs* | Alfred |
| | *The Best in Christmas Sheet Music* | Alfred |

| Costley, Kevin (arr.) | *Be a Star at Christmas* | FJH |
| Evans, Lee (arr.) | *A Musical Christmas for Easy Piano* | Hal Leonard |
| | *A Razzle Dazzle Christmas* | Hal Leonard |
| Faber & Faber | *My First Piano Adventures: Christmas (Books A, B & C)* | Hal Leonard |
| Gerou, Tom (arr.) | *Five Finger Christmas Classics* | Alfred |
| | *Five Finger Christmas Hits* | Alfred |
| Gillock, William (arr.) | *A Young Pianist's First Christmas* | Willis (Hal Leonard) |
| Goldston, Margaret (arr.) | *Christmas Songs and Solos* | Alfred |
| Karp, David (arr.) | *Jewish Festival & Folk Songs* | Alfred |
| Kern, Keveren et al. (arr.) | *Christmas Piano Solos (Levels 1-3)* | Hal Leonard |
| | *More Christmas Piano Solos* | Hal Leonard |
| Lancaster & Kowalchyk | *Christmas Festival (Books 1 & 2)* | Alfred |
| | *Let's Celebrate Chanukah* | Alfred |
| Marlais, Helen | *In Recital With Popular Christmas Music* | FJH |
| Matz, Carol | *Famous & Fun Christmas* | Alfred |
| Mier, Martha | *Christmas Cheer* | Alfred |
| | *Christmas Festival* | Alfred |
| Norton & McBride Smith | *American Popular Piano: Christmas* | Novus Via Music Group (Hal Leonard) |
| Olson, Lynn (arr.) | *A Christmas Gathering* | Carl Fischer |
| | *Happy Holidays* | Carl Fischer |
| | *First Favorite Christmas Carols* | Alfred |
| Pace, Robert (arr.) | *Christmas Music (Book 1)* | Lee Roberts (Hal Leonard) |
| | *Easy Christmas Melodies for Piano* | Lee Roberts (Hal Leonard) |
| | *Favorite Christmas Songs* | Lee Roberts (Hal Leonard) |
| Pace, Cynthia | *Easy Christmas Melodies* | Lee Roberts (Hal Leonard) |
| Vandall, Robert | *Celebrated Christmas Solos* | Alfred |

# Holiday Music: Elementary Level Duet Collections and Sheets

| Composer/Arranger | Title | Publisher |
| --- | --- | --- |
| Alexander, Dennis (arr.) | *Five Christmas Duets* | Alfred |
| | *The Holly and the Ivy* (IPGH) | Alfred |
| Aronson, Sharon (arr.) | *Christmas on the Jazzy Side* | Alfred |
| Bastien, James (arr.) | *The Nutcracker Suite* | Kjos |
| Byers, Rosemary (arr.) | *Sounds of Christmas* (Vol. 3) | Hal Leonard |
| Coates, Dan (arr.) | *Easy Christmas Piano Duets* | Alfred |
| Evans, Lee (arr.) | *Easy Christmas Duets* | Hal Leonard |
| Faber & Faber (arr.) | *Duet Time: Christmas* (Primer & Levels 1 & 2) | Hal Leonard |
| Gillock, William (arr.) | *Christmas Together* | Willis (Hal Leonard) |
| Miller, Carolyn (arr.) | *First Christmas Duets* | Willis (Hal Leonard) |
| Marwick & Nagy (arr.) | *Duets for Christmas* | Lee Roberts (Hal Leonard) |
| Vandall, Robert | *Celebrated Christmas Duets* (Books 1-3) | Alfred |

# Holiday Music: Intermediate Level Solo Collections and Sheets

| Composer/Arranger | Title | Publisher |
| --- | --- | --- |
| Alexander, Dennis | *Christmas Silhouettes* | Alfred |
| | *Especially for Christmas* | Alfred |
| | *The Magic of Christmas* | Alfred |
| Alexander, Leroy | *Sleighride* | Alfred |
| Bastien, James (arr.) | *Christmas Favorites* (Levels 4 & 5) | Kjos |
| Berr, Bruce (arr.) | *The Chanukah Song* | Hal Leonard |
| Bober, Melody (arr.) | *Christmas Memories* | Hal Leonard |
| | *A Contemporary Christmas* | Alfred |
| | *Melody in Christmas* | Willis (Hal Leonard) |

| | | |
|---|---|---|
| Coates, Dan (arr.) | *Christmas* | Alfred |
| | *Simply Christmas* | Alfred |
| Evans, Lee (arr.) | *Christmas: Modern Piano Impressions* | Hal Leonard |
| | *A Joyful Christmas* | Hal Leonard |
| | *Lee Evan Arranges Holiday Jazz* | Hal Leonard |
| Faber & Faber (arr.) | *Christmas: Advance Time Piano* (Level 5) | Hal Leonard |
| | *Christmas: Bigtime Piano* (Level 4) | Hal Leonard |
| Gerou, Tom | *The Christmas Manger* | Alfred |
| Goldston, Margaret (arr.) | *We Wish You a Merry Christmas* | Alfred |
| Hartsell, Randall (arr.) | *Christmas Creations* | Willis (Hal Leonard) |
| Kern, Keveren et al. | *Christmas Piano Solos* (Level 5) | Hal Leonard |
| | *More Christmas Solos* | Hal Leonard |
| Keveren, Phillip | *White Christmas* | Hal Leonard (Irving Berlin) |
| Linn, Jennifer | *Christmas Favorites* | Hal Leonard |
| Norton, Christopher | *Carol Jazz for Piano* | Universal |
| O'Hearn, Arletta | *Christmas Jazzed Up* | Kjos |
| Pace, Helen | *Music for Christmas* | Lee Roberts (Hal Leonard) |
| Rocherolle, Eugénie | *Candlelight Christmas* | Hal Leonard |
| | *Christmas Around the Piano* | Kjos |
| Rollin, Catherine | *Christmas Impressions* | Alfred |
| | *Christmas Pleasures* | Alfred |
| | *Dances for Christmas* (Books 1 & 2) | Alfred |
| | *Deck the Halls* | Alfred |
| | *Jingle 'n' Jazz* | Alfred |
| Vandall, Robert | *Celebrated Christmas Solos* (Books 4 & 5) | Alfred |
| | *The Three Kings* | Alfred |

# Holiday Music: Intermediate Level Duet Collections and Sheets

| Composer/Arranger | Title | Publisher |
|---|---|---|
| Alexander, Dennis (arr.) | *The Magic of Christmas* (Books 1 & 2) | Alfred |
| Byers, Rosemary (arr.) | *Sounds of Christmas* (Vols. 1-3) | Hal Leonard |
| Clark, Sondra (arr.) | *Favorite Carols for Two* | Hal Leonard |
| Cornick, Mike (arr.) | *Sleigh Ride for Two* | Universal |
| Evans, Lee (arr.) | *Jazz Up Your Christmas* | Hal Leonard |
| Gillock, William (arr.) | *Christmas Together* | Willis (Hal Leonard) |
| Haydon & Lyke (arr.) | *Seven Favorite Holiday Duets With Santa Clause* | Lee Roberts (Hal Leonard) |
| Keveren, Phillip (arr.) | *Christmas Cheer* | Hal Leonard |
| Persichetti, Vincent (arr.) | *Appalachian Christmas Carols* | Elkan-Vogel |
| Rocherolle, Eugénie | *Christmas Time is Here* | Hal Leonard |
| | *Christmas Together* | Kjos |
| | *Christmas Side by Side* | Kjos |
| Rollin, Catherine (arr.) | *Carol of the Bells* | Alfred |
| | *The Nutcracker Suite for Two* | Alfred |
| | *Spotlight on Christmas* | Alfred |
| | *We Wish You a Jazz Christmas* | Alfred |
| Vandall, Robert (arr.) | *Celebrated Christmas Duets* (Books 4 & 5) | Alfred |
| | *Duet Fantasy on Carol of the Bells* | Alfred |

# PART TWO
## THE ADVANCING PIANIST

# STYLE PERIODS AND APPROPRIATE REPERTOIRE

# CHAPTER 19

# An Approach to Bach and Scarlatti

## William Heiles

**B**ach's keyboard music is an ideal teaching repertoire, offering pieces of the very highest quality in many different genres and at every level of difficulty. The Scarlatti Sonatas, though less diverse and profound than Bach's keyboard works, are an attractive foil to them, and Scarlatti's more obvious virtuosity and drama appeal to many pianists.

To play and teach Bach and Scarlatti well, one needs a sense of Baroque style and performance practice—not as a rigid set of rules but as a framework in which to explore the musical imagination. A lively and imaginative, though historically wrongheaded, Baroque performance is always preferable to an "authentic" but dull one, and there is no surer route to dullness than an obsession with rules. Fortunately, however, we don't need to choose between lively performances and stylistically appropriate ones, as the best harpsichordists and period instrument ensembles continually prove.

My remarks in this chapter are mostly about Bach but apply in general to Scarlatti as well. I will address several topics: the keyboard instruments of the period, tempo, rhythm and rhythmic freedom, dynamics, articulation and phrasing, ornamentation. Each of these subjects is related to all the others and any good performance must recognize their interrelatedness; for convenience of discussion, however, I will take them up one by one. Finally, I will comment on the choice of editions for playing and teaching.

## The Harpsichord and Clavichord

The full-sized harpsichord is a concert instrument which can project well in a moderately large hall. Its strings are not struck with hammers, as on the piano, but are plucked by small quills, or plectra. A concert harpsichord typically has two keyboards and three registers or stops, allowing for terraced dynamics and tone-color contrasts but not for gradual dynamics. On the clavichord the strings are neither struck nor plucked; rather they are touched by metal tangents. This mechanism makes possible gradual dynamics and even vibrato, though the dynamic range is much narrower than that of the piano, and the overall dynamic level remains very soft.

The revival of historical keyboard instruments has favored the harpsichord more than the clavichord because of its greater versatility and suitability for concert playing; practically all Baroque keyboard music can be played on the harpsichord but much of it (for example, the larger and more dramatic Bach suites, the Italian Concerto, the Goldberg Variations, and most Scarlatti Sonatas) cannot be played effectively, if at all, on the clavichord. Still the clavichord was greatly prized, especially in Germany, for its soulfulness and it remains the only keyboard instrument on which the player can affect the quality of a sound throughout its duration, rather than only at the moment of attack.

There is no substitute for the experience a pianist gains from playing Bach and Scarlatti on the harpsichord. The instrument's transparency makes contrapuntal textures immediately understandable. The vividness of the plucked attack brings out subtleties of rhythm and articulation. The limited number of dynamic levels and tone colors clarifies Baroque forms and enhances the unity of expressive character common to most Baroque pieces. These insights, gained not abstractly but through concrete musical experience, invariably shape the way a pianist subsequently plays Bach or Scarlatti on the piano. It is not that the piano is made to "sound like a harpsichord" (which would be impossible even if it were desirable) but that playing the composer's works on his own instruments opens a window to his musical thinking.

## Tempo

The effectiveness of Bach's music depends always on its content, never (as in some Romantic and twentieth-century music) on speed or slowness for its own sake. Even in the most technically brilliant pieces, virtuosity depends on rhythmic precision, articulation, and clarity of detail, all of which are diminished if the tempo is too fast. On the other hand, expressive playing requires a delicate balance between structure and ornament, rigor and freedom, which is lost if the tempo is too slow. The harpsichord can help teach a pianist to avoid extremes of tempo. Its resonance, rich but more quickly decaying than the piano's, rules out excessively slow tempos; at the same time, the clarity of attack, which makes each individual note vivid rather than fusing many notes into large textures, makes excessively fast tempos noisy and confusing.

An important factor in choosing a performance tempo in Bach is the Baroque emphasis on genre, especially in dance music. Each of the common Baroque dances is defined not only in terms of meter and rhythmic features but also in terms of tempo and character. Any dance title is, in itself, a performance direction; all dances of a given type are played within a rather narrow tempo range. (The same can be said, for example, of Chopin's Polonaises, but not his Waltzes or Mazurkas.)

The six French Suites provide a good illustration of this principle. Of the six allemandes, those in B minor, E-flat Major, and G major can all be played at about the same tempo (I would suggest around 58 to the quarter-note); the more introspective D minor and the more rhythmically complex C minor allemandes demand a slightly slower tempo (about 54) while the lighter E major one might go only a little faster (about 69). The two true Courantes, in D minor and B minor, can be played at the same tempo—about 69 to the half-note or 46 to the dotted half, according to the shifting pulse. Of the four Correntes (imprecisely titled Courantes), those in E-flat major, G major, and E major could all go about 104 to the quarter; the one in C minor requires a faster tempo (about 152) only because of its simpler meter. The Sarabandes in D minor, C minor, B minor, and G major all sound convincing at about 58–60 to the quarter; the E-flat major one, with fewer 16th-notes, would go only a little faster (about 63) and the more heavily ornamented E major one only a little slower (about 54). The Menuets can be played at around 42 to the dotted half. The Gigues, with their differing meters, require more varied metronome settings, but none should be played too fast for clarity; I would suggest that the half measure be taken at about 88–92 for the E-flat major Gigue, 63 for the G major one, and 80–84 for the E major one. The D-minor Gigue, in an exceptional duple meter with dotted rhythms, might be played at about 84 to the quarter or 42 to the half-note.

## Rhythm and Rhythmic Freedom

Many performance practice issues in Baroque music involve the interpretation of notated rhythms, especially dotted rhythms. Some of these issues are still controversial, but many questions answer themselves fairly easily if approached with musical intuition and common sense. The following guidelines may be helpful to performers and teachers:

1.  All musical notation is necessarily somewhat approximate, especially regarding rhythm. Music is played by human beings, not machines, and the rhythmic intuition of any talented performer is too subtle to be expressed in notation. Furthermore, Baroque-period rhythmic notation confronts today's musicians with ambiguities because several conventions now taken for granted (double-dots, dotted rests, precise notation of triplet and sextuplet rhythms, etc.) were not in general use at the time. A pianist who plays a rhythm in Bach differently than it appears on the page is not "altering" the rhythm but rather attempting, despite a misleading notation, to discover and reveal the composer's true intention.

2. In much music representing human movement, including of course much dance music, the contrast between long and short durations tends to be emphasized in performance—that is, long notes are sometimes played longer than written, short notes shorter. This phenomenon is not limited to Baroque music. In the Chopin Polonaises, for example, the first eighth-note of the accompaniment rhythm is often lengthened and the following two sixteenth-notes correspondingly shortened. In habaneras the dotted rhythm in the first beat of the accompaniment is normally overdotted somewhat. This heightened contrast between long and short durations is the impetus behind much Baroque overdotting—not only in explicit dance movements but also in overtures, with their strongly processional character, and in any movements influenced by the overture style (such as the E-flat minor Prelude from WTC I).

3. A Baroque piece or a movement of a larger work tends to be governed by one kind of motion throughout, whether continuous notes of the same value (as in allemandes, courantes, gigues, and most fugues), dotted rhythms (as in overtures), or some more complex measure-long pattern (as in sarabandes). An *occasional* apparent deviation from this consistency of motion should arouse the performer's suspicion. For example, in the G-minor Prelude of WTC II the notated 16th-notes in the left hand of measures 3 and 4 should be played as 32nds to match the rhythm of the other voices. In the Scarlatti Sonata K. 238 (Kirkpatrick edition, Vol. I, p. 98) the very first note—as well as many other notated eighth-notes following eighth-rests—should be played as a 16th-note following a dotted-eighth rest. Similarly, in the first measure of Bach's C-minor Partita the second E-flat in the right hand, apparently an eighth-note, should be played as a 16th, matching the dotted rhythms throughout the opening section. In the Allemande of the G-major Partita the very few notated duplet 16th-notes should be played in conformity with the prevailing triplet rhythm. On the other hand, in the Allemande of the F-major English Suite duplet and triplet 16th-notes both appear so frequently that the duality of rhythm is probably intended.

4. Anything that feels awkward is probably wrong. It would be very uncomfortable, for example, to play the 16th-notes in the Courante of the E-flat Major French Suite *after* the third note of the triplet; common sense dictates that the apparent dotted rhythm be coordinated with the triplet. (This is also true of many passages in Chopin and Schubert, such as the Coda of the Chopin F-minor Ballade.)

5. Anything that sounds unpleasant is certainly wrong. Overture movements such as the D-major Fugue from WTC I sound dull and pompous if not overdotted at all; but if they are double-dotted

(overdotted to an extreme), they sound nervous and jumpy. The best-sounding proportion between the long and short notes in an overdotted rhythm is probably about 5 to 1; this proportion should be felt rather than counted.

The accelerandos and ritardandos so common in Romantic piano music can be employed only very sparingly in Bach and Scarlatti. A more appropriate sort of rhythmic freedom for most Baroque keyboard music is one in which the beat remains fairly steady while the notes within it are played with considerable flexibility. In arriving at this sort of rhythmic freedom the harpsichord is again a helpful teacher. The instrument's clarity of attack and transparency of texture help the player to hear the difference in character between individual notes. One note is more dissonant, another more consonant; one is more stable, another more forward-moving; one is more structural, another more ornamental; etc. Responding to these differences, the player may dwell a little on the more important notes while letting the others move at or slightly above the normal tempo. Thus the notes within a beat can be different in length, while the beat itself remains at about the same tempo. (This kind of rhythmic freedom is related to the *tempo rubato* favored by Mozart and Chopin, in which the melodic line is played freely while the accompaniment, and therefore the tempo, remains steady. Perhaps one reason so few pianists play such a *tempo rubato* today is that the modern piano, richer and thicker in sonority than Mozart's and Chopin's instruments, has dulled our sensitivity to the differences between individual notes.)

# Dynamics

To understand the role of dynamics in playing Bach, it is necessary to distinguish between dynamic *levels* and dynamic *shaping* within any given level. Dynamic levels change only rarely in good Bach playing. A piece of Baroque keyboard music (or an individual movement of a longer work) almost always retains the same expressive character throughout; it does not require frequent dramatic dynamic changes, as in Classical-period music, or large-scale crescendos and diminuendos, as in Romantic music. (One of the worst mistakes a pianist can make with Bach is to impose these sorts of dynamic effects on the music in order to "make it interesting".)

When should a pianist change dynamic levels in playing Bach? Here once again, the harpsichord is the best teacher. A harpsichordist can change dynamic levels only by moving hand stops or jumping from one keyboard to another. Hand stops can be moved only between movements or during the pause between sections of a movement, since the player has to stop playing to manipulate them. A skilled player can jump from one keyboard to another quickly and easily but too much of this jumping destroys unity and dilutes what can be, in small doses, an attractive effect. The spelled-out words *forte* and *piano,* which one finds in the Italian Concerto, French Overture, and other works, direct the player to change keyboards (and indicate that these works should be played on a two-keyboard harpsichord, rather than a clavichord). To judge from these directions, Bach intended the player to change keyboards within a movement for only two reasons: either to bring out the contrasting solo and tutti sections in concerto-based movements or, more rarely, to create echo effects, as in the "Echo" movement from the French Overture or m. 65–68 of the first movement of the Italian Concerto. (Note that in both these cases the "echoes" are varied, rather than literal repetitions!) These two reasons provide excellent guidance for pianists.

In some Scarlatti Sonatas, such as K. 29, 209, 210, and 211 (all in Vol. I of the Kirkpatrick edition), dynamic levels might change more frequently. Sonatas like these anticipate the Classical style in their duality of themes (often based on the contrast between major and minor modes) and their dramatic oppositions and pauses. Within each half of the sonata a pianist or harpsichordist might play the major-mode passages *forte* and the minor-mode passages *piano* (or vice versa), taking advantage of the pauses or fermatas to change levels.

Whereas a pianist should change dynamic *levels* in Bach only sparingly, dynamic *shaping* within a given level must be employed continually. Like all the music of its time, Bach's music requires a sense of rhetoric that brings out the character and shape of each phrase. On the harpsichord articulation and timing create rhetorical shaping quite satisfactorily; on the clavichord subtle dynamics contribute also. On the modern piano articulation and timing are less vivid than on the harpsichord or clavichord but still important, while the role of dynamics in shaping phrases is more critical than on either harpsichord or clavichord. In considering rhetorical dynamics in Bach pianists should keep the following principles in mind:

1. The shape of a phrase is often determined more by rhythmic and harmonic considerations than by purely melodic ones. The climax of a phrase often comes not on the highest note but on the longest or harmonically most dissonant one.

2. Structurally important notes should be emphasized over those that are more ornamental.

3. In Bach's music a phrase often consists of several interrelated smaller units. Each smaller unit must have its own shape, while the smaller units must fit together to create a convincing form for the whole phrase.

4. Most phrases and smaller units in Bach begin on weak beats or between beats and progress toward strong beats or emphasized syncopations.

A slight crescendo often seems a natural response to this forward motion. In this sense a good Bach performance, like the music itself, is dynamically straightforward and goal-oriented.

5. A pianist must be sensitive to the decay of any emphasized long note; such a note is best regarded as containing an automatic diminuendo.

The familiar subject of the C-minor Fugue from WTC I is a good illustration of these points. Example 1 suggests a possible dynamic treatment. I have shown the subject not only in its complete form but also in two increasingly simple versions in which the more ornamental notes are gradually stripped away, leaving only the more structurally important ones. I hope this notation will not only clarify the dynamic relationships but also illustrate the kind of continuous formal analysis a player should apply in interpreting any music.

Example 1

## Articulation and Phrasing

It is essential to understand the meaning of these terms and the difference between them. A phrase is a musical thought; phrasing is the process of clarifying the character of each musical thought and the relationships between them. Articulation is an *aspect* of phrasing involving the connecting (slurring) or detaching of notes. Even in Romantic piano music, with its emphasis on legato playing, articulation is important; many Romantic-period composers, especially Schumann and Brahms, took great care to notate slurs as well as phrases. But especially in Baroque, Classic, and twentieth-century keyboard music articulation is indispensable to the success of any performance. In these styles a tension between articulation and phrasing is often central to the inner life of the music.

Articulation in Baroque keyboard music is best understood as an *aspect* of phrasing, closely related to dynamics. A few principles are easily grasped:

1.  Good articulation is never simply a dichotomy between connecting or detaching notes. Rather it involves a continuum of note-lengths from the most overlapped ("finger-pedalled") legato to ordinary legato, slight detachment, portato, ordinary staccato, and occasionally, subject to the resonance of the instrument, even staccatissimo. Within any phrase, note lengths vary slightly, just as dynamic levels do, in order to create a convincing shape. In a series of detached notes some are longer, some shorter, according to their relative importance. In a series of slurred notes some are more overlapped, others less. Good Baroque keyboard performance demands a flexible and continually varying articulation, not a collection of unvarying "touches".

2.  A note can be emphasized through articulation either by lengthening it or by preparing it with a bried silence and/or delay. A note can be de-emphasized either by shortening it or by covering its attack with an overlap of the preceding note.

3.  The first note of any slur, therefore, will automatically receive an emphasis; the last note of any slur will be weakened. Any short slur will convey a diminuendo. (On the modern piano this effect can be canceled by giving the slurred notes a large enough dynamic crescendo, but a crescendo of the necessary size is impossible on the harpsichord, clavichord, or fortepiano.)

4.  To give a short group of notes a crescendo through articulation each note must be given more preparation—that is, must be preceded by a longer silence—than the one before. Thus the notes leading toward the climax become progressively shorter, not longer, while the climax note itself is probably lengthened.

5.  In general, larger intervals and slower notes are more likely to be detached; smaller intervals and faster notes are more likely to be slurred.

Some of these points can be illustrated by returning to the subject of the C-minor Fugue. Example 2 shows a possible articulation of this subject.

Example 2

I have tried to indicate subtle differences in length by longer or shorter dashes. (A teacher soon finds that it is impossible to adequately notate a good Baroque articulation.) Because of the crescendo to the first A-flat the G is played a little shorter than the eighth-note C; the same relationship occurs in the second and third statements of the motive. A good harpsichordist will probably make an almost imperceptible separation before the eighth-note C in each statement of the motive in order to make this note stronger ("louder") than the preceding two 16ths; on the piano, with its thicker sound, this subtlety may be lost and it is probably acceptable to slur into the eighth-note C. Slurred in this way, the first three notes are felt essentially as a written-out mordent with the emphasis not on the third but on the first note, as would be natural in any mordent. On either piano or harpsichord, the player should not slur into the climax note A-flat. (Note that the *phrase* leads to the A-flat but the *slur* does not.) At the end of the subject the player should not slur into the final E-flat, which, as already pointed out, is more structurally important than the preceding 16th-notes. But here again, the phrase, as opposed to the slur, leads to the final note; it would sound very awkward to pause at the bar line.

To play Baroque music well, a pianist or harpsichordist must be able to separate for articulation without interrupting the flow of phrases. An exercise helpful in developing this skill is suggested in example 3.

Example 3

RH 2  3      3
LH 3  2      2

Play the three notes with a crescendo and imagine legato, while fingering 2-3-3 in the right hand or 3-2-2 in the left. The fingering will automatically produce a separation in articulation that emphasizes the last note, while the crescendo and imagined legato will unify the three-note phrase.

Finger-pedalling, mentioned earlier, is an extension of legato articulation important in Baroque (and Classical-period) keyboard playing. Like foot-pedalling, it adds resonance and warmth to textures that might otherwise sound dry. In playing Bach on the piano, finger-pedalling is always preferable to foot-pedalling. Without the damper pedal, the sonority of the piano remains less thick and therefore closer to the characteristic Baroque sound. Notes can be pedalled more selectively with the fingers than with the foot; more important notes can be held longer than less important ones and non-harmonic notes within a broken chord need not be held at all. Most importantly, doing without the damper pedal helps the pianist understand Bach's musical and technical thinking (since, obviously, Bach could not have thought in terms of damper pedal on his own keyboard instruments).

Example 4 shows finger-pedalling that might be employed in the Allemande of Bach's E-flat French Suite. Notes might be held about as long as the slur marks indicate; dots show slight releases that bring out the rising melodic line B-flat-C-D-etc. In the third beat of measure 2 the F is treated as an eighth-note appoggiatura, slurred to its resolution on the E-flat; the same applies in the first beat of measure 3.

Example 4

# Ornamentation

The brief table Bach wrote for his son Wilhelm Friedemann explains most of the ornaments found in his keyboard music, though it omits the *Schleifer*, a simple upward slide of a third represented by a rather odd-looking sign (see example 5).

Example 5

Since Bach was so highly influenced by French keyboard music, pianists should also study Francois Couperin's ornament table, which is longer and more complete than Bach's. Couperin makes it clear that when a trilled note is preceded by the note one step higher, the trill nevertheless begins on the upper auxiliary (the note preceding the trilled note is therefore repeated at the beginning of the trill). However, if there is a written slur from the preceding note into the trilled note, the trill starts on the principal note (in this case a note repetition would violate the slur).

On both practical and philosophical grounds, I am opposed to the written-out ornament realizations found in some Bach editions. Good ornament playing is guided by sensitivity to melody, rhythm, and harmony and is too flexible to be transcribed in conveniently readable notation. It is much easier for a student to learn to play ornaments by understanding their musical purpose and listening to the teacher and recorded performers than by puzzling over clusters of triplet-32nd-notes in small type at the bottom of a page. Furthermore, a teacher may want to adjust the treatment of ornaments to the abilities of the individual student. A less sensitive or advanced student can play certain ornaments more simply or leave out some of the most difficult ones; a more talented or advanced student can play some ornaments more elaborately or even add ornaments (for example, on repeat of allemandes or sarabandes). This discretion on the part of the teacher is hampered by an edition in which particular ornament realizations are already prescribed.

Ornament realizations are only one of several kinds of editorial suggestions found in non-Urtext Bach and Scarlatti editions; others have to do with dynamics, tempo, slurring and phrasing, etc. Today's "edited" editions are certainly an improvement over those of several generations ago (though the Bischoff Bach edition, a monumental achievement in its time, remains valuable and usable). But all editorial suggestions, even the best-intentioned ones, are problematic. They can represent any really satisfactory treatment of rhythm, dynamics, and ornamentation in only the most approximate way. Because they are printed in the score (even in small or gray type), they acquire an appearance of authority that inhibits the teacher's discretion and discourages students from thinking for themselves. There is no inherent reason why we as educated musicians should trust an editor's opinion over our own. Because of my faith in teachers and students, I advocate the use of Urtext editions in teaching Baroque music.

But even in Urtexts, such as the Henle Bach edition, one must be skeptical regarding an "invisible" form of editorial suggestion—fingering. In any music played with little or no pedal, fingering tends to create articulation. Decisions about articulation should be made first and should then become the basis of fingering choices, not the other way around— and there is no reason for teachers and students to leave these decisions to editors.

The enduring value of Bach's music lies in its universality. The appreciation of a Bach work never depends on a particular emotional state, dramatic program, or extra-musical image (although Bach's music is highly emotional and dramatic and not without extra-musical associations). Rather his is music *about music*. The joy it brings is the joy of purely musical discovery. Its beautiful, rich, and complex structure invites the player and teacher to ask endless questions about interpretation and to find answers that are often new and surprising. The value of any Bach performance is determined not by the correctness of the answers arrived at but by the depth of the questions asked and the integrity of the questioning and answering process. The best teacher of Bach is the one who helps students learn to ask their own questions, preparing them for a lifetime of seeking and finding their own answers.

# CHAPTER 20

## Essential Baroque Repertoire for the Middle School and High School Student

**Reid Alexander**

### Introduction

To prepare students for the challenges of the Baroque style, consider using Baroque-like teaching pieces available in contemporary collections. Contributions such as *Baroque Folk* (Alfred), Terry Owens' *Astrological Preludes* (Harris), Jeanine Yeager's *Baroque Encores* (Kjos), Dallas Weekley and Nancy Arganbright's duet arrangements *Three Baroque Pieces* (Kjos), and Fred Kern's *Brandenburg Notebook I, II* (Alfred) are just a few sets which prepare students for the easier literature of Bach, Daquin, Handel, and Scarlatti.

This educational literature can act as a barometer, helping to determine the student's readiness to play literature from the period. If a student cannot adequately handle one of Owens' *Preludes*, late elementary pieces that imitate the Baroque style, what will transpire if a more challenging Bach composition such as a two-part invention is assigned? The challenge for every teacher is to match repertoire with the student's level of advancement.

### Suggested Baroque Literature by Composer (alphabetized by composer)

| Composer | Title or Volume | Publisher |
|---|---|---|
| J. S. Bach | *Kleine Präludien und Fughetten* *Prelude in C Major, BWV 939* | Wiener Urtext |

Students should study selected Bach *Little Preludes* before moving on to the more difficult *Inventions, Sinfonias*, suite movements, and *Well-Tempered Clavier*. Many editions organize the *Little Preludes* by groups of six, though this is an arbitrary grouping that originated with nineteenth century editors. This *Prelude in C Major* is noted for the left hand pedal point and mordents as well as the ending sixteenth-note flourish. Students may omit the ornaments if they pose coordination difficulties or play only the first beat mordents. Other recommended preludes could include E minor, C minor, C, F, and C; BWV numbers 941, 999, 924, 927 and 933 respectively.

| | | |
|---|---|---|
| J. S. Bach | *Dances of J. S. Bach (Hinson, ed.)* | Alfred |
| | *Gavotte from French Suite no. 4* | |
| | *in G Major, BWV 816/4* | |

This volume represents a unique contribution to the teaching literature as it contains selected movements from the *English* and *French Suites*. Students not ready to play entire suites can become acquainted with particular movements and explore the various dance styles. The informative *Foreword* discusses the various dance forms and reviews the dances that comprise Bach's required and optional suite movements. This well-known *Gavotte* begins on the half measure and has running eighth notes under right hand parallel sixths.

| | | |
|---|---|---|
| J. S. Bach | *Celebrate Bach, Vol. II (Hisey, ed.)* | Frederick |
| | *Invention no. 10 in G Major, BWV 781* | Harris |
| | *Invention no. 14 in B-flat Major, BWV 785* | |

The *Inventions* and *Sinfonias* of Bach represent a Baroque musical bible for the late intermediate or early advanced student. Experiencing equality of hand participation and finger independence is essential for any student who desires to move on to more advanced Baroque literature. Aside from the often-taught C, F, D minor, and A minor inventions (no. 1, 8, 4, 13), the *tempo di Giga* texture of the *Invention in G Major* prepares for the more advanced gigues in Bach's suites.

Bach undoubtedly played inventions on the clavichord. Unlike the harpsichord, the clavichord was capable of producing soft dynamic nuances. With *Invention no. 14*, shape presentations of the subject and practice with consistent phrasing and articulations. Octave canonic imitation occurs between the hands at measures 12 and 16. During practice, identify measures where the hands are rhythmically in unison and use cadences to establish sections for practice. Two recommended *Sinfonias* for initial study are those in the keys of F minor (no. 9) and B minor (no. 15). This edition includes performance notes about each invention.

| | | |
|---|---|---|
| J. S. Bach | *Das Wohltemperierte Clavier,* | Any |
| | *Book I* | Standard |
| | *Prelude and Fugue in C minor,* | Edition |
| | *BWV 847* | |

In this prelude, Bach's use of tempo markings frames the music from the opening perpetual motion texture to the later improvisatory material in the *Adagio* measures. Students will develop an appreciation for the harmonic rhythm and descending motion by blocking during practice. This also will assist learning notes and fingerings.

Ideal for introducing fugal form, this three-voice fugue approximates the same difficulty as a *Sinfonia*. Highlight or bracket the subject throughout the piece and then decide on articulation and touch issues. Studying the preludes and fugues in G minor and B-flat major could follow this work.

| | | |
|---|---|---|
| J. S. Bach | *Celebrate Bach, Vol. III (Hisey, ed.)* | Frederick |
| | *Partita no. 1 in B-flat Major, BWV 825* | Harris |
| | *IV. Minuet I, II, V. Giga* | |

Any single movement of this *Partita* can be selected for study or the entire *Partita* is feasible for a skilled high school pianist. The two minuets should be played in a *da capo* manner. This Italian *Giga* does not follow the imitative style of most gigues and also differs from the French spelling. The crossing hands texture makes this *Giga* an exciting piece to perform.

| | |
|---|---|
| J. S. Bach | *Italienisches Konzert, BWV 971* |
| | *[Allegro], Andante, Presto* |

The opening movement of the Italian Concerto is accessible to talented teenage pianists. The *concerto grosso* allows the student to explore the range of sounds and colors of the piano to create the *tutti/soli* effects. The beautiful arioso (*Andante*) in D minor requires a high degree of interpretive skill and musicianship; the final *Presto* returns to F major and technically challenges the performer when played at tempo.

| | | |
|---|---|---|
| J. S. Bach | *At the Piano With J. S. Bach* | Alfred |
| | *Capriccio on the Departure* | |
| | *of his Beloved Brother, BWV 992* | |
| | *III. Adagissimo (Lamentations of his friends)* | |

This *Capriccio* is Bach's only keyboard work of a programmatic nature. Of the six movements, the *Adagissimo* third movement portrays extreme sorrow. Though not fully realized by Bach (he wrote only the bass line and melody), this intermediate level movement consists of a series of four-measure right hand phrases over a ground bass. The descending seconds and two-note slurs musically represent sobbing or sighing.

| | | |
|---|---|---|
| C. P. E. Bach | *Solfeggietto in C minor, Wq117/2* | Any Standard |
| | | Edition |

A superb late intermediate composition representative of the Rococo style of Bach's sons, *Solfeggietto* (also *Solfeggio*) possesses an etude-like quality and alternates between improvisatory sounding linear writing and homophonic vertical textures. Attaining evenness of touch challenges most students.

Daquin              *Le coucou*                    Frederick Harris

Composed in the popular *Rondeau* style of the late French baroque, Louis-Claude Daquin's *Le coucou* contains repetitions of the main theme separated by contrasting material (couplets). Available in the *Celebration Series* (Repertoire, Level 9), the musical imagery jumps off the page through the repetitive birdcall of a falling third.

Handel              *Celebrate Handel, Hisey, ed.*    Frederick Harris
                    *Gavotte in G Major, HWV 491*

Musicians neglect Handel's intermediate keyboard music in favor of the frequently taught pieces in the Bach notebooks. This volume is an invaluable collection of Handel's intermediate and early advanced teaching pieces which includes *Impertinence, HWV 494* and selected movements from five suites such as the well-known *Air with Variations* (Harmonious Blacksmith) from the *Suite in E Major, HWV 430*. This Gavotte embodies one of Handel's best-known keyboard dances.

Rameau              *Menuet en Rondeau*               Dover
                    *(Complete Works for Solo Keyboard,*
                    *ed. Saint-Saëns)*

One of Rameau's most famous teaching pieces, this late elementary *Menuet* is part of the collection, *Pieces de Clavecin*. It is useful for teaching inequality of note values (*notes inégales*). The well-known *La Joyeuse (Rondeau)* is also contained in this set.

Domenico Scarlatti   *Celebrate Scarlatti, Vol. I, (Hisey, ed.)*   Frederick
                    *Sonata in C Major, L 104, K 159*              Harris

A favorite of pianists, this early advanced sonata is influenced by the Spanish *jota*, a triple meter dance accompanied by castanets. The *acciaccatura* creates the castanet effect. In the return of the A section, Scarlatti was unable to complete the outline of the right hand broken C triad (i.e., C, E, G) in mm. 56-58 because the top note G was unavailable on his harpsichord.

Domenico Scarlatti   *Celebrate Scarlatti, Vol. II, (Hisey, ed.)*   Frederick
                    *Sonata in D minor, L 366, K 1*                Harris

Because of the five-finger motif and imitative two-part texture, this *Sonata* pairs wonderfully well with Bach's *Invention no. 4 in D minor*. To prepare for this level, the study of easier Scarlatti sonatas could include the works in C, B-flat, D minor, G minor, and A; K 73B, 42, 34, 88d, and 83b respectively.

## Suggested Baroque Anthologies

| | |
|---|---|
| *Dances of the Baroque Era, Vols. I, II* (Nagy et al., eds.) | Editio Musica Budapest |
| *Italian Masters of the Baroque Period* | Hal Leonard |
| *Style and Interpretation, Vols. I, II* (Ferguson, ed.) | Oxford |
| *The Baroque Era* (Palmer, ed.) | Alfred |
| *The Pianist's Book of Baroque Treasures* (Banowitz, ed.) | Kjos |

# CHAPTER 21

## An Approach to Classic Repertoire

### Kenneth Drake

For the mature pianist, the music of the Classic period remains the touchstone for testing the basic qualities of his musicianship. The repertoire of the Romantic period offers more notes, a greater exploitation of the piano as we know it today, and therefore a seemingly more exciting pallette of tone and sonority. By contrast, the fabric of a sonata of Haydn, Mozart or Beethoven offers little protection from the cold light of truth, exposing the independence and sensitivity (or lack of it) of the pianist's fingers and the strength of his musical understanding. The present discussion, therefore, is limited to two topics: technique: touches and articulation, and imagination: the relationship of tempo to structure.

The phrase "identifying with the music" may be defined as the experience of oneness with the printed page, when the composer's desires expressed as rhythms, note and rest values, phrasings and dynamics grip the player's mind and muscles, veritably becoming also his desires. In this respect, the intermediate stage of the pianist's development is often one of arrested growth. Unclear, unmusical, unimaginative playing shuffles on through increasingly difficult repertoire, like the catching of a young baseball player of whom Casey Stengel is supposed to have said, "Ten years from now, he will be ten years older." In the mind of the catcher-pianist, however, ten biological years are often mistakenly equated with ten years progress, an illusion which tells him that basic problems are too elementary for him. On the contrary, the inadequacies of adult years are the result of having neglected the daily sharpening of basic skills. Most of that which follows deals with "elementary" matters, and no apology is offered for it, since, to progress technically, one must begin each day's practice with the attitude of learning all over again, to play the piano.

To assess the actual state of one's technical skills, questions such as these might be asked: Does my actual sound fulfill the design of what I hear in my imagination? Can I match sounds? Can my fingers produce on demand the exact lengths of notes of different time values? Do I sense the interaction between tension and looseness, or is my hand, wrist, or arm always tight? Can I reach under the hand with the thumb smoothly? Each of these questions has to do with touch, through which the pianist's immediate sensation of identification is received. Eighteenth-century instruction manuals describe five touch notations: a wedge or dash over the note, indicating that the note is to be shortened to one-fourth its value; a dot, calling for the note to be shortened to half its value; no mark whatsoever, indicating non-legato; dots beneath a slur, a direction for *portato;* and finally a legato slur, for which an overlapping of the notes would be appropriate and, in the case of broken chord figures, required.

Of these, the holding down of the notes of a broken chord beneath a slur may seem strange to our ears and fingers. Following advice given by C.P.E. Bach in "The True Art of Playing Keyboard Instruments",[1] one may assume that the slurred broken chord figures in the Mozart *E-flat Sonata, K. 282* (first movement, bars 4–7 and following),

and the Beethoven *Op. 13* (third movement, bars 1–7),

*Op. 28* (fourth movement, bars 17–27)

and *Op. 27/1* (second movement) should be held down.

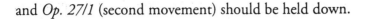

In the first two instances, holding all the notes of the chord permits more subtle pedalling; in the latter example, the phrasing increases the gasping effect produced by separating each group, bar by bar, as Czerny directs.2 The distinction between dashes and dots as staccato indications has little meaning except in an academic sense. Bach remarks that he avoided using the dash because it might be confused with the fingering numeral, adding that the shortness of staccato depended in any case on the speed of the piece, the length of the note, and the dynamic level.3 In order to be this adaptable, one's ears and reflexes must be trained to sense the beginning, middle and end of a note, as would a singer or string player, whose tone is not produced by mallets striking strings. Real color in one's playing is not possible without exploiting the possibilities of these three parts of every sound produced on the piano.

At this point, some observations about the finger, the pianist's brush, may be helpful. The drawing pictures an arm from fingertip to shoulder.

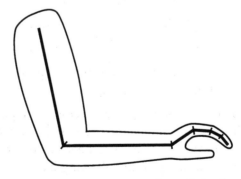

1.  The finger does not begin at the palm of the hand or even at the wrist or elbow, but rather must be considered as beginning at the shoulder.

2.  The arm is balanced in the fingertip of the finger which is playing, implying that the elbow should be free to move away from and back to the body, avoiding any cramped position of the wrist and aiding natural phrasing movements.

3. The greatest tension occurs in the first knuckle above the fingertip, with no tension in the wrist; in fact, the level of the wrist should be determined by the finger's support, the latter felt as pressure varied by the movement of the arm.

4. The tension needed for the supporting action of any one finger should not extend to the entire hand.

The beginning of a note determines not only the vitality of the pianist's sound but also the ability to voice chords. Unless the student is shown a preferable way, he will probably pound the right hand in the following passage, with particularly ugly results in the repeated open fifths.

Mozart, *Sonata in C major, K. 309, first movement*

The student is never too young, or too old, to be shown and reminded that one never touches a keyboard without discriminating between sounds produced simultaneously. To learn how voicing feels under the fingers (and thus to guarantee it the next time), a kind of pretending practice is helpful: Play the note of the chord which is to sound brighter and pretend the others by placing the fingers on the keys without playing. The objective is to hear with the fingertips, as the diagram suggests.

| feel pinch | | feel tone |
|---|---|---|
| | becomes | |
| hear tone | | hear pinch |

(In no case should the words pressure or pinch be interpreted as meaning forceful pushing with the arm.)

Related to voicing is shading, the voicing of a phrase horizontally. Like the open-fifth example above, the repeated notes shown below will immediately sound unmusical if the successive C's are not heard in relation to each other, as a line leading to the following bar.

Mozart, *Sonata in B-flat major, K. 570, first movement*

The playing of two-note slurs is another subtle but accurate indication of the student's sensitivity in playing music of this period.

Every teacher has heard

and equally bad.

The latter almost always results from an editorial staccato placed over the second note. This figure might be a convenient starting point to demonstrate lift figures in this particular movement, for the same drop-lift, down-up arm phrasing movement must be applied to the slurred dotted-eighth (dotted quaver) and sixteenth (semiquaver) figure at the beginning, as well as to short slurred figures generally. If the two-note slurred pattern in the opening of the finale of the Mozart *A-minor Sonata* is realized with such a drop-lift movement, the player becomes a part of the opera, at one with the distraught character who circles about the stage wringing her hands in anguish.

The same pulling effect is produced by the two-note slurs over the octaves at the beginning of the *Allegro in the C-minor Fantasy* of Mozart,

Mozart, *Sonata in A minor, K. 310, third movement*

as well as at the opening of the last movement of the *C-minor Sonata*.

If the opening theme of the Haydn *E-minor Sonata* is phrased as it appears in the Peters Edition, it is difficult to avoid playing the eighth-note (quaver) too short at the end of the slur. The articulation indicated in the Vienna Urtext sounds natural.

(Peters)(Vienna Urtext)

If notes in a slurred line do not match or relate to each other, it is often due to losing the ongoing touch sensation during the middle of a note, or its duration. The pianist, who in his imagination hears ahead, must in his reflexes match finger pressures backward. The problem becomes chronic when two voice lines must be played with the same hand.

Haydn, *Sonata in E minor, No. 53, first movement*

The duration of a staccato note also reveals either sensitivity or carelessness.

Mozart, *Sonata in F major, K. 332, first movement*

Imagining a swell on the single sixteenth-note (semiquaver) and associating it with a drop-lift movement places greater stress on the slurred sixteenths (semiquavers) which follow and heightens the agitated character of the passage.

Mozart, *Fantasy in D minor, K. 397*

The distinction between non-legato and legato has been obscured by the editing of the past century. One reason may be that, early in the nineteenth century, legato had replaced non-legato as the normal touch. Another reason may lie in the editor's purpose to show the student where a phrase begins and ends. The composer, in this case, assumed that the player was musically intelligent and used slurs to indicate stresses and lifts within the phrase. In any event, it is in the articulation of non-legato (unslurred) passages that the consistency of the ends of notes becomes particularly noticeable. For example, listening to scales played with one hand alone, in most instances, will reveal single notes alternating with smears of notes, because of the sluggishness of certain fingers in getting out of the keys. Until this is remedied, there can be no serious attempt at playing the music of the Classic composers. The following diagram is presented to describe the ideal toward which practice for articulation must be directed.

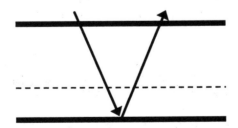

The parallel lines represent the normal key descent of 3/8 inch, the dotted line the point of let-off, or escapement, beyond which the hammer is no longer under control of the finger. The V-shape line represents the finger attack and rebound from the bottom of the key dip, with or without releasing the key completely. The ability to articulate is a lifelong occupation for the pianist and, at the same time, is usually the first quality to disappear with the interruption of practice for any length of time.

There are several complementary methods of practice which may be applied to a passage such as the following to develop articulation.

Haydn, *Sonata in G major, No. 54, second movement*

In drawing-off practice, the finger is pulled back across the key and off (from the hand knuckle) and is returned to a resting position on the key. The finger movement, which necessitates a snappy extra movement of the flexor muscles (and which can be felt by placing the other hand under the forearm), begins from a position of relaxation, passes through friction on the key surface and returns to a position of relaxation. In dotted-rhythm practice, the shorter note is played staccato from on the key surface and must be placed as close as possible to the dotted note which follows, without losing the separation between them.

In finger-tossing practice, the sensation is one of freedom from the hand knuckle and of a tap on the key. This manner of practice is helpful in overcoming heaviness, since, as the arm weight is increased, the fingers must be moved in a proportionately greater arc. Fermata practice affords an opportunity to learn the sensation of arm pressure balanced in the finger, looseness of the hand (non-playing fingers should rest on the keys), and the reaching under the thumb.

Each of the methods described involves some element of exaggeration with as little tension as possible.

The foregoing has been concerned with the identification of the pianist with the piano through touch, the miracle through which a machine of wood, steel and ivory or plastic becomes an extension of human flesh and nerves. The remainder of this essay involves identification through a recognition of structure and the uniqueness of musical ideas. No carpenter could build a house without knowing how to read the architect's plans, but many a pianist, who would not try to walk through a solid wall in his house, strides through a piece apparently without ever noticing the end of one idea and the arrival of another; neither the apex of a phrase nor dynamics or phrasing will ever alter the pace. At worst, such an "interpretation" is the result of not caring; at best, it is the result of a fear of "taking too much liberty." There are no liberties possible in playing a sonata by Haydn, Mozart or Beethoven; there is only a responsibility to recognize differences, make comparisons, and arrive at judgments about the relative importance of this or that detail in the overall plan.

The first movement of the *G-major Sonatina* of Beethoven provides a brief illustration. Although the authenticity of the piece is questioned, it is a masterpiece in its simplicity. The first bar plus one beat constitutes a complete musical thought: I—V—I. Do the slurred eighths (quavers) in the second bar comment on the opening or do they introduce the continuation of the opening bar in bar 3? If one chooses the former, there must be a comma between bars 2 and 3, and the musical effect is quite different from the latter way of playing the passage.

Beethoven, *Sonatina in G-major, first movement*

What effect does the Alberti bass in bars 5 and 6, the two-note slurs in bar 7, the appoggiatura in bar 8, the one-bar phrases in bars 13 and 14, and the new Alberti pattern in bars 24–31 have upon the feel of the tempo? Granted that the whole movement sounds tranquil, even in its tranquility it moves ahead and holds back.

When we ask ourselves whether some feature is important enough to share with the listener, we become involved with time, both as it is measured metronomically and as we perceive it encompassing a succession of events. Neither the ticking of a metronome for five minutes nor random sounds for five minutes will by itself result in a musical work. The pull of the two forces, a perfectly measured pulse on one hand and the unmeasured play of ideas in the imagination on the other, is like the tautness of a rubber band held between two persons moving about independently in a room. Tempo may be said to be the pace at which we are able to experience musical events, with rhythm being the constant presence of pulse within that pace.

Knowing where and why to take time is a perplexing issue for the younger pianist. Too often, students are told what to do before being given the opportunity to exercise their own intuition. If the teacher asks questions to stimulate the student's thinking, he must be willing to risk admitting that at times he himself does not have a definite answer. The respect of our students is not based so much, however, upon our knowing something as upon our ability to learn something new as we work with them. A remark of Buckminster Fuller comes to mind, to the effect that the student cannot have learning injected or pumped into him, but that the learns by working beside "a loving pioneer while he is still pioneering."

One reason for a student's insecurity in this matter of taking time is that we expect good taste to be immediately apparent, when in reality no one ever becomes confident of his own judgment without first going too far one way or the other, realizing it himself, and then correcting it. Rather than stressing "how much", it would foster greater independence to begin with "why". The "why" is that music is the combining of pitches, rhythms, and dynamics into an infinite variety of patterns which expressed ideas and concepts for the composer. The subtlety and depth of the music is a timeless force, uniting the moment of creation with the moment of re-creation—we could as well be physically alive in Beethoven's day as the present, for in performance the essence of the past and the present is immediately the same and therefore independent of time.

For example, one way by which music achieves structure is through an overall plan of departure and return. Each of us has known the experience of returning—the anticipation, the strangeness of change within the familiar, and the feeling of the duration of life and the length of one's days. A reunion with family or friends would not be a matter-of-fact occurrence. The point of recapitulation in a sonata movement epitomizes for a sensitive interpreter all the feelings surrounding that return to the past which we wish to keep forever fresh, as we knew it. Often a holding back prior to the return is written in the score.

Haydn, *Sonata in A major, No. 41, first movement*

Such instances are less common in the Mozart sonatas.

Mozart, *Sonata in C minor, K. 457, first movement*

In the Beethoven sonatas, the reader is referred to the following entrances of the recapitulation: Op. 2/2 I, Op. 7 IV, Op. 10/1 III, Op. 10/2 I, Op. 10/3 I and IV, Op. 13 III, Op. 14/1 I and III, Op. 14/2 III, Op. 22 I, Op. 28 I and IV, Op. 31/2 I, and Op. 31/3 II. As an experiment, one might try the following passage from Op. 49/2 II first played straight, then again with a *tranquillo*.

Beethoven, *Sonata in G major, second movement*

At other times, any relaxation of the tempo would not be appropriate, since the composer prepared the return dynamically (as in Op. 2/1 I) or obviously wanted the return to occur almost unnoticed (Op. 13 I).

As another type of example of the "why" of tempo fluctuations, we organize our thoughts, when writing, by grouping sentences into paragraphs, according to whatever the topic may be. If we imagine a letter being read aloud, it seems natural to expect that the reader will pause at the end of a paragraph, possibly reflecting on what has been related in it, before continuing. One often hears passages such as the following played with all the inflexible routine of a military band marching past the reviewing stand at retreat.

Mozart, *Sonata in C major, K. 545, first movement*

Especially in the case of a more lyrical second theme, the tempo may be held back slightly in deference to the lyrical character.

Mozart, *Sonata in D major, K. 576, first movement*

In an instance such as the following, the tempo seems to move ahead, possibly because of the arrival of the steady sixteenths (semiquavers) in the left hand.

Beethoven, *Sonata in G minor, Op. 49/1, first movement*

A final type of "why" example is less easily categorized. It includes the avoiding of sudden changes of movement when going from one rhythmic subdivision to another.

Beethoven, *Sonata in F major, Op. 10/2, first movement*

Sudden dynamic changes necessitate a tempo adjustment, if only a quick break.

Mozart, *Sonata in A minor, K. 310, third movement*

In the next example, the new phrase comments upon the preceding, suggesting a release from tension and therefore moving ahead.

Mozart, *Sonata in D major, K. 311, second movement*

Occasionally, after a pause the resumption of the tempo sounds more natural if it happens gradually.

Mozart, *Fantasy in D minor, K. 397*

*Expressivo,* or by extension, *con espressione,* indicates holding back the tempo.

Beethoven, *Sonata in F minor, Op. 2/1, first movement*

If the compound appoggiatura in the following example is played on the beat with the G—B-flat in the left hand, as I believe it should be, the crowding which results forces one to hold back the tempo or to stretch the beat.

Haydn, *Sonata in E-flat major, No. 59, first movement*

In summary, touch is the attempt to do the impossible with the piano: to make the immutability of a single note mutable. Tempo is the attempt to do the impossible with time: to make the measured sound unmeasured and the expected sound unexpected. That this can be achieved is a credit to the imagination, the womb of the mind, where the meaning of being human is conceived, whether this meaning is morality or art. What is conceived is full of the purpose for living and the promise of rebirth. Playing, as much as any other discipline of life, is not an act done for the entertainment of others or the gratification of the ego. As Mme. Lili Kraus remarked in an interview, the player and his audience who have been moved by the performance of a Beethoven sonata have experienced a kind of redemption. What better thought could be kept in mind at the beginning of that association between two individuals known as the "piano lesson"?

# References

Badura-Skoda, Paul and Eva. *Interpreting Mozart on the Keyboard.* London: Barrie and Rockliff, 1962.

Bilson, Malcolm. *Some General Thoughts on Ornamentation in Mozart's Keyboard Works.* The Piano Quarterly, Fall 1976, Number 95.

Czerny, Carl. *Uber den richtigen Vortrag der Sämtlichen Beethoven'schen Klavierwerke.* Vienna: Universal Edition, 1963. (Also in English.)

Drake, Kenneth. *The Sonatas of Beethoven as He Played and Taught Them.* Cincinnati: Music Teachers National Association, 1972. (Reissued by Indiana University Press.)

Drake, Kenneth. *The Beethoven Sonatas and the Creative Experience.* Bloomington: Indiana University Press, 1994.

Einstein, Alfred. *Mozart, His Character, His Work.* London, New York: Oxford University Press, 1945.

Geiringer, Karl. *Haydn, A Creative Life in Music.* New York: Norton, 1946.

Lang, Paul Henry, ed. *The Creative World of Mozart.* New York: Norton, 1963.

Newman, William S. *Performance Practices in Beethoven's Piano Sonatas.* New York: Norton, 1971.

Rosenblum, Sandra. *Performance Practice in Classic Piano Music.* Bloomington: Indiana University Press, 1992.

# CHAPTER 22

## Essential Classic Repertoire for the Middle School and High School Student

### Reid Alexander

## Introduction

Teachers and students become absorbed with the development of technique when studying music from the Classic period. Such study might include Czerny studies and work with scales and arpeggios to achieve clarity of sound and touch. Additionally, encourage students to learn about the transition from the harpsichord to *fortepiano*, the general development of the piano, and how differences between our modern instrument and the early *pianoforte* affect interpretation and pedaling. Awareness of style should include understanding form and phrasing, distinguishing between *legato* and non-*legato*, and implementing detailed touch articulations such as *staccato*, wedge marks, and two-note slurs to name a few. Ultimately the production of sound expected from the fingers must match one's musical imagination for realizing the score.

Three indispensable categories of repertoire include the study of easier German dances and bagatelles, sonatinas, and shorter variation sets. Experiencing these miniature forms is the first step in mastering music from the period and preparing for more advanced repertoire. Early intermediate methods like *Music Pathways: Level D Discoveries* (Fischer) will assist transfer students who lack a firm reading foundation in sixteenth-note rhythms. Paul Sheftel's collection, *Etudes Brutus* (Alfred), contains clever studies which imitate the Czerny style but in a contemporary style. Duet collections such as Diabelli's *Sonatinas on Five Notes* (Peters) and educational solos like William Gillock's *Sonatina in Classic Style* (Willis) and Robert Vandall's *Bagatelles* (Alfred) also serve as excellent introductory material.

## Suggested Classical Literature by Composer (alphabetized by composer)

| Composer | Volume or Title | Publisher |
|---|---|---|
| Beethoven | *Celebrate Beethoven, Vol. I* *Sonatina in G Major,* *Kinsky-Halm Anh. 5* *I. Moderato, II. Romanze* | Frederick Harris |

Attributed to Beethoven and in a compact two-movement structure rather than three, this sonatina is a must for the early intermediate pianist. Each movement has a closing *Coda*. Similar freestanding pieces at this level would include compositions from op. 107 (*Ten National Airs*), *German Dance, WoO 42, no. 6, Six Écossaises, WoO 83, and the companion Sonatina in F Major, Anh. 5.*

| | | |
|---|---|---|
| Beethoven | *Sechs Variationen WoO 70* *Über "Nel cor piu non mi sento"* | Frederick Harris |

These six variations, composed in 1795 and based on the popular operatic duet, "No longer do I feel youth sparkle in my heart," by Giovanni Paisiello, are ideal as an introductory variation set. Well balanced, each variation is 20 measures in length with exception of the 47 measure Var. VI. The tuneful theme, rhythmic variety, and an impressive sounding final variation all combine to form a most appealing set of variations. Other recommended variations at this level include the *Six Variations on a Swiss Folk Song, WoO 64* and *Six Easy Variations on an Original Theme, WoO 77.*

| | | |
|---|---|---|
| Beethoven | *Lustig und Traurig* (Happy and Sad), *WoO 54* | Frederick Harris |

The late *Bagatelles* of Beethoven remain under taught. The bagatelle style offers students the opportunity to explore the subtleties of Beethoven's writing but without the complexity of texture and length as seen in the mature piano sonatas and variations. Comprised of two contrasting and expressive sections unified by similar melodic fragments, *Lustig und Traurig* represents the compact bagatelle style.

| | | |
|---|---|---|
| Beethoven | *Für Elise, WoO 59* | Frederick Harris |

Though often taught (and simplified in some publications), there is no denying that students are attracted by the pensive theme, moods, and drama portrayed by the music. Less experienced teachers are cautioned not to assign *Für Elise* too early. Elementary grade pupils often struggle with the more difficult second theme in F major. Composed in 1810, the original title is *Bagatelle in A minor*. The dedication to *Elise* most likely refers to the nickname for Therese Malfatti, the daughter of Beethoven's physician.

| Beethoven | *Bagatelles in G minor, D Major,* | Frederick |
| | *A minor, op. 119, no. 1, 3, 9* | Harris |

The first five bagatelles of the eleven in op. 119 were sketched earlier in Beethoven's life. Number 1 sounds very improvisatory, if not experimental, and reveals the composer's fondness for harmonies a third apart. Though in G minor it ends convincingly in G major.

With the marking *a l'Allemande*, no. 3 should be played in the vigorous manner of a triple meter German dance. The right hand repeated high D is a full 6th higher than earlier compositions written for a piano that only went to F.

In rounded binary form, no. 9 is superb for intermediate students because of the use of a simple waltz bass under right hand broken eighth-note arpeggios. The rocket-like opening theme demands a consistent fingering in measures 1-2. The Neapolitan 6th harmony in measure 3 provides harmonic color.

| Beethoven | *Celebrate Beethoven, Vol. II* | Frederick |
| | (Hisey, ed.) | Harris |
| | *Sonata in C minor, op. 13 (Pathétique)* | |
| | *II. Adagio cantabile* | |

All three movements of the famous *Pathétique* Sonata are valuable for students to learn. However, the middle movement should not be overlooked in favor of learning only <u>one</u> of the outer movements. The incredibly beautiful *legato* theme, voicing challenges within the right hand and between the hands, and variation-like treatment of the accompaniment merit study. The term *Pathétique* (added by editors) means moving or touching rather than pathos or pity.

| Beethoven | *Sonata in C minor, op. 10, no. 1* | Frederick |
| | *I. Allegro molto e con brio* | Harris |

Aside from the easier *Sonatinas* and the two op. 49 *Sonatas*, the first movement of op. 10, no. 1 epitomizes Beethoven's early period. As an entry-level piece for his early sonatas, the first movement may be played instead of, or in addition to, the commonly chosen op. 2, no. 1. The brisk dotted values, arpeggiated figures, and *sfz* indications make this an attractive movement. Initial dynamic marks should be applied to follow-up sequential phrases where not notated. Other recommended introductory sonatas (all in this edition) include op. 2, no.1, the two-movement op. 79, and op. 14, no. 1.

| Clementi | *Celebrate Clementi* (Hisey, ed.) | Frederick |
| | *Preludes, op. 43* | Harris |
| | (from *Introduction to the Art* | |
| | *or playing on the Pianoforte*) | |

Selected Clementi *Preludes* can be found in various period anthologies. Many of these *Preludes* consist of only 4 to 8 measures and resemble short improvisations in the Classic style. They make wonderful "quick learn" pieces or lesson sight-reading material.

| Clementi | *Six Progressive Sonatinas, op. 36* | Frederick |
| | *Sonatina, in C Major, op. 36, no. 3* | Harris |
| | *Allegro spiritoso, Adagio, Allegro di molto* | |

Of the famous op. 36 *Sonatinas*, no. 3 remains a favorite. The first movement is very lively and the transition to the recapitulation reveals striking harmonies. The brief middle movement, in binary form, and final rondo are equally well known. Other recommended works include selected *Waltzes* from op. 28, movements from the *Musical Characteristics, op. 19*, and the *Sonata in D Major, op. 4, no. 1*.

| Haydn | *Celebrate Haydn, Vol. I* (Hisey, ed.) | Frederick |
| | *Divertimento in F Major, Hob. XVI:9* | Harris |
| | *Allegro, Minuet, Scherzo* | |

The Haydn early piano sonatas (called *Divertimenti*) provide a refreshing contrast to the frequently taught Clementi sonatinas. Some editions do not include these early sonatas because of their lower level of difficulty. The lack of dynamic marks suggests that these early "sonatinas" were intended for the harpsichord. The first movements exhibit greater rhythmic variety when compared to the sonatinas of Clementi and Kuhlau. Last movements tend to follow a binary (or rounded binary) structure. From this *Divertimento*, the bright and cheerful one page *Scherzo*, in rounded binary form, is a favorite with students. Other suggested *Divertimenti* include those in D, C, G, and A; Hob. XVI: 4, 7, 8, and 12 respectively.

| Haydn | *Celebrate Haydn, Vol. II* (Hisey, ed.) | Frederick |
| | *Sonata in C Major, Hob. XVI:35* | Harris |
| | *I: Allegro con brio* | |

To introduce Haydn's more mature writing, three sonatas come to mind for secondary students: Hob XVI: 35 (C), 37 (D), and 23 (F). The opening movement of no. 35 is deceptively difficult because of the quick cut tempo and continuous triplet figure that must be played evenly.

| Haydn | *Sonata in D Major, Hob. XVI:37* | Frederick |
| | *I: Allegro con brio* | Harris |

This is certainly a landmark sonata for aspiring students. Find the two themes in the exposition and the transition or bridge material between the themes. Also notice contrasts in the music. For example, the opening measure emphasizes the beat, yet two measures later two note slurs create humorous syncopations. The opening measures also outline adjacent four-measure question and answer phrases.

| Haydn | *Sonata in F Major, Hob. XVI:23* | Frederick |
| | *[moderato], Adagio, Finale: Presto* | Harris |

Dedicated to Haydn's patron Prince Esterházy, this more advanced sonata contains greater technical and rhythmic complexities. On a grander scale than earlier sonatas Haydn composed for his students, the first movement fits the hand quite well and students enjoy playing the richly detailed sonata-*allegro* texture. The second movement, in binary form with repeats, echoes the structure and lyricism of a baroque *sicilienne* while the last movement is framed in a short variation-like structure. Other commonly taught sonatas include B minor, E minor, and E-flat; Hob. XVI: 32, 34, and 49 respectively and the *Andante and Variations in F Minor, Hob. XVII:6*.

| Mozart | *Celebrate Mozart, Vol. I* (Hisey, ed.) | Frederick |
| | *Viennese Sonatina in C* (from *K 439b*) | Harris |
| | *Allegro, Minuet, Adagio, Finale* | |

Mozart's six Viennese piano sonatinas are transcriptions from *Five Divertimenti, K 439b*, originally composed for a trio of wind instruments. The Viennese sonatinas provide excellent preparation for Mozart's solo piano sonatas. The textures challenge the pianist to imagine instrumentation for individual voices. This work is interesting because of the expanded four-movement structure, dramatic first movement, and elegant, expressive writing throughout.

| Mozart | *Sonata in C Major, K 545* | Frederick |
| | *Allegro, Andante, Rondo* | Harris |

The right hand sixteenth-note passagework of this well-known first movement is excellent technique for the late intermediate student. The various ornaments can be measured against the opposite hand to facilitate fluency. Students must be encouraged to play the opening theme in the same tempo of the remaining musical material. Note that the first movement recapitulation begins in the subdominant. The short but tricky Rondo is the most challenging movement. After playing all three movements of K 545, the second movement (*Allegretto*) of K 547a will be enjoyable to play, as it is similar to the third movement of K 545.

| Mozart | *Sonata in G Major, K 283* | Frederick |
| | *Allegro, Andante, Presto* | Harris |

In this early sonata (1774), all of the movements use the sonata-*allegro* form. The first movement combines refined motifs with contrasting octaves and extended sixteenth-note passages. Short two- and three-note figures dominate, and Mozart elaborates melodic fragments when repeated. Careful attention must be given to the right hand two-part texture in both the exposition and recapitulation.

The second movement is particularly beautiful because of the manner in which Mozart varies thematic material in the right hand when repeating a melodic idea. The two voices in the left hand require careful delineation.

Contrast characterizes the classical style. In the *Presto* movement, identify the various themes and spot practice the diminished seventh passages. Other suggested sonatas, in approximate order of difficulty, include those in F, E-flat, A, and F; K 280, 282, 331, and 332 respectively.

Mozart                 *Fantasy in D minor, K 397*          Frederick Harris

This *Fantasy* is popular with students much in the same manner as Beethoven's *Für Elise*. It can be learned in sections, making the learning process less intimidating. Nevertheless, musical demands surface during study. Students have difficulty reading the chromatic left hand passages and maintaining even tempos within sections. Take care not to play the opening *Andante* too slow (in cut time, not 4/4). Scholars note that the final ten measures were not from Mozart's hand.

Mozart                 *12 Variations on*                   Frederick Harris
                       *"Ah, vous dirai-je, Maman",*
                       *K 265*

Based on the familiar theme of "Twinkle, Twinkle Little Star", the hands share technical difficulties throughout these variations. Mozart writes in a variety of styles, including some contrapuntal (VIII, IX) and coloratura (X) variations. The lack of dynamic markings in the score requires guidance from the teacher. This entire variation set is challenging, but the final product is well worth the effort.

## Suggested Classical Anthologies

*Celebration Series Perspectives, Repertoire,*          Frederick Harris
    *Levels 5-10, List B*

*Sonatina Album* (Kohler, ed.)                          Schirmer

*Style and Interpretation-Classical Piano Music, Vol. 3*    Oxford
    (Ferguson, ed.)

*The Classic Period*                                    Alfred

# CHAPTER 23

## Preparing Students for the Romantic Style of Chopin

### Catherine Rollin

When we think of the Romantic era from the perspective of being pianists and piano teachers, the first composer who comes to mind is generally Chopin. Although it is wonderful to play and teach the music of Mendelssohn, Schumann, Liszt and Brahms extensively, Chopin's music is the most gratifying for pianists. Chopin developed a language for the modern day piano that no other composer had done before.

He explored most of the virtuoso possibilities of the piano as well as conceiving of melodies that could inspire one to play a true cantabile. Although many of the characteristics discussed in this chapter apply to all Romantic composers, we are focusing on Chopin because his style was the foundation for piano playing in the Romantic era. He influenced the development of piano music for every composer not only during that era, but all those that followed. Studying Chopin's music and style enables students to develop not only their musical skills, but also their sheer physical comfort at the piano.

Although Chopin's music is idiomatically written for the piano, most of it is still too musically complex and technically challenging for students at earlier grade levels than late intermediate or early advanced. The lack of adequate pieces that prepares students for Chopin's music is one of the primary reasons that I have composed pedagogical music. I will be drawing on examples from my pedagogical pieces as well as many of Chopin's masterworks to explore some of the important elements that comprise the mastery of his music.

# Distinguishing Characteristics of Chopin's Music

1. Beautiful, expressive melodies

2. Distinctive accompaniment styles

3. Use of pedal that emphasizes the harmonies and resonance of the piano

4. Use of rubato and tempo freedom within the same piece

5. Use of florid passages or fioraturas

Understanding these characteristics can help our students play the music of Chopin with conviction and authenticity.

## Beautiful, Expressive Melodies

Chopin instructed his students to emulate singers when they played the piano. He loved the human voice and encouraged all his piano students to phrase and breathe like a singer. Unquestionably, Chopin's strong feelings about "singing" at the piano influenced the kind of melodies that he wrote. They are not only beautiful, but they can inspire students to shape the line and sing from within themselves.

This concept brings to mind a wonderful story about one of my student recitals. My student Rose was going to be performing Chopin's *Fantasie Impromptu, Op. 66*. In the B section, we examined the melodic shape. As I literally sang the melody line, I simultaneously played the notes on my student's hand, demonstrating how I used more arm weight as the melody went up and then conversely used a subtle diminuendo with decreasing arm weight as the melody resolved in a downward motion. I explained that the arm weight must reflect the increasing breath support of the singer as the line goes up and decrease as the melodic shape descended and resolved the phrase.

Example 1                     Chopin, *Fantasie-Impromptu, Op. 66, ms. 41-44*

At the lesson before the recital, I emphasized that the Fantasie-Impromptu was one of Chopin's greatest works and reminded Rose that the B section needed to sing so beautifully that it could almost inspire the audience to sing along if they knew the melody. The following Sunday afternoon we had our recital. Rose was playing the Fantasie-Impromptu more lyrically than I had ever heard her play. When the B section melody returned for the second time, much to my combined happiness and distress, an elderly relative of one of my other students who was sitting right near the front, joined in and was singing along with Rose's beautiful playing! I will never forget that moment. Although it was a distraction, what more could I ask for as a piano teacher than to have my student's playing inspire someone in the audience to spontaneously sing along in a heartfelt manner?

In writing music for students that is preparatory for the Romantic style, I endeavor to write melodies that feel natural to sing. In *Summer's Nocturne,* each phrase of the A section begins with an octave leap followed by descending stepwise motion.

Example 2

## SUMMER'S NOCTURNE

Catherine Rollin

The obvious distance of the octave leap helps students to understand how a singer would naturally have to give a lot of breath support in order to reach the high note of the octave leap. Students understand that they will continue to use arm weight on the upper note of each subsequent phrase's octave leap. It is then easy to make a natural sounding diminuendo on the descending line following the octave leap. With each phrase having a similar shape, it helps students understand the concept of melodic shaping.

In Chopin's *Nocturne in E flat Major Op. 9, No. 2,* Chopin begins the main melodic phrase with an ascending sixth that then drops and resolves. The second phrase begins again with an ascending sixth followed by an octave leap. Measure four has the last large leap of a tenth followed by generally descending motion.

Example 3

As in *Summer's Nocturne*, the Chopin Nocturne's melody will be shaped with the arm weight going to the higher notes and subtle lessening of the arm weight as the line descends.

In *Waltz from Spotlight on Romantic Style*, each phrase unit consists of a melody that uses the notes of either a dominant or diminished seventh chord followed by a half note on the sixth degree resolving down a third. The rising pattern in measure one is easy for students to shape with a natural sounding crescendo. In measures 2 and 4, the half note that resolves down a third creates the natural sigh of a two-note slur.

Example 4

The shape of the melody is reminiscent of Chopin's *Ballade in G Minor, Op. 23* (example 5) which is also based on a dominant-seventh chord. In the Ballade, the melodic idea in measures 8-11 uses a D dominant-seventh in third inversion. This pattern rises, then falls, and is followed by a sighing two-note slur moving from measure 9 into 10.

Example 5                    Chopin, *Ballade in G minor, Op. 23, ms. 8-10*

A student who has played pieces similar to *Waltz* will have a good idea of the natural melodic shape of the seventh chord phrase as well as that of the two-note slur. Ultimately, the best advice we can give our students is to sing melodies with the natural shape and breath of a singer. However, it is helpful to sing and gain experience with preparatory works for piano before studying Chopin.

## Accompaniments

In the Classical era, the most common accompanying patterns are based on a harmonic figure known as an *Alberti* bass.

Example 6

Although there are different accompanying patterns than the standard *Alberti* bass in Classical works, these accompaniment patterns are not indicative of the inventiveness of any of the masters including Mozart and Haydn. Beethoven, however, uses the left hand to provide much more than just an accompaniment pattern. Chopin takes off from what Beethoven began. Chopin develops, explores and hones a new language of accompaniment patterns. Chopin took octaves, arpeggios and scales, and used them to expand the left hand's role into that of an orchestra. Through using a wide expanse of the keyboard, sustained with pedal, the left hand becomes a source of color and musical drama.

In my *Prelude in A Major* (example 7), I use a broken octave pattern that is typical of those used by Chopin. It is important for a student who wants to play Chopin to become fluent and comfortable with this broken octave pattern.

Example 7

**PRELUDE NO. 7 IN A MAJOR**

Catherine Rollin

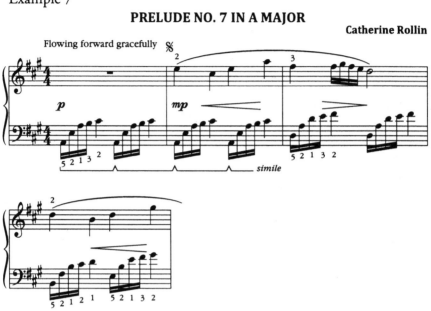

Chopin's *Etude in C minor op. 10, No. 12* (example 8) is one of many instances when Chopin uses this broken octave pattern as the basis of his accompaniment.

Example 8        Chopin, *Etude in C minor, Op. 10, No. 12, ms. 10-13*

These broken octave patterns in conjunction with long pedals create a soaring, full-bodied sound that exploits the piano's harmonic capabilities beautifully.

Two more examples of this broken octave pattern in teaching literature can be found in *Summer's Nocturne* and *Summer's Dream*.

Example 9

**SUMMER'S DREAM**

Catherine Rollin

In *Summer's Dream* the fingering 5, 1, 5, 3, 1 is suggested as an alternative to the more typical 5, 2, 1, 2, 1. The first fingering is, of course, optional, but gives students who are just emerging from primarily five-finger position pieces the opportunity to play in a more sweeping style with the left hand, even if their left hand is very small. *Summer's Nocturne* (example 4) uses the more traditional 5, 2, 1, 2, 1. With this more patterned melody, students who are new to the Romantic style can focus their attention on the left hand movement.

Another characteristic of many Chopin accompaniments is his use of patterns that create a mood or sense of atmosphere, in addition to providing the harmonic basis for the music.

In the B section of Chopin's *Nocturne in C-Sharp Minor, Op. 27, No. 1*, the left hand begins with triplet motion, and each measure is punctuated by a held dotted half note that creates a rising line of tension underneath the murmuring triplets. This accompaniment creates the effect of the rustling leaves shortly before the storm begins. If the performer plays the triplets very quietly before the crescendo begins at measure 33, it will create an ominous mood. Here, the left hand is more than just an accompaniment. It now creates mood and atmosphere.

Example 10

Chopin, *Nocturne in C sharp minor,*
*Op. 27, No. 1, ms. 29-32*

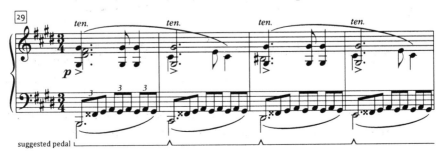

In my piece, *Echo Nocturne*, the left hand part that is intended to create atmosphere and mood, also serves as the harmonic basis for the piece. Understanding the characteristics of the left hand in Chopin will help our students maximize their musical potential.

Example 11                                  Rollin, *Echo Nocturne, ms. 37-40*

## Use of Pedal

One cannot think about accompaniments without also considering the effect of using the pedal to sustain Chopin's patterns. The extensive use of pedal, particularly long pedals that connect the sound from one harmony to the next harmony is one of the most important characteristics in creating the lush sound of Chopin's music. In some ways, Chopin's pianos were quite close to those that we play today. The development of the damper pedal, the una corda pedal, the resonating sound board, etc., were all part of what we think of as today's modern acoustic instrument. Chopin's music makes great use of the sound capabilities of the acoustic piano. It is relatively common performance practice in Chopin's work to pedal in conjunction with the harmonic changes. Although measure one of the example 12 has non-chord tones **in the melody**, we still keep one pedal throughout the measure and only change the pedal at measure two where the accompaniment harmony changes.

Example 12

**VALSE IN B MINOR**

**Frédéric Chopin**

To prepare students for the sound of pedals that follow the left hand harmonies, I wrote my first Romantic style piece *Ballet Beauties*.

Example 13

**BALLET BEAUTIES**

Catherine Rollin

One of the most important elements of pedal that Chopin employed was pedaling through rests. Chopin understood the unique nature of the piano with its resonating soundboard combined with pedal. He understood that if a pianist played a note staccato, but still held the pedal, it would create a different sound effect than simply holding the note.

A fine example of this pedaling concept appears in Chopin's *Scherzo in B flat minor, Op. 31* (example 14). The pedal marking indicates it is to be engaged at bar 5 and continue through bar 8. Although measure 5 is indicated with a quarter note staccato followed by two quarter rests, the pedal holds while the player moves from the low end of the piano to the large chords in the treble. The effect is indeed dramatic. We still hear the staccato release, but the resonant low B flats are in our ear as we play the following chords. The B flats act like a dramatic springboard of sound. Chopin was a true innovator is using the pedal for drama and gathering up the resonating power of the soundboard.

Example 14                          Chopin, *Scherzo, Op. 31, ms. 5-9*

# Rubato and Rhythmic Logic

There are discussions among musicologists as to whether Chopin's rubato consists only of right hand freedom over a strict left hand or if Chopin uses a rubato that pushes the pulse forward balanced with moments that relax the time as the term rubato has commonly become understood today. It is probable that Chopin used both kinds of rubato but only used that term to describe the former. However, it is in the execution of fioraturas (soon to be discussed) that Chopin's own definition of rubato seems to prevail. Here, the accompaniment maintains a strict pulse and the right hand plays the role of an improvising singer. Sometimes, when he wants an increase in energy, Chopin creates instances of rhythmic freedom through his indications of stretto and agitato, and words like cantabile and dolce when he wants the music to relax.

In addition to these specific instances, let us recognize that almost all good music making has some natural give and take in the pulse. For clarity, this type of freedom will be referred to as rhythmic logic, rather than rubato. Any freedom in the pulse has to feel logical. We can determine the logic if we dance to it, or conduct it. Without requiring students to learn the specifics of conducting, teachers can have them play a right hand passage while conducting with the left hand. Generally, if we are going to experiment with rhythmic logic, students can feel if what they are conducting seems too exaggerated, and ultimately physically illogical.

Try this yourself. Take the Chopin Waltz in D flat Major (see the next example), starting at measure 52. Try conducting in one, only pulsing on the downbeats. At measure 52 and 53, the theme is winding down, so relax the pulse slightly. At measure 54 when the main melody of the B section resumes, it feels unnatural to immediately resume "a tempo." Follow the logic of the left arm, and gradually reach "a tempo" in bars 55 and 56. Rely on the logic of the conducting arm to relax the tempo or resume "a tempo" with a natural sounding lilt on beat one. Another great way to feel the logic of the rhythm is to sing the melody and swing the body from side to side on the downbeats. It is guaranteed that if your rhythmic logic is not logical, your body will tell you this. Having students dance and/ or conduct regularly helps them make the connection between logic and rhythm. Often times, famous artists linger on notes in such an illogical manner, that it totally breaks the musical line and interrupts the flow of the music. Perhaps professionals in their quest to sound expressive are often guilty of overstretching the time and lingering on notes in an illogical way that defies rhythmic logic.

Example 15                    Chopin, *Waltz in D flat, Op. 64, ms. 52-57*

In my pedagogical Romantic works, I write in cues to help students see instances that invite some natural give and take in the pulse.

In my piece, *Summer's Nocturne* (example 16), I instruct performers to start to accelerando *poco a poco* at measure 17 until the next ritard; then repeat the same ideas in measures 19 and 20. If a student uses the conducting logic test, they will be able to do a beautiful accelerando that has a natural feel. One of the keys of the conducting logic is that we accelerate either by beats, or larger units like the downbeat. Accelerandos and/or ritardandos do not sound logical when they occur within the beat. In this example, the logical unit for the accelerando and ritardando would be the quarter note. At measure 17, accelerate gradually on every beat starting at beat 3.

Example 16                                    Rollin, *Summer's Nocturne, ms. 17-20*

## Fioraturas

Fioratura is a term that comes from the Italian word for flower. In music, it often refers to highly embellished vocal lines in an aria. It has also become a term used to refer to highly ornamented passages found in works of Chopin including the Ballades and Nocturnes. Often, but not always, these passages in Chopin are notated in small notes. They also can have an uneven number of notes in the right hand relative to the left hand.

We know that Chopin felt that all good musicians should emulate the human voice and sing their melodies while playing the piano. In keeping with this concept, fioraturas are an important part of the coloratura style sung by the most gifted of singers. Many students are intimidated by these passages when they see the unusually large amount of notes. Therefore, I was motivated to include fioratura-like passages in *Nocturne from Spotlight on Romantic Style* (example 17). The goal was to create passages that were comfortable and pianistic enabling students to play them expressively, just as a singer would sing them. Moreover, students could learn in this *Nocturne* that they need not be intimidated by a large number of 32$^{nd}$ notes.

See m.'s 1-12 of this piece.

Example 17

**NOCTURNE**

Catherine Rollin

In measure 3, 8 and 11, the fioratura-like passages are accessible. In measure 3, the fioratura is based on a figure that turns around the note A followed by a descending five-note grouping. In measure 8, the fioratura-like passage is a written-out trill. In measure 11, the 32$^{nd}$ note passage is a descending D major scale.

In the case of Chopin, many fioraturas have a grouping of notes that does not evenly fit with the left hand accompaniment. Not only are students intimidated by these passages, but teachers also feel reluctant to teach them. Some teachers are unsure of how to play these passages themselves. Should they be played with the right hand notes evenly distributed over the left hand or can they be distributed in predetermined groupings over the left hand? The latter makes these passages much more accessible to our students, but is it acceptable practice?

If we analyze fioratura passages performed by several highly respected artists, in almost all cases, one will conclude that these artists are all subtly measuring the notes of fioraturas. In other words, there is a definite number of notes in the fioratura passage in the right hand played in relationship to the left hand accompaniment. These "measured" fioraturas sound effective because they follow the logic of musical shaping and coincide well with the harmony in the left hand.

Let's examine a "measured" fioratura passage from Chopin's *Nocturne in C sharp minor op. posthumous.*

Example 18        Chopin, *Nocturne in C sharp minor, ms. 13* and *46*

The example above shows two measures where the notes are the same in the right hand. However, closer observation will reveal a slight difference in the grouping of the notes. Chopin's students said that he rarely played a piece the same way twice. In measures 13 and 46, he slightly varies the placement of the notes on beats two and three. But in writing out these rhythms, he leaves a clue that one can play the notes that are melodic (beats 1 and 2) more slowly than the notes that continue to fall in one direction (beats 3 and 4). Using this principle, one can use other examples of Chopin's "measuring" of fioratura passages as a guide for deciding how to group the notes. Generally, if the notes are more melodic in shape, rather than ascending or descending in a somewhat scale-like fashion, it is usually the most effective to take more time on the melodic passages.

Ultimately, by "measuring" the notes, we can give the fioratura passage more musical meaning than just playing the notes with even distribution.

A relatively simple unmeasured fioratura-like figure can be found in Chopin's *Nocturne in E minor Op. 72, No.1* (see the example below).

Example 19                                Chopin, *Nocturne in E minor,*
                                          *Op. 72, No. 1, ms. 35-37*

In measure 35 of this nocturne, the ten-note fioratura can be grouped 3 + 3 + 4 against the left hand eighth notes. Putting the faster note grouping at the end creates an exciting sweep as it moves up to the B in measure 36. Similarly, in measure 37, the eleven-note fioratura figure can be grouped most effectively as a 3 + 4 + 4 grouping. This will give a feeling of soaring to the downbeat on measure 38 and is very dramatic.

Some of Chopin's most famous fioratura passages occur in his *Nocturne in B Flat Minor op. 9, No. 1* (see the next example).

The fioratura of measures two and three must be treated as one long idea so what the player does in bar two impacts what happens in bar three. On my score I have several different measured possibilities and I will often play these for my students so they can decide how they would sing this themselves. Most students seem to favor the eleven-note figure in bar 2 divided as 4 + 4 + 3 against each eighth note pair of the left hand. Then in measure three, the twenty-two-note grouping can be grouped 3 + 4 + 4 + 4 + 4 + 3 against each eighth note pairing. The left hand will keep a strict pulse, (as discussed above in Chopin's use of the word rubato) but

Example 20

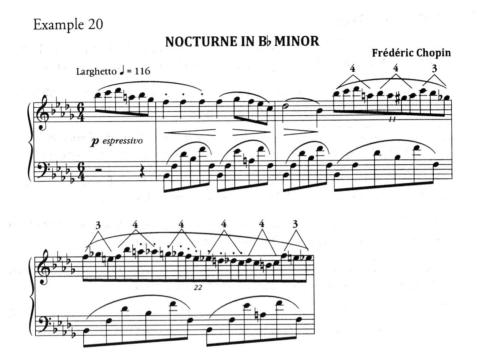

due to the different groupings of the notes, the right hand will feel free. For example, the four consecutive groupings of 4 in measure three will feel like the notes want to pick up a little speed as they descend; then the final grouping of 3 will create a quasi ritardando or sense of winding down at the end of the fioratura passage. In addition, every note should be shaped dynamically to fit the passage. Teachers can encourage students to sing the notes as they play to guide their dynamic choices. Professional pianists seem to either combine measured and unmeasured notes or perform the entire passage measured.

Because Chopin did sometimes compose measured fioratura-like passages, in the case of unmeasured fioratura-like passages, it is the author's opinion that he wants performers to sound like they are improvising. A well shaped, measured fioratura sounds more like a beautiful singer than one that is played evenly over the left hand accompaniment. There are convincing cases for either approach, but measuring these passages makes them much more accessible to students and therefore gives them more opportunities to enjoy Chopin's compositions.

Everyone who studies the piano deserves to have the wonderful experience of playing some of Chopin's masterworks. Students who first have the experience of playing many preparatory Romantic style pieces will ultimately play Chopin's music with confidence and understanding.

# Permissions

Example 2 and 16: *Summer's Nocturne* (from "Lyric Moments 1") by Catherine Rollin. © MCMXCV by Alfred Publishing Co., Inc. All Rights Reserved. Used by Permission.

Example 4: *Waltz* (from "Spotlight On Romantic Style"), by Catherine Rollin. © MCMXC by Alfred Publishing Co., Inc. All Rights Reserved. Used by Permission.

Example 7: *Prelude in A Major* (from "Preludes For Piano 2") by Catherine Rollin. © MCMXCI by Alfred Publishing Co., Inc. All Rights Reserved. Used by Permission.

Example 9: *Summer's Dream* (from "Lyric Moments 1") by Catherine Rollin. © MCMXCV by Alfred Publishing Co., Inc. All Rights Reserved. Used by Permission.

Example 11: *Echo Nocturne* (from "Romantic Gems") by Catherine Rollin. © MCMXCVII by Myklas Music Press . All Rights Reserved. Used by Permission.

Example 13: *Ballet Beauties* (from "Romantic Gems") by Catherine Rollin. © MCMXCVII by Myklas Music Press. All Rights Reserved. Used by Permission.

Example 17: *Nocturne* (from "Spotlight On Romantic Style") by Catherine Rollin. © MCMXC by Alfred Publishing Co., Inc. All Rights Reserved. Used by Permission.

# CHAPTER 24

## An Approach to Romantic Repertoire

### Walter Schenkman

Whether considered from the standpoint of professional or student performance, the Romantic repertoire appears to suffer serious distortion in one direction or another. More often than not, the professional effort ends up in increased technical efficiency, greater speed of delivery, and a sometimes startling streamlining of all emotional involvement. What is more, the critics aid and abet our modern day performers in this rather cold-blooded, calculated operation. The following review, appearing in a syndicated press release not too long ago, is symptomatic of the present plight of much "Romantic" performance:

> *Perhaps there are no better Chopin* Etudes *recorded than these . . . This is Chopin for the modern taste. The pianist lets the composer speak for himself. His fingers enunciate the music . . . Every note is sounded honestly and with authority. (An) enormous intellectual capacity . . . controls every measure. The happy result is* true *Chopin, completely devoid of the exaggeration of excessive emotionalism.*
> (Italics mine)

One can hardly condone or take comfort in the opposite extreme that apparently obtains in many student performances of this same repertoire. After being told that his orientation in Baroque music is wrongly executed, his Mozart is unstylistic, and his Beethoven out of character, it comes as a relief to the understandably bewildered and frustrated student to turn to a music that he rightfully, perhaps, feels that the can call his own. The rationale for this assumption, though not necessarily formulated in so many words, could hardly be simpler. After all, the music *is* Romantic, is it not?

What more can be expected but that one be expressive, pour one's heart out, and play it just as one feels it?

These contrasting approaches, even of one and the same work, result in totally disparate performances, goes without saying. Nevertheless it must be admitted, and deplored too, that both share one very important trait in common: a total and complete disregard for anything even remotely resembling an authentic tradition of Romantic performance. And make no mistake about it, the Romantic repertoire does have its own traditions and conventions, and these are to be respected to every bit the same degree as those of the music of any other period, whether Classic, Baroque, Renaissance, or even Modern!

The performer who blithely ignores these traditions and pays no heed to what those conventions might prescribe, is evading his responsibilities and is in no way likely to present a reading that does honor to the sense of the musical message in question. In the case of the Romantic repertoire specifically, the professional may well thrill his audience with his prowess and dexterity. The student may wallow, and glory in the impressive sonorities he manages to elicit from the keyboard. In both instances, however, the Romantic message is far removed and remains unheard.

There must be an alternative, more satisfactory approach, but what remedies can be proposed, and most important, what can the teacher do to alleviate the situation?

First of all, as with any music, one must be aware that the nub of the problem lies in one's understanding of the peculiarities of a given notation. Perhaps the difficulties of the Romantic notation *per se* have never been sufficiently underlined. Yet the gulf that separates this notation from its realization is probably every bit as great, and certainly as hazardous, as that which divides the notation of Baroque ornamentation, for instance, from its proper actualization. And ambiguities of notation already unclear, become all the more obscure as one admits the use of the pedal, sometimes indicated expressly by the composer, and sometimes simply implied.

In order to help the student achieve a better understanding of the subtleties of this notation, the teacher may call attention to certain specific topics for closer investigation and study. The matter of *texture*, for instance, comes immediately to mind. In the Romantic setting, qualities of texture and relationships between textures of varying quality assume a primary importance. No valid performance of Romantic music is even remotely possible without an acute awareness of these qualities, and a proper sense of perspective over these relationships.

Closely connected with the matter of *texture* is that of *articulation*. This topic would involve a consideration of the separate strands of the textural fabric as independent entities, and would be concerned with stress relationships to be observed *within* these entities. The generally accepted goal of according equal stress to every single note within a given figuration should be reexamined.

Another vexatious problem is that of *tempo* and *tempo fluctuation*. This area is fraught with some uncertainty and much controversy. Rather than setting the metronome at the beginning of a performance and closing one's eyes and ears, it should be feasible, at the very least, to cultivate an appreciation of those liberties that the Romantics themselves so frequently marked into their own scores. Similarly the student would be well advised to heed those markings consciously before he even thinks of introducing (or substituting) his own "instinctive" *tempo rubato*.

With regard to texture it is of interest to trace the typical Romantic setting of a broken chord structure to its simplest origins in the Alberti Bass. The Alberti Bass marked an important crossroad, providing as it did a convenient practical application of Rameau's theories of vertically conceived harmony. And composers who were disposed to abandon Bach's contrapuntal complexities in favor of a richer melodic development, were quick to take advantage of it. The importance of this shift of interest for the performer cannot be overemphasized.

A musical example may serve to illustrate this point. For instance, in considering the Alberti figure of the popular Mozart *C major Sonata*, one would probably take for granted that the right hand melody should receive more emphasis than the accompanying figure of the left hand. But the question also arises concerning this figure itself: is there a further hierarchy of relative importance to be established *within* the four notes of the Alberti or are they to be projected as four independent, evenly stressed rhythmic beats?

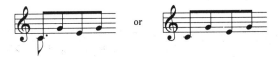

Perhaps herein is to be seen an essential element of the contrast between Rameau's theories and those of Bach. The former take into account the total chordal structure involved in assigning relative importance to individual notes, the latter are more concerned with the contrapuntal, note-to-note relationships between lines. Given Mozart's historical position there is little doubt that his outlook would have conformed more to Rameau's than to Bach's point of view. Certainly in the case of figuration of this type, one might be justified in assuming that a certain stress on the initial note of each group in relation to the three succeeding notes is proper, both from a rhythmic and harmonic point of view.

The situation is more explicitly clarified as one moves on to an examination of a typical Beethoven texture. Here a concept of foreground (melody), middle (filler), and background (bass) is useful. For instance, an example like that of the Adagio of the Pathetique shows a definite three-part texture, with the bass line accorded a part equal in importance and in the duration of its note values, to that of the top line melody. Played on the piano, the full durations of both melody and bass notes can be properly projected only if the intensity of the inner sixteenths (semiquavers) is carefully controlled.

Beethoven, *Sonata in C minor, Op. 13*

The concept of a three-part texture is a valid one for a tremendous quantity of the Romantic keyboard literature. Ever higher levels of sophistication are to be met with in the new and richer forms of textural settings, devised by the Romantics, bringing in their wake correspondingly higher levels of technical difficulty. For example, in his first *Song Without Words*, Mendelssohn inserts a flowing arpeggio pattern in sixteenths (semiquavers) in place of the relatively static and repetitious two-note figure of the Pathetique. From the technical point of view, he accomplishes his purpose by the simple device of dividing the middle part between the two hands, and thereby he achieves a greater fullness of texture altogether. For the rest the outer lines, though spaced further apart, are very similar in both character and notation to Beethoven's setting.

Mendelssohn, *Song Without Words, Op. 19, No. 1*

A subtle distinction is introduced in the notation of the Schumann example quoted below. No phrase marks are drawn over the bass line and eighth-note (quaver) rests actually punctuate its progression. Because of a quarter-(crotchet) beat pedal marking (in this case even though provided by an Editor) one suspects that the end-result in performance would probably closely parallel that of the other two examples.

Schumann, *Scenes from Childhood, Op. 15, No. 1*

The situation becomes even more tenuous as one proceeds to a still higher level of sophistication such as one might find in the setting of the "Harp" Etude of Chopin. In this case Chopin fills both hands with accompanying chordal effects, and at first glance one might be led to analyze the score in terms of an obvious two-part texture. However, closer examination would reveal, and the ear of the sensitive performer would confirm, that a three-part texture of melody, filler, and bass still prevails. It is even indicated in Chopin's indefinite notation as far as absolute durations are concerned, which distinguishes melody and bass from filler by means of larger noteheads. The filler material initially simply duplicates the notes of the six-four in both hands and in general duplicates other chordal combinations as the composition proceeds.

Chopin, *Etude in A flat, Op. 25, No. 1*

Again, as in the case of Schumann's supporting bass, there is room for disagreement as to exactly how legato a connection Chopin intended in the outside voices. Certain it is that oftentimes in this composition, because of the wide stretches involved in many of the figurations, a semblance of legato could only be obtained by a skillful use of the pedal. It is also certain, on the basis of Schumann's first-hand evidence, that Chopin did not permit every one of the small notes to be heard distinctly. "It was rather an undulation of the A flat major chord, here and there thrown aloft by the pedal."[1] So much for our "true" Chopin of the 1970s with "every note sounded honestly."

Perhaps the height of sophistication and technical difficulty is reached in a setting such as that of the fourth *Transcendental Etude, Mazeppa,* by Liszt. It is obvious that Liszt notates this work in a manner literally impossible to achieve with the hands alone, and without the aid of the pedal. From the standpoint of texture, the octave doublings of both melody and bass lend an orchestral fullness that leaves our earlier examples far behind. The interchanging of the hands, in the execution of the middle part, carried Mendelssohn's innovation to its logical extreme. From the standpoint of execution, even with the aid of the pedal, the obstacles to a successful performance are legion. But as is so often true in dealing with Romantic textures, the solution to the many problems involved will never be found in physical stamina alone. Of equal, if not of more importance, is an alert sensitivity to the balancing of sonorities, so that the musical sense of the phrase is not sacrificed to the busy inner activity.

Liszt, *Transcendental Etude in D minor, Mazeppa*

Liszt, too, does not observe the niceties of notation concerning the duration and rests necessary to make up a full bar. A review of our five examples shows some interesting trends in this respect. Whereas both Beethoven and even Mendelssohn are generally scrupulous in this connection, elements of experimentation, vagueness, and even downright carelessness increasingly find their way into the scores of Schumann, Chopin, and Liszt.

Actually, Romantic notation gives the appearance of having been in a constant state of flux. The pedal had removed all reason for the exact and literal voice leading of an earlier period, by injecting an element of indefiniteness into the total picture as far as sonority was concerned. But the pedal did not change, and was not intended to change, the basic perspective over these sonorities. It did allow, however, and even fostered the development of a musical shorthand. Composers were able to take certain matters for granted without bothering to spell them out fully; or they were able to spell them out differently on different occasions.

For instance, had Chopin been absolutely correct in the notation of the A flat *Etude*, he would have inserted stems in an opposite direction for both melody and bass. In the left hand part of the first bar he would have had to include a dotted half note (minim) A flat on the second beat tied over to a whole note (semibreve) in the following bar. The cumbersomeness of this procedure is immediately obvious and Chopin's compromise solution is reasonably satisfactory. But now turn to a similar "undulation over a C minor chord" as is seen in the left hand figuration of the "Revolutionary" *Etude*. To the eye this score presents a simple two-part texture: melody in octaves and sixteenth-note (semiquaver) figuration in the bass. But if one allows for shortcuts of notation, it is perfectly reasonable to assume that the pedal provides the equivalent of a downward stem on the initial C, imparting to it a relatively heavier stress and longer duration, and thereby restoring our typical three-part texture.

A similar situation obtains in Schumann's notation of the opening of his *Phantasy, Op. 17*. Here Schumann notates the initial G of the figuration in the left hand as just another sixteenth note (semiquaver), but he also inserts a *sforzando-piano* marking above it. Though the whole passage is often enough played forte throughout, if one may judge by the dynamic marking and the initial pedal, Schumann's conception more likely intended a rush of soft notes over a resounding bass G. The "foreign" note, A, of the dominant ninth chord was probably intended to add a further element of vagueness to the total sonorous effect, and is very similar in nature to the passing note, D, of the "Revolutionary" which colors, or clouds, the rise and fall of the C minor broken chord figuration, which should not be overstressed.

Figurations from Chopin and Schumann

A conclusive example of Chopin's casual attitude with regard to notation may be seen in the development section of the Allegro movement of the B flat minor Sonata, where the composer combines the initial motive of the *Grave* introduction with that of the *agitato* first theme. The original notation of the *Grave* is |¢ ♩.. ♪| 𝅝 |. This figure is modified in notation almost beyond recognition as shown in the example below, and it is little wonder that the significance of the bass line in octaves, as distinct from the middle chordal figure in sixths, is so often missed in performance.

Chopin, *Sonata in B flat minor, Op. 35, Allegro movement*

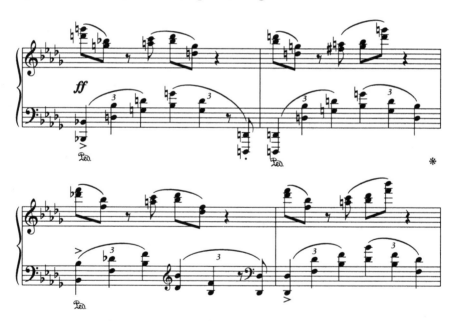

The examples cited so far have dealt primarily with a three-part setting featuring the melody on top, a bass line as foundation, and harmonic filler in between. A popular Romantic variant of this setting exchanges upper and middle parts: the melody line is placed in the middle and the filler on top. (The credit for a "first" in this connection is variously assigned to Thalberg, Mendelssohn, and even some minor earlier composers.) This arrangement is familiar enough to quote a popular Mendelssohn setting of the same melody in both ways:

Mendelssohn, *Rondo Capriccioso,* inner portion

If the performer is able to strike the right balance in the first example, highlighting the melody, underlining the bass progressions, and properly subduing the repeated middle chords, there should be no great problem in reversing roles in the second. Melody and bass line would be clearly projected in the left hand, while the arpeggio figuration of the right would be subordinate, even if scintillating. There is always a temptation, though, in a setting of this sort for the performer to be led by his fingers to change priorities so that the figuration becomes the end-all of the performance.

This temptation becomes all the greater as the sophistication of the figuration increases and the challenge of a "clean" performance of it becomes all the more formidable. Examples like those of the Chopin *Etude in F major, Op. 25, Nr. 5,* or the middle section of the *Mazeppa* of Liszt might illustrate the point very effectively. Musical meaning which so often resides in an unspectacular left hand part, recedes into the background, and honest articulation of every note of the decorative figuration becomes the sole *raison d'être* of the performance. One might say that any projection of a musical message is purely accidental under the circumstances and it is about as likely to occur as in a performance of a fugue where the forceful presentation of counterpoints obliterates any recognition of the subject.

If the predilection for "honest" articulation is allowed to dominate the performance, at least it should be tempered by the reading and pondering of the words of an older-generation mentor of Romantic performance standards. Writing in the introduction of his *Etudes,* which appeared in 1826, which were studied eagerly by Schumann certainly, and most likely by Chopin and Liszt as well, Moscheles states: "Passages consisting of an uninterrupted sequence of rapid notes are to be divided by a moderate accent at the commencement of each group of four notes (three if triplets). This accent is not so much to be effected by force, as by slightly dwelling on the first note (of each group)." Moscheles goes on to remark on the judgment that must be used in this matter "since its abuse will render the passage stiff and mechanical."[2]

It is interesting to consider certain of the Chopin *Etudes* in the light of these remarks. For instance, in the first *Etude in C* and in the eighth in *F of Op. 10,* the composer actually employs an accentuation to this effect on the first sixteenth note (semiquaver) of each group of four. The accented note is often brutally slammed out in performance and thereby produces a harsh effect. A more proper execution, in accord with the sense of Moscheles' remarks, would rather gently sustain the accented note to create an effect of a color wash: the marked note would stand out prominently above its neighbors by means of a judicious balance rather than by brute force. To modern ears this might suggest an element of "dishonest" articulation: in fact, it involves a certain juggling of time values, a miniature *tempo rubato,* as well as variation in stress.

With regard to flexibility versus rigidity of tempo, the words of Moscheles as a moderate precursor of the Romantics, might be given serious heed. After warning the player always to play in time, he goes on to add that there are naturally exceptions: when a composition is marked *agitato, a capriccio, con passione, con anima,* etc., the performer is left "to the dictates of his own taste and fancy."

In conclusion, I have deplored certain current standards of performance of Romantic piano music and have attempted to identify some facets of this music in the hope of establishing a basis for a more authentic performance practice. Certain typical types of texture have been examined and illustrated and the importance of a proper perspective in their regard emphasized. Ambiguities of notation have been considered and their possible consequences discussed. Subtleties of articulation have been touched upon and the importance of flexibility in tempo, at least in accord with the composer's obvious instructions, underlined.

The teacher who ponders these various points and brings them in one way or another to the conscious attention of his or her students right from the start, will contribute greatly to a restoration of more proper values in the performance of the Romantic piano literature. For his part, the student will little by little develop the ability to think of this music in terms of specific types of textures, rather than in terms of scatterings of isolated, unrelated notes.

For example, he will quickly learn to draw a parallel between the left hand accompaniment part of a work like the *E flat major Nocturne* with those of the *C* or *F minor Nocturnes* quoted below. Awareness of the specific character of a given texture will also lead to the realization, for instance, that Chopin's peculiar penchant for those *staccato* markings in his accompaniments need not necessarily be taken in the sense of short, abrupt punctuation points, but rather call for a heavy, *marcato* emphasis, most especially on the low bass note. The resultant piano sonority, full and rich, would exemplify Czerny's apt words regarding the uses of the pedal by means of which "... we are enabled to make the bass-notes vibrate as long as if we had a third hand at our disposal, while two hands are engaged in playing the melody, and the *distant* accompaniment" (Italics mine).[3]

Chopin, *Nocturne in E flat, Op. 9, No. 2,* opening phrase

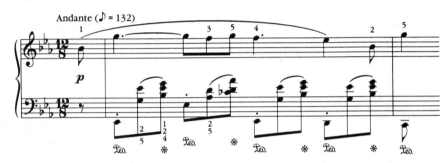

Chopin, *Nocturne in C minor, Op. 48, No. 1*

Chopin, *Nocturne in F minor, Op. 55, No. 1*

When the student approaches his first Chopin *Etude* he may thus have a better understanding of what to look for on the printed page. Though technical priorities may reside in the specific figuration to be mastered, he will be conscious of the fact that musical priorities most likely lie elsewhere: more often than not in an unpretentious left hand part (difficult enough if it is to be rendered convincingly). With regard to the technically demanding figuration itself he will not be misled into taking Chopin's typical accent markings, generally falling on the first note of each group of four (or six) sixteenths (semiquavers) too literally. He will avoid harsh hammer blows that would separate those accented notes from their neighbors placing them out of context with one another.

Finally, he will avoid the all too common temptation to "play it by ear," and insert all sorts of little *rubati* that may even be in direct contradiction to the composer's express markings: "An arbitrary and excessive stretching of the bar continuously applied (*tempo rubato*)," as Hummel, writing in his *Pianoforte Method* of 1828, described it.

The Romantic repertoire does have its conventions and traditions. Let us make it our business, as teachers, performers, and students, to search them out and observe them.

# Tempo Rubato

So much confusion surrounds the subject of *Tempo Rubato* that it is hardly surprising to find that many teachers prefer to avoid the subject altogether. Perhaps they do no worse than those teachers who offer their students a rash of broad generalizations, especially when dealing with the Romantic repertoire, that have little or no basis in fact. The following brief outline attempts to describe some of the salient points to be borne in mind when discussing *Tempo Rubato.*

Suggestive in its own right, the term *rubato,* from the Italian word for "stolen," has been used to signify different things at different times. Today the term is used quite loosely to cover the full spectrum of tempo flexibility. Sometimes referred to as a "full" *rubato,* this type of *rubato* affects the whole musical fabric with its discreet fluctuations around a basic pulse. In Mozart's day the meaning of *rubato* was generally more closely delimited: the term was usually understood to refer to certain liberties allowable in the execution of a melodic line in relation to its accompaniment. Somewhat later the term was used in theoretical treatises to indicate a modification of dynamics rather than of tempo, and to denote an off-beat accentuation of those beats that were normally considered weak, or "bad". One hundred and fifty years before Mozart, Frescobaldi described the practice of *rubato* much as we understand it today, but without using the term at all. And finally, centuries before Frescobaldi and before the use of a metrical notation, one may assume that an equivalent for our *tempo rubato* must have been a dominant force in the various performance traditions that grew up around the execution of the plainchant melody.

We have inherited then, a state of semantic confusion, where the inherent quality of the thing itself is frequently confused with, and by, its nomenclature, and this situation has frequently given rise to many a wild notion. The most preposterous of these, the popular notion of some years back that Chopin "invented" *rubato,* fortunately receives little credence today. A more serious theory to be challenged is that which asserts that Mozart, and more particularly Chopin, did not know *our* type of *rubato,* because they practiced a more specific type which did not include the liberties we associate with the term. *The fact that they might have practiced "our" type of rhythmic freedom, under a different name or different theoretical rationalization, is excluded from consideration altogether.* Thus Virgil Thomson, the distinguished American composer and critic, in his review of a Rubinstein recital of 1942, was able to state with absolute authority that Rubinstein's *rubato* "derives from Paderewski," who, in turn derived it from a supposed Viennese tradition. "I don't believe for a moment it resembles anything Frederic Chopin ever did or had in mind."

The confusion was likewise allowed to spread in the reverse direction. Many of the specific prescriptions for Mozart's type of *rubato,* for instance, were incorporated in the "rules" offered by the popular literature on the subject around the turn of the present century, for the "full" *rubato* of our day. The concept of "paying back" that which was "stolen," logical enough in Mozart's *rubato,* was not to be applied likewise to "our" *rubato,* which affects the total musical texture and is not limited to just the melody. The more extreme tenets in this regard advocated a measure-by-measure "clearing of accounts." The 1905 Edition of *Elsons' Musical Dictionary* defines *rubato* in the following manner: "A slight deviation to give more expression by retarding one note and quickening another, but so that the time of each measure is not altered as a whole."

A somewhat more liberal attitude left open the possibility of delaying the settling of accounts until the end of the particular phrase in question. The 1944 Edition of *The Harvard Dictionary of Music* explains that "under the influence of their study of the treatises of Mozart's time," there were writers who "applied the 'give and take' principle of the 18th century type to the 'full' rubato . . . They maintain here, too, the accelerandi and ritardandi complement one another, so that, after six or seven measures in free tempo, the player arrives at exactly the same moment in time that he would have reached had he played in rigid tempo."

A clear understanding of the principle underlying Mozart's *rubato* is necessary in order to comprehend the lines of thought that lead to such conclusions. The procedure of playing the right hand part *rubato* while the left maintains strict tempo, is initially baffling and seemingly impossible, and we see the results of semantic confusion again; we automatically associate the term *rubato* with complete flexibility and total freedom. The concept is readily grasped in its illustration by the theorists of the time: the realization of a *rubato* by (a) *anticipatio* and one by (b) *ritardatio* are shown in the following self-explanatory examples.

The notation and realization of *rubato*.

This is a far cry indeed from the *rubato* described by Paderewski: "There are in musical expression certain things which are vague and consequently cannot be defined; . . . a musical composition, printed or written, is, after all, a form, a mould. The performer infuses life into it, and whatever the strength of that life may be, he must be given a reasonable amount of liberty, he must be endowed with some *discretional power*. In our modern meaning discretional power is Tempo Rubato." Paderewski's *rubato* includes no strict accounting of the time "stolen"; "what is lost is irrevocably lost." There is a striking distinction to be noted in the term *rubato* as described by Paderewski and the term as described and illustrated by the theorists of Mozart's day, one should not think for a moment that those theorists did not allow for discretional powers on the part of the performer too. *However, as will be seen, these powers of discretion were not necessarily accounted for under the heading of rubato.*

From the middle of the 18th century on, such theorists as Joachim Quantz, Leopold Mozart (whose *Violinschule* appeared in 1756, the year of Wolfgang's birth), J. A. Hiller, Marpurg, and Tuerk were in general agreement on the principle of the so-called "grammatical accents" which distinguished between the "good" and "bad" beats of a bar; i.e., given two successive notes of equal time-value in common time, for example, "one will always be long and the other short" (Hiller, 1774). Or as Marpurg elaborates: "The first and third crotchets (in 2/2) are good, stressed, uneven or accented time-members and the second and fourth are bad, passing, even, or unaccented time-members" (1759). Of course in triple meter situations the first beat remains "good", while the second and third end up by being "bad."

For situations beyond the normal, "rhetorical" and "pathetic" accents, more extreme in character, are added to the vocabulary. For example, in his *Klavierschule* of 1759 Tuerk discusses the necessity not only of emphasizing certain notes, but also of lingering on them. "As to the duration of such lingering, I would make it a rule that no note should ever be prolonged for more than half its proper value." In the same work he speaks of instances where "the expression can be enhanced by exceptional means," among which are counted first of all, "intentionally playing out of time," and secondly, "accelerating or slackening the tempo." It is important to note that these first two categories of exceptional means already include all of the discretionary powers that Paderewski asked for in the name of *tempo rubato*.

The "so-called *tempo rubato*" itself does not figure in Tuerk's discussion until his *third* category of exceptional means, and though it is described as having more than one meaning, "it is most commonly understood to mean the shifting of notes by playing them too soon or too late" (as illustrated in example 1). Mozart categorically states his preference for this type of *rubato* in an oft quoted letter to his father dated October, 1777: ". . . Everyone is amazed that I can always keep strict time. What these people cannot grasp is that in tempo rubato in *Adagio,* the left hand should go on playing in strict time. With them the left hand always follows suit . . ." It is recorded, too, that Mozart actually wrote a letter which gave detailed instructions concerning the way he wanted his C minor Phantasie (K. 475, composed in 1785) to be performed. This letter, unfortunately lost, would have provided us with invaluable insights into Mozart's later style of performance. One wonders whether in his later years he might not have changed his earlier judgments; in the absence of the original letter, one has to turn to the internal evidence offered by the music itself.

It is interesting to note how in the opening of this work Mozart "lingers" over the initial "good" beat on the dotted quarter (crotchet) C and reinforces this lingering by means of dynamic contrast. The performer who slightly expands the duration of this opening dotted quarter (crotchet) in relation to the even eighth note (quaver) motion that follows, and likewise slightly "lingers" over the crying dissonances that follow, for not more than "half their proper value," will probably come closer to a valid performance of the opening statement than the one who gives every beat its exact and literal value. One recalls Burney and his description of C.P.E. Bach's manner of performance: "In the pathetic and slow movements, whenever he had a long note to express, he absolutely contrived to produce a cry of sorrow and complaint from his instrument . . ."

Mozart, *Phantasie in C minor, K. 475,* opening statement

In the directions of the score of the *C minor Sonata* generally associated with the *Phantasie,* Mozart calls for a *calando* at one point leading back to the main theme of the *Adagio,* and gives the performer's fancy free rein at another (the last statement of the Rondo theme is marked "*a piacere*"). Here we have the equivalent of the first two of Tuerk's "exceptional means": intentionally playing out of time, and slackening the tempo. An interesting example of a written out *rubato* may be seen in the notation of the Rondo theme itself. One might consider this a realization, by *anticipatio,* of the "correct" notation proposed below:

Mozart, *Sonata in C minor, Rondo* (in original and proposed notation)

Here incidentally, one sees, perhaps, the beginning of that tradition of *not* playing the hands together, that dominated so much of 19th century performances.

A comparison of the rhythmic treatment of this Rondo theme with that of similar melodic construction in earlier works is likewise revealing. The B flat Rondo theme from the *Sonata, K. 333*, dating from 1778, shows no contradiction of the proper "grammatical" accents; the G major theme from *K. 283*, dating from around 1774, toys with the idea of stressing the "bad" third beat, and thus plays tricks with the listener's conventional sense of proper accentuation. As is so often the case in both Mozart and Haydn (Haydn's popular *C major Sonata* with its offbeat accentuation comes immediately to mind), the matter of "improper" stress is only resolved satisfactorily for the listener's ears at the conclusion of the overall phrase. The *rubato* of the opening theme of the C minor Rondo distorts the grammatical accentuation beyond recognition, and in effect sets up two completely independent spheres of rhythmic activity. For the sake of simpler comparison, the themes below have been transposed into C major.

Mozart, *Sonatas in B flat, K. 333,* and *in G. K. 283,* opening statements (transposed into C)

A comparison of two rhythmic settings of a similar idea, one early the other late, is likewise informative in the case of Beethoven. The example from the early *C minor Sonata, Opus 10* (likewise transposed for the sake of simpler comparison) shows a straightforward rhythmic approach. The "good" quality of the initial melody note C is enhanced by the additional duration bestowed by the dotted quarter (crotchet). The succeeding two notes are weak in nature, and merely serve to prepare for the "good" suspension on the A flat dotted half (minim) of the following bar. The example from the late Opus 110, in addition to its slower pace *Moderato* as opposed to *Allegro con brio,* shows a greater elasticity in rhythmic treatment again by means of the introduction of the *rubato* element. As in the case of the Mozart C minor example, one might imagine this opening bar notated in even quarters (crotchets); a *rubato* performance by *ritardatio* would yield results roughly equivalent to those of Beethoven's actual notation.

Beethoven, themes from *Sonatas, Op. 10, No. 1,* and *Op. 110*

As one approaches Chopin the evidence becomes more extensive . . . and more contradictory. On numerous occasions, Chopin reaffirms his insistence on maintaining a steady tempo, constantly scolds his pupils for any infraction of this rule, and even suggests practice with a metronome! Given the wealth of evidence available, there is no basis for suspecting any change in these expressed attitudes; but there is room for serious debate as to just what Chopin's concept of a steady tempo included. On the other hand, the term *rubato* itself, appearing more often in his early than in his late works, probably referred to the melody alone in Mozart's sense, as described above.

Perhaps embedded in Chopin's sense of "strict time" were those characteristics so often recommended by the writers of the treatises of his day. Kalkbrenner with whom Chopin initially proposed to study upon his arrival in Paris during the late 1820s, tells us that when the strong beat of the measure is emphasized, "l'oreille se trouve de suite satisfaite" (the ear is immediately satisfied as a consequence). He calls for slight retards at "*les terminaisons de phrases*," and the necessity of holding back the movement when there is a frequent change of harmony, or a fast succession of modulations. Hummel, in his *Method* mentioned above, warns that "the contrast between holding back and the movement forward must never appear too striking in relation to the main tempo." As Moscheles tells us, the emphasis on the first beat is also extended to cover passage work in groups of sixteenth notes (semiquavers) where, for example, the first note of each group of four is accorded an extra stress.

Perhaps the contradictions between Chopin's own words about what he was doing, and those of contemporary musicians who witnessed the event, can be better reconciled in the light of certain of these theoretical formulations. For instance, there is the famous argument between Chopin and Meyerbeer as to whether a certain Mazurka as played by Chopin was in 3/4 as the composer maintained, or in 2/4 as Meyerbeer insisted on the basis of what he heard. Charles Halle, a distinguished pianist and founder of the Halle Orchestra, elaborates on this particular peculiarity of Chopin's rhythm and gives an important clue: after commenting on "the entire freedom with which he treated the rhythm," Halle goes on to remark that "most of his mazurkas . . . when played by himself appear to be written not in 3/4 but in 4/4 time, *the result of his dwelling so much longer on the first note of the bar*" (Italics mine).

In any event, this would not be the first or last time that a discrepancy might exist between subjective and objective rhythmic reality. Sternberg recounts how Moscheles once proposed to illustrate how one should play a Beethoven *Adagio* in *strict time,* but yet with expression. "And then he sat down and played a most beautiful rubato, for he was a consummate artist. When he finished he commented upon how strictly he had kept time!"

As in the case of Mozart and Beethoven, it is interesting to note some of the syncopated, *rubato* effects that Chopin incorporates in his own notation. One may cite the lyrical theme of the *B Flat Minor Scherzo,* as an example of a rhythmic treatment very similar to that noted in connection with the Beethoven *Sonata, Opus 110.* The tie over the bar line of the initial melody note exemplifies Chopin's "dwelling" on the strong beat. Again, one might imagine the following "plain" notation before adding the coloring ingredient of *rubato:*

Chopin, *Scherzo in B flat minor, Op. 31, No. 2,* inner portion

The quotation from the *Fantasy in F Minor* shows a typical anticipation of the beat in the right hand showing the tradition of hands not being played together, followed by a whole series of off-beat syncopations.

Chopin, *Fantasy in F minor, Op. 49,* inner portion

The next quotation compares the treatment of a very similarly shaped melody line at the hands of Chopin and Brahms. In this particular example, Chopin again anticipates the initial down-beat in the right hand; but his line thereafter flows with the normal metrical accentuation. Brahms coordinates his melody line with the bass at the outset, but then introduces a chain of off-beat, "hands-not-together" chords. Again, for the sake of convenience, the Chopin has been transposed to the A minor of the Brahms example, and is given in outline form.

Comparison in outline of Chopin, *Nocturne in F minor, Op. 55, No. 1,* and Brahms, *Intermezzo in A minor, Op. 76, No. 7*

Comparison in outline of Chopin, *Nocturne in F minor, Op. 55, No. 1*, and Brahms, *Intermezzo in A minor, Op. 76, No. 7*

Liszt, who introduces the direction *rubato* into his scores not much later than Chopin (at least as early as 1834) seems at first to use the term itself in much the same sense as Chopin, mainly affecting the melody alone. Certainly by the middle of the century at the latest, his use of the term seems more general and appears to convey much the same meaning as we understand it today, i.e., the whole musical fabric is affected, not just the melody.

Consideration of *rubato* in this sense may well produce satisfactory results, too, in the case of an example like that of the section in Debussy's *Clair de Lune* marked by the composer *tempo rubato* (second page):

The bass E flat octave and the succeeding syncopated chord on the eighth beat in both hands would be taken at a leisurely pace. The basic pulse would quicken as the triplet motion begins, and would be relaxed again as the conclusion of the phrase is reached in the duples and quarter note (crotchet).

In certain instances the designation of *tempo rubato* seems to imply a certain irregularity within the bar and, one is almost tempted to accept the definition quoted above, taken from *Elsons' Dictionary* of 1905 "retarding one note, and quickening another . . .". For example, in Gershwin's *Second Prelude for Piano*, the "*poco rubato*" tempo heading prescribed by the composer, might be taken as implying a heavy stress on the first beat of the four even quarter (crotchet) chords of the accompaniment, with a corresponding "quickening" of the remaining three beats. If this interpretation is correct, it is significant that one is back to Chopin's practice of an inordinate "dwelling" on the first beat of the bar, and not very far removed from the 18th century theorists' distinctions between "good" and "bad" beats, except that in this case the third beat has also been consigned to the category of "bad". It is likewise noteworthy that Gershwin assigns the direction of "*ben ritmato*" to his *First and Third Preludes*; no distortion of good, honest beats is permitted here!

Bartók attempts to give the performer certain guidelines in the production of a *rubato,* by suggesting the outer limits of the tempo changes desired. For instance, in the short melodies of the *Hungarian Peasant Songs* of no more than a page in length, the composer might provide a metronome marking such as MM: 90-70. These markings might be further clarified by the use of stress marks, breathing pauses, groupings within phrases, etc. The burden of finding a natural, tasteful performance still comes back to the sensitivities of the performer.

One cannot ever hope to attain a perfect knowledge of "what really existed" in Mozart's day, or in Chopin's; the conclusions one reaches must of necessity lie in the domain of opinion. It appears certain, however, that if one is to introduce an element of flexibility into the performance of Mozart, it should be done on the basis of an awareness of the theoretical principles which governed rhythmic relationships in Mozart's time, as well as on the basis of a sympathetic understanding of the peculiar character of the composition to be performed. The same awareness and understanding must control the introduction of flexibility in Chopin or others of the Romantic composers, *with the added requirement that the performer must take into account the many explicit instructions and verbal characterizations,* i.e., *agitato, morendo, risvegliato,* etc., that are contained in the typical Romantic score, and should familiarize himself with the special peculiarities of the vocabulary employed by the different composers. It is as inexcusable to overlook these directions, which should serve to determine the character of the performance, as it would be, in reading music, to fail to notice the various accidentals added by composers to color their harmonies.

Though many subtle differences may be observed between different ages and different composers, perhaps a common tradition embraces the basic concepts of rhythmic organization over the past centuries. One might proceed on the assumption that any series of regular beats will be arranged in some form of predictable fashion or other; strong or "good" beats will alternate with weak or "bad." The difference between one style and another is probably determined in large part by the exact quantitative and qualitative distinctions drawn between these various beats. Into this realm of established and agreed upon predictability, composers introduce an element of unpredictability with their shifting of accents and contrasts of longer and shorter durations. The phenomenon of *tempo rubato* produces a further element of unpredictability in performance; certain points are singled out for more stress than others, or perhaps the "predictable" stresses, while retained, are exaggerated beyond the normal expectation.

Following the lead of the theorists, one can advise to establish and emphasize a solid first "good" beat of a greater relative duration than the literal-minded will readily accept; one can suggest relaxation at the end of phrases; one can call for special emphasis at the climax of a melody, or one can recommend the bold relief of a dissonance in relation to a succeeding consonance. Perhaps one may suggest an exaggeration of the contrast between the long and the short duration, by extending the one and curtailing the other. And withal, one might caution that all of these distortions and exaggerations must be *imperceptibly* executed— "unbemerklich", as Hummel said. Going back to the original derivation of *rubato* what the good exponent of thievery takes away by sleight of hand will never be missed by his listeners.

The teacher who communicates these concepts of *rubato* to his or her students will have done his share towards a better understanding of a difficult and complex subject and towards the reduction of arbitrary distortions that have no place in honest and valid performance, whatever the music.

# References

Apel, Willi. *Harvard Dictionary of Music.* Cambridge, 1944.

Burney, Dr. Charles. *An 18th Century Musical Tour in Central Europe and the Netherlands.* Vol. II of Dr. Burney's Musical Tours in Europe, Oxford University Press, London, 1959.

Paderewski, Ignace Jan. *Success in Music and How it is Won,* by Henry Finck, with a Chapter on Tempo Rubato by Ignace Jan Paderewski, Charles Scribner's Sons, New York, 1909.

Rothschild, Fritz. *Musical Performance in the Times of Mozart and Beethoven: The Lost Tradition in Music Part II.* Adam and Charles Black, London, 1961.

Schonberg, Harold C. *The Great Pianists from Mozart to the Present.* Simon and Schuster, New York, 1963.

Thomson, Virgil. *Music Reviewed 1940–54.* Vintage Books, New York, 1967.

# CHAPTER 25

## Essential Romantic Repertoire for the Middle School and High School Student

### Reid Alexander

### Introduction

Of the four keyboard style periods, high school pianists immensely enjoy playing Romantic literature of the nineteenth century. The extended range of the keyboard, many descriptive titles, colorful harmonies, brilliant textures, and above all, singing lyricism and extensive use of the pedals, contribute to the special appeal of music from this period.

When preparing for this "essential repertoire," the important role educational music plays cannot be underestimated. For example, collections such as William Gillock's multi-key *Lyric Preludes in Romantic Style* (Alfred), Paul Sheftel's *Interludes* (Carl Fischer), and Eugenie Rocherolle's *Six Moods for Piano* (Kjos) serve a valuable purpose in helping students master pedal technique, voice textures, and read music in a variety of keys.

As mentioned in the baroque section, educational literature again can act as a barometer for the student's readiness to play more difficult compositions. If the student cannot fluently perform an easier Rollin or Gillock *Prelude* with musical finesse, what will happen if a Chopin *Prelude* is assigned? Obviously, the student will need additional preparation before stepping up to the next level of repertoire. Additional sets particularly useful when preparing students for the Romantic style include:

| | |
|---|---|
| *A Splash of Color, Books I, II* (Alfred) | Dennis Alexander |
| *Carefree Days* (Frederick Harris) | Susan Alson |
| *I Remember Gurlitt* (Alfred) | Cornelius Gurlitt |
| *Preludes for Piano, Vols. I, II* (Alfred) | Catherine Rollin |

## Suggested Romantic Literature by Composer (alphabetized by composer)

| Composer | Title or Volume | Publisher |
|---|---|---|
| Brahms | *Celebrate Brahms* (Hisey, ed.) *Waltzes for Piano, op. 39, simplified version* | Frederick Harris |

Brahms composed three versions of the op. 39 waltzes, two solo versions of which one is less difficult but still challenging (referred to as the "simplified version", but hardly elementary) as well as a spectacular arrangement for four-hands one piano. Any of these 16 short waltzes, varied in tempo, mood, and key, and full of cross rhythms are excellent for introducing Brahms' music to secondary students.

| | | |
|---|---|---|
| Brahms | *Klavierstücke (Six Pieces for Piano), op. 118* | Frederick Harris |

A superb introduction to the more advanced writing of Brahms, the second *Intermezzo in A Major*, of op. 118, is particularly beautiful. It requires careful voicing throughout, especially in the contrasting middle section where a canon occurs between the hands. This particular edition also includes the two op. 79 *Rhapsodies* (B minor and G minor) which many talented high school students study.

| | | |
|---|---|---|
| Burgmüller | *25 Easy Études, op. 100* (*Celebrate Burgmüller*, Hisey, ed.) | Frederick Harris |

Burgmüller studies prepare for the harder character pieces of Heller, Schumann, and Mendelssohn. The op. 25 early intermediate studies are particularly useful with middle school students. Familiar titles include *Ballade*, *The Chase*, and *Arabesque*. This edition contains all 25 études of op. 100, frequently played compositions from opp. 105 and 109, and the *Rondo alla Turca*, from op. 68 (no. 3), modeled after the famous Mozart *Alla Turca* (K 331).

| | | |
|---|---|---|
| Chopin | *Preludes, op. 28* (Paderewski, ed.) *Prelude in E minor, no. 4* *Prelude in D-flat Major, no. 15* *Prelude in G minor, no. 22* | Chopin Institute |

When playing selected preludes by Chopin, point out the key relationship that he used for the entire cycle (circle of 5ths alternating major and minor, C, A minor, G, E minor, etc.) In the chromatic E minor prelude, mention that the half steps in the top tones of the final three chords mirror the use of melodic chromaticism throughout. The opening A section of the D-flat prelude requires careful balance between melody and accompaniment. The enharmonic change of A-flat to G-sharp on the repeating tenor note in the B section should not go unnoticed. The impressive sounding left hand octaves and brilliant right hand chords of the G minor prelude will captivate and inspire the aspiring high school pianist.

| Chopin | *Celebrate Chopin, Vol. I* (Hisey, ed.) | Frederick |
| | *Waltz in A minor, posthumous* | Harris |

This edition includes several intermediate solos written during Chopin's youth. In this easier *Waltz* (and others), guide students to "map out" by letter the different sections. Here, the repeating left hand harmonic pattern facilitates memorization. This particular work should be required of any student before attempting more difficult waltzes.

| Chopin | *Cantabile in B-flat, KK IVb, no. 6* | Frederick |
| | *Lento in C-sharp minor, KK IVa, no. 16* | Harris |
| | *Nocturne in E-flat Major, op. 9, no. 2* | |

Chopin's nocturne style can be approached incrementally through these three pieces. The one page *Cantabile*, written at about the same time as op. 9, no. 2, contains a florid operatic melody over a nocturne-like accompaniment. A step up in difficulty, the three-page *Lento in C-sharp minor* quotes musical material from the composer's second piano concerto. The beautiful *cadenza* figures, in measures 57-60, become easier to read if the student perceives the E scale fragments and fingers scale excerpts accordingly. Lastly, the more advanced op. 9, no. 2 requires careful attention to pedaling and right hand detailed phrasing.

| Chopin | *Études* (Paderewski, ed.) | Chopin Institute |
| | *Étude in E Major, op. 10, no. 3* | |

The Chopin studies represent a more advanced level of study. The *Étude in E Major, op. 10, no. 3* can introduce this genre of repertoire. With melody over accompaniment, the opening texture resembles the middle movement of Beethoven's op. 13 and requires the same *legato* phrasing and projection of top tones. The B section, comprised of contrary tritones and sixths, will be a technical challenge. Other Chopin suggestions (in approximate order of musical and technical difficulty) include:

| Chopin | *Preludes, op. 28, no. 6, 7, 9, 20* | Chopin |
| | *Mazurkas, op. 68, no. 3; op. 7, no. 1, 2* | Institute |
| | *Waltzes, op. 69, no. 1, 2; op. 34, no. 2* | |
| | *Nocturnes, op. 15, no. 3; op. 72, no. 1* | |
| | (posthumous) | |
| | *Polonaises, op. 26, no. 1* | |
| | *Études, op. 10, no. 6, 9; op. 25, no. 1, 2* | |
| Field | *Nocturnes* | Any Standard Edition |

As Chopin borrowed the nocturne from John Field, consider teaching an easier Field nocturne before embarking on more difficult Chopin textures. The *Nocturne no. 5 in B-flat Major* (usually published as one of 18) reveals a lyrical right hand melody over an elegant left hand eighth-note accompaniment. Field elaborates the right hand melody when restated.

| Grieg | *Celebrate Grieg* (Hisey, ed.) | Frederick Harris |
| | *Selected Lyric Pieces* | |
| | *Puck, op. 71, no. 3* | |

*Puck* is a superb piece for introducing the key of E-flat minor. The *staccato* left hand *ostinato* figure and spirited right hand eighth-note five-finger sequences highlight the A section. The diminished chords and distant key relationships in the B section make it an attractive teaching piece.

| Grieg | *Notturno, op. 54, no. 4* | Frederick Harris |

The *Notturno* contains cross rhythms that must be carefully taught. Arresting right hand melodies (bird-like) occur throughout and the climatic B section appeals to every listener. The ABA[1] structure facilitates memorization. Slightly more difficult than the Field *Nocturne in Bb*, it should be taught prior to the Chopin *Nocturnes*.

| Grieg | *Wedding-Day at Troldhaugen,* | Frederick Harris |
| | *op. 65, no. 6* | |

*Wedding-Day at Troldhaugen*, composed for Grieg's silver wedding anniversary, can be a "pupil saver" piece at the high school level. The rhythmic left hand accompaniment under a spirited right hand melody make it one of Grieg's most famous piano solos. The ABA *Coda* structure facilitates memorization. The slow and beautiful B section musically depicts a renewal of the wedding vows.

| Heller | *Celebrate Heller* (Hisey, ed.) | Frederick Harris |

Stephen Heller's studies in opp. 45, 46, and 47 are ideal preparation for the harder character pieces of Schumann, Mendelssohn, and others. This edition contains studies not in the older Schirmer edition, *Fifty Selected Studies* (Oesterele, ed.) and clearly identifies opus sources. Students look forward to playing the *Study in D minor, op. 45, no. 15* (subtitled *Warrior Song*) because of the brilliant sounding chordal texture in brisk dotted rhythms.

| Liszt | *Celebrate Liszt* (Hisey, ed.) | Frederick Harris |
|---|---|---|
| | *En rêve (Nocturne or Dreaming),* *S. 207* | |

As with Brahms, much of Liszt's piano writing technically represents a very advanced level. However, several late works are of moderate difficulty and interesting to study from a harmonic viewpoint. This short piece utilizes a dominant pedal point, the damper pedal and upper register of the keyboard, and long treble trills to create a marvelous floating sound. Other teaching possibilities, all in this volume, include *Four Short Piano Pieces, S. 192, Consolations: Six pensées poetiques (Six poetic thoughts), S. 172, La lugubre gondola* (The Mournful Gondola), *S. 200/2*, and at a more advanced level, the *Concert Étude, no. 3, Un sospiro, S. 144/3*.

| MacDowell | *Twelve Studies, op. 39* | Any Standard Edition |
|---|---|---|

MacDowell's collection, *12 Études for the Development of Technique and Style*, contains some of his most popular compositions including *Alla Tarantella, Hungarian*, and *Shadow Dance*. In particular, *Alla Tarantella* contains right hand eighth-note figures over left hand chords. Special attention must be given to the crossing hands texture and right hand four-octave chromatic scale in the B section.

| Mendelssohn | *Celebrate Mendelssohn* (Hisey, ed.) | Frederick Harris |
|---|---|---|

Mendelssohn composed 48 *Songs without Words* organized into eight different opus numbers. Two *Songs*, worthy of mention on any recommended list of teaching repertoire include the *Venetian Boat Song, op. 19, no. 6*, and the *Tarantella (Presto), op. 102, no. 3*. The latter uses a *staccato* texture that requires an easy wrist motion. This edition contains the most often played *Songs Without Words* and Mendelssohn's famous *Rondo Capriccioso, op. 14*.

| Schubert | *Celebrate Schubert* (Hisey, ed.) | Frederick Harris |
|---|---|---|
| | *Four Impromptus, op. 142* *(D 935)* | |

These *Impromptus* provide a wonderful port of entry to Schubert's early advanced writing. No. 2, in A-flat major, appeals to high school students because of the dignified hymn-like opening and the flowing triplets in the dramatic B section that shift between major and minor and climax in a brilliant *fortissimo*. Though the entire piece is in three, notice the consistent rhythmic emphasis on beat two much like a Baroque *Sarabande*. Blocking chord patterns in the B section assists in securing position shifts and fingerings. Other Schubert possibilities that secondary students frequently learn and perform would include selections from the six *Moments musicaux, op. 94/D 780* as well as the *Four Impromptus, op. 90/D 899* (specifically no. 2 in E-flat and no. 3 in G-flat), and individual movements from the less difficult *Sonata in A Major, op. 120/D 664*.

| Schubert | *Twelve Ländler, D790/op. 171* | Frederick Harris |

Schubert wrote over 400 short dances organized somewhat haphazardly in different collections. This opus, however, is one of the few dance collections that remains intact as intended by the composer. The diversity of melodic ideas and accompaniment patterns combined with astonishing key relationships make this opus incredibly rewarding to learn and perform.

| Schumann | *Celebrate Schumann* (Hisey, ed.) | Frederick Harris |
| | *Wilder Reiter* (Wild Rider) | |

This edition includes an interesting variant (written by Schumann) of this enormously popular intermediate solo. In the variant, Schumann treats the return of the A section differently, making the piece slightly harder. Schumann's entire *Album for the Young* should be remembered for the many outstanding intermediate solos including *Soldier's March, Happy Farmer, First Loss,* and *Knight Rupert.*

| Schumann | *Kinderszenen* | Frederick Harris |
| | (Scenes from Childhood), *op. 15* | |

Selected movements of the *Kinderszenen,* such as *About Strange Lands and People* and *Important Event,* may be individually taught to students. *About Strange Lands and People* uses a three-voice texture, bass, moving eighths shared between the hands, and right hand melody, similar to Grieg's *Arietta, op. 12. Important Event* is a short, robust sounding piece with brilliant left hand octaves in the middle section. Both of these scenes use a descending melodic tetrachord that musically unifies the entire set.

| Schumann | *Fantasiestücke* | Frederick Harris |
| | (Fantasy Pieces), *op. 12* | |

*Fantasiestücke* represents one of Schumann's most famous collections. From these eight pieces, teachers often assign *Warum?, Grillen,* and *Aufschwung* to secondary students. The impressive *Grillen* uses an ABA[1] sonata-like structure with aggressive chordal textures intermixed with jumping position shifts. The B section (development) contrasts with slower lyrical material.

| Tchaikovsky | *Album for the Young, op. 39* | Peters |

For the intermediate student, selections from Tchaikovsky's *Album for the Young* are a must. Well-known titles from this opus include *Mazurka, Dolly's Funeral* and *French Song.* The *Mazurka* right hand melody contains dotted rhythms and second beat accents--perfect study material leading to Chopin's *Mazurkas.* Another Tchaikovsky teaching possibility is the *Seasons, op. 37a,* specifically no. 6, *June (Barcarole).*

# Suggested Romantic Anthologies

*Celebration Series Perspectives,*                          Frederick Harris
    Repertoire Albums 5-10 (List C)

*Contemporaries of Schumann* (Hermann, ed.)                Hinrichsen

*Late Romantic Treasures* (Banowetz, ed.)                        Kjos

*Masters of the Romantic Period* (Hinson, ed.)                 Alfred

*Style and Interpretation, Vol. 4* (Ferguson, ed.)             Oxford

# CHAPTER 26

## An Approach to Twentieth Century Music and Beyond

### William Heiles

Although music of the twentieth century differs from earlier music in many ways, its continuity with the past far outweighs these differences. The harmonic language of twentieth-century music is not a break with the nineteenth century but a logical extension of it. Seemingly new twentieth-century rhythmic practices may have roots in traditional *tempo rubato* and cadenza performance or even reach back to the Middle Ages and Renaissance. The interest shown by many twentieth-century composers in folk and indigenous music from Europe, the Americas (including American jazz), Asia, and Africa has a precedent in the nationalism of late nineteenth-century art music.

Although composers look to the musical past for influence and inspiration, they interpret the past in light of the present and from unique points of view. For example, Ravel's *Sonatine* reinterprets the Classical sonata and sonatina from an early twentieth-century vantage point; Schönberg's piano pieces continue and modify the Romantic character piece; Ives' sonatas explore New England's traditional popular and religious music in the light of late Romanticism and a strikingly modern imagination; Ligeti's *Etudes* bring Romantic and Impressionistic piano technique into contact with a new rhythmic polyphony. Twentieth-century composers, like all composers, seek not merely to entertain but also to engage, challenge, and move performers and listeners. They wish to be understood, but not *too* easily! And they take pride in their craft.

As pianists and teachers, therefore, we should approach twentieth-century music in the same way we do music of earlier centuries. This means, first of all, knowing the major repertoire, whether or not we actually teach it. All of us are familiar with major works (not only keyboard works) of Bach, Mozart, Haydn, Beethoven, Schubert, Schumann, Chopin, Liszt, and Brahms, and have studied and played representative pieces by these composers. To teach twentieth-century piano music effectively we need a similar familiarity with composers such as Debussy, Ravel, Bartok, Stravinsky, Hindemith, Prokofiev, Berg, Schönberg, Webern, Ives, Copland, Barber, Carter, and Ligeti. We should have heard music by many of these twentieth-century giants, and we should have played representative pieces by at least a few of them. Some of these composers have written beginning- and intermediate-level piano music; all of them are essential to a realistic perspective on piano music of our century.

Choosing teaching (and performing) repertoire involves utilitarian decisions: For example, is this piece the right level of difficulty for my student (or will it fit well on my next recital program)? But the selection also involves value judgments: For example, is this piece *worth* teaching (or playing)? Earlier generations of pianists and teachers have made such judgments again and again, gradually determining what repertoire has withstood the test of time and what has not. As we make our own judgments regarding music of our era, gradually determining what repertoire will survive beyond us, we bear an inescapable responsibility to future generations of pianists and teachers.

The criteria that determine the *value* (as opposed to the mere *utility*) of teaching repertoire are timeless. A piece has value not because it uses some particular compositional or pianistic technique but only to the extent it rises above that technique to create a significant musical experience. To judge the value of a piece you are considering teaching, you might ask yourself questions like these:

- Do I myself enjoy playing this piece? After playing it once, do I want to play it again, better?

- If I play through this piece during the day, do I remember something about it that evening or the next day?

- Does the content of the piece justify the level of complexity? Is there an underlying musical motivation that I can convey to a student? Is there an interpretive richness that allows the piece to be approached in more than one way?

- Do I admire the composer's craftsmanship?

- Does the piece connect with and reinterpret the musical past in meaningful ways? On the other hand, does it merely repeat an already well-established musical style or experiment merely for the sake of experimentation?

- Is the piece written well for the piano as an instrument? Do I enjoy the *feel* of playing it? Will it help students acquire and improve technical skills that they can apply to other music, including eighteenth- and nineteenth-century music?

The pedagogical value of any music depends on the interpretive and technical challenges it poses for the player. In twentieth-century piano music these challenges, though new in some respects, are often extensions of those already present in earlier periods. The nineteenth century's emphasis on piano virtuosity has been continued and heightened. In fact, sheer enjoyment of motion is available in twentieth-century piano music as never before. Debussy's "*L'isle joyeuse*", "*Reflets dans l'eau*", "*Poissons d'or*", and "*Feux d'artifice*," for example, require unprecedented technical spontaneity and flexibility. Ravel's highly sophisticated piano writing calls for rational planning of every aspect of technique on a level that is both meticulous and adventurous. Many of Prokofiev's piano works require an athletic, almost machine-like, rhythmic precision. Later twentieth-century composers, while continuing these approaches, also invent (and often subsequently discard) novel ways of attacking the keyboard and other parts of the piano.

Timbre has been a primary musical element in the twentieth century, leading to an extraordinary interest in the piano's various sonorities. All three pedals have been exploited with great effect. (The *sostenuto* pedal, however, is not used in Debussy and Ravel!) Dynamics also appear with a greater range, precision, and subtlety than ever before. Similarly, accents and subtle gradations of accents have become more important than ever (consider Bartok's discriminating notation of them).

From Debussy onward (see "*Minstrels*", for example), a flexible and varied articulation reclaims the important role it played in Baroque keyboard music. Most twentieth-century composers take care to indicate dynamics, pedaling, and articulation precisely. (Do not assume legato unless specifically indicated!) This precision, along with the rhythmic and harmonic unfamiliarity of more recent music, means that pianists must study the scores with greater thoroughness than they may (unfortunately) be used to doing with earlier music.

Students approaching twentieth-century piano music tend to be most troubled by two kinds of problems; rhythmic complexity and the difficulty of memorization.

## Rhythmic Difficulties

Rhythmic complexity did not begin with twentieth-century music. The pacing of a Beethoven sonata and the rubato in a Chopin ballade or mazurka require great rhythmic sensitivity. But the counting-out of notated duration in most eighteenth- and nineteenth-century music seems elementary compared with newer music. In the twentieth-century, as the common-practice harmonic system has loosened or dissolved completely, the impact of harmonic forces on rhythm has correspondingly weakened. To achieve rhythmic interest composers have naturally tended to notate more complex rhythms that demand more counting skills from performers.

Counting skills can be learned with practice. These are the most important ones:

- While the pulse remains at the same tempo, switch from one kind of subdivision to another. For example, while maintaining quarter notes at a steady tempo, switch back and forth between pairs of eighth notes and eighth-note triplets, or between eighth-note triplets and sixteenth-note quintuplets.

- While the subdivision remains at the same tempo, combine different numbers of subdivisions to form pulses of different lengths. This technique underlies Bartok's "additive" rhythms (e.g., the Bulgarian Dances from *Mikrokosmos,* Vol. VI).

- Subdivide the same pulse in two different ways at the same time. For example, play two against three or three against two, five against three or three against five, seven against three or three against seven, and so forth.

Playing polyrhythms, that is, combining different subdivisions of the same pulse, is the most difficult of these three skills. The most common polyrhythm in nineteenth-century music is two against three, in which the player counts the *three* and fits the second note of the *two* into it. A three-against-two (in which the player counts the *two* and fits both the second and third notes of the *three* into it) is more difficult. Most piano students have trouble with m. 66 of Debussy's "*Reflets dans l'eau*" (see example 1) or m. 36 of Gershwin's *Second Prelude* (see example 2). In each of these cases the problem can be solved by translating the larger triplet mentally into two smaller triplets with ties (see examples 3 and 4).

Example 1

Example 2

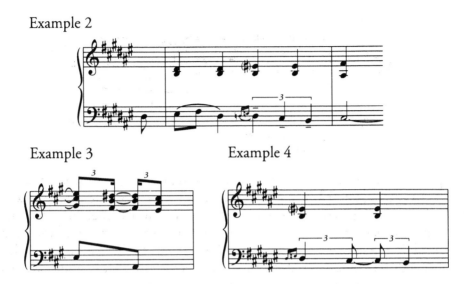

Example 3                          Example 4

With a more complex polyrhythm, the procedure remains the same: To play five in the time of three, for example, a pianist can mentally translate the large quintuplet into three quintuplets, each one-third as long, again using ties. (It isn't necessary to count to 15, only to 5; see example 5).

Example 5

Polyrhythms should be approached intuitively and physically as well as arithmetically and mentally. A good method is to practice the individual hands or voices separately at first, emphasizing the physical feel of each rhythm. Then put the two rhythms together, first playing either one of them silently while letting the other one sound. Some calculated "cheating" can be helpful at this stage; for example, the first three notes of a five-against-two, as in the Bartok improvisations, Op. 20, no. 6 (see example 6) can be played as a "lazy" or dragged triplet (this is quite appropriate to the tipsy feeling of the Bartok passage). In m. 13 of Samuel Barber's Excursion No. 3 (see example 7) you might approach the left-hand quintuplet by first

Example 6

Example 7

*senza ped.*

playing four even eighth notes against the right hand, leaving out the last B-flat. Then play the measure several more times, "rushing" the left hand by different degrees, until you are able to "rush" it just enough so that the third left-hand note comes between the two sixteenth notes of the right hand. If the left hand continues playing the rest of the quintuplet in this "rushed" tempo, the last B-flat should fit comfortably between the last two right-hand sixteenths. (This intuitive approach to a polyrhythm will work best if you have first figured out, using elementary fractions, how the notes of the two hands align with each other.)

Counting skills can be practiced away from the piano, of course, by tapping or clapping with the hands or feet and counting aloud. Alone or in combination, the skills discussed above suffice for almost all twentieth-century music. And once learned, they enhance the player's rhythmic awareness in eighteenth- and nineteenth-century music as well.

## Memorization

For most pianists, twentieth-century music is harder to memorize than music of the Classic and Romantic periods. The harmonic language is less predictable, the rhythm more complex. Phrasing is less symmetrical and, as in Bach, phrases tend to overlap one another, rather than separating clearly. But, fundamentally, the process of memorization is the same in all music. The skills a player develops in memorizing twentieth-century music will be useful for memorizing music of all other periods.

Memorization is not a separate process but rather an aspect of total learning. Like other aspects of learning, it takes place gradually throughout a pianist's experience with a piece. From the earliest stages, any note that isn't sightread at the moment it is played must be either remembered from a previous sight-reading (perhaps with the aid of some cue in the score) or predicted on the basis of recognized patterns. Because patterns in twentieth-century music are less familiar than in older music, prediction is less useful; therefore memory becomes the principal alternative to sight-reading (for this reason, in fact, some pianists find twentieth-century music *easier* to memorize than more traditional music.)

A player can monitor and encourage the continuous process of memorization long before being ready to play without the score. After some experience with a new piece, close your eyes (at least figuratively) and ask yourself what you remember about it. Pursue general observations first. What can you remember, in general, about the *harmonic* language? What tonality or tonalities, if any, are present? Is the harmony primarily chromatic or diatonic? Do certain intervals seem to predominate? What are the important *rhythmic* characteristics? What are the *textures?* Where (on what pages, on what parts of the page) do climaxes or other important *formal* events occur? What are the main musical ideas (themes, motives) and what can you remember about them? If you can't remember the exact notes, can you remember shapes or other characteristics? After asking yourself general questions like these, then see whether you can remember any more specific details—for example, the beginning, the ending, or some unusual event during the piece. Repeat this self-examination from time to time as you continue to work with the piece. Gradually the gaps in your memory will close.

Encourage your memory to make use of cues. Can you play both hands in a passage while reading only one (covering one staff so that you cannot see it)? Seeing one measure, can you play the next one or the next few without seeing them? Gradually expand your ability to remember *without* cues. Can you begin playing from memory at the most important structural points (double-bars, climaxes, recaps)? After any cadence? After any phrase ending? At the beginning of any measure? Can you play either hand without the other at any point of the piece? Your memory is most likely to grow through these stages if your practice habits include beginning at many different spots and frequently playing hands separately.

*Physical* memory, crucial in all music but perhaps most crucial in music of the twentieth century, can take place successfully only if we fully understand the physical processes of playing a piece. This means, to begin with, knowing the fingering. Often, when a passage refuses to settle into our memory or our fingers, we discover that we don't really know how we're fingering it. In complicated passages try reciting out loud the finger-numbers in each hand. Do not play—do not move your hands or fingers at all: you will then be engaged in mental practice, which is one of the best approaches to learning and memory. (It is no paradox that the physical processes of playing can be fully understood only through mental effort.) Larger-scale physical processes—hand positions and motions, gestures and choreography in general—must be thought out just as carefully. We need to continually ask ourselves questions about the physical aspect of playing a piece, just as we do regarding the interpretive aspect; in fact the physical aspect of playing must be directly, intrinsically, related to the interpretive aspect or else technique is meaningless.

In twentieth-century music, as in all music, do not try to memorize a piece by first perfecting measure 1, then adding the measure 2, and so forth. A performer learns and memorizes a piece not linearly but *spatially.* The process is like a painter working on a canvas. First the outline is conceived and sketched; then, as the artist's attention moves freely between areas of the canvas and between closer and more distant views, the relationships among the various parts of the work become gradually clearer, the details are filled in, and the painting takes shape.

Effective memorization depends on, and in turn supports, the gradual development of musical understanding and technical control. In music, as in life, we remember best those things that are most important to us, that stimulate our thoughts and feelings. If we have convictions, or at least opinions, about how notes, chords, and phrases should sound, we will be more likely to remember them and (more importantly) we will play them better as we try to communicate these convictions to listeners.

As performers, we discover, renew, and broaden our convictions about musical interpretation through experimentation, self-questioning, and decision-making; we need to keep these processes alive in ourselves and inculcate them in our students. Despite the relative precision and thoroughness of twentieth-century musical notation, the most important and intimate decisions are still left to the performer's imagination. The score, as always, is not a series of commands but rather an invitation to collaborate in the composer's endeavor.

There are many important reasons to play and teach twentieth-century music, but perhaps the most important is its essential oneness with music of previous centuries. The best twentieth-century works reaffirm traditional musical values in untraditional ways; the open-mindedness, inventiveness, and sense of adventure that these compositions require of performers and teachers is an invitation to rediscover the newness of great music of the past.

# CHAPTER 27

## Essential Modern Repertoire for the Middle School and High School Student

### Reid Alexander

## Introduction

Such a wide range of composers, musical styles, and strands of literature exist for the twentieth and to date twenty-first centuries, that it is challenging to assimilate a "must list" for teaching purposes or even give proper recognition to the many deserving composers from the period. However, one intermediate set recommended for the study of alternate notation forms is the three-volume collection titled *Amusements* (Frederick Harris) by Stephen Chatman. The carefully graded volumes include pieces using chance, 12-tone, whole tone, random pitch, and cluster writing techniques. More importantly, the music is attractive to hear and serves as interesting, even novel studio recital material for younger students. Elementary students can easily work from level one which has titles such as *Lonesome Cowboy* and *Monkey Business*. Secondary students will be challenged by the musical events in level 3.

## Suggested Repertoire by Composer (alphabetized by composer)

| Composer | Title or Volume | Publisher |
|---|---|---|
| Samuel Barber | *Love Song (1924)* | Alfred |

The most accessible of Barber's solo compositions, this little known gem is in spirit a song without words at the late intermediate level.

Samuel Barber          *Excursions, op. 20*                    Schirmer

The four *Excursions* represent advanced material feasible for the skilled high school pianist. The first, written in a rondo format, is very appealing because of the left hand perpetual motion *ostinato* imitating the boogie-woogie style. The fourth, a Hoedown in duple meter, is also recommended.

Béla Bartók          *Celebrate Bartók* (Hisey, ed.)      Frederick Harris
                     *Bagatelles, op. 6* (Sz. 38)

Usually only one or two pages in length, the less familiar fourteen *Bagatelles* characterize Bartók's very early writing (1908). Busoni commented, upon hearing the pieces, "Finally, something new." These miniatures generally increase in difficulty and vary considerably in texture and compositional approach. Numbers 1, 3, 4, and 6 are excellent for exploring the collection.

Béla Bartók          *Rumanian Folk Dances, Sz. 56*      Frederick Harris

These six dances, written in 1915, provide an excellent introduction to Bartók's music. Individual dances can be studied or the set can be taught in its entirety (approximately 5 minutes in length). The last two *Allegro* dances are noticeably more difficult than the first four. Transcriptions for piano and violin as well as string orchestra popularized the work.

Béla Bartók          *Sonatina, Sz. 55*                  Frederick Harris

Bartók's *Sonatina* comprises three movements *(Bagpipers, Bear Dance, Finale)* and is closer in difficulty to Ravel's *Sonatine* than earlier classical sonatinas. The work was fashioned on five Hungarian folk tunes distributed throughout the movements. The *Finale* is the most challenging musically and technically. Other Bartók works often studied by high school pianists include the *Suite, op. 14, Sz. 62, Dances in Bulgarian Rhythm (Mikrokosmos, Book VI, Sz. 107/6), Allegro Barbaro, Sz. 49, and Three Rondos on Slovak Folktunes, Sz. 84.*

Tony Caramia          *Adventures in Jazz Piano, Vol. I, II*      Bärenreiter

Written by one of America's foremost composers of jazz teaching pieces, *Adventures in Jazz Piano* is a most attractive collection that includes a wide variety of styles for the intermediate student including blues, boogie-woogie, and ragtime.

Aaron Copland          *The Cat and the Mouse*            Boosey and Hawkes
                       *(Scherzo humoristique)*

One of Copland's most successful piano solos, this piece was written very early in his career when he studied with Nadia Boulanger. The musical imagery and programmatic story line make the work incredibly popular with students. Not marked in some editions, use the *sostenuto* pedal for the low tone beginning in m. 72. The damper pedal can then change with the shifting harmonies above.

| Aaron Copland | *Four Piano Blues* | Boosey and Hawkes |

Similar to Barber's *Excursions* but slightly less difficult, these four pieces are superb for the student with an interest in jazz. Composed between 1927 and 1946, each requires a feel for the blues style. The first, *Freely Poetic*, is highly recommended. For smaller hands, redistribute the wide left hand reaches between the hands.

| Claude Debussy | *Celebrate Debussy, Vol. I* (Hisey, ed.) *Page d'album* | Frederick Harris |

One of the last piano solos Debussy composed (1915), *Page d'album* was written to raise money for the French red cross during World War I. Debussy inscribed the manuscript with the words, *Le Vêtement du Blessé* (The Dressing of the Wounded). A stunningly beautiful slow waltz of only one page, it is an ideal piece for introducing Debussy.

| Claude Debussy | *The Little Shepherd* | Frederick Harris |

*Doctor Gradus ad Parnassum* and *Golliwog's Cakewalk* are well-known movements from Debussy's *Children's Corner*. However, the easier *Little Shepherd* can be used to introduce Debussy's style. The opening flute-like theme conjures up musical imagery and the prolonged cadential chords allow the player to listen to lingering harmonies.

| Claude Debussy | *Préludes* (Book I) | Frederick Harris |

Ideal for exploring Debussy's prélude style, the *Des pas sur la neige* score reveals subtle voicing challenges along with triplet and sixteenth cross rhythms. Another possibility, *La fille aux cheveux de lin* contains beautiful pentatonic sounds and streams of parallel chords for which Debussy is famous. Assign difficult préludes such as *La cathédrale engloutie* after the student has had some experience with the Debussy style. At a more advanced level, consider the two *Arabesques*, *Prélude* to *Suite Bergamasque*, *Pour le Piano*, and the *Estampes* (III. *Jardins sous la pluie*).

| Norman Dello Joio | *Lyric Pieces for the Young* | Marks/Hal Leonard |

This collection contains six early intermediate teaching pieces, each a miniature gem. *The Prayer of the Matador* uses a habanera rhythm throughout and possesses a marvelous Spanish flavor.

| George Gershwin | *Gershwin at the Keyboard* | Alfred |

Pianists often teach Gershwin's *Preludes* and the *Rhapsody in Blue*. The less familiar 18-song arrangements represent Gershwin's own written-out improvisations of popular show tunes. Technically less difficult arrangements include *Do It Again* and *Somebody Loves Me*. Most of the song arrangements are two pages in length with the well-known *The Man I Love* and *I Got Rhythm* longer and considerably more challenging.

Alberto Ginastera    *Twelve American Preludes*    Carl Fischer

Ginastera made a lasting contribution to the teaching literature with these preludes. They focus on a variety of textures and sounds and range in difficulty from intermediate to early advanced. *For Accents* and *Sadness* introduce the set nicely. The rhythmic and brilliant sounding *Creole Dance* closes a student recital perfectly. A more advanced recommendation is the gorgeous slow middle movement, *Danza de la moza donosa* (Dance of the Beautiful Maiden), from the set titled *Danzas Argentinas*.

Scott Joplin    *Celebrate Joplin* (Hisey, ed.)    Frederick Harris

Secondary students benefit technically and musically by studying the compositions of this talented American composer. This edition includes favorites such as *Maple Leaf Rag* as well as lesser-known titles deserving of more attention.

Dimitry Kabalevsky    *Twenty-Four Preludes, op. 38*    MCA

Kabalevsky is best known for his many elementary and early intermediate teaching pieces such as *Clowns* (op. 39, no. 20) and *Toccatina* (op. 27, no. 12). Composed during the second world war, this set of *Preludes* represents Kabalevsky's advanced writing and borrows the key arrangement used by Chopin in his preludes. Numbers 1 and 15 serve as an excellent introduction to this opus.

Aram Khachaturian    *Toccata*    Schirmer

Khachaturian is famous for pieces in the intermediate set, *Adventures of Ivan*, such as *Ivan Sings* (i.e., Melody) as well as this more advanced *Toccata*. A virtual warhorse of the preparatory repertoire, the *Toccata* appeals because of the energetic rhythms, repeating technical patterns, and brilliant *forte* colors. Specific attention must be given to the complex rhythms in the middle section.

Olivier Messiaen    *Huit préludes pour piano (1929)*    Durand
                     *Prélude no. 7 (Gentle Sorrow)*

This two-page *prélude* is definitely approachable by secondary students and useful for introducing this French composer's style. Not nearly as complex and dissonant as his later piano works such as the *Vingt Regards sur l'Enfant Jésus*, the highly expressive writing uses repeating material and demonstrates the use of mixed meter.

Robert Muczynski    *Collected Piano Pieces*    Schirmer
                    *Six Preludes, op. 6*

These moderately difficult preludes have earned significant recognition. Recommended for introducing the set, the first prelude uses a bright ascending melody over left hand *staccato* and accented chords. The sixth is a brilliant *forte* and *staccato* study incorporating right hand chromatic melodies over left hand bass syncopations and octave accents.

| Linda Niamath | *A Zoo For You* | Frederick Harris |

Linda Niamath is one of Canadian's premiere educational composers. *A Zoo For You* contains 10 highly original early intermediate solos similar to Previn's *Impressions*. A favorite among students, *Penguins* uses A-flat and C major tonalities and a left hand *ostinato* interspersed with sliding chromatic tritone passages.

| Christopher Norton | *Microjazz Collection* | Boosey & Hawkes |

The British composer Norton (born New Zealand) has made a significant contribution to contemporary teaching literature through the multiple levels of *Microjazz* and the more recent *Connections* (Frederick Harris) and *American Popular Piano* (Novus Music). He explores a kaleidoscope of contrasting styles blending contemporary sounds with jazz and pop.

| Octavio Pinto | *Scenas Infantis* | Schirmer |

These five descriptive miniatures epitomize attractive explorations of childhood scenes. No. 1, *Run, Run!*, is a triadic study which necessitates a loose, flexible wrist. No. 5, *Hobby-horse*, uses energetic rhythms and sounds more difficult than the score suggests. The ending broken chord patterns impress student recital audiences.

| Francis Poulenc | *Mouvements Perpétuels* | Chester |

The opening movement uses a pleasing left hand *ostinato* under a charming right hand descending melody. The shorter, middle movement, *Trés modéré*, requires careful voicing. The final movement, *Alerte*, is the most challenging.

| André Previn | *Impressions* | Alfred |

Previn's 20 *Impressions* (character pieces), unfamiliar to many pianists, are appropriate for the progressing intermediate student. The sounds are very original and the writing compact. Suggested titles include *Roundup*, *Poodles*, and *Desert Flowers*.

| Sergei Prokofiev | *Music for Children, op. 65* | Boosey & Hawkes |

One of Prokofiev's most famous collections, *Music for Children* contains well-known late intermediate level pieces such as *The Rain and the Rainbow*, *Tarantella*, and *Waltz*. The opening of the *Waltz* is similar to Grieg's *Waltz in A Minor, op. 12*. *The Rain and the Rainbow* presents wonderful imagery. The left hand shifts physically outline rainbows in the air.

| Sergei Rachmaninoff | *Preludes, op. 3, no. 2; op. 23; op. 32* | Boosey & |
| | *Prelude in C-sharp Minor, op. 3, no. 2* | Hawkes |
| | *Prelude in G Minor, op. 23, no. 5* | |

These two preludes are accessible to skilled students. An early work, the immensely popular C-sharp minor is one of the most often performed works in the entire literature. Care must be taken to achieve *forte* colors without attacking the keyboard and to achieve technical fluency in the contrasting middle section. The more complex G minor texture is more difficult than it appears because of the arpeggios and subtle voicing required in the B section. Beyond these two preludes, consider the witty *Humoresque, op. 10, no. 5.*

Maurice Ravel          *Prélude*                    Any Standard Edition

This two-page miniature in ternary form (ABA¹*Coda*) may be the only solo piano composition by Ravel accessible to the late intermediate student. Originally, it was written as a sight-reading piece for Paris conservatory auditions. The beautiful writing mixes elegant melody with interesting harmonies throughout.

Maurice Ravel          *Sonatine*                   Any Standard Edition
                       *I: Modéré*

Much of Ravel's piano music is too difficult for secondary students. The early advanced *Modéré* movement to the *Sonatine* is a notable exception and represents a rare example of the sonata form in an impressionistic style. The use of the term *sonatina* refers more to the brevity of the work than a simplistic level of difficulty.

Vladimir Rebikov       *Silhouettes, op. 31*                    Alfred

Known as the father of Russian impressionism, Rebikov's use of whole tone and pentatonic colors prepares younger students for impressionism. Familiar titles from this early intermediate set include *Shepherd Playing On His Pipe* and *Playing Soldiers.*

Erik Satie             *3 Gymnopédies*                          Alfred

These three forward looking compositions, which share thematic material, have a unique, distinctive sound and should be remembered as possible teaching material. Each requires careful voicing and pedaling.

Arnold Schönberg       *Sechs kleine Klavierstücke, op. 19*    Universal

Suitable for the serious secondary student, this opus represents the least difficult pieces of Schönberg's piano output. Though musically abstract, numbers 2 and 6 are quite easy technically and best for introducing the opus.

Dmitri Shostakovich    *Three Fantastic Dances, op. 5*         Alfred

Composed when Shostakovich was still a teenager, these three early advanced dances, arranged in a fast-slow-fast order, provide much variety. No. I (*Allegretto*) introduces the set with its rhythmic melody and left hand jumping bass all in a march-like texture and ABA structure. The second movement is a waltz and the latter resembles a lively polka incorporating clever harmonies.

Robert Starer          *Sketches in Color, Vol. I, II*          Alfred

These two sets (seven pieces each) of short sound explorations have gained significant recognition among pianists. Set two is more difficult than set one and the composer notes that the sketches may be performed without titles, individually or in groups.

Alexander Tcherepnin *Bagatelles, op. 5*          Any Standard Edition

Firmly entrenched in the 20th century late intermediate repertoire, these ten bagatelles individually can serve as contrasting recital material to earlier bagatelles by Beethoven. No. 1 (*Allegro marciale*) is best known for the *forte* martial-like texture, dissonant intervals, and brilliant octave texture.

Christos Tsitsaros     *Cinderella Suite*          Frederick Harris

Tsitsaros writes in a highly original and creative style. *Cinderella Suite* contains eight late intermediate programmatic pieces. Students musically can follow the fairy tale's story line by playing titles such as *The Dance of the Mice* and *At the Prince's Ball*. The titles are well suited for pre-collegiate recital programs. The lyrical *Cinderella's Sorrow* best introduces the collection.

Robert Vandall        Preludes, Book III          Alfred

Robert Vandall is known for his remarkable contribution of elementary solos and duets for younger students. Significantly more involved than his preludes in Books I/II, the seven preludes in the third book (each in a different key) display varied and original writing at the late intermediate to early advanced levels.

## Suggested Modern Anthologies

*12 x 11, Piano Music of 20th Century America* (Hinson, ed.)          Alfred

*Bravo Brazil!, Vols. I, II* (Appleby, ed.)          Kjos

*Celebration Series Perspectives,*          Frederick Harris
  Repertoire, Levels 5-10, Lists D/E

*Contemporary Piano Literature, Vols. I-VI*          Alfred
  (Clark and Goss, eds.)

*Impressionism* (Twelsiek, ed.)          Schott

*Music of our Time Series, Vols. I-VIII*          Waterloo

# CHAPTER 28

# Introducing Jazz to the Intermediate Student

## Geoffrey Haydon

Exposing piano students to jazz can be an eye opening experience for both teachers and students. From a pedagogical perspective, there is not yet an established method that enables one to acquire the knowledge and skills necessary to become a proficient jazz musician. Therefore, many teachers and students are unable to approach this idiom with the same confidence and determination they do with classical music. However, teachers can no longer ignore jazz or other types of popular music if they wish to offer students exposure to other genres of music besides those of the European tradition. The United States Congress has declared jazz a national treasure and many students are afforded opportunities to become involved with jazz. Including jazz in piano students' musical diet will:

1. Give them another reason to learn about chords, scales, rhythm, form, etc., for they cannot competently deal with this idiom without this kind of knowledge.

2. Give them more performing and/or career opportunities.

3. Enable them to learn the art of improvisation through the medium of jazz.

4. Enable those who become involved in the school jazz band the knowledge necessary to participate in a competent manner.

5. Provide motivation to stay involved with music after leaving the teaching studio.

6. Make piano teachers more marketable.

Piano teachers, no matter what age, can learn enough about jazz to competently teach it. With the kind of background that is necessary to teach classical music, teaching jazz may not be as difficult as it might seem; however, teaching jazz (as is the case with any other kind of music) should not be taken lightly. Much of jazz has to do with the concept of improvisation.

## What is Jazz Improvisation?

Jazz improvisation is the spontaneous expression of musical ideas according to a set of given rules based strictly or loosely on the jazz tradition. Many people think jazz musicians are free to do "whatever they please, whenever the please." In reality, there is much discipline involved in learning to become a competent jazz improviser. He/she must develop a deep understanding of the materials being used and a keen sense of time.

## Form

Before teaching jazz improvisation, teachers must become familiar with certain concepts that are of central importance to a jazz improviser. First, there is form. We teach form in classical music to better understand how composers organize the material in a composition. Jazz improvisers use form to keep track of where they are at any given moment in a composition. Most jazz improvisations are based on a given popular tune that is repeated as many times as desired. For example, George Gershwin's *I Got Rhythm* has been the basis for countless numbers of jazz improvisations. To simply play the melody is not considered improvisation. It is what happens after the melody has initially been played that is usually improvised. However, in order for all the musicians (assuming there is more than one) to stay together they must agree on a "road map" they will all follow. In the case of *I Got Rhythm*, its AABA 32-bar song form will be the "road map" that is cycled through many times until all those who wish to improvise have had their turn. [An analogy might be starting on a walk at your home and going around the block many times. Each street represents an A or B section and each time you return home you may either stop or continue around the block for another revolution.] Even though the melody may no longer be present, there is a chord progression that helps the musicians keep their place. If the chord progression begins to change (this can happen sometimes), then the timing of each section (8 measures per letter, for example) still keeps everyone together. Even today, many jazz improvisations follow one of three common forms: 1) AABA (32 bars) [such as *Somewhere Over The Rainbow*]; 2) ABAC (32 bars) [such as *All Of Me*]; 3) AAB (12 bars) [any 12 bar blues such as *Blue Monk*, *C Jam Blues*, or *Now's The Time*]. By mastering form, high quality jazz musicians from different parts of the world who may not even speak the same language can immediately begin playing a composition without rehearsal and sound as though they have been playing together for years.

## Jazz Syntax

Another important concept is syntax. All jazz musicians not only need to learn how to read traditional notation but also interpret chord symbols. Even though jazz history is full of people who aurally learned the tradition and often never learned to read music at all, today's jazz musician can benefit greatly from developing good reading skills. Moreover, it is more difficult to teach jazz to students who don't know how to read music. Many jazz compositions are written in a *lead sheet* format that features a combination of traditional notation and chord symbols. Lead sheets can be intimidating for classical musicians because most of what is actually played is not on the page. The page only offers a general musical outline and it is therefore up to the performer(s) to complete the picture musically speaking. For keyboard players, it is extremely important they learn the content of each chord symbol because more often than not, they will be expected to provide the harmonic content of the chord progression of a jazz composition. However, any improviser will want the content of his/her improvisation to be compatible with the relevant chord progression. This cannot be accomplished without either intellectually or aurally knowing the content of chords.

## Chord Voicing

Keyboard players not only need to know about chord content, but also about how to voice chords. Voicing chords, in the jazz sense, is the art of arranging the notes of a chord for a certain kind of sound. For example, a Cmaj$^{7(9)}$ (C$^{\Delta 7(9)}$) chord contains the notes C, E, G, B, and D. However, a jazz keyboard player will almost never play this chord with all the notes arranged in thirds in root position. Actually, there are many possible ways to voice a Cmaj$^{7(9)}$ chord, most of which do not contain the root since it is assumed the root will be supplied by a bass player (See example 2).

Example 1                    Example 2

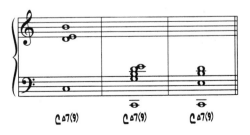

Voicing is a concept of which all jazz musicians are aware, but keyboard players must master this important skill. Actually voicing is one of the determining qualities when assessing style. The way Mozart voiced major triads is quite different from that of Chopin; and different from that of Brahms, etc.

# Chord-Scale Relationship

Associated with chord knowledge comes chord-scale relationship. Improvising jazz musicians match a particular scale or group of scales to a particular given chord. Moreover, they are not limited to the major and three forms of minor scales. The Greek modes, whole tone scales, and many others are also considered viable scales from which to derive improvisational material. Therefore, in dealing with a chord progression in a given composition, jazz improvisers need to have scales available for immediate recall that relate to each chord. Of course, it doesn't happen overnight, but it has to begin somewhere. For example, the C major scale can be played over a Cmaj$^7$ chord; then patterns can be formed using the notes of a C major scale. The same procedure can be done with a C Lydian mode over a Cmaj$^7$ chord, a C natural minor or C dorian scale over a Cmin$^7$ chord, or a C mixolydian mode over a C$^7$ chord. This kind of information is of premier importance for jazz improvisers.

# Jazz Rhythm

Another concept for jazz musicians is rhythm. All musicians, of course, must deal with this concept. However, in addition to what all musicians must master regarding rhythm, jazz musicians have the added complexity of mastering swing rhythm. The term swing can appear to be vague at times due to the fact that it has several different musical connotations. First, there is the capitalized "Swing" that refers to a style and/or historic period of jazz known more completely as "Big Band Swing." Second, there is a slang usage that usually indicates a general positive feeling towards something (i.e., "This band can really swing!"). Then there is the rhythmic connotation that specifically refers to a subdivision of the beat (i.e., swing eighth-note). Many books, arrangements, and/or methods of the past have described the swing eighth-note concept as an uneven subdivision of the beat that has a ratio of 2 to 1 with the first eighth-note getting the larger portion (See example 3).

Example 3

While it is sometimes true, it is actually not always the case. If it was, then jazz could be notated accurately. However, it cannot. The way an improviser chooses to "swing" the rhythm is dependent not only on the beat subdivision but also articulation. The result is a particular kind of "swing feel" unique to the individual performer. Charlie Parker's swing feel was different from that of Louis Armstrong; or from that of John Coltrane, etc. Even though each is different, their sense of swing is equally valid. All of these individuals learned swing rhythm by listening. Today's students can learn swing rhythm by both listening and studying it, and by learning to first sing using SCAT syllables. Then they can sing and play, transferring the swing feel from their voices to their instrument (See example 4).

Example 4

doo bah doo bah doo bah doo bah    doo

By using the syllable *doo* on the first eighth-note and *bah* on the second eighth note of each beat, a swing rhythm will occur more naturally. In opposition to what is normally taught in classical music, students must be taught to articulate swing eighth notes by emphasizing the second eighth note (off the beat) more than the first. Also, it is helpful to slur the second eighth note into the first eighth note thus grouping them across each beat. The proportion assigned to each of the two eighth notes is not important and generally ranges from a 1 to 1 ratio (equal) to beyond 3 to 1 (unequal). What IS important though is that the speed of the beat is not sacrificed and therefore remains consistent (in the groove). Many jazz students struggle with learning to create a swing feel without sacrificing the groove.

# Using the Ear

It has always been important that aspiring jazz musicians develop their aural abilities. They must continually improve their ability to identify aurally whatever is occurring at the moment. Then, they can react to whatever their ears encounter during a given improvisation. Because they will sometimes be providing the harmonic background for an improvising soloist, keyboard players especially need this skill so they will be equipped to react to what is being played at any given moment. The best way for students to develop their aural abilities is to begin using their ears as a means of identifying music. Methods by which ear training is taught at universities and conservatories have not proven themselves effective or reliable in seeing to it that the aural abilities of music majors significantly improve. However, find someone who has a good ear and it is likely this person has spent a significant amount of time "picking out music" by ear. It is granted some people do this more easily than others, but this skill CAN be acquired and developed. Piano teachers should require their students to learn familiar songs complete with harmonic accompaniment by ear. Christmas carols or nursery rhyme tunes are always a good place to begin since most students are familiar with this kind of music, and the melodies and harmonies are usually basic. After students can play a tune by ear, it is extremely helpful for them to transpose it to different keys. They will begin to learn what different keys feel, look (on the keyboard), and most importantly sound like.

Related to developing one's aural ability is the concept of listening. It is unreasonable for us to assume we could ever learn to play jazz without having at least heard it. The same is true for classical music. Our students should be made aware that listening to a live performance or recording can often answer many questions about their approach to learning music. It is astonishing to realize that many students think all the music is on the page. That is to say that they think all they need do is follow the directions on the page. However, this statement is even less true for jazz musicians since very little, including the notes, is written down. Therefore, it is important that our students be listening to jazz regularly if they wish to develop into jazz musicians.

## Jazz Styles

As they listen, students can become familiar with the different stylistic categories of jazz. The history of jazz has given birth to many different styles and today's jazz musician benefits greatly from acquiring knowledge about these styles. Some of these jazz styles include Be Bop, Big Band Swing, Dixieland, Latin, etc. If you think about it, this concept is also true of classical music. Knowing about the Baroque, Classical, Romantic, Impressionistic, etc. styles of music is beneficial in much the same way. Therefore, studying the history of jazz will benefit students in the same way acquiring knowledge about the history of classical music does. There are numerous jazz history texts available in libraries and bookstores. Each gives a different perspective so it is recommended that more than one be consulted. After becoming more knowledgeable about jazz history, one can achieve more depth by reading the biographies of jazz musicians of the past.

## 12 Bar Blues

Introducing the twelve-bar blues is a good way to escort students into the world of improvisation. The twelve-bar blues consists of a twelve-measure chord progression that can first be reduced to just three chords: $I^7$, $IV^7$, and

$V^7$. The basic chord progression is best organized in three four-measure units. The first four measures use only the $I^7$ chord; the second four measures use the $IV^7$ and $I^7$ chords; and the last four measures use the $V^7$, $IV^7$, and $I^7$ chords (See example 5). This progression is a good one to begin with because it is a basic twelve-bar blues chord progression that is easily recognized by Americans and many other cultures.

Example 5

This progression can be established with some kind of bass pattern. The following example uses a simple bass line for the twelve-bar blues when played in the key of C (see example 6).

The chords in example 6 correspond to the twelve-bar blues when played in the key of C. Notice all chords are dominant sevenths (major-minor seventh). The right hand chord voicings in example 6 represent one way the notes can be arranged for a more appropriate jazz sound. Examples 7 and 8 illustrate how root position chords can be re-arranged. In example 8, the bass is moved away from the right hand voicing, and the 3rd and 7th are combined with an extension tone (9th or 13th) to create a three-note right-hand chord voicing.

Example 6

Example 7

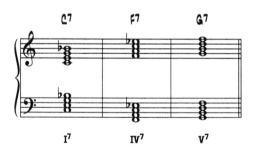

Example 8

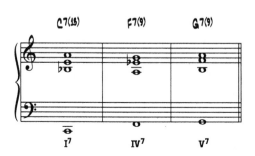

Once students are comfortable combining the right hand chords on the first beat of each measure with the left hand bass line, they can begin to "comp" the chords. "Comping" is an important aspect of chord accompaniment (in fact, "comp" is short for "accompany") all jazz keyboard players must learn. When keyboard players comp, they create (compose) various rhythms by jabbing chord voicings mostly off the beat (on the *bah*). If done tastefully, there will be plenty of space left for the improvising soloist. Example 9 below is one possible way the last four measures of a twelve-bar blues chorus might be comped.

Example 9

Over the chord progression the improvising soloist plays melodies using the blues scale for a source to choose notes. Example 10 gives the blues scale in the key of C.

Example 10

This blues scale "blankets" the entire twelve-measure progression. In other words, any of the notes in this blues scale will sound good at any time. It is not necessary to change to the F blues scale in measures 5-6 or the G blues scale in measure 9. After students are fluently able to play the blues scale up and down at least two octaves, have them pick out three adjacent notes in the blues scale and create interesting motives (usually called "riffs" by jazz and blues musicians, See example 11).

Example 11

# Learning Jazz Standards

Although the blues is an important aspect of jazz, it is only a small part of a much larger picture. Students must spend a portion of their practice time learning jazz standards. Jazz standards are compositions that have established themselves in the ever-growing body of standard jazz repertoire. Many of these compositions are "Tin Pan Alley" songs by American popular songwriters such as Jerome Kern, Irving Berlin, Cole Porter, George Gershwin, Richard Rodgers, Fats Waller and many others. Some are by jazz musicians such as Duke Ellington, Charlie Parker, Miles Davis, etc. Jazz standards are available in lead sheet format in fake books. After learning a jazz standard, jazz musicians should know internally (from memory) its form, melody, chord progression, and perhaps even lyrics (if there are any). After studying a significant amount of jazz standards, one begins to sense many similarities in the chord progressions. First, most harmonies include the third and the seventh as well as the option of including tones which extend beyond the octave (i.e., 9$^{ths}$, 11$^{ths}$, and 13$^{ths}$) or tones that are considered altered (i.e., raised or lowered 5$^{ths}$, raised or lowered 9$^{ths}$, raised 11$^{ths}$, lowered 13$^{ths}$). Secondly, the ii$^7$ – V$^7$ – I$^{\Delta 7}$ and ii$^{7(b5)}$ – V$^{7(b9)}$ – i$^7$ progressions are as common as the V$^7$ – I and V$^7$ – i progressions in classical music. In fact, through analysis if one circles all the ii$^7$, V$^7$, I$^{\Delta 7}$, ii$^{7(b5)}$, i$^7$ chords (essentially 4 different types of seventh chords) found in standard jazz tunes, very few chords will be left without a circle. Therefore, learning these basic chord progressions in every key makes the harmonic realization of jazz standards much easier.

# The ii$^7$ – V$^7$ – I$^{\Delta 7}$ Chord Progression

The ii$^7$ – V$^7$ – I$^{\Delta 7}$ progression consists of a minor seventh chord; followed by a dominant seventh chord; followed by a major seventh chord. Each chord's root is a perfect fifth below the preceding one. Learning this progression in every key makes the realization of jazz compositions much easier. In order to establish this progression, the minimum essentials each chord needs are the root, 3$^{rd}$, and 7$^{th}$ (See example 12):

Example 12

These chord-voicings can then be expanded to include the 5th, 9th, and 13th. Keyboard players should learn to play these chord-voicings with either the right hand (so a bass line can be provided) or the left hand when a bass player is present (leaving the right hand free to add extensions to the left hand chords or improvise a solo). Example 13 contains three-note chord-voicings with roots in the bass.

Example 13

After learning the above $ii^7 – V^7 – I^{\Delta 7}$ voicings in every key, one can apply them to chord progressions from jazz standards like the one below in example 14.

Example 14

Rather than choosing any one voicing and using it exclusively, it is best to establish smooth voice leading by using the closest position available. The voicings in the treble clef can be played by the right hand when a bass line needs to be played by the left hand. At other times, such as when a bass player is present, keyboard players can play the voicings in the treble clef with the left hand leaving the right hand free to play a prescribed melody or improvise a solo.

Keyboard players have to learn to play within many different contexts. They will find themselves in a big band, a combo, or by themselves as keyboard soloists. As soloists, keyboard players must supply the harmony, rhythm, and melody while only being given a lead sheet as a guide. At the professional level, this skill can be quite complex. However, the basic components are easily learned by students who already have some experience getting around the instrument. Since the 3rd and 7th are the most important tones in a seventh chord (perhaps with the exception of the root, although when sounded together, the 3rd and 7th can imply the root without it actually sounding), these tones should not normally be omitted. By using only these two tones combined with the bass and melody of a jazz composition, one can learn a basic approach to playing from a fake book. Normally all that is on the page is the melody and chords (See example 15).

Example 15

Example 16 below demonstrates the basic components needed to realize a lead sheet. It features the melody in the top stave, the 3rd and 7th of the relevant chord in the middle stave, and a bass line that uses the root and 5th of the relevant chord on beats one and three respectively to establish a rhythmic feeling of two beats to the bar. The top and middle staves should be played with the right hand, and the bottom stave with the left hand.

Example 16

Eventually one can comp the middle stave chord-voicings and move a few melody notes to the off-beat eighth note position to help establish a swing feel, and create a melodic bass line playing quarter notes changing the rhythmic feel to four beats to the bar (See example 17).

Example 17

Teachers can make use of instructional materials when teaching jazz. There are many kinds of books and/or methods available. Some address the art of improvisation; some address chord-voicings; some cover the jazz vocabulary (i.e. jazz theory); some are methods complete with play-along materials; and some contain transcriptions of well-known jazz artists. When considering what books are best suited to your needs, remember that no method or book will contain all that is needed. Any method or book can and should be used along with supplementary materials.

There is no mystery to learning to play jazz. It takes the same dedication and perseverance as any other kind of music. There are many ordinary people possessed with a modest amount of talent who have developed into wonderful jazz musicians. What these people have done is spend their practice time developing areas of musicianship vital to playing jazz. The following is a partial list of activities that helps lead to an eventual mastery of jazz.

- Listen to well-known jazz artists; analyze their playing and determine what makes them effective.

- Work on melodic patterns in every key.

- Pick out familiar tunes by ear; learn some music directly from a recording

- Attend live jazz performances.
- Listen to jazz on radio stations; use the internet to access jazz performances
- Study chord progressions; develop an understanding of how each chord progresses to the next.
- Learn about the principles of chord substitution.
- Practice with a metronome set on beats two and four (in 4/4 time) and beat 2 (in ¾ time).
- Keep a notebook of patterns; sequence them through different keys and through jazz standards.
- Build your own jazz recording library.
- Read through jazz fake books.
- Learn what scales and/or modes go with what basic seventh chord.
- Read about the history of jazz.

# CHAPTER 29

## Taking You From
*I Can't Get Started* to
*Over the Rainbow*

### Tony Caramia

I hope my thoughts and suggestions below will be very useful and inspiring for teachers. This genre of music is motivating and fun for our students, but many of the important stylistic, theoretical, and technical issues that arise in jazz/pop music are often not addressed in "traditional" music training.

It is my desire that the teacher who confesses to know relatively little about how to perform or teach jazz/pop can come away from this discussion with a clearer picture of the nature of this remarkable kind of music, and feel enabled to teach it with more authentic and stylistically accurate results.

## Jazz Resources on the Internet

We live in an age of information, and for those interested in learning more about jazz, the internet offers a multitude of resources. In fact, there are so many sources of information currently, it is hard to know where to begin! But let me offer a few:

**www.claviercompanion.com:** this amazing amalgamation of *Clavier* and *Keyboard Companion* magazines is a must read for all teachers. For those interested in learning about Jazz, the editors offer a Jazz and Pop Department with articles written by a team of jazz experts, on topics ranging from jazz harmonies ("***just a second***", Summer, 2007; "***the ii-V-I progression***", Sept./Oct., 2009); to teaching familiar and unfamiliar jazz ("***Gershwin's Blue Lullaby***", Spring, 2008; and "***A Classic Case of the Blues***", March/April, 2010).

**www.allaboutjazz.com:** Jazz reviews, interviews, news, forums, videos, downloads, photos, clubs, calendar and much more.

**www.allmusic.com:** An amazing sight, where you can explore in depth, many forms of jazz, from Blues to Swing; from Latin to Contemporary. A highly recommended place for students to read about and listen to styles they're performing.

**www.downbeatjazz.com:** The online version of the popular and long-lived magazine all serious jazz musicians have read for decades.

**www.last.fm/tag/jazzpiano:** An interesting site where you can compare many recordings of the same song, like Duke Ellington's *Take the "A" Train* (83 *pages* of tracks or sampled interpretations to listen!)

**www.jazzbooks.com:** THE source for play-along CDs, music, books, hardware and software, history and bibliography texts, and information about upcoming festivals and workshops for teachers and students alike.

**www.jazzstandards.com:** Musicians, educators, researchers, and disc jockeys, use this quick reference site for the standards jazz performers play the most! I cannot recommend this highly enough—this is THE most informative site on jazz repertoire.

**www.npr.org/music:** In addition to podcasts of shows devoted to Jazz, one of the links is "Basic Jazz Record Library", a very useful guide to starting a fun journey of listening.

**www.youtube.com:** On this popular site anyone can post videos of almost anything. While you can find many interesting videos here, be advised that the quality and content can vary. Type in "jazz piano" in the *search for* box. You'll be amazed, delighted, amused, and overwhelmed at the diversity of approaches. I especially recommend searching for performances by the Jazz Piano greats, such as Duke Ellington, Oscar Peterson, Chick Corea and Marian McPartland.

**www.itunes.com:** A terrific place to compare many versions of the same song.

# Instructional

**www.berkleeshares.com:** Berklee Shares offers individual self-contained music lessons developed by Berklee faculty and alumni. It is free and open to the music community around the world and contains a library of MP3 audio, QuickTime movie, and PDF files, as well as a glimpse into the educational opportunities provided by Berklee.

**www.playjazznow.com:** The world's only source for downloadable play-along tracks.

Of course there are innumerable other links to jazz information, as well as traditional text books, method books, fake books, sheet music, recordings, videos, and so much more (a list of text resources will follow later in this chapter). It is daunting and certainly difficult to decide what source is perfect for one's specific needs. Some typical questions might include: Which site, book, or recording will help a student perform William Gillock's **New Orleans Jazz Styles** in a more authentic style? Does the printed score provide all the interpretative clues? Haven't I heard somewhere (you might ask) that a good jazz pianist doesn't try to play what's on the page? Do I instruct my student to avoid the markings on the page? If so, then why are there markings on the page if I'm only going to change them? In this chapter we will try to provide answers to questions like these as we explore this unique and popular body of repertoire.

# Choosing Repertoire for Your Students

As with any style of music, choosing the right piece for your student is an important step in leading to a successful experience. Before we discuss aspects of jazz as they relate to specific pieces, there are a few general items to consider when selecting pieces for your students to play:

When choosing repertoire for any student at any level, good teachers should consider the following points most carefully:

- SOUND: Is it "jazzy"? Does the piece sound idiomatically accurate and would it appeal to students, teachers, parents, and an audience?

- FEEL: Does the music fit the hand at the appropriate level? Is it pianistic?

- TECHNIC: Does the music involve unnecessary or unwarranted technical problems? Is the student prepared to handle all the technical challenges, or will new techniques need to be learned for this piece?

- STYLE: Does the music teach something about a form or style (such as swing or blues?) What will the student learn from the piece? Is the piece contrived or musical?

In addition to the above parameters, I try to be mindful of other factors when choosing *jazzy* repertoire:

- What does the music teach about Jazz? Does it evoke the sound of a particular artist or recording?

- Does it employ such jazzy elements as blue notes, grace notes, blues form, walking bass, etc.?

- Does the fact that it is a jazz piece contribute unnecessary or unwarranted technical problems, simply because it's in the jazz idiom?

As with all music, playing jazz well is all about **_sound_**. After choosing a jazz piece for a student, it is vital to become familiar with jazz performance practice, as defined by performances of jazz by great artists such as Louis Armstrong, Duke Ellington, Oscar Peterson, and many others. (Many of their performances are documented on YouTube and *iTunes*). It is these artists who created the 'rules', and they did so *not* from written scores, but from aural experiences. ***It is these performances that jazz teaching repertoire tries to capture***. Jazz inescapably comes from **an aural tradition**, creating a different source to consult when teaching a jazz piece—not the printed page, but the actual performances and/or recordings.

# "New Rules": Jazz Interpretation vs. Classical Interpretation

Most of us are familiar with traditions of performance practice, style, tempo selection, and overall sound in the various style periods (Baroque, Romantic, etc.) in "traditional" piano repertoire. In jazz, the approach is often very different. You'll see that these next points about jazz differ considerably from classical repertoire and must be understood if one is to create authentic jazzy performances.

- TEMPO: You can and should use ANY tempo, from very slow to very fast. There are no tempo indications or metronome suggestions in Ellington's *Prelude to a Kiss*. Tempo markings and especially metronome markings in a jazz teaching piece are, unfortunately, misleading. To illustrate this point, try an experiment: Find a student who has downloaded *iTunes,* or download it for free to your home computer (Mac or PC).

  o Click **music store**

  o In the **Search Music Store box**, type in the song title, ***Autumn Leaves***

  o You'll see that over 30 albums containing the song appear; and far more single recordings are available (you can listen to 30 seconds for free; for a small fee you can purchase the entire section). The point is: if you were to listen to even half of these recordings of *Autumn Leaves,* you would **not** hear the same version, the same tempo, or even the same key.

If you were able to attend several jazz concerts in which *Autumn Leaves* was performed, the same phenomenon would occur: from different approaches to arrangements from solo to small combo, big bands, vocals, and many other combinations of sound; interpretations might explore multiple keys or several tempos and moods; rhythmic treatments could range from bossa nova to waltz to ad lib.

***There is no urtext in jazz.*** We are not obliged to follow the composer's wishes when interpreting jazz—and this performance practice aspect of jazz is the same when interpreting a jazz teaching piece. This doesn't excuse poor musicianship; rather, it *enhances* musicianship, as it invites creative and personal approaches that might possibly change what a composer such as William Gillock or Philip Keveren had in mind. This is not only good, but is actually expected and encouraged in the jazz world. Therefore, I often try 3 different tempi with a blues or swing piece, and the results are frequently amazing. I simply ignore any reference to tempo or metronome. After all, Duke Ellington *never* performed his own *Satin Doll* the way he wrote it, nor the same way twice.

- SWING RHYTHMS: These are often written as straight 8th notes

  ; dotted 8ths and 16ths ;
  or quarter eight triplet . Unfortunately, *there is no*
  *accurate way of notating swing.* It simply boils down to a long sound followed by a shorter sound. It must be felt and performed in a relaxed manner, with an articulation that incorporates a smooth melodic line occasionally interrupted by accented sounds. The best aural models for students to learn how swing should sound are the recordings of John Lewis and Bill Evans.
  Suggestion:
  - Go to **www.allmusic.com**
  - Click Jazz
  - In the GO box, type in John Lewis; underneath that box, click Artist/Group
  - Click the top name, John Lewis
  - Continue reading, but eventually click Discography
  - You should see a range of recordings from 1956-2006, with several available to hear short (10 second) excerpts. My recommendations for students (and teachers) as an aural guidance for swinging are *Evening with Two Grand Pianos (1979), Evolution* (1999) and any recording with his seminal group, The Modern Jazz Quartet, especially *Beginnings (1952), The Wonderful World of Jazz (1960), Kansas City Breaks (1982),* and *The Complete Last Concert (1992).*

  Doing the same for Bill Evans will yield many wonderful sounds:
  - Go to **www.allmusic.com**
  - Click Jazz
  - In the GO box, type in Bill Evans; underneath that box, click Artist/ Group

- o  Click the top name, Bill Evans (piano)

- o  Continue reading, but eventually click Discography

- o  I recommend them all, but especially *Conversations with Myself (1963); Bill Evans with Symphony Orchestra (1965); Alone (1969); You Must Believe in Spring (1977);* and *Marian McPartland's Piano Jazz with guest Bill Evans, (1978),* as prime examples of a truly personal jazz that swings.

- GRACE NOTES: A cursory listening to the samples from the two artists mentioned above will also give the listener many examples of the jazzy use of grace notes. The important point here is: jazz artists don't add grace notes because the score tells them to; they add grace notes because their *ear* tells them to and the style they're using, like swing, dictates grace notes. You'll hear that jazz musicians automatically add grace notes before roots, major 3rds, 5ths, and 7ths, especially if the note that is 'graced' is a longer duration, or on the beat, and if the principle note is a white key and the grace note is a black key. This facilitates the sliding sound guitarists or singers often employ. So students should freely add grace notes before these principle scale degrees whenever the 'spirit moves them', as long as it doesn't interfere with the tempo or cause a technical problem. And students should feel free to add grace notes *even if the composer hasn't written them.*

Finally, perhaps the most important point of all: **_Jazz Interpretation is defined by the Rhythm._** Correct interpretation and articulation of swing rhythms in a jazz piece—whether notated or improvised—is dictated by the rhythms one uses, *not* the editor, *not* the edition, and *not* what is notated. This is often the most difficult aspect for classically-trained musicians to understand. Jazz performance comes from an **aural** tradition, not a notated one. Those who compose jazz teaching literature: William Gillock, Christopher Norton, Philip Keveren, Bill Boyd, Walter Noona, Glenda Austin, Melody Bober, Catherine Rollin, Lee Evans, et al., are influenced directly or indirectly by jazz musicians *who attempted to create a different interpretation each and every time they played the same song.* George Shearing never played his *Lullaby of Birdland* the way he wrote it or the way he performed it the previous night!

For example, go to **www.allmusic.com:**

- o  Click Jazz

- o  In the GO box, type in George Shearing; underneath that box, click Artist/Group

- o  Click the top name, George Shearing (piano)

- o  Continue reading, but eventually click Discography

o Listen to Shearing's own interpretations on *The Swingin's Mutual* (1961; *An Evening with George Shearing and Mel Torme* (1982); *Dexterity* (1987); *Perfect Match* (1988); *George Shearing in Dixieland* (1988); *That Shearing Sound* (1994)*, and many more.

It is this world of constant experimentation that permeates jazzy repertoire, whether it is W. C. Handy's *St. Louis Blues* or William Gillock's *New Orleans Nightfall*. It must be different from the score; the idiom of jazz allows—demands—that we alter the performance each and every time, that we seek yet another way of playing the notes

Now let's examine a few key points. The following are answers to the popular are frequent questions I've heard:

# Style and Interpretation

## Question:

*I can teach students the notes and rhythms to notated pieces like William Gillock's New Orleans Jazz Styles or Christopher Norton's Microjazz, but what do I need to know about style and interpretation in these works?*

## Answer:

You do need to know something about style and interpretation. You wouldn't want to play Mozart in the style of Prokofiev, so you want to approach a jazz piece with a good sense of what is appropriate for that particular style or genre. As explained above, the printed score in jazz is *a point of departure* not the goal to be realized faithfully, as in a Chopin *Prelude*. Aural support, from listening to recordings, attending jazz concerts, and watching videos (such as those found on **www.jazzlegends.com** and **www.legendsofjazz. net**) can help immeasurably in understanding how to interpret various jazz styles represented by these pieces. These and other videos can help shape the sound as you watch the hands of jazz artists, and hear how they approach a song or solo.

## Question:

*What are some of the basic jazz styles that my students should be aware of, and how do I apply them to pedagogical pieces?*

## Answer:

A majority of the jazz teaching repertoire can be placed into the following categories: blues, ballads, swing, and Latin jazz. Each has its own particular style and approach, but there can be some overlapping characteristics.

- *Blues* is, of course, a form (12 measures in length, with an adherence to placing the I, IV, and V chords in key points within the 12 bar framework). Blues can also rely heavily on grace notes and minor 7ths.

The classic blues sound and mood is created by mixing minor 3rds in the melody against major 3rds in the accompaniment.

Example:

The key is F; the use of A♭ and E♭ create a typical 'bluesy' sound.

- **Ballads** showcase the rich harmonic world of jazz, without necessarily observing a specific form (one can find Blues ballads or other jazzy slow pieces). The use of complex rhythms like swing is usually not prevalent in Ballads.

Examples:

- *Swing* refers to both a rhythmic component in jazz as well as the prevailing style of jazz in the 1930s as played by Teddy Wilson, Benny Goodman, and Count Basie. In the jazz teaching world, one encounters swing rhythms in many compositions—it is the friction between what this rhythm looks like and what it sounds like that frequently frustrates teachers.

Examples:

This is a good piece to develop an easy, relaxed sound so necessary to proper swing. Be sure to lightly emphasize each syncopation, and keep the touch smooth.

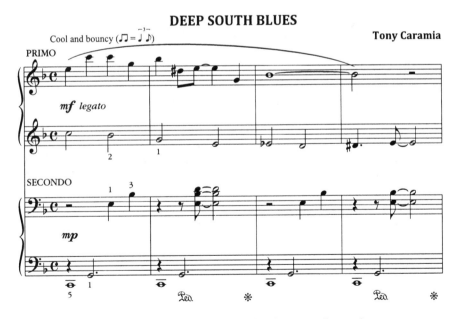

This duet features swing rhythms in both secondo and primo parts. Again, be sure the touch is smooth, especially in the Primo right hand melody; gently emphasize the syncopations in the secondo right hand part.

### DO IT AGAIN
Secondo

George Gershwin
*arr.* **Caramia**

Sometimes dotted 8ths and 16ths are used to indicate swing (secondo part). This notation is used for easier reading, to remind the player that the 1st note is longer than the 2nd. The swing sound should always sound like a quarter-eighth triplet: , *never* a dotted 8th and 16th:

- *Latin Jazz*, in the form of bossa novas, tangos, or rumbas are a welcome change from swing and other more common forms in jazz teaching pieces and can vitality to a student's repertoire.

Examples:

### BOSSO NOVA FOR FOUR HANDS

**Tony Caramia**

### TANGO

**Céline Bussières-Lessard**

This excellent, well-crafted piece has much to teach about style, especially the gentle, lilting tango rhythm in the left hand.

## Question:

*Do some of the same style issues of "traditional" music like articulation, voicing, dynamic range, and rubato apply to jazz playing?*

## Answer:

Yes: good sounds at the piano (voicing top notes of chords, judicious pedaling, a strong sense of proper articulation, and steady pulse when indicated) are part of jazz as well as classical literature.

Examples:

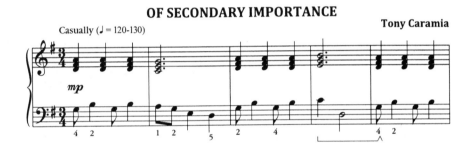

OF SECONDARY IMPORTANCE

Tony Caramia

AFTER YOU'VE GONE

Turner Layton
arr. Lyke

# Rhythm

## Question:

*Are there any rules about when to swing and when not to swing?*

## Answer:

I presume this question comes from a piece in which the composer has not specifically indicated that rhythms should be swung. In this case one's ear comes into play. Some pieces can sound good either played straight (not swung) or swung, but no, there are no rules.

Examples:

There is no indication that this piece must swing, but it could. Whether one swings or not, the tempo must be steady.

Although this suggestion here to swing, I believe the piece sounds very nice without swing, achieving a kind of meditative quality.

## Question:

*How would you teach "swing" to a student for the first time?*

## Answer:

The first aspect of swing is that, no matter how it is represented in the page, it must sound long-short and smooth. It must NEVER sound as a ♪. ♪, but more like ♩ ♪. I divide each beat into 3, with a slight emphasis on 3; the students count 1-2-**3**-1-2-**3**-1-2-**3** (think of a song like "I've Been Working on the Railroad": it has a natural 'swing'. Another song to study for its 'swing' potential is "Row, Row, Row Your Boat": if you compare how it is usually written with the way everyone sings it, you'll see that we 'swing' this song even though it is notated with 'straight' 8th notes.)

Students need to *hear* swing, so duets are a good start. Bill Boyd's *Jazz Prelims* (Hal Leonard) and Lee Evans' *Razzle Dazzle, Jazzmatazz and Jazz Pizzazz* (Hal Leonard) are good examples. Students hear the swinging teacher part and then can mimic the sound of those rhythms in later pieces.

## Question:

*Where should I place emphasis when rhythms are syncopated?*

## Answer:

In jazz all syncopations are to be emphasized or accented, whether notated as such or not. If a chord or single note is syncopated, it is articulated with more weight than a note that's on the beat. Also of extreme importance: if a note ends on an off-beat *and before a silence*, it must be strongly articulated *whether it is notated with an accent or not.*

Example:

Make the sound on the and of 1 (in measures 1 and 2) short and emphasized, *because this sound appears before a rest.*

## Question:

*Are there other rules or conventions for accenting (or not accenting) specific beats?*

## Answer:

In general beats 2 and 4 are emphasized in a swing environment.

Example:

Here is another example where a player could elect to swing or not. If one does, then the emphasis should be on beats 2 and 3.

## Question:

*Is it ever appropriate to use rubato in jazz repertoire?*

## Answer:

Of course! Jazz is not defined only by swing. Jazz pianists' approach to ballades can be a sublime listening experience. I recommend the following albums as superb examples of the kind of gentle and sensitive musicianship jazz pianists are capable of producing:

**Bill Evans** (in addition to the examples mentioned earlier)
  *Quiet Now (1969)*
  *You Must Believe in Spring (1977)*

**Fred Hersch**
  *Evanescence (1990)*
  *Dancing in the Dark (1992)*
  *Live at Maybeck Hall (1993)*
  *Plays Rodgers and Hammerstein (1995)*
  *The Duo Album (1997)*
  *Songs and Lullabies (2003)*

# Text and Method Resources

*Play-a-Long Recordings* by Jamey Aebersold; Aebersold Jazz, Inc.

One of the 1st of its kind (first published in 1967), it is extremely user-friendly, with more than 160 volumes currently available. Recommended order for study:

**Vol. 24: Major and Minor.** Covers all major and minor keys in comfortable tempos

**Vol. 1: How to Play Jazz, 1992, 6th ed.** Thorough in its preparation of the player to improvise

**Vol. 2: "Nothin' But the Blues"** Beginning-Intermediate level. 11 blues tunes in various keys and tempos.

**Vol. 3: "The ii-V progression"** Intermediate level. This is the most important musical sequence in jazz.

**Vol. 54: "Maiden Voyage"** 14 jazz standards at easy tempos. Includes *Autumn Leaves* and *Satin Doll*

**Vol. 70: "Killer Joe"** 13 Easy standards for beginning improvisers

**Vol. 76: "How to Learn Tunes"** Memorize melodies and chord changes for any tune, any key

For further study, explanations, and to order online, visit **www.jazzbooks.com**.

***How to Play from a Fake Book*** by Blake Neely (Hal Leonard)

Ever wondered how to create better accompaniments for the melodies in your favorite fake books? This "teach yourself" book introduces you to chord building, various rhythmic styles, and much more, so that you play the songs you like just the way you want them. Keyboard players with a basic understanding of notation and sight-reading will be on their way to more fun with fake books. The relaxed tone of the text and selection of fun songs keep *How to Play from a Fake Book* entertaining throughout—perfect for amateur musicians, or as a supplement for keyboard teachers and their students.

***An Introduction to Jazz Chord Voicing for Keyboard - 2nd Edition*** by Bill Boyd (Hal Leonard)

This book and CD package will provide the contemporary pianist with the tools necessary to improvise accompaniments with chord voicings characteristic of today's jazz sound. Learn how to "comp" from a fake book, including how to incorporate the melody within contemporary jazz chord voicing styles. The accompanying CD includes several of the examples in the book recorded in a jazz combo context.

***Jazz Works*** by Ann Collins (Alfred)

Ann has crafted a superb book, one of the best on the market for teaching beginning jazz techniques for intermediate to advanced pianists. She writes "*this text attempts to bridge the gap between traditional piano study and advanced level jazz instruction*" and she does this very successfully. There are CD arrangements (with trio accompaniment: drums, bass, piano); 7 chapters that cover material including triads, 6th and 9th chords; dom. 7ths and diminished chords; ii-V-I and ii-V-i progressions. The appendices include a list of jazz melodies; chord spellings; and glossary. Highly recommended!

***Jazz Piano*** by Liam Noble (Hal Leonard)

An In-Depth Look at the Styles of the Masters, featuring lessons, music, historical analysis and rare photos, this book/CD pack provides a complete overview of the techniques and styles popularized by 15 of the greatest jazz pianists of all time. All the best are here: from the early ragtime stylings of Ferdinand "Jelly Roll" Morton, to the modal escapades of Bill Evans, through the '70s jazz funk of Herbie Hancock. CD contains 15 full-band tracks.

***Jazz Piano from Scratch*** by Charles Beale (Hal Leonard)

A How-To Guide for Students and Teachers *Jazz Piano from Scratch* is a complete step-by-step guide to playing jazz with confidence and style. Designed for the absolute beginner, it breaks down the process into simple yet fun activities, with many musical examples to illustrate the points made. The accompanying CD provides examples, activities and some great trio playing to use as a backdrop to the student's own work. Together with a range of other supporting materials—pieces, scales, quick studies, aural tests and more—this book/CD pack provides a comprehensive introduction to the world of jazz.

***Classical Approach to Jazz Piano Improvisation*** by Dominic Alldis (Hal Leonard)

This keyboard instruction book is designed for the person who is classically-trained and wants to expand into the world of jazz improvisation. It provides clear explanations and musical examples of pentatonic improvisation; the blues; rock piano; rhythmic placement; scale theory; major, minor and pentatonic scale theory applications; melodic syntax; the language of bebop; left-hand accompaniment; walking bass lines; thematic development; performance tips; and more.

***The Complete Jazz Keyboard Method*** by Noah Baerman (Alfred)

This series from Alfred and the National Keyboard Workshop reveals all the secrets to playing jazz keyboard. It provides a fun way for the player with intermediate-level or above note-reading and keyboard experience to gain valuable playing and improvisational skills. The *Beginning* book goes from major scale and basic triad theory all the way through 7th chords, pentatonic scales and modulating chord progressions, and the book features a full etude or tune demonstrating every new concept. The *Intermediate* book includes a review of book one, a continuation of modes, chord extensions, changes, chromatic tones, guide tones, chord substitution, rhythm changes, the blues, altered dominant chords, and more. The *Mastering* book starts with a review and quickly moves on to the more advanced concepts of chord voicings, modal soloing, substitution, reharmonization, modes of the minor scales, diminished and whole tone scales, walking bass, stride piano technique, non-diatonic progressions, and much more. The optional CD demonstrates examples and gives the student an opportunity to play along. The optional *Beginning* DVD offers instruction so any keyboardist with basic keyboard skills can dig right in and begin learning jazz right away.

***Hal Leonard Keyboard Styles Series***. Book & CD (Hal Leonard)

The Hal Leonard Keyboard Style Series serious books by different authors for the keyboardist at the early-advanced level or above. The titles include:

*Blues Piano*

*Jazz-Blues Piano*

*Gospel Piano*

*Salsa Piano - The Complete Guide with CD!*

*Smooth Jazz Piano*

*Post-Bop Jazz Piano - The Complete Guide with CD!*

*Bebop Jazz Piano*

*Country Piano*

*Jazz-Rock Keyboard - The Complete Guide with CD!*

*Intros, Endings & Turnarounds for Keyboard*

***How to Play Chord Symbols in Jazz and Popular Music*** by Lee Evans & Martha Baker (Hal Leonard).

This book instructs the student on playing chord symbols simply and effectively more than any book available. It only deals with keys up to one sharp or four flats in a key signature. Divided into two parts, the first part outlines basic chords, from triads up to and including 7th chords and altered chords, one key at a time. Part two covers extended chords: 9th, 11th, 13th chords and additional altered chords. This book is intended for the intermediate level pianist looking for a way to learn chords to improvise, play by ear, and read lead sheets.

***The Jazz Piano Book*** by Mark Levine (Sher Music Co.)

Over 300 pages with complete chapters on intervals and triads, the major modes, ii-V-I, 3-note voicings, suspended and phrygian chords, adding notes to 3-note voicings, tritone substitution, left-hand voicings, altering notes in the left-hand, stride and Bud Powell voicings, block chords, comping and more.

***Essentials of Jazz Theory*** by Shelton Berg (Alfred)

Alfred's Essentials of Jazz Theory is designed for jazz enthusiasts and musicians who want to have a better understanding of the language of jazz. To successfully navigate this all-in-one jazz theory course, one should be versed in basic music theory concepts. Concepts covered in Book 1 include: swing feel, swing eighth-notes, syncopation, chord changes, voice leading, modes, pentatonic scales, grace notes, blue notes, blues scales, and more. Includes a glossary and index of terms and symbols.

Before reading any text (and before teaching any jazz), I urge you to find aural examples to listen to and study. They are so readily available on the Internet, on recordings, on the radio, in a library, and best of all, in live concerts and clubs. Happy listening and happy teaching!

# Permissions

All musical examples used in Chapter 29 are by permission of Stipes Publishing L.L.C.

# APPROACHES TO TECHNIQUE, PRACTICING, MEMORIZING, PEDALING, FINGERING, AND RECITAL PERFORMING

# CHAPTER 30

## Technique and Artistry

### Catherine Rollin

It is the primary goal of this chapter to get teachers to think about what actually constitutes technique. Then, they can think about what type of skills they want to develop in their students and how they can go about developing them. The given examples only touch upon a few of the skills and physical vocabulary that is so important to develop in our students. For a more exhaustive overview of specific physical vocabulary please refer to my series *Pathways to Artistry Technique, Books 1, 2 and 3*.

In order to develop technique in our teaching studios—we need to have a clear definition of technique. Is technique the ability to play fast, mechanically and loudly? Usually, this seems to be what people are referring to when they say someone has a great technique. Most of the time, the people that are perceived as having great technique are those who play with percussive tone and high finger action. The loudness comes from a fast, abrasive throwing motion of the fingers. Very often, the people who play like this end up with severe arm and hand injuries if they practice too much. Most importantly, the majority of the time, this kind of technique has little to do with arm weight and almost nothing to do with tonal beauty. The listener hears notes, octaves and trills that are impressive, but not integral parts of the music. Ultimately—this kind of technique does nothing to serve the art of music.

> Technique: 1. *method of performance, esp. in artistic work.* 2. *technical skill, esp. in artistic work.*

These two primary definitions from the American College Dictionary don't support the kind of idea of technique as described in the first paragraph. According to these dictionary definitions, technical skill is something that serves the artistic medium.

Based on these dictionary definitions, players who play with an abrasive tone quality and whose only skill is to impress listeners with the pure athleticism of their playing are doing the opposite of what a musician should be doing and the opposite of what we teachers should be teaching. These pianists are developing skills in a vacuum. Their skills are not skills that are supportive of beautiful music making. And worse, these "skills" often lead to debilitating injuries.

True technique leads to performances that are musical and shine with artistry. True technique also involves a great deal of athleticism, but the athleticism involves physical skills that are one hundred per cent supportive of the music making. In other words, the physical movements help make the playing more musical and are not tension producing. Here are some of the skills that contribute to true technique. This list is not all inclusive, but it is a helpful outline for teachers to follow and understand when trying to develop technical mastery in their students.

1. **Tone Quality**: Without good tone quality a musician cannot convey the beauty of the music.

2. **Unity of Ideas Through Physicality**: There are several different physical movements, each one resulting in connecting individual notes into cohesive ideas or units of thought. The particular skill or combination of skills used are determined by the specific musical passage. As pianists, we are always trying to overcome the basic percussive nature of the instrument and make it sing. Unity of notes is one of the greatest challenges for pianists.

3. **Variety of Touch for Character:** As good musicians, we need to develop the physical movements that result in sounds that have variety and character. The different ways we use our physicality can lead to sounds that evoke moods and feelings, and also paint pictures. The way a pianist plays a note or a series of notes can bring to mind images that are cute, fun, sad, serious, playful, agitated, dramatic, etc. The variety that pianists can bring to their playing strongly impacts their overall artistry. For example, having only one sound for staccato to be used in every single piece of music would be like a great painter having only one shade of blue with nothing to mix the colors. This would take away the painter's ability to create endless varieties of blue to fit each scenario.

4. **Command of Elements That Comprise the Acoustic Piano:** Every instrument has its idiosyncratic qualities. The piano, with its three distinct pedals and resonating soundboard, has a myriad of sound possibilities that are unique to it. Understanding the acoustic properties of the piano and developing the ability to use all of the pedals creatively and with good control, is a large part of playing the piano with the technical skill.

# Tone Quality

A student's first instinct in playing the piano is usually to play each key from the fingertip down. Teachers have to help the students to understand the role of the fingertip itself. The fingertip is just the recipient of the weight of the arm. Teachers can explain this concept to their students by comparing playing the key to hitting the ball with a tennis racket. Good tennis players swing both the arm and racket as one long, continuous delivery system. The swing back is for the purpose of gathering momentum and power for the hit, and then the swing continues to follow through after hitting the ball. Without the follow through, the momentum is lost and the ball is hit with a short, musically speaking "percussive" hit. Although the head of the racket is what actually comes into contact with the ball, it is the entire apparatus of the arm and racket together, coupled with momentum and follow through that constitutes the technique of hitting the ball. The actual moment of when the ball is hit is just part of a whole process of preparation and follow through. Similarly, at the piano the weight of the arm needs to get behind the playing finger, prepare, and follow through in order to produce a good sound.

When writing my technique series, *Pathways to Artistry* I gave years of thought to what primary physical elements contribute to good tone (the equivalent of the good hit of the tennis ball). The essential ingredients include: arm weight, elastic wrist and strong fingers. Every player, even young children, have adequate arm weight to produce a good sound. To continue with the tennis analogy, the fingertip is the delivery point of the arm weight. The first segment of the finger must be strong in order to receive the weight of the arm. It is like the head of the tennis racket having taut stringing so the ball will bounce well off it. The arm acts like the arm-racket combination in tennis—preparing to play the key with the slight upward preparatory movement of the "elastic" wrist. The weight is delivered to the key and then follows through with a slight give of the "elastic" wrist. The wrist is the most subtle of the ingredients. The preparatory upward motion is generally small and helps raise the arm slightly to prepare for its eventual drop. Once the finger reaches the bottom of the key, the wrist acts as a shock absorber for the arm weight. If the initial movement into a phrase is begun without any give of the wrist, the forearm will react with tension and the resulting sound becomes harsh.

Although it is easier for teachers to allow their students play with their fingers only, the use of the "elastic" wrist will help deliver the arm weight and keep the forearm relaxed. The "elastic" wrist can be summarized very simply:

Lift to prepare, drop the weight of the arm on to the strong finger as it depresses the key—letting a slight give of the wrist absorb the arm weight, lift out—or keep weight in the keys depending on what is to follow musically.

If we teachers demonstrate and teach the above skills from the very early stages of piano study, our students will be made aware of the importance of good tone quality. This awareness will help the students develop the connection between listening and playing from the start. It might seem obvious, but most technique studies emphasize mindless repetition that is antithetical to the kind of listening that develops the connection between body movement and the sound that is produced.

# Unity of Ideas

The piano is described as a percussion instrument because each note is produced by an individual hammer blow on the strings. One of our most challenging goals as pianists/musicians is to achieve legato and unity of melodic ideas on this basically percussive instrument. The best way we can create the semblance of legato is through dynamics. Thus, even if we are not trying to actually crescendo, as pianists we must make a very subtle gradation of sound (usually a crescendo) as a line rises to help create the legato connection. If each note is played at the same dynamic level, the hammered aspect of the instrument is impossible to mask. If we are going to do subtle crescendos and diminuendos—what I refer to as shaping the musical line—we have to have very fine control of the weight that goes into each key. The ability to finally control the arm weight from key to key is one of the most important elements of good technique. Students are rarely instructed to think about subtle musical shaping while practicing scales or Hanon, but it is this kind of training that is crucial in developing their technique correctly.

In my *Pathways to Artistry Technique 1, 2, and 3*, I have described in detail many physical skills that should be part of every pianist's physical vocabulary. These skills lead to the mastery of delivering subtle arm weight and/or changes in the arm weight to fit specific musical situations. Among these many skills are: elastic wrist, rotation, (wrist rotation), rolling wrist, under-over wrist rolls, finger pivots, compass pivots, arpeggio arches, etc.

In each piece of music, certain physical vocabulary will fit the specific musical situation. A student who has some introductory familiarity with the above physical skills can determine which physical skills they will need to use for that particular piece. It is the role of the teacher not only to demonstrate and explain each physical skill, but to help students analyze which skills they will use for each musical situation. Many pieces will require a specific skill to be used repeatedly throughout the piece or a large section of the piece of music.

Each time students develop more mastery of a skill, they will be better able to use that skill with each subsequent piece of music. To use another tennis analogy, once a player develops the basic form for the backhand, with every backhand shot they make, they will further hone that skill. In my *Pathways to Artistry Technique* series, I show the different skills and give short musical examples for the students to practice and transpose. That way, when the specific skill arises in a piece of music, the student will already have some familiarity with the corresponding physical skill that supports the musical shape.

For this chapter we have already discussed the elastic wrist as a means of initial weight delivery. For shifting of weight delivery from note to note within a united idea, let's consider the "under-over wrist roll" as one of the crucial skills within our "physical vocabulary."

In preparation for using the "under-over wrist roll," place your right hand fourth finger on the closed fallboard of the piano. With the strong finger tip acting as the axis of the circle, create very small counter clockwise circles on that strong finger tip. Now try this same movement on the fifth finger of the right hand.

Now feel both the fourth and fifth finger acting together as the axis of the circle. As you bring the arm around on the under portion of the counter clockwise circle feel the weight of the arm transfer from the fourth to the fifth finger as you circle on that axis.

To illustrate the "under-over wrist roll," let's look at Chopin's *Waltz in C sharp minor Op. 64, No. 2* (example 1).

Example 1

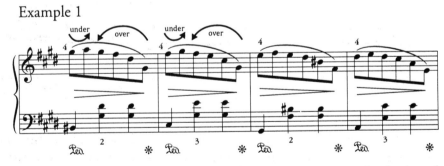

Transfer this counterclockwise circular movement onto the keyboard using the right hand of the musical example. Play the first G♯ with the fourth finger. As you start to turn on the axis of the fourth finger, transfer the weight of the arm to the fifth finger playing the A. (The G♯ and A form the **under** part of the circle). After you have played the fifth finger, continue the circle. Once you have played the fifth finger, the circle starts to rise in the counterclockwise circle and the weight of the arm comes out of the key. This leads to less arm weight on the subsequent eighth notes covering beats 2 & 3. (These notes form the **over** part of the circle.) Thus, the most arm weight is on the offbeat eighth note of beat 1 that is the high point of the pattern. Beats 1 and 2 have a similar amount of weight and the offbeat eighth note of beat 2 as well as the same for beat 3 have the least amount of weight. As the sequence continues in bars 34, 35, 36, etc., we repeat this motion. This physical motion helps to distribute the arm weight to match the musical shape of the music. Using this under-over motion in each measure of the sequential pattern gives not only a beautiful shape to each bar, but also creates an aural unity to the pattern. If we were to sing this sequence, each measure would have the same musical shape with the offbeat eighth note of beat 1 having the most breath support. Through the skill of under-over wrist rolls we are helping make the dynamic shaping that makes our percussive instrument sing.

Here are two other examples using the "under-over" wrist roll from preparatory level music:

Example 2                                    *Waltz* by Catherine Rollin

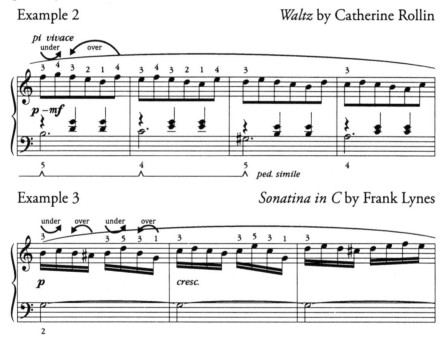

Example 3                              *Sonatina in C* by Frank Lynes

Developing skills like the "under over wrist roll" helps all pianists come to the repertoire with an understanding of what is physically necessary to effectively shape the musical passage. This physical understanding is at the service of the music and is part of achieving true technical mastery. With each new piece, students will become more adept with each skill used. This growing assurance and command of skills that support the music's beauty constitutes true technique.

## Variety of Touches for Character

As a composer myself, the most important thing performers can do is get to the essence of the musical composition. Therefore, it is a good idea to ask students the following questions: What is the composer trying to say? What is his message? What is the feeling you would like to evoke in your listener? Without addressing these questions, it is difficult for anyone to become a great musician. Performing music requires communication, and we cannot communicate without knowing what we want to say. Therefore talk to your students about creating character. Is this piece light hearted, is it angry, etc? What can we do physically to produce the sound that will help create the character we desire? Is character created only by dynamics? We know the answer to this question is no. So how do we create character? One of the key ingredients is the ability to touch the key with different amounts of weight and speed to create a wide variety of sound coloration. Can we create a staccato that is sharp and biting, cute and distinct, gentle and thoughtful, or fun and full bodied? The answer for the above would be respectively: yes, yes, yes and yes! Furthermore, the techniques respectively for the above four moods would be push-off staccato, wrist staccato, portato, and forearm staccato. In addition, we can combine these following four staccatos and create hybrids that blend into different resulting sounds and then have a different musical purpose. Without this wide variety of weight and speed, we cannot create the interesting palette of sound characters needed for being good musicians.

Next, let's use the wrist staccato to illustrate how we can create different sounds based on the physical motion, and the weight and speed with which the note is played.

To explain the physical movements required for the wrist staccato, imagine the following: your forearm is the neck of a woodpecker. Your whole hand is the woodpecker's head and the fingertip is the beak. Keep the forearm stationary, and throw the hand and fingertips as one unit (imagine how a woodpecker thrusts his head and beak). This throwing motion creates a very short, distinct sound. When played with little arm weight, it creates an ideal staccato that we might describe as cute. When throwing the hand with more momentum and weight, this touch can be used for very pointed, strong individual sounds.

In Mozart's *Sonata in C K. 309* (example 4), students can use a light throw on the wrist staccato to create a distinctively cute and sweet character.

Example 4

Example 5 is another example of a wrist staccato where students can use a faster throw of the wrist staccato to create a more crisp and slightly agitated sound adding to the distinct character of this piece.

Example 5

**THE WILD HORSEMAN**

Robert Schumann

If pianists have a clear idea of how specific physical movements result in specific sounds, they can effectively use these physical skills to create the sound that fits the musical situation. This wide variety of sounds will result in a wide variety of moods and characters in one's playing. Even students in the very early stages of playing the piano can confidently create these varied characters if teachers have shown them how to do it. This a very attainable and crucial part of acquiring a true technique and even a second or third year student can use their physicality to achieve more character than a professional who doesn't use their physicality creatively.

# Command of the Elements that Comprise the Acoustic Piano

When listening to pianists, both students and professionals, I often feel that the pedals, particularly the damper pedal and una corda pedals are rarely used to their fullest extent for the respective level of the performer. The resonance of the piano soundboard creates a glorious sound that is only possible with the acoustic piano. But beyond the resonance, we can use the una corda to totally change the color of a passage of music. We can use the damper pedal to retain the ringing of a bass note, and flutter the foot without losing the bass sound. We can even sustain isolated notes with the sostenuto pedal and then use the damper pedal freely while keeping certain specific notes sustained. Helping our students understand the capabilities of the pedal and helping them to develop the technique of foot and ear working together is one of the most important elements of technique that are generally overlooked in the piano teaching studio.

Listening to most students, I rarely think of the word color as something that stands out in their playing. But we do think of color usually as one of the most important features in accomplished musicians that we admire. I have found that if students are shown how to use the pedals, particularly the damper pedal, they can produce coloristic playing quite readily.

Very often, teachers don't even introduce the use of pedals for several years, often waiting until a student can reach the pedals comfortably. All teachers of small children should invest in a pedal extender; hopefully one that can control both the damper and una corda pedals. Parents can buy these for their children. Without using the damper pedal, students are missing one of the most special aspects of playing the piano.

In my piece: *Rainbow Fish* (see example 6), the student will put down the damper pedal at the beginning and never change it throughout. Hearing all the whole-tone scale notes resonate simultaneously automatically captures the imagination of students. I rarely see a beginning student listen more closely than when they are enchanted by the sound possibilities of the acoustic piano resonating with a damper pedal.

Example 6

hold the damper pedal down throughout

Once students are familiar with the damper pedal, teachers have to teach them that there is more to do than just play the damper pedal up and down. If you speak with anyone who is performing professionally, they are going to speak about using quarter, half, and flutter pedals. If students are never told that there is such a thing as gradation of pedal depth, they are rarely going to discover it for themselves. Students might be told not to use any pedal in Bach because of the multiple moving voices. In reality, use of a tasteful quarter pedal at every fourth sixteenth note in Bach's *Sinfonia in E minor* (example 7) helps the legato of that voice continue, or the constant fluttering (what I call just wiggling their big toe on the pedal surface) of the pedal on each 16th note might give a beautiful resonance to the tone.

Example 7

very shallow pedal every fourth 16th note        very shallow toe wiggle (flutter pedal) every 16th note

If teachers introduce these pedaling concepts at an early stage, most of their students will embrace it and develop refined pedal technique. If we do not underestimate what our students can do if shown how to do it—the results in intermediate students with artist level pedaling skills can be quite amazing. The use of the pedal is not something that is commonly considered part of technique, but the student who has the ability to combine the use of the foot and ear for color and sonority possesses one of the most important technical skills for playing piano artistically.

The longer I teach, the more I am convinced that what usually is considered technique has very little to do with the real skills needed to play the piano well. In fact, the commonly taught high finger, digitally focused approach to technique generally results in sound production that is antithetical to beautiful music making. It is my hope that through chapters such as this one and series such as my *Pathways to Artistry* Technique Books, teachers will give much more thought to technique and consider the importance of the development of skills that truly build technique and contribute to artistry.

# Permissions

Example 2: Waltz (from "Spotlight On Romantic Style"), by Catherine Rollin. © MCMXC by Alfred Publishing Co., Inc. All Rights Reserved. Used by Permission.

Example 6: Rainbow Fish (from "Bean Bag Zoo") by Catherine Rollin. © MM by Alfred Publishing Co., Inc. All Rights Reserved. Used by Permission.

# CHAPTER 31

## Artistic Damper Pedaling:
## A Master Lesson in
## "Piano Pedal-gogy"

### Steven Hesla

Damper pedaling may well be the least-developed pianistic skill. Yet, nearly every pianist has learned good, basic pedaling. This chapter, through the experiences of a student named Will, offers suggestions for transforming ordinary, good pedaling into artistic pedaling. Artistic pedaling involves detailed listening that draws students into new ways of managing and coloring sound. It can be exciting to learn and rewarding to teach, with positive benefits for every aspect of musical interpretation.

## Exploring the Elements of Artistic Pedaling

When Will, a high school senior, came to study with me, I asked him to pick a piece he might enjoy learning and work on it the week before his first lesson. He chose *Milonga del ángel* by Argentine composer Astor Piazzolla.[1]

Example 1                                        *Milonga del ángel*, mm. 1-4

At his lesson I was impressed to see how much Will had accomplished on his own. The phrasing was musical, with an already intuitive sense of the romantic underpinnings of the piece. Fingering was mostly observed or well-chosen. The pedaling was thoughtful and normal, with changes correctly erasing one harmony precisely as new harmonies were produced.

However, his pedaling was also more generous than necessary. Will provided full pedaling at every change, quickly releasing and immediately reengaging the pedal to the bottom, gathering an overly abundant mixture of the next measure's melodic and harmonic tones. Even so, the somewhat murky pedaling would have passed as acceptable for most students.

After complimenting Will on his fine work, I played a few measures of the piece and asked what differences he heard. He noticed how clearly I brought out the layers of melody and accompaniment, and how much dynamic shading there was within each layer. He didn't notice that I was using a somewhat shallower pedal with totally quiet pedal changes, but he liked that the piece sounded more expressive and detailed.

Then, I played the first few measures again with a thicker pedal, thumping slightly at every change. He noticed how much wetter it sounded, even though he still appreciated the more layered and shaded phrasing that I retained. When I pointed out the thumping noises, he heard them. When I returned to the inaudible pedal changes, he noticed how much more beautiful and seamless the music sounded. With new sounds fresh in his ear, Will was eager to explore more sophisticated possibilities, and we launched our work together.

We discussed how the shapes of melody and accompaniment could be practiced hands separately and then hands together, and considered a variety of solutions for balancing the various musical forces at work. Will caught on quickly as his ear assessed and then increasingly guided each attempt to achieve musical refinements. Soon his ear was fully engaged in managing the musical quality of every note. The pedaling was still overly generous, but the piece sounded increasingly beautiful. Will was pleased not only to make these improvements, but also to learn how and why each improvement made a tangible difference in the beauty of each phrase.

As for pedaling, Will noticed the little thumps his right foot made, but he found it difficult to make adjustments. His pedaling habits were ingrained. He heard the extra resonance in the sonority; however, in order to catch the first notes of each harmonic change, it seemed the foot needed to get back down as quickly as it had come up. He was intrigued with how I had played the same passages with seamlessly quiet pedal changes.

Thus, we proceeded with the refinement of Will's pedaling. Through a series of exercises, Will's musical ear became further developed, and a transition toward artistic pedaling took place within an hour.

## Practicing Intentional Pedal Thumps

With nothing played on the keyboard, I demonstrated pedal thumps by snapping the release of the damper pedal and then quickly putting the pedal back down. Next, Will took a turn. While watching the dampers of the grand piano, he abruptly released the pedal to induce snappy noises as the dampers slapped the strings. Then, he caught ghosts of the thumps by immediately driving the pedal to the bottom. He had no idea the damper mechanism could make so much racket. It was fun and even amusing to explore these extraneous sounds.

Example 2                                         Exploring Pedal Thumps[2]

Notational Pedal Line
Rest = Pedal Up
Notation = Pedal Down

- Using the notational pedal line, release the pedal with an exaggerated snap at each rest, reengaging the pedal immediately at each indicated rhythm for the duration of the note values. Make as much noise as possible and try to catch ghosts of each thump in the next pedal. Play nothing on the keyboard. Watch the dampers if possible. The purpose of the exercise is to explore and transgress the boundaries of silent pedaling.

## Practicing Inaudible Pedal Changes

After reviewing the noisiest possible pedal changes, I demonstrated changes where only a slight brushing sound could be heard as the dampers lifted and then settled gently back onto the strings. Will described these brushing sounds as "calming and mysterious." He watched the dampers rising and falling, and then observed my foot, noticing that the pedal came up and went back down more gradually than was his habit. He also observed that the dampers were closer to the strings when the pedal was not driven to the bottom.

Then, Will practiced making inaudible pedal changes. With no notes to worry about, he was able to focus completely on the movements of the pedal and dampers, and he achieved these adjustments quite readily. Will's foot had located the damper pedal's "point of change," which is the precise point where the dampers are fully resting on the strings, but poised to lift with the slightest downward movement of the foot on the pedal.

Example 3                           Exploring the Damper Pedal's Point of Change

Notational Pedal Line
Rest = Pedal Up
Notation = Pedal Down

- With the heel on the floor and the foot in normal pedaling position, explore the damper pedal's free-play, which is the top eighth inch or so of movement on a well-adjusted pedal before it begins to lift the dampers. The foot can feel a slight pressure as the pedal meets the rail which lifts all of the dampers. Start this exercise with the foot in that position, perched at the "point of change." Then, playing nothing on the keyboard and watching or imagining the motion of the dampers, gradually put the pedal down. Explore various depths of the pedal. Practice returning the pedal inaudibly to the point of change and no farther.

- At first, this exercise is more about listening and less about counting. Hear the brushing sounds as the dampers are lifted and then returned to the strings. The strings will actually vibrate a little when the dampers leave the strings. Hear these vibrations. When releasing the pedal to the exact point of change, let the foot rest there for a considerable moment, making sure that all vibrations in the strings have ceased. Savor the silence.

- A variety of rhythmic or non-rhythmic executions may be explored, but equal durations of pedal-up and pedal-down can help establish inaudible releases and unhurried reengagements of the pedal.

- Shallower pedal depths facilitate both clearer musical textures and quieter pedal changes.

- Repeat this exercise until the point of change is fully memorized by the ear, foot, and mind.

Next, to provide Will with a model of artistic pedaling, I demonstrated the following smoothly pedaled white-key triads:

Example 4                                    Consecutive Triads, Pedaled Artistically

By now, Will could hear how inaudibly I released the pedal to the point of change and how comfortably I reengaged the pedal once the previous triad had cleared and each new harmony was clean. He was intrigued, and his attempts to reproduce these smooth, quiet changes were successful in many ways. He played the triads with good tone and released the pedal with less thumping than usual. However, his foot still wanted to go back down immediately. It was his *modus operandi* to reengage the pedal too soon and too deeply. He felt as if there was some kind of reflex over which he had little or no control. I assured him it was just a habit that could be replaced by new and improved skills.

## Developmental Exercises for Artistic Damper Pedaling

As an antidote for Will's too-quick pedal reengagements it was helpful to rehearse several simpler exercises. I mentored Will through each step of the following exercise until he felt totally comfortable: "Play the triad; now add the pedal; now release the keys while keeping the pedal down; absorb the rich sonority; *taper* the pedal smoothly to the point of change; and finally, absorb the silence before playing the next triad." I wanted Will to consciously experience each element of the exercise.

Example 5                                    Tapering Pedaled Triads into Silence

- As in example 3, this exercise is initially more about listening than counting. The teacher can guide students to master each step before moving on to the subsequent event on the next beat.

- After all elements are comfortable, the teacher or student may count aloud or internally. A metronome may be used. Play each triad on beat one; catch it with the pedal on beat two; release the keys on beat three; and finally, release the pedal inaudibly to the point of change on beat four.

- Listen to the sound *taper* into silence as the dampers return to their resting point. Keep the foot poised exactly at the point of change, where the pedal will begin to activate the dampers with the slightest movement of the foot downwards.

- To highlight a particular element of this exercise, a fermata may be added to any of the four beats. For example, a fermata on the fourth beat will enhance hearing both the erasure of the triad and the silence that follows.

Soon, Will was tapering the release of the pedal smoothly rather than abruptly. He described it as a "continuous release," and pictured a graph depicting an upward-curving line. Will had never thought about pedaling in such detail and found it exciting to be developing tapered pedal releases.[3]

Will was now ready to synchronize the erasure of one triad with the playing of the next one.

Example 6                    Combining Two Events: Concluding One Triad
                                While Introducing the Next

- Play each triad on beat one, catching it with the pedal on either beat two or the second half of beat one.
- Release the keys on beat four while keeping the pedal engaged.
- On beat one of each measure, release the pedal inaudibly to the point of change at the exact moment the new triad is sounded.
- Reengage the pedal on either beat two or the second half of beat one.
- Counting aloud or internally is recommended once each element is comfortable.

It proved more difficult than expected for Will to listen for the tapered erasure of the previous harmony while playing the new triad. In addition, he kept putting the pedal back down immediately after playing each new triad. We laughed together as long-ingrained habits took over, yet again. After a few awkward tries, Will simultaneously heard the tapered release of the pedal and the clarity of each subsequent chord. His right foot was no longer in such a hurry. The snaps, thumps, and blurs were gone, and Will was advancing toward artistic pedaling.[4]

## Practicing on the Keyboard without Pedal

Practicing pedaled music without the pedal is always beneficial. Artistic pedaling is as much about what happens on the keyboard as it is about what happens with the damper mechanism. Stripping away the pedal can reveal what solutions might be better addressed on the keyboard. It can also reveal where the use of the damper pedal would be essential for a successful interpretation.

Will was unknowingly playing the triads of example 6 a bit stiffly while concentrating so intently on pedaling. So, we removed all pedaling from the exercise and examined components of physical and musical flow from one triad to the next. We discussed how every note is comprised of three basic components:  a beginning, duration, and an end (release).

Because a note played on the keyboard can be sustained by merely holding down the key or the pedal, pianists are often under-involved in the duration and releases of notes. Duration should be experienced much like bowing a stringed instrument, blowing air through a wind instrument, or sustaining air and vocal support in a song or aria. A well-timed, simultaneous release of all notes in a triad can ensure a beautiful beginning of the next triad, much like a swimmer's graceful departure from a diving board portends a graceful entry into the water.

Will had never considered that there is often silence between notes. For example, every time the same fingering is used on two consecutive triads, some degree of silence exists between the end of one triad and the beginning of the next. This silence can be included in the flow; it can be "bridged." By practicing the flow of un-pedaled triads, Will learned not only to concentrate on the beginning, duration, and end of each triad, but also to flow across the bridge of silence.

Example 7            Bridging Silence Between Un-Pedaled,
Consecutive Triads

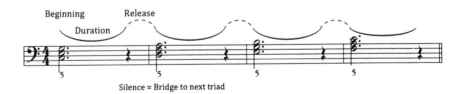

Silence = Bridge to next triad

- Play each triad in either or both hands with a smooth, simultaneous beginning. Listen intently and experience the duration of each triad with no heaviness or pressure in the keys.

- Prepare the simultaneous release of all notes on beat four in anticipation of the next triad, so the silence actively flows to the beginning of the next triad. Hear and experience the "bridge of silence."[5]

- Teachers may discuss a variety of supple arm, wrist, and finger movements in conjunction with this exercise. Physical and musical aspects of artistic interpretation are always intertwined.

The previous exercise applied perfectly to measures 33-36 of *Milonga del ángel*.

Example 8                                    *Milonga del ángel*, mm. 33-36

Will had mentioned this passage was difficult for his right hand. Soon, he realized he had only been thinking about the beginnings of the notes, with no awareness of duration, release, or bridging of silence to the next chord. Thus, his body felt stiff, the sound was brittle, and the phrase failed to flow. We discussed how a stiff release of one chord invariably results in a stiff attack of the next chord, and how stiff playing can be disguised, but never mitigated, by good pedaling.

By applying the principles learned in Ex.7, Will rehearsed the un-pedaled flow of the right-hand chords. He could sense how the exercise applied directly to this phrase, and promised to practice both the exercise and the music at home to further develop physical comfort and musical flow.

## The Benefits of Finger-Pedaling for Artistic Pedaling

We moved on to the final project for Will's first lesson: pedaling sequential notes rather than solid or blocked harmonies. Arpeggiating the diatonic white-key triads of Ex.4 provided a useful vehicle for practicing finger-pedaling, which is the sustaining of selected notes, often beyond their indicated note value. Finger-pedaling the left-hand notes in this exercise would provide ample time for tapered releases and unhurried reengagements of the damper pedal.[6]

Example 9        Practicing the Components of Pedaled, Broken Triads

Add finger pedaling to each set of LH triads to allow unhurried reengagement of pedal.
PEDAL LINE

- Without using the damper pedal, practice the left hand alone, sustaining the root, third, and fifth to form a complete triad. The student may pause temporarily on the last note of each triad, thus absorbing the collective sonority. Teachers can guide students to feel comfortable in selectively sustaining notes.

- Concentrate on the simultaneous and tapered release of all three sustained notes on beat 4. After the releases are comfortable, use beats 4, 5, and 6 to bridge the silence to the next finger-pedaled triad.

- Practice the right hand with no pedal, but also *without* finger-pedaling. Because the pedal will already be engaged, the right hand will not need to be finger-pedaled in this instance.

- Practice the hands together without pedal until each hand is comfortable with its task. Consider that one hand is bridging the silence while the other hand is playing. It is challenging, but highly beneficial, to sense this bridging while also focusing on the notes being played.

- Finally, add the pedal with the same tapered releases and graceful reengagements that were rehearsed with the blocked triads in Ex.6.

Will did quite well with this exercise. However, his final right-hand note wanted to hang over into the next pedaled harmony. Once he focused on clarifying the first left-hand note of each measure, he was able to release each right-hand note at the proper moment, and the hands and pedal worked together to create smooth, clean changes.

This exercise proved immediately beneficial to measures 1-4 of *Milonga del ángel*, where we reexamined the whole notes at the beginning of each measure.

Example 10                    *Milonga del ángel*, mm. 1-4, left hand only

We considered that the whole notes in the left hand could be:

1. Showing a layer of voicing so the foundational B-natural of each measure might sing out a little more than the eighth notes.

2. Suggesting finger-pedaling the B-natural so the pedal would not have to be reengaged quite so quickly.

3. Indicating pedaling for an entire measure, since the B's could not be held past the third eighth note.

Our first lesson together covered a great deal of material.[7] Many of the events took only moments to experience. Others took more time and repetitions to clarify issues and come up with solutions. Will took home a recording of the lesson to review all these considerations.

# Results, Refinements, and Additional Elements of Artistic Pedaling

Will's second lesson proved that he understood the primary components of artistic pedaling. *Milonga del ángel* had improved significantly, and beautifully quiet pedal changes were now the norm. We spent much of our second lesson reviewing, clarifying, adjusting, and further exploring artistic pedaling.

### The Benefits of Delayed Pedal Reengagements

During his first lesson, Will had been blurring the melodic notes of measure 10 by reengaging the pedal immediately after the downbeat. I demonstrated delaying the pedal reengagement until after the right hand's second F-sharp was played. Then, Will practiced this solution, making sure to sustain the bass, tenor, and alto notes of the F-sharp dominant seventh chord harmony as indicated, catching them in the delayed pedal reengagement. We refined this solution even more during his second lesson.

Example 11a                                *Milonga del ángel,* mm. 10-13

Example 11b                        Delayed Pedaling for Melodic Clarification
Suggested execution:

- Practice the first two beats of measure 10 without pedal to be sure all keyboard issues are solved:
  - o  Sustain the lower three notes of the harmony while playing the melody cleanly with voicing and dynamic shading.
  - o  Stopping on beat two, listen for the F-sharp seventh harmony outlined by the four sustained notes.
- Repeat the exercise, adding the pedal on beat two after the E-natural in the melody has cleared.
- Note: the E-natural in the left hand is the defining note of the F-sharp seventh harmony and belongs in the pedal. However, the E-natural in the right hand is melodic and sounds more beautiful when it is not sustained by the pedal.

## Refining the Arpeggiated-Triad Exercise

We also reviewed and refined the arpeggiated-triad exercise (example 9). Will had become adept at making sure the last right-hand note of each measure did not hang over into the first left-hand note of the next measure, but there was no musical connection. I had him play only the first and last notes of each measure without pedal until he could create flow from the right hand into the left hand. Once this slur was internalized, he added the pedal. Finally, he played example 9 as written with smooth pedaling and much-improved musical flow.

Example 12          Refining Musical Flow in Pedaled, Broken Triads

- Without using the pedal, practice a legato slur across each bar-line from right hand to left hand. Feel the flow across the bar-line and feel the legato connection of widely-spaced notes, more than one octave apart.
- Remember to sustain the left-hand eighth note longer on each downbeat to ensure its presence when the pedal is added.
- Then, add the pedal as indicated, sustaining the root of each triad until the downbeat of the next measure.
- Finally, play Ex.9 as written, making sure the final eighth note of each measure flows musically into the next cleanly-pedaled downbeat.

## Exploring Incremental Pedaling

During his second lesson, Will learned to add smidges of pedal to a Hanon exercise he already knew. We reviewed "Hanon Number One" with no pedal. Then, with his foot poised at the point of change, Will added the barest hint of pedal. The goal was to add the least amount of pedal possible. After a couple of blurry attempts, he found this sparing sonority, and we explored adding and subtracting percentages of pedal while playing through the entire exercise.

Example 13                     C. L. Hanon, *The Virtuoso Pianist*, Part I, No.1

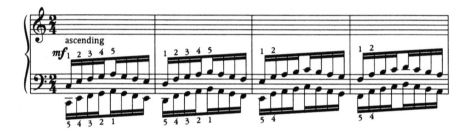

- With the foot poised at the point of change, begin the exercise with no pedal.

- As the exercise progresses, add the least amount of pedal possible by moving the foot minutely downwards.

- Find and retain the position of the pedal where all notes have the slightest glimmer of pedal, with none too wet or too dry.

- Practice returning to the point of change, easing back and forth between 0% and 1% pedal.

- Explore increasing and decreasing percentages of pedal until the ear is comfortable with guiding any desired degree of wetness or dryness.

A number of metaphors can be used to describe various depths of pedal. Students can imagine:

1. Dairy pedaling: skim, 1%, 2% , or whole.

2. Miles per hour pedaling: 10, 20, 30 MPH.

3. Percentage pedaling: from 1% to 100%.

4. Faucet pedaling: from a trickle to a wide-open flow.

## Refining the Bridge of Silence

Will's chords in the right hand of measures 33-36 of *Milonga del ángel* (Example 8) had improved notably since his first lesson. His technique was clearly more comfortable, as he listened carefully for the beginning, duration, and release of each right-hand chord. We reviewed the flow of un-pedaled chords across the bridge of silence and discussed the importance of retaining that flow when using the pedal. Refining this ability would positively impact all of Will's playing, both pedaled and un-pedaled.

## Conclusion: Artistic Pedaling, Summarized

Will was all smiles when I affirmed that he had acquired the essential components of artistic pedaling, which, with practice, would be with him for his whole life. He knew it was true, and expressed surprise that it seemed not all that difficult to make the transition. I suggested it was partly because we had broken the large ideas into tiny components, each of which made sense. Will concurred that the exercises helped clarify the core elements of artistic pedaling, and that each exercise simultaneously engaged and developed his ear, mind, fingers, and foot.

The core elements of artistic pedaling may be summarized as:

1. The ability to taper pedal releases inaudibly to the point of change.
2. The ability to engage the pedal intentionally rather than habitually.
3. The ability to vary the depth of the pedal for an infinite variety of wetter or drier sonorities.

Of equal importance is what happens on the keyboard. Hands and damper pedal must work together inseparably to create each desired musical effect. The ear will determine increasingly refined results.

Fortunately, artistic pedaling can be incorporated at any age and any level of development. Both elementary and advanced pianists will benefit from learning or reviewing the exercises in this chapter. Acquiring artistic pedaling, a most worthwhile endeavor, can lead to a lifetime of musical advancements and achievements. Gladly, it's never too early to learn these skills; thankfully, it's never too late.

## Endnotes

[1] Astor Piazzolla. *Milonga del ángel.* Publisher: Editorial Lagos (Warner/Chappell Music), Buenos Aires, © 1987. Used by permission. Included in *Celebration Series Perspectives*®, Piano Repertoire 08. Mississauga: The Frederick Harris Music Co., Limited, 2008. www.frederickharrismusic.com. The milonga, a traditional song genre from the Río de la Plata region of Argentina, Uruguay, and Southern Brazil, served as a source of inspiration for the tango.

[2] Audio tracks of this chapter's musical examples are available at www.stevenhesla.com

[3] The tapered pedal release may be the most critical element of artistic damper pedaling. When students are learning to release the pedal inaudibly, they may at first slice (or cut off), rather than taper, the ends of notes. To illustrate the difference, have students intentionally slice the ends of the triads into silence with abrupt pedal releases. Try this with and without pedal thumps. Then, explore a variety of tapered pedal releases until a nuanced erasure of each sonority feels natural. The physical motions of hands and feet are mirror images of each other during pedal-changes: as the foot comes up, the hands go down. Therefore, thumpy pedal releases will invite thumpy attacks on the keyboard, corrupting both technique and tone. Sliced pedal releases will produce slicing effects on the keyboard. And artfully tapered pedal releases will promote graceful entries into the next notes and harmonies. Artistic pedaling will invariably and positively influence the pianist's touch.

[4] While there are exceptions, it is generally important for previous sonorities to be completely damped (silenced) at the moment subsequent tones are gathered into a new pedaled event. Also, quick pedal reengagements may be necessary for a particular musical effect, but there are more circumstances where a somewhat delayed reengagement would serve the music at least as well, if not better. Tapered pedal releases and unhurried pedal reengagements can make a huge difference in musical artistry, equipping pianists with highly pliable tools to enhance rather than obscure musical intentions.

[5] The release of un-pedaled triads should have the same tapered effect as the release of pedaled triads in Ex.5 (*cf.* endnote 3). The sound should evaporate, rather than slice, into silence. While the duration of silence will vary greatly according to articulation, note values, and tempos, the principle of bridging silence is uniformly applicable in all circumstances.

[6] Finger-pedaling has been an important means of sustaining notes on keyboard instruments since the Baroque period and earlier. A familiar example of finger-pedaling is notated in J.S. Bach's famous *Prelude in C Major* from the first book of *Preludes and Fugues*, where longer durations are indicated for the initial sixteenth notes in the left hand. Its benefits to pedaled and un-pedaled music on the modern pianoforte are enormous.

[7] It would be appropriate and productive for younger or less experienced pianists to rehearse these exercises over the course of several lessons. Any given exercise might become an assignment for one week or longer. Other exercises could be created to meet students' needs.

# CHAPTER 32

# Practice Techniques for the Intermediate Student

## Geoffrey Haydon

Teachers and students spend many hours in the teaching studio during the intermediate stages of development. It is here that much critical feedback is given concerning interpretation, fingering, technical approach, note accuracy, balance, etc. For certain rare students, this kind of information is all that is needed to insure consistent progress towards pianistic improvement. However, most students not only need this type of information but they also require specific information about what kinds of practice activities in which to engage in order to insure consistent, high-quality progress.

In fact, much good teaching is communicating to students how to practice. The activities a student pursues in a practice session can lead directly to accomplishing a desired goal. Unfortunately, there are activities students often pursue that lead away from a desired goal. In essence, we must recognize that time spent at an instrument does not necessarily insure improvement will occur. It is *how* the time is spent that seems to dictate the quality and rate of progress. Therefore, students who understand the importance of developing practice strategies, organizing each practice session, and monitoring their own progress will be much more likely to make consistent improvement. As teachers, it is our responsibility to help students create a productive practice environment where consistent growth occurs.

## Structuring the Practice Session

Structuring the practice session is a step in the right direction. The student begins by defining both long and short-range goals. Long-range goals will generally take a week to one month to accomplish. Anything spanning a longer period of time can and should be monitored by the teacher who sees the big picture (from beginning through intermediate through advanced levels) more clearly. Long range goals might include memorizing a certain amount of repertoire, refining and polishing a given amount of repertoire, making progress with an identified technical problem, increasing the tempo while maintaining control, etc. Teachers can make it clear how much progress is expected from one week to the next (the amount should be reasonable yet challenging).

Short-range goals are things students can accomplish within each practice session or over the course of two or three sessions. Defining short-range goals might include choosing fingering, practicing for fingering reliability and/ or consistency, making progress with a technical problem, spending time finding different ways to practice a passage, theoretical analysis, and many more. Eventually students become conditioned to plan, in a detailed manner, activities for a practice session. However, it is more common for students to begin their practice session by playing through a piece and waiting for flaws to surface. Then, rather than developing strategies for solving each problem, they simply play the piece again hoping that mindless repetition will lead to perfection. This mode of practice behavior is rarely effective in bringing about consistent, qualitative progress. Instead, students should have a definite idea of exactly what activities they will pursue in a given practice session and more importantly how much time will be devoted to each activity.

Another way students don't get the most out of their practice time is by spending too much time on any one activity. It may seem that the more time spent on mastering a problem, the quicker one will master it. However, in reality this statement is rarely true. The most obvious example is the age-old adage that it is better to practice one hour each day of the week than to practice seven hours for one day per week. A better strategy would be to spend a given amount of time solving a problem and then leave it for the next practice session. Usually some progress even happens in the interim provided, of course, the time between sessions is not too long. The idea, then, is that students engage in a variety of practice activities during each practice session rather than spending the entire time on any one activity.

The intermediate level is a crucial time for most students. They will often be at a musical age where they are beginning to think for themselves rather than blindly following instructions. The habits formed at this time will most likely follow them into the advanced levels of study. Therefore, it is important good practice habits are established.

# Listening

Most students need help learning to listen carefully to their own sound. They should be actively listening to others make music, too. Having students play for each other is often an effective way to get them to listen more critically. Having them then give positive feedback can also be instructive. If students learn to be supportive and constructively critical listeners, they can create a competitive atmosphere while building camaraderie.

Using the inner ear is also an important aspect of listening. Hearing the music inside your head means you already know what to listen for when you play. It is helpful to imagine other instruments playing a piece and hear the result in the inner ear. Words are often inadequate tools to describe sound. Hearing a string or wind instrument perform a legato melody can be indispensable in enabling students to understand how to transfer this concept to the piano. Since much piano music is conceived as instrumental and/or vocal music transferred to the piano, it is imperative students hear how other instruments and singers make music. It is even better if they experience singing or playing other instruments for themselves. For example, a good way to teach articulation involves having the students first sing an articulation such as a two-note slur. After hearing them sing, the teacher gets a clear reading of their concept of articulation. Once the concept is right, students should be able to apply it to the piano more easily and with better, more accurate results.

# Performing Versus Practicing

Performing and practicing are two different concepts. Students must understand the difference between them. An athlete expects to engage in activities that relate to, but are not the same as, playing the sport. For example, basketball players spend some of their practice time running up and down stairs to build endurance even through they will never do this in a game. Piano students often spend too much time playing a piece instead of working on it. Many think playing a piece IS practicing. While it is true that playing in basketball games will make you a better player, you will not improve very much if that is all you do. Piano playing is much the same. Time must be spent mastering various techniques and solving problems in order for a reasonable amount of improvement and reliability to occur in performance situations.

# Practice Strategies

It is important that teachers help students arrange for success when they set out to solve a problem. The problem must be identified and isolated. Then practice strategies can be developed that will lead to an eventual solution. There will be students who "stop and start" when playing, going back to "correct" a flaw. However, no flaw can be corrected once it has occurred. In fact, stopping creates another flaw since the flow of the music has been interrupted. In a performance, this philosophy is obvious. But it should be equally apparent in practicing. Most flaws will only occur when in context and stopping to "correct" the flaw doesn't do anything to see to it that it doesn't occur again. Teachers can sometimes encourage this approach by stopping students as soon as a flaw occurs. A better strategy involves finding a practice tempo where the least amount of flaws can surface (preferably none). Students should quickly find the tempo at which everything can be done correctly at least three times in a row. This tempo will almost always be much slower than anticipated. Then the tempo can be gradually increased to a speed that eventually surpasses the performance tempo while still adhering to the same standards. The metronome is an excellent aid when employing this practice strategy. Without a metronome, most students cannot discipline themselves to keep the tempo slow. No matter how hard they try without the metronome, the slow tempos accelerate to tempos too fast for the mind to process all the new information. As a result, many flaws begin to happen. It is better to begin with a product that is as close to perfection as possible so that not much time is spent undoing bad habits or correcting flaws.

Practicing from the end of a segment back towards its beginning is a strategy that produces positive results. Students often choose a segment to practice and then begin by working out the first part of it. Next, they play the worked out segment but, instead of stopping to work out the next segment, they continue on into less familiar territory with possibly poorly planned fingering and other flaws. If this occurs several times, then a habit forms that eventually must be broken once the part is worked out. Fingering, articulation, and dynamics must be determined in the beginning stages of work on a segment. Then students must be sure they are practicing what has been worked out consistently. If they begin by practicing the last segment; then work on the next to last segment; and continue in this manner until they reach the beginning segment, they will always be playing into familiar territory. Therefore, good habits will be reinforced rather than bad ones being created.

A certain percentage of practice time should be devoted to approaching problematic material in a variety of ways that involves manipulating the notes to facilitate mastery. This kind of information can be most helpful since there is usually nothing written in the music itself that would indicate how to manipulate the material in an effort to solve problems.

Intermediate students often find it difficult to deal with two different articulations distributed between the hands. There are many occasions when a staccato or a two-note slur articulation is indicated in one hand while legato is marked in the other. It is often beneficial to allow students to first deal with these problems in the context of something familiar and non-intimidating such as a scale or five-finger pattern (See examples 1 & 2).

Example 1

Example 2

After having mastered these skills in a familiar environment, it will be much easier to apply them in their repertoire.

Another useful way to practice is called blocking. It involves intelligently combining notes into clusters allowing students to conceive of a passage of individual notes in groups. For example, scales and arpeggios can be blocked according to finger groups. This kind of practice helps students learn the fingering more quickly and facilitates playing the scales and arpeggios at fast speeds. Example 3 demonstrates this practice strategy using an A major scale and arpeggio. It blocks the finger groups (alternating groups of three and four fingers) and then isolates the final or ending finger since it is not consistently a member of a finger group.

Example 3                        A major scale and arpeggio blocks

The blocks can then be seamed together by isolating the thumb as in example 4.

Example 4        A major scale and arpeggio blocks with isolated thumb

The passage below from Clementi's *Sonatina in D Major, Op. 36, No. 3* can be blocked in the right hand (See example 6).

Example 5 Clementi – *Sonatina in D Major, Op. 36, No. 6 (ms. 9-10)*

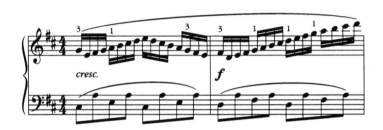

Example 6

The left hand can be blocked several different ways. Both example 7 and example 8 establish the harmonic basis and rhythm of the material.

Example 7

Example 8

Example 9 and example 10 are designed to facilitate the technical difficulty of an Alberti bass figure.

Example 9

Example 10

Bach's *Minuet in G Major* (see example 11) can be blocked in both hands to help students assimilate the notes in groups (see example 12). Moreover, students will more easily recognize the harmonic content.

Example 11

Example 12

Another step in the process would be to have students block less notes at one time as they progress towards playing the piece as written (see example 13).

Example 13

Example 15 blocks the material in Schumann's *Wild Horseman* (see example 14) considering both the harmonic and melodic content.

Example 14          Schumann – *The Wild Horseman, Op. 68* (ms. 1-4)

Schumann, The Wild Horseman, Op. 68 (ms. 1–4)

Example 15

Another useful way to manipulate a passage involves changing the rhythm. The following excerpt is often problematic for intermediate students (see example 16).

Example 16    J. S. Bach – *Two-part Invention in F Major* (ms. 30-34)

J.S. Bach, Two-Part Invention in F Major (ms. 30–34)

This passage can be manipulated in countless ways. The following dotted rhythm helps isolate notes in groups of twos with the first note being long and the second short (see example 17).

Example 17

This dotted rhythm simply reverses the long and short notes (see example 18).

Example 18

Practicing a passage using different articulations helps students isolate different aspects of the passage and allows them to experiment with different articulation possibilities. It leads them to a deeper understanding of the passage in all respects. Examples 19-21 gives some suggested articulation possibilities with the same Bach Invention.

Example 19

Example 20

Example 21

The same passage can also be practiced accenting chosen notes. This method brings attention to the accented notes eventually helping students to develop control in shaping the passage. There are many ways to practice using accents such as: 1) accenting every two, three (see example 23), or four notes; 2) accenting a particular finger every time it plays; 3) accenting the off-beat notes as in example 22 below:

Example 22                                    accenting the off-beat notes

Example 23                                    accenting every three notes

Another way to practice a passage is to stop on chosen notes. This method allows students to concentrate on only a few notes at a time. Students can practice in this manner at performance tempo almost immediately thus accelerating the process of learning to successfully perform the passage up to tempo. The following excerpt demonstrates stopping on every first note of a group of four using the same Bach Invention:

Example 24

Students should be made aware that they can practice stopping on every second, third, or fourth notes as well. As they put the passage back together they will want to take the same approach with larger groups of notes such as eight or sixteen.

# Damper Pedal Technique

Using the sustain (damper) pedal is often a problematic issue with intermediate level students. Before exploring the stylistic applications of its use too much, students should learn basic information about when and why it is used. Many methods introduce the pedal by demonstrating how it can cause the notes of a given arpeggio to sustain even though the fingers are not holding the keys down.

Example 25

Unfortunately, many methods don't go beyond this concept of sustaining arpeggiated harmonies and therefore take it for granted students will learn other pedal applications on their own. The most frequent reason for using the pedal is to connect notes and/or harmonies that cannot be connected by the fingers alone. Many students are never taught this simple concept. They are instead told to use their ear and operate their foot accordingly. Sometimes this approach works but it is important to recognize the information is vague. While it is true our ears play an important role in pedal use, students will greatly benefit from knowing precisely how to connect notes and/or harmonies in a clear, reliable manner. The following pedal exercise (see example 26) demonstrates a basic pedaling technique using the concept of *syncopated pedaling*.

Example 26

The foot is lifted on beats two and four while the hands play on beats one and three. It is important that the hands not lift until the foot goes back down or else a break in the sound will occur. Students should listen carefully for a smooth connection of one harmony to the next with no break in sound. The foot should not go back down until the ear hears a clear, well-defined harmony. The register of the piano will affect how the pedal is used. As the register becomes lower, the strings have more bulk and length. Therefore, it takes longer for them to be silenced. Playing this pedal exercise in different registers of the piano will illustrate how subtle changes in pedal use must occur in order to attain consistent clarity (see example 27).

Example 27

Students should be encouraged to come up with their own practice methods. They can use their imagination in attempting to solve musical and technical problems. Teachers can suggest and advise them in their quest to develop reliable practice techniques.

When students are by themselves practicing, the task of mastering a piece of music can seem overwhelming. They are confronted by a variety of musical and technical problems that need to be solved. Therefore, teachers must be sympathetic to a student's perspective without lowering standards. Marking in the score with pencil (or using post-its) is an effective method to remind students about how and what to practice. Simply telling them does not insure the information will be remembered after leaving the studio. After a new concept is introduced, it should be reinforced until the teacher is satisfied it has been fully integrated into the student's practice methods. Teachers should regularly ask students: 1) how they practice; 2) in what specific activities they engage when practicing; 3) how much progress has occurred as a result of a particular practice activity. This information is useful in refining students' practice habits.

Students need to realize that the product presented at the lesson is a direct reflection of the work done at home. The notion "I played this better at home" cannot be taken into account. It is what happens in the teaching studio and later on the stage that indicates reliability (and therefore usefulness) and depth of understanding. Once students honestly assess their performance in the teaching studio, they can effectively evaluate their practicing. Anything done well in the teaching studio most likely indicates successful practice strategies. Anything not done well needs to be reconsidered and perhaps restructured.

Eventually teachers want their students to become independent learners and have the ability to solve problems without much outside help. This transformation does not happen overnight. At first only the teacher can monitor progress accurately but eventually students should learn to monitor their own progress. As they come closer to this goal, they will be closer to becoming independent musicians who can produce a first rate product.

# CHAPTER 33

# Fingering Principles for the Intermediate Student

## Geoffrey Haydon

For piano teachers, teaching fingering is a little like teaching good manners. There are many ways of going about something, but only a few are the best and most efficient means. Just as there are people with bad manners, there are also those with bad fingering habits. Both learn to get along but not without undue struggle. Learning what ways are best and most efficient requires experience, discipline, and an acquired knowledge of principles. Piano teachers must see to it that students learn principles of good fingering to help assure their future independence as good players.

It is important to decide on fingering as early as possible in the process of learning a piece. Choosing fingering early gives students an opportunity to reinforce a good product for a longer period of time than if they wait and therefore spend unnecessary time undoing bad habits. Many students don't pay attention to what fingers they are using; often a reason for awkward fingering choices. Once students make a conscious decision about a fingering, they should carefully monitor what fingers they are using. Teachers can help make them more aware of their fingering by observing it in the lesson and correcting it when it is wrong. It is also important that once a fingering is chosen, it be executed that way consistently. Reinforcing one way to do something means it will eventually become second nature. The reinforcement must be frequent and consistent for this second nature process to happen.

The fingering should be indicated in the score until it is no longer necessary to do so. Most intermediate students will need finger indications in the music. It is best to have them write their own fingering in their music. Some students will want to indicate a finger over most notes. It is all right to allow them to do so at first; however, eventually they should learn to rely on less frequent finger indications.

How important is it that the published fingering indicated in the score be followed? The answer depends on whether the fingering serves its purpose for the particular student. Editors create most published fingering (not the original composer). It therefore represents one person's opinion at best and cannot be guaranteed to work for anyone but perhaps the editor himself. There is no harm in trying the published fingering but students should not feel obligated to use it. While it is true that we all have eight fingers and two thumbs, the similarity stops there. Everyone's hand has important differences in size, the proportion of fingers to each other, and stretching potential. Therefore, there are often several possible fingering choices. Students must find the fingering that is best for them. The only time they might want to be more loyal to a published fingering would be when they know the composer put it there. It can be revealing to consider a composer's fingering because it might lead to a better understanding of the desired sound and/or interpretation. In the end, however, students should determine what fingering best suits their needs.

Having said all of the above, an acquired knowledge of good fingering principles facilitates choosing appropriate fingering in a piece. Learning good fingering principles begins with scale and arpeggio fingering. All major and minor scale fingerings follow the basic rules below:

1.  The thumb is not used on a black key.

2.  The basic finger pattern will alternate a group of three fingers (1, 2, 3) with a group of four fingers (1, 2, 3, 4).

3.  When beginning on a white key (on the first scale degree) and ascending, begin on 5 in the left hand and 1 in the right hand. The reverse is true when beginning on a white key (on the first scale degree) and descending.

4.  Within a finger group, the fingers occur in successive order.

If these rules are followed, only a few scales will generate more than one possibility for a correct fingering.

# White-Key Majors

The C major scale is commonly considered a point of departure when first learning scales. Its fingering can be directly applied to 5 white-key major scales in both hands (C, G, D, A & E). Moreover, 6 out of 7 white-key major scales in the right hand (C, G, D, A, E & B), and 6 out of 7 white-key major scales in the left hand (C, G, D, A, E, & F) use the C Major scale fingering.

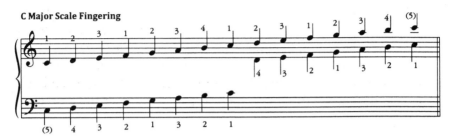

The above C major fingering is based on the simple principle of a group of three fingers followed by a group of four fingers thus accounting for the seven *different* notes in the scale. The direct application of this fingering applies to G, D, A and E major scales in both hands. For example, the D major scale is performed using the exact same fingering:

The F and B major scales reverse the order of finger groups in one hand. In the right hand, F major utilizes the group of four fingers first, followed by the group of three fingers when ascending. The same is true for B major in the left hand when descending. In this case, the ending finger is the fourth finger instead of the usual fifth finger. Note, therefore, that the fourth finger "wears two hats" in this scale fingering:  1) a regular finger within a 1234 finger group; 2) an ending finger at the top or bottom of the scale.

At this point, it must be noted that seven out of twelve possible major scales have been fingered using just two finger patterns. Now it is time to consider the five remaining black-key major scales. In the left hand, four out of five scales have the same fingering (D♭, E♭, B♭ & A♭) while the right hand generates five different fingerings. Therefore, all left hand major scale fingerings can be performed utilizing only four different finger patterns.

## Black-Key Majors

In the left hand, four black-key major scales (D♭, E♭, B♭ & A♭) begin with the group of three fingers followed by the group of four fingers when ascending. The remaining black-key scale (G♭) begins with the group of four fingers followed by the group of three fingers when ascending. At the top of the scale, it is recommended that the third finger be used as a final finger; however, some people prefer the second finger. The fourth or fifth fingers are not considered suitable left hand final fingers in these scales.

In the right hand, it is best to consider D♭ and G♭ as a pair. While their fingerings are different, the existence of only two white keys per octave dictates the fingering because the thumb must play on these notes.

B♭ and E♭ are similar because the thumb plays on the second note (the first white key when ascending); however, the order of finger groupings is reversed in each scale.

The Ab major scale has the most interesting fingering of all since it begins in the middle of a four-note finger group when ascending. However, most people do not use the fourth finger when beginning this scale since it is not really needed. Instead they use the second and third fingers. In this case, the fourth finger is not actually used until the second octave. In addition, because the top of the scale finishes with an incomplete four-finger group, the illusion of two three-finger groups in succession is created when descending from the top note.

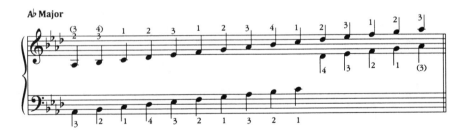

# White-Key Minors

Minor scale fingerings can also be categorized into white-key minors and black-key minors. White-key minors are simple: All white-key minors (all forms: natural, harmonic, melodic) finger exactly like their parallel major. For example, C minor (all forms) uses the same fingering as C major or B minor (all forms) uses the same fingering as B major (see the following examples).

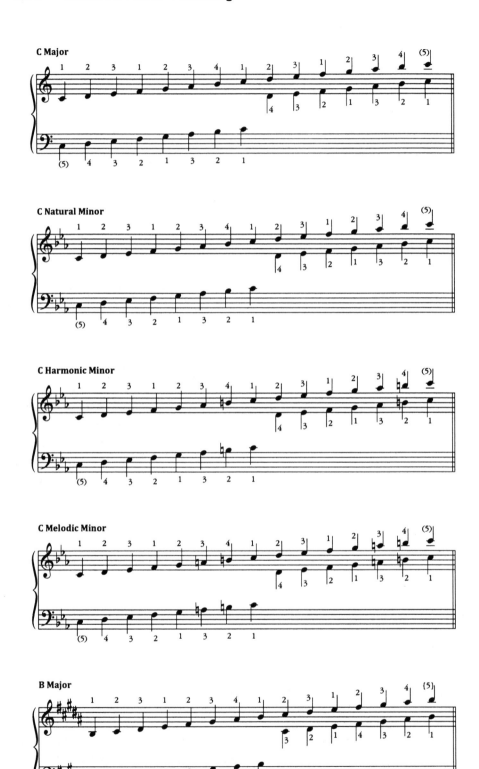

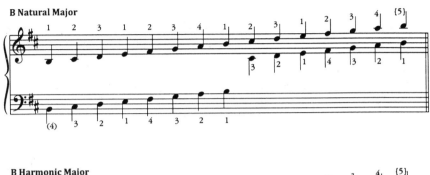

# Black-Key Minors

Black-key minor scales generate several different fingerings. In the right hand, there are quite a few different fingerings; however, they can be categorized.

In the left hand, all forms of F♯ and C♯ minor scales are fingered the same as their parallel majors. In the right hand, C♯ natural and harmonic minor scales use A♭ major fingering while C♯ melodic minor is fingered like D♭ major. Note that the third finger must be used at the top of this scale so as to initiate the correct natural minor fingering for the descent. In the right hand, F♯ natural and harmonic minor are also fingered like A♭ major. F♯ melodic minor has a unique fingering that is similar to A♭ major but not exactly the same. It begins with an incomplete three-finger group rather than an incomplete four-finger group. Note that the third finger must also be used at the top of this scale so as to initiate the correct natural minor fingering for the descent.

Bb and Eb minor scales each have one left-hand fingering (different from their parallel majors) that remains the same for all three forms of minor. In the right hand, all forms of Bb minor finger exactly like its parallel major. Eb natural minor's right hand fingering is essentially borrowed from Gb major (the two white keys dictate where the thumb must play). The other two forms, harmonic and melodic, also use the same fingering.

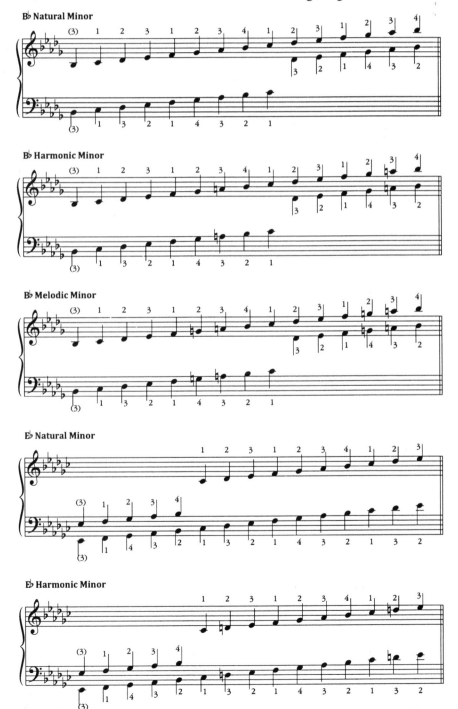

**E♭ Melodic Minor**

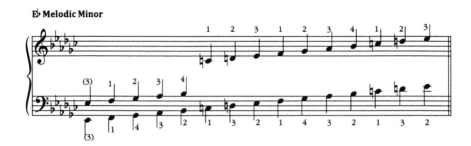

In the right hand, all forms of G♯ minor finger exactly like its parallel major. G♯ minor has two left-hand fingerings: 1) G♯ harmonic and melodic minor are the same as A♭ major; 2) G♯ natural minor borrows its fingering from B major. Note that the second finger can be used at the top of this scale so as to facilitate the natural minor fingering for the scale descent.

**G♯ Natural Minor**

**G♯ Harmonic Minor**

**G♯ Melodic Minor**

# Chromatic Scale

The chromatic scale generates many fingering possibilities. The first one to teach uses only the thumb and second finger on white keys and the third finger on all black keys. This fingering is the most likely to produce clear articulation. However, due to how often the thumb is used, it is the least likely to attain speed.

If a faster, more legato effect is desired, then the following fingering, which adds one four-finger group, is recommended.

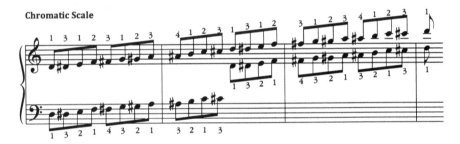

The fingering below, which regenerates itself every two octaves, makes use of alternating groups of three and four fingers (with one instance of repeating a three-finger group) for when extremely fast speeds are desired.

In some situations, the fifth finger can be employed in chromatic scales for the highest possible speeds.

# Major and Minor Arpeggios

Major and minor arpeggio fingerings are based on the *all white key* arpeggios such as C, F, and G major or D, E and A minor. All of these arpeggios and their respective inversions use consistent finger patterns. Therefore, they are used as an important point of departure in generating all major and minor arpeggio fingerings. Let us first consider C major arpeggio fingerings to establish this "point of departure." Notice that all positions (root, 1ˢᵗ inversion, 2ⁿᵈ inversion) are included. There are several reasons to teach all positions: 1) the difficulty of each is about the same; 2) knowing all three adequately prepares students; 3) 1ˢᵗ and 2ⁿᵈ inversion occur more often in piano repertoire than root position.

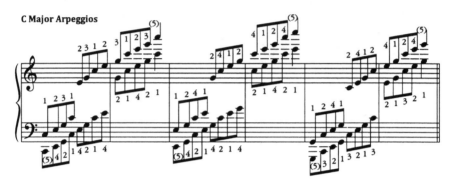

The above fingerings are based on the following principles. These principles, listed below, apply to all major and minor arpeggios that begin on a white key:

1. When ascending and the first note is a white key, always begin on the thumb in the right hand and fifth finger in the left hand. The opposite occurs at the top of the arpeggio when turning around to descend: the arpeggio will end its ascent on the fifth finger in the right hand and thumb in the left hand.

2. In both hands, all first inversions beginning on a white key will use the fingering: 1, 2, 4, (5).

3. All right hand root positions beginning on a white key will use the fingering: 1, 2, 3, (5).

4. All left hand second inversions beginning on a white key will use the fingering: (5), 3, 2, 1.

After considering the above rules, there are only a few positions left to discuss in covering the C major arpeggios. The second inversion in the right hand is fingered: 1, 2, 4, (5). And the root position in the left hand uses the same fingering (but in reverse, of course). Many intermediate students (and some advanced) will want to use the third finger in place of the fourth for these positions but it is not recommended. There will be occasions when it will be better to use the third finger in these positions, but it should be the exception rather than the rule.

To gain a better understanding of arpeggio fingering, it is helpful to form arpeggio "chord blocks."

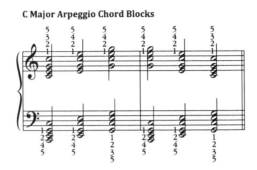

C Major Arpeggio Chord Blocks

Play the root position arpeggio chord block in the right hand and the second inversion one in the left hand. Notice that the position of both hands is exactly alike. The thirds occur between the first, second, and third fingers while the fourth occurs between the third and fifth fingers. These similarities are due to the symmetry of the right and left hands. By moving both hands inward to the next position (inversion), the finger positions (hand shapes) continue to be identical in both hands. Move inward one more time and the same result occurs. These "all white-key" arpeggio fingerings apply not only to C major but D minor, E minor, F major, G major, and A minor, too, since they contain all white keys.

It is now time to consider arpeggios that contain black keys. First, remember that **as long as an arpeggio contains at least one white key, the thumb is not used on a black key.** Therefore, the fingering must be adjusted when the beginning note is a black key. The subsequent fingering is generated following these rules:

1.  When beginning on a black key in the right hand, the thumb will be used on the first white key when <u>ascending</u>.

2.  When beginning on a black key in the left hand, the thumb will be used on the first white key when <u>descending</u>.

Moreover, certain positions will use the third finger instead of the fourth. However, there is a simple logic in choosing the fingering if it is based on the "all white key" arpeggio fingering (discussed above) as a point of departure. For example, in the right hand, the second inversion of C major (an "all white key" arpeggio) is fingered: 1, 2, 4, (5). In changing the E natural to an E flat for C minor, you are getting further away from the fifth finger; therefore, the third finger is used instead of the fourth. In the left hand, the root position of C major is fingered: 1, 2, 4, (5). In changing the E natural to an E flat for C minor, you are getting closer to the fifth finger; therefore, the fourth finger is retained.

**C Minor Arpeggio Chord Blocks**

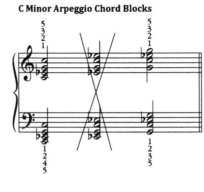

**C Minor Arpeggios**

*C major and minor arpeggios have the exact same formation as F major and F minor as well as G major and G minor. Therefore, F major and minor, and G major and minor arpeggios finger the same as C major and minor arpeggios. It therefore makes sense to group these three keys together.*

D major demonstrates the same logic but in the opposite hands. In the right hand, the second inversion of D minor (an "all white key" arpeggio) is fingered: 1, 2, 4, (5). In changing the F natural to an F sharp for D major, you are getting closer to the fifth finger; therefore, the fourth finger is retained. In the left hand, the root position of D minor (an "all white key" arpeggio) is fingered: 1, 2, 4, (5). In changing the F natural to an F sharp for D major, you are getting further away from the fifth finger; therefore, the third finger is used instead of the fourth.

**D Minor Arpeggios**

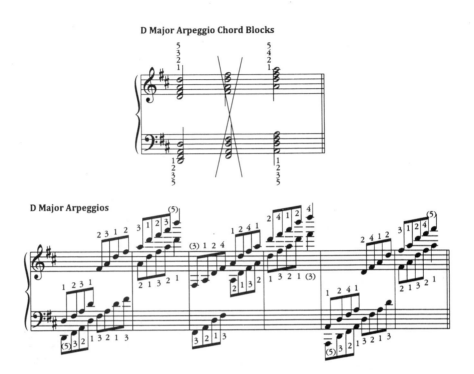

*D major and minor arpeggios have the exact same formation as E major and E minor as well as A major and A minor. Therefore, E major and minor, and A major and minor arpeggios finger the same as D major and minor arpeggios. It therefore makes sense to group these three keys together.*

Arpeggios containing two black keys and one white key use the thumb on the white key and arrange the rest of the fingers accordingly. For example, B major has only one white key (the note B); therefore, the thumb is used on B no matter what position (inversion) is being performed. All positions (inversions) of B major arpeggios use the root position fingering.

It follows that the fingerings of D♭ major, C♯ minor, E♭ major, F♯ minor, A♭ major, A♭ minor, and B♭ minor are based on the same principle. All of these, except B♭ minor, use the *first inversion* position. B♭ minor uses the *second inversion* position.

B minor and B♭ major are much like D major or C minor because there is only one black key in their respective triads. The fingering is generated following these basic principles (already stated earlier):

1.  In the right hand, all root positions beginning on a white key are fingered:  1, 2, 3, (5)

2.  All first inversions in both hands beginning on a white key are fingered: 1, 2, 4, (5).

3.  When beginning on a black note, the thumb plays on the next white note: 1) in the right hand ascending; 2) in the left hand descending.

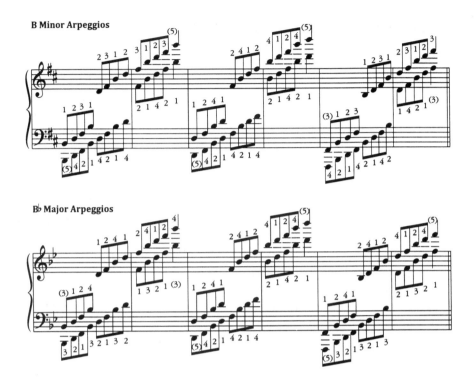

Since G♭ major and E♭ minor contain no white keys, the all white key "point of departure" fingering is used. The thumb playing on a black key is not a problem since there are no white keys in the arpeggios.

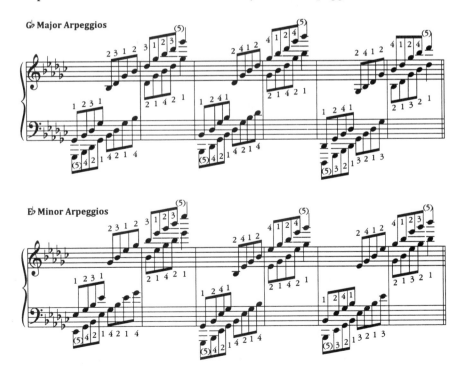

# Diminished Seventh Arpeggios

Diminished seventh arpeggios provide us with a good basis for all seventh chord arpeggios. Since seventh chords contain four notes, the fingering is not a complicated issue. We use the first four fingers leaving the 5th finger for beginning and/or ending notes in seventh chord arpeggios beginning on white keys. In many ways, these arpeggios are easier than major or minor arpeggios and might be taught first if students are familiar with the chords. One unique aspect of diminished seventh chords is that their inversions have the same exact notes as a root position diminished seventh chord by the beginning note name. In other words, the first inversion of a C diminished seventh chord has the same exact notes as a root position E♭ diminished seventh chord. Therefore, students do not need to learn more than the root position of each of the twelve possible diminished seventh chords. Since this circumstance is not true for any other kind of seventh chord (such as dominant, minor, or half-diminished seventh chords), all inversions should be learned with any seventh chord except that of the diminished seventh. The fingering principles discussed below for diminished seventh arpeggios can be easily applied to all seventh chords and their inversions. The C diminished seventh arpeggio below provides the fingering for all diminished seventh (and all other kinds of seventh chords) arpeggios that begin on white keys.

Diminished seventh arpeggios that begin on black keys follow the same rules as those stated earlier with regard to major and minor arpeggios:

1.  When beginning on a black key in the right hand, the thumb will be used on the first white key when <u>ascending</u>.

2.  When beginning on a black key in the left hand, the thumb will be used on the first white key when <u>descending</u>.

The five diminished seventh chords that begin on a black key can be grouped (C♯ & F♯, B♭ & E♭, and G♯) according to fingering:

C♯ and F♯ diminished seventh arpeggios finger the same.

C# Diminished 7th Arpeggio

B♭ and E♭ diminished seventh arpeggios finger the same.

B♭ Diminished 7th Arpeggio

G# Diminished 7th Arpeggio

# Trills

An entire chapter could be devoted to the execution of trills. There are two basic types: measured and unmeasured. Measured trills are most likely going to last a short period of time while unmeasured trills last for longer periods of time. Students will encounter both in intermediate repertoire. They should practice trills using any possible combination of two fingers in both hands. Sometimes it will be necessary to play a trill with the third and fourth, or fourth and fifth (or other combinations) fingers. However, most trills can be performed using one's best "trill fingers." Most students will favor a trill with either the second and third fingers or the thumb and third (or second) fingers. Therefore, it is recommended they include in their technical practice measured trills in a variety of rhythmic subdivisions covering all the possible black and white key combinations for both half steps and whole steps. Below are two examples of such exercises. Once students are comfortable with these trill exercises, they can do the same drills using different combinations of the third, fourth, and fifth fingers.

## Octaves

Dealing with octaves involves learning how to use more than just the thumb and fifth finger. Except in the case of unusually small hands, pianists should endeavor to make use of the fourth and perhaps even the third fingers when playing octave passages. When playing scales in octaves, using the fifth finger on white keys and the fourth on black keys makes it easier to play fast and/or legato. Moreover, because the fourth finger generally has more flesh than the fifth finger, it will be less apt to slip off a black key and it will be stronger.

As students choose fingering in a piece, they will rely on the above principles for guidance. However, more often than not, adjustments need to be made when applying the above scale and arpeggio fingerings to a given piece. Articulation should always play a role in influencing a fingering decision as well. A staccato line can be fingered is if it were legato for a more safe approach. If possible, avoid using the thumb on the second note of a two-note slur in order to avoid bumping the resolution.

## Chord Fingerings

Students are often careless in their approach to fingering left hand oom-pah and/or oom-pah-pah patterns. Some students will use the third or second finger on the single bass note and employ the fifth finger in the ensuing chord. Therefore, the distance between the bass note and chord tends to be maximized, and students miss an opportunity to find the bass note by measuring the octave from the thumb an octave above the indicated bass note. The fifth finger should be used for the single bass note and it should be avoided whenever possible in the chord.

Grieg, Album Leaf, Op. 12, No. 7 (ms. 1–3)

Chopin, Waltz in A Minor (ms. 1–4)

## Repeated Notes

Fingering repeated notes brings up several questions. Should repeated notes warrant the same finger being used over and over or should different fingers be used on the same note or key? Several factors should influence the decision. First and always of premier importance, what kind of sound is desired? Using one finger to repeat the same note will involve the wrist and arm. Therefore, the natural tendency will be to produce a sound that is strong and percussive. A less percussive, soft sound is possible using only one finger but much care must be taken to avoid the natural tendency of the arm and/or wrist moving too much. Using a combination of different fingers will involve the wrist and arm much less, and in a more horizontal way. A less percussive, softer sound will most likely be the result. A combination of different fingers can help build in a dynamic shape of the melodic line. Many students tend to hammer each note with the same intensity when using the same finger to play repeated notes. The result is often an uninteresting melodic line. Using a combination of different fingers creates varied intensities on each note due to the differences in each finger. For example, the opening of the first movement of Clementi's *Sonatina in C Major, Op. 36, No. 3* has repeated eighth-notes as an integral part of the melody. Speed is not a factor here since the difficulty of the repeated notes is the same whether one finger or a combination of different fingers is used. Therefore, there are two distinct possibilities. The first uses the same finger to play the repeated note figures:

Clementi, Sonatina in C Major, Op. 36, No. 3: I. Spiritoso (ms. 1–4)

The result with the above fingering could be quite percussive, heavy, and shapeless unless the student knows how to use the arm to play lightly and with varied attacks. The second possibility uses a combination of different fingers to play the repeated note figures:

Clementi, Sonatina in C Major, Op. 36, No. 3: I. Spiritoso (ms. 1–4)

Here, the result will more likely be a light, less percussive melodic line that subtly varies the notes.

The second factor in choosing a repeated note fingering is speed. How quickly do the notes repeat? Performing fast repeated notes is only possible using a combination of different fingers. The point or speed where one must rule out using only one finger will depend on the level of student and his/her physical talent. Once the decision is made to use a combination of different fingers, then the question of which fingers to use must be addressed. A good preparatory technical exercise involves practicing repeated notes with every different possible combination of fingers. For example, we can use the following finger combinations when using just one hand:

| | |
|---|---|
| 2, 1, 2, 1 . . . | 3, 5, 3, 5 . . . |
| 1, 3, 1, 3 . . . | 4, 5, 4, 5 . . . |
| 1, 4, 1, 4 . . . | 3, 2, 1, 3, 2, 1 . . . |
| 1, 5, 1, 5 . . . | 4, 3, 2, 4, 3, 2 . . . |
| 2, 3, 2, 3 . . . | 5, 4, 3, 5, 4, 3 . . . |
| 2, 4, 2, 4 . . . | 4, 3, 2, 1, 4, 3, 2, 1 . . . |
| 2, 5, 2, 5 . . . | 5, 4, 3, 2, 5, 4 ,3, 2 . . . |
| 3, 4, 3, 4 . . . | 5, 4, 3, 2, 1, 5, 4, 3, 2, 1 . . . |

These should be practiced on both white and black keys. Moreover, the above fingerings can be combined or done in retrograde. Once facility and speed are developed, fast repeated notes are no longer a problem. Students will also learn which of the above fingerings are easier and which are more difficult. The easier combinations will be chosen whenever possible but having practiced all the different combinations means students are better equipped to deal with any situation. For example, Scarlatti's *Sonata in D Major, K. 96* has many repeated sixteenth note figures. They all require a combination of different fingers due to their fast speed. Here are two possible fingerings:

Scarlatti, Sonata in D Major, K. 96 (ms. 33–41)

**Scarlatti, Sonata in D Major, K. 96 (ms. 33–41)**

Rhythm can also play a role when choosing repeated note fingerings. Students can base their choice of fingering combination on its compatibility with the rhythmic organization of the repeated note figure. The following exercise illustrates this concept:

There is also the possibility of alternating hands to perform repeated notes. Drummers and percussionists are familiar with this method. The most common application is known to percussionists as *singles*—alternating each attack between the hands. There is also *doubles*—alternating two attacks between the hands. Drummers execute doubles by bouncing each stick but pianists have the option of either bouncing the arms or wrists (using only one finger per hand) or using a combination of different fingers in each hand. Singles are generally used for a more percussive effect whereas doubles can be less percussive, especially if a combination of different fingers is employed. For example, the fingering indicated in measures 68 and 69 of Bartok's *Dance No. 6 in Bulgarian Rhythm* from the *Mikrokosmos*, Bk. VI uses singles in the left hand and doubles in the right hand effectively combining both methods in a strong, percussive manner:

**Bartók, Dance No. 6 in Bulgarian Rhythm (ms. 68-69)**

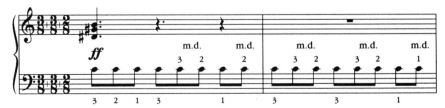

Most intermediate students will default to using the same finger rather than a combination of different fingers when confronted with a repeated note figure (even when a combination of different fingers is indicated in the score). The reason is obvious. It is easier and quicker to decide to use one finger in the early stages of learning a piece. However, students should not base fingering decisions solely on the above factors. They should be taught to weigh all of the factors and make intelligent, musical decisions. Then they should be open to perhaps changing their minds as the piece comes into focus if the original fingering decision appears to be inappropriate.

Eventually students should not need much help in choosing appropriate fingering. Having them pencil in their own fingering first, which teachers can soon afterwards edit, helps them achieve independence. It is important teachers explain the reason for changing a student's fingering choice. The student will then be more likely to make the right choice the next time. As students become more and more independent, the teacher will have less editing responsibility. Eventually students can be encouraged to be creative in choosing fingering. In other words, the best fingering cannot always be found taking a textbook approach. Experimenting with different possibilities can be fun and illuminating.

# CHAPTER 34

## Memorization via Internalization for the Intermediate Student

### Geoffrey Haydon

Memorization is a concept that conjures up a variety of reactions in a piano student. By simply mentioning the word, some students will immediately tense their body and utter statements about unreliability. Other students do not flinch and return the following week with the assigned music memorized. Still others seem to memorize in a natural manner and do not even need to be told "now it's time to memorize . . ." Whatever the case, memorization should be taught in the studio and all students should be led to the realization that it can be developed and improved as each day, week, month, and year goes by.

For a moment, let us digress and discuss why memorization is important. Some students will argue that not all instrumentalists are required to memorize their repertoire and therefore it is not very important. Historically speaking, Franz Liszt and Clara Schumann were among the first keyboard artists to perform entire programs from memory. Before Liszt and Schumann, it was not uncommon for keyboard soloists to use a score when performing although Mozart was well known for not only performing works from memory but also writing them down after the fact. There is also the argument that if the audience does not see the performer and simply listens with eyes closed then it should not make any difference whether the work is being performed from memory or being read from a score.

All of the above arguments present good points and perhaps one day there will be universal acceptance of performers and/or performances regardless of whether the repertoire is memorized. However, the fact remains that in today's world, pianists are expected to perform solo works from memory with the possible exception of occasional twentieth century works. Therefore, tradition has established this expectancy and in order to adequately compete, the aspiring solo pianist must face the reality of developing reliable memory skills. However, this fact alone is neither the only nor the best reason for developing the ability to play from memory.

To understand why memorization is important we need to understand the concept itself. The definition of *memorize* deals with having the power to remember. What does it mean to remember? The Merriam-Webster Dictionary gives several definitions relevant to our topic:

1. The power or process of reproducing or recalling what has been learned and retained especially through associative mechanisms

2. The store of things learned and retained from an organism's activity or experience as evidenced by modification of structure or behavior or by recall and recognition.

To remember, then, means having the ability to recall some event or sequence of events. What is missing in these definitions is the existence of an understanding of what is being recalled. This part is omitted because it is not necessary to have an understanding of something in order to *memorize* it. Memorizing something is best done through association, but what one chooses for an association may or may not be based on an understanding of it. For example, remembering the multiplication tables of grade school might be a process of association with a pattern of numbers rather than an understanding of the multiplication process itself. What should be realized is that if students understand the multiplication process then they will be less likely to forget the tables because they can recreate them at any time should they draw a blank trying to recite from the tables.

This analogy applies to music as well. Many students set about memorizing a piece of music without bothering to develop an understanding of the basic principles at work in the piece. Therefore, the memory work is done only on the surface level and is normally retained for a relatively short period of time. In addition, this kind of memorization is often unreliable under pressure. However, there are other students who have a deep understanding of the work being memorized and can tell you about not only the theoretical content but also the reason for why the notes are arranged the way they are on the page. These students perform more reliably under pressure and will most likely retain this information for a much longer period of time (sometimes an indefinite period of time).

The reason for this kind of reliability is that these students have not only memorized the information, they have *internalized* it. To internalize is to "incorporate within one's self [information] as guiding principles."

Therefore, if one is to internalize music, one must discern the guiding principles of the music. This internalization, of course, means developing an understanding of the music on an intellectual level. Therefore, the idea of memorization is not really a complete concept when applied to piano performing. Internalization is actually a much better concept to teach and apply.

How do students set about internalizing piano repertoire? First, we can identify different systems (at least five) of retaining and recalling musical information that can be used when performing:

1. kinesthetic,

2. aural,

3. theoretical,

4. photographic,

5. and keyboard choreography

## Kinesthetic System

Kinesthetic memory deals with muscle memory—that is, what it physically feels like to play a piece. The kinesthetic memory is perhaps the most important system of memorization but it is important to realize that it is also the most unreliable. It is unreliable because our bodies eventually react kinesthetically on a sub-conscious level. We cannot avoid getting to know our repertoire kinesthetically because, as we practice, our muscles develop a kinesthetic memory of what we are doing. Eventually, muscles develop the ability to execute given tasks in an "automatic pilot" mode. (Understanding this concept is also important in developing a well-disciplined, reliable system of practice.) However, muscles contain no intelligence—our brain is not located in the muscles. Muscles rely on the brain to tell them what to do. But when they are operating on automatic pilot, if a "wrong turn" is taken, they alone lack the necessary tools to find their way back where they are supposed to be.

The majority of children rely mostly on the kinesthetic system when performing without written music. They are operating on a different level of consciousness than that of adults who have a much greater awareness of what they are doing. Children are actually often able to perform incredible feats partially because they are not aware of either the specific mechanics or the difficulty involved. Later when they reach adulthood, a painful transition is sometimes necessary for them to continue performing at a high level. Some people never make this transition successfully. There will be some students who, around the age of 16 to 22 (depending on the person), will suffer from memory problems when performing after having had no problems with memory before this time. Such students will complain, "I never used to have memory problems. What is wrong with me?" There is usually nothing "wrong." The solution to the problem lies in no longer relying solely on a kinesthetic system of recall.

# Aural System

The ear (aural system) is also an important aid when performing from memory. The aural system of memory is also an involuntary aspect of internalization. We cannot avoid getting to know our pieces aurally because we hear them as they are being practiced. The sounds are then stored in our aural memory. This system's reliability depends on the level of development of a student's aural perception. Some student's level of aural perception enables them to find their way through a "memory slip." However, no matter how developed one's level of aural perception is, it is dangerous to rely solely on this system when playing from memory.

# Theoretical System

The most reliable system of internalization involves using an intellectual process that deals with a theoretical analysis and understanding of the musical material. Identifying what is in the score and using specific terms is the first step of this process. Then recognizing relationships through analysis will bring about an understanding of the work in question. There can be many different levels of theoretical analysis and to be absolutely thorough, the student must attempt to be familiar with as many as possible.

On the macro level is form. To have an understanding of a work from a bird's eye view facilitates identifying the basic structural components. Most musical forms employ the element of repetition. Recognizing repetition, whether it is exact repetition, repetition at another pitch level, or variation on an established idea, can greatly facilitate memory recall not to mention saving numerous hours of practice time. For example, in a sonata form, the exposition's first theme material is often repeated verbatim in the recapitulation. The exposition's second theme material is normally repeated in another key with some possible changes. The development explores more distant key areas using mostly material based on the first or second theme material presented in the exposition. All that is left is transitional material and an optional coda and/or introductory section. What if a sonata form movement or piece was internalized with this structure in mind? The pieces of the puzzle would undoubtedly fit more easily together. It would then make sense to internalize some sections together: the two first themes (exposition and recapitulation) since they are identical; and the two second themes (exposition and recapitulation) since they are similar but have differences related to them being in two different keys.

Working towards the micro level one would want to identify key areas, prevalent themes, sequences, intervallic unity, and other smaller devices. Identifying the main key centers in a work eventually leads to an understanding of how each key area is created and/or established. Then, students can analyze the prevalent themes indentifying harmonic relationships and intervallic unity. Eventually, the smallest level of analysis will reveal each interval, chord voicing, articulation marking, dynamic marking, tempo indication, and other markings on the page. All of these elements can be internalized but an understanding of their purpose within the context of a composition must be attained in the process.

## Photographic System

Another system of internalizing music involves the photographic memory. Some people are apparently born with the ability to remember, with great detail, anything that is put before them that they view with their eyes. Occasionally we hear about someone who, after viewing a magazine, can immediately recall all that is on a randomly selected page. These people are indeed amazing but also rare. However, all of us have some kind of photographic memory—we remember people's faces, for example. At a given moment, many pianists know where on the page the music they are playing exists. For some it might be as vague as "in the middle of the page," for others it could be as precise as "the third measure of the fourth line." Everyone's photographic memory can be developed and improved by recognizing its existence and then using it. One must first look at a page of music being as observant as possible about details. Then one must look away and attempt to see, in the mind, the page of music. Each time this process is repeated, the individual will identify something new that wasn't noticed before. Eventually a clear picture should emerge. A good way to check the photographic memory is to recreate the page (from memory) on a separate piece of paper and then compare it with the original.

## Keyboard Choreography System

The last system of internalization is difficult to put into words; however, all pianists have either a conscious or subconscious understanding of it. It is a system that involves the general makeup of the keyboard itself (referred hereafter as "keyboard choreography"). Since the keyboard is the medium through which we play the piano, then there is knowledge acquired that consists of a sequence of keystrokes associated with each piece learned. Pianists seem to naturally develop an inner sense of the keyboard—that is, they photographically see the keyboard in their mind. Beyond this concept, it is possible to imagine a piece of piano music as a sequence of key descents, what finger or fingers were used, how much force, and how they were released. For example, seeing a root position B major triad (see example 1) on the page would conjure up a white-key, black-key, black-key formation in a pianist's imagination.

Example 1

A sense of keyboard choreography actually combines the aural, theoretical, photographic, and kinesthetic aspects of internalization. The same root position B major triad also sparks, in the pianist's mind, a particular sound (aural), the knowledge of its content (theoretical), what it looks like on the page (photographic), and what it feels like to play it a certain way (kinesthetic). Therefore, it is possible to go through an entire composition away from the keyboard by only imagining it happening on the keyboard.

Internalizing a composition using only one of the above systems will not insure retention and therefore may prove to be unreliable under pressure. However, if students internalize a composition using all five systems, then they will know it five different ways. Each system supports the other so that when one or two break down, there are still the other three to back them up. The end result is much more memory security thereby producing a better quality and convincing performance.

How does one go about internalizing a composition using the above systems? What is the correct way to internalize a piece? There are actually many variations on the above methods of internalization. What works for one person does not always work for another. In the end, students must develop their own unique method. However, this statement makes the assumption that students have an organized, well-planned method or system of internalization. Most intermediate students do not and this statement may well apply to many advanced students, too. Therefore, it is important teachers help students develop a clear, consistent, and reliable method of internalization. Students should be warned about the danger of using mindless repetition (rote) as a means of memorizing a composition. Using repetition to remember a piece does not necessarily lead to any deep understanding of the material. Therefore, this method has never proven itself to be reliable and more often than not leads to problems.

## Visualization

One method that can be effective in internalizing a composition is known as *visualization*. It is an extremely challenging way to internalize music and confronts students immediately with issues pertaining to internalizing the material. First, place the score somewhere away from the instrument. This placement insures that students do not yet use playing the keyboard as a method of internalization. Students instead study a small amount of music; perhaps one or two measures (the amount will depend on the piece). At this point, students use anything and everything at their disposal to store the information in their memory.

For example, the first four measures of Edvard Grieg's *Arietta, Op. 12, No. 1* (example 2) can be divided into three parts: 1) bass; 2) broken chords; 3) melody.

Example 2

Grieg, Arietta, Op. 12, No.1, (ms. 1-4)

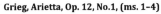

First, students might block the broken chords revealing two harmonies: a four-note E♭ major triad in second inversion, and a D diminished seventh chord in third inversion. The harmony moves from I to vii07 to I again (see example 3)

Example 3

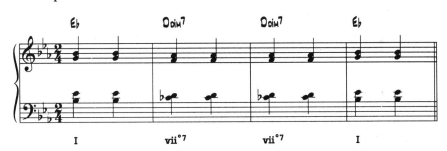

Then they can reconstruct the original version by realizing that these harmonies are arpeggiated from bottom to top. Second, in the bass, there is a pedal point E♭ that lasts four beats (two tied half notes) and is reiterated in the third measure. Third, the melody contains a rhythmic motive:

Example 4

and a melodic motive; both are repeated in measures 3 and 4. The melodic motive repeats the same intervallic sequence one step lower in measures 3 and 4 (see example 5).

Example 5

After students can verbalize this information, they might return to the instrument without the music and immediately try playing one of the three parts (arpeggiated chords, bass pedal point, or melody). What usually occurs at this point is either students can play it correctly with no problems or they have some "black holes" in their recollection of the excerpt. In other words, they know there is something they don't know. Then they return to the music to answer the question(s). Next they go back to the piano for another try. They can repeat this procedure with each part separately and then in different combinations with one another. Eventually, this excerpt solidifies in the memory and students can move on to the next "chunk" of material to be internalized. It is important that this work be reinforced at the very next practice session and subsequent sessions. After these reinforcements, it should only require a little "touch up" work to easily retain the material. It may seem a little ridiculous to be getting up and sitting down so much while learning a piece. However, it is necessary in order to avoid the temptation to rely on the kinesthetic or aural system. After learning the process, it is possible to use this method without leaving the piano bench but it takes great discipline not to play while looking at the music. Students should adhere to the following two rules:

1.  If the eyes are looking at the score, the hands must be in the lap (not touching the keys).

2.  If the hands are touching the keys (i.e. playing the instrument), the eyes must not be looking at the score.

## Challenging the Memory

It is always helpful to engage in activities that challenge the different systems of internalization. Playing a passage using the same finger on each note or perhaps using a different fingering than usually done will rule out the kinesthetic memory and cause students to rely on other systems. Playing at an extremely slow tempo will force students to rely on the theoretical, photographic, and keyboard choreographic systems. Even the ear might have trouble when going extremely slow. Verbalizing the material can be very challenging—particularly if you are away from the instrument. Can you say from memory, for example, the harmonies of the first four measures of J.S. Bach's *Prelude in C Major, W.T.C., Bk. I*? What about the entire piece? Playing a piece hands separate is quite challenging; especially if the entire piece is played from beginning to end with just the left hand part or just the right hand part. Suddenly the ear is hearing something different, the hand that is playing cannot depend on the other for reference, and most likely the complete picture is not there. Many memory slips occur due to a problem that occurs in one hand rather than both at the same time. If each hand depends on the other in order to know what to do next, then when one hand has a problem, the continuity of the piece is in jeopardy. However, if students can play each hand separately from memory (as well as together), then they will be much better equipped to deal with any problems that occur.

Transposing music without the score is perhaps one of the greatest memory challenges. Although time consuming, transposition leads to a much deeper understanding of the material. Many questions will arise while trying to play something in a different key that otherwise would not necessarily surface. The questions will, for the most part, deal with either the distance between the notes (intervals) or the harmonic content. These are good questions to have answered before walking on the stage to perform a piece from memory. Even the ear seems to benefit from this kind of activity because, with each new key, it hears the same relationships in a different context. Getting an intermediate student to transpose may not be as difficult as one might expect. It begins with taking a small amount, perhaps two to four measures, and transposing it to three or four keys. With each key, the process becomes easier and the understanding becomes deeper. A fringe benefit with transposing is a development of familiarity with each of the twelve keys (if students eventually transpose material to all twelve keys). If, on the other hand, students attempt to transpose an entire piece, it will most likely take too long and be too big of a task. They will most likely be intimidated and give up on the process.

Internalization is a concept that involves developing a deeper understanding of the material than surface memorization requires. However, once internalized, any material can be recalled from memory with confidence and reliability. The secret lies in finding more than one way to know the material and then storing the information through a variety of associations.

# Sources

Danziger, Kurt. *Marking The Mind: A History of Memory* (Cambridge: Cambridge University Press), 2008.

Gieseking, Walter and Karl Leimer. *Piano Technique* (New York: Dover Publications, Inc.), 1972.

Middleton, David and Steven Brown. *The Social Psychology of Experience: Studies in Remembering and Forgetting* (London: Sage Publishing), 2005.

Schacter, Daniel L. *The Seven Sins of Memory: How the Mind Forgets and Remembers* (Boston: Houghton Mifflin Publishing), 2002.

Snyder, Bob. *Music and Memory* (Cambridge: MIT Press), 2001.

# CHAPTER 35

## Thoughts on Memorizing, Pedaling and Practicing

### Ruth Slenczysnka

One of my more frustrating moments as a music teacher occurred when a student to whom I had given a memorizing assignment said to me, "I tried my best to memorize this music *but it just wouldn't come!*" Thinking back to my youthful student days, my teachers always decided when and what they wanted me to memorize, but never told me how. I had to succeed in this determined effort alone. By speaking to many teaching colleagues I found that few, if any, had a working technique for memorizing music above the elementary level where ear, eye and hand coordination plus a smattering of harmony are encouraged. After that introduction, all instruction on memorizing ceased.

And yet every young student is given excellent memorizing skills when he or she learns a first little piece that requires a bass line to support a treble melody. The melodic component is first taught to the right hand alone after which the left hand is taught the supporting bass line. After each hand's assignment is clearly established, the teacher carefully, slowly, patiently guides the student to play both hands together until a triumphant entry into a new world of two-hand piano playing is experienced. Perhaps the embryonic elements of a useful memorizing technique can be found in this story.

Pianists over the age of 18 particularly need to have a memorizing technique to use when they become serious about learning more difficult music. At that age their keen children's ability to quickly absorb knowledge begins to atrophy. This may be the reason why so many promising child prodigies fail to become mature artists; they never learned a workable memorizing technique. In this chapter I hope to present some ideas that work for me. Perhaps some of them will work for you too.

It is important to use only *urtext* editions to ensure that what you learn was written by the master composer and that you are building from a reliable source. Once you have decided on the edition you will use, try to obtain an overall picture of the entire composition you wish to learn. Examine the musical form, identify the themes, and appreciate how the composer has developed them. Learn the general harmonic substructure. Many great pianists, Sviatoslav Richter and Claudio Arrau among them, studied J. S. Bach's 48 Preludes and Fugues to learn how this music was crafted. Sergei Rachmaninoff and Artur Schnabel studied Beethoven's 32 Piano Sonatas to learn about structure. Bach wrote his Two Part Inventions and Three Part Sinfonias for the express purpose of teaching serious musicians how to develop small musical ideas. Analyzing how carefully these various pieces are put together will help any pianist to think musically and this kind of understanding will help you to memorize.

Listening to someone else perform the piece is a totally different experience, almost unrelated to making the music yourself. When doing so, start to imagine how you will phrase this masterwork. As a teenager I remember hearing songs and ballads on the radio and thinking to myself, "that singer is certainly not expressing the true meaning of the lyrics as I would, if only I had a voice!" Some of the following directions will give you the means to express what you feel in the music you wish to play.

# Getting Acquainted

The following three steps will help to get your eyes, ears and hands acquainted with the new composition.

## Step One

Read the new composition ten times slowly, all the way through, with the right hand alone (if the composition is quite long then divide it into sections.) Set your metronome at a slow pace to keep you steady as you perform mistake-free and mark your progress using a pencil and pad, giving yourself a check for every good performance. False starts don't count, nor do readings with errors. If too many mistakes creep into your performance then you should lower your metronome level by another five or ten numbers. You are aiming for ten consecutive mistake-free performances, each one metronome marking higher than the last. After successfully accomplishing this you will begin to feel in your right hand, and to hear with your inner ear how the new piece will sound.

If you run across an awkward passage then isolate it and work on it separately. Rework the fingering, if necessary, until you find a practical solution. Slow down the metronome to what might seem to be a ridiculously slow tempo then slowly raise the level until you are able to play the passage, free of mistakes, at the uppermost metronome marking required by the instructions above. You may then restore the corrected passage to the context of the music.

## Step Two

Follow the same procedure with your left hand alone, but lower the metronome level by at least five, perhaps ten numbers. It takes longer to become familiar with left hand sound and you will begin to hear supporting material that you might not recognize without the melody. Most people's left hands are not as highly skilled as their right hands and it will take more time to learn coordination with the ear.

Look and listen especially for the lowest bass line, the highest notes played by the left thumb and, perhaps, a middle inner voice. Often what appears to be a simple accompaniment becomes a valuable addition to the master composer's harmonic plan. When you understand every detail try to achieve a first left hand performance free of mistakes. Monitor your progress as the left hand climbs your ten-performance ladder.

## Step Three

Now you are prepared for your first two handed reading. Psychologists tell us that the left side of the the brain guides the right hand, and the right side of the brain guides the left hand. Use plenty of time to slowly encourage all of these newly educated parts of you to coordinate seamlessly. Start at a tempo ten metronome levels below that of your left hand's first successful reading. You will be listening with a microscope, so to speak, and opening up your ears to lush harmonies and complex details. You may feel a sudden "click" as the left and right hands' newly learned efforts come together. This can be a thrilling moment whether you are studying a Bach Prelude, a Chopin Mazurka, or a section of a Prokofieff Sonata. Continue to monitor your progress as you complete all ten mistake-free performances. Keep raising your tempo by one metronome level until you reach your goal, ten metronome numbers higher than where you began.

Steps one, two and three might take you a day, three days or even a week to complete, depending on how much practice time you are able to put in. You will gain skill as you repeat these steps several times. Every few days, begin all three 10-time ladders two numbers higher, and end them two numbers higher. Your music will grow within you; your inner ear will sing parts of the music while your fingers will begin to know instinctively where to go. You will begin to be comfortable with the composition and musical shapes will emerge that will inspire new ideas about how to build long musical lines.

Think about the music. Are you observing all the composer's phrasing, articulation markings and dynamic signs? Where there are no composer directives you might test a few basic ideas: a crescendo where you think the music asks a question, a decrescendo where you think a phrase ends an idea. Should these repeated motifs be *fp* or *pf*? Should there be a crescendo where there is an ascending progression or possibly a decrescendo where similar motifs descend? Experiment! Breathe life into your music. You can always change an idea you don't like. The important thing is to say something musically.

One day a small mistake will occur while you are completing your ten hands together performances. You examine the area with each hand and with both hands; nothing seems to be wrong. Yet another mistake happens in another area but again, nothing seems to be really wrong. Your new accomplishment seems a bit like an eggshell cracking in many places because the baby chick is fighting to be born. Your new music is asking to be memorized. Wait for this signal. Most people try to memorize too soon, before the piece is sufficiently ready. Because the composition isn't really in your mind yet, results will be marred by inaccurate notes and note values. Articulation and dynamic marks may be overlooked. All of these musical details must be at least partially in place prior to beginning your determined effort to memorize.

"What's all this about learning everything hands alone? I'm a good sight-reader and have read everything both hands together for years." Quite commendable -Bravo! "And working with each hand alone seems to be a waste of time and effort. My teacher wants me to learn quickly and directs me to memorize assignments for each lesson." Sadly, there are many non-performing teachers who make this cruel and unnecessarily punishing requirement. Parents and many teachers may say, "The trouble with you is you don't concentrate!" Not true. Concentration, or lack of it, is not the problem.

Good readers are often poor memorizers. They coordinate eye, ear and kinetic skills without getting their minds involved. Think of an expert typist who looks at the information she is typing but has no idea of its content or meaning. A good reader has a wonderful skill, extremely helpful to any pianist, but memorizing is a mind-directed art. Be respectful; this art requires a thorough knowledge of every musical detail in the score while the mind supervises every move made by each of two hands simultaneously planning beautiful results, and all this on demand!

To train your mind for this task, you must be aware of what *each hand* is doing because: 1) The left hand plays half the music but this music is far more obscure. 2) The left hand needs to be strengthened to be as dependable as the right hand. 3) During performance the mind sometimes focuses on the beautiful line of one hand *or* the other. 4) Each hand must be in a position to function on "automatic" if need be for a few seconds.

This kind of thorough learning cannot be done both hands together in a hurry. There is genuine reward for patient effort.

# Divide and Conquer

Learning a long poem by heart can be daunting but extracting the true meaning from a single line can be satisfyingly pleasurable. Utilizing this learning method requires dividing the entire composition into many small segments, each no longer than a four to six bar phrase. Slow your tempo level and count by eighths instead of quarters. Find the appropriately slow metronome level to focus your aural "microscope." Play the first phrase with the right hand alone. You've heard this phrase many times. Now you must listen to it at this slow pace. Musically, what does this phrase say to you? Play it many times in various ways until you determine the underlying quality. Is it hopeful, auspicious or possibly happy? Can you put words to the melody or imagine a setting? Have you a picture or a story for the whole composition?

Many of the composer's tempo markings can help: *Grave* = serious, *Calmado* = calm, *Tranquillo* = quiet or tranquil, *Sostenuto* = sustained or hopeful, *Andante* = moving, *Andantino* = moving a little, *Allegretto* = a bit light-hearted, *Allegro* = happy, *Allegro Assai* = quite happy, *Vivace* = with spirit. Use whatever the composer wrote as a starting point for your imagination. Setting a mood does not depend entirely upon tempo; use tone quality and color to convey the musical message during the learning period. You can certainly communicate an *Andantino* or *Allegro con Fuoco* while still playing slowly. Meanwhile, create a mental image of how you wish to present this composition so that an audience will fall in love with it. This image will keep you focused through the memorizing hours.

How will you play the first note? Fingertip, finger pad, weight touch from above, push toward the fall board, side of the little finger, side of the hand, two fingers together? Try each possible way many times in order to identify the sound you want. Does the overall direction of your phrase express a crescendo? Are you making every long and short melody note contribute to the crescendo? My wonderful teacher Alfred Cortot said, "Never waste a note!" If there is a staccato do you prefer clipped finger pizzicato, a wrist-directed quick upward motion or an arm-directed slow upward motion? Which of these staccatos best contributes to the musical line? Listen to the last notes of the phrase; do they end the musical thought softly or does the first phrase lead into the next phrase, or is the first phrase the beginning of a musical paragraph? Do you leave the last note with the wrist high or with the wrist down? Is the last note accented or staccato? Many musical decisions can be made at this very slow level. It is during this early phase of learning that you test ideas that will make your interpretation unique. Make many mind-directed musical repetitions while listening carefully. *You are memorizing!*

When you produce ten consecutive memorized performances of the first phrase at ten progressive slow tempo levels, you must study the next phrase in the same meaningful way. The slow tempo invites mind participation. After musically mastering four phrases this way, you might have a memorized sentence. Return to the earliest slow metronome level and try to contain the entire memorized sentence free of mistakes. Your thinking and your breathing are changing; your musical line is growing! If an error occurs in one of the phrases you've already learned, correct it with another ten step "ladder" and return to the musical sentence. Again master this sentence at ten extremely slow tempi. You've made a strong step forward.

Your left hand needs to memorize the first phrase the same careful way. Play the lowest bass line. Beethoven called this voice a "second melody." Brahms' father played the double bass, and this composer wrote a marvelous bass melody into all of his piano pieces. After you've memorized the lowest melody, use your left thumb to play all the high notes and memorize this little supporting voice. Next, make chords of the thumb melody and inner notes to hear the harmonic progression. Listen to each little change while naming the intervals made by the thumb and index finger: "major third, perfect fourth, minor third," etc. Feel with your fingers and know with your mind what you are doing. After this preparation, begin your ten mistake-free performances with your left hand, carefully guiding this process with your mind. Your left hand must not depend on kinetic reaction, repetition, or clues from your right hand.

When you work with both hands together, lower your metronome level to ten numbers below that of your first successful left hand alone tempo (remember you're counting in eighths.) Listen to each finger in each hand contribute to the musical content of your first phrase. This sensation is a bit like watching a sunrise: slow, majestic, and quite marvelous. Does your melody sing? Is the secondary melody in the bass contributing? Is there an inner voice that enhances the music? Continue on with your ten consecutive perfect performances. You are on your way!

Why all this slow practice? You are building memory circuits in your mind, ears and hands that must work reliably under pressure from nerves or unusual circumstances. As a competition jurist I have compassion for the highly gifted candidates for whom insufficient preparation can cause performance mishaps. Part of every fine artist's workday is invested in building memory circuitry. When an artist performs, the mind anticipates where the hands will go but performance is often so rapid that if the mind is on the hands there will be a breakdown. Slow and steady mind training will encourage a comfortable, healthful anticipation. This is your great goal. To oversimplify, most potentially great piano students practice far too quickly and with insufficient thought. Professional artists work much more slowly and build musicality into every note. I've heard them!

1. On a transatlantic ocean voyage in the mid 1930's Robert Casadesus could be heard by fellow passengers as he quietly practiced in his stateroom Daquin's *Le Coucou* slowly and staccato.

2. During a busy concert season in the early 1960's Rudolf Serkin and I were both performing in San Francisco at different venues. We crossed paths at the Fairmont Hotel and he graciously invited me to share breakfast with him in his suite. There was a console piano and on it was an old triangular metronome. He was painstakingly practicing the left hand alone of the *Rondo* from Beethoven's Op. 26 *Sonata*.

3. Before I first met Sergei Rachmaninoff in 1934, I stepped off the elevator in the Hotel Villa Majestique in Paris and heard a piano. "What a slow student!" I thought. When my father knocked at his door the music stopped. The master pianist answered the door in his shirtsleeves. No one else was in the room.

## Shifting Accents

Nearly every composition at the advanced level includes technical passages of consecutive sixteenths or thirty-seconds that cause you to stop, slow down or otherwise interrupt the flow of the music. Select the most bothersome of these passages and work on it with one hand alone slowly, experimenting with various fingerings and hand positions until you've found a workable solution.

You are ready to use "shifting accents", a versatile practice tool that promotes evenness and fleetness by accenting every note in turn. This technique of shifting accents is effective on an entire Chopin Etude, on an octave passage in a Tchaikovsky Concerto, to produce a limpid or crisp Scarlatti Sonata or even to improve a small ornament or long trill. Here is a sketch of how to use them:

| If passage is in groups of 4 or 8: | | If passage is in triplets: | |
|---|---|---|---|
| First: | **1** 2 **3** 4  **5** 6 **7** 8 | First: | **1** 2 3    **4** 5 6 |
| Second: | 1 **2** 3 **4**  5 **6** **7** **8** | Second: | 1 **2** 3    4 **5** 6 |
| Third: | 1 2 **3** 4  5 6 7 8 | Third: | 1 2 **3**    4 5 **6** |
| Fourth: | 1 2 3 **4**  5 6 7 **8** | Fourth: | 1 2 3    **4** 5 6 |
| Fifth: | 1 2 3 4  **5** 6 7 8 | Fifth: | 1 2 3    4 **5** 6 |
| Sixth: | 1 2 3 4  5 **6** **7** 8 | Sixth: | 1 2 3    4 5 **6** |
| Seventh: | 1 2 3 4  5 6 **7** 8 | | |
| Eighth: | 1 2 3 4  5 6 7 **8** | | |

Mme. Isabelle Vengerova, the legendary Russian pedagogue who produced many fine pianists at Curtis Institute, taught a similar practice technique which featured "shifting rhythms": LONG short LONG short, etc. and then, short LONG short LONG etc. I prefer shifting accents to this approach because there is no LONG that can tempt the hand and mind to rest. This would be counter to building the steady pace we need. Ten times with each shifting accent will, over a period of time, give your passage clarity and assurance. Meanwhile, the kinetic exercise will reinforce your mind-directed memorizing and bring the tempo up to performance level, perhaps a little beyond!

First, conquer all the right hand's difficult passages in the composition with the shifting accents. Then start at the beginning of the piece and as you reach each relevant passage use the first accent of the series on it and continue in this way until the end. Repeat several times until it is comfortable. Then do the same with the second accent, repeating as many times as necessary until you can do it easily. Continue until you work through the entire composition with all eight shifting accents many times without mistakes.

Go through the left hand work in the same way; even an Alberti base will be much improved after using this technique. First isolate the difficult passages of running notes and work through each of them using all of the accents. Now start with your left hand at the beginning of the composition and as you reach each sixteenth or thirty-second note passage use the first accent in the series and continue until you reach the end of the piece. Repeat this as many times as it takes to do it comfortably and without errors. Proceed in the same way with the second accent, repeating until it seems second nature. Keep at this until you've conquered the entire memorized composition with all eight accents. You need to be more meticulous with your left hand than with your right because most "derailments" originate with a faulty left hand. Continue to monitor your progress.

When you put both hands together there will be some places where only the right hand will employ the shifting accents, other places where only the left hand will and still others where both hands will use the shifting accents together. Work on each of these passages with all eight accents (or all six if the passage is in triplets) before negotiating the whole composition, just as you did with each hand alone. Certain of the accents may take more repetitions to master than others. Stick with the work and you will master it. You are constantly learning and succeeding.

# Useful Tips

### 1. **Listen Carefully.**

Young Clara Schumann was inspired by the "pearls on black velvet" quality of Franz Liszt's scale work. How does one obtain this sound? It is not speed! Create a musical line that will crescendo as you ascend and use the wrist or the arm and elbow together to direct your downward motion and to help avoid an uneven sound. Think of a coloratura soprano. Use a twenty-performance metronome ladder at a comfortable-to-fast tempo many times. As your tempo advances, you will recognize this special sound of "liquid silver."

## 2. **Keep the Score Handy.**

Always keep the score open in front of you and refer to it whenever you have the slightest question. You might not be looking at it any longer but the score contains all the answers. You never outgrow the need to refresh your memory. Take the score with you on walks and review the music in your mind. Whenever you hit a snag, open the score to find the right answer. Take the score to bed at night and mentally review the music, opening the score when needed for the right answers. When we both lived on the Rue Faraday in Paris during the 1930's, Shura Cherkassky went wild about the great International Exposition that was held in that city and visited there almost every day but *always* with a score in his pocket of some music he practiced at night. In airplanes between concerts and backstage from Bombay to Buenos Aires I would refer to the score. Many times during a performance I would follow an inspiration to make a crescendo or a ritardando and look at the score during intermission to learn if it was "legal" (either written by the composer or left blank.) On some occasions my inspirations were counter to the composer's written indication but in *every* case the score was my teacher.

## 3. **Know Your Intervals.**

There are times when one hand or the other lifts off the keyboard such as at the end of a phrase or musical section. Recognize the harmonic interval formed by the note you left and the note where you return your hand to the keyboard to play. Often the interval is simply an octave higher or lower, or a perfect fifth; whatever it is, you must know it. Sometimes the lift is in the right hand, sometimes in the left, on other occasions in both hands. In every case, *know your intervals.* One year I opened my programs with the great Frank Martin Prelude No. 1. During performances my ear would tell me one thing, but my trained mind knew the intervals and kept me safe from disaster! Classic composers often change keys in their sonata recapitulations. You must know your intervals in the expositions as well as in the recapitulations. Know in what key you're playing at all times. Derailments happen unexpectedly and trying to remember harmony in a split second is too slow. But planting an interval in your conscious mind is nimble and reliable.

## 4. **Know All Motivic Variations.**

Classic and romantic composers often repeat motifs, each with a small difference. Beethoven particularly liked to write groups of three "almost" repetitions, each with its own small variation and color. Many middle movements in Mozart and Haydn sonatas are themes with small variations. Chopin's nocturnes sometimes will include as many as six repetitions of the same small musical idea, each with its own special ornament or bass harmony. Give each repetition a number: "One", "Two", "Three", "Four" etc. and work on each one many times. Then call out loud at random, "Four", play it, "Six", play it, "Two", play it and so on. The great Spanish pianist Alicia de Larrocha works in this way, exasperatingly calling out the numbers in Spanish. This is a very useful numbers game.

5. **Count!**

Always count to yourself as you play. Often there will be an important small change, an interesting chord, or an ornament on a second, third, or fourth beat. Note these situations as landmarks to look forward to.

6. **Contrary Dynamics.**

All master composers present pianists with melodic material that calls for a simultaneous crescendo in one hand and a decrescendo in the other. To master contrary dynamics, try practicing scales with the two hands moving in opposing directions. For example, the right hand starts on C and moves upward one octave and then back to the starting note while the left hand starts on C and moves downward one octave before returning. While doing this, slowly count, "1 and 2 and 3 and" etc. as you shape the contrary dynamic lines, carefully listening with both ears. Keep the two lines smooth, gradual, and free of accents. Lengthen the scale to two octaves and make your two dynamic lines longer. When you are able to feel, hear and comprehend this indispensable skill, transfer to slowly creating this special sound to the context of the music where it is needed.

# Revolving Learning Techniques

Mind directed memorizing and shifting accents each have certain advantages. In recent years, when I've had too little practice time due to a multitude of other obligations, I've combined the two techniques with good results: 1) 1st practice session: Right hand mind-control 2) 2nd practice session: Left hand mind-control 3) 3rd practice session: Both hands mind-control 4) 4th practice session: Right hand shifting accents 5) 5th practice session: Left hand shifting accents 6) 6th practice session: Both hands shifting accents.

Revolving in this way you enjoy a change of pace, different sound and a fresh and useful approach to each practice session. When I practice each day I receive an insight, like a precious small gift, every ten days or so. These six-way practice sessions can revolve as long as you need them.

When relearning music, this revolving technique is especially effective. For this purpose, the first three mind-control sessions need to be almost as slow as they were at first learning. After three six-way cycles you can move the beginning and ending metronome numbers up by four levels each time you revolve. Relearning will be a happy experience and you will reach greater heights musically and technically. Your musical lines will be much longer, elevating your understanding of the work.

## About Pedal

Pedaling is an ear-controlled art. Its purpose is to enhance what your hands, inner ear, and imagination want the music to convey. Such diverse pianists as Julius Katchen, Jorge Bolet, and Dinu Lipatti pedaled the same composition differently every time they performed. One piano will sound better with a lot of pedal and the next will sound better with very little pedal. In a living room, a little pedal will go a long way while in a dry hall you may need a lot of pedal. When you play a composition slowly, you can enhance it by pedaling every melody note. When you play that same composition quickly, your pedal can enhance the harmonic structure with long strokes while your fingers take care of the melody. Most recording studios ask a pianist to use as little pedal as possible. I never practice with pedal because it feels good to get into the keys and make every sound and color myself and then add enhancement when and if my ear requests it.

I use the *una corda* pedal sparingly because pressing it down changes the quality of sound on most pianos. When a composition begins very softly, put the *una corda* pedal down *before* you play and lift it on an accent or a strong beat where the change won't be heard. Cultivate a good pianissimo without *una corda*. Vladimir Horowitz practiced on his fully opened concert grand in his living room until he was happy with the sound without using the *una corda* pedal. But know that it is there just in case you need it!

Here are a few important uses of the pedal with which to experiment:

1. Use pedal to enhance every melody note, especially those your fingers can't connect. First try to achieve your long musical line, then enhance with pedal.

2. Use pedal to enhance harmonic structure; think bottom to top. Break all chords with the lowest note on the beat so that the pedal catches all harmony. You must be clever with fingering and ear-hand control to keep the melody notes *legato*.

3. Use pedal to enhance rhythmic accents and add bounce or lilt to dances such as waltzes, mazurkas, polonaises, gavottes, and ethnic songs. Often, short pedal strokes on accents can help the music.

4. Use pedal to enhance orchestral color in chords, to amplify high-register long trills, and to enhance cadence chords.

5. Use pedal when the composer writes it into the score.

6. Use pedal imaginatively to accomplish specific sounds and effects. There are so many different types of pedaling that a pianist can use at the necessary time and place: <u>pedal reclaiming</u> is especially useful in French impressionistic music, <u>quarter pedaling</u> can be used to enhance scales and add color and sheen, <u>half pedaling</u> in a dry hall, <u>flutter pedaling</u> when playing a legato in one hand and staccato in the other, <u>sostenuto pedaling</u> is useful in Liszt and Busoni transcriptions of Bach and also in impressionistic music.

Walter Gieseking's early master classes on Debussy ignored sostenuto pedaling until his first North American tour in the 1930's when he discovered the sostenuto pedal on the American Steinways! European instruments didn't include this pedal but when Gieseking discovered it he experimented with it, liked it, and later advocated its use.

Pedal is best learned *after* memorizing. Create long musical lines and give motion to your musical shapes first. You can then enhance with pedal as your ear directs you to. When in doubt, pedal less rather than more. Make your legato, fingering, and strong hands take the music as far as they can. Your ear and experience will guide you as you experiment. Vladimir Horowitz tried to imitate the sound and phrasing of the "bel canto" tenors with his hands only!

# Controlled Dynamics

This is especially helpful to the budding professional who must adjust to any instrument. Use a medium tempo ten-speed metronome ladder and practice: 1) Right hand loud, left hand soft. 2) Left hand loud, right hand soft. 3) Both hands nicely balanced with attention to long musical lines and motion.

Perform your composition these three ways at each of the ten metronome levels. Playing in these ways can be challenging at first but after you master it your hands will become fearless of bass-heavy pianos or those with a shrill upper register. Your sound will be in *your* hands.

# Performing New Repertoire

It is normal and natural to be apprehensive of performing a new piece. Seasoned professionals often deal with this by including newer repertoire as an encore in smaller towns. All good teachers should have recital classes where young pianists can overcome inexperience, stretch their imagination, and encourage their peers. Listed below are some effective methods for bringing new repertoire up to performance level.

1. During one week go through the new piece from beginning to end three times *after* every practice session. Make note of every mishap so you'll know where to do special remedial work.

2. Begin your practice session with as many performances as you need to obtain a conservative performance, free of mistakes and with attractive musical lines. Listen and look for ways to make these lines longer. On some days you may need ten tries and on others perhaps you'll succeed with three. Give this practice at least a week during which the way you perceive the composition musically should change.

3. Open the piano and give the new composition a full-fledged recital hall level performance at the tempo you intend to play it. You may find that it sounds and feels different in many ways that you'll want to think about while consulting the score. You will become musically flexible and discover new colors as you are able to experiment with new insights. Do this several times daily for at least one week. Keep up your routine practice, especially on any new problem areas that you might notice.

4. Turn on a television or talk radio show and sit uncomfortably high or low as you go through your composition many times with distractions. Violinist Yehudi Menuhin practiced standing on one foot with the other straight out in front of him!

5. Every few days make an unbreakable date with your tape recorder or high quality digital recorder for a single, recital hall level performance and then carefully and critically listen to the results as you follow the score. Examine the playing as if you were a rival pianist in the next room. Can you hear long musical lines? Are your lines persuasive according to your story or setting for the composition? Does your music flow to a climax? You should aim for shaping the composition into a musical whole.

6. Explore the local schools and churches for uprights on which to play your new piece whether there are people around or not.

7. Visit your local music store and play on every piano there. By now you should be crossing the line from trying to get through the piece as well as you can to performing the composition elegantly with long lines and a magnificent climax. The music store staff will love you and invite you back!

8. There is often a piano to be found at retirement homes and rehabilitation centers where the residents will love a small performance at which you can feature your new composition. It probably feels fairly seasoned at this point and you may already be planning your next new acquisition for your repertoire.

# Postlude

Arthur Rubinstein said that he never walked onstage without taking chances. As a compliment he would ask me, "Did you take a chance in the finale of the fourth ballade last night?" and wink approvingly.

Conductor Leonard Slatkin always says before walking onstage, "Enjoy yourself!"

Vladimir Horowitz's idea of a compliment: "I heard many beautiful moments."

At every lesson with Sergei Rachmaninoff he would say "Small musician, small musical line. Big musician, big musical line!"

Advice to fill a musical lifetime! But my favorite is Rodgers and Hammerstein: "A song is not a song until *you* sing it." Sing your heart into the music. You loved this composition enough to give it life, now it is yours to love always, to enjoy and to share.

# CHAPTER 36

## Preparation for Performance: Ensuring Student Success

### Gail Berenson

What exactly are we teaching during a piano lesson? Although much of our focus is on teaching students a specific skill, helping them achieve the highest caliber performance level and reaching their musical potential, piano mastery is only a small portion of what we teach. There are many things we can do to ensure our students' success and their development of a love of music. As skilled and knowledgeable teachers, we want to provide our students a nurturing learning environment, help them develop productive work habits, educate them to approach the instrument in the most efficient and ergonomically effective manner, keeping them injury-free, help them discover the inspiration in the music to play musically and experience the joy of sharing their music making with others.

## Teaching Environment

### Meeting the Primary Needs of the Student

As a result of cumulative piano lesson experiences, students develop attitudes and beliefs about music, learning and themselves. We must remember that we are dealing with multi-dimensional individuals who have thoughts and feelings that extend beyond the lesson environment. We all possess five basic psychological needs: self-esteem, acceptance, success, status, and independence, of which every teacher must be cognizant. Although it is unlikely that all five will be evident within every piano lesson, the two needs that should remain consistently present and never at risk are the student's sense of self-esteem and the teacher's acceptance of that student. There may be times when a teacher will be unhappy with a student's behavior or performance, but this should not place the student's feeling of being accepted and respected as an individual in jeopardy. A supportive, non-threatening environment motivates and encourages productivity, independence and self-esteem.

Pursuit of a "perfect" performance is an essentially futile, if not never-ending, task. It may be preferable to set more realistic goals: building an appreciation and love of music, encouraging productive attitudes such as striving to do one's best and the desire to work hard, fostering an excitement for exploring and solving musical and technical problems, and cultivating a joy of learning. A nurturing atmosphere can produce outstanding, creative well-rounded performers without the need for ruthless, super-critical and dictatorial behavior from the teacher. Although a few may remain, most of the autocratic demagogues of the past are vanishing, supplanted by teachers who emphasize high musical standards, yet are still capable of being caring mentors and positive role models for their students. A relaxed, supportive and inspiring environment fosters an active, highly motivated, self-reliant student who is willing to explore new ideas without fear of being ridiculed. A "team" approach of teacher and student working together will help the student minimize psychological stress, as well as tension that can promote physical injuries.

Building a comfortable rapport with each of our students is a fundamental teaching objective. The most important element for establishing a trusting student-teacher relationship is honesty. Without trust a student can never feel totally secure. Students need to know that the feedback given them by their teacher is accurate and honest. The challenge for teachers is in differentiating between product and effort, rewarding effort while providing a candid, constructive appraisal of the performance product. Thoughtless feedback can create hurtful feelings and loss of self-esteem that can have devastating psychological effects on a piano student of any age or level of skill.

Below are several suggestions for establishing a healthy teaching environment and some techniques to facilitate constructive communication. These challenges can be used as a teaching checklist.

**Challenge No. 1: Have I encouraged my students to be active participants in their lessons?**[1]

*The lesson environment should enable students to:*

1. Have a say in articulating the lesson's goals, based on what worked or didn't work in their practice.

2. Have a voice in selecting the repertoire to be learned and the order in which the compositions will be covered in the lesson (particularly appropriate with older students.)

3. Be given the opportunity to assess their performance in the lesson, helping to determine the direction the lesson might go.

**Challenge No. 2: Have I given my students the chance to demonstrate what they have accomplished since their last lesson?**

*The lesson environment should enable students to:*

1. Play what they've practiced without excessive interruptions.

2. Articulate how they worked through any difficulties encountered in their practice, clueing the teacher in on their work habits.

3. Have a second chance to play through all, or a portion of a piece if nerves or difficulty adjusting to the instrument prevent the students from playing as well as they are able.

**Challenge No. 3: Have I stimulated my students to think for themselves?**

*The lesson environment should enable students to:*

1. Have ample opportunities to discover and to experiment with solutions to any problems they might encounter.

2. Make comments and respond to questions, comfortable in the knowledge that the teacher will hear, respond, and build upon these ideas.

3. Receive encouragement when they attempt to make an independent decision.

**Challenge No. 4: Have I imparted some new information?**

*The lesson environment should enable students to:*

1. Leave the lesson with a new way of approaching an on-going piece.

2. Leave the lesson with a new musical/technical concept that builds upon what the student already knows.

3. Leave the lesson with additional practicing suggestions.

4. Leave the lesson eager to return to the piano to try out what they have just learned.

**Challenge No. 5: Have I provided a non-threatening environment that motivates and encourages productivity, independence and self-esteem?**

*The lesson environment should enable students to:*

1. Have fun and enjoy the lesson.

2. Make an error, experiment or stumble without fear of humiliation.

3. Be able to accept feedback without the need for defensiveness.

4. Not be overloaded with too many corrections and no clear way to incorporate them into their performance.

5. Feel supported and encouraged by their teacher.

6. Find their efforts honestly rewarded.

**Challenge No. 6: Have I thought through the best way to communicate an idea: appropriateness, priority, awareness of student's learning style, respond in the form of a question or statement, pacing, clarity, non-verbal communication, use of imagery?**

*The lesson environment should enable students to:*

1. Clearly grasp an idea.

2. Put it into use fairly quickly.

3. Transfer the idea to similar but different situations.

**Challenge No. 7: Have I inspired musicality, creativity, and an understanding of styles?**

*The lesson environment should enable students to:*

1. Explore a variety of sounds—how they are produced and how and when they are used.

2. Have the opportunity to experience repertoire from the different musical style periods.

3. Have a say in musical decision-making.

4. Experiment with the skill of improvisation.

**Challenge No. 8: Have I provided my students with the learning tools to be independent?**

*The lesson environment should enable students to:*

1. Understand how musical/technical decisions are made. (Teach concepts rather than simply providing the necessary information—i.e. exploring fingering concepts as opposed to writing in the fingering.)

2. Experience the most efficient and beneficial approaches to practicing.

3. Have the opportunity to make decisions while still under the guidance of the teacher.

**Challenge No. 9: Have I sent my student home with a clear understanding of how to best utilize their practice time?**

*The lesson environment should enable students to:*

1. Try a new idea out several times, in different contexts, to insure that they understand and can repeat this on their own.

2. Watch the teacher demonstrate, if appropriate, the specific musical/ technical concepts so that the students can go home remembering the proper sound and gesture.

3. Review what was accomplished in the lesson to reinforce important details that need to be included in the coming week's practice.

4. Periodically practice within the lesson itself, under the supervision of the teacher, to insure that they know what to do at home.

**Challenge No. 10: Am I serving as a positive role model for my students?**

*The lesson environment should enable students to:*

1. View their teacher as a caring, dedicated, energetic, organized, knowledgeable, fun loving, ethical, enthusiastic, poised and confidant professional.

2. See their teachers continuing to improve themselves by attending professional meetings, reading professional journals, practicing and performing.

# Essential Beginnings

Though it isn't essential to know the names of every muscle in the body, all teachers need to educate themselves about the basic principles of physiology and efficient movement, and possess a rudimentary knowledge of the mechanics of the piano. This is necessary to be able to impart a solid technical foundation to each student. As pianists we need to be aware of the most biomechanically efficient approach to the instrument, remembering that every student is unique in physical make up, so each must be evaluated and approached in a personalized way designed to handle his or her distinct needs.

For beginning students, a "total body" approach to music making, using techniques such as Dalcroze Eurhythmics, helps students develop a more innate, physical response to music and builds greater physical coordination. The focus on larger musculoskeletal systems (arms/legs) versus smaller musculoskeletal systems (fingers) is especially appropriate for younger students, enabling them time to mature and gain a greater degree of coordination, as well as an internalized rhythmic sense.

## Posture

The initial physical approach to the instrument sets a pattern for the future. Some teaching series and approaches focus on this in great detail, others mention nothing, leaving it totally to the teacher to include or not within the context of the lesson. An observant teacher should maintain an awareness of the following: 1) The student's back and shoulder girdle stability: Attention should be given to a student's posture, insuring flexibility to freely move from side to side, as well as forward and back. These motions can be introduced through the use of hand-over-hand arpeggios and reinforced later through scales. 2) The height of the bench: When the hand is placed on the keyboard, the forearm should be level with the keyboard, or possibly just "slightly" elevated. 3) The distance one places the bench from the instrument: The upper arm should be slightly forward of the body, providing room for freedom of motion. 4) How one is seated at the bench: Sit on the edge of the bench, feet on the floor (or on a box if feet are too short to reach the floor), with the right foot slightly forward to maintain stability and balance.

Some teachers may want to learn about the Alexander technique, a way of looking at body alignment, developed by actor, Matthias Alexander. This approach attempts to reeducate individuals to be able to perform simple, everyday activities without excess muscular tension. Musicians and actors frequently seek out Alexander practitioners, incorporating what they learn into their performing and teaching.

Since the piano cannot be downsized for younger, smaller students, as are stringed instruments, we must find ways to adapt to the piano. Teachers should provide adjustable footstools to provide stabilization for dangling feet and a sense of feeling grounded. An adjustable piano bench (or stacks of carpet samples to place on top of a low bench) is an essential piece of equipment for every piano studio. Many teachers also find it useful to visit the home of a student to see exactly what the piano set up is. At the very least, ask the student to describe the home conditions for practice and offer suggestions for improving it, if advisable.

## Hand Position

The natural hand position looks much the same as when the hand hangs naturally at the side of the body—wrist level with the hand, slightly curved fingers, natural hand arch. Teachers should pay attention to collapsing finger joints and work toward gradually strengthening the muscles that support them, a particularly important factor for students with hypermobile joints. Teaching series that begin with the use of five-finger pieces help strengthen the concept of hand position by keeping the hand small and helping the student learn how to maintain the hand arch. Having the student feel the transfer of weight from finger to finger, keeping fingers close to the keys, and using circular motions to maintain a flexible wrist will help promote a fluid, relaxed technique. It is advisable not to move from five-finger pieces to those with extended ranges until the hand position seems fairly secure. Reading should not be attempted until the student is physically comfortable at the keyboard, with the basic hand position well established before the added demands of reading are presented.

# Extending Beyond Five-Finger Range

Improper fingering is one of the major causes for an inaccurate, technically flawed performance, as well as a primary reason for injury. Students need basic guidelines to help them know how to solve a fingering problem. Present fingering in the form of transferable concepts, preferable to writing out the "correct" fingering for the student, or automatically insisting that the student follow what is printed in the score. Fingering concepts include: changing hand position (moving from one 5-finger position to another, with the move made between phrases); stretching (initially introduced using thirds, fourths or fifths, moving to or from the thumb; substitution (changing to another finger on a repetition of the same note); crossing over and under (moving by step, crossing over from a white key to a black key and crossing under from a black key to a white key); and contracting (anything that contracts the hand to less than one finger per key). Provide unedited pieces that incorporate one or two fingering concepts at a time, giving the student the chance to figure out the appropriate fingering that is best suited for his or her hand. Then be sure to provide the student additional opportunities for transferring these newly learned concepts to other repertoire. As teachers we must realize that what works well for us may not be best for the student due to a different size and shaped hand.

## Selection of Repertoire

The choice of inappropriate repertoire is another common catalyst for injury. If the literature is too difficult the student feels inadequate and becomes frustrated and overwhelmed. Repertoire that contains large chords or continuous octaves may create excessive physical demands for a student with a small hand, resulting in an injury. Repertoire selection is one of the most important choices we make for our students. Select a composition the student likes (students are unlikely to practice a piece they dislike), is within his or her ability to play well, yet presents a challenge and is appropriate for his or her hand shape and size.

## Healthy View Toward Technique

Technique serves as a tool that permits the performer to express his or her musical ideas. Since our movements at the keyboard always correlate to the sounds we want to create, technique should never be taught in a sound vacuum or as a separate entity. Some students practice "technique" by the clock, moving their fingers without even listening to what they are doing. Mindless practice creates the perfect circumstances for generating boredom and potential injury. Even when practicing technical exercises, attention should be given to dynamics, creating a musical line, experimenting with sound, touch, etc. Listed below are a few guidelines to help promote a healthier approach to dealing with technical issues:

1. Think of gravity as a useful mechanism, which can be much more effective than force in producing a quality sound. Learn about the proper use of weight and relaxation and connect this information to how one selects which fulcrum to utilize. In our upper extremities these are: wrist, elbow or shoulder. Strive also to achieve an instantaneous release upon striking the key, avoiding the accumulation of held tension.

2. To maintain a fluid technique, the playing mechanism should never remain static. The arm, wrist and fingers move in continuous, synchronized gestures, often mirroring the direction of the musical line. Check to ensure that the arm is aligned behind the finger that is playing at the moment. Twisting of the hand should be avoided.

3. Encourage students to visually "choreograph" their performances. Students may want to experiment with circular motions while playing passage work, vertical motions for octaves, rotation for Alberti bass, trills, double thirds, etc. Stress efficiency of motion, with the gesture always tied to what is necessary to produce the appropriate sound. Use every day images to make these motions more accessible—bouncing a basketball for forearm motions; turning a doorknob, shaking salt out of a saltshaker, or the doing the "Miss America" wave for rotation, etc. Follow through when playing big chords to produce a more ringing sound. The follow through works in much the same way a golfer or tennis player follows through on a swing after striking the ball.

4. Have students build speed by working in groups (musical, physical or rhythmic), not one note at a time, choreographing their gestures, checking for the most efficient fingering and experimenting in small sections "at tempo" to determine if the choreography and fingering will work "at speed."

5. The use of technical exercises can be controversial, with some teachers using repertoire as the vehicle for teaching technique, others preferring the use of published etudes, and still others inventing exercises of their own. If teachers choose to assign exercises, they need to exert special caution in using those that isolate specific fingers as these can produce extreme physical tension. The hand is an integrated unit, making it unnatural to isolate an individual finger. Always provide very detailed instructions about how technical work should be practiced: Advise the student to warm up prior to practicing, varying the exercises or repertoire to avoid using the same muscles consistently, to combine practice with frequent breaks, and to listen and remain focused on the sound produced, paying close attention to how the hand/arm/body functions as a unit to create the sound.

## New Advancements

Diagnostic software: Progress has been made in the development of technology that will enable students and their teachers to assess exactly how much physical tension they are holding as they play. Through combined input from video cameras and physiologic monitoring (surface electromyography), which measures the amount of electrical activity the muscles release when they are contracting, the performer and the teacher have concrete evidence of what is taking place. Just as in all forms of biofeedback, this visual input makes it so much easier for an individual to enact change. Research is ongoing, including the expanded use of this equipment on all musicians, not just pianists. It is proving to be a highly effective tool in guiding students toward playing in a more efficient and effortless way. More information can be found at: http://www.pianoperceptions.com/technology.php.

## Reduced-Size Keyboards

There are many gifted students with exceptionally small hands who want to be able to perform the same major repertoire as their peers. However, the size of the standard keyboard creates an obstacle that restricts their options, even if they explore the alterations one can make to the music (re-voicing notes, breaking and rolling chords, eliminating notes). Although the piano itself cannot be downsized, a possible solution exists for these frustrated students. Reduced-size keyboards are currently being manufactured. David Steinbuhler and his company, Steinbuhler & Company, located in Titusville, Pennsylvania, retrofit grand pianos with smaller keyboards. They also sell new upright pianos that have been built with a reduced-sized keyboard. With a number of universities purchasing these actions, research is ongoing and continues to demonstrate the clear benefits for individuals with small hands of learning on a reduced-size (7/8th and 15/16th) keyboard. For those small-handed pianists who have suffered playing related injuries, these keyboards have proven to be life changing. More information can be found at: http://www.steinbuhler.com.

# Efficient and Healthy Practicing Strategies[2]

Practicing is a time of experimentation, yet too many students regard it as drudgery, thinking of it as a time to drill, adhering to the philosophy that "practice equals repetition." How long one practices is all too frequently determined by the clock rather than by what is accomplished. Although they spend nearly all of the week at the piano playing without the supervision of their teacher, most students do not have the innate ability to determine what should take place between lessons. Therefore, from the very first lesson, the teacher must take the initiative to provide each student with some basic guidelines for developing good practice habits that will develop and grow throughout each student's studies.

By teaching our students the crucial skill of how to practice, we are helping to ensure them a lifetime of injury-free playing. Instilling a creative, positive attitude toward practicing is an important first step. Creative practicing offers students a time when they can sort out their ideas and learn to problem solve. It becomes a period of self-discovery. Learning to listen, experimenting with sound and physical gestures, and approaching practice with an imaginative attitude is far more important than mindlessly exercising our fingers. Resourceful, intelligent practice is more likely to result in an artistic performance.

Students tend to be more excited about their practicing if they take a more active role in their lessons. Encourage students to become active, independent learners, coming to the next lesson with their own questions and lesson agenda. Provide guidelines so they can eventually discover the answers on their own. Ask students to demonstrate within the lesson exactly how they would go about practicing a specific piece or concept, using this as an opportunity to teach them how to figure things out independently. Allow students to take part in deciding what they will prepare for the next week's lesson. Even young students know how much they can practically handle. Encourage creativity, in making musical decisions, figuring out technical problems and exploring the instrument through composing or improvising.

Below are some common sense strategies that concentrate on healthy, productive practicing:

## Most basic are the items that deal with creating an environment that is conducive to quality practicing.

1. Make sure there is good light and a quiet setting.

2. Adjust the bench for height and distance.

3. Be aware of the tendency to overplay a stiff, dull-sounding piano. The art of listening is the most important skill one can learn that leads to successful music making. Of course, an in-tune, regulated instrument is a basic necessity.

## We reap the most benefits from our practice if we are healthy and rested.

4. Encourage students to maintain a healthy diet and get enough rest. Practicing when overly tired, either due to insufficient sleep or practicing late at night, can lead to inattention to proper posture and hand position or loss of concentration.

5. Practice posture should simulate performance posture (feet on floor, back in a neutral position, shoulders relaxed).

**As teachers we have specific responsibilities to insure that our students are adequately prepared before we send them home to work on their own.**

6.  Make sure the repertoire selected is appropriate to the needs and abilities of the student. Compositions should present a challenge to a student, but should also be suited to the student's hand shape and size and within the student's range of ability.

7.  Assist the student in deciding upon an appropriate fingering, a necessity for physical ease and musical fluidity. Inappropriate fingering frequently results in excessive stretching of the hand, creating tensions that can lead to injury. Fingering is a very personal decision and should not be determined by automatically following those printed in the score, nor by what feels most comfortable to the instructor. Learning how to finger is a critical concept that should be taught as early as possible, usually as soon as students begin extending beyond 5-finger range.

**One of the most important lessons we can all learn is how to use our practice time efficiently. Although there are times when we need to repeat a passage to "get it in our hands", repetition strictly for the sake of repetition is to be avoided.**

8.  Vary the activity or repertoire to be practiced so the same muscles are not used throughout. Avoid overuse of one set of muscles.

9.  Excessive, continuous, and unconscious practice breeds injuries. You can practice for as long as you wish providing you can maintain concentration. Break up your practice into 30- minute segments (with 3 to 5 minute relaxation breaks) so that there is no pain or excessive fatigue. Older, more experienced students may be able to continue up to as long as an hour without a break.

10. Repetition in practice should serve a purpose. Repeat a passage only if you are making a specific physical or musical change; avoid mindless practice. Sometimes we need to repeat a passage to gain physical security. Be sure to maintain concentration rather than going through the motions.

11. Constant metronome practice (moving from slow to fast, notch by notch) encourages mindless practice. Use the metronome with a specific purpose in mind.

12. If any change is made in your technique, work in those changes gradually.

13.  Increase practice time in small increments. A frequent cause of injury is a dramatic increase in practice time within a relatively brief period of time.

**Learning how to work out difficult passages and increase speed requires special practice techniques.**

14.  When a difficult passage occurs, stop, isolate and analyze the problem. One shouldn't repeat an isolated passage for more than 5 or 10 minutes. Rather than repeating the same passage over and over, work in smaller, more manageable segments that allows for quicker synthesis.

15.  Slow playing uses muscles differently than fast playing. Both types of playing are necessary during each stage of the learning process. Continuous use of only fast tempi can overwork the muscles, in addition to not achieving the desired musical effect.

16.  Divide the composition into small, musical working sections. Focus on natural physical gestures (rather than note to note) as a way of building speed.

17.  Focus on fluid motion and sound, phrasing, and physical ease.

**Students need to learn the warning signs of an impending injury. They should be encouraged to be aware of how things feel as well as how they sound.**

18.  If there is any evidence of excessive muscular fatigue or any degree of discomfort, STOP IMMEDIATELY. Allow time to take a break, stretch and relax. Stop working on that passage temporarily. Pain is a message that something is not quite right! LISTEN TO YOUR BODY!

19.  If there is a build up of physical tension, you are overworking that set of muscles. Stop and analyze what you are doing. Work even smaller sections. Experiment with other gestures to dissipate the tension. Allow the music to breathe, and remember to breathe deeply.

20.  There should always be a warm up period before tackling anything that is physically demanding. Warming up may consist of playing current repertoire, if played slowly. It does not have to include scales or exercises. Anything that does not over-stress the muscles and tendons is acceptable.

# Frequent Causes of Physical Injury

A frequent consequence of placing excessive demands on the musculoskeletal system, going beyond what an individual's body is able to tolerate, is an overuse, or repetitive strain type of injury. Overuse is the most common cause of injury and is frequently the direct result of improper practice habits. Teachers are a student's first line of defense against injury, and are usually the first to hear if a student is having a problem. For that reason, today's teachers need to be aware of the most common types of injuries and how those injuries can occur. The following items can individually or more often, cumulatively, initiate the circumstances that can precipitate an injury.

1.  A genetic weakness that can become aggravated, in part by the demands of playing the piano, resulting in an injury.

2.  Excessive tension—physical, psychological, or a combination of both.

3.  Poor practice habits:
    *   Improper use of practice time (time management).
    *   Excessive repetition of a physically demanding section.
    *   Overplaying the instrument.
    *   Lack of proper warm-up.

4.  Faulty technique:
    *   Inappropriate fingering.
    *   Improper use of weight (forearm/shoulder/back)
    *   Excessive stretching of the hand.
    *   Etc.

5.  Inappropriate repertoire:
    *   Too difficult.
    *   Not suited to individual's hand.

6.  Individual's lifestyle:
    *   Not enough rest.
    *   Inadequate diet.
    *   Practicing late at night.

7.  Poor quality instrument:
    *   Stiff action.
    *   Dull sound, encouraging individual to overplay.

# What to do if an Injury Occurs

In spite of the best teaching and most careful practicing, an injury can occur, not infrequently due to non-playing related causes. As musicians we must be particularly cautious about the extracurricular tasks we undertake. We need not live life in a bubble, but, like an athlete, we use our body and must take care of it.

Listed below is a description of the stages of overuse:

A.  Stage 1:

Discomfort during OR after activity but no performance disability.

Analogous to post exercise muscle soreness. Pain is usually felt in only one site.

B.  Stage 2:

Discomfort during AND after the activity but no performance disability.

The pain lasts for only a short period after the activity and can be felt in multiple sites. There is some pain during other activities of the hand. Palpable tenderness is present.

C.  Stage 3:

Discomfort during and after the activity and there is performance disability.

Pain will last for a longer period after the activity (greater than 2 hours). Pain will be present at rest and during many daily activities.

D.  Stage 4:

Discomfort that is incapacitating due to continuous pain, weakness, and inability to coordinate.

As teachers it is our responsibility to assess the seriousness of an injury and, if possible, determine the cause. We essentially function as detectives, asking questions and trying to figure out what caused the injury. Is it due to a non-playing related activity or is it due to playing-related overuse or misuse? It is also important for us to be aware of our limitations. If a student arrives at your studio describing injuries similar to those in stage three, this cannot be ignored. Insist that your student seek professional medical intervention as soon as possible.

If you are working with an injured student, carefully observe the student, making sure the student is seated properly at the piano and playing in a tension-free, fluid manner. Before sending a student home to practice, impress upon him/her that pain is a signal that something is wrong and should never be ignored. "If something hurts, stop whatever you are doing immediately!"

Teachers need to be flexible when a student arrives with an injury. Depending upon the type of injury, it is frequently important to keep the hand small, temporarily avoiding compositions that have large stretches or distort the natural position of the hand. Repertoire may need to be adjusted by eliminating excessively demanding compositions or slowing down the tempo to reduce the physical demands or even, in some cases, briefly or permanently dropping a piece.

If an injury is severe enough, it may be necessary to rest the hand and avoid practicing for a few days. When practicing is resumed, the student should begin with short practice periods (5-10 minutes). It might be necessary to insert rest periods every 5 minutes. "Just stand up and stretch, walk around, and return to the piano. Limit the consecutive time to 15 minutes, repeating that time period two or three times, spaced throughout the day. Remember, if you experience pain or excessive fatigue, stop immediately. Increase time gradually!"

Mental practicing, working away from the instrument, can be a way to extend practice time without the physical demands of working at the instrument. This allows for focused, concentrated practice in which the student hears and recreates the sounds in their head—audiation. Even though not moving their fingers as they play through their repertoire, research has shown that many of the same benefits are derived. Athletes have used visualization for many years as a way to enhance their performance.

If students are not allergic to over-the-counter medications, they may want to take either aspirin or one of the many non-steroidal anti-inflammatory medications on the market. Students may also want to ice the injured part after practicing to reduce inflammation. Teachers should learn the proper way to ice an injury and relate this information to the student.

Young piano students are frequently injured in non-playing related sports injuries. One common example is the twelve-year old boy who breaks his wrist while playing hockey. If a student has been immobilized in a cast, it is critical that the return to previous repertoire be handled in a gradual fashion, building strength and flexibility in small increments. Often physical therapy, prescribed by a physician, proves helpful in assisting the student in a rapid recovery. A word of caution about sports activities: Any activity that uses the bare hand as a racket, such as volleyball, basketball, handball, etc., is particularly risky.

# Dealing with Performance Anxiety[3]

Since some students view even a lesson as a performance, a student's potential may never be achieved because of the intrusion of excessive performance anxiety. Adults who admit to catastrophic recital experiences in their youth and a resulting negative feeling toward music and music instruction might feel differently today if their teachers had known how to help them cope with performance anxiety. A major issue for countless music students, performance anxiety very likely was the determining factor influencing many young students in terminating their lessons before they could even begin to assess their talent.

Anxiety is universal. Going on a job interview, making an important phone call, taking an exam—all of these are situations in which we want to excel and, for that reason, makes them stress-provoking, It is the degree to which the apprehension exists and the extent that it interferes with accomplishing our goals that determines if it is a problem. The object is not to eliminate performance anxiety but to discover ways to channel those feelings so they work for, not against us. Rather than derailing a performance, the electricity of the moment can create a spontaneous, thrilling and memorable experience for the performer and the audience.

Performance anxiety has always been around, but acknowledging it is recent. It is our responsibility to help our students feel more comfortable in the performance situations we decide is appropriate for them. Performing can constitute "playing for family" to "entering international competitions", with a multitude of diverse options in between. Students who accept the challenge of placing themselves in a suitable performance environment frequently feel an overwhelming sense of accomplishment and boost to their self-esteem, as well as the joy of experiencing the music and synergistic relationship with the audience.

A workable solution is very personal. Seven strategies are listed below, allowing individuals to experiment, discovering what combination of approaches works best. Many of these strategies are also presented in a Podcast on Performance Anxiety, which can be heard on the MTNA website http://www.mtna.org.

## Breathing

Under stress of performance our heart rates soar well beyond what the physical circumstances demand. Heart rates of marathon runners at the end of a race and performers who have just walked out on stage may be identical! "Pounding hearts" is one of the most common symptoms affecting musicians, making them feel out of control. One goal is to reduce our heart rate. This can be accomplished two ways:

1.  Become more fit so that your resting heart rate is lower to begin with. Achieve a minimum level of cardiovascular conditioning by doing some kind of aerobic activity four times a week for at least 20 minutes each time. Any activity that is continuous, yet not so strenuous that you cannot carry on a conversation, is acceptable. Explore walking, running, swimming, rowing, cross country skiing, bicycling, etc. This will help lower your resting heart rate, thereby beginning your performance at a lower level. Although everyone's heart rate will increase, fit individuals will recover faster.

2. Reduce your heart rate doing breathing exercises prior to or during stressful times. Controlled breathing is the quickest way to achieve control over the autonomic nervous system. Reduce your heart rate just prior to performance by concentrating on breathing. Exercises that focus on diaphragmatic breathing can be found in numerous books dealing with relaxation. Some people use meditation or yoga to slow their breathing and focus concentration.

## Relaxation

It is difficult to separate physical and emotional tension; both can place performers at risk of injury and, at the very least, impede their technique. One of many methods for relaxing consists of tensing individual muscle groups, then releasing. Contrast creates a greater awareness of those muscles. For musicians, the shoulder area is especially vulnerable to excess tension. Here is an example of this technique: Lift your shoulders up toward your ears and hold for several seconds, then release, perhaps doing this several times to achieve relaxation. It is possible to work systematically through the body, beginning with the forehead, working toward the toes. This activity can be undertaken backstage while waiting to perform, providing a specific, calming activity that can help the performer relax.

## Cognitive Thinking

Stage fright is the natural human response to fear. If we <u>perceive</u> performance as threatening, the mind prepares our body to flee the danger, even though it is a recital, not a life-threatening situation. For sufferers of performance anxiety, this may be the most crucial area on which to focus. Being adequately prepared is one of the best ways to reassure ourselves that "we can do it". Other approaches to positive thinking are:

1. Set realistic goals. Pressured by unrealistic goals, we are less likely to do well because we are continuously judging ourselves, striving to emulate a basically unachievable image. View a specific performance as one in a long string of performances. This takes the "everything hinges on what I do today" quality out of each performance. Believe that "whatever happens in this performance will make the next better". There is always room for improvement; think of each performance as a vital link in the learning chain.

2. Stay in the present. "What if I forget and have to stop? What if I look foolish?" Negative thinking diverts our concentration from the natural unfolding of the music, isolating our focus onto a specific note or physical gesture, or away from the music entirely. As a pianist, I try to center my attention on my senses, concentrating on the **feel** of my hands on the keyboard, sinking into the key bed, **hearing** the melodic line unfold and noting how it balances the other voices, **seeing** my

hands move effortlessly over the keys in fluid gestures. Think and hear the music as a whole entity, allowing it to evolve in a natural way. This is why I never try thinking through a composition while waiting backstage without looking at the score. Without aural and kinesthetic cues prompting me from note to note, I am more likely to forget, especially when anxious.

3. Assign positive attributes to the physical sensations that accompany performance anxiety. Many performers have cold hands, butterflies in the stomach or dry mouth prior to an important performance. Rather than worry about these symptoms, tell yourself these are signals from your brain to your body indicating that you perceive this as an important occasion. Excitement will heighten awareness and enable you to achieve a more spontaneous, electrifying performance. Convert frightening physical sensations into the belief that they can assist rather than hinder your performance.

## Imagery

Athletes have been using imagery for years, utilizing this technique to focus their attention in situations where they have one chance to accomplish their goals. Imagery permits them to rehearse their movements and insure a more successful outcome.

This technique can be used to build a memory of positive experiences, making the real thing less foreign and threatening. Just before going to bed, when relaxed, "play through" your pieces away from the instrument, looking at the score, without actually moving your fingers, hearing in your head all of the musical nuances you wish to project. While doing this, think about how good you'll feel during the performance, achieving your goals. (See Guided Imagery On The Day Of A Performance for a sample format. Use this as a guide to devise your own positive thoughts, suited to your individual circumstances.)

Imagery can also serve the practical purpose of warming your hands. If you notice that your hands are cold while waiting backstage, imagine yourself sitting beside a warm, glowing fire, relaxing in the cozy environment of the room, allowing the warmth of the fire to raise the temperature of your hands. Many individuals locate biofeedback centers to learn how to control their blood pressure, muscle tension or hand temperature. This has proven to be quite effective in training people to make this body/mind connection.

## Desensitization

Frequently used in helping individuals overcome phobias, this technique is often associated with fear of flying. Individuals are taught relaxation techniques, then brought in contact with the feared activity in gradual stages. Musicians can devise their own hierarchy, listing their least stressful to most stressful performance situations. It is important that students create their own list, which will differ from other persons. As teachers we can provide students a variety of opportunities to explore the items on their lists. They can play for each other in group lessons or overlapping lessons or play duets with a friend . . . how about performing in a studio/ performance class? . . . higher on the scale might be a recital or competition. For some students, playing into a tape recorder might be a first step. I encourage students to play in nursing homes where audiences are totally non-judgmental, thrilled to have someone visit, bringing the added bonus of knowing you are giving something special to the nursing home residents. Remember that before any major performance, students need at least four dry-runs in a performance setting that is less stressful than the "real" thing. This is the only way that the "bugs" can be discovered and eliminated.

## Medical Advances

Historically, anxious performers used alcohol and tranquilizers, often greatly impairing the quality of their performances. More recently, musicians have discovered the existence of beta blockers, sometimes prescribed as an adjunct treatment for performance anxiety. Available by prescription, this these drugs prevent adrenalin from combining with specialized beta receptors in the autonomic nervous system, eliminating or alleviating the anxiety responses that would ordinarily occur. A violinist auditioning for a position with a major orchestra, fearful that his bow will shake on the string, might find beta blockers the solution. This individual may be more nervous about the possibility of the bow shaking than the performance itself. For those individuals who are caught in a vicious cycle of being nervous because they are nervous, beta blockers can help. However, performers need to keep in mind that beta blockers will not eliminate the negative thoughts that sometimes occur prior to or in the midst of performance.

The most commonly prescribed beta blocker for performance anxiety is Propranolol or Inderal (brand name), otherwise prescribed for various heart conditions. In those instances, the medication is taken regularly in higher doses. For performance anxiety it is taken in a single, small dose (10-20 mg) 60-90 minutes prior to the performance. Entering and exiting the blood stream quickly, it is physically non-addictive, although some may find them psychologically addictive. For some students, taking beta blockers may be medically contraindicated. It is critical for teachers to recognize that it is never appropriate to dispense any kind of medications to their students. If you think a student might benefit from this medication, refer them to a physician.

Several articles that provide information on the types and uses of beta blockers can be found in various issues of *Medical Problems of Performing Artists*, (Science & Medicine, Inc. Narberth, PA). This refereed journal is an outstanding resource for information related to music medicine, musician wellness research and preventive approaches to remaining healthy. As stated on their website,

> *"MPPA is the first clinical medical journal devoted to the etiology, diagnosis, and treatment of medical and psychological disorders related to the performing arts. Original peer-reviewed research papers cover topics including neurologic disorders, musculoskeletal conditions, voice and hearing disorders, anxieties, stress, substance abuse, disorders of aging, and other health issues related to actors, dancers, singers, musicians, and other performers."*

There is much controversy over the use of beta blockers. Under special circumstances, it might make good sense to take advantage of a medication to control the physical manifestations of performance anxiety, although most individuals are able to overcome anxiety by combining the other strategies listed earlier. If, however, someone suffers from severe performance anxiety and feels it necessary to take medication prior to each performance, it might be advisable to seek out a medical professional to discover what is at the root of this anxiety. Because each individual approaches performance in his/her own unique fashion, the decision to take or not take medication must be made in consultation with a physician and, in the case of a student, with a physician, the teacher and the parents.

### Practical Advice

Teachers play a major role in assisting their students in dealing with performance anxiety. There are many simple, practical things we can do to provide students successful performance experiences.

### Teacher Do's

1. Select appropriate repertoire that is challenging, but within a student's capabilities.

2. Encourage thorough preparation, beginning repertoire far enough in advance to allow for security and mastery of material.

3. Assist students in developing self-confidence. A positive self-image will transfer to performance situations.

4. Provide a variety of performance opportunities that build a foundation of positive experiences, including lots of early low-pressure opportunities.

5. Encourage, but never force performance. A teacher can also serve as a role model as one who enjoys performance.

6. Assist students in working on concentration and relaxation skills. Offer a bibliography of relevant books to those students who might find this information useful.

7. Practice stage presence and provide opportunities for dry runs. Try out concert clothing, especially shoes for women.

8. Focus on the naturalness of the music unfolding and conveying the meaning of the music—less emphasis on mistakes or wrong notes.

9. Encourage students to take good care of themselves, emphasizing healthy diet, exercise and adequate rest. Reduce caffeine and include more complex carbohydrates in the diet.

10. Emphasize the joy of performing—having fun!

## Teacher Don'ts

1. Don't force students to perform.

2. Don't tell them they shouldn't be nervous.

3. Don't criticize a student's performance just prior to the recital when adequate time is unavailable for the student to act on the feedback. Comment only about what can be comfortably corrected in the remaining time.

4. Immediately following a performance, don't offer negative feedback, even though constructive. Allow the student to bask in the glory of the performance.

Whatever the performance, the goal is enjoyment, not fear or dread. Try experimenting with this guided imagery for the day of a performance. Create your own image that matches your performance situation, using this template below as a guide.

# Positive Thinking: Guided Imagery for the Day of a Performance

I look up at the clock—time to get up. Then I remember what day it is—today is my recital! It seems only yesterday that it was a month away. I feel excited and yet, ready, as I start this special day.

I move at a relaxed pace all day. After breakfast I spend some time warming up at the piano.

As I begin to feel my muscles grow more supple, I start each composition and then slowly play through some of the more difficult spots. I will go through this process several times today. I will play just enough to feel comfortable since I want to save my energy for tonight, not wishing to wear myself out in rehearsal.

As the day progresses, I feel more and more exhilarated. The day passes quickly, and soon I begin to dress for the performance.

As I dress I feel a flutter of nervousness. It is OK for me to be a little nervous—it is heightening my self-awareness, and will allow me to present a more sensitive performance. I have learned to relax—I can control my nervousness and turn it into a positive factor.

Warming up at the piano in the recital hall, all dressed up, I am very aware that my recital is merely minutes away. This is my night! Having practiced for those short periods spaced throughout the day, I already feel warmed up. Now I begin to feel even more flexible and comfortable as I try out the piano this last time. The sound of the piano in the empty hall resounds in my ears—a new sound, created by the excitement of this moment.

The microphones have been put in place, the lights adjusted, the piano positioned. The stage manager has just told me that he is ready to open the house. This is it!

I retire backstage and visit for a while with a few close friends until they leave to find their seats. Now, while I'm alone is a good time to take one last look at my music, and to rethink my first piece, focusing on what I want to express in this composition. All the little details and decisions I made in my practice have become an integral part of my conception of this piece. I have special feelings about this music that have grown since selecting it, and I want to share these feelings with my audience.

Five minutes to go, and then—the door is opened for me, and I'm walking onto the stage. I feel a charge of excitement and anticipation. I move with ease and purpose toward the piano. All my practice and hard work has brought me to this moment where I can communicate my feelings about this music.

As I acknowledge the applause of the audience, I am aware of their energy and support. The warmth of the lights and the sound of the applause make me feel welcomed to the stage.

I feel comfortable as I sit down at the piano. I have spent so many hours at the piano, it now feels very much like "home." I look out at the expanse of the instrument—the bare strings, the open lid, and I feel a sense of power and mastery. The keys feel warm from the lights. The cone of light makes me feel as if I were ensconced in a cocoon—warm, safe and secure.

I position my hands, take a deep breath and begin to play. Sinking deeply into the keys, I feel assured by the solidity of the bottom of the key bed. My arms feel relaxed, my hands steady. I know I am well prepared.

Although I feel a rapport with the audience, my concentration is on my music—listening, allowing the piece to unfold by itself, through me. Memory will remain intact since I will allow one musical idea to naturally follow another. Ideas unfold like the telling of a musical story I know very well.

My hearing is sharper now than it has been in my practice. The presence of an audience creates a heightened awareness and sensitivity toward my playing. As I respond to the sounds I am creating, I feel as if I am hearing the music in a new, fresh light, stimulating a more intense interpretation of the music. My hands feel very supple. I play with an ease and fluidity that makes me feel as if my hands are "dancing" on the keys.

Each piece is over so soon! What took so long to prepare is going by so quickly—one piece, then another. I can hardly believe that it's already intermission, with only half the program remaining. As I wait backstage, I am eager to get back on stage. My hands are tingling—I can feel the blood surging through my hands—I feel hot and flushed. Turn off the houselights! Let's start the second half!

Back on stage, I realize that as I complete each piece, I grow nearer and nearer the end of the recital. I wish it could go on forever. And then, it's over! I hear a burst of applause, and it feels wonderful. The sound rolls toward me like a wave, enveloping me. It is as if the audience is reaching out to me.

Very important to me is knowing that I have played as well as I can at this moment. This was a good performance! I greet my friends and relive the excitement of the performance with them. I know why I play recitals—it's because I love to perform! Another reason is because I love the celebration afterwards!

# Final Thoughts

The broad range of skills we need as teachers can be staggering, especially for young, novice teachers. Regardless of our level of experience, it remains vital for us to continue to our own education by attending workshops and conferences, reading books and journals, going to concerts and continuing to enjoy and make music. What we learn is conveyed directly to our students.

# Endnotes

[1] Reprinted in part from, "Challenges for Teachers: What do my students hear when I speak?" written by Gail Berenson, from the *Proceedings and Reference of the National Conference on Piano Pedagogy*, The Chicago Conference, 1988.

[2] Reprinted in part from the article, "Perfect Practice" written by Gail Berenson, September/October, 1993 issue of *Piano and Keyboard*.

[3] Reprinted in part from the article, "Beating Stage Fright" written by Gail Berenson, January/February, 1994 issue of *Piano and Keyboard*.

# PART THREE
# RESEARCH AND
# THE PIANO TEACHER

# CHAPTER 37

## Musician Wellness and Today's Piano Teacher

### Gail Berenson

The demand for information on the subject of musician wellness has grown exponentially over the past two decades. Whether an experienced professional artist or a young student just beginning lessons, the need for approaching the instrument and performing in a healthy manner is crucial. It is this knowledge and awareness that enables individuals to enjoy a lifetime of healthy, joyous music making.

This makes the role of the teacher even more critical since teachers are the ones responsible for passing wellness information on to their students. In 2004 in Fort Worth, Texas, The Health Promotion in Schools of Music (HPSM) Project brought together professionals from both performing arts medicine and music, including a unique set of partnerships of over 20 professional organizations. HPSM was a collaborative effort between the University of North Texas System and the Performing Arts Medicine Association (PAMA). That conference resulted in the drafting of key declarations and recommendations relating to the health and well being of music students. Specific details summarizing the results of this significant meeting can be found at the following website: http://www.unt.edu/hpsm/.

The leadership from the HPSM conference took their recommendations to the National Association of Schools of Music (NASM), the accrediting association for many of the Schools of Music in the United States. Responding to the powerful request from this expert body of professionals and recognizing the critical need for ensuring the well being of future generations of musicians, NASM embraced this issue and has strongly encouraged Schools of Music to include wellness information in every music curricula. A more recent positive indicator is a June 2010 statement listed on the NASM website that reflects a partnership between NASM and PAMA that will focus on the health and wellness of musicians.

> *NASM and the Performing Arts Medicine Association (PAMA) have agreed to cooperate and lead in the development of studies and projects focused on the health and wellness of musicians. The primary goal is the production and dissemination of information for students, faculty, and administrators. Hearing issues will be the first area of emphasis.*
>
> *The agreement enables the knowledge, skills, and contextual understandings of medical doctors and music administrators to be combined and coordinated at a new and more formal level. NASM and PAMA will consult with their respective memberships and other interested organizations as projects develop.*

As a result of this recommendation from NASM, underscored further by the growing number of students dealing with musculoskeletal injuries, hearing loss and/or psychological issues, music programs are integrating either specifically designated wellness courses into the curriculum or incorporating this information into their pedagogy course curricula.

Providing an example of how this key information might be assimilated into a pedagogy curriculum, the Wellness Committee, a standing committee of the National Conference on Keyboard Pedagogy, has designed a wellness component for use in a piano pedagogy class. Originally created in 2003, the committee revised the document in 2007. The updated document is located on the Frances Clark Center website: http://www.francesclarkcenter.org.

It is important to incorporate both physiological and psychological information into the curriculum since both areas are integral to maintaining the health and well being of a musician. To provide teachers access to a wide range of wellness information, Music Teachers National Association (MTNA) offers an annotated, searchable database of books, journals and websites. MTNA's wellness bibliography, researched and annotated by Professor Linda Cockey, Salisbury University, and assisted by Kathryn Kalmanson, Head of Research Services, Blackwell Library, Salisbury University, can be accessed on the MTNA website: http://www.mtna.org This extensive bibliography provides ample evidence of the growing number of musicians and medical professionals who have devoted much of their lives researching these topics, authoring articles, books and/or creating DVDs that provide clear guidelines to musicians for staying healthy and happy.

MTNA has been involved in providing wellness information for its members and the general public for quite some time. At a December 2003 MTNA Board of Directors meeting, a list of ten essential skills was presented to the Board by an ad-hoc committee. The decision was made to develop them into a series of articles. Although inclusive of a more diverse range of important learning objectives, several of the skills, and the ensuing articles, relate specifically to wellness issues.

## Essential Skills for Promoting a Lifelong Love of Music and Music Making

- Ability to internalize basic rhythms and pulse.
- Ability to read—musical literacy.
- Ability to perform with physical ease and technical efficiency.
- Ability to hear the notes on the page.
- Ability to work creatively—improvise, compose, harmonize and play by ear.
- Ability to understand basic elements of theory, form harmony, etc.
- Ability to respond to the interpretive elements of the composition to express the emotional character of the music.
- Ability to conceptualize and transfer musical ideas.
- Ability to work independently and to problem-solve.
- Ability to perform comfortably individually and with others in a variety of settings.

The "Essential Skills" articles were published in the February/March 2005 through August/September 2005 issues of the American Music Teacher and are now available on the MTNA website.

## Prevention is Key

As a result of all the ergonomic research due to the onslaught of injuries resulting from extended computer use, medical professionals have learned a great deal about proper positioning at a keyboard to avoid injuries. Many of these same "keyboard" guidelines are equally effective for pianists. This reinforces the importance of educating today's teachers in injury preventive strategies to help their students avoid future injuries and to aid in the development of troubleshooting approaches should an injury arise.

Understanding how the body operates most efficiently and developing a natural, efficient technique is crucial to achieving effortless performance. While building a certain degree of endurance is necessary, musicians now recognize that becoming knowledgeable about body mechanics and allowing the music and the physical mechanism to breathe will result in a natural performance that enables them to project the emotions of the music and not tax the body beyond what it can physically handle. Happily, the "no pain, no gain" motto is disappearing in both sports and music.

Perhaps a student is wrestling with a problem that is psychological in nature, performance anxiety being the most often cited. Envision a young pianist who, after a major memory slip is unable to recover and leaves the stage in tears in the middle of her performance, now fearing future performances of any kind. There are times when some students, and professionals as well, may require the help of a mental health professional to overcome their fear of performing. For other students, a knowledgeable, sensitive teacher can offer sufficient support and assistance. It is important, however, to recognize the boundaries of the teacher/student relationship. Distinguishing the fine line between thinking that we have the skills to help a student prevent or solve a problem and recognizing when it is more appropriate to encourage a student to seek medical help may be difficult but vital.

While teachers should be alert to the situations that require medical intervention and steer our students to the appropriate expert, we also need to move beyond thinking only of "treating" an injury, striving instead for an emphasis on "prevention". For the majority of teachers, their principal teaching objective is to assist students in achieving a lifetime of musical enjoyment, wherever that ultimately takes them. Some students may pursue the concert stage and others will seek teaching positions. However, a large percentage may not select music as a career at all, choosing instead to play for personal enjoyment and self-fulfillment. Students who possess self-confidence, an efficient, healthy technique and a fundamental understanding of musicality will be able to achieve whatever goal they select. This demands a more holistic teaching approach, in addition to students to taking a more active role in their lessons. Injury-preventative and wellness information also needs to be a part of every competent and informed piano teacher's pedagogical arsenal. Whether used in the first lesson of a three-year old beginner or a lesson with a doctoral performance major, this information is relevant. This pragmatic view of music wellness places a strong focus on prevention and is applicable to everyone.

# New Directions

An unexpected group of students is making the decision to study music, with the fastest growing "student" population age forty or above. These individuals, most often beginners, are fulfilling a dream, to play an instrument. Recreational Music Making offers a different kind of instruction. Taught in a group setting, the primary goals of this music instruction are to have fun and to enjoy the process of learning how to make music. The social aspects and the group support benefits that are a natural occurrence in this setting, extend beyond what the students achieve musically. Research has documented the wide range of health benefits for those participating in these music classes. Although typically taught as piano classes, music instruction can also take place within a drum circle or on other instruments.

Even some cruise ships are offering piano instruction on board, offering an enrichment activity that is both fun and provides the subsequent outcome of learning to play the piano. In 2004, Yamaha Corporation of America and Crystal Cruises partnered to launch their "Passport to Music" program as part of Crystal's Creative Learning Institute. By the time the "passengers/ students" disembark the ship, they are able to play several pieces for their friends and relatives when they return home.

For more information about RMM and to learn more about the research that documented a variety of health benefits for RMM participants, please consult the National Piano Foundation website: http://pianonet. com/recreational-music-making/about-rmm/ or the National Association of Music Merchants website: http://www.wannaplaymusic.com/rmm. A number of teachers have become RMM specialists, offering RMM instruction and authoring several RMM method books, which have been published. The teachers who pursue this type of teaching indicate that it is as rewarding and as much fun for them as it is for the students!

# Resources

Numerous books, videotapes and websites on the subject of musician wellness are proliferating the marketplace, providing extremely beneficial information. Physicians and psychologists are establishing practices specializing in music and arts medicine, with many affiliated with performing arts medical clinics, serving the music community of all ages. And, universities are heeding the recommendation of NASM and integrating wellness courses into the music curricula.

# Kudos

I want to commend all the teachers who serve as individual "beacons of light" doing research, promoting healthy approaches to the instrument and advocating for broader dissemination of wellness information. Many of these individuals are also contributing members of wellness committees that are connected with the various associations listed below, and many have authored articles or books or produced videos and DVD's. All of these teachers are making a difference one student, one presentation and one class at a time. I would mention them by name but do not want to risk inadvertently leaving someone out. I wish all these dedicated individuals continued success in their work!

# Associations

More and more associations are including wellness sessions on their conference programs and wellness articles in their journals. Workshops, sponsored by music teacher organizations, are also increasingly common.

**ISME** (International Society of Music Education) presents a biennial world conference in even numbered years, with locations rotating around the world. To provide a bit of information about this organization, the following historical background is posted on the ISME website,

> *The International Society for Music Education was formed at a conference convened by UNESCO in 1953 'to stimulate music education as an integral part of general education'. This has been ISME's main concern over the past decades and continues to be our most important source of motivation. In the years that followed its formation, ISME gradually evolved to what it is today: a worldwide service platform for music educators who want their profession to be taken seriously by educators in other disciplines, by politicians and policy makers, by international organizations that promote culture, education, conservation and durable development of cultural heritage.*

In 2008, the ISME Board of Directors approved a Forum for Vocal and Instrumental Studio Performance. This Forum presents sessions in connection with the World Conference. Its sessions will encompass all aspects of instrumental and vocal teaching and learning that may take place in the home or school on a one-to-one or small group basis. As part of its vision, the Forum includes a focus on arts medicine as it relates to keeping students injury-free, helping them develop an effortless and efficient technique, manage and recover from playing or non playing-related injuries, and discover strategies for coping with performance anxiety. More information about this association and its activities can be found at: http://www.isme.org.

**ISSTIP** (International Society for the Study of Tension in Performance) was founded in 1980 in London, England. Its founder, Carola Grindea (1914-2009), was a piano pedagogue and pioneer in the study of releasing tension. Professor Grindea was ahead of her time in recognizing the importance of discovering ways to handle musicians' excessive tension and painful injuries sustained by the misuse of the muscles and by partnering with medical professionals to offer workshops and clinics for musicians in the United Kingdom. According to the ISSTIP website, www.isstip. org, ISSTIP aims to study and enhance awareness on the various physical and psychological problems of the performing artists. ISSTIP's greatest concern is the increased number of performers around the world who are suffering from physical or physiological dysfunctions. The work of ISSTIP continues with annual round table discussions on wellness issues included in each EPTA (European Piano Teachers Association) conference with seminars on health topics in the United Kingdom, and worldwide through the activities of its international members, and with the publication of its journal, *Tension in Performance – The ISSTIP Journal* (formerly *The ISSTIP Journal* with 14 issues edited by Carola Grindea before her death). ISSTIP offers membership to health professionals, performing artists, teachers, and students. More information about this association and its activities can be found at: http://www.isstip.org.

**MTNA** (Music Teachers National Association) has been mentioned many times in this chapter as a major contributor to the field of musician wellness. A recent addition to its wellness offerings is its Wellness Forum, established in 2008 to provide a medium for open discussion and expression of ideas on this topic and to recommend initiatives, projects and services to the MTNA Board of Directors. More information about this association and its activities can be found at: http://www.mtna.org.

NCKP (National Conference on Keyboard Pedagogy, formerly the National Conference on Piano Pedagogy—NCPP) holds a biennial conference (held in odd-numbered years). The conference is sponsored by the Frances Clark Center for Keyboard Pedagogy, a not-for-profit educational institution located in Kingston, New Jersey. The work of the Center is based on the philosophy of music educator Frances Clark (1905-1998) whose life work revolutionized the field of music education in the twentieth century. With its long time support of a standing committee on wellness, NCKP has made considerable contributions in the area of musician wellness. More information about this association and its activities can be found at: http://www.francesclarkcenter.org.

**PAMA** (Performing Arts Medicine Association) is an association comprised of dedicated medical professionals, artists, educators, and administrators with the common goal of improving the health care of the performing artist. PAMA was founded in 1989, with a membership from around the world. Their annual symposium is attracting significant attention from musicians throughout the United States, and their refereed journal, *Medical Problems of Performing Artists*, published four times per year, serves as a tremendously valuable resource. More information about this association and its activities can be found at: http://www.artsmed.org/.

**WPPC** (World Piano Pedagogy Conference), under the direction of Benjamin Saver, has held an annual conference since 1995. Since its inception, each conference has had an emphasis on technique and wellness. Its online "webzine" also contains a number of wellness-related articles. More information about this conference and its activities can be found at: http://www.pianovision.com.

# NCPP's Pioneering Efforts

As far back as 1988, what was then the National Conference on Piano Pedagogy (NCPP) created a number of standing committees, one of which was the Committee on the Prevention of Medical Problems. In 1990 the committee compiled a list of ten essential principals to help preserve musician wellness. Those principals are listed below and are written about in greater depth by committee members in a "Position Paper on Musician Wellness", published in the 1994 NCPP Conference Proceedings.

# Teachers Need to

1.  Understand the basic principles of physiology, i.e., how the body functions.

2.  Understand the mechanics and acoustics of the instrument and how these apply to the production of sound.

3.  Understand the function of the human body in relation to the instrument for achieving optimum comfort. Although each student's physical makeup is different, there are specific issues which need to be addressed at the beginning stages of learning, such as posture (position of neck, torso, arm, hand, and fingers in relation to the keyboard), balance and economy of motion.

4.  Create effective learning environments for socializing students and dealing with performance anxiety. Group instruction provides a supportive learning environment in which students are encouraged to listen to and comment on one another's performances.

5.  Provide humanistic experiences to a) foster in students a love for music, b) expand students' scope of knowledge at the elementary and intermediate levels of instruction, and c) better prepare students for a lifetime involvement in music. Such experiences are attending concerts, going to art museums, and listening, moving (Dalcroze), and drawing to music. Provide music majors realistic career counseling.

6.  Be aware of resources which increase students' focus or concentration when practicing and performing (i.e. meditation, biofeedback, and visualization). Regular aerobic exercise should also be encouraged.

7.  Be aware of a variety of practice techniques which allow students to efficiently manage their time and increase their speed of learning. The skill of practicing must be taught. When working with children, parents must also be educated about their role in the practicing process.

8. Be willing to investigate the causes of problems with students when they are more deeply rooted in psychological issues rather than physiological ones.

9. Be aware of risk factors which may lead to medical problems, such as performance anxiety, physical risk factors (e.g., joint laxity, hand span), fatigue, stress, improper organization and use or selection of repertoire, and ineffective patterns of communication which do not address the needs of students.

10. Implement, at the university level, courses in pedagogy that would make prospective teachers more aware of the above issues.

Readers are encouraged to consult the 1994 Conference Proceedings to see the committee's recommendations on the guidelines listed above.

## Conclusion

It is reassuring to note the progress made over the past two decades in educating musicians on wellness issues. It is equally exciting to see the number of medical professionals and musicians who have chosen to dedicate their careers to researching and exploring strategies for keeping musicians healthy and able to joyfully continue their music making. A wealth of information is available on a wide range of wellness topics. Dedicated teachers need only look online to learn about books, websites, journals, DVD's and a host of workshops available worldwide to continue to expand their knowledge in this critical area.

One can only hope that the current and continuing advancements in the field of musician wellness will result in countless individuals of all ages pursuing music making and enjoying the experience throughout their lifetime.

# CHAPTER 38

# An Introduction to Brain Research and Learning for the Piano Teacher

## Suzanne Schons

Piano teachers often wonder what is going on inside students' brains. For example, why is it that certain types of practice make playing easier, and why are mistakes so hard to fix? How do students' brains process new learning, and what makes them more likely to remember (or not remember) concepts and skills? What impact do piano lessons have on children's brains? Perhaps most importantly, what can teachers do to help students' brains maximize learning and retention? Although the answers to these questions are complex and not fully known yet, research in the fields of neuroscience, psychology, and education is providing valuable information that helps to shed light on how students learn.

With new brain imaging technologies becoming available in recent decades, neuroscientists have unprecedented access into the brain's inner workings. Before the advent of these technologies, researchers lacked safe ways to explore healthy human brains, so they were limited to observing behavior as a way to develop theories about mental processes. As imaging technologies have developed in recent decades, however, scientists can now actually see what happens in the brain as people think, learn, and perform tasks. The field of neuroscience is expanding at a breathtaking rate, and new findings about the brain are coming out every day. Many studies have even been conducted specifically on musicians and music-related tasks. These developments are exciting for educators, who have a high stake in understanding how the mind works. Piano teachers today have exponentially more information available to them about how the brain learns than piano teachers of past generations and are fortunate to be able to benefit from that knowledge.

Applying brain research to piano teaching can be challenging because the field of brain research is evolving rapidly, and findings are constantly changing and being updated. Also, neuromusical research is complicated by the fact that making music involves very complex mental activities that can be difficult to study. However, combining research from neuroscience, psychology and education provides a wealth of practical information on the brain for piano teachers. The brain is the focus of our work as teachers, so it is essential to know how it functions. Studying the brain will help teachers understand how students learn, assist them in advising students on sound practice strategies, and it helps explain and provide a more solid foundation for effective pedagogical practices.

## Brain Overview

What exactly is this organ inside our heads called the brain? The human brain weighs about three pounds. It is very soft tissue. Neurosurgeons often compare its consistency to toothpaste or tofu. Although it makes up just 2% of our overall body weight, the brain consumes about 20% of its calories! (Unfortunately for the academic world, thinking hard is not a practical weight control strategy.) While it is beyond the scope of this chapter to go into great detail about brain anatomy, a basic knowledge of brain structure and function is helpful for understanding how the brain learns.

The brain stem, located at the base of the brain, is responsible for basic survival functions such as breathing and heartbeat. The cerebellum rests in the back of the brain, near the brain stem, and coordinates balance, movement, and posture. The cerebellum is one of the key areas when it comes to developing the motor skills needed to play the piano. It monitors the speed, direction, force, and steadiness of the motions. Recent findings have also indicated that the cerebellum is involved in emotional responses to music.

Deep inside the brain are some notable structures, including the thalamus, hypothalamus, hippocampus, and amygdala. The thalamus takes in sensory information from the body and directs it to other parts of the brain for processing. The hypothalamus lies just under the thalamus and senses blood temperature and controls hunger and thirst. It also plays a key role in regulating sleep cycles, and triggering the fight-or-flight response. The hippocampus, named for the Latin word for seahorse because of its shape, is a center for memory formation, including that of musical memory. The amygdala also contributes to the fight-or-flight response, and is central to emotional reactions, especially negative emotions. If you have ever felt terrified before a performance and started thinking irrational thoughts, for example, "I have no idea how to play this piece," even when you have practiced and learned the piece thoroughly and effectively, your amygdala is probably signaling your hypothalamus to release a cascade of stress hormones.*

The cerebrum is the large, topmost part of the brain, and the cerebral cortex is the covering, containing the ridges (*gyri*) and grooves (*sulci*) that give the cerebrum its wrinkled appearance. The cerebral cortex is where higher order thinking takes place. The four lobes of the cerebral cortex are the frontal lobe, temporal lobe, parietal lobe, and occipital lobe. Conscious thought, personality, planning, reasoning, risk assessment, and self-control are products of the frontal lobe. (It may not surprise teachers and parents of teenagers to know that the frontal lobe does not fully mature until about age 25.) The temporal lobe, located on the sides of the head, near the ears, is involved in auditory processing and musical perception. The parietal lobe, at the crown of the head, is essential for processing touch, temperature, and spatial orientation of the body, and the occipital lobe, towards the back of the head, is responsible for visual processing. There is also a strip of cells along the back of the frontal lobe called the motor cortex, that initiates voluntary muscle movements. The motor cortex, cerebellum and a group of nuclei deep inside the brain called the basal ganglia, work together to coordinate the gestures and movements needed for piano performance.

The brain is divided into two halves, the right hemisphere and left hemisphere. Although brain regions are often referred to in the singular, for the sake of simplicity (for example, *frontal lobe*), nearly every brain part is actually a pair (for example, *right frontal lobe* and *left frontal lobe*). Each hemisphere of the brain controls the opposite side of the body. For example, your right hemisphere controls your left hand on the piano and your left hemisphere controls your right hand. The corpus callosum is a thick band of fibers that connects the two hemispheres and allows them to communicate.

Music has often been referred to as a "right brain" activity, for various reasons, but current research indicates music making is actually a very complex whole-brain activity. Daniel Levitin, author of the book *This Is Your Brain on Music*, writes, "Contrary to the old, simplistic notion that art and music are processed in the right hemisphere of our brains, with language and mathematics in the left, recent findings from my laboratory and those of my colleagues are showing us that music is distributed throughout the brain. Music listening, performance and composition engage nearly every area of the brain that we have so far identified, and involve nearly every neural subsystem."[1]

# Neural Connections

All learning can essentially be attributed to the brain's neural connections. The two types of cells that make up the central nervous system are *neurons* and *glial cells*. Neurons, or nerve cells, are the cells that make connections to form our thoughts, memories, ideas, feelings, and actions. Glial cells play a supporting role, by insulating and protecting the nerve cells. The brain has about 100 billion neurons (about as many stars in the Milky Way!), and while that is certainly a lot of neurons, glial cells are even more abundant, as they outnumber neurons by 10 to 1. The brain is a busy place!

Neurons have thousands of branches emerging from their core, called dendrites, which are for receiving communication from other neurons. Neurons send out signals to other neurons along a fiber called the axon. There is normally one axon per neuron, and it can be very short or very long—even several feet! Neurons do not physically connect with one another or touch one another. Between each axon and dendrite is a small gap, called a synapse, and it is about a millionth of an inch wide. Communication between neurons takes place through the synapses.

When the brain receives sensory input, certain neurons communicate with each other and form a neural pathway. A neuron sends out an electrical signal that causes brain chemicals called neurotransmitters to be released. As the neurotransmitters cross the synapse and bind to a receiving neuron, they spark a series of reactions that cause the second neuron to generate a signal, or to "fire." The reaction continues and causes other neurons to fire in a particular pattern as well. The firing might last only a brief time. If the sensory input is not repeated again, the neural pathway that was activated will stay in a state of readiness for hours, or maybe even days, but eventually it will decay and the memory of it will be lost. On the other hand, if the sensory input is repeated again, the tendency for the associated group of neurons to fire together is increased, and it does not take as much stimulation for it to fire the next time. Neurons become conditioned to respond more efficiently to signals they have received many times before. Ultimately, when one neuron is triggered, the whole network fires, and is strengthened, thereby consolidating a memory and making it easier to retrieve in the future.

To illustrate how neural communication might happen in the context of piano practice, let's imagine a pianist practicing a phrase. The first time the pianist plays the phrase, it takes considerable effort and concentration to do so. However, with each repetition of the phrase, the neural networks associated with playing it fire more rapidly and become more efficient, and the phrase becomes easier to play. The repeated use of neural pathways that happens during practice is what makes a concept or skill easier—it strengthens those neural pathways in the brain. Furthermore, there is a fatty substance called myelin (made of glial cells) that coats the axons of neurons. Myelin insulates the axons, allowing communication to happen more rapidly, and protects the axons from interference from nearby neural reactions. Myelin thickens on frequently used axons, and practice enhances myelination.

It is important to know that when students practice incorrectly, for example by playing incorrect pitches, rhythms, using inefficient technique, or ignoring dynamics, they strengthen the neural connections to play incorrectly. Unfortunately, the brain cannot distinguish between what a person *meant* to do in practice, and what he or she *did* do! Each repetition of a wrong note makes the neural pathway for that wrong note fire and get stronger. This is why the phrase "practice makes permanent" (revised from "practice makes perfect") really rings true! It is imperative that teachers help students understand the brain basis for why it is so hard to fix a mistake that has been practiced, and why they should be so careful to practice pieces correctly and conscientiously from the beginning.

## Brain Plasticity

The amazing brain is constantly rewiring itself. Every new bit of learning, however small or seemingly insignificant, changes the brain by reorganizing its neural networks. Your brain will be different tomorrow than it is today. The ability of the brain to continuously change is called *neural plasticity*. A newborn baby's brain already has most of the neurons it will ever have, but the connections between neurons are relatively few. A young child's brain grows very rapidly after birth, and creates far more neural connections than an adult brain holds. Because of this overgrowth of synapses, the brain begins the process of pruning unused synapses. Neural connections that are used, as a result of the child's activities and environment, will be maintained and strengthened, and those that are not used will be discarded. Hence, the value of a safe and stimulating learning environment in childhood, including that of a rich musical environment, cannot be underestimated.

Childhood and adolescence are especially active times of neural plasticity, and this is probably why there seem to be windows of time after which it becomes more difficult to learn to speak a language or play a musical instrument with fluency. Recent research is providing astounding information on how musical training changes the brain. Studies have found professional musicians to have larger corpus callosums than non-musicians, perhaps due to the rapid communication between hemispheres needed for musical performance, and/or the bimanual demands (using both hands) of instrumental performance.[2,3,4,5] Studies have also found that musicians have enlarged auditory and motor areas compared to non-musicians.[6,7,8] The research strongly indicates that these brain differences are a result of training, rather than in-born differences. Generally, such brain differences in professional musicians compared to non-musicians are most pronounced in people who began musical instruction before the age of seven years old. While these studies cannot tell us the best age at which to begin music lessons and exactly what the resulting brain changes mean in terms of later musical abilities, it is intriguing information to be aware of when considering musical experiences for children. Teachers will need to look to future research to provide more information on these issues.

As an adult reading this text, perhaps you are starting to feel down about your most plastic brain years being behind you, or are wondering how on earth you are going to explain all this to your adult piano students . . . but take heart! While brain plasticity is most dynamic during one's youth, the process of making and eliminating neural connections in response to a person's environment is continuous throughout life. Adults still have tremendous power to shape their brains and develop knowledge and skills by study, practice, and other choices about how they live their lives and use their time. Adults even have certain advantages in learning by having extensive previous learning to draw upon, and by having mature, optimized neural networks in place. Furthermore, motivation and degree of personal importance greatly influence brain plasticity. Adult piano students should never feel it is too late to learn!

# Human Memory

Human memory is a very complex concept, and our understanding of it is continually evolving. The basic categories of memory are *sensory memory*, *short-term memory/working memory*, and *long-term memory*. Sensory memory takes in sensory data and holds it for only a moment, where it is either transferred to working memory or it is discarded. We are not even aware of what is going on in most of our sensory memory— so many sights and sounds and other sensory information that we encounter go unnoticed by our consciousness, so that we can focus on what is important.

Short-term memory temporarily stores several chunks of information for a short time. Working memory is an extension of short-term memory, with which we consciously process information and give it our attention. When music teachers present new concepts in a lesson to students, students deal with those concepts in their working memory. Teachers want students to take important concepts in working memory and encode and store them into long-term memory, and to be able to retrieve and use them again in the future. It should be noted, however, that long-term memories are not always intact blocks of information that are neatly recalled when needed. Rather, memories are frequently reconstructed and modified, sometimes incorrectly. After all, if memory were perfect, no one would ever start playing the recapitulation of a sonata movement and mysteriously end up back in the exposition. Luckily, there are many things teachers can do to help students improve their memory of piano-related concepts and activities.

# Teaching and Practice Suggestions for Better Learning

## Attention

It is no surprise that the degree of focus and attention that a student gives to a concept in working memory plays a huge role in whether or not that concept will get encoded and stored into long-term memory. Teachers sometimes complain about students not paying attention, but actually there is no such thing as not paying attention. The brain is always paying attention to something, but it may not be directed towards the item the teacher thinks is important! There are several things teachers can do to help students focus on piano activities.

One is to do everything possible to avoid unwanted distractions. Children's brains are very sensitive to distractions, so teachers and parents should be careful to set up a lesson and practice environment that is not cluttered, noisy, or prone to interruptions. If a student cannot deal with a concept in working memory because there are too many other stimuli competing for attention, the concept will likely not end up in long-term memory.

Another consideration is to be reasonable about how long children spend on one activity before switching to another, or before approaching the activity in a different way. Children's brains are not fully developed enough to allocate attention to the degree that adults can, and attention span can also vary greatly from one child to another. A child who is losing focus on an activity may not be able to help it, and should not be admonished for it. Novelty is a big attention-getter for the brain. A student can be happily focused on a learning task, but if something new and novel comes along, such as a phone ringing or a light going out, the brain cannot help but pay attention to the novel stimulus. Teachers can use the brain's response to novelty to their advantage by approaching learning with different activities and sensory approaches. For example, if a student is working on a piece that uses tonic and dominant chords in the accompaniment, the teacher might break for a moment to do a quick ear training game or writing activity using the same chords. Another fun way for students to shift gears is to have the student figure out a familiar tune by ear that uses only tonic and dominant chords, such as "Alouette" or "Skip to My Lou." The songs can then be transposed to other keys. Creative skills can be brought into play by improvising a short piece using tonic and dominant chords. Students can switch the melody and accompaniment to the opposite hands. Using multiple sensory approaches in teaching has the added benefit of engaging more neural networks in the brain, which also enhances memory.

## Elaborative Rehearsal

Teachers should attempt to help students connect new concepts to previous learning, a concept cognitive psychologists refer to as *elaborative rehearsal*. Connecting new information to already known information makes learning easier and retention stronger. Examples of elaborative rehearsal in a piano lesson could include relating a new concept of constructing an augmented triad to a known concept of constructing a major triad, or comparing a new concept of rounded binary form to the previously studied concept of simple binary form.

## Distributed Repetition

The field of cognitive psychology has done extensive research on the effects of *massed repetition* (lots of practice all at once), versus *distributed repetition* (practice spaced out over time). As piano teachers might expect, distributed repetition is usually much more effective for long-term learning. Many current piano methods incorporate distributed repetition techniques into the method by reinforcing and revisiting concepts in subsequent pieces. However, teachers must also be conscientious that students are reviewing concepts learned in the past. For example, a student who learns to write or play a minor scale needs to keep reviewing that scale periodically. Teachers should not assume that because a student seemed to learn something sufficiently well at one time, that it will be remembered in the future without regular review.

## Chunking

Chunking (or *recoding*) techniques are essential for helping the brain process more information at once, and knowledge of music theory is key to chunking musical information. If a student never learns how to spell and recognize minor chords, for example, the pitches D, F, and A will be processed as three chunks rather than as one chunk (D minor triad) in working memory. Teachers might illustrate this to students who do not appreciate the importance of theory (hard to imagine), by playing a memory game, such as asking them to memorize a series of letters quickly, such as ETBHUCRS. See how well the student can recall the letters again a few minutes later, and then try again with a familiar rearrangement of the letters: SCHUBERT. Surely the student will be more successful the second time, when the letters are perceived as one chunk, rather than as eight random letters! This activity demonstrates how quickly and easily the brain can remember information that is chunked.

## Motivation and Emotions

Motivation and emotions are critical to the brain's learning and memory processes, as emotions and cognition are closely connected, and share brain circuitry. The brain treats learning that has an emotional component to it as very important. Teachers should always strive to create a positive emotional climate in the lesson not only for obvious ethical reasons, but also because it supports learning so much. When learning is relevant and interesting and produces positive feelings, it does not seem like work. Someone who loves baseball will gladly spend hours learning names and statistics related to the sport that non-fans would find dull and meaningless. Not every child will come to piano lessons intensely interested in the subject, but teachers should strive to find ways to make musical activities as meaningful as possible to students. As an example, practicing chords can be a part of learning a lead sheet for a pop song that the student finds personally motivating and relevant.

## Modeling

As any experienced piano teacher knows, demonstrating a principle at the piano for a student is often more effective and efficient than verbally explaining it, and educational research has also supported the use of modeling in teaching.[9] It is now thought that the presence of a mirror neuron system is an important factor behind the effectiveness of demonstration and modeling. A fascinating discovery found in monkeys in the 1990s, and later in humans, mirror neuron networks are neural systems in motor and other areas of the brain that fire not only when one performs an action, but also when one observes or hears an action. In pianists, such a mirror neuron system becomes activated when observing and listening to piano performances, and the more experience a person has with the piece being performed, the more strongly the mirror system becomes activated.[10] Thus, when a student observes a teacher modeling gestures and other aspects of piano playing, his brain is actively learning. A reasonable implication is that teachers should not only model frequently, but also do so with their best artistry and precision each time. The student's brain is always taking note!

## Healthy Habits

It is helpful for students to stand up and move periodically, whether during a lesson or practice session. During periods of extended sitting, circulation slows down, which can cause decreased alertness. Standing up and moving gets blood circulating more and carrying oxygen to the brain, and adding movement to music also provides extra sensory input to the brain. (Although it will be hard to put it down, you might want to stand up and stretch or move from time to time while reading this book.) Humor can also help to stimulate alertness. Laughing not only increases circulation, but it also decreases stress hormones, lowers blood pressure, relaxes muscle tension, and provides an endorphin surge that can create a positive climate. Finally, a healthy diet and adequate hydration are vital for optimal brain functioning, and physical exercise also appears to improve cognition and learning. Teachers cannot control what students eat or drink, and whether they exercise, of course, but teachers can issue occasional reminders about how healthy habits contribute to their brain's performance.

## Timing of Practice

*When* a student practices after a lesson has an impact on retention of new skills and concepts. New learning and memories are unstable, and it is helpful to consolidating and stabilizing them to rehearse and practice within the first 24 hours of a lesson. Even if a student cannot schedule a full practice session in that time frame, a brief review of portions of the week's assignment can be beneficial. Remember that distributed repetition is also needed to consolidate learning, which is why additional regularly spaced practice between lessons has been found by generations of piano teachers to be essential for optimal progress.

## Take Breaks and Get Some Sleep

Playing the piano is an exceptionally complicated task for the central nervous system. It combines auditory, visual, and sensorimotor components, and requires attention, planning, logic, timing, and frequent quick physical adjustments based on multi-sensory feedback. Not many piano teachers will be surprised to hear that deliberate practice and thoughtful repetition are necessary for developing motor skills at the piano that become refined and reliable. However, much of the consolidation that happens in the brain for motor skills occurs during breaks between practice. Motor skills become more consolidated and automatic about six hours after the activity stops, and memory of motor skills is further established during sleep.[11] This is probably why piano playing often feels easier the next day after practicing. Students should be aware of this information so that they understand that cramming in practice right before a lesson or performance does not work! Also, practicing when mentally or physically fatigued can lead to poor technique habits and making and reinforcing mistakes.

## Mental Practice

Immediately after reading this sentence, take a moment to close your eyes and imagine yourself at the piano, playing just the first few notes of a piece you know. Although you have not actually played the piano, many regions of your brain just became activated as if you did. Many pianists have had the experience of visualizing a performance, perhaps reading though the score away from the piano as they do so, and found that their memory and understanding of the piece increases. Studies using brain imaging technologies have found that mental practice and visualization activate nearly all of the same neural circuitry as physical practice.[12,13] Because the brain treats mental practice very similarly to physical practice, neural connections are strengthened and reinforced as a result. Most teachers are already familiar with mental practice, but students may have an easier time getting motivated to add it to their arsenal of practice techniques when they understand the brain basis for its effectiveness.

## What Does the Future Hold for Music and Brain Research?

It is an exciting time in brain research, and many new and useful discoveries about how the brain processes music are undoubtedly on the horizon. Studies are continuing to explore how the brain learns and how it performs tasks specific to music, such as how it perceives music, how it performs and creates music, and how studying music changes the brain. Much more investigation needs to be done on how various pedagogical approaches and practice techniques impact brain activity and learning. As research advances, teachers will need to make informed decisions about when and how to apply findings to their teaching. The insights gained into students' learning processes from brain research are tremendously interesting, and often reaffirming, and it will be an exciting ride to see what the future holds for brain research.

## Suggested Reading

Blakemore, Sarah-Jayne, and Uta Frith. *The Learning Brain: Lessons for Education*. Malden, MA: Blackwell Publishing, 2005.

Edwards, Richard. "The Neurosciences and Music Education: An Online Database of Brain Imaging and Neuromusical Research." PhD diss., University of North Carolina at Greensboro, 2008. https://libres.uncg.edu/ir/uncg/f/umi-uncg-1523.pdf. (accessed July 7, 2010).

Gruhn, Wilfred, and Frances H. Rauscher, eds. *Neurosciences in Music Pedagogy*. New York: Nova Biomedical Books, 2008.

Hodges, Donald A. "Can Neuroscience Help us do a Better Job of Teaching Music?" *General Music Today* 23 [2010]: 3-12.

Levitin, Daniel. *This Is Your Brain on Music: The Science of a Human Obsession*. New York: Penguin Group, 2006.

Robinson-Riegler, Bridget, and Gregory Robinson-Riegler. *Cognitive Psychology*. 3rd ed. Boston, MA: Pearson Education, 2012.

Svard, Lois. "The Musician's Guide to the Brain: From Perception to Performance." *MTNA e-Journal* 1, no. 4 (April 2010): 2-11.

Sweeney, Michael S., *Brain: The Complete Mind: How it Develops, How it Works, and How to Keep it Sharp*. Washington, D.C., National Geographic, 2009.

# Endnotes

\* See chapter 39, page 491, "Performance Anxiety Management" by Vanessa Cornett-Murtada, for more information on the causes of performance anxiety.

[1] Daniel Levitin, *This Is Your Brain on Music: The Science of a Human Obsession*. (New York: Penguin Group, 2006), 8-9.

[2] Sara L. Bengtsson et al., "Extensive Piano Practicing has Regionally Specific Effects on White Matter Development," *Nature Neuroscience* 8, no. 9 (2005): 1148-1150.

[3] Gottfried Schlaug et al., "Increased corpus callosum size in musicians," *Neuropsychologia* 33 [1995]: 1047-1055.

[4] Gottfried Schlaug et al., "Effects of Music Training on Brain and Cognitive Development," *Annals of the New York Academy of Sciences* 1060 (2005): 219-230.

[5] Gottfried Schlaug et al., "Training-Induced Neuralplasticity in Young Children," *Annals of the New York Academy of Sciences* 1169 (2009): 205-208.

[6] Thomas Elbert et al., "Increased Cortical Representation of the Fingers of the Left Hand in String Players," *Science* 270, no. 5234 (1995): 305-307.

[7] Gottfried Schlaug et al., "In Vivo Evidence of Structural Brain Asymmetry in Musicians," *Science* 267, no. 5198 (1995): 699-701.

[8] Robert J. Zatorre et al., "Functional Anatomy of Musical Processing in Listeners with Absolute Pitch and Relative Pitch," *Proceedings of the National Academy of Sciences* 95 (1998): 3172-3177.

[9] Roseanne Kelly Rosenthal, "The Relative Effects of Guided Model, Model Only, Guide Only, and Practice Only Treatments on the Accuracy of Advanced Instrumentalists' Musical Performance," *Journal of Research in Music Education* 32 (1984): 265-274.

[10] Amir Lahav, Elliot Saltzman, and Gottfried Schlaug, "Action Representation of Sound: Audiomotor Recognition Network While Listening to Newly-Acquired Actions," *Journal of Neuroscience* 27 (2007): 308-314.

[11] Stefan Fischer et al., "Motor Memory Consolidation in Sleep Shapes More Effective Neuronal Representations," *Journal of Neuroscience* 25, no. 49 (2005): 11248-11255.

[12] Alvaro Pascual-Leone et al., "Modulation of Muscle Responses Evoked by Transcranial Magnetic Stimulation During the Acquisition of New Fine Motor Skills, *Journal of Neurophysiology* 74, no. 3 (1995): 1037-1045.

[13] Ingo G. Meister et al., "Playing Piano in the Mind—an fMRI Study on Music Imagery and Performance in Pianists, *Brain Research. Cognitive Brain Research* 19 (2004): 219-228.

# CHAPTER 39

## Performance Anxiety Management

### Vanessa Cornett-Murtada

## Why Study Performance Anxiety Management?

For any performing musician, mental wellness is a vital part of success. Yet, how often do we take time in a piano lesson to discuss or practice strategies for managing performance fear? Most teachers will agree that, regardless of the length of the lesson, it is difficult or impossible to fit everything in. At the very least, we make time for repertoire study, technique, theory, and sight reading. Many teachers are able to include elements of ear training, composition, improvisation, or even music history. But the one element which is often absent from the lesson curriculum, performance anxiety management, is the reason many musicians quit lessons or give up performing altogether!

The hard truth is that most teachers were never taught the basic facts about performance anxiety, such as how it is manifested in the brain, what triggers it, and what techniques have been scientifically tested and found to manage it effectively. We usually do the best we can, drawing from what our teachers told us, or from what works for us. Has anyone ever told you that you have nothing to be worried about, or that the more you perform, the less fear you will experience? By the end of this chapter, you will understand what many music instructors do not: why these strategies *don't* work.

This chapter begins with some important disclaimers, because any discussion of anxiety management assumes three characteristics of the performer. 1) She is well-prepared for the performance, through smart and sufficient practice. *There is no anxiety management technique that can substitute for adequate preparation.* 2) She possesses adequate technical and musical ability, and her repertoire is not too difficult for her to play confidently and artistically. 3) She is not physically or psychologically challenged in a way that would make a comfortable performance experience impossible.

## The Anatomy of Anxiety

Performance anxiety is like a juvenile delinquent in that it has a bit of a checkered past. Decades ago, "stage fright" was a common term used to describe the fear of public performance. Because this field was virtually unexplored by scientists, most people viewed stage fright as a stigma that a performer was not talented enough or was unable to master performance fear on her own. Most performers chose to hide their anxieties in shame. Those who did have the courage to seek treatment from an analyst may have been diagnosed with a variety of phobias, social disorders, or psychological complexes!

Fortunately, therapists today are beginning to understand the universal nature of anxiety, and performing artists now benefit from excellent research in the field, resulting in more opportunities for support, understanding, and effective solutions. Today, most professionals use the more acceptable terms for stage fright: performance anxiety or musical performance anxiety.

The range of performance anxiety, from mild jitters to crippling fear, can often take the joy and spontaneity out of performing. Advanced and professional musicians are not immune, and we now know that little truth exists in the axiom that more performance experience will result in fewer feelings of anxiety. Musical performance anxiety usually involves a fear of how others will judge our performance and perhaps even judge us as individuals. It can start minutes, hours, days, or even weeks before that important performance. Obviously, music performance is not a life and death situation. Why, then, do performers experience such fear when faced with the possibility of sharing music for an audience? To fully understand, we must go back in history… about 25,000 years.

Imagine that you are a Neolithic Age hunter-gatherer, foraging in the woods for delicious wild berries for your dinner. Now imagine that when you look up, you realize that you are face to face with a fierce saber-toothed tiger! You have been looking at berries, but the tiger has been watching you, and has decided that you would make for an excellent snack. What would you do in this situation?

Most likely, you will immediately act on one of three options: you will run away as fast as you can, you will face your enemy and fight for your life, or you will freeze and perhaps even "play dead" the way a possum might. Many people refer to this as the powerful *fight or flight* response to stress. We have all heard stories of mothers who are able to lift a car to save a trapped child; this seemingly super-human ability is made possible through a stress response which bypasses our rational mind.

We are fortunate that our brains and bodies have always been well-equipped to deal with such immediate life-and-death situations. Deep within our brains is contained primitive, automatic genetic wisdom that alerts us to danger. When a threat occurs, a small almond-shaped part of the brain, the amygdala, reacts immediately by sending signals to other parts of the brain in a complex and instantaneous chain reaction. The hypothalamus gland, when stimulated by the amygdala, sends an immediate message to the adrenal glands, and initiates a sequence of chemicals released in the blood stream. The most significant of these chemicals is epinephrine, also known as adrenaline. This primitive fear response actually bypasses the rational part of your brain. When faced with a life-threatening fear, you will react before you even have time to think about your situation.[1]

# Physical Symptoms of Performance Anxiety

Let's take a closer look at some specific physical manifestations of the fight or flight response. The following chart explains why we experience certain symptoms when under pressure. Demystifying uncomfortable physical responses can be the first step toward becoming a more confident performer.

| Physiological response to increased adrenaline | Reasons for this response | Resulting symptoms |
|---|---|---|
| Respiratory rate increases | Increased need for oxygen | Shallow breathing<br>Quickened breathing |
| Pulse quickens;<br><br>Blood is redirected to large muscles in the arms and legs | Increased strength to fight or run from threat | Pounding or racing heartbeat<br>Rising blood pressure<br>Cold hands or feet |
| Blood vessels in the digestive system close | Digestion slows or stops | Fluttering stomach<br>Upset stomach; nausea<br>Dry mouth |

*(continued)*

| | | |
|---|---|---|
| Pupils dilate | Sharpened sight | Hypersensitive visual awareness<br><br>Sensitivity to bright lights |
| Capillaries under the surface of the skin close down | Reduced chance of excess bleeding in battle | Cold hands |
| Perspiration increases | Reduced chance of skin cuts | Clammy hands<br><br>Excessive sweating |
| Increased firing of neurons in the brain | Increased focus | Awareness intensifies<br><br>Hyperfocusing |
| Muscles tighten | Physical preparation to fight or run | Excess tension<br><br>Headache |
| Excess waste eliminated | Decreased body weight offers the ability to run faster | Increased urge to use the bathroom |

For many students, simply understanding the information in this chart is a tremendous step forward. We begin to understand that the fear response is a natural, normal reaction to stress. We recognize that there is nothing wrong with us, because each of these symptoms is meant to help us, and possibly save our lives!

The problem arises when we are faced not with a saber-toothed tiger, but with a shiny Steinway grand piano. If we fast-forward to the present day, we see that our stressors are not usually life threatening: rush-hour traffic, a bounced check, oversleeping through an important appointment, or playing a recital piece from memory. Nevertheless, these stressors still trigger the fight or flight response, pouring stress hormones into our bodies. Our brains don't distinguish sources of fear: wild animal or a mysterious bump in the night, a threat is a threat. The difference is that in the twenty-first century, the threats we experience are mostly psychological rather than physical. Not only that, but in our culture it is no longer reasonable in most instances to fight or run away... if your boss yells at you for being late to work, it is generally not acceptable for you to respond by punching him in the nose or running away and jumping out of the window. No, in today's society you are expected to control your reactions and simply "deal" with it.

How unfair! The brain has just dumped a whole cocktail of chemicals in your blood stream, and rather than get rid of them by running away or engaging in battle, you are forced to smile and pretend that everything is okay. This is like drinking six cups of coffee and then trying not to feel wide awake or jittery; you can't simply will those chemicals out of your blood stream. This is why the following phrases, while well-intended, will never really help an anxious musician: "Don't be nervous," "Just try to calm down," or "You have nothing to worry about." This is so important. Our first, most intuitive response is to soothe a frightened student by suggesting the fear isn't real. But teachers who do that unwittingly communicate that the student's feelings are invalid or, even worse, imagined.

For some students, the physical symptoms of performance anxiety represent the greatest cause of distress, because they can interfere with the ability to perform well. A pianist, for example, may fear that his hands will shake visibly, be too cold to move with agility, or perspire enough to cause him to slip on the keys. For many, though, the emotional and psychological effects of anxiety can be even more devastating.

# Psychological and Hidden Symptoms of Performance Anxiety

The psychological manifestations of anxiety can be crippling to a performer. During the fight or flight response, the inner judges of the mind can become overactive. On the surface, a performer may fear making a mistake, having a memory lapse, or not getting a good contest rating. On a deeper level, a student may begin to question her own competence and self-worth. Those negative thoughts might be working hard to convince her that she isn't good enough, that she will humiliate herself, will never succeed, will be revealed as a phony, or even will be unable to continue. Many performance issues can be rooted in fears of the unexpected, the unknown, or the loss of love or approval by others. Even professional performing musicians can fear disappointing their audience, a special coach, colleagues, rivals, or newspaper critics.

It is important to remember that these fears are not restricted to music recitals and festivals. As human beings, we experience a wide range of "performances" in life. Raising your hand and asking a question in a class or workshop is a performance... how often have you mentally rehearsed the question while waiting for the instructor to call on you? Other types of life performances include picking up the phone and calling a stranger, taking an exam, mingling at a party, and going out on a date. In each case, the "performer" perceives that he is being evaluated, and the need to live up to an unnamed set of standards is a significant source of stress.

Anxiety can also manifest itself through a multitude of hidden symptoms which may go completely unrecognized by both the student and teacher. Sometimes behavioral problems and excuse-making are rooted in fear. General agitation, indecisiveness, self-disparagement, and withdrawal may also be indicative of anxiety. By far the most common manifestation of anxiety is *procrastination*. People of all ages tend to avoid what they fear, and may be surprised to learn that anxiety about the quality of a performance, lesson, paper, or exam may be behind the urge to put the project off until later. Students who tell you they aren't ready, don't feel like it, can't do it, can't see the point, or don't feel well may be secretly afraid of failure.

# Solutions for Performance Anxiety Management

We must remember that in the large scheme of things, performance anxiety is not entirely a bad thing. Those little jitters can give a performer that extra edge needed for an especially outstanding performance. Not only is it possible to perform well while experiencing anxious symptoms, but it is unrealistic to expect all those symptoms to vanish. Adrenaline may remain in the bloodstream, but students can learn to minimize the most distracting physical and psychological symptoms, and reinterpret nervous energy as enthusiasm, excitement, and the opportunity to enjoy an optimal performance.

It is essential that a performer try these techniques well in advance of the performance, preferably for three to six months, although four to six weeks of regular practice is often enough to result in noticeable improvement. When a student regularly engages in an anxiety management technique, she is often creating a conditioned response in the brain. This means that after a while, her brain immediately recognizes the technique, and her body begins to relax much more quickly and automatically. A student would ideally practice these exercises regularly, and always before a lesson or practice performance in front of a teacher or peers. If regular practice performances are impractical, performing for an audio or video recording device can simulate a performance experience. It will *not* help if a student decides to try one or more of these techniques for the first time right before a performance. The brain needs to learn and practice new techniques when it is calm.

Every performer is different, and solutions for performance anxiety management can be very personal. Remember, a technique which works well for the teacher may not always work for the student.

# Breathing Techniques

If I had to choose the quickest, most accessible, and most immediately effective anxiety management technique, it would be the simple act of diaphragmatic breathing. Breathing is the only function we do either completely consciously (voluntarily) or unconsciously (involuntarily), which means that breathing is the only function with which we can influence the involuntary nervous system. Deep, diaphragmatic breathing can lower the blood pressure, slow the brainwaves, and reduce any sort of anxiety. Breathwork has been used successfully to treat people with high blood pressure, digestive disorders, irregular heartbeat, and even psychological disorders.

Piano students are at a bit of a disadvantage in that proper breathing is not really necessary to be able to play the instrument well. As a result, unlike their peers taking wind, brass, or voice lessons, piano students are not often taught how to breathe correctly. During the fight or flight response, the breathing will often become shallow and rapid, and feelings of anxiety will increase. When under stress, piano students will sometimes hold their breath without realizing it. It is a good practice for teachers to observe the breathing patterns of an anxious student while he performs in the lesson.

The easiest way to teach proper breathing is to ask a student to place her hand on her abdomen, watching and feeling it rise and fall as the belly expands and contracts. It also helps to lie down flat on the floor, balancing a book on the stomach, and watching the book rise and fall with correct diaphragmatic breathing. When practicing breathwork for anxiety management, it is not necessary to close the eyes, but it can be very helpful. Blocking out visual stimuli encourages calm, restful activity in the brain, and can bring about feelings of deep relaxation more quickly. Conscious breathing should ideally be a part of every lesson, every practice session, and every performance.

Some students prefer to have a more structured approach to breathing for stress relief. Observing and counting breaths is easy to do and can be very effective. To observe the breath, try not to control the rate of inhalation and exhalation. You may choose to see if you can gradually make the breathing deeper, slower, and quieter. If you decide to count breaths, be sure only to count from 1-5 or 1-10 and then start over, rather than continuing to count up. Eventually you can let go of the counting and focus on the natural experience of breathing.

It can be very helpful to use the exhale to help release anxiety. Even if we wanted to get rid of every bit of anxiety, that sort of goal is impossible.

But we could agree to release half the anxiety on each exhale. After inhaling deeply, if you slowly think "release half" on the exhale, you can visualize letting half of the tension go away. After another inhale, you may think "release half" on the exhale, thus releasing half of what was left of the remaining anxiety. This is a wonderful exercise to decrease anxious feelings slowly and realistically. You may also choose to think "I am" on the inhale, and fill in the exhale with a word or phrase that describes how you would like to feel. For example, after thinking "I am" on the inhale, you may think "quiet and relaxed" on the exhale. Other good examples for the exhale are words such as "safe," "prepared," "fine," and "content."

# Progressive Relaxation Techniques

Emotional tension feeds off physical tension, and vice versa. It is like the chicken and the egg: when we are nervous, we feel tense, and the physical tension makes us feel even more anxious, which causes more tension. Students who learn to relax their muscles systematically often experience an immediate decrease in the physical and psychological symptoms of anxiety.

One helpful way to encourage muscle relaxation is to tense each muscle group one at a time, then relax. If you clench your fist as tightly as possible, you will notice that the arm muscles behind it will begin to quiver. When you suddenly stop clenching and allow the arm to drop, the muscles will be even more relaxed than before you applied the tension. Shrugging the shoulders high, holding them briefly in a position of tension, and then letting them drop is a particularly useful exercise for pianists. The large muscles which tend to hold the most tension are the thighs, abdominal muscles, arms, and shoulders. Smaller muscle groups in the neck, jaw, and forehead are also targets of excess tension.

Another way to ease tension is through suggestion, allowing the muscles to relax by simply noticing how they feel and by encouraging them, in your mind, to relax. This technique can be very effective, and can be done without drawing any attention to the performer. Observe how your body reacts when you read the following sentence slowly and deliberately. "My shoulders feel warm, loose, and heavy, and I allow gravity to gently pull them down into a place of comfortable relaxation." To practice this type of relaxation, find a quiet place and sit comfortably so that your back is supported. Breathe deeply from the diaphragm as you visualize each part of your body. Feel yourself grow warm and relaxed as you repeat phrases such as the following two or three times: "I feel quiet. I am beginning to feel quite relaxed. My feet feel heavy, warm, and relaxed. My ankles feel warm, relaxed, and comfortable. My knees feel warm, relaxed, and comfortable…" You may slowly work your way up the body from the feet to the scalp. With practice, this technique can be more effective and calming than tensing and relaxing each muscle group.

## Creative Imagery and Visualization

Athletes have known about the performance-enhancing power of visualization for many years, and musicians are only recently beginning to catch up. The mind is more powerful than most of us realize, and we now know three very important facts about the effects of creative imagery. First, the brain and nervous system are unable to distinguish between an event that was imagined and one that actually occurred. Second, when a person is clearly visualizing a specific movement, all the nerves involved in making the muscles move are stimulated as if the movement were physically taking place. Finally, we know that visualization enhances performance for athletes and performing artists. The essence of creative visualization is to consciously focus the imagination on an objective with the intention of achieving that objective.

The four elements of a successful visualization activity are relaxation, concentration, suggestion, and positive expectation. When visualizing a performance experience, it is important always to emphasize a positive experience. A student has the power to imagine the most wonderful performance possible! The more sensory modalities a musician uses, the more powerful and effective the visualization will be. For example, a performer can imagine the look of the stage, the piano, and the green room or backstage area. She could recreate the sound of the audience talking before the performance, the sound of the applause, and of course the music itself. She could imagine what the warm stage lights would feel like, how the smooth keys would feel beneath her fingers, and how positive and excited she would feel on the inside. She might even be aware of the scent of the performance venue, whether it is musty, or if flowers are near the piano.

It is important to realize that while the vast majority of people can close their eyes and create or follow along with a visualization activity, some students are not especially visual and have great difficulty visualizing. With these students, emphasis should be placed on the other senses, particularly the kinesthetic sense of how the performance feels. Gail Berenson has written a fine example of a visualization exercise in her chapter "Preparation for Performance: Ensuring Student Success."

## Mindfulness Practice

Mindfulness, in its simplest form, is nonjudgmental moment-to-moment awareness. Observing the breath, as mentioned earlier, is a form of mindfulness practice. With this technique, a performer might learn to become a peacefully detached observer of her own mental activity, without reflecting on the past or worrying about the future. She might learn to accept mistakes without judgment and to separate her negative thoughts from the reality of the situation. Mindful awareness can be practiced anywhere, at any time, or may be cultivated as a form of meditation.

Many mindfulness techniques are based on a meditation practice in which the meditator strives for a clear awareness of what is happening as it happens from moment to moment. Usually the breath is the primary focus of attention in mindfulness meditation. The practitioner is encouraged to observe any changes in his thoughts, feelings, and physical experiences. The identifying characteristics of this type of meditation include non-judging, acceptance, patience, trust, and letting go. Mindfulness meditation is different from other human activities because it has no goal other than for one to be oneself!

The practice of mindfulness is widely used in clinical settings in the United States because of its documented benefits in reducing stress and anxiety, and coping with chronic pain. At many hospitals and university medical centers, meditation is used as an effective treatment for anxiety disorders such as phobias and the fear of public speaking. Research also indicates that this form of meditation can reduce anxiety in children and adolescents.

Neuroscientists have found evidence that people who have practiced meditation throughout their lifetime are effective in controlling their emotions and physical reactions to stressful situations, an obvious benefit for performing musicians. The effects of regular mindfulness meditation include a decrease in blood pressure, diminished respiratory rate, lower pulse rate, diminished oxygen consumption, increase in the calming brain waves associated with relaxation, and an improved sense of well-being.

A simple sitting meditation can be as short as ten minutes at first. Try to find a quiet location where you will not be disturbed, and be sure phones and e-mail alerts are turned off. One does not need to sit cross-legged on a cushion, because a chair or sofa will be just as effective. The back can be unsupported or supported, but it is important not to recline or lie down in order to avoid falling asleep. The eyes can be closed or remain open, although closing the eyes will automatically invite slow, calming brainwaves. Breathe in a calm, effortless way, rather than attempting to control the breath or breathe "correctly." Simply observe the thoughts that wander into the mind, and gently let them go. The goal is not to control these thoughts (which is impossible, anyway), but to simply observe them, focusing on one thing at a time. Through observation, racing thoughts will often slow down, although this is not the goal. In fact, there is no goal other than gentle, non-striving observation.

Other types of meditation involve replacing the observed thoughts with a single point of focus, such as a mantra or affirmation. Some students use part of their meditation to practice creative visualization. Others may wish to identify critical thoughts in a non-judgmental way. All of these are effective tools for performance anxiety management, particularly if practiced every day. A student may even learn to become a detached observer of unexpected problems that may arise during a performance, such as a memory lapse, by acknowledging the slip with non-judging awareness before refocusing his attention back on the music.

## Affirmations

Affirmations are short, prepared, powerful statements that help a student focus on a positive performance experience. Affirmations can be specific to a particular piece ("My Mozart sonata is cheerful, light, and very steady") or to the performance experience as a whole ("I am well-prepared and confident"). Statements for performance anxiety management may focus on the student's love of the piece, the supportive and encouraging family members in the audience, or the goal of having fun. It is important to remember that to be effective, an affirmation must be truthful and realistic, because the subconscious mind will reject any suggestions that do not align with one's personal belief system. Therefore, a statement such as "My performance will be flawless" is much less realistic than "I am ready to do my best." Negatively-motivated affirmations such as "I will play this piece faster than Amy did last year" are to be discouraged in favor of positive ones that focus on personal development. The student should take part in creating an affirmation that feels good to him. Short affirmations such as "I can do this!" tend to be more effective than long lists of goals. More mature performers sometimes enjoy using an especially well-crafted literary quote for inspiration.

Prayers differ from affirmations in that they are often based on an established faith tradition. They may be written by the student, or they may come from a sacred text. While affirmations usually involve personal statements of intent, prayers may also include a supplication or request to a higher power. Of course, it is very important to be sensitive to every student's particular faith tradition. If a student wishes to include his personal faith as a part of an affirmation, it is often best to allow this suggestion to come from the student.

## Cognitive Psychology Techniques

In Western psychology, the use of rational thinking to cultivate good mental health became widespread in the mid-twentieth century with the development of various forms of cognitive therapy. While a music teacher should never attempt to psychoanalyze or counsel a student, understanding some basic concepts of cognitive psychology can be very useful. The main premise behind cognitive restructuring is that all stress is the result of one's own thinking. Mark Twain illustrated this beautifully when he said, "I've experienced many terrible things in my life, a few of which actually happened." In other words, what happens to you is not the source of stress, it's how you interpret that stress. One of the reasons this approach has worked so well in the last fifty years is because cognitive restructuring returns power and control to the individual, and encourages people to suspend negative judgment of themselves.

Cognitive therapists assert that we are largely responsible for the way we feel and act by the beliefs we hold about the events in our lives. Events contribute to the way we feel and act, but do not cause these reactions, which are mostly determined by our beliefs about these events. Rational beliefs may be described as beliefs which are logical, consistent with reality, and promote psychological wellbeing and the pursuit of meaningful goals. Conversely, irrational beliefs would be those which are rigid, illogical, inconsistent with reality, and which interfere with psychological wellbeing, obstructing the pursuit of personal goals. Some examples of irrational thoughts include "I should never make a mistake in a recital" and "I'll never be able to play this right." Rational thoughts, on the other hand, might include "If I happen to make a mistake, it won't be the end of the world" or "I can't play this well yet, but I will improve if I practice well." Learning to identify irrational thoughts is not particularly difficult. A few words to listen for include: must, should, need, and never. For example, an anxious musician may think he *should* never have a memory lapse, he *should* never disappoint his teacher, he *must* not fail, or perhaps he will *never* be good enough.

Irrational thoughts may be disputed by using honesty and common sense. Music teachers can help students develop healthy mental habits by gently encouraging rational thinking. If a student says "I just have to get a higher rating at the festival this year," we can identify this as an irrational thought if we understand that "have to" is a form of "must." A teacher might ask the student if the two of them can explore that sentence together. (Must he get a higher rating? What terrible thing will happen if he doesn't? Is a rating the only measure of success?) After some discussion, they might rephrase the thought to make it more rational. "I really *want* to get a higher rating at the festival this year, I like the idea of challenging myself, and I know what I need to do to practice well. But every performance is different and every judge is different, and a rating is simply one opinion of how I play. If I don't get a good rating, it won't be the end of the world. I really want to do my best." This sort of healthy thinking is an essential part of performance anxiety management. Students who are able to identify and dispute irrational thinking successfully tend to have a more positive and realistic outlook about performing. They are better able to censor the negative mind-chatter that results from the body's fear response.

Human beings are the only animals on the planet who are capable of meta-cognition, the ability to observe and evaluate our own thought processes. In other words, we are the only beings who can think about our thinking. We can begin to realize that we experience whatever we focus on, whether positive or negative. As an example, try not to think about a fat, waddling purple porcupine. As you continue to read, simply erase that image from your mind. Don't think about the purple you-know-what at all. (If you are a normal human being, you are most likely reading this with the image of a purple porcupine in the back of your mind. Your brain did not accept the condition that you were *not* supposed to think about it.)

This simple concept can be quite powerful and effective. Daydreaming about a purple porcupine won't cause any harm, but imagine the result of a student telling himself *not* to rush the tempo, *not* to forget the beginning of his piece, or *not* to trip and fall on the way to the piano. If the mind focuses on whatever we give it, a healthier solution might be for the student to remember to establish the perfect tempo ahead of time, to affirm that her memory is quite secure, and to make sure she walks to the piano carefully and confidently. Students are quite good at listing all the things they don't want to happen in a performance, and sometimes it takes practice to turn those thoughts around into expressing what they do want. I once ran into a friend of mine at a state park, where he had brought his eight-year-old daughter to play. As she ran across slippery wet river rocks, he called out, "stay upright!" When I asked him about his unusual choice of words, he explained that if he said "don't fall!" she would immediately, and without exception, fall down.

Since people often fear the unknown, gradual desensitization is another very effective method for encouraging students to perform without fear. Teachers should be sensitive to anxious students who may not be ready to perform in a public recital or adjudicated contest. For many of these students, performing for parents, friends, or even a video camera can be an excellent first performance goal. Sometimes a practice recital in a non-threatening venue such as a retirement home or church is a good next step. The more positive performance experiences, the better!

Students and teachers can use a technique called detachment training to help reshape negative thoughts. Anxiety is often triggered by low self-esteem, and students with low self-esteem will often assume that people will judge them based on their performance. To practice detachment training, a student would say and believe: I perform music, but I am not my performance. I am separate from my performance, I am different from my performance, and most importantly, I am more than my performance.[2]

# Reflective Writing Techniques

Reflective writing, also called journaling, can be an extremely effective technique in exploring the mind, learning about the self, practicing exercises in mindfulness, and overcoming fears and anxieties. Students often show tremendous progress when required to keep a practice notebook or journal to record personal reflections and observations about their practice sessions, overall progress, and feelings about music in general. Without prompting, many students who keep practice journals begin to express their deepest feelings, questions, hopes, and fears. Every student will express herself in a different way. Journaling is a very effective way for students to identify symptoms of anxiety and unhealthy thought patterns such as irrational self-talk. As a student becomes more comfortable with reflective writing before and after practicing, a teacher may begin to incorporate small assignments such as breathing or mindfulness exercises.

Journaling assignments should be specific and simple. For example, you might ask a student to take five deep breaths before every practice session and record how he feels afterwards. He could keep track of the distractions that make his mind wander during practice or performance, create solutions, and comment on the results. He might write two positive affirmations for each piece, one for the music and one for himself. Another assignment that can be fun is to have a student write a playfully nasty letter to the critical judges inside his head.

Younger children who experience performance anxiety may not be able to keep a journal. Using art as a form of expression, these students can draw a picture of the critical little monster who thinks he lives in their head. They can even give it a name. This is a wonderful way to teach children that the fear is separate from the self, and therefore under their control. Stuffed monsters or puppets work well, too. A child can do many things with a nasty mind monster: she can talk to it, yell at it, laugh at it, stomp on it, or make peace with it.

# Physical Activity

If the brain's automatic fight or flight response occurs in order to prepare the body for vigorous action, it makes sense that moderate physical exertion can send chemicals into the bloodstream which counteract the fear response. In fact, it only takes five minutes of physical activity (or enough to break a mild sweat) to begin to ease the symptoms of anxiety. Sometimes musicians will pace back and forth or jiggle their legs before a performance, without knowing that the body is working to counteract the fight or flight response naturally. Running is not often logistically practical before a performance, but jumping up and down, doing jumping jacks, or jogging in place will more than do the trick. It is important to give the body enough recover time before performing, so that the performer will be calm rather than sweaty and panting. Children, especially in a group setting before a recital, often appreciate and have fun engaging in a physical game to get the jitters out, but need a few minutes to calm down and focus before it is time to perform. The idea is to counteract the fight or flight response and then allow the body to return to a normal state.

On the other hand, some musicians choose to practice performing immediately after physical exertion. If you think about it, the most intense performance anxiety symptoms mirror the symptoms of physical exertion: pounding heartbeat, perspiration, breathlessness. If a student were to get his heart rate up, immediately sit down at the piano, and be able to play well despite the distracting physical symptoms, he might be able to handle any physical symptom when on stage. It is also helpful for a student to learn that it is possible to give an excellent performance even when feeling physically uncomfortable. This practice technique is not for everyone, but can be especially helpful for students who need to practice choosing an appropriate performance tempo while under the pressure of increased adrenaline. Of course, in an actual performance, one would not want to walk out on stage breathless and sweating.

## Medication

Much has been written about the use of prescription beta blockers such as Inderal (propranolol) for performance anxiety management. These medications prevent adrenaline from binding to beta receptors in the brain, and are normally prescribed for patients with heart conditions. Performers who take small doses of beta blockers before a performance may experience fewer physical symptoms of anxiety, such as pounding heartbeat, but this medication does nothing to alleviate the psychological symptoms of self-criticism or self-doubt.

Beta blockers must be prescribed by a doctor, and should never be passed from teacher to student or from one performer to another. The side effects can be dangerous, particularly among students who suffer from asthma or diabetes. Many professionals agree that the use of medication should be used as a last resort, after the student has *regularly practiced* other management techniques such as breathing, relaxation, visualization, cognitive restructuring, or mindfulness. In all fairness, some adult professionals suffer from such severe anxiety that they are not able to perform without beta blockers. While the use of medication should be generally discouraged, particularly among students, we should not criticize performers who are obliged to rely on beta blockers, just as we would never judge a person who must rely on prescription antidepressants. Of course, the use of alcohol or tranquilizers for performance anxiety management can be hazardous, and are not recommended for performers of any age.

# Other Anxiety Management Techniques

## Healthy Rituals

The need for ritual is deeply ingrained in all human beings. In fact, healthy rituals, not to be confused with superstitions, can help calm and center the anxious mind. For many performers, recital-day preparations become part of a ritual, including what they eat before performing or how they warm up. Others carry good-luck charms with them, repeat specific prayers or affirmations before performing, or engage in a calming visualization exercise. It is important to remember that we do not perform well *because* of these rituals! Eating a banana before you walk onstage does not insure a fearless performance, and the fact that a student forgot her lucky pet rock will not cause a memory slip. Rituals in and of themselves have no power, but the soothing regularity may help prepare and focus the mind for an optimal performance.

## Biofeedback

This technique trains people to improve their feelings of tension or anxiety by monitoring and learning to control some of the signals from their bodies. A biofeedback technician can help a performer learn to relax certain muscles quickly and easily, or to raise his own skin temperature, creating a feeling of warmth in the hands. Some professional equipment such as feedback thermometers or a biofeedback machine is usually necessary at first.

## Yoga and Tai Chi

Some researchers have found that a combined form of yoga and tai chi increases states of alertness and relaxation in the brain, decreases symptoms of anxiety and stress, and enhances certain types of performance. Musicians may also find that the gentle stretching of yoga practice will make them stronger and more resilient to performance-related injuries.

## Hypnotherapy

For anxiety sufferers, hypnotherapy can be effective as a form of visualization or imagery guided by a licensed therapist. A hypnotherapist will generally lead the performer in deep breathing and relaxation exercises before offering suggestions about cultivating confidence on stage and transforming anxious thoughts into excitement and positive energy.

## Essential Oils

The scent of lavender has been found to encourage slow, relaxing brainwaves and a feeling of well-being in some people. Aromatherapy combined with massage therapy has also been helpful for some anxiety sufferers. Other scents which have shown promise include jasmine, chamomile, and pine.

# When Should a Student Seek a Therapist?

Sometimes a student's anxiety may stem from deeper personal or family issues. Although the teacher-student relationship is often a close and personal one, most music teachers are not trained psychologists, and should not attempt to psychoanalyze a student. Sometimes the best choice is for a student to see a professional licensed therapist in addition to practicing regular performance anxiety management techniques learned in the music studio.

The following are a few signs that a student should see a counseling psychologist or doctor:

1. If anxiety symptoms related to music performance are severe or persistent, despite regular practice of the techniques discussed in this chapter.

2. If the student's anxiety seems to affect more areas of her life than music performance. Examples could include recurring issues of self-esteem or self-worth, persistent irrational thoughts, social phobias or other fears. Some students may exhibit excessive and constant worry, tension, irritability, restlessness, or insomnia.

3. If the student exhibits signs of depression in addition to performance anxiety. These include regular feelings of hopelessness, pessimism, worthlessness, emptiness, or loss of interest in hobbies and other activities. Depressed students may experience fatigue, a change in eating or sleeping habits, difficulty concentrating or remembering details, and general fatigue or loss of energy.

4. If the student has expressed interest in using beta blockers or other anti-anxiety medications.

# Conclusion

Teachers of the twenty-first century have the advantage of new breakthroughs in the areas of psychology and neuroscience. Anxiety management has become a major topic of research in past decades, and it is our responsibility to be aware of exciting new trends in this field. Sometimes we forget how powerful our words can be, and we should be as sensitive and thoughtful as possible about how we speak to a student, especially before a performance. Remember that it takes great courage for a student to admit that he is scared. Rather than minimize or trivialize a student's expressed fears ("Don't worry, you have nothing to be nervous about"), instructors should always acknowledge and validate his feelings ("I know you feel nervous, and I completely understand. Lots of other performers get nervous, too! Maybe we can find some solutions together").

The greatest challenge to most teachers is finding a way to fit performance anxiety management techniques into the limited studio time. With creative planning and an understanding of the positive long-term effects, however, we can usually find a way. It would only take a few seconds to begin each lesson or practice performance with a moment of silence and some deep breathing. Gentle stretching or short relaxation exercises can become part of the regular practice routine. A teacher can always include techniques such as journaling, writing affirmations, or composing personal visualizations as part of the weekly assignment. Some of the activities mentioned in this chapter work well in a group lesson or performance class. Of course, the best thing a teacher can do is to serve as an excellent model for students. An instructor who is able to incorporate some of these techniques into her own practice, demonstrate and practice them with the student, and share personal experiences and insights, will become an important partner in the personal development of each young pianist.

Every piano teacher will, at some point in her life, meet an adult who will be quick to share that he quit music lessons years ago because of acute nervousness or fear. As our pedagogy evolves, hopefully more and more instructors will share some of these indispensable tools with their students. Performance preparation is an essential part of excellence in piano teaching. If teachers were as well-trained in performance anxiety management techniques as they are in teaching staccatos and scales, imagine what a difference it would make in the lives of their music students!

# Recommended Reading

Benson, Herbert, with Miriam Z. Klipper. *The Relaxation Response.* William Morrow and Co., Inc., 1975. Also: *Beyond the Relaxation Response: How to Harness the Healing Power of Your Personal Beliefs.* Times Books, 1984.

Carson, Rick. *Taming Your Gremlin: A Surprisingly Simple Method for Getting Out of Your Own Way.* Quill, 2003.

Gawain, Shakti. *Creative Visualization: Use the Power of Your Imagination to Create What You Want in Your Life.* New World Library, 2002. Also *The Creative Visualization Workbook*, 1995.

Green, Barry, with W. Timothy Gallwey. *The Inner Game of Music.* Doubleday, 1986. Also, Green's *The Mastery of Music: Ten Pathways to True Artistry.* Broadway Books, 2003.

Greene, Don. *Fight Your Fear and Win.* Broadway Books, 2001. Also *Performance Success: Performing Your Best Under Pressure.* Routledge, 2002.

Klickstein, Gerald. *The Musician's Way: A Guide to Practice, Performance, and Wellness.* Oxford, 2009.

Maisel, Eric. *Performance Anxiety: A Workbook for Actors, Singers, Dancers, and Anyone Else who Performs in Public.* Back Stage Books, 2005. Also *Coaching the Artist Within.* New World Library, 2005.

Ristad, Eloise. *A Soprano on Her Head: Right-Side-Up Reflections on Life and Other Performances.* Real People Press, 1981.

Werner, Kenny. *Effortless Mastery: Liberating the Master Musician Within.* Jamey Aebersold (book and meditation CD), 1996.

# Endnotes

[1] Teachers are beginning to understand that knowledge of how the brain works is essential to all teaching, not just performance anxiety management. For more information, see Suzanne Schons' chapter "An Introduction to Brain Research for the Piano Teacher."

[2] This method of disidentification and other helpful cognitive techniques may be found in the performance anxiety workbook by Eric Maisel.

# PART FOUR
# THE ADULT PIANIST

# CHAPTER 40

## The Adult Beginner in the Studio and College

### Denise Edwards

The first chapter of Ivan Turgenev's 1862 novel *Fathers and Sons* introduces Nikolai Petrovich Kirsanov, one of the fathers in the title. He is described as advanced in years, a "grizzled, slightly bent, stoutish, elderly gentleman." Nikolai Petrovich Kirsanov is 41 years old. Turgenev's novel illustrates just how much ideas of old age have changed since the nineteenth century. In his day, 41 was the beginning of old age. Today, it is almost the prime of life.

In 1900, the average man spent most of his lifetime working and a relatively brief time, two to three years, in retirement. Because of increased life expectancy and earlier retirement, the average individual today spends more than 20 percent of his or her life in retirement.

America's population is "aging." In 1980, the median age of Americans was 30.0 years. By 2015, the median age is expected to be 37.1, and the percentage of residents 18 years and older will be 76.0. The age structure of the population has been affected by the baby boomers, persons born between 1946 and 1964. About 75 million baby boomers were born in the United States. By 2015, all of the boomers will be over the age of 50.

Adult education in the United States is flourishing. Whether by necessity or for personal enrichment, Americans over the age of 18 are participating in formal education more than ever before. As the United States economy has shifted from manufacturing to information and services, institutions of higher learning have adapted to this change by tailoring their curricula to the older adult learner, in addition to continuing to serve the needs of the traditional college student.

Adults have more discretionary income than they used to for pursuits such as piano lessons, and the availability of inexpensive electronic keyboards has made piano lessons accessible to more adults.

The increasingly high median age of the general population, longer lifespans, more retirement years, and an interest in lifelong learning are sociological factors that have affected the business of piano teaching. Adult piano study is a prospering market for both the independent studio teacher and the community college music program.

# Physiology

As a person ages, certain physiological changes take place, although these can vary greatly from one individual to another. Muscle strength declines after age 40. There is a loss of muscle mass, which is replaced by fat. Muscles become less flexible, as do their supporting tendons and ligaments. Handgrip strength decreases, and the ability to do physical work diminishes.

By the mid-forties, the eyes may have difficulty focusing on objects that are close up (presbyopia), an increased sensitivity to glare, and problems adjusting to varying levels of light.

Half of all people have some degree of age-related hearing loss (presbycusis) by the age of 75. The ability to hear high-frequency sounds diminishes, which affects speech discrimination. Men's voices may be easier to understand than women's. There is difficulty hearing in noisy situations. Hearing loss may result in "tinnitus," or ringing in the ears.

The brain shrinks as it ages. Also, there is a loss of neurotransmitters, the chemicals that help send signals across synapses, which are the spaces between brain cells. Memory becomes less efficient. It may take longer to learn new things. The level of dopamine, a neurotransmitter that affects fine motor function, declines. The brain retains "neuroplasticity" throughout a person's lifetime, however. In response to stimuli, the brain continues to "rewire" itself by deleting old connections and creating new ones.

Learning to play the piano as an adult is similar to learning to play a new sport as an adult. Initially, every move is a conscious act requiring great effort and concentration, with the greatest brain activity occurring in the cerebral cortex. The motion becomes more natural as the cerebellum, where the capability for such unconscious movements as walking is stored, gradually takes over. "Practice makes permanent." As repetition makes the motion less conscious, the cortex should be freed up for strategizing and planning. However, the adult cortex becomes occupied with other thoughts such as, "This is hard." Also, instead of focusing on the task at hand, the adult student often focuses internally, resulting in a high level of anxiety. Mind games such as visualization can improve physical performance.

# Learning Characteristics

Adult learners exhibit several common characteristics. Being aware of these characteristics can assist the studio teacher and the college teacher in working with adult students.

Adults are highly motivated to learn. This motivation and commitment can compensate for a late start and less than agile fingers.

Adults may lack confidence in their ability to learn. Adults need to feel successful. They need short-term manageable goals. Adults learn best when they know why they are learning and toward what goal they are working. It is important that they understand what steps are necessary to reach the goal and in what order.

Adults learn more effectively when they set their own pace. The emphasis should be on the amount of improvement in relation to the individual's initial proficiency. Adults learn best when they have feedback. They can be highly critical of their own playing. They need to know how they are doing.

Adults also learn best when the learning atmosphere is people-centered, supportive, and informal, more than it is music-centered. Many adults enjoy the warm social atmosphere of group instruction. A recent trend in adult music education is Recreational Music Making (RMM). Whether in a private or in a group setting, the emphasis is on musical self-expression and personal enrichment rather than performance.

Teaching adults is not the same as teaching children. While many of the long-term goals--the ability to read music fluently, the development of technical facility, having a good theoretical foundation, etc.-- are the same, the means of achieving these goals are different.

In selecting materials, the teacher should avoid juvenile books and select materials that present the same concepts in a more mature way and with more explanation. Adults quickly grasp the cognitive. They can absorb more cognitive information and more explanation than can children. Adult texts differ from juvenile method books in that the concepts are presented more quickly and with more explanation.

The beginning adult piano student has high expectations of himself and can be very critical of his own performance. The teacher, by selection of materials, pacing, and verbal encouragement, can provide the student with successful experiences. The more competent the student becomes, the more confident he becomes.

## Common Problems

One problem the adult beginner commonly experiences is difficulty in playing rhythmically. Rhythmic problems are sometimes difficult to solve, particularly if the student seems to lack an innate rhythmic sense. Often, the problem is due to careless practice habits. Insistence on establishing a beat and tapping out rhythms before playing will often remedy the situation. Isolating the rhythm of a piece and playing it on one key can help. The teacher should gradually introduce new note values and time signatures.

Another problem common to adult beginners is difficulty in playing with a legato touch. Difficulty arises especially if the student cannot aurally distinguish between legato and non-legato playing. The teacher must emphasize how legato playing sounds and how it feels. This problem is compounded when repeated pitches are present in the melodic line. In the initial stages, working on the transfer of arm weight from one finger to the next and playing melodies that do not have repeated notes may promote a good legato touch. The piece below, "Sadness," from the beginning adult piano text *Keyboard Fundamentals*, Book One, is an example of such a piece.

**SADNESS**

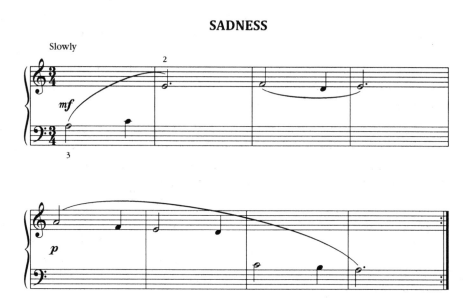

Muscular tension is another problem of the adult piano student. He must remember to keep his shoulders down and wrists free and to maintain a good playing posture throughout his practice sessions. Stretches and warmups can help the adult piano student. Also, classes in yoga or the Alexander Technique can help the student use his body more naturally.

For students over 45, presbyopia can be a problem when reading music. Bifocal and trifocal lenses do not accommodate the distance between the student's eyes and the music. Glasses prescribed for computer use may work, or students can have glasses prescribed for music reading.

Older students may have age-related hearing loss. Hearing aids do not fully compensate for hearing loss. In both the private and the group setting, the teacher should try to face the hearing-impaired student when speaking to him. Even people with normal hearing lip read to some extent. Hearing-impaired students may have difficulty understanding speech when speech and other sounds occur simultaneously. The group piano teacher should discourage students from "noodling" on the keyboard "on speaker" when he is giving verbal instructions to the class.

## The Private Studio

Young piano students are often amazed when they discover that adults, too, take piano lessons. They say, "My mother says she is too old to learn to play the piano," or, "Why didn't that man take piano lessons when he was a kid?" There does seem to be an optimal age for learning to play a musical instrument. One study found a significant difference in the left hand technique of violinists who began instruction before the age of 12 and those who began it after. Piano teachers often observe a marked difference in the technical capabilities of their adult students who had any piano instruction as a child and those who had none. However, piano instruction for even the "absolute adult beginner" can be rewarding for both the student and the teacher.

There are many reasons for the studio teacher to teach adult students. One is increased income. Many adults are able to schedule lessons during the daytime or the late evening hours, when children are unable to come.

Adults have good attitudes. No one is making them take lessons. They are paying for the instruction and want to get their money's worth. They didn't grow up in the world of "fast food" and the "eight-second sound bite," and they have the discipline to postpone immediate gratification for a long-term goal.

Adults probably won't provide the studio teacher with anecdotal material for the dinner table, but they usually don't talk back. They don't ask such questions as, "How old are you?" or, "Do you ever dust?" Adults aren't known for bending backwards over the piano bench or tipping a vertical piano forward with their knees.

The studio teacher should interview any prospective adult student. Adult students have definite goals in mind when they take lessons. The teacher needs to determine if the goals are realistic and if the teacher has the expertise to help the adult reach these goals.

Many of the "beginning" adults in a studio are not, literally, beginners. Many had instruction years ago but have not kept up their playing and want to "start over." The fingers of an adult student with childhood piano instruction are more facile than those of the adult with no experience. However, any "bad habits" acquired during that time are difficult, if not impossible, to change. Problems with hand position, fingering, and pedaling are common. The studio teacher should explain to the student why he thinks something should be done a certain way, but he should also be very understanding if the student is unable to break a habit.

The experience gained from teaching adult students makes the studio teacher realize even more the importance of establishing good habits from the outset of a child's musical training. The teacher will also realize the importance of developing sight reading skills. Those adults who "come back" to the piano are those who read well.

Teaching adult students does present some problems. It is easy for the lesson to become a "therapy session" for the student. Some adults even call their lessons "therapy." They can easily talk an entire lesson away. The teacher, who has probably been without adult company all day, has to be careful not to become a party to this. Sometimes, it is difficult to "stay on task" when the teacher and the student have become friends.

Occasionally, there is an adult student for whom playing the piano is extremely difficult. The student struggles at his lesson week after week even though he has been practicing diligently. The teacher tries to be as encouraging as possible. Working with this adult student reminds the teacher of how fortunate his young students are to be taking lessons at their age and makes him wish they would realize that.

Teaching adults in the studio is interesting and gives the piano teacher a perspective on teaching that he or she would not have had otherwise.

The remainder of this chapter addresses the adult beginner in the community college piano class.

# The Community College

A community college is a two-year collegiate institution that serves the residents of a specific geographic area. This area encompasses several public school districts and may include several counties. The purpose of the community college is to meet the educational needs of area residents through vocational-technical, collegiate transfer, and continuing education programs.

Community colleges offer both daytime and evening classes. Some colleges offer courses on the weekend. Depending on the geographical size of the district, courses may be offered at "off-campus centers," including correctional facilities.

Admission to the community college is generally open to all district residents who are 18 or older. Some colleges allow younger students to enroll in regular classes or offer dual credit in conjunction with their high school courses. The student body is composed of many part-time students in addition to full-time students. The majority of all community college students hold jobs, and many commute long distances to attend classes.

In addition to employing full-time faculty, the community college usually employs many part-time instructors, which enables the college to offer more diverse and specialized courses than it could otherwise. The college taps the expertise and experience of people who are "in the field," whether it be business, a trade, or a profession.

Besides having regularly scheduled classes, the community college offers non-credit seminars and workshops for the purpose of personal or professional development. These workshops might include such titles as "Stress Management," "Financial Planning," "Creative Writing," and "Assertiveness Training." Community colleges often have programs designed for pre-college-aged children and senior citizens. Community service, whether through a traditional college curriculum or through other means, is the top priority of the community college. The community college is very attuned to the job market and works with local employers when expanding existing programs or adding new ones to its curriculum.

The typical community college music curriculum offers four semesters of group piano instruction. (Sometimes, piano classes beyond the fourth semester can be given as workshops or continuing education courses.) Students enrolled in these group piano classes include music majors who intend to matriculate at a four-year institution, but for whom piano is not the major instrument; students enrolled in collegiate transfer programs and vocational-technical programs who are fulfilling humanities requirements; and continuing education students who are not seeking a degree but wish to pursue piano study for their own enjoyment. The student composition of the group piano class is diverse in musical experience, motivation to learn the instrument, innate ability, and age. This diversity is interesting but can create problems in developing a group piano curriculum. The community college group piano teacher must meet the needs of both the music major and the "recreational" pianist, and often within the same class period.

The group piano course requirements and expectations for a music major might easily intimidate the beginning recreational pianist. Because the music major is studying music theory, may have had prior piano experience, or may have acquired some digital dexterity from studying his major instrument, he will usually progress at a faster rate than will the non-major. The music major knows standard musical notation, even if he can read only one clef. His musical ear is more developed than the non-major's, so he possesses some "ear-hand" coordination. Indeed, any kind of musical experience (band, choral, or keyboard), even though it may have been many years earlier, gives a group piano student an advantage over his classmates who have no musical background. The group piano student who is a music major needs to develop proficiency in performing functional skills such as harmonization, improvisation, and transposition. While the non-major should be exposed to these, he is more interested in developing his reading, repertoire, and technique.

The best solution to the problem of trying to meet the needs of both music major and non-music major group piano students is to offer separate sections for music majors and non-majors, or to conduct "placement" tests and fill sections accordingly. If there are only a few music majors enrolled in group piano, the teacher might be able to meet with them as a group once a week through a college's "independent study" option. If none of these options is feasible due to scheduling or the number of course offerings, other alternatives should be considered. Competency-based testing is one option. A piano proficiency test as a degree requirement might also spur the music major on to greater achievement than can, realistically, be expected of his less-experienced classmates. The music major with prior piano instruction might be placed in a higher level of group piano or could take private applied piano lessons through the college.

## Designing the Group Piano Curriculum for the Non-Music Major

The student body of a community college must be considered when designing a group piano curriculum. The curriculum should meet the needs of the students. Although the recreational pianist will be exposed to functional keyboard skills, he is more interested in developing his sight reading and technique. More than anything, he wants to play pieces. Until the instructor has met a particular level one piano class, he or she must assume that the individual student knows absolutely nothing about music or playing the piano. The students need reassurance that the class is designed for the absolute beginner. Most classes are a combination of students who have virtually no musical experience and those with varying degrees of experience in such organizations as band, orchestra, and choir. Some will have had a few years of piano lessons in grade school and now wish to play again. Others have had the desire, but not the opportunity, to study. Most of the students are eager and motivated to learn. Only a few take the course because they need "easy credits." These students usually drop the class after a few weeks. The students bring varying degrees of maturity and life experiences to the class. Many students have jobs and families. The demands on the student's time may be great, but he still wants to learn to play the piano.

As well-intentioned as their efforts may be, some students are not prepared for the discipline and time commitment required to learn the instrument. They need to be made aware of the necessity of daily practice and having "access" to a piano. Those students who have pianos in their homes or are able to practice at the college tend to experience more success in the piano course than do those students who must seek a place to practice. Many students own keyboards, which are usually adequate, but a student should be encouraged to practice on an acoustic piano as often as possible, especially if the keyboard he owns is not touch-sensitive.

# Meeting the First Class

At the first class meeting, the instructor should give each student a copy of the course syllabus. It should include the instructor's contact information, the catalog course description, and a list of the required text(s) and supplies. The syllabus should state the learning outcomes, have an outline of the course, and describe the course requirements. It is important that the student know what is expected of him in terms of practice time, class attendance, and examinations. The instructor should be as specific as possible about grading procedures and what the student must do to earn an "A" in the course.

It is helpful for the instructor to know something about the student's musical background. A short questionnaire would serve this purpose. This information is also useful for recruiting students for band, orchestra, and choir classes.

It is important that the course begin well. The instructor should be enthusiastic about teaching and should also try to help the students feel at ease. He should have a lesson prepared for the first class meeting, especially if the class meets only once a week. The lesson plan would include familiarizing the students with a digital piano lab. This might include individual experimentation with the sampled sounds the pianos will produce and other features of the instruments. The instructor can demonstrate how he can use the lab to group students so that they can work together. He can also show them how he can listen to students individually as the rest of the class works in groups or practices independently.

Concepts to be covered at the first class should include keyboard registers, up and down, black key groupings, the letter names of the white keys, and finger numbers. The instructor should demonstrate how to sit at the piano and should also explain why it is important to maintain a good hand position. The staff may or may not be introduced, depending upon the course text and the instructor's philosophy. The instructor should explain basic note values and have the students clap and count simple rhythmic patterns. The following example is from *Keyboard Fundamentals, Book One.*

## Note Values

Some common note values are shown below. These note values will be used in playing your first melodies.

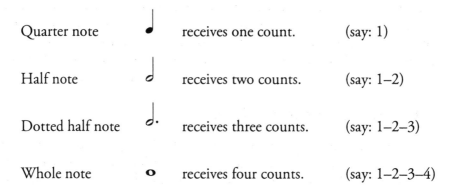

| Quarter note | ♩ | receives one count. | (say: 1) |
| Half note | ♩ | receives two counts. | (say: 1–2) |
| Dotted half note | ♩. | receives three counts. | (say: 1–2–3) |
| Whole note | o | receives four counts. | (say: 1–2–3–4) |

## Rhythm Drills

Tap and count aloud the following rhythm patterns.

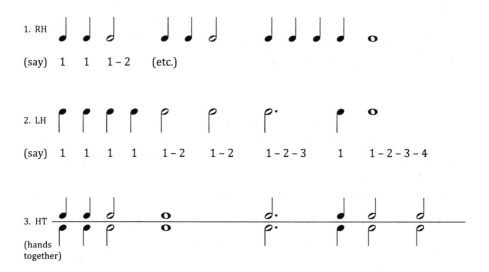

1. RH

(say)   1    1    1 – 2    (etc.)

2. LH

(say)   1    1    1    1    1 – 2    1 – 2    1 – 2 – 3    1    1 – 2 – 3 – 4

3. HT
(hands
together)

It is important that the student leave the first class with a piece he can play. The instructor can introduce an easy "black-key piece" to be taught by rote or in a simplified notation. It should be patterned, be rhythmically simple, and move around the keyboard. The student might experiment with holding the damper pedal down throughout the piece. The following selections, from *Keyboard Fundamentals*, Book One, are examples of such pieces.

## A Two-Note Black Key Tune for the Right Hand

Play the tune pictured below using RH fingers 3 and 2. An arrow indicates the starting key. Begin with the two black keys in the middle of the keyboard. Move to the right twice, as indicated. Find each new set of two black keys very quickly. Count aloud as you play.

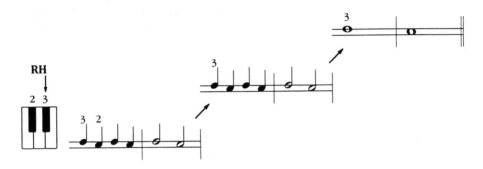

**Teacher Accompaniment**

## A Two-Note Black Key Tune for the Left Hand

Play the tune below using LH fingers 2 and 3. An arrow indicates the starting key. Begin with the two black keys in the middle of the keyboard. Move to the left twice, as indicated. Find the next set of two black keys very quickly. Count aloud as you play.

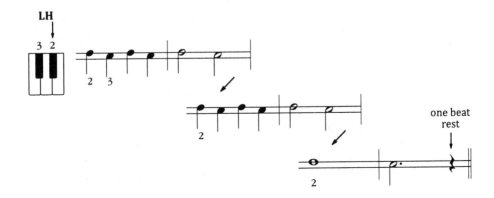

**Teacher Accompaniment**

The instructor should avoid overwhelming the students by not teaching too many concepts at the first class meeting. Some students are easily intimidated. The instructor should plan to "review" at the next class meeting. Undoubtedly, there will be new students at the next class who registered late. It is wise to review previously introduced concepts every week. The students are appreciative of this, too.

## Classroom Management

The "pacing" of a class period is very important. Pacing becomes easier with an instructor's increased experience. Each class period should include a variety of activities that relate to the concepts and materials being studied. Such activities as sight reading, improvisation, theory drills, ensemble playing, technical drills, and repertoire practice provide reinforcement of these concepts. The instructor should always "follow through" on the previous week's assignment.

More music theory must be taught in the non-music-major piano classes than in the classes of music majors. The use of take-home drill sheets and in-class board work will reinforce theoretical concepts. Having students work at the board gives the instructor immediate feedback as to whether or not the students understand the material. Board work also adds variety to the class session and provides relief from sitting for long periods of time. Also, the instructor can direct the students to computer programs that are available online and in the college's computer labs.

The instructor should use several activities to reinforce the same concept. For example, when studying tonic and dominant chords, the students could name the tonic and dominant chords in a particular key, play the chords on the piano, write the chords on the staff, analyze the chords in a score, and identify the chord functions aurally.

## Student Evaluation

Frequent evaluation keeps the students and instructor up-to-date on student progress and detects problems before they become uncorrectable.

Students should have a performance "quiz" every two to three weeks. To save valuable class time, especially in large classes, students can record their performances for the instructor to critique outside of class. At other times, it is useful for students to have immediate feedback.

Quizzes requiring written responses check the student's knowledge of symbols, terms, and theoretical concepts. Students tend to do well on these quizzes, which can be morale boosters. Instructors can also utilize the college's computer labs when assigning theory exercises and in evaluating the student's understanding of theory concepts.

## Piano Classes for Senior Citizens

Classes for older adult learners (those over 50) can attract students who otherwise might not enroll in group piano classes. Materials and approaches suitable for the recreational aspect of the classes can also accommodate any special needs class members may have. These older students are some of the most devoted group piano students and return for subsequent levels of instruction. Older students prefer daytime classes that meet once a week. Reduced or free tuition and socialization with peers are other incentives for senior citizens to enroll in a group piano course.

## Recruiting Students

In developing a community college group piano program, an instructor may discover that he doesn't have a ready body of students from which to draw, particularly if the piano classes are elective. He may find it necessary to recruit students in order to keep sections filled. The best advertising is generated by former students. However, many district residents may be unaware that the college even offers piano instruction. The group piano instructor should have a faculty web page that links to the college's website. The page should have information about course offerings and can include video clips of classes. Also, an ad placed toward the front of the college's printed semester course schedule can increase group piano enrollment. These schedules are often mailed to district residents, who might notice the ad while leafing through the schedule. Another way to reach the community is through newspaper articles, television and radio announcements, and "community calendar" listings. Support staff at the college can assist the instructor with advertising.

## Equipment

The instructor should work with the college administration to provide the most up-to-date electronic technology possible. Sometimes, instrument dealers, in conjunction with a capital leasing company, will lease piano lab equipment to colleges. This helps the college to "stay current." In some situations, it may be in the college's best interests to purchase the equipment. The group piano teacher needs to keep a "wish list." Being able to justify educationally the expense of a proposed purchase is essential. Regardless of the sophistication of the pianos and other equipment, using them to their fullest potential is important.

## Other Considerations

The instructor should make the class as enjoyable and interesting as possible. Students who attend a Saturday morning class or who, after a long day at work, rush to an evening session, should feel that their efforts are being rewarded.

The instructor should learn the names of the students as quickly as possible. He should become acquainted with each student personally, without being intrusive. He should be understanding of personal and professional problems that may interfere with the week's preparation. The instructor should have a positive attitude about each student and know that he or she can succeed. The instructor should be available for help, should the student need it.

It is important for the instructor to establish a good rapport with the students, not only for the success of the piano class, but also for the good of the community college. The group piano instructor may be a student's only contact with the college. His opinion of the entire community college may be based solely upon his group piano experience. Having good public relations with the community is vitally important for the institution.

If the college has a tutoring program, the group piano teacher can select applied piano students who would be suitable tutors. Group piano students needing extensive outside help would be referred to these tutors.

A lending library in the piano lab can provide materials for those students who need additional or more challenging work.

The group piano instructor should provide an aural and visual model for the students by frequently playing assigned pieces. He should avoid "showing off," but he should encourage sensitivity and expressiveness in the students' playing through his demonstrations. The students will want to hear the instructor perform "his" music, so he should play a short selection later in the semester.

For those community college students who cannot or do not wish to enroll in group piano classes, or who have completed the group piano curriculum, private piano lessons are often available from full-time or adjunct music faculty members.

Not all college students who are preparing for a career in piano teaching are suited for community college teaching. But for those who exhibit warmth and friendliness and have a sincere desire to help people, teaching group piano at a community college can be very rewarding.

# References

"Aging Baby Boomers in a New Workforce Development System." http://www.doleta.gov/Seniors/other_docs/AgingBoomers.pdf.

"Aging: What to Expect as You Get Older." *mayoclinic.com*. 7 August 2010. http://www.mayoclinic.com/health/aging/HA00040.

Bock, Linda. *Teaching Adults in Continuing Education*. Urbana-Champaign, IL: The University of Illinois, 1979.

Hastings, John. "Old Dog, New Tricks," *The State Journal-Register* (Springfield, IL), December 26, 1994.

"Introduction to Neuroplasticity." *memoryzine.com*. 2 July 2010. http://memoryzine.com/2010/07/02/introduction-to-neuroplasticity/.

Langan, Michael. "Age-related hearing loss." *nlm.nih.gov*. 4 November 2008. http://www.nlm.nih.gov/medlineplus/ency/article/001045.htm.

Lyke, James and Denise Edwards. *Keyboard Fundamentals*, Book One. Champaign, IL: Stipes Publishing Company, 2006. CD included.

"Resident Population By Sex and Age: 1980 to 2006." *census.gov*. 2008. http://www.census.gov/compendia/statab/2008/tables/08s0007.pdf.

"Resident Population Projections By Sex and Age: 2010 to 2050." *census.gov*. 2008. http://www.census.gov/population/www/projections/summarytables.html.

Rozien, Michael F. and Mehmet C. Oz. *You Staying Young: the Owner's Manual for Extending Your Warranty*. New York: Free Press, 2007.

Schwerin, Susan. "The Anatomy of Movement." *brainconnection.positscience.com*. http://brainconnection.positscience.com/topics/?main=anat/motor-anat2.

Starnes, Dorothy. "The Process of Aging (Gerontology)." *essortment.com*. http:// www.essortment.com/all/agingprocessge_roqp.htm.

Turgenev, Igor. *Fathers and Sons*. Various editions, 1862.

# CHAPTER 41

## Tips for Teaching the Adult Piano Student

### Peter Jutras

The twenty-first century piano studio is increasingly populated with non-traditional students of varying ages, abilities, and needs. Adult students are one of the fastest-growing groups of piano students, and an understanding of how to teach adults can allow a piano teacher to serve this growing clientele.

Adults are living longer, healthier, and wealthier lives than any previous era of human history. Many of them are retiring at a younger age, and they are increasingly looking for meaningful hobbies and activities. Music study is one of those sought-after activities, and the experience can be equally rewarding for the teacher.

Adult students often arrive at piano study with a wide range of prior musical experiences, preferences, modes of learning, and goals for their study. The successful teacher of adults will need to balance a general understanding of adult learning with specific details about each individual student's aspirations.

The most important factor in teaching adults is *understanding*. Understanding who the students are, what their backgrounds, how they learn, what their goals are, and what they value in the experience is crucial to the success of the lessons or classes. Teachers must understand that adults are very different from traditional pre-college students, and this chapter will outline some of those differences.

# What Are Adult Students Looking for?

This is a crucial question for any teacher of adults, and it is one that has driven my own research on adult music students. When I first began teaching adults (as a young teacher), I quickly noticed that different adult students were seeking different experiences and outcomes from their piano study. Finding many of these goals fascinating and interesting, I decided to investigate the perceived benefits of adult piano study. [i]

Adult piano students are choosing to invest a great deal of their own time, energy, and money in piano study, and they do so without any expectation of fame, riches, or a celebrity career as a concert pianist. Many adult students are already successful in other areas of life (home, career, family), yet they still want to undertake what can be a humbling experience. An understanding of what adult students seek in their piano study is crucial, as it allows teachers to offer instruction and experience tailored to those goals. Adult students are quick to "vote with their feet"—if they are not getting what they hope for out of piano study, they will quit or look for a different teacher.

# The Benefits of Adult Piano Study

The range of benefits derived from music study can vary greatly, and adults will value and seek different benefits. Of course anyone studying piano will want to improve fundamental musical skills, but the degree of importance assigned to skill improvement can vary by student. Many adults will also be seeking to satisfy a dream they have always had, escape from their everyday routine, find an outlet for stress reduction and relaxation, or simply have some fun. Others will be looking for social outcomes, happy to forge relationships with the teacher and other adult piano students. Some adults will see piano study as a means to improve their mental and physical health, keeping their brains and muscles active and engaged throughout the aging process. There will also be adult students who are intently focused on improving specific musical skills such as technique, sight-reading, and public performance.

In my research with over 700 adult piano students across the U.S., the highest-rated benefit was Dream Fulfilled. [ii] Participants in the study were rating the statement "Studying piano fulfills a dream that I have always had." The personal meaning and importance of piano study to adults is something teachers must know, but they must also realize that the "dream" is unique for each student. One of the most important steps in successful teaching of adult students is having initial conversations with your students to ask them what their goals and aspirations are. What do they want to get out of piano study, and what do they envision that they will learn?

For some adults, the answers will be clear. For others, the act of discussing goals and thinking broadly will help lead them to realizations that may have been unclear in the past. Some may not have much to say and will be happy to have you direct the course of study in a traditional manner. Unlike children, adult students are able to think critically and articulate broad reasons for wanting to study piano. With this information in hand, the teacher will be able to design a course of study that will be fulfilling and satisfying for the student, and rewarding for the teacher.

## Types of Adult Students

As you discuss goals with your adult students, you will quickly realize that there are different types of adult students. While each individual will be unique, it is not unusual to see some categories emerge. Understanding the tendencies of different types of students can help you both adjust your teaching and provide targeted group activities that are comfortable for everyone involved.

There are a variety of labels and types of adult students proposed in research on adult learning. Recent research by Thomas Swenson gives an interesting account of different types of adult piano students. [iii] These categories are often broad-based, differentiating among levels of commitment and dedication, for example, serious vs. casual students.

In addition to the types established by others, I've noticed a range of different adult students in my own experience. Taking the time to understand the different approaches and goals of these students is invaluable to the teacher. There will be new beginners who don't have any experience, "beginners" who have some prior knowledge (some of which may need correction), beginners who played as children but have forgotten most everything, and beginners who have taught themselves some basic concepts with books or videos. You will also encounter a wide range of intermediate and advanced adult students who have been playing for years.

Students may vary widely in their goals and expectations, from those who want a more casual, recreational experience to serious amateurs who will practice hours each day, perform advanced repertoire, and maybe even enter the growing world of amateur competitions. Adult students may arrive on your doorstep with specific topics and goals they wish to explore. Perhaps they want to learn jazz harmonies, how to improvise offertories and preludes for church, or how to improve "traditional" skills such as sight-reading and technique.

Understanding some of the basic types of adult piano students can help you improve instruction, but it can also help you match your adult students in social settings such as studio classes and adult recitals. Adults will appreciate being around like-minded students, allowing them to share goals and solutions to common problems. While social gatherings are usually healthy for adult piano students, mixing the wrong type of students can cause problems. New beginners who feel tentative and are not ready to perform may not appreciate attending a studio class where advanced students are playing advanced repertoire. Instead, it might be best to keep the beginners together where they feel like they are interacting with equals and can share common concerns and fears.

A typical adult student really *wants* to learn the piano and is already directed towards specific goals. These goals may vary widely from student to student. Some may be there to learn specific repertoire and hone performance skills, others may be looking to complete an unfulfilled experience from childhood, and still others may be simply curious about how to play basic songs and read music. Taking the time to understand these goals is invaluable to the teacher, and it will help the student stay motivated and focused.

# Adult Learning

It is important for teachers to understand that adults learn and interact with the world in a way that is completely different from children. While this statement may seem obvious, it is common to hear adult students complain of a failed attempt at piano study, in which the teacher tried to teach the adult just like the children in the studio. It is true that adults will have to learn the same basic material as children, but they are likely to learn that material in a very different fashion.

## Andragogy

In the second half of the twentieth century, Malcolm Knowles, a pioneering figure in adult learning theory, brought the word *andragogy* into use. In contrast to *pedagogy* (the art and science of teaching children), *andragogy* is the art and science of teaching adults. In his work, Knowles outlines some basic assumptions of adult learning, contrasting these characteristics with those of children. [iv] The five basic ways in which Knowles posits that adult learning differs from that of children are:

1. Adults are more self-directed than younger students.

2. Adults have a rich reservoir of experience.

3. Adults' readiness to learn is based on social roles.

4. Adults are more problem centered.

5. Adults are intrinsically motivated.

## Prior Experience

Unlike children, adults arrive in our studios with a rich reservoir of life experience, potentially stretching over several decades. These experiences typically include various jobs, travels, relationships, families, and learning experiences. All of this experience colors how an adult perceives the world, and this perception will have a large impact on learning.

It is important for a teacher to take the experience of adult students into account and design instruction accordingly. For example, adults who have spent most of their lives in the military may expect a certain degree of detailed order and structure to each learning activity, while those who have spent most of their lives teaching in a classroom will have expectations and ideas about learning that are colored by their own professional lives.

In addition to life experience, music experience also factors into adult study. When children begin music study, they typically have very little prior musical knowledge or experience. It is not uncommon, however, for adult beginners to arrive with pre-conceived ideas and notions about music. They may have had a limited amount of study as children, they may have experience on other instruments, or they may have done some study on their own. While it is often best for these students to start at the beginning and proceed thoroughly (and correctly) through the fundamentals of piano study, teachers should be prepared to answer questions about topics the students have explored on their own. Teachers should also be prepared to clear up misconceptions and correct errors. For example, I sometimes encounter adult students who believe that minor always means black keys, that stem direction always indicate which hand plays the notes, that the hands must always set up in a five-finger position, and that dots add one beat of rhythm to every note.

## Self-Direction and Readiness to Learn

Unlike most children, adult students are self-directed in their learning. Research in this area of adult learning has shown that adults prefer to learn on their own terms. [v] While this may seem to diminish the role of the teacher, it is important that teachers help facilitate adults' self-directed learning. Teachers need to equip students with the necessary skills and practice strategies that will allow adults to make progress on their own. When properly motivated, adults can do very well with self-directed theory workbooks, sight-reading projects, and other activities. The teacher is still important: proper preparation and sequencing from the teacher will help ensure that the students have success and establish good habits in their self-directed learning.

Self-direction also relates to adults' readiness to learn. For most adults, true learning will not take place until they have decided that something is worth learning. Frustrating as it may be for the teacher, it often doesn't matter whether or not the teacher thinks a topic is significant—the student must be convinced before learning will take place. Therefore, in addition to discussing goals with adult students, teachers will often have to do a little bit of "selling," explaining why something is important and worth studying. The teacher must help align everyday activities with the larger goal. For example, explaining why doing a certain technical exercise will actually help the student play a piece of repertoire, or why learning about music theory will help the student memorize repertoire.

## Immediacy of Application

Learners of every age are interested in immediate and tangible results, but this is particularly true for adult students. Adults want to play, and they want to see their learning translate immediately into piano playing. Adult students often have little patience for abstract learning and exercises that don't demonstrate an immediate benefit. When teaching beginning adult piano students, it is important to get them playing as soon as possible, with rote songs, off-staff notation, and other pre-reading activities. This allows them to experience concepts on the piano without getting bogged down in academic definitions and explanations. When a new concept is taught, it should come with useful pieces or excerpts that illustrate the concept, allowing the student to apply it right away. When long-term projects are undertaken, adults should be reminded of the usefulness of the work. When possible, these long-term projects should be broken down into a series of short-term goals that allow the student to see real progress.

## Intrinsic Motivation

This aspect of adult learning is very rewarding for teachers. Adult students make their own choices, and they want to be studying piano. They typically bring a great deal of energy and enthusiasm to their study, and this can be very advantageous. The only disadvantage that can arise from this is an unreasonable sense of what might be accomplished in a given time frame. If the teacher can help adults set reasonable goals, choose repertoire that will result in musical success, and focus on the interests of each individual student, lack of motivation will usually not be an issue.

# Suggestions for Teaching Adult Beginners

## Play Early and Often

Have your adult students play pieces as soon as possible. When teaching an adult beginning piano class, I typically have the class playing a rote song in the first 20 minutes of class, before I have explained anything about posture, rhythm, setup, reading, names of the piano keys, etc. Thus they are given an immediate sense that they are playing the piano, and it builds their motivation and inspires them to learn. Many adult beginners don't realize how "complex" music can be, and they *expect* to play right away. Boring these students with lots of explanations can be a sure way to turn them off to learning.

## Repetition, Repetition, Repetition

Adults often find themselves understanding a concept perfectly well yet failing to execute it with their fingers accurately. While adults can pick up academic learning quickly, this doesn't mean that they can develop muscle memory, coordination, and other movement skills faster than their younger counterparts. In fact, it may take adults longer than children to master some physical movements. Seniors may have a more limited range of motion, and adults often over-think their movements and are more inhibited and hesitant when trying new motions. When teaching rhythm, technique, and especially hands-together coordination, repetition is very important for adults. Remind them of the importance of repetition and help them understand that needing to repeat motions does not mean they are slow learners. They should also be aware that repetitions of mistakes will ingrain bad habits and be damaging; students need to practice *accurate* repetitions. This often means playing slow and taking small sections to ensure accuracy. Teachers should be prepared to repeat pieces week after week to help them build security and consistency.

## Have a Toolbox of Practice Strategies

Teachers can take advantage of the thinking capacity of adults when helping them develop practice skills. Adults are better equipped to analyze problems and employ practice strategies that go beyond just "playing it again." Teachers can help adults learn how to identify errors and recognize common problems such as fingering, position moves, coordination, rhythm, etc. The teacher and student should then work together to develop a variety of practice techniques to address those problems. From tapping and counting on a tabletop to spot practice, adults will make good use of your suggestions for work.

## Use Familiar Repertoire

For the most part, adults want to learn music they already know. While style preferences will vary from student to student, they will often arrive with specific ideas. Make use of these preferences, and generously sprinkle your teaching with melodies from familiar folk songs, classical themes, and popular songs. The motivational power of tunes such as *Happy Birthday, Jingle Bells,* or *Amazing Grace,* to name three examples, can be quite meaningful to the student. Adults will appreciate the familiarity and feel like they are learning something useful to play for non-musicians. In addition, they will be much more successful at identifying and correcting errors in their practicing when they are playing familiar tunes.

## Be Ready to Adjust the Curriculum

Most teachers have an established idea of what should be taught to lead students towards complete musicianship. Adults may not always be interested in all of these subjects, and, if part of what you want to teach doesn't meet their goals, then you may have a tough time getting learning to happen. This doesn't mean that all of our teaching has to be defined by the student, but we may want to consider the value of what we're teaching to an adult who may never perform in public or study certain styles of repertoire. Does an adult who wants to learn to play simple hymns need to learn all twelve harmonic minor scales? Of course, it is always part of the teacher's job to expand the horizons of the student. Anytime you can convince an adult student why a certain topic is beneficial, it will be worth the effort.

## Be Prepared for Questions

Adults love to ask questions, and if something doesn't fit within their conceptions of what makes sense, they are likely to become stuck on that concept until they find a satisfying explanation. When I was a young teacher teaching my first adult beginning classes, I remember getting quite flummoxed by questions about why stems went up or down, why there were seven notes in the alphabet, why the "middle" note was C and not A, why the black keys didn't just have their own names, why there was a space between the staves, why there was a need for time signatures if quarter notes always got one beat, and why a composer would ever write pickup notes— why not just start on beat one? They will also ask fundamental questions, such as what is a scale, what does it mean to be in a key, and what are major and minor? There are good answers to all of these questions, but I wasn't always prepared to articulate those answers in a simple, easy-to-understand manner! As the years have gone by, I've learned that these questions are quite routine and predictable—adults have a thirst for knowledge, and they genuinely want to know the *why* of what they are learning. I have also learned that there are times when I just have to tell my students to be patient waiting for an answer: explaining a concept they aren't ready to understand can lead to more confusion.

## Set the Stage for Success

Many adults will come to piano study with big ideas, wanting to play advanced pieces that they have heard for years. While the motivation and desire is admirable, adult students can get swept up in a challenge that is too far above their skills—a challenge that will take a long time and may always be a struggle. Encourage your adult students to play repertoire that they can play well, so they can truly make music and be an artist at the keyboard. In the long run, it is much more satisfying than barely being able to get the notes in a more difficult piece. Help your students realize the joy of playing beautifully, and choose repertoire that will allow them to do so.

## Don't Forget Memory Strategies

Memory can present a variety of challenges to adult students. For example, research has shown that as adults age, they are much less effective at using mnemonic strategies to remember new materials. Many of the mnemonics that might work well for younger students (e.g., Every Good Boy Does Fine or Fat Cats Go Dancing...) actually may be more difficult for older students. Instead of spending time and energy on a mnemonic approach, time might be better invested in learning the concepts of key signatures and the circle of fifths. Adults are likely to have a better ability to understand and process the intellectual side of concepts than children. If they understand the concept, fact memorization can be less important or even unnecessary. In teaching reading, I prefer an intervallic approach. Freed from the stress-inducing need to feel like they must memorize every note on the grand staff (and perhaps some associated mnemonics), my adult beginning students learn to focus on the relationships between the notes. Understanding these relationships will help them read fluidly in any range and move with facility between notes in the treble and bass clefs.

Today, many professional pianists choose to perform with the score, and this can be a helpful and useful tool for adult piano students. In addition to alleviating anxiety about memory lapses, it can free adult students from worry in their practicing and allow them to focus on accuracy and artistry. If an adult student insists on performing from memory, then the employment of a variety of analytical, aural, and visual strategies can help them feel more secure than simple reliance on muscle memory.

## Coordinating Technical Progress

Coordination is another area where adults, particularly adult beginning students, may encounter frustration. I often hear adults complain, "I know what I was supposed to play, but my fingers didn't get there!" It may be important to spend more time with your adult students on basic coordination activities, and remind your adults that repetition is not remedial, but very important to learning these motions. I often remind students of the degree to which professional athletes continue to repeat basic motions when practicing. From the very first lessons, I encourage my adult beginners to do a lot of tabletop "tapping" of different finger combinations to help develop coordination and control. For many students, piano is the only activity they've ever done that requires detailed and specific control of individual finger numbers. Developing this skill takes time and repetition, and adults should learn to be patient with themselves during this process.

As students advance, coordination can remain an issue in technically difficult repertoire. For these students, spend considerable time working on the physical motions of piano playing. Breaking complex gestures down into a series of movements to be practiced, repeated, and internalized helps students who have hit a physical plateau. Developing meaningful drills and exercises geared towards specific spots in a piece of repertoire gives adult students targeted and meaningful technique practice.

## Fun, Fun, Fun

In my research on the benefits of adult piano study, "fun" benefits such as Play/Fun, Escape from Routine, and Stress Reduction are consistently among the highest-rated benefits for adults. They want to learn, but *enjoying* the learning is very important. When teachers lose sight of this and piano study becomes a struggle, adults may begin to question whether they want to continue. Teachers should be prepared to adjust goals, choose enjoyable repertoire, and honor students' preferences to keep the lessons fun for the student.

## Let Adults Learn From Each Other

Creating social experiences for the adults in your studio helps set up new avenues for learning and reinforcement. Have adult students talk to each other and realize that they share many of the same concerns, fears, and frustrations. Adults may feel quite isolated, particularly if their lessons are scheduled around children rather than other adults. Knowing they are not alone in their experiences boosts their confidence. At one point, many of my advanced adult students met weekly (without me) to play for each other and discuss learning and practice strategies. They reported that this greatly enhanced their piano experience, and they were clear in assuring me that this didn't replace my instruction, it just gave them another avenue for learning. Many adults may not take the initiative to establish such events on their own, but they will respond to structures already in place.

## Teach Appreciation

One of the most rewarding things about teaching adults is their level of *appreciation* for music. Unlike very young students, adults have an extensive working knowledge of history, culture, politics, travel, and customs. This knowledge can be related to the lives and stories of the composers and repertoire that they study, and adult students will love to learn more about the context of what they are playing. Adults will often enjoy reading composer biographies and other writings. Therefore, you can present lectures on topics that might not be appreciated by most children.

This knowledge not only helps adults understand their music better, but it also helps to satisfy their natural desire to understand *why* music is the way it is. These discussions can provide great material for studio classes and other group gatherings, and I always enjoy doing the research, often learning new things and expanding my own understanding of a topic. "Field trips" can be organized around interesting concerts or lectures. If those don't happen frequently in your area, you can organize your own concert night with DVDs or internet-based videos of great performers.

In addition to learning about the lives of the composers, adults will also be fascinated to learn about the history and workings of the instrument itself, the lives of famous performers, and the everyday life experiences of professional musicians. Many of your students will have collections of recordings, be regular concertgoers, and listen to music on the radio and other broadcast media. Your discussions about music appreciation need not be limited to the piano repertoire or specific styles that may be under study—on the contrary it can be useful to expand the horizons of your students and examine chamber, symphonic, and opera literature, along with jazz, blues, gospel, and many other music styles.

## Help With Time Management

Given their intrinsic motivation, most adults are willing to practice as necessary to progress, especially when they value the goal. The busy life of an adult, however, can often interfere with practicing and cause challenges. Business travel, increased workloads, and unexpected family situations can all wreak havoc with an adult's schedule. Teachers should be prepared to deal with these disruptions and counsel students not to get too frustrated or discouraged over what they cannot control. In addition, the teacher should be ready to offer a variety of solutions, from short practice activities that can be done in 5-10 minutes, to listening, singing, and mental practice tasks that can be done away from the piano. Dedicated adults may be willing to practice on hotel pianos or other locations when they are traveling, but they may need some practical advice and ideas from the teacher to help them accomplish this.

Life's disruptions can affect the regular lesson time as well, and teachers of adults should be prepared for cancellations from their adult students. When it is clear that the circumstances are beyond the adult's control, teachers may consider being more flexible with their adult students on both regular scheduling and makeup policies. Amy Greer proposed an interesting system of *a la carte* lessons for adult students. [vi] The disruptions will eventually pass, so the teacher should do what is necessary to keep the student motivated and ready for the eventual return to normalcy.

## Teach With Empathy and Understanding

This final suggestion may be the most important: always teach adult students with empathy and understanding. We've discussed the importance of understanding who your students are, what their goals may be, what music they enjoy, how they learn, and how their life experiences may color their learning. This information helps you to understand your adult students when they first arrive in your class or studio, but it is also important to be sympathetic throughout the learning process.

For many adult students, particularly adult beginners, simply entering your studio is already an act of courage and humility. Adult students have listened to music for years, and they often have a fairly sophisticated sense of what good piano playing sounds like. They are well aware that their own playing doesn't match this model of perfection that they hear in recordings and media, and they are very self-conscious about what they perceive to be shortcomings and failures.

Teachers should provide some perspective, reminding the student that progress takes time and commitment. Adults often expect a level of performance that takes professionals years of practice to achieve. This lack of perspective may cause them to be frustrated when pieces don't improve after one or two days of practice—they may not have any idea that you expect them to spend three or four weeks working on that piece.

Talk to your students about challenges in your own practicing, how long you spend learning difficult repertoire, and how far ahead you prepare music for performances. Let them know that you understand their frustrations, and that you're there to help. Explain to your students that there are aspects of piano study that you struggle with as well, and then present your strategies for dealing with those struggles.

While many of the things you teach to adults will be very easy for you, take care not to let them appear that way to your students. Think back to how you learned certain techniques and conquered difficulties in your repertoire. Relate these stories to your students and talk about how they can apply similar solutions to their own struggles. Adults will appreciate the inside information, and it will help allay concerns they might have about slow progress. Your flexibility and understanding as a teacher will send the right message and help develop a healthy relationship.

Some adult students are apprehensive when they have to miss a lesson, have had a poor week of practice, or haven't been able to conquer a challenge. Teachers may feel bad about this apprehension, as they certainly never intend there to be anything frightening about piano lessons! Many adults are truly unsure if teachers will empathize with issues that might get in the way of piano study, not to mention the fact that many students also place unreasonable (and uninformed) expectations on themselves. Your understanding and caring during these times will help develop trust, and students will enjoy their study more when they realize that they shouldn't worry about these issues.

# Conclusion

Teaching adults can be rewarding and fulfilling. As the generation of Baby Boomers retires, more and more adults will be seeking music study, and piano is likely to remain a popular choice. With a little thought about how adults learn, and a lot of time spent talking to your students and understanding their dreams, preferences, learning styles, and past experiences, teachers can tailor programs that will keep adult students motivated and help them achieve their musical goals.

# Suggested Readings for Adult Piano Students

Adams, N. (1997). *Piano Lessons: Music, Love, and True Adventures.* New York: Delta.

*Clavier Companion.* Bi-monthly publication for pianists and piano teachers with regular column on Adult Piano Study. www.claviercompanion. com.

Holt, J. (1991). *Never Too Late: My Musical Life Story.* Cambrige: Perseus (Originally published 1978, New York: Delacorte.)

Maris, B.E. (2000). *Making Music at the Piano: Learning Strategies for Adult Students.* New York: Oxford University Press.

# Endnotes

[i] Jutras, P. (2006). The benefits of adult piano study: As self-reported by selected adult piano students. *The Journal of Research in Music Education* (54) 2, 97-110. (Based on 2003 Ph.D. Dissertation, University of North Texas.)

[ii] Ibid., p. 105.

[iii] Swenson, T. (2006). Profiles of career-aged keyboard students: Attitudes, preferences, and demographics (Doctoral dissertation, The University of Oklahoma, 2006). *Dissertation Abstracts International 67* (03), AAT 3211367.

[iv] Knowles, M.S., Holton, E.F., & Swanson, R.A. (2008). *The Adult Learner: A Neglected Species.* (6th Ed.). New York: Elsevier, Butterworth-Heinemann.

[v] Tough, A.M. (1979). *The Adult's Learning Projects: a Fresh Approach to Theory and Practice in Adult Learning.* (2nd. Ed.). Toronto: Ontario Institute for Studies in Education.

[vi] Greer, A. (2009). À la carte lessons. *Clavier Companion* (1) 6, pp. 46-48.

# CHAPTER 42

## The Music Major in the College Piano Class

This chapter examines college group piano programs for music majors in various emphases such as music education, applied music (performance), music history/literature and music theory/composition. Students in these programs generally study piano in a lab situation for two years to satisfy National Association of Schools of Music (NASM) and departmental requirements. The aim of group piano study is to assist non-piano majors in achieving at least a respectable intermediate level of proficiency. Special topics which concern those preparing to teach in a piano lab include 1) a brief history of college group piano, 2) the college adult beginner, 3) the piano lab, 4) teaching in a piano lab, 5) the objectives of group piano study and 6) the advanced piano class.

## A Brief History of College Group Piano

Raymond Burrows (1906-1952) laid the groundwork for establishing adult piano study in classes. A professor at Teachers College, Columbia University, he taught pedagogy classes and authored several publications including *The Young Explorer at the Piano, Young America at the Piano* and *The Adult Explorer at the Piano*. Burrows' 1944 publication, *Elementary Piano Instruction in the College*, contained useful ideas for establishing college piano classes and planning a curriculum of study. His materials for adults stressed singing, playing by ear, analysis and and understanding of chords used in practical ways such as the harmonization of folk melodies.

Burrows incorporated the principles of developmental psychology in music learning. These principles were reflected not only in his teaching but in his various method books for adults. Certainly his work in piano pedagogy firmly established Teachers College as a center for piano education, especially during the years immediately following World War II. At that time colleges were flooded with students studying on the G.I. Bill. And college administrators were looking for ways to offer quality piano instruction to music students. They looked to pianists trained by Robert Pace at Teachers College, Columbia University.

After Burrows' untimely death in 1952, his successor, Robert Pace (1924-2010), continued to refine adult piano study in classes. With a Juilliard background and a keen interest in educational psychology, Pace stressed group interaction and high musical standards. He preferred the term *group piano* to *class piano*. He trained teachers to *question* rather than *tell*. Students in groups were encouraged to listen critically, verbalize reactions, support one another and discuss the musical and technical points of repertoire being studied. Group piano lessons, according to Pace, needed to be musically integrated. Practical piano skills (reading, harmonizing, improvising, etc.) received equal emphasis along with the study of repertoire and technique. Pace also published extensively for the adult pianist from the 1950's until is death in 2010. His numerous students (including me) were placed in important colleges and universities throughout the United States where they developed model programs in group piano for adults (and children.)

The late 1970's and throughout the 1980's witnessed a virtual explosion of piano pedagogy degree programs, especially at the master's degree level. An important component of these programs focused on adult study in groups and in particular the impact of the digital piano lab. New technology demanded new methods of instruction.

## The College Adult Beginner

Teaching adult beginners in a college group situation is enjoyable from many standpoints. College-age adults are highly motivated to learn and want to move ahead. They want things to happen quickly and they want whatever they learn to be immediately useful. They vary markedly from each other and generally are full of spirit and good humor.

College-age adults tend to be very busy students with many competing demands made upon them. For instance, they might be playing in an opera orchestra every night for two weeks, or off on a choir tour for a week or swamped with term papers midway through a semester. For these reasons, it is wise for the group piano teacher to plan realistically, select meaningful materials, schedule assignments well in advance (in writing or via email) and most importantly to make every minute of the lesson count. Outside practice will be minimal at best considering the student's work on a major instrument or voice and demands from other music and academic courses.

Music majors at the piano have a head start. They generally possess a fine rhythmic sense, especially instrumentalists. And they know one clef well. But they are often frustrated by coordination difficulties because their intellects generally run far ahead of their hand agility. Most music majors beginning piano study will cover in a sixteen-week semester what an average child might learn in two years. Music majors are fortunate in that they are enrolled in theory classes concurrently with piano classes. This gives them an opportunity to apply music theory knowledge directly to the keyboard.

Adults need as much help with efficient practice routines as children. Group piano instructors should never assume that music majors know how to practice. It is a common experience to find that they have no organized plan even when practicing their major instrument.

For the secondary pianist (non-piano major) the two most important skills for life-long learning are sight reading and technique. Therefore, a sequential program focusing on reading and fluent playing needs to be considered when planning curriculum and materials.

## The Piano Lab

During the 1950's through the 1970's college piano classrooms consisted of 8 to 12 studio upright pianos. That is what I faced as a young instructor at the University of Illinois—a basement room with unbelievable cacophony. One can imagine the difficulty of sorting out the sound. My teaching aid consisted of a Diller (Angela) wooden keyboard that was used to show where to place the hands. Fortunately, acoustic pianos were being replaced by electronic piano laboratories. This necessitated a new kind of teacher training which brought the group piano specialist face-to-face with the world of electronics. Companies which manufactured these labs, such as Wurlitzer and Baldwin, became heavily involved in teacher education as well as publication of materials suitable for this new type of instruction.

The electronic piano lab solved many problems associated with the acoustic multiple piano classroom. The noise problem disappeared with the use of headsets and teacher control centers improved instructor communication with students. Audio aids, including cassette tape decks and turntables, operated directly from the teacher control center. Things began to look up!

Visual aids were also developed for lab teaching and included, depending on the make of the lab, visualizers and television monitors as well as overhead projectors with accompanying transparencies of scores and text pages.

The visualizer, developed by Wurlitzer, was perhaps the most effective visual aid of all. It attached to the teacher control center and was programmed to light up notes on a large staff, a large keyboard or both. All this was accomplished by simply touching teacher piano keys. This invention revolutionized class presentations and enhanced learning. Piano lab educators, such as Dr. Larry Rast of Northern Illinois University, showed teachers throughout the country how to use the lab efficiently. Currently, George Litterst's *Classroom Maestro* has replaced the visualizer.

In the 1980's, many American electronic piano companies ceased manufacturing since Japanese companies such as Yamaha, Roland, Kawai and Korg introduced superior digital keyboards and digital technology. The MIDI revolution of the later 1980's was being felt. The old electronic piano labs were being replaced in favor of digital piano labs outfitted with high quality teacher control centers, keyboards with sampled sounds (piano, harpsichord, organ, etc.), sequencers and in many cases computers interfaced with student pianos.

The digital revolution silenced critics of the former electronic piano lab. The digital piano's sound coupled with its touch (weighted action), represented a vast improvement over former instruments. For example, the Kawai digital piano with its wooden keys simulated the feel of a traditional acoustic piano. Transferring from a digital keyboard to an acoustic instrument became an easy adjustment.

## The Typical Two-Year Program

Most four-year colleges with music departments offer at least a two-year sequence of group piano instruction for music majors whose principal performing medium is voice or an orchestral instrument. Normally, this is divided into four semesters of about 15 weeks each. Many music schools require students to take a piano proficiency exam at the end of the two year period.

## Objectives of Group Piano Study

Teachers are fortunate to be able to select from many excellent texts listed at the close of this chapter. These texts follow a similar plan, that of supplying unified musical materials stressing the fundamentals of musicianship. These materials reflect a common objective: to develop well-rounded musicians at the keyboard. Most texts are structured sequentially and include studies in reading, transposing, harmonizing, playing by ear, improvising, arranging, repertoire from different eras and technical studies which further an understanding of how the body works in an efficient manner at the keyboard. Structuring syllabi and examinations becomes easy for the teacher with a strong text.

# Proficiency Exams

Once syllabi are determined for each semester of study, structuring an examination covering all the important elements becomes essential. There will always be students with prior piano experience who want to "test out" of early levels. The proficiency exam provides an opportunity for students to be placed in a proper level or section. In some schools, credit is granted upon successful completion of a proficiency test.

# Class Size and Scheduling

The effectiveness of group teaching appears to be in direct proportion to class size. Leaders in the group piano teaching field testify that extremely large classes (twenty-four in some piano lab situations) are awkward. First-year classes held to a maximum of ten work well. Second-year classes of six to eight students allow ample time to cover more complex assignments and longer repertoire pieces.

College piano classes generally meet two or three times a week for fifty-minute periods. A fifty-minute instructional period permits the instructor to plan several activities within any one period - an improvement over the typical half-hour private lesson which preceded the advent of college piano classes.

# Practicing

Daily practice is essential for the college piano lab student. Most schools provide practice rooms for these students. Access to an acoustic piano enables a student to experiment with a different (but similar) piano action and fine gradations of touch. Use of the pedals on an acoustic piano becomes quite different (and more controllable) than the pedals on a digital piano. If a student can practice 30 minutes daily with good concentration, progress can be assured. This is preferable to cramming on weekends or for an exam.

When not in use for instructional purposes, piano labs can be opened up for supervised practice. Teaching assistants may be assigned to monitor practice. Supervised practice is especially helpful for students with special problems such as poor reading skill. Monitor sessions of this nature allow students to log practice time. This helps teachers to determine which problem students are actually seeking help.

# Teaching In a Piano Lab

Effective piano lab lessons demand that the teacher plan each class, evaluate each session and make reasonable assignments. Some suggestions for the novice teacher follow.

Since most of the teaching in a piano lab involves headphone work either in lecture mode (for the whole class) or in individual mode, a well-modulated voice is appreciated. An occasional break to loudspeaker function can liven up a lesson. This becomes useful when a teacher might want the entire class to hear a model harmonization or a well-prepared solo.

Students need to be kept busy with various tasks while a teacher is working with an individual student. A teacher begins to develop a fine ear in lab work, one which detects problems quickly. Solutions need to be offered and tried. Specific practice steps can be jotted down by the student.

When new work is presented, a step-by-step approach works best. For example, if a new chord pattern is introduced, teach the bass line first. Discuss a good fingering. Then teach the right hand chords and have students find common tones. Once again, allow the students to develop a logical fingering. Then combine both parts but move slowly. When the pattern is secure, try it in another key. Let students do some practicing. While they practice, a teacher can either tune in to students individually or move around the room observing hands on the keyboard. At the next lesson, follow through work in the form of review and checking is important. Using these chords in other ways deepens harmonic understanding and interrelates activities. For example, these same chords might be analyzed in sight reading studies or employed in a harmonization assignment and used as a background pattern for improvisation.

Students are intrigued with various sampled sounds available on digital pianos. Allow them to use them to full advantage. A simple Bach piece on the harpsichord sample gives students an appreciation of an instrument of the Baroque era. A harmonized melody with flute and organ opens up all kinds of instrumental possibilities. Teach students to orchestrate. Jazz majors like using the sounds of vibes, electronic piano, jazz organ, slap bass and various percussion sounds. In many cases, students can teach the teacher.

Assignments which are reasonably paced will find favor with students. Class work and tests should equate equally in determining grades. Once a block of work in many areas appears to be in good shape, it is time for a test. Then it is time to move on to new units or chapters.

Remember to spend a little time on sight reading during each class. That, in addition to technical warm-ups, gives students a lifetime gift - the ability to read and approach the keyboard in a natural way. Non-pianists will use the keyboard as a tool for learning scores. They will also play simple accompaniments and pieces. Lab teaching, if successful, should provide experiences which lead to a lifetime of using the keyboard in practical ways.

# Teaching Assistants

Most music departments depend upon graduate teaching assistants for a good share of college group piano teaching. The supervisor of teaching assistants assumes the role of teacher trainer. Solid supervision of teaching assistants assigned to the group piano program pays huge dividends. The assistant essentially acquires on the job training. At regularly scheduled meetings with the supervisor, the assistant receives feedback on his teaching skills and learns how to evaluate, plan, give exams and grade his group piano students.

Moreover, the teaching assistant learns valuable lessons in classroom management. Christopher Fisher, in his excellent book *Teaching Piano In Groups* (Oxford), devotes a chapter to "Group Piano and the University Music Major." Fisher offers many samples of forms that college group piano instructors will find very useful. He also explains points on record keeping and mentions software programs that replace the attendance and gradebooks of the past. This chapter (and the book) is highly recommended for the novice. Foreign assistants, in particular, need help with the group concept and need to gain familiarity with American music including jazz. Assistants represent the future. They become the next generation of group piano teachers in the college and/or studio.

# Advanced Piano Classes

The impact of comprehensive keyboard musicianship programs for non-piano majors has been so great that many music departments have initiated advanced courses for keyboard majors. Advanced Class Piano, Keyboard Skills for Piano Majors and Advanced Group Instruction in Piano are titles found in current music school catalogs. Music Education piano majors, as noted earlier, receive good training in piano performance and piano technique, but often lack keyboard skills which are relevant for public school music teaching. The future music teacher must function in a variety of keyboard situations. He needs, first of all, to be an excellent sight-reader. He is frequently called upon to accompany vocalists and instrumentalists for contests and programs. In general music classes at all levels, he must be proficient in realizing harmonies with a given tune and chord symbols. And he must often create music for movement - on the spot - with no music on the piano rack. Warm-up choral rehearsals require him to transpose exercises, and even short sections of the works being prepared. The advanced piano class serves as an excellent elective course for the applied or piano pedagogy major who wishes to broaden his keyboard training. In short, the advanced piano class fills in the gaps and rounds out a piano major's proficiency at the keyboard.

A curriculum for the advanced piano class needs to be flexible and take into account the varied ability levels and skills each student brings to class. Free from the time-consuming demands imposed upon the applied piano professor, namely the teaching and checking of solo repertoire and technical work, the advanced class piano teacher is free to develop a "crash course" approach to sight reading, ensemble playing, harmonizing folk and popular melodies, transposing, learning to play by ear, chord pattern playing and score reading. The development of these skills (at an appropriate advance level) prepares the piano major for any variety of musical situations he or she faces in the future.

Most advanced piano classes are a year in length (two semesters) with varying emphases. The materials in these classes vary. Some use Art Song collections for sight reading and transposition practice. Most include vocal and instrumental scores for score reading and reduction. Almost all consider the realization of lead sheets important and various fake books are adopted. More complex harmonizations using 9ths, 11ths, 13ths and alterations accompanies the use of a typical fake book. Students learn appropriate jazz voicings and become familiar with a rich body of American musical theatre repertoire.

Arranging tunes for piano/four hands or two piano/four hands tests the creative ability of students. Any number of projects will come to mind once a teacher assesses students and their backgrounds. Some suggested materials conclude this chapter on lab teaching.

## Suggested Group Piano Texts for College Music Majors

Hilley, Martha and Olson, Lynn. *Piano for the Developing Musician* (6th ed.). Belmont, CA: Wadsworth Publishing Company, 2005.

Lancaster, E. L. and Renfrow, Kenon. *Alfred's Group Piano for Adults, Books One and Two*. Van Nuys, CA: Alfred Publishing Company, 2004/2008.

Lyke, James, Caramia, Tony et al. *Keyboard Musicianship: Piano For Adults, Books One and Two*. Champaign, IL: Stipes Publishing Company, 2009/2010.

## Suggested Materials for Advanced Piano Classes

Evans, Lee and Baker, Martha. *How to Play Chord Symbols In Jazz and Popular Music*. Milwaukee: Hal Leonard Publishing Company, 1991.

Evans, Lee. *The Professional Pianists Fakebook*. Milwaukee: Hal Leonard Publishing Company, 1990.

## Any Publisher

Books of art songs, various one piano/four hands and two pianos/four hands collections at the early advanced level, score reading collections, etc.

# CHAPTER 43

## Standards in Piano Proficiency

### Geoffrey Haydon

What does it mean to be proficient at playing the piano? When one is proficient at something, it usually means they have achieved a high level of skill. The piano offers an unusually large variety of skills one can acquire in learning to play the instrument. Over the years, the piano pedagogical tradition has emphasized some skills while perhaps de-emphasizing others. Moreover, the emphasis of certain skills has had something to do with what aspects and/or styles of playing the piano are relevant. For example, most aspiring solo concert pianists might spend a great deal of time developing technical skills, while an aspiring jazz pianist might spend that same time developing a thorough knowledge of chord progressions and chord-scale relationships. An aspiring collaborative pianist, while still desiring technical skills similar to a concert pianist, will spend time developing advanced reading skills.

The above skills as well as others are often not consistently addressed in the private studio lesson at either the pre-college or college level of study. Therefore, many music departments have implemented a keyboard proficiency test for keyboard majors. Keyboard proficiency standards are already part of the National Association of Schools of Music (NASM) standards for all music majors whether they are keyboard majors or not. It is recognized by NASM that certain fundamental keyboard skills are necessary to develop a well-rounded musician no matter what instrument they play. However, if keyboard is your principal instrument, then it is assumed that fundamental keyboard skills are developed in the private studio lessons. More often than not, these skills are not taught. There are many piano majors who are already performing Beethoven Sonatas, Liszt Concertos, or Chopin Etudes, but yet cannot harmonize a simple melody, perform basic chord progressions with good voice leading in all twelve keys, or transpose a simple accompaniment to a variety of different keys. While the ability to play advanced repertoire can be impressive, the mastery of keyboard skills develops a much deeper level of musicianship, makes learning repertoire a quicker and easier process, and can make a musician more marketable. The real world often requires musicians to adapt quickly to a given situation. Pianists with these kinds of skills are equipped to take advantage of such opportunities that can then lead to future successful endeavors.

Keyboard skills can be organized into categories: Sight-Reading, Scales, Arpeggios, Chord Progressions, Harmonization, Transposition, Score Reading, Playing By Ear.

# Sight-Reading

Sight-reading is one important aspect of piano proficiency. Developing the ability to play something well the first time you see it is an extremely beneficial skill. Good sight-readers generally learn repertoire more easily and quickly than those who are not. They can function competently in ensemble situations, and become familiar with a greater amount of repertoire. Remember many students we teach will never become professional musicians. It is likely that, years later they will only be able to play a handful (if that) of pieces they studied while in our studio. However, if they have become good readers, they will take this skill with them for the rest of their life, using it to make music with others or to enjoy playing through new and old music while entertaining themselves and/or those around them.

Developing good reading skills comes mostly with acquiring experience doing just that. It is important that new material is encountered on a regular basis. How is text reading taught in grade school? It is taught by consistently reading something new rather than reading the same material over and over. Applying this analogy to music, we must realize that once we have played a piece several times, we are no longer sight-reading. Therefore, to develop good sight-reading skills, something new must be read regularly. In pursuing good sight-reading skills, students should keep the following guidelines in mind:

1. **Avoid looking down at the keyboard unless it is absolutely necessary.** Work to develop a keen tactile sense of the keyboard so the eyes can stay on the page the majority of the time. Once you look down, then eventually you must look up again at the music and find your place. This loss of orientation with either the keyboard or the score is a contributing factor in interrupting the flow of the music when sight-reading.

2. **Do not sacrifice the flow of the music in trying to play every note on the page.** Good sight-readers know how to make quick decisions

about editing complex material to make it immediately playable or not letting occasional inaccuracies get in the way of the flow. Do not go back and "correct" a mistake; let the wrong notes go by, most people won't notice unless the flow of the music is interrupted.

3. **Count, either inside your head or out loud**, depending on the situation, to be sure of rhythmic accuracy and to aid in knowing where you are in the score. This guideline is especially important when playing in ensemble situations because the pulse is the common ground on which everyone meets.

4. **Read ahead of what is occurring at the moment.** If what you see is what you are playing at the moment, then there will be problems. A good sight-reader reads at least one measure (or more) ahead of what is being played.

One of the best ways to accomplish good sight-reading skills is to have students participate in ensemble situations such as piano four-hand, two piano, or piano plus instrumentalist(s) or singer(s). For a piano student to survive in an ensemble situation, following the above guidelines is imperative.

## Scales and Arpeggios

Technique is also an important component of keyboard proficiency. In developing technique, students are expected to acquire proficiency in performing scales, arpeggios and chord progressions. These have been confirmed building blocks of keyboard proficiency for a long time. However, today's student is rarely thorough or organized in attaining a high level of proficiency regarding scale and arpeggio technique. Students should aspire to develop both quality and speed in playing scales and arpeggios in all keys. The order in which they are presented should be based on logic and the particular student's strengths and weaknesses. It is best to be flexible yet creative in deciding what order to present them. Most likely, students will first become familiar with the major and minor scales (all forms), as well as major and minor arpeggios hands together in unison. See Chapter 33 for the fingerings of the above scales and arpeggios. Next students can learn scales in thirds, sixths, and tenths between the hands. Eventually, they can learn scales in thirds, sixths, and octaves in each hand. After learning major and minor arpeggios, students can progress to the seventh chord arpeggios, including the diminished seventh, the dominant seventh, the minor seventh, and the half-diminished seventh. Students who thoroughly cover the above scales and arpeggios will be equipped to deal with almost any situation in their repertoire.

# Chord Progressions

Chord progressions are essential to developing a keen understanding of harmony. Learning basic chord progressions in every key means students are becoming familiar with given harmonies in different contexts. For example, a G major triad can function as a I chord in G major, a IV chord in D major, a V chord in C major, a III chord in E minor, and a VI chord in B minor. As they become familiar with chord progressions in all keys, students will sense how any chord depends on context to indicate its relationship to the chords around it. Moreover, teaching chord progressions using Roman numerals to indicate function helps students to think "in the key" rather than memorizing a seemingly arbitrary series of different letter names. The following chord progressions (see examples 1-6), universally used to teach harmony, are arranged with good rules of voice leading in the right hand and a bass line in the left hand. Students should learn these in every key.

Example 1

Each chord progression can also be learned with chords in the left hand and the bass line in the right hand. This arrangement equips students to harmonize melodies with block chord voicings in the left hand.

Example 2

Chord progressions are frequently taught with chords in both hands presumably to save time. However, this method is not recommended. Playing chords in both hands will produce a thick, unmusical sound that is rarely used in music. Therefore, rather than breed that kind of sound, it is better to teach good rules of voicing chords with bass lines, and learn something closer to what will be encountered in pieces.

Example 3

i  iv  i⁶₄  V⁷  i    i  iv  i⁶₄  V⁷  i    i  iv  i⁶₄  V⁷  i

Example 4

I  IV  ii⁶  V⁷  I    I  IV  ii⁶  V⁷  I    I  IV  ii⁶  V⁷  I

Example 5

I  IV  V⁷/V  V⁷  I    I  IV  V⁷/V  V⁷  I    I  IV  V⁷/V  V⁷  I

Example 6

I  vi  ii⁷  V⁷  I    I  vi  ii⁷  V⁷  I    I  vi  ii⁷  V⁷  I

# Harmonization

Each of the above examples begin and end with a root position, first inversion, and second inversion triad respectively due to smooth voice leading. If students learn each progression starting from each of the three right hand positions, then they are ready to harmonize melodies in keyboard style (melody and chord in the right hand; bass line in the left hand).

There are many ways to harmonize a melody, each one creating a style of its own. Two styles are discussed here because they are especially good approaches due to their simplicity and reliability. The best style to teach first is the left-hand block chord style. This style features a chord in the left hand with the melody being played above with the right hand. As a straight-forward approach, students can extract many of the progressions from examples 1-6 in harmonizing simple melodies. Example 7 illustrates the left-hand block-chord approach.

Example 7

I    V⁷    I    IV    I    V⁷/V    V⁷    I    IV    V⁷    I

From this point, students can easily learn different styles by experimenting with various accompaniment patterns such as an Alberti bass pattern (see example 8):

Example 8

Or an oom-pah pattern (see example 9):

Example 9

The second approach is called keyboard style. This style puts the chord and the melody in the right hand and only a bass line in the left hand. Therefore, students must base the choice of inversion used in the right hand on generating the top note as the melody note. Notice that not every note needs to have a chord put with it.

Example 10

Once the style has been chosen, there are four steps that lead students to being ready to harmonize a melody:

1. Determine what key(s) the melody is in.

2. Spell and play I, IV, and V$^7$ in the key(s).

3. Decide on the basic harmonic rhythm; that is, how often a chord should change or be reiterated. For example, in 4/4 time, one could have a harmonic rhythm of one harmony to a bar thus changing chords on the first beat of each measure (one chord slot per bar), two harmonies to a bar thus changing chords on the first and third beats of each measure (two chord slots per bar), or four harmonies to a bar thus changing chords on every beat of each measure (four chord slots per bar). There will always be more than one possibility, but after some investigation one choice will usually reveal itself as best. Then there is still the possibility of changing the harmonic rhythm by either doubling it or halving it. For example, many cadence points in music are approached with a doubling of the harmonic rhythm.

4. Go through the melody and assign I, IV, or V$^7$ (I, iv, or V$^7$) to each chord slot. Make your decisions based on establishing a relationship between melody notes and the relevant chord tones.

5. (Optional) After having decided on I, IV, and V$^7$ chords, go through the melody substituting or inserting chords other than I, IV, or V$^7$, such is ii$^6$, ii$^7$, V$^7$/V, etc. Since all of these chords lead directly to a V$^7$ chord, the most logical place to substitute or insert them would be before an already chosen V$^7$ chord.

The following melody is harmonized first with only I, IV, and V$^7$ (see example 11). The chords change at the rate of twice per measure. All melody tones, except one escape tone near the end, will agree with the chosen chord because they are contained in the chord.

Example 11

I   V$^7$   I   IV   I   IV   V$^7$   I   IV   V$^7$   I

Then the melody is re-harmonized by inserting or substituting vi, ii⁷, and V⁷/V.

Example 12

$$\text{I} \quad \text{V}^7 \quad \text{vi} \quad \text{ii}^7 \ \text{V}^7 \quad \text{I} \quad \text{V}^7/\text{V} \quad \text{V}^7 \quad \text{I} \quad \text{V}^7/\text{V} \quad \text{V}^7 \quad \text{I}$$

# Transposition

Another important skill is transposition. To possess the ability to transpose material to any other key means one has a deep theoretical understanding of its content. When transposing, students learn to deal with such elements as interval relationship, chord function, and key relationship. They must identify the distances between the notes and apply that information to the new key. Most people use one of the following two methods when transposing. The first involves identifying the interval of transposition and applying that interval to all notes encountered. For example, if the melody was originally in G major and it was being transposed to C major, students would "think up a perfect fourth." This method will work, but it is not recommended because it involves no real analysis of the material. Moreover, it is not easy to think this way because the interval of transposition will generally be arbitrary, therefore almost always different. The second method involves identifying and applying to the new key the intervals between the notes both harmonically and melodically. This method is best because the key of transposition does not matter (if you are familiar with all keys). Below are four steps that describe this method:

1.  Determine the key of the piece.

2.  Determine the scale degree of the beginning note(s).

3.  Go to the key of transposition and find that scale degree or those scale degrees.

4.  Read intervals and apply the information to the key of transposition.

What is important about the above method is that students must learn to recognize intervals on the page and then "think" them in the new key. It is helpful to realize all even numbered intervals are arranged in one of two related formations: a) a line note to a space note (see example 13); b) a space note to a line note (see example 14).

Example 13

2nd          4th          6th          8th (octave)

Example 14

All odd numbered intervals are arranged in one of two related formations: a) a space note to a space note (see example 15); b) a line note to a line note (see example 16).

Example 15

Example 16

Applying this information becomes easier as one acquires experience doing it. Having students verbalize the interval and its direction is useful in guiding them to recognize the intervallic content when looking at the score rather than only seeing note names.

Example 17

The above excerpt begins the right hand on the fifth scale degree in G major. Transposing it to the key of E♭ major would involve finding the fifth scale degree of E♭ major (which is B♭). Then, by identifying each interval and its direction (up or down), the melody is generated using E♭ major's key signature.

Example 18

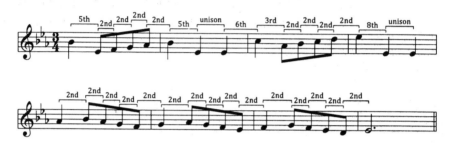

The same is true in the left hand. The first note is the third scale degree of G major. One simply finds the third scale degree of E♭ major. Then the same interval reading procedure is used to generate the bass line in E♭ major (see example 19).

Example 19

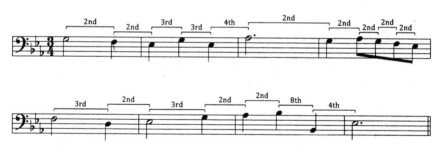

The advantage to this method of transposing is that the key of transposition does not matter. Since you are reading intervals and thinking in the key of transposition, only your familiarity with the key of transposition will be an issue.

## Score Reading

Many teachers do not include score reading as a part of lesson content. Developing the ability to score read can be challenging, yet the rewards justify acquiring this skill. Some students will have the opportunity to accompany a choir perhaps in church or school. Most likely they will be asked to play the individual parts of a Soprano, Alto, Tenor, Bass (SATB) score in various combinations during rehearsal to help singers learn their parts. Other students may be interested in reading a symphonic or string quartet score. Not all students will find a practical use for this skill but exposing them to it will help them become good readers and well-rounded musicians.

When score reading, students are required to combine sight-reading, intervallic recognition, and the process of interpreting more than two staves at once. They will encounter transposing instruments and/or instruments which use clefs other than the bass and treble clef. Therefore, transposing skills will play a role in how well they can score read. Moreover, score reading helps students widen their field of vision. As they become comfortable dealing with three or more staves simultaneously, their grand staff reading will improve remarkably.

Score reading is a skill that can be acquired mostly through experience. Teachers should have string quartets and SATB scores available for students to sight-read. It is usually best to use harmonically oriented material in the early stages of learning to score read. Then students can progress to material that is more contrapuntal.

## Playing by Ear

Part of becoming proficient at the keyboard involves developing the ability to use the ear to play something. While most of the skills discussed above require some kind of reading, playing by ear uses the ear (both the inner and outer ear) rather than the eyes as the primary medium of communication to and from the brain. It is tragic that many teachers actually discourage students who play by ear. In doing so, they deny students the opportunity of developing one of the most useful tools in music.

The best way to develop the ear is to use it. There are students who appear to be naturally gifted with the ability to rely on the ear to play something. While they may possess talent in this area, closer observation will usually reveal these people have already spent a great deal of time using their ears to make music. Even though some teachers discourage playing by ear, there are some methods (such as the Suzuki method) that teach students to learn music by ear first. The best method is to have students both learn to read music and play by ear rather than letting one take precedence over the other.

If you use it, the ear *will* improve but, just like sight-reading, it must be done on a regular basis. Teachers can make regular assignments of melodies for students to learn by ear. Nursery rhyme songs or Christmas carols are good starting points since they are familiar to most people. It is important students learn these melodies in more than one key. Eventually they can add chords to the melodies helping them to hear harmonically as well as melodically.

Using the ear to play means students are venturing into the world of improvisation. They must make decisions regarding range, chord voicing, style, etc. There is nothing wrong with improvising as long as students understand when it is appropriate to do so. In fact, Beethoven, Mozart, Chopin, Liszt, Bach, and many great composers were reputedly wonderful improvisers. Improvisation was a part of their musical upbringing and most likely contributed to their eventual mastery of music. Therefore, if students learn to improvise, they are in good company.

Achieving high levels of keyboard proficiency helps build will-rounded, solid musicians. Students who develop proficiency in all of the skills discussed above become fluent in the language of music. Therefore, learning and interpreting music will come more easily and quickly. In addition, their ability to adapt to different musical situations will be greatly enhanced making them functional and marketable in today's competitive world of music.

# PART FIVE
## HISTORICAL
## PERSPECTIVES

# CHAPTER 44

# A Short History of Piano Pedagogy in the United States

## Vanessa Cornett-Murtada

Piano pedagogy is a fascinating and ever-changing field of study. Approaches to teaching piano, perhaps more than any other instrument, have changed dramatically over the last hundred years. Investigating the history of piano pedagogy can help teachers understand important advancements in teaching methods and philosophies, and appreciate the rapid progress of excellent piano teaching in America.

## Piano Teaching in the Early Twentieth Century

What must it have been like to take piano lessons in the U.S. a hundred years ago? A student in the early or mid-1900s might have walked to her weekly piano lesson in a nearby neighborhood after school. She probably paid the teacher a few cents for each lesson, which was most likely a half hour in length. The teacher was in all likelihood a woman who taught part-time in her home, and who probably received no piano teacher training beyond how she had been taught as a child or young adult. The lesson undoubtedly consisted of numerous scales, perhaps a recital piece, and much repetition of mechanical finger exercises. While many an instructor was kind and encouraging, more often she was viewed as an exacting disciplinarian who balanced pennies on the backs of her students' wrists or taught with a ruler in one hand. And woe to the student who neglected his practice or forgot to curve his fingers and lift them high!

Piano teaching trends in the first half of the twentieth century generally followed a strict, authoritarian approach. As was the case in the nineteenth century, rapid finger technique was valued above all else, and teachers often demanded motionless wrists and unyielding finger independence. Many of these teaching philosophies had their roots in the European conservatory approach of the previous century, where the primary goal of instruction was to produce a virtuoso performer.

It was during this time, however, that esteemed teachers in Europe and America began to embrace new philosophies of piano instruction. These included the use of the whole body, especially the arms, to produce a beautiful tone and a more natural approach to technique. With new advances in the fields of education and human development, lessons gradually became less authoritarian and more child-centered, with an emphasis on music as a life-enriching experience.[1] As pianos became more and more accessible in the home, many piano teachers adjusted their approaches in order to reach a broader range of students.

## Piano Methods and Teaching Approaches

The history of piano teaching in the United States may be traced in the growth and development of various piano "methods," instructional books for beginning students. The first piano instruction books developed and printed in America included the *Modern School for Piano-Forte* (1853) and *New Method for the Piano-Forte* (1859), both by Nathan Richardson. Some books contained titles which were amusing by modern standards, such as Septimus Winner's *Perfect Guide for the Piano in Which the Instructions Are So Clearly and Simply Treated, as to Make It Unnecessary to Require a Teacher* (1861). More popular, however, were books which addressed the earliest fundamentals of playing for young students, such as W.S.B. Mathews' *Standard Graded Course of Studies* (1892), Dorothy Gaynor Blake's *Melody Book* (1916), and the *Diller-Quaile First Solo Book* (1918) by Angela Diller and Elizabeth Quaile.

In the early 1900s, piano production reached its peak. The popularity of the instrument, combined with increased activity by the printing industries, resulted in a dramatic increase in the publication of piano instruction books. The methods most widely used during the first part of the twentieth century included *William Berold's Piano Course* (1904) by William Berold, *Modern Graded Piano Course* including the book *Teaching Little Fingers to Play* (1936) by John Thompson, *Michael Aaron Piano Course* (1945) by Michael Aaron, and the *John W. Schaum Piano Course* (1945) by John Schaum. The middle-C method of music reading, in which the student begins with both thumbs on middle C, was the most common way of teaching music to beginning students. For young beginners, the limited range of the keyboard offered by the middle-C method was a very accessible way to begin reading music. Later methods which used this approach included *Beginning Method for Children* (1967) by David Carr Glover.

Frances Clark introduced a different way of teaching music reading, often called the landmark approach, with the publication of her *Frances Clark*

*Library for Piano Study* (including the primer *Time to Begin*) with Louise Goss in 1955. Using the primary pitches of bass clef F, middle C, and treble G, students learned to read intervals up and down from those landmarks. Clark also used an effective method of pre-reading, using off-the-staff notation as well as partial staves. The series *Music Pathways* (1972) by Lynn Freeman Olson, Louise Bianchi, and Marvin Blickenstaff employed the same method of intervallic reading, but used the five Cs on the staff as landmarks. The landmark approach developed very fluent sight readers who were able to utilize an extended range of the keyboard. Other methods stressing landmark reading include Clark's influential *The Music Tree* series (1972).

A different approach to music reading, the multiple key (also called multikey) method, was introduced by Robert Pace in 1961, in his series *Music for Piano*. With this approach, students learned five-finger positions in all twelve keys, enabling them to read music in a multitude of key signatures very quickly. In the *Bastien Piano Library* (1976) and later *Bastien Piano Basics* (1985), James and Jane Smisor Bastien presented this reading method at a more gradual pace, creating a reading approach that is sometimes referred to as gradual multiple key. Both strategies stress five-finger positions for reading elementary pieces, as well as early study of diatonic chords. *The Young Pianist Series* (1981) by Walter and Carol Noona also employs a gradual multiple key approach.

More recent piano methods are eclectic in their approach in that they combine middle-C, landmark, and/or multiple key strategies for music reading. Some of these include *Piano Adventures* (1993) by Nancy and Randall Faber, the *Hal Leonard Student Piano Library* (1996) by Barbara Kreader, Fred Kern, Phillip Keveren, and Mona Rejino, *Alfred's Basic Piano Library* (1981) by Willard A. Palmer, Morton Manus, and Amanda Vick Lethco, and many other excellent series. Over the past several decades, new methods for preschool-aged beginners, adult beginners, and group piano classes also became available to meet the needs of the growing diversity of students and teachers.

As piano methods evolved to accommodate new teaching styles and the needs of beginning students, authors began to publish additional books to supplement the primary teaching method or lesson book. Early technique supplementary books included John Schaum's *Hanon-Schaum* (1946) and Edna Mae Burnam's *Dozen a Day* (1950). Theory supplements included Leila Fletcher's *Theory Papers* (1943) and a number of note spellers by various authors. The use of supplementary books for topics such as ear training, sight reading, creative activities, recital solos, ensemble music, or music of a specific style, became more popular. Advances in music technology certainly affected piano teaching materials, and supplements such MIDI discs, CDs, theory software, and companion websites are widely available today.

One important new approach to music reading was the growing popularity of pre-reading, in which a student learns to read from symbols before the staff is introduced. More and more teachers emphasized singing in the lesson, Dalcroze eurhythmics and other movement activities, and the importance of functional skills such as harmonization. Because of the influence of rote-teaching methods such as the Suzuki approach, more teachers began to use occasional rote teaching to develop a student's ear and sense of musicality. Creative activities such as composition and improvisation became a part of many lessons, allowing students to apply music concepts actively and in a way that was personally gratifying.

The music in early elementary-level books included many American folk tunes and patriotic songs. As the trend towards multiculturalism grew, more non-European folk tunes appeared in method books and supplements, and publishers were more sensitive about omitting pieces whose titles might seem overly religious or offensive to some students.[2]

## Piano Teacher Training

During the first half of the twentieth century, the peak of piano production and the increased publication of piano methods and materials encouraged the development of piano teaching approaches. As the popularity of piano lessons increased, so did the need for well-trained piano teachers. Colleges and universities eventually became the most reputable place for American piano teachers to receive structured training in various piano methods and teaching strategies. At the same time, a new philosophy of educating the whole musician emerged as many universities offered courses and programs in "comprehensive musicianship."

Public school group piano courses exploded in popularity after World War I, and finding qualified piano instructors to teach these classes became a challenge for schools, since few private instructors were adequately trained to teach piano to groups of students. Colleges began to offer group piano classes as well as courses in class piano pedagogy, and pioneering group piano methods were developed by Robert Pace, Frances Clark, Guy Duckworth, and Raymond Burrows.[3] Robert Pace's workshops on class piano instruction attracted hundreds of teachers to Teachers College, Columbia University. James Lyke, one of the first to author a comprehensive adult text for teaching keyboard skills, remembers those early classes with Pace. "Observing his work with children in groups was a revelation to me. These children not only played pieces wonderfully, but also were interacting with one another and actually learning how music was put together. They were phenomenal. These youngsters took dictation, improvised, sight-read, harmonized melodies, etc. It was the unification of so many musical elements that impressed me. Robert Pace changed my life. He was a real pioneer."[4] Pace recalled the demand for these classes after the Second World War. "In 1945 the war had ended. We had thousands of young people coming back in '46 and those next years or so, returning to college after being away for several years. The colleges were flooded… If you can imagine 20 out-of-tune uprights playing a Bach minuet, and they were about a couple measures apart before they got to the end of it, it was quite an experience!"[5]

The cacophony of multiple upright pianos began to subside as electronic piano labs were gradually introduced in the late 1950s and early 1960s. Companies such as Wurlitzer began to manufacture electronic keyboards designed specifically for group piano instruction. The first Wurlitzer electronic piano weighed one hundred pounds in 1954. Two years later, piano lab options included keyboards with headphones and an optional teacher's monitoring unit. Because of the increased use of electronic keyboards, more and more teachers began using the word "keyboard" instead of "piano." Although piano sales and the demand for piano lessons had declined sharply, the sudden popularity of electronic keyboards and synthesizers in the 1980s sparked new interest among musicians, and kept many Americans interested in keyboard training in the later part of the century. Influential community music schools such as Frances Clark's New School for Music Study served as models of teaching excellence for both private and group instruction. Today, the New School continues to fulfill its role as a popular teacher training center.

As course offerings in piano pedagogy rapidly developed and diversified, the National Association of Schools of Music (NASM) developed standards for a B.M. degree with a teaching major in applied music, compiled in conjunction with the Music Teachers National Association (MTNA). At that time, performance requirements were less rigorous than in B.M. performance degrees. As piano pedagogy degree programs quickly grew in popularity, educators recognized the need to raise standards and develop consistent guidelines. In the 1980s, Marienne Uszler and Frances Larimer published two volumes of "The Piano Pedagogy Major in the College Curriculum: A Handbook of Information and Guidelines" which considered recommendations from NASM, MTNA, and several other national organizations. One important change in these guidelines was that they emphasized a high standard of performance for piano pedagogy majors. The most prevalent degrees today include the B.M. in piano performance with some training in pedagogy, the M.M. in piano pedagogy, the M.M. and D.M.A. in piano performance and pedagogy, and the Ph.D. in music education with an emphasis in piano pedagogy.

In addition to these undergraduate and graduate degrees, a number of colleges and universities offer piano pedagogy certificates, often two-year non-degree programs. These programs typically offer training in business strategies, learning theories, curriculum and lesson planning, method book evaluation, and techniques for private and group teaching. Some programs require applied lessons, studio or classroom teaching observations, and/ or a supervised teaching practicum. Most pedagogy degree and certificate programs offer a diverse curriculum in order to address the needs of ever-multitasking independent music teachers.

# Professional Opportunities

As higher standards in piano teacher training continue to develop, so does the need for increased professionalism in the field. Instructors depend on opportunities to network with other teachers, continue their own music education, and be aware of current trends in research and technology. Two of the most effective ways for teachers to keep up with important developments in the field are through professional music publications and organizations.

One of the first magazines for musicians was *The Etude* which was founded in 1883 by Theodore Presser, and was published monthly until 1957. Each issue contained articles about classical and popular music, advice columns about teaching, and scores of piano pieces, etudes, and songs. While *The Etude* was by far the most influential and popular music publication of its time, other magazines included *The Musician, Perry's Music Magazine,* and *The Echo.* The Music Teachers National Association, founded in 1876, began publishing the journal *American Music Teacher* in 1951. The articles, regular columns, and reviews of new music continue to educate music teachers throughout the United States. *Piano Quarterly* (1952-1992) was one of the few scholarly piano journals dedicated to research, historical and analytical studies, and conference reports. *Piano Quarterly* was resurrected in 1993 as *Piano and Keyboard,* a magazine for professional and amateur classical and jazz pianists. In 1962, The Instrumentalist Publishing Company began publishing *Clavier* magazine, which was a popular resource for many years. In 1990, Richard Chronister founded the magazine *Keyboard Companion,* devoted to elementary-level teaching and later published by the Frances Clark Center for Keyboard Pedagogy. *Clavier* and *Keyboard Companion* merged in 2009 to form a new bimonthly publication, *Clavier Companion,* which offers practical teaching advice, interviews, features, book and music reviews, and regular columns. Thousands of piano teachers take advantage of the excellent publications currently in print.

Professional organizations are essential to continued professionalism in the area of piano pedagogy. The Music Teachers National Association (MTNA) continues to be an outstanding resource for music teachers. Among the many programs offered by MTNA, one of the most valuable is the program for national certification. Becoming a Nationally Certified Teacher of Music (NCTM) is an important way for instructors to develop excellent credentials while promoting a high level of competency in the field of music teaching. Members of MTNA may also join the state and local chapters, which usually offer high-quality conventions and piano teacher workshops. The National Conference on Keyboard Pedagogy (NCKP), held every other year in the Chicago area, offers outstanding teaching demonstrations and sessions devoted to new research and practical teaching advice. In addition, teachers may choose to join the American College of Musicians/ National Guild of Piano Teachers or the National Federation of Music Clubs, both of which offer performance opportunities for students of all levels. Other options include The National Group Piano and Piano Pedagogy Forum (GP3), the World Piano Pedagogy Conference, and a variety of international music organizations and conferences.

## Piano Pedagogy in the Twenty-First Century

A piano lesson today may be an entirely different experience from what it was a hundred years ago. Today, a student may go to a teacher's home, a community music school or college preparatory program, or may have access to piano instruction at her school. The instructor may have professional degrees or certifications in music, may own and operate his own music business, and might teach piano as a full-time career. Lessons might be private lessons of any duration, or may include partner lessons or group classes. Students may record their performances on digital keyboards, notate their original compositions using music notation software, play music theory games and complete assignments on a lab computer, or post videos of their recitals on a studio website.

As researchers continue to make breakthroughs in the areas of psychology, neuroscience, technology, human development, and other areas, teachers must learn to adopt the best possible teaching practices. The following statements summarize some of the recent philosophical trends in American piano teaching:

1. Technique is inseparable from musical interpretation.
2. Whole body coordination is essential to piano performance.
3. Rhythmic control helps to achieve musical organization and continuity.
4. Effective practice and performance require mental concentration, aural awareness and frequent self-evaluation.
5. The success of piano students depends on the humanistic facet of piano teaching.[6]

We have certainly come a long way from the strict conservatory approach of a hundred years ago to a more humanistic, student-centered approach to learning. Today, more and more teachers embrace the idea that they must first understand their students as diverse individuals, then work to engage the mind as well as the body for an enjoyable and fulfilling experience. With the breathtaking rate of change that took place over the past century, it is exciting to think of what the future of piano teaching may bring!

# Recommended Reading

Allen, Doris. "Women's Contributions to Modern Piano Pedagogy." In *The Musical Woman: An International Perspective, ii: 1984-1985*, ed. Judith Lang Zaimont, 411-444. Westport, CT: Greenwood Press, 1987.

Brubaker, Debra. "A History and Critical Analysis of Piano Methods Published in the United States from 1796 to 1995." Ph.D. diss., University of Minnesota, 1996.

Burns, Debra Brubaker, Anita Jackson, and Connie Arrau Sturm. "Unsung Heroines: Contributions of Selected Early Twentieth-Century Women to American Piano Pedagogy." *American Music Teacher* 52 no. 3 (December-January 2002-2003): 24-28, 93.

Fisher, Christopher. *Teaching Piano in Groups.* Oxford University Press, 2010.

Mueller, Sheryl Maureen Peterson. "Concepts of Nineteenth-Century Piano Pedagogy in the United States." Ph.D. diss, University of Colorado at Boulder, 1995.

Sturm, Connie Arrau, Michael James, Anita Jackson, and Debra Brubaker Burns. "Celebrating 100 Years of Progress in American Piano Teaching, Part I: 1900-1950." *American Music Teacher* 50, no. 2 (October-November 2000): 29-32.

Sturm, Connie Arrau, Michael James, Anita Jackson, and Debra Brubaker Burns. "Celebrating 100 Years of Progress in American Piano Teaching, Part II: 1950-2000." *American Music Teacher* 50, no. 3 (December-January 2000-2001): 24-28.

Uszler, Marienne. "American Piano Methods" in *The Well-Tempered Keyboard Teacher*. Second Edition. New York: Schirmer Books, 2000, 339-354.

# Endnotes

[1] Connie Arrau Sturm, Michael James, Anita Jackson, and Debra Brubaker Burns, "Celebrating 100 Years of Progress in American Piano Teaching, Part I: 1900-1950," *American Music Teacher 50, no. 2* (Oct.-Nov. 2000), 30.

[2] Sturm, et. al., "Celebrating 100 Years of Progress in American Piano Teaching, Part II: 1950-2000," *American Music Teacher 50, no. 3* (Dec.-Jan. 2000-2001), 25.

[3] Maria Isabel Montandon, "Trends in Piano Pedagogy as Reflected by the Proceedings of the National Conference on Piano Pedagogy (1981-1995)" (Ph.D. diss., University of Oklahoma, 1998), 24.

[4] Ronald Chioldi, "Reflections on a Remarkable Career—An Interview With James Lyke," *Clavier Companion 1, no. 3* (May/June 2009).

[5] "Forward Thinkers Looking Back: The Coming of Age of American Piano Pedagogy." (Panel discussion, National Conference on Keyboard Pedagogy, Chicago, July 30, 2009).

[6] Michael J. James, "The Evolution of Pedagogical Thought in American Piano Teaching of the Twentieth Century" (D.M.A. diss., University of South Carolina, 1994), 73-74.

# CHAPTER 45

## Ruth Slenczynska
## Remembers Her Teachers

### Introduction by James Lyke

In her book, *Forbidden Childhood*, Ruth Slenczynska recounts how her domineering father sought to collect celebrated musicians and coerce them into teaching his daughter--usually without a fee. This provided Ruth with a golden opportunity to study with many great pianists of the 20th century. To a child prodigy of the 1930s, these legendary figures passed on strong opinions about how music should be played. Her friendship with these great musicians plus the encouragement they gave her made an indelible impression.

Ruth Slenczynska stresses the importance of learning from more than one teacher. She describes study in terms of painting, adding many changes along the way. Working with a discerning teacher, she states, allows a pianist to generate ideas of his own. After a period of time, it is wise to move on to another teacher for more ideas. Finally, one arrives at the point when confidence will allow the writing of one's own signature in the lower right hand corner of the painting.

### Josef Lhévinne

He actually came to our house in Berkeley when I was five. Even at that age, I already had a reputation for perfect pitch. He tested my knowledge of harmony by asking me to play the dominant chord of D major on the piano. I played the chord he requested and then, whether by design or forgetfulness, he replied, "No, that's not what I meant. I asked you to play the dominant seventh chord - this." And he played it for me. I corrected him firmly: "You didn't ask for the dominant seventh" and I played it for him. "If you had asked for it, I would have given it to you." I'm sure my parents were shocked at my cheek!

Soon after that, I remember a concert that Mr. Lhévinne gave in a stadium at the University of California. For an encore he played Liszt's *La Campanella*. I remember being tremendously excited and crying over and over, "I want that piece!" It became my signature piece and a favorite encore that I played frequently in concerts right to the end of my career. After that particular concert, I met Mr. Lhévinne backstage and he wrote on my program, "To my young colleague Ruth."

# Josef Hofmann

He played another of the earliest concerts I can remember from my childhood. It was at Alameda, and he performed Chopin's second sonata. I remember the powerful rhythms that dominated the *Marche Funèbre*. It made such a vivid impression on me that I tried to picture how it might be at my father's funeral. I could envision the drums, the solemn march, the eulogy, and then the steady, relentless tread resumed again and the howling of the wind over the grave. I pictured myself in that scene too!

When I played on his piano in Philadelphia, the sound had no depth. He taught me how to lean into the keys on the soft parts of my fingers to produce the desired sound. As he was often on tour, I actually studied more often with his Russian assistant, Madame Isabelle Vengerova. We did a lot of arduous work with the metronome. My classmates at the Curtis Institute included Shura Cherkassky, Jorge Bolet, and the budding composer Samuel Barber.

# Artur Schnabel

I was six at the time, and I most remember his lessons for their length (sometimes 2 ½ hours) and for their utter meticulousness. Every note had to be accounted for. After I played a piece through for him, he would proceed to analyze my playing of it in great detail, often taking up to 30 minutes. In all that time he never touched the keyboard. He could make more points without pressing a single key than any teacher I ever studied with. I remember he helped me get the feeling of a difficult passage in Mozart's F major sonata [K.332] by softly singing "ein-e blum-e, ein-e blum-e" to me as I played.

# Egon Petri

When I went to study with Mr. Petri in his opulent studio with two big concert grands in Berlin, I had no finger dexterity. To remedy this, he had me work on scales and arpeggios using dramatic dynamics. We worked on the proper movement of hands, arms and body. He showed me how to put all this together to sound deliciously musical in a piece like Schubert's *Impromptu In E-flat*.

# Alfred Cortot

At eight I studied with Mr. Cortot in Paris. He was a revelation. He looked at music *as music,* not just ideas written on paper. For Schnabel, one always went back to what the composer wrote, but for Cortot that was just the starting point. "Music is like poetry", he told me. "It will say different things to you the next time you play it, or three days or three months from now." One never played the same piece twice in exactly the same way.

There were always surprises in his lessons. He would write dynamic markings in pencil all over the score of a piece he wanted me to practice. When I came for my next lesson, he would erase all the markings he'd written and inscribe new ones in their place: *piano* instead of *forte, crescendo* instead of *diminuendo,* and so forth. He as always experimenting, turning a piece upside down to see what treasure it might hold. He was continually prodding me: "Don't you have any ideas of your own?  Express them!"

# Sergei Rachmaninoff

At the same time I was studying with Cortot, I went to take lessons from Rachmaninoff. But he never described them as "lessons."  He said he detested teaching, having done some of it in his earlier years and finding it distasteful. Our sessions were always "social visits", with discussions of music as the main topic of interest. Delicious, steaming cups of hot tea with lemon and a piece of cinnamon were my rewards!

He had no theories. His instruction consisted of showing me something on the piano and then turning to me with the invitation: "Let's see you do that." By then, I'd absorbed enough technique from my other teachers to pull off almost everything he showed me. It seemed I was a great source of amusement to Rachmaninoff, like his favorite plaything. When I played something to perfection, he would pace the room, chuckling and laughing merrily.

Once, I prepared something for him that was beyond my capability. It was the opening of his second piano concerto, and those widely-spaced chords were physically more than my childish hands could reach. When I got through the passage by playing the bottom note in each instance, and then the chord on top of it, Mr. Rachmaninoff looked at me with dismay: "You sound like a lame duck!"  Then he proceeded to show me how to break the chords in such a way that they would not sound like broken chords beyond the sixth row of the audience.

He always stressed the importance of forming a musical line. "Small musician, small musical lines," he would say. "Big musician, big musical lines!"  He emphasized color, too. Once, when I was not bringing forth enough color in a particular passage in his *Prelude in D Major, Op.23/4,* he took me by the arm and led me to the window. It was the time of year when the mimosa trees were in bloom all over Paris, and we could see their riot of color all down the avenue. "I want that gold color in your sound," he said. "Not pale white." To this day, I think "gold" whenever I play this work.

I have, as one of my treasures, the score of the second movement of Beethoven's *Piano Concerto in C Major* with four straight lines in Mr. Rachmaninoff's handwriting over the notes of that sad, beautiful theme indicating where I should put the weight of my whole arm. He also taught me how to apply the entire arm, but with a considerably lighter touch, in Chopin's *Nocturne in F-sharp Minor*.

"Who is your teacher?" Mr. Cortot asked me suspiciously when I saw him next after a number of sessions with Rachmaninoff. When I told him, he shrugged in a resigned way and said: "A great musician and composer, but a pianist...?" Rachmaninoff felt much the same way about Cortot, "Impossible, always playing wrong notes." Neither had much good to say about the other, yet I learned from both. For some time each had praised elements of the other's work in me, but neither suspected that I was studying with the object of his detestation!

## Wilhelm Bachaus

Thanks to Bachaus, I am now very particular about the edition I use. When I brought my treasured Schnabel edition of Beethoven's Sonatas to a session with Bachaus one day, he sniffed, "Which way do you want to play, Schnabel's way, or Beethoven's?" I'd never given any thought to the importance of an *ur*-text. Now, I work from originals whenever possible. Bachaus made perfect sense to me. If you work with any editor's edition, even when the editor is Artur Schnabel, you can't help but do what the editor has written in.

## Nadia Boulanger

Even though I did not aspire to become a composer, studying with Madame Boulanger enriched my piano playing. If you don't know the harmonic structure behind a composition, you're just playing notes on paper. Rachmaninoff had always placed a major emphasis on working towards the climax of a piece, and then receding from it. If you don't know the harmonic structure of the work, you can't do this and the point is lost.

## Isidor Philipp

He was a wonderful little man who had an old fashioned way of goading you to do your best by holding up someone else (in this instance, his star pupil

Guiomar Novaes) as a shining example. He encouraged me to electrify my audiences by emulating her. It was not meant to be destructive, but at that time of my life I was going through a period when I wasn't terribly sure of myself and I'm afraid I didn't learn as much from him as I might have.

## Vladimir Horowitz

He was a friend whom I consulted for advice on problems, rather than a teacher in the usual sense. When I asked how he projected *pianissimos* to the last row of the audience, I was fascinated by his reply. He told me that he practiced on his own concert grand in his Manhattan townhouse, closing all the doors of his living room and opening the cover of the piano as far as it would go. He started with a big, full sound and gradually refined it until the tone was so soft and sweet that it was clearly audible in the next room but would not offend anyone who heard it.

He also refined his *pianissimos* during the time of his famous, self-imposed exile from the concert stage, when he was living with his wife Wanda on a farm in Tuscany. At that time, he was fascinated by the sound of the lyric tenors of the Golden Age, whom he heard on records that his brother-in-law Walter Toscanini found for him. When he returned to his New York townhouse he worked hard to imitate on the piano the Bel Canto sound that he loved in those old tenors, slowly melting 2 to 3 notes at a time into one another. It worked!

## Books by Ruth Slenczynska

*Forbidden Childhood* (with Louis Biancolli). New York: Doubleday & Co., 1957. Out of print.

*Music At Your Fingertips: Advice For The Artist And Amateur On Playing The Piano* (with Anne M. Lingg). New York: Da Capo Press, 1961.

ACA Digital Recording: CM10010 *"Live."* Ruth Slenczynska, piano. Notes by Phil Muse.

# PART SIX
## ORGANIZATIONS
## FOR PIANO TEACHERS

# CHAPTER 46

## Benefits of Belonging—Priceless: Music Teachers National Association

### Gail Berenson

Becoming a member of a professional association is the wisest decision we can make as a music teacher. In doing so, we are accessing a wealth of resources while also providing our students invaluable benefits. Music Teachers National Association (MTNA), a non-profit 501 C3 corporation, is America's oldest professional music teachers' organization and provides a broad network of educational and support services for its members. A special and perhaps unexpected benefit of membership is the formation of many valued and lifelong friendships.

Theodore Presser and sixty-two colleagues founded music Teachers National Association in 1876 during the Christmas holidays in Delaware, Ohio. At the time, this fledgling organization drew little attention, even within Ohio. Earlier that year, another dedicated group of music teachers decided to initiate a state (Ohio) music teachers' organization, unaware that a national association was already in existence. It wasn't until 1877 that the Ohio group became aware of the newly founded MTNA. Deciding that it would be advantageous to affiliate themselves with the national association, they made plans to dissolve their own organization and become an MTNA affiliate. That dissolution was completed in 1877 and in 1879 the Ohio Music Teachers Association became the first state affiliate of Music Teachers National Association.

MTNA now has a membership of approximately 24,000 music teachers representing all fifty states. It is regarded as one of, if not THE pre-eminent music teacher association in the world, providing support and serving as a pedagogical resource for independent and collegiate music teachers throughout the United States. Belonging to MTNA automatically connects members at the local, state, division and national levels, and extends a wide and diverse range of services and resources that provide countless opportunities for its members and their students to grow both professionally and personally.

> MTNA's motto: *Working for a more musical tomorrow.*

> MTNA's mission: *To advance the value of music study and music making to society and to support the professionalism of music teachers.*

# Local Affiliates

With over 550 local affiliates, an MTNA-affiliated association is easily accessible to most of its members. The local affiliates regularly hold their own teacher enrichment activities that include a variety of educational workshops and conferences that bring an array of clinicians and performers into their communities. Many also host discussion groups, repertoire sharing and other topic-based meetings, providing teachers the chance to exchange ideas and develop a social support network. Not limiting their activities to teacher education, a wide range of student activities are also offered—recitals, various competitive and non-competitive events, large piano ensemble concerts, master classes, etc. Members of local associations enjoy the camaraderie of their peers, performance opportunities for their students and numerous avenues to share ideas, network and continually broaden their knowledge and teaching skills. They can also volunteer for leadership positions leading to possible positions at the state and national levels.

# State Affiliates

The next tier of affiliates is at the state level, providing an educational network of professional peers no matter where your work or family takes you. An annual conference is the event common to all of the states. These conferences provide outstanding educational experiences for their members, offering sessions and performances that stimulate, re-energize and provide the latest information to enhance one's teaching. The state affiliates also offer competitive and non-competitive performance events for students, many of which are the progression of local events that advance to the state level. Some states offer student certificate programs and statewide ensemble performances. In addition, all state members have access to a state newsletter. Volunteering at the state level offers the opportunity to further develop leadership skills, become more involved in the workings of the association, and get to know and work with members throughout the state.

# Divisions

The national association is divided into seven Divisions for purposes of determining representatives to serve on the Board of Directors and to provide another tier of competitions that determine the finalists that compete at the national level. Besides serving a two-year term on the Board, each Division Director chairs one of MTNA's seven Forums: Arts Awareness and Advocacy; Collaborative Performance; College Faculty; Collegiate Chapters; Independent Music Teachers; Local Associations and Wellness. Each of these Forums meets at the national conference and provides members a venue to share ideas in each of these areas. Each January, all Divisions host the penultimate level of the MTNA competitions, with the winners continuing to compete at the national finals.

# National

## Conferences

National meetings provide the entire membership the opportunity to gather for several days to learn, socialize, be inspired and revitalized.

## MTNA National Conference

MTNA's most significant activity is its annual National Conference, held in a major metropolitan area that rotates throughout the country, drawing between 2,000 to 3,000 attendees. Filled with a wide range of exciting sessions, concerts, master classes, an extraordinary exhibit area and the final rounds of the national competitions, there is literally something for everyone.

## Group Piano/Piano Pedagogy (GP3)

In even numbered years, MTNA hosts a two-day conference for collegiate teachers involved in class piano and piano pedagogy instruction. This more intimate event with a limited enrolment allows for an intensive focus on each topic for one day.

## Competitions

MTNA Competitions are well known and respected throughout the world as highly competitive, high calibre, well-run and well-organized competitions. As stated on the MTNA website,

> *The purposes of the Music Teachers National Association Performance competitions are to provide educational experiences for students and teachers and to recognize exceptionally talented young artists and their teachers in their pursuit of musical excellence. The state competitions are considered the primary educational level with the division and national levels showcasing outstanding performance and honoring significant pedagogical achievement.*

There are performance competitions (junior, senior and young artist) on nearly every instrument. In addition, there is a high school level duo-piano competition and a collegiate level chamber music competition. Composition competitions are held at the elementary, junior, senior and young artist levels. Prize money for these competitions is quite generous, and the young artist piano competition winner is the recipient of a very unique prize—a Steinway piano.

## Publications

The American Music Teacher and the MTNA E-Journal are the two major publications available to all members; both are refereed. The AMT, published six times per year, offers readers outstanding educational articles, in addition to providing pertinent association news and trends in the music field. The online E-Journal, recently added to the roster of MTNA publications, is published four times per year and is made available to the general public. It contains longer, interactive and more research-oriented articles.

## MTNA Foundation

The MTNA Foundation Fund, established in 1989, supports programs to financially assist teachers and students with their educational pursuits and provides funds for student competition awards. The Foundation also provides an opportunity for individual and corporate support of MTNA and its programs. It is the source of funding for many of the awards presented by MTNA, including prestigious awards such as the MTNA Achievement Award, the Distinguished Service Award, the Frances Clark Keyboard Pedagogy Award and the MTNA Teacher of the Year Award. MTNA state and local-affiliated associations may apply for grants for projects that benefit teachers, their students and their communities. The Fund also supports the Commissioned Composer program. The MTNA Fellow program provides a vehicle for the states to recognize individuals who have made significant contributions to their state and the field of music.

## Professional Certification Program

MTNA offers a Certification Program to provide verification to the public of an individual's teaching qualifications and identify competent music teachers in their communities. It also strives to improve the level of professionalism within the field of applied music teaching. Based on five standards that demonstrate a teacher's knowledge and skill, teachers become certified after successfully completing the outlined process. Members report that going through the steps to become certified becomes a positive growth process in and of itself. Once certified, teachers will need to annually submit a list of activities in which they have participated to show that they are continuing to fulfill the program's standards and are updating their skills.

## Collegiate Student Membership

The key to the successful future of an association is a diverse and vital membership. Drawing in the younger generation will help ensure the longevity and strength of an association. MTNA promotes the benefits of membership to college students, providing a professional link with other music professionals and a support network to help them bridge the gap from student to professional life. Many universities and colleges have established Collegiate Chapters. Many of today's collegiate pedagogy programs are incorporating the MTNA Certification Standards and the correlating certification projects into their pedagogy curriculum, enabling students to become certified after successfully completing their course.

## Professional Development Resources

A broad range of resources is available through MTNA, many arising as a response to requests from MTNA members. A few of these are listed below:

- Insurance offerings – this extends from medical to musical instrument insurance.
- Annotated Bibliography on Musician Wellness – an extensive listing of books, journals and websites that are accessible through a searchable database.
- Professional Support Line – answered by a knowledgeable teacher who will research any questions she is unable to answer.
- Legal Consultation – providing answers to professional legal issues that arise.
- Intermediate Chamber Music Repertoire Database – a searchable database that includes works for a minimum of three performers, normally consisting of piano plus other instruments, unconducted, one-on-a-part.

## MTNA Website

The MTNA website continues to evolve as MTNA makes it easier for its members and the general public to access information online. Whether it is locating the name and contact information for a state officer or finding a book on the topic of performance anxiety, MTNA is the "go to" source. It continues to become more interactive, offering different constituencies the opportunity to exchange ideas with one another. The MTNA website is the place to search for more up-to-date information on all MTNA activities.

# Conclusion

Being a positive role model for our students is one of the most challenging tasks we undertake when we decide to pursue a teaching career. For that reason, it is especially important for our students to see us continuing to improve ourselves. We want them to understand that the learning process never stops as long as we remain involved in our profession. That means attending professional meetings and taking an active role in professional organizations, reading professional journals, practicing and continuing to make music. It is reassuring to know that we do not have to travel this road alone in our pursuit of greater knowledge. MTNA is here to serve as our pedagogical and musical partner in our quest. There is no better way to continue our own personal and professional growth than to engage in a professional organization that is making a difference and offers so much to so many people.

It was an honor and a privilege for me to serve MTNA as its national president. I have enjoyed taking on a variety of offices that ranged from the local to the national. Volunteering has taught me how to handle a wide array of responsibilities, to learn a great deal about MTNA and, best of all, has provided me the chance to meet so many wonderful individuals, many of whom have become lifelong friends. If you are not a member of MTNA, please join. If you are already a member, consider volunteering. Becoming an active, contributing member is guaranteed to help you grow as an individual as well as help cultivate your organizational and leadership skills. What you give to the association comes back to you in spades!

# Post Script

It is impossible to include complete information for every program and service offered by MTNA in this brief chapter. Under the wise and thoughtful stewardship of the MTNA Board of Directors and the efforts of the incredibly dedicated and talented staff, MTNA continues to evolve. All MTNA offerings are continually re-evaluated, expanded and sometimes changed. I urge readers to go to the MTNA website http://www.mtna.org to access the most current information.

# CHAPTER 47

# The National Conference on Keyboard Pedagogy

## Vanessa Cornett-Murtada

The National Conference on Keyboard Pedagogy (NCKP) is a biennial meeting of keyboard music teachers, researchers, and industry leaders from the United States and around the world. This conference has been an essential part of excellence in the field of piano pedagogy for over thirty years.

## History

Richard Chronister (1930-1999) was a leading teacher and pedagogue in the twentieth century. Among his many accomplishments, he founded the first university degree program in piano pedagogy, developed a new piano method for students, founded and edited a magazine for piano teachers, published prolifically, and co-founded the first national piano pedagogy conference in America. In 1979, Chronister contacted James Lyke, now Professor Emeritus at the University of Illinois, about organizing a new National Conference on Piano Pedagogy (NCPP). Those first conferences were held in Missouri, Illinois, Wisconsin, Ohio, and Michigan, before settling on a regular central location of the Chicago area. The attendance grew from 80 pedagogy teachers in 1979 to over 900 in 1994.

Thirty years after its inception, Lyke reflected on organizing the first National Conference on Piano Pedagogy. "One thing that we decided early on was to have music making be a big part of each conference. Headliners in the concert world, applied piano teachers, and piano pedagogy teachers participated in these musical programs. And later on, students became featured in brief musicales."[1] Lyke and Chronister hoped the conference would build bridges between applied piano instructors and piano pedagogy teachers through demonstration lessons, papers, and reports by specialized committees.

By the time the NCPP reached its peak of activity in the mid-1990s, the topics most frequently addressed at the conference were practice teaching, pedagogy curricula, technology, learning theories, literature, and performance.[2] Some topics emphasized at the earlier conferences, such as group instruction and teaching materials, were gradually replaced by topics such as medical problems of performing artists, collaborative performance, internships, independent music studios, and music industry. The conferences tended to emphasize practical topics and activities, and curriculum decisions tended toward a teacher-centered approach. Practice teaching demonstrations were essential to each gathering, and became the central focus of every conference, according to Richard Chronister.[3]

In 1995, NCPP was discontinued because of challenges related to funding, resources, and the growing size and complexity of the organization. Five years later, through the leadership of Marvin Blickenstaff, Louise Goss, Samuel Holland, and many other respected pedagogues, the National Conference on Keyboard Pedagogy (NCKP) was founded to continue the mission of NCPP. The Frances Clark Center for Keyboard Pedagogy continues to sponsor this event, which is held every two years in the Chicago area. Executive Director of the Frances Clark Center, Samuel Holland remembers that in planning the first NCKP gathering in 2000, the committee decided to return to the basics of outstanding teaching. "Some teachers are effective; others are not. Some teachers have students who study for years; others have students who drop after a few lessons. Some teachers' students always seem to perform well in contests and festivals; others do not. Some teachers' students make music after lessons end. Others don't. And so on down the line. What is the difference? Whatever it is should be the core of what piano pedagogy should be all about."[4] NCKP continues to grow and adapt to accommodate the changing field of piano pedagogy. Frances Larimer, chair of the NCKP Task Force on Pedagogy Curricula, observes that "more recent additions have included contributions by the music industry through exhibits and showcases, sessions on the use of technology in piano performance and pedagogy teaching including hands-on demonstrations, and the introduction of pre-conference seminars in specialized areas."[5]

The National Conference on Keyboard Pedagogy Lifetime Achievement Award is presented periodically on behalf of the Frances Clark Center for Keyboard Pedagogy. This recognition is awarded to an individual who has made substantial and enduring contributions to the field of piano pedagogy over a lifelong career. James Lyke was honored with this award in 2009, Nelita True in 2005, and Richard Chronister posthumously in 2001. Between 1979 and 1994, NCPP recognized Louise Bianchi, Frances Clark, Guy Duckworth, William Gillock, Marguerite Miller, Lynn Freeman Olson, and Robert Pace with Lifetime Achievement Awards.

# The Committees of NCKP

Since the inception of NCPP, a variety of committees were formed to explore various topics and research trends in piano pedagogy. Five committees existed for the duration of all seven NCPP conferences: Practice Teaching (later called Intern Teaching), Learning Theory, Performance/Pedagogy Teacher, Administration, and Independent Studio Teaching. Various committees have been formed or discontinued to further the mission of the conferences, and at this printing in 2011 the committees of NCKP are: Collaborative Performance, Historical Perspectives, Independent Teachers, Internships/ Practica, Music in Early Childhood, The Pedagogy Students, Research, Special Needs Students, Teaching Adults, Technology, and Wellness for the Pianist.

In 1984, the Task Force on Pedagogy Curricula was instrumental in establishing standard guidelines for undergraduate and graduate programs in piano performance and pedagogy in the United States. They outlined curricula for an undergraduate major, emphasis, or concentration in piano pedagogy, as well as pedagogy competencies for the B.M. degree in piano performance and the M.M. and D.M.A. degrees in piano performance and pedagogy. Marienne Uszler and Frances Larimer co-authored the landmark publications "The Piano Pedagogy Major in the College Curriculum: A Handbook of Information and Guidelines." Volume one, The Undergraduate Major, was published in 1984, and volume two, The Graduate Major, was published in 1986. These handbooks, which are available on the Frances Clark Center website, follow the guidelines recommended by the accrediting National Association of Schools of Music (NASM), and emphasize a high standard in piano performance. They have assisted numerous colleges and universities in developing or revising degree programs in piano performance and pedagogy.

Other NCKP committees have been active in contributing to the dissemination of important research in the field of piano pedagogy. The Committee on Historical Perspectives has produced detailed bibliographies of sources on the legendary teachers Frances Clark and Rosina Lhévinne, and an annotated bibliography of sources on the history of piano pedagogy. The Committee on Wellness for the Pianist created a complete wellness curriculum outline and bibliography, and the Committee on Teaching Adults has produced helpful bibliographies on adult learning and adult teaching methods. The Committee on Research has sponsored conference poster sessions on recent research, among other projects.

# The Frances Clark Center for Keyboard Pedagogy

The National Conference on Keyboard Pedagogy is organized and sponsored by the Frances Clark Center for Keyboard Pedagogy. Frances Clark (1905-1998) was one of the most esteemed piano teachers in the United States during the twentieth century. She developed pedagogy programs at Kalamazoo College, Westminster Choir College, and The New School for Music Study, and with Louise Goss she created an outstanding piano method for beginners, *The Music Tree*, part of the *Frances Clark Library for Piano Students*. After her death, Richard Chronister worked to establish a non-profit center for piano pedagogy in her name. The mission of the Frances Clark Center is to continue her influence by conducting research, developing teaching methodologies, and sharing information through seminars, conferences, and publications. The goals of the Center are to enhance the quality of music-making in the lives of students, to educate dedicated music teachers, and to develop outstanding teaching materials for students of all ages and levels.

Each year the Music Teachers National Association (MTNA) presents the Frances Clark Award for Keyboard Pedagogy to an individual who "has made a significant contribution through the creation and development of products or publications that further the field of keyboard pedagogy." The Center fulfills its mission in part through The New School for Music Study, the bi-monthly publication *Clavier Companion*, and journals of conference proceedings.

An outstanding non-profit community music school founded by Frances Clark and Louise Goss, the New School for Music Study serves keyboard students of all ages and abilities. In addition to offering private and group lessons, it is a teaching laboratory for new teaching methods and materials and serves as a model for university preparatory departments. Their mission states, in part, "We believe there is music in every child, and that all children, through music, can become happier, more confident and more creative human beings."

In 2009, the magazine *Clavier Companion* was formed through the merger of two other publications, *Keyboard Companion,* founded by Richard Chronister in 1990, and *Clavier.* It is published six times per year by the Frances Clark Center and contains interviews and articles of interest by nationally-known pedagogues. Regular departments include Repertoire and Performance, Rhythm, Adult Piano Study, Perspectives in Pedagogy, Technology, Music Reading, Technique, and News and Views. The mission of *Clavier Companion* is "to increase the quality and longevity of music-making and music education at the keyboard throughout the global community."

The National Conference on Piano Pedagogy published eight volumes of conference Proceedings and Reference journals from 1980-1994. These publications documented the most important events of the NCPP, including keynote addresses, committee reports, papers on various topics, and summaries of teaching demonstrations and performances. More recent conference archives and some proceedings from NCKP meetings are available online at the Frances Clark Center.

# Conclusion

The National Conference on Keyboard Pedagogy serves many functions as a communication forum for the piano pedagogy field, a platform to present current practices and foster the exchange of ideas on the piano teaching training area, and a reference from which colleges and universities could build and refine their piano pedagogy programs.[6] Samuel Holland remembers, "Richard Chronister's hallmark was to get people together, start them talking, ask provocative questions, lob occasional hand grenades… and then allow the discussion, the concerns, and the needs of the constituency to define the organization and the actions that ensued. We don't have Richard anymore, but I guarantee that we will pursue this course."[7] Chronister himself believed that "this is a sharing conference, a give and take between presenters and participants, and even between presenters themselves… Our aim is to create a situation in which those we have come to respect in various areas of expertise are willing to talk to each other, discuss their points of view, even question the premise they hold, instead of giving another lecture or master class. We've heard them do that; we want something different here."[8] Today, the National Conference on Keyboard Pedagogy continues to be one of the most important organizations for piano teacher training in the United States.

# Recommended Resources

Clark, Frances. *Questions and Answers: Practical Advice for Piano Teachers.* The Instrumentalist Company, 1992.

*A Piano Teacher's Legacy: Selected Writings by Richard Chronister,* ed. Edward Darling. The Frances Clark Center for Keyboard Pedagogy, Inc., 2005.

Montandon, Maria Isabel. "Trends in Piano Pedagogy as Reflected by the Proceedings of the National Conference on Piano Pedagogy (1981-1995)." Ph.D. diss., University of Oklahoma, 1998.

## NCKP Committee Publications (available online)

"Annotated Bibliography of Sources on the History of Piano Pedagogy."

"Bibliography of Adult Teaching Methods."

"Bibliography of Dissertations on Adult Learning for Teachers of Piano and Piano Pedagogy."

"Bibliography of Sources on Frances Clark."

"Bibliography of Sources on Rosina Lhévinne," 2007.

"Periodicals for Adult Learning Committee." Music Articles on Teaching Adults; Non-Music Articles on Adult Learning, 2003.

"The Piano Pedagogy Major in the College Curriculum: A Handbook of Information and Guidelines." Vol. 1, The Undergraduate Major, 1984. Vol. 2, The Graduate Major, 1986.

"Wellness Curriculum Outline," 2007.

http://www.francesclarkcenter.org/NationalConference.html

# Endnotes

[1] "Forward Thinkers Looking Back: The Coming of Age of American Piano Pedagogy." (Panel discussion, National Conference on Keyboard Pedagogy, Chicago, July 30, 2009).

[2] Maria Isabel Montandon, "Trends in Piano Pedagogy as Reflected by the Proceedings of the National Conference on Piano Pedagogy (1981-1995)" (Ph.D. diss., University of Oklahoma, 1998).

[3] Montandon 123.

[4] Samuel S. Holland, "Toward a Pedagogy of the New Millennium." (Keynote address, National Conference on Keyboard Pedagogy, Oak Brook, IL, July 18, 2001).

[5] NCKP panel discussion, 2009.

[6] Montandon 171.

[7] Holland.

[8] Richard Chronister, Opening Remarks, Proceedings and Reference of the National Conference on Piano Pedagogy, USA, 1994, 24.

# PART SEVEN
# THE INSTRUMENT

# CHAPTER 48

# What Piano Teachers Need to Know About Their Instruments

## Geoffrey Haydon

Pianists, along with other kinds of keyboard players, are perhaps the only instrumentalists who generally know very little about the inner workings of their chosen instrument. This lack of knowledge can often lead to improper care and maintenance. It also means that in a performance situation, the pianist is often at the mercy of both the instrument and the available piano technician (if there even is one) who sees to it that everything has been properly prepared. Piano students (or their parents) usually make the assumption that their piano teacher knows pertinent and accurate information regarding the acquisition, tuning, servicing, and quality of a piano. Unfortunately, this is not always the case. In addition, some teachers either do not admit their ignorance or are themselves unaware of their general lack of this kind of knowledge.

If you are taking tennis lessons, you would expect the tennis pro to not only know all about the game itself but also about the equipment that is used to play the game. Piano teachers should also know the same kind of information about the piano. While it would be unreasonable to expect piano teachers to become piano technicians, it makes good sense that they should become knowledgeable about the various aspects of piano technology. Piano teachers who have been educated about the different facets of the piano are equipped to:

A. See to it that their instrument is maintained properly.

B. Deal with minor problems that don't require the expertise of a piano technician.

C. Advise students about caring for their own pianos.

D. Advise students about buying pianos, perhaps steering them in the direction of the best quality instrument for the budget allotted.

E.  Communicate effectively with a piano technician in dealing with a
    particular problem that exists in a piano.

Understanding the piano begins with knowing about its history. Much
has happened to the piano since Bartolomeo Cristofori invented the
instrument around 1700. Since the basis for Cristofori's invention was the
harpsichord, then learning about its history as well as that of other early
keyboard instruments such as the clavichord and organ is also relevant. The
piano underwent many transformations from approximately 1700-1900
before arriving at what we know to be today's modern piano. There are
many books (such as *Giraffes, Black Dragons, and Other Pianos* by Edwin M.
Good or *Men, Women and Pianos* by Arthur Loesser) that thoroughly cover
this information and it is highly recommended that piano teachers become
knowledgeable about the history of the piano. In addition to gaining an
understanding of the piano's parts and their development, one also gains
insight regarding what kind of instrument the composers of the past had in
mind when composing for the keyboard. This kind of information answers
many questions concerning technique, range, texture, balance, etc. when
approaching repertoire composed during the transitional years.

After becoming acquainted with the history of the piano, teachers
can become familiar with how today's pianos operate. Learning about
the different components of the piano can appear to be an intimidating
experience. A piano has literally thousands of working parts inside, yet the
pianist sees mostly keys going up and down. The piano's components can
be broken down into four basic areas:

1.  **The Housing**

The outside case that is usually designed as a piece of furniture. On a grand
piano, the housing includes three legs, the lid (which can be raised or lowered),
and the shell. An upright piano has a lid, a shell that is usually box-shaped,
and legs (they differ in design from one model and/or make to another) that
are usually limited to just two. Since the case is almost always made of wood,
one might assume that the sound of a piano is greatly affected by its housing.
However, the case of a piano has very little, if any, affect on the overall sound.
Therefore, judging a piano by examining its outside appearance will not reveal
much more than an assessment of its quality as a piece of furniture.

2.  **The Sound Board, Bridge(s), and Pin Block**

The **SOUNDBOARD** is the most important sound producing component
in the piano. It is usually made of narrow pieces of wood (high quality spruce
is ideal) glued together. The soundboard amplifies the sound of the piano in
much the same way the hollow body of a violin or acoustic guitar amplifies
their sound. One only has to compare the unamplified sound of a solid-body
electric guitar to that of its acoustic counterpart to appreciate the importance

of the soundboard in a piano. Therefore, in order for the piano to sound good, the soundboard must be in good condition. Things like soundboard cracks or warping can render an otherwise good piano useless.

Glued on top of the soundboard is the **BRIDGE**. Usually made of maple or beech, it acts as a *middleman* between the strings and the soundboard; in essence, it transfers the vibration of the strings to the soundboard. There are many (two for each string) small pins (bridge pins) glued into the bridge that determine one of two terminating points for the vibrating length of each string. Since the bridge is where the crucial transfer of vibration (i.e. sound) takes place, it plays a major role in determining the quality of sound.

The **PIN BLOCK**, located near the top of an upright or near the front of a grand, is a large block of laminated wood (usually beech or maple in the better quality pianos) which houses **TUNING PINS**. Each tuning pin is able to hold the tension of its respective string because it is hammered into a hole in the pin block whose diameter is predetermined for a snug fit; tight enough to hold approximately 150-200 pounds of tension but loose enough for the tuner to manipulate in fine increments when adjusting each string's tension. Although the pin block has nothing to do with the tone quality, its role is still a crucial one because it must be reliable in allowing the tuning pins to maintain the tension of the strings. When the pin block is no longer able to perform this function, a new one is necessary. However, replacing the pin block is a major and costly job. It would be unwise to replace the pin block in all but the highest quality pianos.

### 3.  The Plate, Strings, and Tuning Pins

Inside the case is a large, heavy, harp-shaped cast-iron molding that is bolted into the piano's housing. This one-piece cast-iron molding makes it possible for the strings to be stretched at high tensions (18 to 20 tons total) without the wood components buckling. Moreover, the **PLATE** is positioned so as to ensure that the strings produce a **DOWN BEARING** on the bridge for the purpose of transferring the strings' vibrations to the soundboard. The amount of down bearing greatly affects the tone quality and although it can be measured, once the strings are brought up to pitch, it cannot be changed. Too much down bearing will produce a "choked" quality of sound and reduce sustaining time. Not enough down bearing will weaken the overall sound and sometimes cause the sound to be unfocused. Since the plate is shouldering most of the burden of string tension, it has hitch pins on the backside that are strong enough to maintain the tension on the opposite side of the tuning pins. In addition, close to the front of most grand pianos, the plate determines the terminating point of each string which is opposite from the bridge pins. The plate creates terminating points in two ways. In the upper register there is a bar (sometimes referred to as the Capo d'astro) that produces a down bearing on each string thus producing a termination point. The strings in the middle and lower register are individually passed through metallic holes (agraffe) to produce the termination point. If the above method is not used in uprights, then either the bar or the bridge pin method is used instead.

Discussing **PIANO STRINGS** is a complex issue. There are two basic types: 1) steel strings; 2) steel strings that are copper wound. The design of a piano is based on complex mathematical formulas that take into account string mass, length, and tension. A basic pattern emerges that is common to all pianos. The string length and mass is smallest in the uppermost register. The length and mass increase as the register descends. Eventually it becomes necessary to attach copper winding to the strings in the bass register in order to give them the proper amount of mass rather than giving them impractical lengths (the lowest A string would require a length of more than 30 feet if it were not copper-wound; thus the piano would have to be an impractical 30 feet long or tall). The increments by which the strings increase in mass and length as well as where the copper winding begins differ with each model and make of piano. This aspect is often referred to as the **SCALE OF THE PIANO**.

The steel strings (treble strings) are used in such a way that one strand actually functions as two strings. One end of a string is attached to one **TUNING PIN**, stretched across the bridge, wrapped around the hitch pin, and stretched back across the bridge to another tuning pin. In essence, one string makes a big loop around the hitch pin to create two strings. When a string is broken, it will appear to the casual observer that two strings have broken. A broken string may not be so obvious when playing because there are actually three strings per key everywhere but in the lower register in most pianos. When one string breaks, one of two things happens. Either two adjacent notes lose one string or one note looses two strings. The copper-wound strings, on the other hand, use one strand as only one string. They are simply attached to their corresponding hitch pin opposite the tuning pin.

One other point must be made clear when discussing piano strings. Using copper-wound strings is an imperfect solution to a space problem. However, we have become used to the different timbre of this kind of string in the bass register and all pianos make use of this method. If one listens carefully, the point at which the copper windings begin can be distinguished. With some pianos, this *breakpoint* will be quite subtle, while with others, it will stick out like a sore thumb. The shorter the piano, the less space there is for the longer strings (bass strings). Therefore, the size of a piano plays an important role in determining the tone quality, especially in the lower register.

### 4. Piano Action

The action is by far the most complicated component and contains the most working parts. It is beyond the scope of this chapter to list all the different parts or their functions. However, most pianists need only know about the basics of the action. The way an action works in any piano begins with the key. Only the front part of the key is normally visible (usually about half of it) while the back portion connects to the action through a small metal button called the **CAPSTAN**. There is a center point on which the key rests (**BALANCE RAIL**) thus allowing it to operate like a seesaw. As the front end goes down, the back end goes up raising the capstan; which then engages the **WHIPPEN**.

The **WHIPPEN** pushes the **JACK** into the **HAMMER BUTT** and propels the hammer towards the string(s). Just before the hammer strikes the string(s) (about 1/16 inch), the jack disengages (**ESCAPES**) from the hammer butt thus allowing the hammer to rebound freely from the string(s). [The concept of **ESCAPEMENT** is the principle on which the piano action is based and has remained so since the days of Cristofori's invention.] Therefore, the performer has complete control over how the hammer approaches the string until it is about 1/16 of an inch away. However, once the escapement occurs, the action returns the hammer to a resting position without the performer having to do anything special. As the key is released, the action resets everything so the process can be repeated when appropriate. Today's grand action has a **REPETITION LEVER** incorporated into the whippen that makes it possible for everything to be reset without the key being completely released. This lever facilitates the repetition of one key, particularly at fast speeds.

The **DAMPERS** are also considered part of the action even though in grand pianos they are not permanently connected to the keys. Each damper consists of some kind of felt connected to a wooden head. The wooden head is moved on and off the string(s) by a thin but sturdy wire that is manipulated by the key going up and down. Moreover, it is possible for the entire set of dampers to move, as a unit, on and off the strings when the right pedal (**DAMPER** or **SUSTAIN PEDAL**) is depressed and released. If you look inside a grand piano, you can clearly see the dampers performing their task. If you observe the dampers from the backside of a grand piano, you will notice that, as the strings get longer, the shape of the felt changes from a flat surface to a wedge-like formation. Sometimes a wedge-like damper will come "out of the groove" thus leaving the string(s) to freely vibrate. This problem is best solved by the piano technician but occasionally, if one is gentle, the damper can be nudged back into its groove and may not become a problem again. Notice also that there are no dampers in the upper-most register of any piano.

The above descriptions of the basic parts and their respective functions could be much more detailed. However, most piano teachers can be satisfied that understanding the above information will equip them to adequately deal with issues regarding the piano. Moreover, there are a few tasks teachers can learn to perform that can save time, money, and the inconvenience of arranging for a piano technician's visit. It is not advisable to attempt any servicing of a piano without first learning how from a qualified piano technician. There are two ways to learn. One is to hire a technician and have him/her teach you; it should not take more than one visit amounting to the price of one tuning and could perhaps be combined with the regular tuning visit. The second way involves taking a basic piano technology course that some college music departments offer.

All piano teachers can learn how to use a tuning hammer to tune a unison (match pitch with each of the three strings that are assigned to a note). This skill is not very difficult. It can be very useful because when a string has been replaced, it will need to be brought up to pitch at least three or four times over the course of several months before being able to hold pitch with the consistency of the other strings around it. Acquiring this skills means you can "touch up" an occasional note without having to: 1) wait for the tuner to come; 2) pay the tuner for the visit. One should not take this concept too far though and assume they can tune the entire piano. That is a much more complex task.

All piano teachers can learn how to get inside the piano where the action resides and, in the case of a grand piano, take the action out. Frequently, loose items such as pencils, pens, paper clips, etc. fall inside a piano. While it will almost never cause any kind of serious damage, having the ability to remove them allows for the alleviation of a potentially irritating problem. Moreover, many problems such as sticking keys or rattles are caused by things obvious to the eye. Once the action is visible, these problems can sometimes be dealt with quickly and easily. If not, then you can feel comfortable that a visit from a qualified piano technician is necessary.

## Piano Maintenance

We can now turn to the issue of properly maintaining a piano. Due to the fact that many of the crucial components are made of wood, a piano reacts to changes in **temperature** and **humidity**. Questions concerning whether a piano fairs better in a humid climate versus a dry one or a hot climate versus a cold one are quite common. As humidity and temperature change, wood expands or contracts. Therefore, the answer lies in arranging an environment with a consistent temperature and humidity. This arrangement can be accomplished in a variety of ways. The temperature of a room can be controlled with a thermostat. However, most homes only have one or two thermostats; therefore, the temperature tends to vary from room to room. Also, the amount of insulation and the location of windows and outside walls can greatly influence the rise and fall of temperature. Humidity, on the other hand, can only be controlled with a humidifier and dehumidifier. It is best to have a device that controls humidity in the same room as the piano. **The safe range for humidity is between 40% and 60%.** If your area experiences below 40% or above 60% humidity, chances are good that local qualified piano technicians have special ways to deal with these extremes. In addition, placing the piano away from heating and/or air conditioning vents as well as windows, direct sunlight, and outside walls can help keep both the humidity and temperature consistent. In the end, it is not possible to completely control these two elements so it is generally counterproductive to become overly concerned about humidity and temperature. Pianos are designed with climate changes in mind.

## Piano Tuning

What is involved in tuning a piano? By strict definition, tuning a piano involves adjusting the tension of the strings so that each note sounds its respective pitch clearly. How often should a piano be tuned? The answer depends on several factors. First, is the piano new? A new piano needs much more attention in the first two to three years due to the fact that its strings are still stretching and it is adapting to its new climate. Even if it was bought in the same area, the climate in your home can be quite different from that of the dealership. Most new pianos will need tuning three to four times during the first year, two to three times in the second, and twice the next year. This important fact is not always clearly stated by piano salesmen. In their effort to make a sale, they are not always ready to volunteer information concerning money that will have to be spent after the initial purchase. Most good dealerships offer one, two, and sometimes three free tunings with a purchase. However, this amount is still not enough to adequately break in a new piano. After its break in period, the appropriate amount of tunings a piano needs depends on how much it is used, how much climate change it experiences, and what the discerning ear tells you. The average student's piano at home should be tuned at least once a year and preferably twice annually in order to adequately keep up with yearly climate changes. A piano teacher's instrument, due to the heavy use it probably gets, should be tuned three to four times a year. All pianos should be tuned at least once a year. The adage "Hardly anyone ever plays the piano so it doesn't need tuning" holds no water. In fact, just like a car, within reason, it is better for a piano to be played than to sit idle.

# Piano Regulation

Making adjustments in the action so that it operates efficiently is known as REGULATION. During a tuning visit, a piano technician will not generally make adjustments in the action unless asked to do so. Usually a piano's action will not need to be regulated as often as the piano needs tuning. The frequency of regulation depends on how much a piano is used and, again, how much climate change it has experienced. A new piano should be regulated within a year after it is purchased because there is some settling that takes place in the action. Afterwards, a piano will normally need regulating about every five years. A piano teacher's instrument will normally need regulating about every two to three years. The procedure involves making many small adjustments and possibly replacing some parts. It may cost as much as three or four tunings.

# Voicing Piano Hammers

Some people may wish to change the tone of their instrument. The tone of a piano is often described as either bright (loud or brilliant) or dead (not loud or dull). Piano hammers play an important role in determining the tone quality. The different mallets a marimba or vibraphone player uses provide a good analogy to the hammers in a piano. The harder mallets produce a loud, brilliant, sharp tone while the softer mallets produce a softer, rounder tone. Piano hammers are made of dense felt that are wrapped around a piece or wood. They are designed to produce brilliance when striking the string with a great amount of force and to produce a softer, rounder tone when striking the string with less force. However, over the course of time, hammer felt becomes packed down and hardened thus producing a sharp, brilliant tone no matter what. At this point, a technician can perform a procedure known as *voicing* the piano. It involves loosening the hammer felt to restore the original consistency. This process is an art in itself, and requires much experience on the part of the technician. Since the tone is being changed when voicing the hammers, an inexperienced technician might create inconsistencies from one note to the next causing the piano to sound uneven. When a piano is voiced down, most players will think the action has been tightened because suddenly it is more difficult to get the same brilliance out of the instrument. However, before long, these players will adjust and be satisfied with the greater dynamic range and rounder tone. Once in a while, an occasion will arise when it is desirable to make the tone quality more brilliant. In this case, the technician will apply a chemical solution to the hammers to make them harder and more compact. This process should not be done unless absolutely necessary because it is difficult to reverse.

# Cleaning a Piano

What about cleaning a piano? The outer case of a piano is like a piece of furniture. The dealer or a furniture expert should be consulted regarding its care. The keys can be wiped with a dry or slightly dampened cloth. Remember that anything liquid is an enemy of the piano. Therefore, cleaning solutions, oil, or wet cloths should be avoided. Moreover, it is a good idea to keep anything containing liquid (including flowers or drinks) off the piano where it can never be spilled on or inside. This rule of thumb can prevent hundreds of dollars in damage. Cleaning anything else in the piano should, at the very least, be done in consultation with a qualified piano technician and, at the most, be left up to him/her.

# Buying a Piano

There will times when students will ask for a teacher's advice about purchasing a piano. It is best to be honest and straightforward regarding quality. Pianos come in many shapes and sizes. There are principles to keep in mind. Size can be an important factor in determining the quality of sound especially in the bass register. Since the bass strings are the most affected by length, the smaller the piano, the greater the bass register is compromised. Sometimes more emphasis is placed on appearance. At other times a piano may not look particularly attractive, but the sound may be quite good and the workmanship of high quality.

Upright pianos range from 36 to 60 inches in height and come in three general sizes. Those that are less than 40 inches are generally called spinets and are of the lowest quality. They have an indirect action, they are difficult to service and/or repair, and their small size compromises the overall tone quality. Most companies have discontinued the spinet model upright piano for the above reasons. Upright pianos that are 40 to 48 inches in height are known as console or studio uprights. They tend to differ in quality from one model and/or brand to another. They have a direct blow action and are much easier to service and/or repair than spinets. Upright pianos taller than 48 inches are known as full size uprights and generally represent the top of the line models. Upright pianos are the best purchase when the buyer either cannot afford a grand piano or hasn't the space for one. The upright piano was originally designed as a compromise of space and money. It will never compete equally with a grand piano, but it can be adequate especially if students can find ways to practice on a grand piano periodically.

Grand pianos range in size from 4 to over 9 feet. The 9-foot grand piano, called a **concert grand**, is usually purchased for large concert halls. It is the top of the line model grand piano. In the case of many companies, there is a large difference in quality between the concert grand and those that are smaller. In general, the smaller the instrument, the lower the quality. Most serious pianists will want a grand piano that is 5 feet, 6 inches to 7 feet in length, sometimes called *studio grand*. These pianos are made for the home yet they are also designed to approximate the sound and feel of a concert grand piano. Anything less than 5 feet is called a *baby grand*. Due to its small size, the quality of sound in a baby grand piano is greatly compromised. In fact, most full-size upright pianos sound better than baby grand pianos. As a general rule, the action of a grand piano is superior to that of an upright piano but if the tone quality is not good, then it is better to avoid purchasing the instrument.

When purchasing a new piano, negotiating with a dealer becomes an important part of the process. Most piano dealers operate in a similar manner to car dealers. The amount of mark up on the advertised price is very high. However, just as it is with car dealers, piano dealers will always accept a lower amount of money than what is indicated on the price tag. It will take some work on the part of the buyer to talk the dealer down, but, in the end, it is usually worth the trouble. Hiring a qualified piano technician (who has no loyalty to any dealership or brand name) will almost always save a buyer money in the long run because he knows better how to justify a lower price than indicated. Some dealerships and/or salesman offer piano teachers a percentage of the commission on sales made due to their recommendation. However, it seems unlikely that anyone (teachers or technicians) could give objective advice regarding a piano purchase if they know they are receiving a monetary reward for steering someone in a particular direction. Once the purchase has been made, it is a good idea to make a note of the piano's serial number BEFORE leaving the store. Then check the instrument once it has been delivered to insure the piano delivered was the same one selected.

When purchasing a used piano, teachers can aid students by looking at the newspaper advertisements or talking on the phone to the piano's owner about the instrument in question. These activities can save time and trouble by eliminating instruments obviously not worthy of consideration. Some good questions to ask include the instrument's age, its history of care and maintenance, whether every note works, its brand name, its model, its size, and the reason why it is being sold. Once a piano has been deemed worthy of purchase by the student and/or teacher, it is highly recommended that a qualified piano technician be brought in for a final consultation to be sure the instrument has no serious problems. In addition to peace of mind, a piano technician's opinion can possibly save a buyer a significant amount of money thereby justifying the expense of his/her expertise.

## Piano Technicians Guild (www.ptg.org)

Finding a competent piano technician is not always an easy task. One cannot simply look in the yellow pages or on the internet, and be sure they are getting someone who can do the job adequately. Moreover, most piano technicians have more expertise in one area than another. In other words, some will be better tuners than regulators or rebuilders. Others will excel at tone voicing but not at tuning or regulating. It used to be necessary to do research mostly by "word of mouth" to distinguish between good and less accomplished piano technicians. While this method can still produce good results, there is a professional organization known as the *Piano Technicians Guild* that is a good resource for people interested in finding a piano technician. Their mission statement speaks for itself:

> *. . . to promote the highest possible standards of piano service by providing members with opportunities for professional development, by recognizing technical competence through examinations and by advancing the interests of its members.*

Those that are members of the organization must pass rigorous examinations to be given the rank of RPT (Registered Piano Technician). Their website (www.ptg.org) has numerous resource materials intended to help piano technicians; but these resource materials are also designed to help piano teachers and the general public in numerous ways. For example, one can find the piano technicians in their particular area or they can obtain contact information for piano movers. There is even an extensive listing of books about the piano.

Learning about the piano can have many benefits for the piano teacher. Communicating better with the piano technician, solving minor problems as they occur, helping students with advice regarding the care and maintenance or purchase of a piano, and saving money are some of the reasons why becoming knowledgeable about piano technology can be advantageous.

## Selected Bibliography

Dolge, Alfred, *Pianos and Their Makers* (Covina Press c 1911, Dover c 1972).

Fine, Larry. *The Piano Book* (Brookside Press), 1987.

Gaines, James R., *The Lives of the Piano* (Holt, Rinehart and Winston, 1980).

Gurlik, Philip. *The Piano—A Piano Technician's Guide for the Piano Owner* (Potter Press: Bend, OR), 2000

Leverett, Willard, *How to Buy a Good Used Piano* (Potter Press, 1980, 1993).

McCombie, Ian, *Piano Handbook* (Charles Scribners Sons, 1980).

Pierce, Bob, *Pierce Piano Atlas* (Bob Pierce, Tenth Edition, c 1997. P.O. Box 20520, Abuquerque, New Mexico, 87154-0520.)

Reblitz, Arthur, *Piano Servicing, Tuning and Rebuilding* (Second Edition Vestal Press), 1993.

Schmeckel, Carl D., *Piano Owners Guide* (Charles Scribners Sons),1974.

Smith, Virgil E. *Your Piano & Your Piano Technician* (Kjos West; Dan Diego, CA), 1981

# ABOUT THE AUTHORS

James Lyke served on the faculty of the University of Illinois from 1959-1993 as chairman of the Group Piano and Piano Pedagogy Division. In 1980 he established an MM in Piano Pedagogy along with a Piano Laboratory program for children and adults. Dr. Lyke also supervised graduate teaching assistants in studio and class work. During summer sessions, he taught workshops for piano teachers and was in charge of Illinois Summer Youth Music Piano Camps for middle and high school students. In 1993 he accepted a professorship at Georgia State University and taught there through the end of 1999. Dr. Lyke then retired to Manhattan continuing his work with arranging, composing and publishing.

In 2009, he was presented with a Lifetime Achievement Award from the National Conference On Keyboard Pedagogy. Other honors: Frances Clark Keyboard Pedagogy Award (2002), Contribution To Music Award from The University of Northern Colorado (2002), and Outstanding Alumnus Award from SUNY, College at Fredonia (1979). Throughout his career, he was an active performer. Workshop tours have taken Dr. Lyke throughout the United States and to Australia, South Korea, Cyprus, France, Switzerland and Austria. He may be reached at his website: www.jameslyke.com.

Catherine Rollin is a pianist, composer, clinician and teacher of prize winning students. She has over three hundred original works published by Alfred Music Publishing Co., Inc. Rollin developed her groundbreaking series: "Pathways to Artistry" to help pianists play with greater artistry, physical relaxation and good tone production. The three level series includes technique, original repertoire and masterworks edited by Rollin. This series is available in the U.S., Canada and Europe and has also been translated into Japanese and Chinese.

Catherine Rollin has given over 200 workshops in the U.S. and Canada. Additionally, she was featured on a seven city tour of Japan in 2006.

Rollin has presented at the National Conference on Keyboard Pedagogy, the Music Teachers National Association Conference and numerous state conferences. Her topics range from technique insights to mastery of Romantic, Impressionist and Jazz Styles. Additionally, Rollin's versatility and ability to work with students playing pedagogical music through advanced masterworks has made her a sought after master class presenter.

Rollin's pedagogical music has been prominently featured on various prestigious "required" lists including the National Federation of Music Clubs Bulletin which has featured her solo, duet, concerto, and one-hand works. She has received numerous commissions including those from the Goshen College Piano Workshop, The Hattiesburg Music Teachers Association, Clavier Magazine and the Southwest District of the Ohio Music Teachers Association.

More than 40 of Catherine's students have placed in the three divisions of the Michigan Music Teachers Association state finals in the last twenty years – including eighteen first place awards. This is an unprecedented record for the state. Additionally, Rollin's students have been recognized at state, regional and national level competitions both in performance and composition. Her students have been featured soloists with the Warren, Rochester, Detroit, Pontiac-Oakland and Ft. Worth Symphonies.

Contact Catherine Rollin at www.catherinerollinmusic.com.

**Dr. Geoffrey Haydon** has successfully bridged both classical and jazz styles of performance. Currently, Dr. Haydon coordinates the piano faculty at Georgia State University where he teaches applied piano, piano literature, jazz history, and jazz theory. Known as a classical and jazz artist, he has received rave reviews in his solo, chamber, and concerto performances given throughout the USA, in Europe, Russia, China, Japan, South America, and Central America. He is also a member of the Haydon/Parker Duo, Joe Gransden Big Band, and Georgia State University Faculty Jazztet. He has performed with well-known jazz artists such as Eddie Daniels, Joe Henderson, Eddie Gomez, Bobby McFerrin, Freddie Cole, Bill Watrous, Jerry Weldon, Randy Brecker, Indugu Chancler, Conrad Herwig, and Hal Crook. Dr. Haydon regularly performs with the Atlanta Ballet Orchestra and has performed with touring shows including *The Phantom of the Opera*, *The King and I*, *The Producers*, *Hairspray*, *Sister Act*, and *Grease*.

Dr. Haydon is in demand as a clinician and adjudicator. He has numerous publications with Alfred Publishing, Stipes Publishing and is co-author of *Jazz History Overview*, a textbook by Kendall Hunt Publishing. *Beginning Jazz*, a book of Dr. Haydon's jazz piano compositions, is published by Lee Roberts Publications. Both include MIDI accompaniment tracks available on CD. In collaboration with James Lyke, Dr. Haydon has co-arranged American popular songs for solo piano in a book titled *Oldies But*

*Goodies*, and a Christmas piano duet book, both published by Lee Roberts Publications (distributed by Hal Leonard Publications). Dr. Haydon regularly contributes articles published in Clavier Companion and reviews appearing in *American Music Teacher*. He has developed an impressive reputation as someone with a high level of expertise using technology in the areas of performance, composition, arranging, and pedagogy. Giving workshops and clinics around the U.S., Dr. Haydon is an artist/clinician with RolandUS. Dr. Haydon can be heard on *Cabin Fever*, a jazz CD by the McLean-Haydon Jazz Quartet, and *My Foolish Heart*, a jazz piano/vibraphone CD by the Haydon/Parker Duo. Both CD's are available on the ACA Digital label. Dr. Haydon received his Bachelor of Music degree from the University of Richmond and studied three summers at the Aspen Music Festival. He received his Master and Doctorate of Musical Arts degrees from the University of Texas at Austin where he studied with Nancy Garrett and Gregory Allen.

**Reid Alexander**, Professor of Music (piano and piano pedagogy) at the University of Illinois (Urbana-Champaign), is an accomplished pianist and dedicated teacher. Earlier in his career, the University of Illinois honored Professor Alexander as a faculty recipient of an all-campus award for teaching excellence, recognizing his teaching versatility with pianists of all ages. Each year Dr. Alexander works with a talented class of international and domestic students. A finalist in the first Gina Bachauer Piano Competition, his early piano study was with the Arthur Loesser student, Gerald Snyder, and later the well-known Schnabel student, Stanley Fletcher. Additional coaching has occurred with Jack Radunsky, Kenneth Drake, Ruth Slenczynska, and Mieczyslaw Horszowski. Credits include recitals and presentations throughout the United States and abroad. A doctoral graduate of Vanderbilt University, his publications encompass many widely used editions of keyboard music (Frederick Harris), academic piano texts (Stipes), and articles in professional keyboard journals. During 1999-2000, he served as Professor of Piano and Director of Piano Pedagogy at the University of Oklahoma-Norman.

**Gail Berenson** is Professor of Piano at Ohio University, Athens. She is a dedicated teacher, active performer, passionate chamber music collaborator, and noted expert on musician wellness issues. She has performed and lectured in over thirty states and eight countries. Ms. Berenson is one of the co-authors of *A Symposium for Pianists and Teachers: Strategies to Develop Mind and Body for Optimal Performance*. She is a former President of Music Teachers National Association.

**Tony Caramia** is Professor of Piano at the Eastman School of Music, where he is Director of Piano Pedagogy Studies and Coordinator of the Class Piano Program. In May 2003, he was a guest on Marian McPartland's

"Piano Jazz" on NPR. He has adjudicated at the American Jazz Piano Competition for the American Pianists Association, and for the Crescendo Music Awards. In September of 2007, he was privileged to participate in the dedication concert on the new "Sorel" Steinway at SUNY Fredonia, in honor of his former teacher, Miss Claudette Sorel.

He received the 2010 Outstanding Achievement Award from SUNY Fredonia. Mr. Caramia is featured in the Yamaha *Clavinova on Campus* series; a Contributing Editor for *Clavier Companion* Magazine, and on the Editorial Committee of *American Music Teacher.*

He has conducted numerous workshops in jazz piano for teachers at MTNA National and State Conventions; the International Association for Jazz Educators (IAJE) Teacher Training Institutes; the National Piano Teachers Institute, and the International Workshops. He has lectured and performed at the European Piano Teachers Association International Conference in London; the Australian Piano Pedagogy Conference in Adelaide; the Institute of Registered Music Teachers National Conference in New Zealand, and the International Stride Summit in Switzerland.

A strong advocate of theme recitals, he has presented multi-media tributes to composers Harold Arlen and Richard Rodgers, and the extraordinary pianist, Cy Walter. He was a featured performer at the prestigious Rochester International Jazz Festival, and the 2007 and 2009 National Conference on Keyboard Pedagogy in Chicago, and the 2010 50th Anniversary Celebration of the New School for Music Study.

**Richard Chronister** (1930-1999) was active in the field of piano teaching and teacher training for over 40 years. He founded, edited and published *Keyboard Companion*, a magazine that focused on elementary level piano teaching from 1990-1999. Mr. Chronister held a variety of teaching positions at colleges and universities as well as The New School For Music Study at Princeton, NJ. Among his many achievements, he co-founded National Keyboard Arts Associates to test, develop and publish materials for elementary and intermediate piano students. He also co-founded the National Conference on Piano Pedagogy (NCKP) in 1979 and served as Executive Director until 1995. He later became a founding member of the Frances Clark Center for Keyboard Pedagogy in Princeton, NJ.

**Ann Collins**, Western Illinois University professor emeritus, maintains a busy schedule as an instructor of jazz piano clinics for classically-trained piano teachers.  She has made numerous presentations at MENC and MTNA National Conferences, the International Association for Jazz Education, the National Group Piano Symposium, and the National Piano Pedagogy Conference, where she was twice selected as a demonstration teacher. She has served as a member of the IAJE resource team and has been a featured clinician on numerous state convention programs and university seminars.

Ann is the author of the *Sing and Play* preschool piano series (Stipes) and *Lead Lines and Chord Changes* (Alfred). Her publication *Jazz Works* (Alfred) is designed to help bridge the gap between traditional piano study and jazz instruction, and her most recent publication *Jazz Piano Projects: Pre-Jazz Level* (FJH) presents ear-training, improvisation, and harmonic activities for young students, as a supplement to traditional lessons in preparation for jazz piano study. Ms. Collins was also a co-author of the MTNA *Jazz Studies Guide*.

Her jazz trio recordings *6:05 Central Standard Time* and *Re: Romance* are available through www.CDBaby.com; www.AnnCollinsJazz.com or from ACollinsJz@aol.com.

**Vanessa Cornett-Murtada** is the Director of Keyboard Studies at the University of St. Thomas in St. Paul, Minnesota, where she teaches piano and piano pedagogy. A licensed hypnotherapist, she serves as a performance anxiety coach for students and professional musicians. She has given lectures and workshops on the topic of performance anxiety management throughout the U.S., Europe, and the Far East. She chairs the Historical Perspectives Committee of the National Conference on Keyboard Pedagogy.

**Jo Ellen DeVilbiss** has been associated with The Conservatory of Central Illinois in Champaign, IL since its inception and founding in 1986. Currently she serves as the school's Executive and Artistic Director and member of the piano faculty. As Director, she oversees programming reaching over 600 students each year. DeVilbiss has been active in the leadership of the National Guild for Community Arts Education having served as a peer mentor, site evaluator and member of its national Board of Trustees. She holds an Arts Management Certificate from that organization's AMICI Institute. In 2009, DeVilbiss was the recipient of the prestigious ACE Award for Arts Advocacy presented by the 40N/88W Arts Council of Champaign County.

With music degrees from Drake University (B.M.E.) and the University of Illinois (M.M.), DeVilbiss is in frequent demand as an accompanist and performs as a duo-pianist with her musical partner and husband, Reid Alexander. She has served on the music faculties of Lawrence University, University of Wisconsin-Fox Valley, University of Illinois, Parkland College, and Indiana University in Indianapolis (IUPUI). An active clinician and adjudicator, DeVilbiss also has authored software for piano instruction and multi-media platforms and authored articles for professional keyboard journals. A member of Sigma Alpha Iota, she received the Rose of Dedication (2007) from that organization recognizing excellence in leadership.

**Denise Edwards** teaches adults and children in her home studio in Springfield, Illinois. She is on the adjunct faculty at Lincoln Land Community College, holds national certification from Music Teachers National Association, and is a co-author of *Keyboard Fundamentals*, a text for adult beginners.

**Lee Evans**, Ed.D., is Professor of Music at NYC's Pace University. He is the author/composer/arranger of over 90 music books published in the United States by Hal Leonard Corporation, plus a considerable number of books published in Japan; not to mention numerous music magazine articles that have appeared over the years. His most recent solo-piano books for The FJH Corporation in the U.S. include the late-beginner level *Color Me Jazz, Books 1 and 2*, and the intermediate/upper intermediate level *Ole! Original Latin American Dance Music, Books 1 and 2*.

**Carole Flatau** is recognized as a teacher, clinician, writer, editor, adjudicator, and arts advocate. She has presented music workshops and seminars throughout the United States and Canada, and is a frequent contributor to professional music magazines. A charter member of NDMTA, she has been active in MTNA and has held national positions in the National Federation of Music Clubs.

After fifteen years in the corporate world as keyboard editor for Columbia Pictures Publications, CPP Belwin, and Warner Bros. Publications, she returned home to Valley City, North Dakota, where she re-established her teaching studio and formed *Noteworthy Publications*. In addition to her teaching, she is a church organist, a frequent speaker and program presenter, and a story lady at the local library.

**William Heiles** is Professor of Music and Chair of the Piano Division at the University of Illinois at Urbana-Champaign, where he joined the faculty in 1968. He received his bachelor's degree at the Oberlin Conservatory of Music and, after further study in Munich as a Fulbright scholar, earned his master's and doctorate at the University of Illinois. An active pianist and harpsichordist, his performing repertoire spans all styles from the early Baroque to the present, with special emphasis on the music of Bach, Chopin, and the twentieth century. He has performed cycles of the complete harpsichord music from the *Clavierübung* of J. S. Bach, as well as the entire *Well-Tempered Clavier, Vols. I and II,* and *The Art of the Fugue* on both piano and harpsichord. As pianist he has presented numerous local and regional premieres of major works by Pierre Boulez, Elliott Carter, György Ligeti, and Donald Martino. Following his critically praised New York debut in 1977, he recorded the complete piano music of Boulez in a series of lecture-recitals broadcast over public radio. His performances on CD include Martino's *Pianississimo* and *The Laughing Third* by Herbert Brun. Heiles has taught and performed in such festivals as the Chautauqua Music Festival (New York) and Skálholt Summer Music Festival (Iceland). While maintaining an international class of students, he has given many workshops and master classes for regional and national associations of piano teachers, adjudicated numerous piano competitions, and contributed articles, reviews, and interviews to *Clavier* and the *Journal of the American Liszt Society.*

**Steven Hesla**, University of Montana Professor, received his Bachelor of Music degree from the Oberlin Conservatory of Music and his Master of Music degree from the University of Illinois at Urbana-Champaign. A recipient of The University of Montana's Distinguished Faculty Award for the College of Visual and Performing Arts, Hesla has been the teacher of many state, divisional, and national finalists in MTNA and other competitions. He has performed both nationally and internationally as soloist and with the Montana Piano Trio.

His recording of David Maslanka's *Concerto No. 2 for Piano, Winds and Percussion* is available on the Albany Records label, and his solo CD *Music and Spirit* was released in 2006. He appears in Gershwin's original two-piano version of *Rhapsody in Blue* with pianist Margery McDuffie Whatley, as released on the ACA Digital Recording label (Atlanta) in 2010. A popular performer and clinician, Professor Hesla has served as Conference Artist for MTNA and RMTA conferences in both the United States and Canada.

**Pete Jutras**, Ph.D., NCTM, is the Piano Pedagogy Specialist at the Hugh Hodgson School of Music at the University of Georgia in Athens, GA. He is Editor-in-Chief of *Clavier Companion* magazine, a leading piano pedagogy journal, and he served as Editor-in-Chief of *Keyboard Companion*. His writings have been published in *The Journal of Research in Music Education*, *American Music Teacher*, and *Keyboard Companion* magazine.

Dr. Jutras is a frequent presenter at international, national, state, and local conferences, including the ISME World Conference, the National Conferences of CMS, MENC, and MTNA, the National Conference on Keyboard Pedagogy, the World Piano Pedagogy Conference, the National Group Piano and Piano Pedagogy Forum, and multiple state and local events. He has conducted extensive research on adult music study, specifically on the benefits of adult piano study and the benefits of participation in New Horizons Bands.

**Karen Koch**, NCTM, maintains a teaching studio in Trenton Illinois and founded the Music Educators' Marketplace in 1999. She holds a B.A. from

Knox College, and an M.A. in Piano Performance and Pedagogy from Webster University St. Louis. She is active in Illinois and Missouri MTNA chapters, Piano Guild, and as a clinician, and church musician. Email: kk@musicedmarket.com. Website: www.musicedmarket.com.

**Karen Ann Krieger** is Associate Professor of Piano and Piano Pedagogy and Collegiate Piano Chair at the Blair School of Music, Vanderbilt University. Krieger is the author of instructional piano books and solo piano compositions published by Alfred and FJH.

**George Litterst** is a nationally known music educator, clinician, author, performer, and music software developer. A classically-trained pianist, he is also a MIDI musician who works extensively with the high-tech pianos in his performing, teaching, and other professional activities. As a software developer, Mr. Litterst is the co-author of the intelligent accompaniment software program, *Home Concert Xtreme*, the electronic music blackboard program, *Classroom Maestro*, and the long distance teaching and performance program, *Internet MIDI*, from TimeWarp Technologies (www.timewarptech.com).

**Walter Schenkman** served as Professor and head of the Piano Department at the University of Northern Colorado for a number of years. He has written extensively on a variety of musical subjects and given concerts and workshops throughout the United States. He studied in Paris and earned degrees from Harvard University, Yale University and Indiana University.

**Suzanne Schons** is on the music faculty of the University of St. Thomas in St. Paul, Minnesota and teaches piano at the K&S Conservatory of Music in Woodbury, MN. She holds a Ph.D. in Music Education-Emphasis in Piano Pedagogy from the University of Oklahoma.

**Paul Sheftel** is a leader in keyboard studies and has performed, lectured, and conducted workshops in nearly every state. His published materials and software are widely used throughout the USA, as well as in Europe and Asia. A pioneer in the creation of instructional materials using MIDI technology, he has also composed electronic orchestrations to support Carl Fischer's "Music Pathways" piano method by Olson, Bianchi, and Blickenstaff, as well as the Bastien Piano Method.

Paul has appeared both as part of his two-piano team, Rollino and Sheftel, and in solo recitals in many of New York's leading concert halls including Carnegie Hall, Town Hall, Alice Tully Hall, Merkin Hall, and Hunter College. The team performed widely throughout Europe and the USA appearing as soloists with such renowned orchestras as the

Berlin Philharmonic, The Concertgebouw of Amsterdam, The Royal Philharmonic, The Chicago Symphony among many others.

He has served on the faculties of the Manhattan School of Music and Hunter College, has been piano editor for Carl Fischer and is currently on the faculty of The Juilliard School where he teaches Piano Pedagogy. He maintains a private teaching studio in New York City.

**Ruth Slenczynska**, American pianist, gave her debut concert in Berlin at the age of six and made her orchestral debut in Paris at the age of eleven. She became a sensational child prodigy in Europe and America. Constant practicing, touring and a very demanding father resulted in strain. She withdrew from performing at the age of fifteen, studied at UC Berkley, and resumed her concert career in 1954. She held an Artist-in-Residence position at Southern Illinois University in Edwardsville from 1964-1987. Recent years have taken her to Taiwan (another Artist-in-Residency position) and to Japan for a series of concerts and recordings. She moved to New York in 2001 and established herself as a teacher, still giving master classes and serving on competition juries. Her book, *Forbidden Childhood*, recounts her child prodigy years and another book, *Music At Your Fingertips*, gives advice on piano technique.

**Dr. Christos Tsitsaros** is Professor of Piano Pedagogy at the University of Illinois at Urbana-Champaign. Prior to moving to the United States, Dr. Tsitsaros studied in Poland (Frédéric Chopin Academy of Warsaw) and France, where he graduated from the Ecole Normale de Musique de Paris with distinction. He continued his studies at the Jacobs School of Music of Indiana University (M.M, Artist Diploma 1986)) and later at the University of Illinois (DMA in Piano Performance, 1993). Dr. Tsitsaros is active both as a pianist and composer. His collaboration with Hal Leonard Corporation and Frederick Harris Music has resulted in a series of educational piano works that have been included in examinations for the Music Teacher National Association, the National Federation of Music Clubs and the Royal Conservatory of Canada. In addition, he is a regular editor and recording artist for the G. Schirmer Performance editions and has produced two individual piano CDs with his original piano works (Centaur Records Inc.).

He frequently appears in workshops and conferences as a performer and lecturer in the United States, Russia, and Canada.